Lecture Notes in Artificial Intelligence 7102

Subseries of Lecture Notes in Computer Science

LNAI Series Editors

Randy Goebel
University of Alberta, Edmonton, C
Yuzuru Tanaka
Hokkaido University, Sapporo,
Wolfgang Wahlster
DFKI and Saarland University,

LNAI Founding Series Editor

Joerg Siekmann
DFKI and Saarland University, Saarbrücken, Germany

Sabina Jeschke   Honghai Liu
Daniel Schilberg (Eds.)

Intelligent Robotics and Applications

4th International Conference, ICIRA 2011
Aachen, Germany, December 6-8, 2011
Proceedings, Part II

 Springer

Series Editors

Randy Goebel, University of Alberta, Edmonton, Canada
Jörg Siekmann, University of Saarland, Saarbrücken, Germany
Wolfgang Wahlster, DFKI and University of Saarland, Saarbrücken, Germany

Volume Editors

Sabina Jeschke
RWTH Aachen University, IMA/ZLW & IFU
Dennewartstraße 27, 52068 Aachen, Germany
E-mail: jeschke.office@ima-zlw-ifu.rwth-aachen.de

Honghai Liu
University of Portsmouth, School of Creative Technologies
Intelligent Systems and Biomedical Robotics Group
Eldon Building, Winston Churchill Avenue, Portsmouth, PO1 2DJ, UK
E-mail: honghai.liu@port.ac.uk

Daniel Schilberg
RWTH Aachen University, IMA/ZLW & IFU
Dennewartstraße 27, 52068 Aachen, Germany
E-mail: daniel.schilberg@ima-zlw-ifu.rwth-aachen.de

ISSN 0302-9743   e-ISSN 1611-3349
ISBN 978-3-642-25488-8   e-ISBN 978-3-642-25489-5
DOI 10.1007/978-3-642-25489-5
Springer Heidelberg Dordrecht London New York

Library of Congress Control Number: 2011941364

CR Subject Classification (1998): I.4, I.5, I.2, I.2.10, H.4, C.2

LNCS Sublibrary: SL 7 – Artificial Intelligence

Typesetting: Camera-ready by author, data conversion by Scientific Publishing Services, Chennai, India

Printed on acid-free paper

Springer is part of Springer Science+Business Media (www.springer.com)

Preface

Robots are increasingly being used for service duties, exploring inaccessible areas and for emergency and security tasks, besides their conventional application in industrial environments. The trend toward intelligent and autonomous systems is uninterrupted and poses new challenges for the interaction between humans and robots. Controlling robots is far beyond conventional programming specific tasks and cooperation between humans and robots becomes crucially important. As a result, the behavior of modern robots needs to be optimized toward these new challenges.

Against this background, the 4th International Conference on Intelligent Robotics and Applications picked "Improving Robot Behavior" as its central subject. Building on the success of the previous ICIRA conference series in Wuhan, China, Singapore and Shanghai, China, the renowned conference left Asia for the first time and took place between December 6–8, 2011 in Aachen, Germany. On the one hand, ICIRA 2011 aimed to strengthen the link between different disciplines developing and/or using robotics and its applications. On the other hand, it improved the connection between different perspectives on the field of robotics - from fundamental research to the industrial usage of robotics.

The response from the scientific community was great and after an extensive review 122 papers were selected for oral presentation at the conference. These high-quality papers from international authors cover a broad variety of topics, resembling the state of the art in robotic research. The papers accepted for the conference are presented in this volume of Springer's *Lecture Notes in Artificial Intelligence*. The volume is organized according to the conference sessions. The sessions cover a wide field of robotic research including topics such as "Robotics in Education", "Human–Robot-Interaction" and "Bio-inspired Robotics" as well as "Robotics Assembly Applications", "Parallel Kinematics" or "Multi-Robot Systems".

We would like to thank all authors and contributors who supported ICIRA 2011 and the organization team under the direction of Max Haberstroh and Ralph Kunze. Our special gratitude goes to the International Advisory Committee and Program Chairs for their help and guidance, as well as the many external reviewers who helped to maintain the high quality the conference demonstrated in the past three years. Our particular thanks goes to the keynote speakers Rüdiger Dillmann (KIT, Germany), Dennis Hong (Virginia Tech, USA) and Bradley Nelson (ETH Zürich, Switzerland) for their inspiring talks.

December 2011

Sabina Jeschke
Honghai Liu
Daniel Schilberg

Conference Organization

Conference Chair

Sabina Jeschke   RWTH Aachen University, Germany

Conference Co-chair

Xiangyang Zhu   Shanghai Jiao Tong University, China

Program Chairs

Ulrich Epple   RWTH Aachen University, Aachen
Stefan Kowalewski   RWTH Aachen University, Aachen

Program Co-chairs

Honghai Liu   University of Portsmouth, UK
Jangmyung Lee   Pusan National University, Republic of Korea
Chun-Yi Su   Concordia University, Canada

International Advisory Committee

Tamio Arai   University of Tokyo, Japan
Hegao Cai   Harbin Institute of Technology, China
Toshio Fukuda   Nagoya University, Japan
Klaus Henning   RWTH Aachen University, Germany
Huosheng Hu   Essex University, UK
Oussama Khatib   Stanford University, USA
Jurgen Leopold   Huazhong University of Science and
       Technology, China
Ming Li   National Natural Science Foundation of China,
       China
Peter Luh   Connecticut University, USA
Jun Ni   University of Michigan, USA
Nikhil R. Pal   Indian Statistical Institute, India
Grigory Panovko   Russian Academy of Science, Russia
Mohammad Siddique   Fayetteville State University, USA
Xinyu Shao   Huazhong University of Science and
       Technology, China
Shigeki Sugano   Waseda University, Japan
Michael Wang   Chinese University of Hong Kong, China

Kevin Warwick   University of Reading, UK
Bogdan M. Wilamowski   Auburn University, USA
Ming Xie   Nanyang Technological University, Singapore
Youlun Xiong   Huazhong University of Science and
                                Technology, China
Lotfi Zadeh   California University of Berkeley, USA

Conference Area Chairs

Andrew Adamatzky   University of the West of England, UK
Shamsudin H.M. Amin   Universiti Teknologi Malaysia, Malaysia
Nikos A. Aspragathos   University of Patras, Greece
Philippe Bidaud   Université Pierre and Marie Curie, France
Darwin G. Caldwell   Italian Institute of Technology, Italy
Jan-Olof Eklundh   Center for Autonomous Systems, Sweden
Ashraf M. Elnagar   University of Sharjah, United Arab Emirates
Hubert Gattringer   Johannes Kepler University Linz, Austria
Vladimir Golovko   Brest State Technical University,
                                Republic of Belarus
Jwusheng Hu   National Chiao Tung Universty, Taiwan
Karel Jezernik   University of Maribor, Slovenia
Petko Kiriazov   Bulgarian Academy of Sciences, Bulgaria
Heikki Koivo   Helsinki University of Technology, Finland
Krzysztof Kozłowski   Poznan University of Technology, Poland
Maarja Kruusmaa   Tallinn University of Technology, Estonia
Dirk Lefeber   Vrije Universiteit Brussel, Belgium
Yangmin Li   University of Macau, Macau
Bruce MacDonald   University of Auckland, New Zealand
Eric T. Matson   Purdue University, USA
Ivan Petrovic   University of Zagreb, Croatia
Miguel A. Salichs   Universidad Carlos III de Madrid, Spain
Jim Torresen   University of Oslo, Norway
Laszlo Vajta   Budapest University of Technology and
                                Economics, Hungary
Holger Voos   University of Luxembourg, Luxembourg
Cees Witteveen   Delft University of Technology,
                                The Netherlands
Changjiu Zhou   Singapore Polytechnic, Republic of Singapore

Conference Special Session Chair

Naoyuki Kubota   Tokyo Metropolitan University, Japan

International Program Committee

Fakhreddine Ababsa, France
Ehsan Aboosaeedan, Iran
Sadek Crisóstomo Absi Alfaro, Brazil
Cihan Acar, Japan
Carlos Antonio Acosta Calderon, Singapore
Nitin Afzulpurkar, Thailand
Mojtaba Ahmadi, Canada
Andika Aji Wijaya, Malaysia
Otar Akanyeti, Italy
Berkant Akin, Turkey
Mohammad Al Janaideh, Jordan
Mohamed Al Marzouqi, UAE
Ahmed Al-Araji
Amna AlDahak, UAE
Khalid A.S. Al-Khateeb, Malaysia
Kaspar Althoefer, UK
Erdinç Altug, Turkey
Farshid Amirabdollahian, UK
Cecilio Angulo, Spain
Sherine Antoun, Australia
Silvia Appendino, Italy
Philippe S. Archambault, Canada
Kartik Ariyur, USA
Panagiotis Artemiadis, USA
Joonbum Bae, USA
Feng Bai, China
Subhasis Banerji, Singapore
Sven Behnke, Germany
Nicola Bellotto, UK
Cindy Bethel, USA
Richard J. Black, USA
Misel Brezak, Croatia
Elizabeth Broadbent, New Zealand
Magdalena Bugajska, USA
Darius Burschka, Germany
Qiao Cai, USA
Berk Calli, The Netherlands
Jiangtao Cao, China
Zhiqiang Cao, China
David Capson, Canada
Barbara Caputo, Switzerland
Guillaume Caron, France
Auat Cheein, Argentina

Xiaopeng Chen, China
Ian Chen, New Zealand
Zhaopeng Chen, Germany
Wenjie Chen, Singapore
Youhua Chen, USA
Dimitrios Chrysostomou, Greece
Xavier Clady, France
Burkhard Corves, Germany
Daniel Cox, USA
Jacob Crandall, UAE
Robert Cupec, Croatia
Boris Curk, Slovenia
Marija Dakulovic, Croatia
Konstantinos Dalamagkidis, Germany
Fadly Jashi Darsivan, Malaysia
Kamen Delchev, Bulgaria
Hua Deng, China
Ming Ding, Japan
Hao Ding, Germany
Can Ulas Dogruer, Turkey
Haiwei Dong, Japan
Zhenchun Du, China
Hadi ElDaou, Estonia
Martin Esser, Germany
Andrés Faíña, Spain
Yongchun Fang, China
Faezeh Farivar, Iran
Ehsan Fazl-Ersi, Canada
Ying Feng, Canada
Lucia Fernandez Cossio, Spain
Manuel Fernandez-Carmona, Spain
Kevin Fite, USA
Antonio Frisoli, Italy
Zhuang Fu, China
Velappa Gounder Ganapathy, Malaysia
Zhen Gao, Canada
Antonios Gasteratos, Greece
Yiannis Georgilas, UK
Hu Gong, China
Dongbing Gu, UK
Liwen Guan, China
Lei Guo, China
Alvaro Gutierrez, Spain
Norihiro Hagita, Japan

Hassan Haleh, Iran
Kenji Hashimoto, Japan
Mitsuhiro Hayashibe, France
Patrick Hénaff, France
Sophie Hennequin, France
Dominik Henrich, Germany
K.V. Hindriks, The Netherlands
Vesa Höltta, Finland
Masaaki Honda, Japan
Tianjiang Hu, China
Yong'an Huang, China
Cong-Hui Huang, Taiwan
Mathias Hüsing, Germany
Detelina Ignatova, Bulgaria
Atsutoshi Ikeda, Japan
Akira Imada, Belarus
Mircea Ivanescu, Romania
Edouard Ivanjko, Croatia
Yumi Iwashita, Japan
Patric Jensfelt, Sweden
Seonghee Jeong, Japan
Li Jiang, China
Bahram Jozi, Australia
Takahiro Kagawa, Japan
Yasuhiro Kakinuma, Japan
Kaneko Kaneko, Japan
Pizzanu Kanongchaiyos, Thailand
Shigeyasu Kawaji, Japan
Eunyoung Kim, USA
Chyon Hae Kim, Japan
Balint Kiss, Hungary
Andreja Kitanov, Croatia
Bin Kong, China
Petar Kormushev, Italy
Akio Kosaka, USA
Volker Krueger, Denmark
Naoyuki Kubota, Japan
Chung-Hsien Kuo, Taiwan
Bela Lantos, Hungary
Kiju Lee, USA
Kristijan Lenac, Croatia
Gang Li, China
Kang Li, UK
Zhijun Li, China
Qinchuan Li, China
Bin Li, China

Feng-Li Lian, Taiwan
Geng Liang, China
Chyi-Yeu Lin, Taiwan
Wei Liu, China
Jindong Liu, UK
Jia Liu, China
Xin-Jun Liu, China
Bingbing Liu, Singapore
Benny Lo, UK
Yunjiang Lou, Macao
Leena Lulu, UAE
Dominic Maestas
Elmar Mair, Germany
Takafumi Matsumaru, Japan
Jouni Kalevi Mattila, Finland
Johannes Mayr, Austria
Abdul Md Mazid, Australia
Emanuele Menegatti, Italy
Qinhao Meng
Huasong Min, China
Lei Min, China
Seyed Mohamed Buhari Mohamed
   Ismail, Brunei Darussalam
Hyungpil Moon, Republic of Korea
Rainer Müller, Germany
Hyun Myung
Hiroyuki Nakamoto, Japan
Lazaros Nalpantidis, Greece
John Nassour, France
Andreas C. Nearchou, Greece
Samia Nefti-Meziani, UK
Duc Dung Nguyen, Republic of Korea
Hirotaka Osawa, Japan
Mohammadreza Asghari Oskoei, UK
Chee Khiang Pang, Singapore
Christopher Parlitz, Germany
Federica Pascucci, Italy
Fernando Lobo Pereira, Portugal
Anton Satria Prabuwono, Malaysia
Flavio Prieto, Colombia
Hong Qiao, China
Md. Jayedur Rashid, AASS, Sweden
Sushil Raut, India
Nilanjan Ray, Canada
Robert Richardson, UK
Roland Riepl, Austria

Jorge Rivera-Rovelo, México
Fabrizio Rocchi, Italy
Stephen Rock, USA
Andreja Rojko, Slovenia
Juha Röning, Finland
Anis Sahbani, France
Sébastien Saint-Aimé, France
Elsayed Sallam, Egypt
Marti Sanchez-Fibla, Spain
Ingrid Schjolberg, Norway
Kosuke Sekiyama, Japan
Naserodin Sepehry, Iran
Xinjun Sheng, China
Desire Sidibe, France
Ponnambalam Sivalinga G., Malaysia
Jorge Solis, Japan
Kai-Tai Song, Taiwan
Peter Staufer, Austria
Giovanni Stellin, Italy
Chun-Yi Su, Canada
Anan Suebsomran, Thailand
Jussi Suomela, Finland
Yoshiyuki Takahashi, Japan
Yuegang Tan, China
Li Tan, USA
Bo Tao, China
Kalevi Tervo, Finland
Ching-Hua Ting, Taiwan
Federico Tombari, Italy
Aksel Andreas Transeth, Norway
Nikos Tsourveloudis, Greece
Akira Utsumi, Japan
Kalyana Veluvolu, Republic of Korea
Ivanka Veneva, Bulgaria
Aihui Wang, Japan
Xiangke Wang, China
Hao Wang, China
Shuxin Wang, China

Furui Wang, USA
Guowu Wei, UK
Stephen Wood, USA
Hongtao Wu
Xiaojun Wu, Singapore
Xianbo Xiang, China
Elias Xidias, Greece
Rong Xiong, China
Caihua Xiong, China
Peter Xu, New Zealand
Xipeng Xu, China
Kai Xu, China
Jijie Xu, USA
Xin Xu, China
Guohua Xu, China
Bing Xu, China
Xinqing Yan, China
Wenyu Yang, China
Zhouping Yin, China
Masahiro Yokomichi, Japan
Kuu-Young Young, Taiwan
Hanafiah Yussof, Malaysia
Massimiliano Zecca, Japan
Jianguo Zhang, UK
Wenzeng Zhang, China
Xianmin Zhang, China
Xuguang Zhang, China
Yingqian Zhang, The Netherlands
Dingguo Zhang, China
Yanzheng Zhao, China
Xiaoguang Zhao, China
Yi Zhou, Singapore
Huiyu Zhou, UK
Chi Zhu, Japan
Limin Zhu, China
Chun Zhu, USA
Chungang Zhuang, China
Wei Zou, China

Organizing Committee

Max Haberstroh
Ralph Kunze
Christian Tummel
Alicia Dröge
Claudia Capellmann

Katrin Ohmen
Richar Bosnic
Robert Glashagen
Larissa Müller
Kathrin Schoenefeld

Table of Contents – Part II

Self-optimising Production Systems

Computational Intelligence

Robot Control Systems

Human-Robot Interaction

Manipulators and Applications

Stability, Dynamics and Interpolation

Evolutionary Robotics

Bio-inspired Robotics

Image-Processing Applications

Table of Contents – Part I

Robotics Assembly Applications

Rehabilitation Robotics

Mechanisms and their Applications

Multi Robot Systems

Robot Mechanism and Design

Parallel Kinematics, Parallel Kinematics Machines and Parallel Robotics

Handling and Manipulation

Tangibility in Human-Machine Interaction

Navigation and Localization of Mobile Robot

Biomechatronics for Embodied Intelligence of an Insectoid Robot

Axel Schneider, Jan Paskarbeit, Mattias Schäffersmann, and Josef Schmitz

Universität Bielefeld, DFG Center of Excellence *Cognitive Interaction Technology*,
Universitätsstr. 25, 33615 Bielefeld, Germany
http://www.cit-ec.de, http://www.emicab.eu

Abstract. In this paper, the design and development of the new hexapod robot HECTOR is described. To benefit from bio-inspired control approaches for walking, it is fundamental to identify the most important morphological and biomechanical aspects and to associate them with biological control approaches whose function principles rely on those special body features. In a second step, these pairs can be transferred to the robot to lay the foundation for embodied intelligence. According to this idea, the main characteristics of HECTOR as presented here are the muscle-like elasticity in the self-contained joint drives with integrated sensor processing capabilities, actuated 2D body segment drives, the layout and orientations of the legs and joint-axes and a lean bus system for onboard communication.

Keywords: hexapod robot, six-legged walking, compliant joint, elastic actuation.

1   Introduction

The multiplicity of behaviours which are demonstrated even by putatively simple animals and the associated ability to adapt to different environmental situations are still superior to those found in technical systems like robots. Given this starting point, the design of bio-inspired robots seems to be a well suited strategy to approach the abilities of biological systems. However, at the beginning of a design process, the question which inspiration should be taken from the biological example and transferred to the technical system and which inspiration should be left out – perhaps for the sake of suitable simplification – is most important. In this work we report on such a process which resulted in the design of a novel bio-inspired hexapod robot named HECTOR (**HE**xapod **C**ognitive au**T**onomously **O**perating **R**obot). The robot follows the example of the stick insect *Carausius morosus* by utilizing important aspects of the morphology, biomechanics and neurobiological control.

With respect to biomechanics, current research in bio-inspired walking robots aims at improvements of leg constructions as it can be seen for instance in LAURON [15], modularisation of drive technology for limb joints as in the SPACECLIMBER [1] and also improvement of attachment organs like in the STICKYBOT [11]. Investigations of vertical movements led to the optimisation

S. Jeschke, H. Liu, and D. Schilberg (Eds.): ICIRA 2011, Part II, LNAI 7102, pp. 1–11, 2011.

of leg geometry and control for climbing robots as shown e.g. in RISE [18]. An important feature in biological systems is intrinsic compliance in the actuation system and in parts also in the limb structure. An extreme example of the latter is the setup of elastic limbs e.g. in octopus which currently also finds its way into robotics [6]. HECTOR integrates some of the above mentioned inspirations like modular, elastic joint drives, additional body segment drives and the adoption of the leg geometry of stick insects.

With respect to control of walking robots, early successful implementations of coordinated walking behaviour was based on the subsumption architecture as proposed by Brooks [4] and implemented in the robot GENGHIS [5]. This architecture divides control hierarchically into several layers in which the lower layers have a reflex-like character and can be subsumed by higher layers. An early distributed neural network approach which takes into account that individual legs have their own rhythmic behaviour and are weakly coupled to neighbouring legs was embedded in ROBOT I by Beer and colleagues [3]. The principle idea that individual legs operate as autonomous agents which generate cyclic changes between swing and stance phase during walking mainly triggered by proprioceptive sensory inputs is also the foundation for the WALKNET controller [8,16]. HECTOR will use the WALKNET controller as a foundation to raise bio-inspired, reactive walking to a cognitive level while at the same time introducing and investigating sensor-actor loops for the sake of more stable gait generation in challenging walking situations. To support these sensor-actor loops, a novel, lean bus system (BioFlex Bus) for communication with those robot components related to walking has been developed.

For the current robot design we decided in favour of a hexapedal rather than for instance a bipedal setup because in two-legged walking much attention has to be paid to secure dynamical stability of the robot already during walking on flat terrain. The resulting careful operation impedes the exploration of an otherwise large parameter space. In contrast, static stability in a six-legged machine can be guaranteed in most situations. The number of DoF (Degrees of Freedom) is large enough to allow redundant postural solutions in different movement situations. Section 2 describes the transfer of morphological features to the robot, Sect. 3 introduces the implementation of bio-compliance in the construction of the self-contained, elastic joint drives and describes a concept for body segment actuation to increase manoeuvrability. Section 4 contains a description of a lean bus system for communication between on-board computer and all drive- and sensor-components. The paper finishes with a discussion and an outlook in Sect. 5.

2   Biomechatronic Transfer of Morphological Features

Besides bio-inspired control concepts for the coordination of legs and leg joints during walking [16], the transfer of important morphological features is a prerequisite for the analysis of the concerted interplay between function/control on the one side and shape/morphology on the other. HECTOR is modeled on the

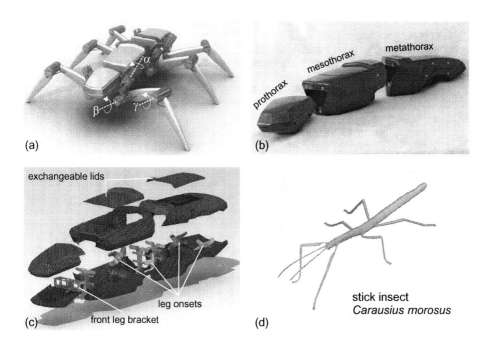

Fig. 1. (a) Rendered image of the robot HECTOR with three axes of rotation for one leg. (b) Real image of the three housing parts for pro-, meso- and metathorax of the robot made from CFRP to achieve a lightweight construction. (c) Exploded view of the three housings showing the self-supporting structures, load transmission points of the leg onsets and exchangeable lids for the meso- and metathoracic segments. (d) The stick insect *Carausius morosus* which serves as biological example for the robot.

stick insect *Carausius morosus* which is shown in Fig. 1(d). A rendered version of HECTOR is depicted in Fig. 1(a). Body and leg lengths were scaled-up by a factor of approximately 20. This results in an overall length of the robot of $\sim$950 mm and leg lengths without tarsi of $\sim$572 mm (coxa $\sim$32 mm, femur $\sim$260 mm, tibia $\sim$280 mm). For comparison, dimensions of average stick insects can be found in [7]. In stick insects, the body is divided into a head, three thorax (pro-, meso- and metathoracic) and further abdominal segments. For the robot, only the three leg-carrying thorax segments were copied. The relative distances of the leg onsets of front-, middle- and hind legs were maintained. A real image of the three housing parts for pro-, meso- and metathorax made from CFRP (Carbon Fiber Reinforced Plastic) is shown in Fig. 1(b). Figure 1(c) shows an exploded view of the housings for pro-, meso- and metathorax. Meso- and metathorax have a self-supporting structure like exoskeletons of insects. At the leg onsets the leg forces are introduced into the CFRP-structure. The prothorax segment is not self-supporting but is mechanically connected to the bracket which holds the front legs. The configuration of the three leg-joints is also depicted in Fig. 1(a). The first joint is the α-joint which is mainly responsible for protraction and retraction of the leg during swing and stance. The second joint is the β-joint,

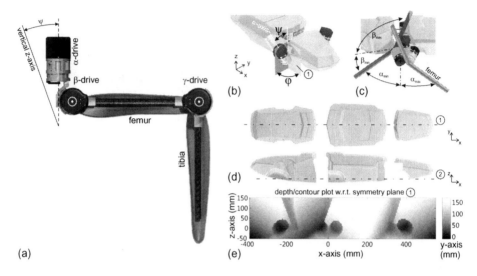

Fig. 2. (a) Section view of one of HECTOR's legs. Each leg has three axes (and drives) and three segments. The axis of the α-drive is inclined by the angle ψ with respect to the vertical z-axis. (b) Pro- and mesothorax of the robot including α-drives. The α-drives' axis of rotation is first revolved around the z-axis by an angle φ relative to a plane ① that is parallel to the x-z-plane. Subsequently it is revolved by an angle ψ relative to the z-axis [also shown in (a)]. (c) Maximal positions of β-drive and femur for the right middle leg. (d) Top and side view of the robot housings. (e) Maximal outline for the robot housings relative to the symmetry plane ① depicted in (d). The point of origin for the z-axis is depicted in (d) as line ②.

mainly responsible for elevation and depression of the whole leg. The third joint is the γ-joint, primarily responsible for the excursion of the leg. The rotational axes of the leg joints are not aligned with the three spatial dimensions but are rather slanted and have the same spatial orientation as found in stick insects. Details of the leg configuration are shown in Fig. 2(a). The mounting angle of the α-drive is inclined with respect to the vertical z-axis. Figure 2(b) shows the exact orientation of the α-drive in space. Each of the six α-axes can be characterised by fixed φ- and ψ-angles as indicated. A work plane [① in Fig. 2(b)] is assumed that is parallel to the x-z-plane in the body with a lateral offset that is defined by the point of the leg onset. This plane is rotated around the z-axis erected at the leg onset by the angle φ. The axis of the α-joint lies in the resulting plane, cuts the point of the leg onset and is tilted by the angle ψ relative to the vertical. The housing in the vicinity of the leg onsets had to be designed such that enough room for internal components is available and at the same time the maximum and minimum postures could be reached. This was done by a sequential process in which the α-joint was rotated from front to rear accompanied by synchronous up and down movements of the β-joint [cmp. Fig. 2(c)]. In this process, the femur segment cut through a virtual volume and deleted those voxels which were not part of the later housing. The results are shown in Fig. 2(e). The point of origin

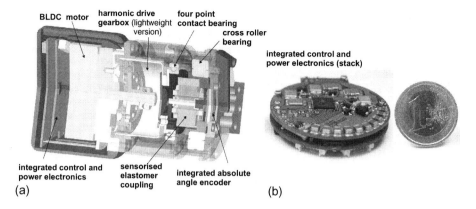

Fig. 3. (a) Section view of the elastic joint-drive used in the 18 leg joints. Technical data: length: ~90 mm, diameter: ~50 mm, max torque: ~15 Nm, weight: ~0.39 kg, power/weight: ~170-400 W/kg. (b) Image of the power- and control-electronics stack integrated into the elastic joint drive as indicated in (a). One Euro coin to compare size.

for the x- and z-axis corresponds to the lines ① and ② in Fig. 2(d), respectively. The three black round areas in Fig. 2(e) indicate those volumes which the β-actuator penetrates during the above described process. The outer shape of the final robot housings is given as top and side view in Fig. 2(d).

3 Bio-inspired Drive Technology for Leg and Body Joints

Joints in biological systems are driven by at least two antagonistic muscles. Muscles are non-linear, compliant actuators with a velocity-dependant damping function. Their intrinsic compliance – which is also found in stick insects – is not only important because of its inherent shock protection effects with respect to the mechanical structure they are integrated in but also for the function of fundamental biological control principles like Local Positive Velocity Feedback [17] and positive force feedback [14,13] in movement regulation. In robotic systems, compliance can be generated by integration of a physically existing elastic element, by pure control or by a mixture of both [10]. For HECTOR a new type of self-containing compliant joint-drives (BioFlex Rotatory Drive) is used in the leg joints. These drives are designed to generate nonlinear compliance based on an integrated serial elastic element represented by a novel sensorised elastomer coupling. A section view of the joint-drive is shown in Fig. 3(a). Technical details are given in the caption. The joint-drive consists of a brushless DC motor (BLDC) with external rotor, a lightweight harmonic drive gearbox, a serial elastic element in the form of a sensorised elastomer coupling in the mechanical output and further sensors for proprioception. To utilise the advantages of the BLDC motor, miniaturised compact electronic boards have been developed to fit into the back of the joint-actuator. Besides the power electronics, the board

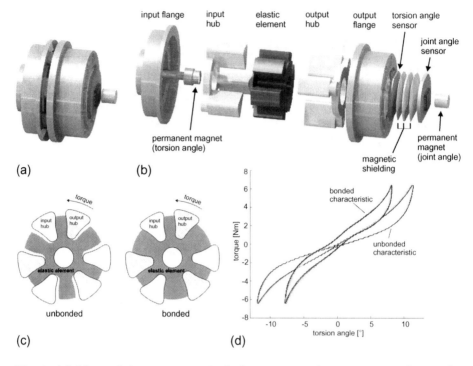

Fig. 4. (a) View of the new, sensorised elastomer coupling as integrated into the BioFlex rotatory drive [see Fig. 3(a)]. (b) Explosion view of the sensorised elastomer coupling. (c) Schematic view of the cross section of the elastic element and the two hubs. (d) Plot of the acting torque as a function of the torsion angle for the bonded and the unbonded version.

stack also contains the control electronics for processing of multiple sensory inputs and a microcontroller that is able to host local implementations also of bio-inspired control approaches. The board stack is depicted in Fig. 3(b). The incorporation of a serial elastic element is essential at least in three different ways. First, it protects the mechanical structures like the gearbox from torque peaks during sudden ground or object contact. Second, a real elastic element reacts in real time as opposed to elasticity due to pure control which is only effective in those load conditions whose time responses lie in the range of the finite control response time. Third, a real elastic element can store energy. The latter plays a subordinate role in statically stable walking as it is the case for HECTOR.

The details of the sensorised elastomer coupling as integrated in the BioFlex Drive in Fig. 3(a) is shown in Fig. 4. In order to maintain a lightweight and small-sized drive construction with integrated compliance the new sensorised elastomer coupling has been designed following the principle idea of jaw couplings. The coupling is depicted in Fig. 4(a). Figure 4(b) contains an explosion view of the coupling. The input flange is mechanically connected with the output of the

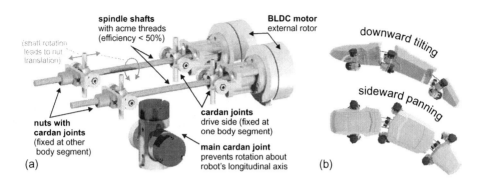

Fig. 5. (a) 2 DoF spindle drive which allows panning and tilting of two adjacent body segments. (b) Maximum downward tilting and right panning is achieved by using both spindle drives with the same/opposite rotational directions.

motor/gearbox combination [pivoted in a four point contact bearing in the drive, see Fig. 3(a)]. The output flange is mechanically connected with the output disc which is pivoted in a cross roller bearing [see Fig. 3(a)]. The input hub with three teeth is fixed to the input flange and the output hub with three teeth is fixed to the output flange (form closure). The torque between input and output is transmitted via the 6-armed elastomer inlay which is inserted in between the hubs. The torsion (twist) between input hub and output hub is measured by means of a Hall-effect based torsion angle sensor. This sensor faces a diametrically magnetised permanent magnet which is connected to a pin that itself is connected to the input flange. When assembled, the magnet on the pin dives through holes in the hubs and the elastomer inlay and resides closely in front of the torsion angle sensor. The joint angle sensor board is mounted back-to-back to the torsion angle sensor and faces a second, diametrically magnetised permanent magnet to measure the joint angle. Because both sensors can each be influenced by the other magnet, three layers of magnetic shielding have been added between the sensors. Figure 4(c) focusses on function of the jaw coupling. A radially cross section through the groove visible in Fig. 4(a) is depicted. During manufacturing of the coupling, the elastic element can be pressed between the teeth of the input and output hub without any bonding effect of the elastomer and the metal surface (unbonded) or with a bonding effect. The first version is depicted on the left side of Fig. 4(c). It can be seen that only three lobes of the elastic element contribute to the stiffness during a torsional twist (the other three have no mechanical contact with the teeth anymore). In the bonded version as shown on the right side, all six lobes of the elastic element contribute to the stiffness of the coupling when a load is acting. Figure 4(d) shows real data of the relation between the acting torque and the torsion angle between input and output hub of the sensorised elastomer coupling. It can be seen that the bonded version has a higher stiffness than the unbonded version. The hysteresis indicates the inherent damping of the polymer material.

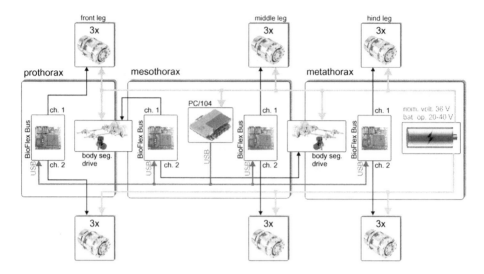

Fig. 6. Schematic depiction of the robot from above showing the pro-, meso- and metathorax. Each thorax segment has two legs with three joint drives. The joint drives communicate with a bus master (BioFlex Bus) in each thorax segment. Each bus master has two channels (2 Mbit/s each). The bus masters are connected to the host computer (PC/104) in the mesothorax via high-speed USB.

In their natural habitat, stick insects have to overcome different types of obstacles mostly represented by twigs and leaves. In these cases the animals make use of their ability to pan and tilt their leg-carrying thorax segments to increase manoeuvrability. To introduce this ability also to HECTOR, a novel 2 DoF spindle drive has been constructed as depicted in Fig. 5(a). The main cardan joint connects the adjacent thorax segments and restricts the freedom of movement to panning and tilting. Four additional cardan joints (two on the drive side, two nuts with cardan joints in the adjacent segment) are allocated in pairs at their respective thorax segment. Two spindle shafts with acme threading (efficiency slightly below 50 % to achieve self-locking) connect the four segmental cardan joints. The spindle shafts are driven by BLDC motors. Rotation of both shafts in the same direction generates tilting. Whereas, rotation of both shafts in opposite direction generates panning of the adjacent segments as shown in Fig. 5(b). Different rotatory combinations lead to arbitrary panning and tilting.

4   Lean Communication on the Robot

A small-sized bus system to exchange control and sensor information with other parts of the robot had to be developed for a direct integration into the drive systems introduced in Sect. 3. The schematic depiction of the communication setup is shown in Fig. 6. A host computer (PC/104) is situated in the mesothorax for high-level control of all actuators (leg and body joint-drives). The communication between PC/104 (host) and the drives and other clients is realized with a

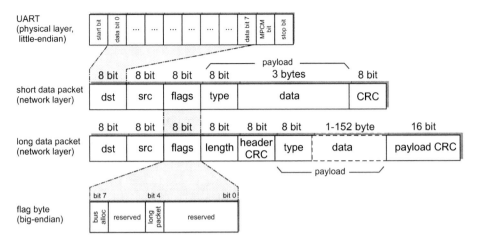

Fig. 7. Configuration of the physical and network layer of the BioFlex Bus. The BioFlex Bus master is connected to a PC via USB and is treated as a virtual serial port. This enforces segmentation of data into 8-bit chunks which make an 11-bit UART packet (shown in the top row). The two middle rows show the configuration of a short (4 byte payload) and long packet (up to 153 bytes payload). A flag-byte (bottom row) in the preamble informs the client of the packet length (short or long) and whether an answer is expected (bus allocation).

newly developed bus system, the BioFlex Bus. Its hardware consists of a miniaturized bus master board which is connected to the host via high-speed USB. On the client side, the BioFlex Bus master possesses two galvanically decoupled channels which allow half duplex, single access communication via a differential RS-485 connection with 2 Mbit/s each. Since the bus system has to operate in electromagnetically noisy environments close to BLDC motors, bus systems like I^2C are not an option. The BioFlex Bus system was developed for several reasons. First, small size communication components had to be chosen on the client boards, especially in the self-contained joint-drives. Second, high-speed bus operation with short data packets (4 bytes payload, 4 bytes overhead) as well as medium-speed bus operation with long data packets (up to 153 bytes payload, 7 bytes overhead) was desired. Third, the BioFlex Bus uses an asynchronous master-controlled single access bus-sharing scheme that allows simple implementation as well as generation of real-time sensorimotor functions. Also, the communication of clients connected to the same channel is possible without packet repetition by the bus master.

The packet design and the configuration of the physical and network layer of the BioFlex Bus is visualised in Fig. 7. The BioFlex Bus master is connected to the host computer via USB and is treated as a virtual serial port on the host. Data segmentation happens in 8-bit chunks and is supplemented by start-, stop- and MPCM-bit (MPCM = Multi Processor Communication Mode, sometimes called Multi-Drop Mode). This elementary frame is shown in the top row of Fig. 7. The two middle rows show a short and a long packet with a 4 byte and an up to 153 byte payload container. A flag byte in the preamble (bottom row) contains the information whether the current packet is short or long and if the receiver is allowed to respond (permission for bus access).

5   Discussion

In this paper we have introduced the new hexapod robot HECTOR. The robot is inspired by the stick insect *Carausius morosus*. In the robot design, important morphological and functional parameters of the stick insect have been considered. The main characteristics are the compliance in the self-contained joint-drives based on a sensorised elastomer coupling, a novel 2D body segment drive, the layout and orientations of the legs and joint-axes and a lean bus system for onboard communication. In contrast to state of the art walking machines like Scorpion [19] and Scarabeus [2] which use inelastic joints, HECTOR's compliant joints allow a passive adaptation to uneven substrate. In addition, compliant joints allow the application of bio-inspired control approaches which rely on elasticity and adaptivity on the joint level like Local Positive Velocity Feedback [17]. The new segment drives increase the manoeuvrability of the robot by introducing two actuated DoF per body joint. Other robots like Whegs II [12] use one DoF for climbing and tunneling. The Walknet control system for leg coordination [9] is based on low bandwidth signal exchange between neighbouring legs. The lean BioFlex Bus System, which was also introduced in this work, allows high frequency communication down to the hardware level of the drives with short packet lengths. This system is tailored to the requirements of biological control approaches. In the future, it is intended to approach walking tasks which contain complex foothold positions and situations which require torque reserves for gap crossing and steep walking. Within the new EU EMICAB project, the robot will be equipped with additional distributed proprioceptors, allowing for novel, highly adaptive, neurobionic control strategies. The control system of HECTOR will be expanded by planning capabilities for instance to decide wether an obstacle is traversed or avoided to reach predefined goals or – more body centered – to invent strategies to cope with coordination problems on the level of leg coordination.

Acknowledgments. This work has been supported by the DFG Center of Excellence "Cognitive Interaction Technology" (EXC277), by the Federal Ministry of Education and Research (BMBF BIONA programme, ELAN-project to A.S.) and by an EU-FP7 grant (ICT-2009.2.1, No. 270182).

References

1. Bartsch, S., Birnschein, T., Cordes, F., Kuehn, D., Kampmann, P., Hilljegerdes, J., Planthaber, S., Roemmermann, M., Kirchner, F.: Spaceclimber: Development of a six-legged climbing robot for space exploration. In: Robotics (ISR), 2010 41st International Symposium on and 2010 6th German Conference on Robotics (ROBOTIK), pp. 1265–1272. VDE Verlag GmbH, Berlin (2011)

2. Bartsch, S., Planthaber, S.: Scarabaeus: A Walking Robot Applicable to Sample Return Missions. In: Gottscheber, A., Enderle, S., Obdrzalek, D. (eds.) EUROBOT 2008. CCIS, vol. 33, pp. 128–133. Springer, Heidelberg (2009)
3. Beer, R.D., Chiel, H.J., Quinn, R.D., Espenschied, K.S., Larsson, P.: A distributed neural network architecture for hexapod robot locomotion. Neural Computation 4, 356–365 (1992)
4. Brooks, R.A.: A robust layered control system for a mobile robot. IEEE Journal of Robotics and Automation RA-2, 14–23 (1986)
5. Brooks, R.A.: A robot that walks; emergent behaviors from a carefully evolved network. A.i. memo 1091, Massachusetts Institute of Technology (1989)
6. Calisti, M., Giorelli, M., Levy, G., Mazzolai, B., Hochner, B., Laschi, C., Dario, P.: An octopus-bioinspired solution to movement and manipulation for soft robots. Bioinspiration and Biomimetics 6(3) (2011)
7. Cruse, H.: The function of the legs in the free walking stick insect, Carausius morosus. J. Comp. Physiol. A 112, 235–262 (1976)
8. Cruse, H., Brunn, D., Bartling, C., Dean, J., Dreifert, M., Schmitz, J.: Walking - a complex behavior controlled by simple networks. Adaptive Behavior 3(4), 385–418 (1995)
9. Cruse, H., Kindermann, T., Schumm, M., Dean, J., Schmitz, J.: Walknet - a biologically inspired network to control six-legged walking. Neural Networks 11(7-8), 1435–1447 (1998)
10. Eiberger, O., Haddadin, S., Weis, M., Albu-Schäffer, A., Hirzinger, G.: On joint design with intrinsic variable compliance: Derivation of the DLR QA-Joint. In: Proc. of the IEEE/ICRA, pp. 1687–1694 (2010)
11. Kim, S., Spenko, M., Trujillo, S., Heyneman, B., Santos, D., Cutkosky, M.: Smooth vertical surface climbing with directional adhesion. IEEE Transactions on Robotics 24(1), 65–74 (2008)
12. Lewinger, W., Harley, C., Ritzmann, R., Branicky, M., Quinn, R.: Insect-like antennal sensing for climbing and tunneling behavior in a biologically-inspired mobile robot. In: Proc. of the IEEE/ICRA, pp. 4176–4181 (2005)
13. Prochazka, A., Gillard, D., Bennett, D.J.: Implications of positive feedback in the control of movement. J. Neurophysiol. 77, 3237–3251 (1997)
14. Prochazka, A., Gillard, D., Bennett, D.J.: Positive force feedback control of muscles. J. Neurophysiol. 77, 3226–3236 (1997)
15. Roennau, A., Kerscher, T., Dillmann, R.: Design and kinematics of a biologically-inspired leg for a six-legged walking machine. In: Proc. of the IEEE/BioRob, pp. 626–631 (2010)
16. Schmitz, J., Schneider, A., Schilling, M., Cruse, H.: No need for a body model: Positive velocity feedback for the control of an 18-DOF robot walker. Applied Bionics and Biomechanics 5(3), 135–147 (2008)
17. Schneider, A., Cruse, H., Schmitz, J.: Decentralized control of elastic limbs in closed kinematic chains. The Int. J. of Robotics Research 25(9), 913–930 (2006)
18. Spenko, M.J., Haynes, G.C., Saunders, J.A., Cutkosky, M.R., Rizzi, A.A., Full, R.J., Koditschek, D.E.: Biologically inspired climbing with a hexapedal robot. J. Field Robot. 25(4-5), 223–242 (2008)
19. Spenneberg, D., Kirchner, F.: The Bio-Inspired SCORPION Robot: Design, Control & Lessons Learned, pp. 197–218. Climbing & Walking Robots, Towards New Applications, I-Tech Education and Publishing, Wien, Austria (2007)

Novel Approaches
for Bio-inspired Mechano-Sensors

Alin Drimus and Arne Bilberg

Mads Clausen Institute for Product Innovation,
University of Southern Denmark, 6400 Sønderborg, Denmark
{drimus,abi}@mci.sdu.dk

Abstract. In this paper, we present novel approaches for building tactile-array sensors for use in robotic grippers inspired from biology. We start by describing the sense of touch for humans and we continue by proposing different methods to build sensors that mimic this behaviour. For the static tactile sense we describe the principles of piezoresistive materials, and continue by outlining how to build a flexible tactile-sensor array using conductive thread electrodes. An alternative sensor is further described, with conductive polymer electrodes instead. For the dynamic tactile sense, we describe the principles of PVDF piezoelectric thin films and how can they be used for sensing. The data acquisition system to process the information from the tactile arrays is covered further. We validate the proposed approaches by a number of applications: classifying a number of fruits and vegetables using only the haptic feedback during their palpation, recognizing objects based on their contact profile and detecting gentle contact and vibrations using the piezoelectric sensor. We conclude by showing what needs to be improved and addressed further to achieve human-like tactile sensing for robots.

Keywords: tactile sensors, piezoresistive materials, piezoelectric materials, object recognition.

1 Introduction

Humans use their five senses in order to observe and get information from the surrounding environment. Tactile sensing is very important for humans in manipulating tools or objects, as well as for feature exploration and interaction. Touch provides information about contact forces, torques and contact distribution and by the means of exploration it provides object properties such as geometry, stiffness and texture. Research in this area has gradually shifted from structured environments in manufacturing plants toward unstructured everyday life environments like the real world [11]. When addressing the complex problems that may arise with the unstructured environments and unknown objects, robot designers have been using vision systems and image processing techniques to provide the robot with information about its surrounding and objects to be manipulated. Although vision provides important information, it is not always

S. Jeschke, H. Liu, and D. Schilberg (Eds.): ICIRA 2011, Part II, LNAI 7102, pp. 12–23, 2011.

trivial to obtain, and the accuracy is limited, due to imperfect calibration and occlusions. In addition, vision does not provide all information about object properties such as deformability or material properties. Errors in estimation of object shape are common even for known objects and these errors may cause failures in grasping. Mechanical compliance is a very important characteristic of an object, and it is essential in grasping of fragile items. Hardness, thermal conductivity, friction, roughness are also very important for humans in object manipulation and determination of its properties. Information about the object properties could be used to improve grasping in terms of contact locations and constellation of the robotic gripper as well as forces applied by different fingers. Therefore, introducing a tactile sense for robots could improve their abilities in achieving tasks that humans do so easily.

1.1   Inspiration from Biology

The tactile sense of humans is both accurate and sensitive and is the biggest inspiration when designing sensors for robots. A good overview of the psychophysics of touch can be found in [9]. Mechanoreceptors convert the mechanical deformations caused by force, vibration or slip of the skin into electrical nerve impulses. Glabrous human skin contains four different types of tactile sensors; a list of their properties is given in Table 1. These mechanoreceptors can be classified into two main categories: *static* and *dynamic* and the distinction between them is that dynamic sensors do not react to temporally constant pressure, but only to changes in the applied stimuli. The *Ruffini corpuscles* and *Merkel* receptors react to static pressure, while *Meissner cells*, the first dynamic type, roughly measure the speed of skin indentation, and *Pacini corpuscles* preferably react to vibrations or changes of indentation speed [14].

The dynamic sensors are of special importance for actively checking surface properties of objects that humans interact with, for example the texture of a coin can only be distinguished by sliding of the finger across its surface. Movement is an integral part of touch sensing for recognition and exploration. Determining imperfect grasp is also given by dynamic sensors as well as detecting unexpected contact, release or slip of the object. On the other hand, the static sensors are needed for accurate force feedback during manipulation and the spatial distribution of pressure enables us to maximize the area of contact and even perform simple shape recognition. Therefore a combination of both types of sensors, static and dynamic, achieving similar performances with that of our sense of touch has been the focus of the research in this area.

2   Related Work

MEMS (micro electro mechanical systems) based technologies are capable of fabricating miniaturized biological inspired sensors, but also bioMEMS (hybrid artificial-biological micro-structures) based on a combination of organic and inorganic materials are considered for different applications [6]. Recent advancements consider tissue engineering, which deals with growing tissues in a physiological environment. The trend in biomimetic sensor technology is to move from technologies suitable for developing discrete sensors to technologies suitable for composite structures including tissues, with integrated sensing, actuation and signal processing. In terms of tactile-array sensors for static stimuli, such as pressure, there are a range of technologies that have been used with various results [11]. There are a few technologies that can be used for manufacturing tactile-array sensors, and the most used are piezoresistive (rubbers or inks), piezocapacitive, piezoelectrical, and optical [4]. [17] propose an industrial tactile-array sensor using a piezoresistive rubber. However, this sensor has a low spatial resolution and does not have any flexible capabilities. A flexible 16x16 sensor array with 1 mm spatial resolution was developed for minimal invasive surgery, but the sensor fails to give steady output for static stimuli, and has a high hysteresis and non-linearity [8]. A combination of static and dynamic sensors was developed in [5] to address both pressure profiles and slippage, but the design has only 4x7 cells, and a number of wires equal to the number of cells. Flexible sensors based on pressure conductive rubber with 3x16 cells were developed using a stitched electrode structure, but the construction method and the leak currents brought high variations in the measurements [15]. [14] propose a tactile sensor with high sensitivity based on capacitive elements and an array of dynamic sensors. However the prototype is not very robust and the resolution is not comparable with the human skin. For dynamic sensors, most literature considers the use of piezo-electric PVDF films [4]. Using this type of material for dynamic sensing has shown promising results in determining the texture of cloth [16] or measuring vibrations and detecting slip [4]. Tactile sensors are mainly used in improving grasping of robots, exploration and for recognition or classification of objects [4]. [12] used tactile information to estimate the state of an object in order to discriminate between different cans and filled bottles, and obtained similar results with the ones obtained from recognition tests done by humans. A different approach is described in [2], where multiple grasps are performed on a set of household objects in order to classify them according only on tactile information at the points of contact with the considered objects. In some studies, grasp generation is based on visual input and tactile sensing is used for closed-loop control once in contact with the object. For example, the use of tactile sensors has been proposed to maximize the contact surface for removing a book from a bookshelf [1]. The application of force, visual, and tactile feedback to open a sliding door has been proposed in [10]. Tactile information can be also used to reconstruct the shape of unknown explored objects as proposed in [3].

3   Approaches for Developing Tactile Sensors for Static Stimuli

3.1   Building Tactile Sensor Arrays Using Piezoresistive Materials

After previous investigations on different technologies and methods for building tactile sensors, as described in [7], we have chosen the piezoresistive rubber as the most suited to build a flexible tactile-array sensor. The CSA material is a pressure-sensitive conductive rubber, a material made of non-conductive elastomer, with a homogeneous distribution of electric conductive particles. When there is no force applied over the material, the particles do not touch each other, exhibiting a high electrical resistance. When external force acts, the particles come into contact with each other and more paths for a flowing current would be created. The resistance of the material drops as the result of strain into the material and the percolation theory [8]. Due to the percolation theory the Force-Resistance characteristic shows a non-linear behaviour and because of the elastomeric nature of the base polymer, it shows also hysteresis and creep. The characteristic of the material is depicted in Figure 1a) for a number of 20 trials, where linearly increased force up to 400 grams-force and then decreased to 0 grams-force was applied to a test sample of the material. The circuit used for measuring the electrical resistance is based on the voltage divider principle and is illustrated in Figure 1b). Even though non-linearities and creep effects are present in the behaviour of the material, we do not consider these as being a major disadvantage, as the human skin also shows them [8]. Given its flexibility, cost, sensitivity and robustness we consider this material a very good candidate for building a tactile-array sensor.

Table 1. Summary of tactile fingertip units and their properties (adapted after [9] and [14])

Property	FAI	FAII	SAI	SA2
Endings	Meissner	Pacinian	Merkel	Ruffini
Location	shallow	deep	shallow	deep
Number/unit	12-17	1	4-7	1
Adaptation	fast	fast	slow	slow
Mean receptive field	13 mm^2	101 mm^2	11 mm^2	59 mm^2
Spatial resolution	poor	very poor	good	fair
Frequency range of response	10-200 Hz	70-1000 Hz	1-200 Hz	1-200 Hz

3.2   Flexible Tactile Array Sensor Using Conductive Thread Electrodes

Array sensors are problematic in terms of wiring complexity, requiring a large number of wires to address all elements. Therefore we are considering a simplified design based on a matrix structure with n columns and m rows. We will use a multiplexing method using electrodes arranged in rows on one side and as columns on the other side of the sensor device, as depicted in Figure 2a). In this way, by selecting only one column and one row, the information from a single element can be read. Such a readout circuit would reduce the wiring to $n + m$ wires, which is a desirable improvement. By iteration through all combinations of columns and rows, we would read all the values of the pressure applied onto the sensor. A tactile image is the set of these values at a given time instant.

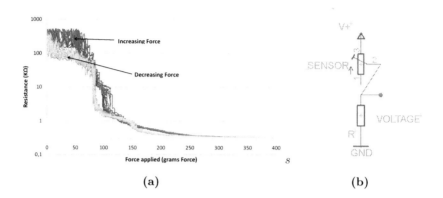

Fig. 1. a) Force vs. Resistance characteristic for the piezoresistive material, measured over 20 trials of applying increasing and decreasing force and **b)** Voltage divider principle used for measuring the electrical resistance of one single piezoresistive element

Another big challenge in building flexible tactile sensors is the need of flexible electrodes to pick up the resistance at different points on the flexible material and which should withstand a wide range of forces and bends. We propose a very simple prototype that allows for the construction of a robust sensor. From our previous results [7] we have concluded that there should not be any permanent electrical contact between the electrodes and the piezoresistive rubber patch, as this reduces the sensitivity for the low-forces range. Our manufacturing method starts with a thin flexible substrate (PVC) covered by an adhesive layer. On top of this substrate, we lay conductive threads spaced 2.5 mm apart in a series of 8 parallel lines. On top of the threads, we add a piezoresistive rubber patch, which is 0.5 mm in thickness, and has a 20x20 mm size. Next, a similar layer as the base layer is added on top, only this time, the conductive threads overlap the bottom ones perpendicularly. These steps are illustrated in Figure 2a). The conductive threads ensure the flexibility and maximum compliance of the whole structure. The conductive threads show a resistance of about 10 Ω per 10 cm, and they are about 40 cm long. The resulted prototype is roughly 25x25 mm, 1 mm in thickness and has a number of 64 taxels. It's main advantages are flexibility, robustness, simplicity and cost.

3.3   Flexible Tactile Array Sensor Using Conductive Polymer Electrodes

This approach stars with a flexible polymer (PVC) substrate as the base layer covered with an adhesive layer. A conductive paint (flexible polymer with silver particles) is applied in a thin layer through a mask with patterns for electrodes. After the mask is removed, the paint becomes thicker and bound to the base substrate because of the adhesive layer. After the paint cures, we add the piezoresistive patch on top of the base layer with electrodes and we complete the "sandwich" like structure with another layer similar to the base layer, only this time with the electrodes facing inwards and rotated so that the top electrodes overlap the bottom electrodes perpendicularly. This method is depicted in Figure 2b). The main advantage of such a method is that using high precision patterns ensures a very good uniformity of the structure, therefore the taxels will have the same response for the same applied stimuli. Also, because the paint traces are somehow more flat than curve as in the previous design, there is more contact between the electrodes and the piezoresistive material, therefore the sensitivity is increased, especially in the low forces range. The main disadvantage of this method is that after a number of bends and stretches, followed by ageing, the electrodes are prone to cracking, which can compromise the design. Nonetheless, it is a promising fabrication method, which could be improved by a different conductive paint composition.

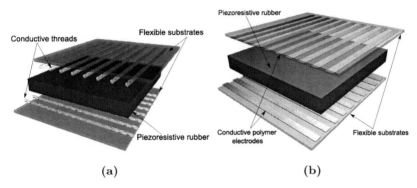

(a)   **(b)**

Fig. 2. Sensor prototypes for static stimuli: **a)** with conductive thread electrodes and **b)** with conductive polymer electrodes

4   Approaches for Developing Tactile Sensors for Dynamic Stimuli

PVDF (Polyvinylidene fluoride) film is a flexible and thin kind of macromolecule piezo materials. The response is quite similar to the signal variation of the Pacinian corpuscle sensory receptor in the dermis [16] and the output is characterized by the temporal differential property. The output follows a brief potential wave when a pulse of pressure is applied and a similar pulse when pressure is released. However, there is no response if the pressure stimuli is stationary.

The PVDF polymer piezo-films have many advantages, mainly due to their mechanical properties: flexibility (can adapted to non-planar surfaces), high mechanical resistance, dimensional stability, homogeneous piezo-activity within the plane of the film, high piezoelectric coefficients for high temperatures up to 80°C (PVDF) or 110 °C (copolymer) and high dielectric constant. They are both sensitive and have a large electrical output. Commonly available with thickness from 9 to 100 μ m, PVDF films are inexpensive, commercially available in thin flexible sheets, durable and rugged. An important limitation is the sensitivity to temperature or pyroelectricity and the fact that only dynamic loads can be sensed [8].

For the preliminary experiments, a PVDF piezoelectric thin film transducer manufactured by Measurement Specialties Inc. was attached as an extra layer to the tactile array sensor. The output of the transducer was coupled as the input of a charge amplifier using a high impedance input op-amp and a current integrator to amplify the charge accumulated at the input, avoiding thus parasitic capacitance of the wires from the sensor to the amplifier circuit. The structure of the transducer is depicted in the Figure 8a).

5   Experimental Results and Applications

5.1   Data Acquisition

In order to address an array of n x m resistive cells, we use the simple voltage divider principle as illustrated in Figure 1b) to measure the resistance of one taxel combined with multiplexing the rows and the columns. For a high multiplexing speed and a high number of inputs we use a dsPIC33FJ256, a digital signal controller developed by Microchip.

The scanning procedure works as follows: for each row_i from $(row_1, ..., row_n)$ we apply a voltage over the row_i ($V_{applied}$) and all the others are kept to ground (0V). We use n Digital Output ports $(O_1, ..., O_n)$ to control which row will be enabled and which not, by setting $O_i = 1$ and all others $O_1, ..., O_{i-1}, O_{i+1}, ..., O_n = 0$. At this point, we use m Analog Input ports $(I_1, ..., I_m)$ corresponding to the m columns, $column_1, ..., column_m$. We start by converting the voltage on I_1 by ADC, followed by the conversion of the I_2 and so forth, until we reach I_m. After this point we have obtained m values, $V_{i1}, V_{i2}, ..., V_{im}$ that represent the voltage difference between row_i and all m columns. Doing so will result in a matrix of n x m voltage readings. Each such matrix represents a frame or a *tactile image*.

The implemented data-acquisition module scans the tactile array providing 100 frames per second, with 8 bit data for each taxel, 64 or 100 taxels depending on the proposed sensor and thus providing a tactile image every 10ms.

5.2   Classification of Fruits and Vegetables Using Haptic Feedback

The aim of this application is to demonstrate the ability to recognize with a high degree of confidence deformable objects (fruits and vegetables) only using haptic feedback from the 8x8 sensors during a palpation procedure. The palpation takes 8 seconds and consists of squeezing the object for 4 seconds and de-squeezing the objects for the other 4, closing and opening the gripper with 1mm/s. The start (time t_0) is considered when both gripper jaws are in contact with the object, which is given when the tactile-sensor data is above a specified threshold. The procedure ends at time t_N, where N represents the number of frames (tactile images) recorded from the tactile sensors. In our case the data-acquisition system provides a tactile image each 20ms, thus in total about 400 frames. A frame is an array of 64 values (8×8), x_1, x_2, ..., x_{64}, each representing an 8 bit value that encodes the pressure applied over the taxel. Examples of such frames are illustrated in Figure 4 for the palpation of a lime and a mushroom.

In order to reduce the dimensionality, we extract just the first two moments of each tactile image as two independent features. These extracted features are not correlated and are related to the overall pressure and shape of contact. The average of the tactile image gives a good estimate of the overall pressure applied to the contact area, which increases with the number of contact taxels and with the pressure over each taxel. The standard deviation is a rough estimate of the number of contact pixels, describing a wider or narrower contact area. Even though more features can be extracted, we limit the discussion to the first two as they encapsulate most of the information and to reduce the computational complexity. The dimensionality of the resulting data becomes N values for each feature. An observation Z is therefore represented as:

$$Z_\mu = \{\mu_1, \mu_2, ..., \mu_N\} \tag{1}$$
$$Z_\sigma = \{\sigma_1, \sigma_2, ..., \sigma_N\} \tag{2}$$

In Figure 3, different time series depicting the μ and σ sequences for the kiwi fruit are represented.

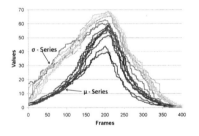

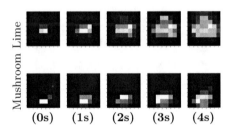

(0s)   (1s)   (2s)   (3s)   (4s)

Fig. 3. Different series for μ (dark blue) and σ (light blue) describing the palpation procedures of the Kiwi fruit. The graphs show that the different time series are consistent despite squeezing the object at different positions.

Fig. 4. Example tactile images for the Lime and Mushroom sampled every 1s during the palpation procedure

We use a k-nearest neighbors (k-NN) classification method to classify the time series resulting from the palpation procedure. We store a number of training examples for each object and a new observation is compared to the training data. Based on a distance metric, the k-nearest neighbours are found, and the new observation is assigned the label that is most frequent in this set. In order to calculate the distance between the time series, we use the Dynamic Time

Warping algorithm [13], which is widely used in different areas for measuring the similarity between time series. We use two distance metrics, one that considers only the first feature and the second that considers both features:

$$dist_1(z_1, z_2) = DTW(Z_{1,\mu}, Z_{2,\mu}) \cdot w_\mu \qquad (3)$$
$$dist_2(z_1, z_2) = DTW(Z_{1,\mu}, Z_{2,\mu}) \cdot w_\mu + DTW(Z_{1,\sigma}, Z_{2,\sigma}) \cdot w_\sigma \qquad (4)$$

where DTW is the distance measure of dynamic time warping for the considered observation for the specific time series, μ or σ and w_μ and w_σ represent a normalizing weight factor for the specific time series. The recognition rates for using one feature (the first moment) and both features for classification are shown in Table 2 and were computed using 10 fold Cross Validation for a number of 70 palpation observations. Figure 5 represents the confusion matrix (vertical axis represents the truth and horizontal represents the output of the classification), where a clear diagonal can be observed for both considered distances. The results are better if we consider the second distance, and we can be see that it is possible to discriminate with high confidence the test objects, even though grapes turned out to be mushrooms (and vice-versa) in a small number of cases and a plum showed sometimes similarity with a grape or a tomato with a mushroom.

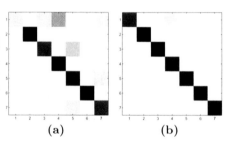

(a)   (b)

Table 2. Classification results for one and two features using 10 fold Cross Validation, 95 % confidence interval, for the tested objects: Grape, Kiwi, Lime, Mushroom, Orange, Plum and Tomato

kNN	One Feature	Two Features
1NN	74.29 ± 6.63 %	92.86 ± 5.94 %
3NN	68.57 ± 6.63 %	88.57 ± 6.63 %
5NN	61.43 ± 10.51 %	84.29 ± 4.77 %

Fig. 5. Confusion Matrix for 1-NN classification for the test objects: : **a)** using one feature and **b)** using two features

5.3   Determination of Tactile Contact Profile of Small Objects

This application considers different small objects (such as washers, bolts and a tip of a screwdriver) in order to illustrate the advantage of increasing the spatial resolution of a tactile array sensor. For this prototype, the area of a taxel is comparable in terms of size with the area of the mechanoreceptor in the human fingers. The small objects were pressed with an evenly distributed pressure against the surface of the 10 x 10 sensor with painted polymer electrodes described in the previous section. A number of tactile images recorded from the sensor are displayed in the Figure 7, where the contact profiles given by the sensor are depicted next to images of the tested object. Using different image

Fig. 6. Experimental setup a) sensors mounted on the Schunk Parallel Gripper, b) the objects considered for palpation and c) gripper performing the palpation of an orange

processing techniques invariant to rotation and position it would be possible to detect which object is touched, irrespective of the force applied, position of the object and its orientation, but this is beyond the scope of this paper.

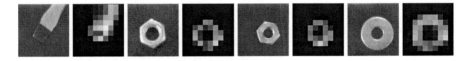

Fig. 7. Tactile images for different small objects (a screwdriver head, nuts and a washer) pressed against the flexible sensor with conductive polymer electrodes

5.4 Determination of Gentle Contact and Vibrations

The intent of this application was to detect similar events that are observed by the fast adapting sensors from the human skin for dynamic stimuli. The establishment of contact can be problematic for the previously described sensors especially due to the high sensitivity threshold, thus making gentle contacts (as the drop of a needle) impossible to detect. The release of contact is important for the robot to define the state of current interaction with the object. Another aspect refers to the active sensing, where a robotic finger equipped with a piezo-electric sensor slides over different object surfaces to recognize their texture. This is caused by the exploration method that induces small vibrations which can be picked up using the sensor. The output from the amplifier stage having the DC and high frequency components filtered out is depicted in Figure 8b. Gentle contact and release was established by applying light objects (less then 20 grams in weight) over the transducer and removing them. Active exploration was achieved dragging a rough textured object against the surface of the piezo-electric layer. However, different signal processing techniques should be further employed to recognize the texture properties of the explored objects, which are beyond the scope of this paper.

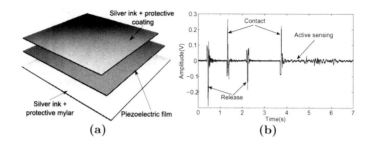

Fig. 8. PVDF piezoelectric thin film sensor for measuring dynamic stimuli: **a)** structure and **b)** output signal during different events: contact, release and sliding the surface against a rough object

6   Conclusions

In this paper we have presented a few novel approaches for developing flexible tactile array sensors inspired from the human sense of touch and that can be used to add the sense of touch to robotic grippers. We have considered the piezoresistive principle as the most suitable for building array tactile sensors for static stimuli and proposed two approaches for sensor manufacturing. For the dynamic stimuli we consider the PVDF piezoelectric films as the most suitable technology. We have described the implementation of a real time data acquisition and signal conditioning for the proposed approaches as well as we validated the properties of the sensor prototypes in applications that classify a range of fruits and vegetables only based on haptic feedback with good recognition results, discriminate between small objects based on their tactile contact profile and are able to determine contact events and texture of the touched objects using active exploration. Even though some of the challenges of mimicking the sense of touch have been addressed, there is still a long way before we could be able to make a usable "artificial skin" that can add a human like sense of touch to the robots. Future work will consider improving the manufacturing methods for increasing the robustness of the sensors, increasing the size and addressing advanced signal processing for active exploration or detection of slip.

Acknowledgments. This work is supported by the Danish Handyman Project and by the EU project EMICAB (FP7-ICT, No. 270182).

References

1. Morales, A., Prats, M., Sanz, P.J., Pobil, A.P.: An experiment in the use of manipulation primitives and tactile perception for reactive grasping. In: Science and Systems, Workshop on Robot Manipulation: Sensing and Adapting to the Real World, Atlanta, USA (2007)
2. Schneider, A., Sturm, J., Stachniss, C., Reisert, M., Burkhardt, H., Burgard, W.: Object identification with tactile sensors using bag-of-features. In: IEEE/RSJ International Conference on Intelligent Robots and Systems (2009)

3. Bierbaum, A., Rambow, M., Asfour, T., Dillmann, R.: A potential field approach to dexterous tactile exploration. In: IEEE/RAS International Conference on Humanoid Robots, Humanoids (2008)
4. Cutkosky, M., Howe, R., Provancher, W.: Force and tactile sensors. Springer Handbook of Robotics, pp. 455–476 (2008)
5. Goeger, D., Göger, N., Woern, H.: Sensing for an anthropomorphic robotic hand: Hardware and signal processing. In: IEEE International Conference on Robotics and Automation (2009)
6. Dario, P., Laschi, C., Micera, S., Vecchi, F., Zecca, M., Menciassi, A., Mazzolai, B., Carrozza, M.C.: Biologically-Inspired Microfabricated Force and Position Mechano-Sensors. In: Sensors and Sensing in Biology and Engineering, pp. 109–125. Springer, Berlin (2003)
7. Drimus, A., Marian, N., Bilberg, A.: Tactile sensing for object identification. In: Research and Education in Mechatronics, Glasgow, UK (2009)
8. Goethals, P.: Tactile feedback for robot assisted minimally invasive surgery:an overview. Tech. rep., Department of Mechanical Engineering K.U.Leuven (2008)
9. Lederman, S., Browse, R.: The physiology and psychophysics of touch. NATO ASI series Sensors and Sensory Systems for Advanced Robots F43, 71–91 (1988)
10. Prats, M., Sanz, P.J., del Pobil, A.: Vision-tactile-force, integration and robot physical interaction. In: IEEE International Conference on Robotics and Automation, Kobe, Japan, pp. 3975–3980 (2009)
11. Lee, M.H., Nicholls, H.: Tactile sensing for mechatronics - a state of the art survey. Mechatronics 9, 1–32 (1999)
12. Chitta, S., Piccoli, M., Sturm, J.: Tactile object class and internal state recognition for mobile manipulation. In: International Conference on Robotics and Automation (2010)
13. Sakoe, H., Chiba, S.: Dynamic programming algorithm optimization for spoken-word recognition. IEEE Transactions on Acoustics, Speech and Signal Processing 26(1), 43–49 (1978)
14. Schmidt, P.A., Maël, E., Würtz, R.P.: A sensor for dynamic information with applications in human-robot interaction and object exploration. Robot. Auton. Syst. 54, 1005–1014 (2006)
15. Shimojo, M., Namiki, A., Ishikawa, M., Makino, R., Mabuchi, K.: A tactile sensor sheet using pressure conductive rubber with electrical-wires stitched method. IEEE Sensors Journal 4(5) (October 2004)
16. Tanaka, Y., Tanaka, M., Chonan, S.: Development of a sensor system for collecting tactile information. Microsyst. Technol. 13, 1005–1013 (2007)
17. Weiss, K., Woern, H.: The working principle of resistive tactile sensors cells. In: Proc. IEEE International Conference on Mechatronics and Automation (2005)

Helping a Bio-inspired Tactile Sensor System to Focus on the Essential

Sven Hellbach[1,2], Marc Otto[1], and Volker Dürr[1,2,*]

[1] University of Bielefeld, Faculty of Biology, Dept. Biological Cybernetics
[2] CITEC Center of Excellence Cognitive Interaction Technology
Universitätsstrasse 21–23, 33615 Bielefeld, Germany
http://www.uni-bielefeld.de/biologie/Kybernetik/
{sven.hellbach,marc.otto,volker.duerr}@uni-bielefeld.de

Abstract. Insects use their antennae (feelers) as near-range sensors for orientation, object localization and communication. This paper presents further developments for an approach for an active tactile sensor system. This includes a hardware construction as well as a software implementation for interpreting the sensor readings. The discussed tactile sensor is able to detect an obstacle and its location. Furthermore the material properties of the obstacles are classified by application of neural networks. The focus of this paper lies in the development of a method which allows to determine automatically the part of the input data which is actually needed to fulfill the classification task. For that, non-negative matrix factorization is evaluated by quantifying the trade-off between classification accuracy and input (and network) dimension.

Keywords: Active Tactile Sensing, FFT, Material Classification, Object Localization, Acceleration Measurement, Non-Negative Matrix Factorization NMF, Dimension Reduction.

1 Introduction

Insects are a widespread group of animals, inhabiting a wide range of ecosystems and hence being confronted with variate living conditions. One of the reasons why insects are able to adapt to such different living conditions is their ability for rapid and parallel object recognition and scene analysis. For near-range sensing in animals, the active tactile sense often is of central importance. Mammals like cats or rats use active whisker movements to detect and scan objects in the vicinity of their body. Similarly, many insects actively move their antennae (feelers) and use them for orientation, obstacle localization, pattern recognition and even communication [1]. Here we use the antenna of the stick insect *Carausius morosus* [2] as the biological model for a bionic sensor for reasons summarized by Dürr and Krause [3]. Beyond the understanding of nature's principles, the research offers a new type of sensor for mobile robot systems. In particular, in environments where other sensors are not able to provide reliable data,

---

* This work was supported by the EU project EMICAB (FP7-ICT, No. 270182).

S. Jeschke, H. Liu, and D. Schilberg (Eds.): ICIRA 2011, Part II, LNAI 7102, pp. 24–33, 2011.

e. g. vision sensors in dusty or dark environments, a tactile sensor is able to provide additional information. Apart from advantages in dim or dusty environments, tactile sensors can detect cues that are not amenable by vision. For example, is difficult for vision sensors to determine material properties, whereas the sensor described here is able to classify materials with high reliability. Furthermore it can measure object distance or at least confirm the position of a visually detected obstacle.

It could be shown in [4] that an artificial neural network based approach generates reliable results in tactile material classification. Additionally, the experiments suggested that it might be possible to reduce the input dimension without deteriorating performance. The objective of the present study is to reduce the input dimension, the size of the neural network and, hence, calculation efforts as much as possible without affecting classification performance too much.

The following section provides a short overview on the field of tactile sensing. The sensor hardware is introduced in section 3, while the software part is discussed in section 4. Afterwards, experimental results are presented in section 5. Finally, the work is concluded in section 6.

2   Previous Work

When thinking about scene interpretation, particularly the recognition of individual scene objects, the use of tactile sensors in the broadest sense is playing an increasing role [5,6]. Insect-like tactile sensors have been pioneered by Kaneko and co-workers, who used either vibration signals [7] or bending forces [8], both measured at the base of a flexible beam, to determine contact distance. In contrast, we use a single acceleration sensor located at the tip of the probe [9]. Contact distance is determined by using the peak frequency of the damped oscillations of the free end. Beyond the focus on single antenna-like sensors, their integration with vision has been researched, for example, in the AMouse project [10], which used rat-inspired whiskers instead of insect-like antennae. In contrast to our approach, whisker vibration was not measured at the tip of the sensor but at its mounting point. Other than these early works, our system is able to detect 3D contact position with a single antenna by measuring its vibration. The interpretation of the sensor readings is done in a bio-inspired way using neural networks. The input for the network is pre-processed using non-negative matrix factorization (NMF) for dimension reduction.

3   Sensor Hardware

The biological counterpart is equipped with a large number of sensors. Handling such a large number of sensors is a challenging task. In particular, integrating all types of sensors into a single antenna-like device would be very demanding. Instead, here we regard the antenna at a higher level of abstraction. One of the basic features of the biological archetype is the ability to detect the position of potential obstacles and to analyse their properties. A first step to be able to mimic these abilities is to use a two-axis acceleration sensor (Analog Devices ADXL210E), which measures the vibration characteristics during object contact. The used sensor is mounted at the tip of a 33 cm poly-acrylic tube. The antenna is designed in a way that the entire probing rod, and hence the the sensor, can be exchanged easily [11].

The robotic feeler is based on major morphological characteristics of the stick insect antenna, such as two rotary joints
that are slanted against the vertical plane. The scale is approx. 10:1 compared to the stick insect to match that of the
Bielefeld insectoid walking robot TARRY (Fig. 1). The actuator platform consists of two orthogonal axes. Two 6V DC
motors (Faulhaber 1331T 006SR) were used rather than servo
motors to minimize vibrations of the probe due to discrete
acceleration steps. The linkage of the hinges was designed to
mimic the action range of the stick insect, amounting to 90° in
the vertical range, centred 10° above the horizon, and to 80°
horizontal range centred 40° to the side. Positioning accuracy
is limited by slack in the motors and amounts to approx. 5
mm at the tip of a 40 cm probe (approx. 7°).

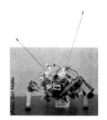

Fig. 1. The stick insect inspired walking robot TARRY

Both hinges are equipped with a position sensor (muRata SV01A). Hence the orientation of the sensor rod is known in two dimensions encoded in po-lar coordinates. Since the hinge axes are orthogonal, no additional coordinate transformation is necessary. As yet, the description of object position in 3D space requires an additional coordinate. This is obtained by determining the contact position along the probe, as described in section 4.

The control of the motion of the antenna as well as the sensor read out is implemented on an embedded system (ATMEL AT90CAN128). The raw sensor signal is available via RS232 for further processing.

4   Interpreting Sensor Readings

In the following, a method is described for the interpretation of the sensor sig-nals following a simple physical relation. Depending on the position of contact, the free oscillating segment of the sensor tube differs. This results in damped oscillations of different frequency composition. Either the two predominant fre-quency components or the entire frequency spectrum of the damped oscillation are taken into account for estimating the position of contact. As an intuitive ex-ample, one can imagine a guitar string gripped at different position for playing different tone pitches.

In addition, the damped oscillation also carries information about the mate-rial involved. Back to the guitar string analogy, this might be compared to the different tone caused by nylon or steel strings. For a clearer understanding, the different steps of the proposed method are depicted in Fig. 2.

Sensor Data Alignment. The used acceleration sensor is able to measure the acceleration in two orthogonal dimensions. Hence, the data coming from the

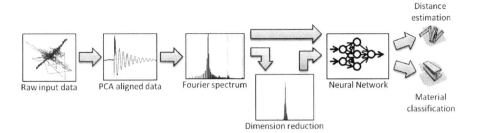

Distance
estimation

Raw input data   PCA aligned data   Fourier spectrum

Neural Network

Material
classification

Dimension reduction

Fig. 2. The flow chart illustrates the basic idea of the sensor signal processing architecture. The raw signal coming from the acceleration sensor is aligned using a PCA, breaking it down to a one-dimensional signal. From this signal the Fourier spectrum is computed and either presented directly to the particular neural network or being pre-processed by a dimension reduction algorithm. The neural networks are able to classify the signal to determine the material property or to estimate contact distance.

sensor is the projection of the actual oscillation onto both dimension vectors. This leads to different sensor readings, depending on the rotation of the antenna with respect to the axis defined by it. To align the rotated oscillation with one of the axes PCA[1] is applied. PCA [12] computes a set of eigenvectors which are oriented with respect to the principal axes of the data distribution. The matrix of eigenvectors E can be used directly as an affine transform matrix applied on the data X:

$$X_{rotated} = E \cdot X. \tag{1}$$

The first dimension of the rotated data $X_{rotated}$ contains the part of the data with the largest variance. For the time being, solely this part is used for further processing.

Detecting the Contact. As a next step, it is necessary to know at which time a contact occurred. On a static system this is a trivial task, which can be solved with a simple threshold. However, it becomes more challenging while the active tactile sensor is in motion, since the motion induces an oscillation into the sensor rod as well. At the moment we stick to the threshold, keeping in mind that more elaborate techniques may improve performance even more. For detecting the end of the oscillation the local maxima over time are considered. The end point is defined as the time, at which these maxima begin to drop below a dynamic threshold. The threshold is chosen to be 10% of the global maximum of the current damped oscillation. The window from the detected start to end point is taken into account for further processing after removing the mean.

As described above the basic idea is to analyse the frequency content of the damped oscillation. Hence, the frequency spectrum of the time series within the window is computed using Fast Fourier Transform (FFT) [13].

---

[1] Principal component analysis.

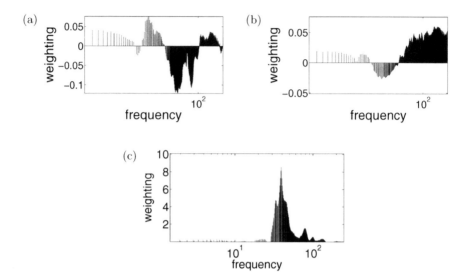

Fig. 3. Each of the three plots shows an exemplary basis vector for the three tested dimension reduction approaches (a) PCA, (b) PLS, and (c) NMF. The basis vector defines the new coordinate system with respect to the original high-dimensional space, which actually is a representation of the Fourier spectrum. Hence, those basis vectors can be illustrated as a spectrum, as it is done here.

Dimension Reduction. Using the entire Fourier spectrum would result in a very high-dimensional input space for the neural network. Moreover, the number of network parameters, i.e., synaptic weights is large. This makes it necessary to provide a sufficiently large data set and, therefore, results in a long training time. Assuming that material classification could still be sufficiently good without using the entire spectrum, the question arises which part of the spectrum should be selected as input? In biological systems, the filtering of the input spectrum is done already by the sensory organs themselves, many of which function as band pass filters. As a result, natural sensory systems often use a relatively small number of neurons, each one responding to a preferred range of pattern frequencies, e.g. the auditory system in the human inner ear. To avoid a design process that specifies the band pass filter characteristics, we opted for a data-driven approach. To maintain the bandpass filter analogy, the demand for such an algorithm would be a filter system with positive weights only. Note that such a filter system does not need to be orthogonal. This would allow to generate overlapping filter system and hence would result in highly specialized neurons in the consecutive neural network architecture.

Three methods of dimension reduction were tested: principal component analysis (PCA), Partial Least Squares (PLS) [14], an algorithm similar to PCA, and non-negative matrix factorization (NMF) [15]. The first two are based on an optimization algorithm tries to find a set of orthogonal vectors that describe the new coordinate system. The vectors are chosen so as to describe the largest possible fraction of total variance with each subsequent dimension. The PLS algorithm extends the PCA constraints by not only using the input data, but also the output data.

Both, PCA and PLS, result in a set of basis primitives with negative components, which contradicts our demand for generating a set of band pass filters. This is not the case for NMF. For NMF there is no orthogonal constraint for the set of vectors. The only limitation is that all the data, including the basis vectors, needs to be non-negative, thus meeting our main requirement.

Fig. 3 shows representative single basis components for each oneof the three algorithms tested. Each solution was gained from processing the entire Fourier spectrum. The results of NMF are the most suitable ones with respect to a data-driven band pass filter approach. The resulting basis primitves basically look like band pass filters with different characteristics. Due to the non-orthogonality, they overlap much like it would be the case with overlapping tuning characteristics in sensory organs of animals. Based on these considerations, the subsequent analysis is confined to the NMF algorithm only.

Distance Estimation and Material Classification. The distance estimation and material classification tasks are performed by two simple multi-layer perceptrons (MLP). Both networks receive either the entire Fourier spectrum or the results of the dimension reduction algorithm as an input. The network showing best results for distance estimation is a 3-layer network with 20 neurons for the first hidden layer and 5 for the second one. For material classification a 2-layer network with 51 neurons in the hidden layer is sufficient. Both networks were trained by use of a gradient descent method.

5   Results

The experiments show, that the active tactile sensor is able to discriminate different types of materials as well as to derive the position of contact. Hence, eight cylindrical objects with identical diameter were presented to the sensor, consisting of different materials, namely aluminium, stainless steel, wood, copper, brass, POM[2], PVC, and acrylic glass. These materials were chosen to represent a wide spectrum of materials with different damping characteristics. The selection includes samples that are expected to be discriminated easily, e. g. aluminium and PVC, as well as samples that are expected to be much harder to distinguish, e.g. the two kinds of plastic. The impact of the antenna occurred at 16 positions along the sensor tube, ranging from 80mm to 360mm in steps of 20mm, and at 375mm, as measured from the centre of rotation. Each impact was repeated 100 times, yielding a total of 1600 sample measurements per material and 80 per contact distance.

In order to test the optimal performance of the active tactile sensor, the experiments in this paper are limited to a stationary case, i. e. all used data sets are recorded with a stationary antenna. To do so, the antenna was mounted on

---

[2] Polyoxymethylene.

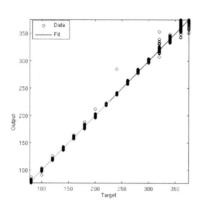

Fig. 4. The plot shows a regression plot, which indicates the relation between the network output distance and the desired target distance (both in mm). Each data sample is represented as a circle. An optimal solution would be located on the bisectrix $y = x$.

a working desk with the objects to be probed fixed in the desired distance. The contact at different distances always occurred with the same angle of impact. In the experiments presented here, the algorithm controlling the movement of the antenna ensures that the antenna stops and keeps applying a constant pressure to the probe, as soon as the probe has been hit. The application of a constant pressure is necessary to avoid rebounding of the antenna.

Performance is expected to deteriorate towards the most distal contact sites because the signal-to-noise ratio decreases severely if only a small part of the rod is able to oscillate freely. This can be confirmed by the regression plot for contact distances beyond 300 mm in Figure 4. The network performance results in a root mean squared error (rmse) of 1.71 mm, amounting to approx. 0.4% of the length of the probe.

Exceeding the results of [4], that material classification works with very high accuracy. The confusion matrix in Fig. 5 thus confirms earlier results for different network parameters than in [4]. Beside the overall classification accuracy, the differences between the material characteristics are revealed in the matrix. For example wood and aluminium show only a small number of false classifications, while brass and wood seem to be more similar to each other.

As described in section 4, the input of the multi-layer perceptron was the Fourier spectrum after systematic reduction of dimension by pre-processing with NMF. We wondered how many input dimensions are really necessary for still being able to provide a sufficient accuracy for classification? To answer that question, the NMF was applied several times, producing a data set with different numbers of dimensions. This data set was presented to the network leading to the results depicted in Fig. 6. For each number of dimensions, the training was performed several times, in order to avoid random effects. We determined the best performance for each number of input dimensions, plotted as a solid line in Fig. 6. The best performance is used as reference, since our intention is not

			Target Class						
	Aluminium	Stainl. steel	Wood	Copper	Brass	POM	PVC	Acrylic glass	
Aluminium	1567	15	2	1	4	1	1	9	97,9%
Stainl. steel	22	1481	19	19	32	10	6	11	92,6%
Wood	9	6	1468	23	50	15	21	8	91,8%
Copper	3	3	18	1517	35	10	9	5	94,8%
Brass	6	9	54	35	1462	13	14	7	91,4%
POM	6	6	14	4	11	1495	58	6	93,4%
PVC	6	4	22	20	14	38	1488	8	93,0%
Acrylic glass	3	0	5	4	5	7	1	1575	98,4%
	96,6%	97,2%	91,6%	93,5%	90,6%	94,1%	93,1%	96,7%	94,2%
	3,4%	2,8%	8,4%	6,5%	9,4%	5,9%	6,9%	3,3%	

Fig. 5. Confusion Matrix for material classification: The matrix summarizes the number of data samples assigned to a specific class by the network (output class) broken down into their target classes. The diagonal entries (light grey) contain the number of the true positive classifications. The border columns and rows (dark grey) indicate the percentage of the correct and incorrect classified elements per class, while entries in the lower right right corner tell the overall performance. Both results are computed without applying NMF-based dimension reduction.

to evaluate the random nature of the optimisation approach, but to show the possible content of information for each number of dimensions. In addition, the figure contains the results for a classification using the entire spectrum as input. The results for reduced input dimension asymptotically approach the results of the entire spectrum. For dimensions larger than 30, the system with reduced input achieves at least 86% correct assignments. From dimension 30 onwards, the increase of performance becomes smaller. Compared to the network applied on the entire spectrum of 509 frequencies (dashed line in Fig. 6), which reached 94.2% (compare Fig. 5, this is a reduction of only 8% of accuracy while the amount of data is reduced by 95%.

6   Conclusion

A bio-inspired tactile sensor was presented. The system is able to measure the position of a possible obstacle and is able to classify its material properties. With as little as 8

For the presented approach, solely one axis of the two-axes acceleration sensor is actually used. For increasing the system performance, it would be interesting to integrate the second dimension as well.

The experiments show that distance estimation reaches an accuracy of 0.4

However, before being able to mount the antenna onto a mobile robot, it is necessary to extend the pre-processing algorithm in a way that is able to handle self-induced noise by the motion of the robot.

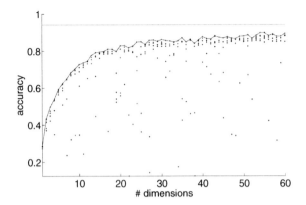

Fig. 6. The network was trained and tested with a different number of input dimensions derived by the NMF. For each of that number the plot shows the classification results. The dashed line indicates the best network with unreduced input and serves as a reference. For each trained network, the result is plotted as a single dot. The solid line connects the best results for each number of dimensions.

So far, we have applied multi-layer perceptrons. However, the data being processed is data with temporal characteristics, which suggests to apply recurrent neural networks. Using recurrent networks helps to eliminate the start/stop-detection, which is done as a pre-processing step. In that way distance estimation and material classification could run in an on-line system.

As a further perspective, it is desired to integrate multiple sensors onto a mobile platform. In doing so, a monocular vision-based system would benefit from the additional use of tactile sensors. The hypotheses gained from the vision system could be augmented with further information, like the detected material or the object's exact location in 3D Cartesian space. Additionally, the system would be able to verify the visual object detection hypotheses.

References

1. Staudacher, E., Gebhardt, M.J., Dürr, V.: Antennal movements and mechanoreception: neurobiology of active tactile sensors. Adv. Insect Physiol. 32, 49–205 (2005)
2. Dürr, V., König, Y., Kittmann, R.: The antennal motor system of the stick insect Carausius morosus: anatomy and antennal movement pattern during walking. J. Comp. Physiol. A 187, 31–144 (2001)
3. Dürr, V., Krause, A.: The stick insect antenna as a biological paragon for an actively moved tactile probe for obstacle detection. In: Proc. of CLAWAR 2001, pp. 87–96 (2001)
4. Hellbach, S., Krause, A.F., Dürr, V.: Feel Like an Insect: A Bio-Inspired Tactile Sensor System. In: Wong, K.W., Mendis, B.S.U., Bouzerdoum, A. (eds.) ICONIP 2010. LNCS, vol. 6444, pp. 676–683. Springer, Heidelberg (2010)

5. Bebek, O., Cavusoglu, M.C.: Whisker sensor design for three dimensional position measurement in robotic assisted beating heart surgery. In: ICRA, pp. 225–231 (2007)
6. Kaneko, M., Kanayma, N., Tsuji, T.: Vision-based active sensor using a flexible beam. IEEE-ASME Trans. Mechatronics I 6, 7–16 (2001)
7. Ueno, N., Svinin, M.M., Kaneko, M.: Dynamic contact sensing by flexible beam. IEEE-ASME Trans. Mechatronics 3, 254–264 (1998)
8. Kaneko, M., Kanayma, N., Tsuji, T.: Active antenna for contact sensing. IEEE Trans. Robot. Autom. 14, 278–291 (1998)
9. Lange, O., Reimann, B., Saenz, J., Dürr, V., Elkmann, N.: Insectoid obstacle detection based on an active tactile approach. In: Proc. of AMAM (2005)
10. Fend, M., Bovet, S., Hafner, V.: The artificial mouse - A robot with whiskers and vision. In: Proc. of the 35th ISR (2004)
11. Dürr, V., Krause, A.F., Neitzel, M., Lange, O., Reimann, B.: Bionic Tactile Sensor for Near-Range Search, Localisation and Material Classification. In: AMS, pp. 240–246 (2007)
12. Pearson, K.: On lines and planes of closest fit to a system of points in space. The London, Edinburgh, and Dublin Philosophical Magazine and Journal of Science. 6, 559–572 (1901)
13. Bochner, S., Chandrasekharan, K.: Fourier Transforms. Annals of Mathematics Studies 19 (1949)
14. Schwartz, W., Kembhavi, A., Harwood, D., Davis, L.: Human Detection using Partial Least Squares Analysis. In: ICCV (2009)
15. Lee, D.D., Seung, H.S.: Learning the parts of objects by non-negative matrix factorization. Nature 401, 788–791 (1999)

Robust Dataglove Mapping
for Recording Human Hand Postures*

Jan Steffen, Jonathan Maycock, and Helge Ritter

Neuroinformatics Group, Faculty of Technology,
Bielefeld University, Bielefeld, Germany

Abstract. We present a novel dataglove mapping technique based on
parameterisable models that handle both the cross coupled sensors of
the fingers and thumb, and the under-specified abduction sensors for the
fingers. Our focus is on realistically reproducing the posture of the hand
as a whole, rather than on accurate fingertip positions. The method proposed in this paper is a vision-free, object free, data glove mapping and
calibration method that has been successfully used in robot manipulation
tasks.

1 Introduction

The generation and acquisition of sufficiently accurate hand posture data as a
basis for learning dextrous robot grasping and manipulation is a complex and
time-consuming task. Several analyses have used optical markers to extract hand
posture data from camera images [1,12]. These approaches are capable of providing very accurate joint angle data under optimal conditions, however, they
can struggle in poor lighting conditions and especially in the case of grasping
and object manipulation, occlusions of one or several of the markers pose additional problems. An alternative is to use data gloves that measure joint angles
directly using in-built sensors. Whereas the problems associated with using a
vision system are bypassed, the mapping of raw sensor values to joint angles and
the resultant calibration of the mapping becomes important.

Some approaches to glove calibration benefit from the incorporation of vision
systems that can generate a large amount of highly accurate training data in a
relatively short time [3,2]. However, they have to struggle with the same problems
that purely vision-based approaches have, at least during the calibration phase,
and they require the use of a usually expensive vision system. Other approaches
do not require any additional hardware than the glove itself, but do rely on
calibration objects [4,13,7].

The method proposed in this paper is a vision-free, object free, data glove
mapping and calibration method that has been successfully used in robot manipulation tasks [11,10]. The aim of our work is to use the data glove to gain an

---

* The authors would like to acknowledge support from the German Collaborative
Research Centre "SFB 673 - Alignment in Communication" granted by the DFG, and
the German Center of Excellence 277 "Cognitive Interaction Technology" (CITEC).

S. Jeschke, H. Liu, and D. Schilberg (Eds.): ICIRA 2011, Part II, LNAI 7102, pp. 34–45, 2011.

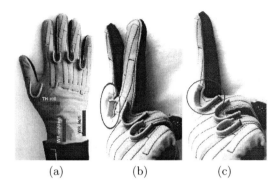

(a)   (b)   (c)

Fig. 1. The Immersion Cyberglove II Wireless. **(a)** The bend sensors are placed on top of the joints. Wrist and thumb roll sensors (red bars) are placed inside the top layer of the glove. **(b)** Forefinger / middle finger abduction sensor in the zero-abduction position **(c)** The fingers are once again not abducted, but the abduction sensor is heavily twisted due to the flexion of the middle finger.

insight into how people perform complex manual interaction tasks and to aquire data for the field of robot grasping and object manipulation. Our focus is not on having an accurate reproduction of the fingertip positions, but on imitating the demonstrated hand posture as a whole. Although these two approaches may sound similar, depending on the robot hand size and kinematic design, they can yield significantly different results.

Our work is related to the work of Kahlesz et. al [7], but, unlike Kahlesz, the calibration is based on explicit, parameterisable models for the cross coupled sensors of the fingers and the thumb, which are derived from analyses of recorded sensor data. This allows us to adapt to the data glove's intrinsic sensor dependencies caused by the design of the glove. By using a flexible data model and fitting it to the recorded data, user-specific model parameters are reduced to the minimal and maximal values of the sensors. Once the glove specific parameters are calculated , the calibration itself can be performed simply by moving the worn glove to its extreme positions. The IMMERSION CYBERGLOVE [3,2,4,13,7], widely accepted as the current most accurate data glove, is used.

The work in this paper is part of ongoing research that seeks to complement the current, strongly control- and physics-based approach for the synthesis of robot manual actions with an observation-driven approach [8]. To this end a "manual intelligence" multi-modal database is being constructed in which direct recordings of humans performing various interactive manual tasks is its main focus. A robust mapping from a dataglove to a physics based model is crucial if we are to transfer human manual interaction skills to robots.

2   The Human Hand Model

The *human hand model* [see Figure 2] was designed to represent the CyberGlove sensor readings in the form of a vector of joint angles. This vector describes the

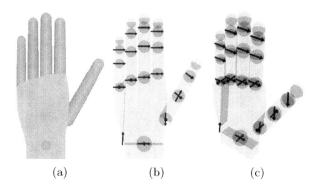

(a)   (b)   (c)

Fig. 2. The human hand model. **(a)** Visualisation in simulation. **(b-c)** The kinematic model from two different angles: the finger segments are depicted in gray whereas the hinge joint axes are visualised as black arrows.

hand posture including the wrist. To keep the representation simple and close to the design of the data glove, the model exclusively consists of only hinge joints. The complex kinematics of the human thumb [5,6] are especially simplified: all joint axes are orthogonal or parallel to each other. These simplifications also facilitate a possible further mapping onto other hand models and in particular onto robotic hands, which usually only feature hinge joints since ball-and-socket joints are difficult to control.

The glove itself has 22 sensors placed on top of the corresponding finger/hand joints [see Figure 1]. Each sensor returns integer values in the interval [0; 255], with 0 representing no bending and 255 representing maximum bending. Due to the natural joint limits of human finger joints, the whole range of possible values is usually not used. In this form, most of the 22 bend sensors in the glove can be directly associated with a single joint in the kinematic structure of the hand model as visualised in Figure 2 (b-c). Exceptions to this direct correspondence are the finger abduction joints, for which only indirect sensors are available in the CyberGlove design.

3   Mapping from Cyberglove to Human Hand Model

In general, the design of the CyberGlove (Figure 1) allows for a simple linear mapping between minimal and maximal sensor readings and the corresponding minimal and maximal finger joint values. Three exceptions to this simple case render the generation of an overall mapping a less trivial task. Firstly, the thumb abduction and roll sensors mutually influence each other [Sec. 3.1]. Secondly, a general shortcoming of the sensor placements needs to be handled, as the glove features only three spread sensors for the four fingers. The corresponding absolute joint positions cannot be fully specified [Sec. 3.2]. Lastly, readings of the finger spread joint sensors do not only depend on the spreading degree of the two corresponding fingers, but also heavily depend on the finger flexion of the neighbouring fingers [Sec. 3.3].

3.1 The Thumb Abduction / Roll Sensor Mapping

There are two bend sensors in the CyberGlove that measure the thumb abduction and roll angles: the "Thumb roll sensor" and the "Thumb-Forefinger abduction sensor". Contrary to what their names suggest, they do not only measure one effect, but are correlated and depend on each other. However, since the two sensors do not affect other movements, it is possible to generate a mapping from their sensor values onto the two roll and abduction angles.

To create this mapping, a data set from the "Thumb roll sensor" and the "Thumb-Forefinger abduction sensor" was recorded using ten different roll positions ranging from 0° to 90° with a constant step size of 10°. In each step, the thumb was moved from the minimal towards the maximal abduction limit. Figure 3 (a) depicts the resulting 1116 sensor readings, where the marker colours encode the corresponding roll angles from 0° (bright red) to 90° (bright blue).

An approximative mapping can be constructed by fitting the data points into an "approximatively bounding" parallelogram as shown in Figure 3. The sides of the parallelogram can be interpreted as non-orthogonal axes of an askew compressed frame. Projecting the sensor values onto these axes yields relative positions in the valid value ranges for the abduction and roll angles of the thumb (with outliers getting cropped). The absolute angle values can be obtained by

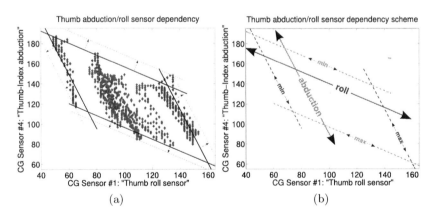

Fig. 3. Data-driven thumb mapping model: visualisation of the thumb roll/abduction dependency ("Thumb-Forefinger abduction" and "Thumb roll sensor"). **(a)** Recorded thumb data from abduction movements while keeping the roll angle fixed (different colours correspond to different roll angles). Solid black lines represent approximated data borders , the green arrows illustrate the calibration process (see text for details) and the dashed grey lines depict the corresponding calibration result. **(b)** Model of the abduction/roll sensor dependency extracted from the data recordings shown in (a).

linearly interpolating between the minimal and maximal values. Alternatively, minimum and maximum borders and the current sensor values can be projected onto the sensor axes using the askew axes as projection directions. This yields intersection points $x_0^{min}, x_0^{curr}, x_0^{max}$ on the horizontal "Thumb roll sensor" axis and $y_0^{min}, y_0^{curr}, y_0^{max}$ on the vertical "Thumb-Forefinger abduction sensor" axis. Therefore, the thumb abduction angle, α, and the thumb roll angle, β, can be written as:

$$\alpha = \frac{y_0^{min} - y_0^{curr}}{y_0^{min} - y_0^{max}} \cdot (\alpha_{max} - \alpha_{min}) \tag{1}$$

$$\beta = \frac{x_0^{curr} - x_0^{min}}{x_0^{max} - x_0^{min}} \cdot (\beta_{max} - \beta_{min}) \tag{2}$$

where $\alpha_{min}, \alpha_{max}$ and β_{min}, β_{max} denote the minimal and maximal values for the thumb abduction and roll angle, respectively.

The data recordings depicted in Figure 3 can be viewed as an example of the general dependency and behaviour of the glove sensors. A general trend is reflected in the form of the bounding parallelogram and can be described by the gradients of its bordering lines.

In order to capture this general behaviour and to adapt it to a new subject, only the gradients m and y-axis intercepts b of the bordering lines are fixed, and the values $x_0^{min}, x_0^{max}, y_0^{min}$ and y_0^{max} (that are used in Eqs. (1) and (2)) are computed after the calibration.

Since the gradients m_1 (the left border) and m_3 (the right border) are the same, and the gradients m_2 (the top border) and m_4 (the bottom border) are also the same, they are labeled $m_{1/3}$ and $m_{2/4}$, respectively. The corresponding y-axis intercepts b_1 to b_4 have to be stored separately.

Calibration can be performed using this model by moving the thumb to its extremal abduction and roll positions and replacing the bordering lines of the parallelogram such that it completely bounds the recorded data. Figure 3 (a) visualises such a process (green arrows) and the result (dashed grey lines) and Figure 3 (b) shows the resultant model extracted from the recorded data.

3.2   The Finger Spread Sensor Mapping

The finger abduction sensors are placed on top of the glove [see Figure 1], between the fingers. In the zero-spread position, the sensor strips are fully bent and spreading of the fingers results in less bending. Since each sensor is connected to two fingers and therefore describes the spread angles of two joints, each single sensor measures the angle between the fingers rather than the two angles of the underlying finger spread joints. Furthermore, since only three such sensors are provided to describe the angles of four spread joints in the hand, the sensor-to-angle mapping is under-specified. This means that no absolute specification of the angle values can be made. To compensate for this, Turner [13] fixated the middle finger in the zero-spreading position, which provided an absolute landmark to orientate the relative finger positions can be oriented. Whereas Turner reports accurate mapping results for the evaluated movements, an important drawback of this method is that no spread movements of the middle finger can be recorded.

Our approach aims at realising a model in which all fingers can perform abduction movements. Since one of the aims of our approach is to use the CyberGlove as an input device for dexterous manipulation tasks by robots and the spread movements of the middle finger can grately affect manipulation movements, we pursued a different way to resolve the problem of the under specified sensor mapping. In our model the forefinger and little finger are assumed to be always spread at the same angle. While this new assumption does not significantly improve mapping errors, it enables the model to capture side-movements of the middle finger and thus enhances its flexibility.

The computation of this constraint is straightforward. The absolute sensor values s_i of three sensors (where $i = 1$ is the sensor between the forefinger (FF) and the middle finger (MF), $i = 2$ is the sensor between MF and ring finger (RF), and $i = 3$ is the sensor between RF and little finger (LF)) are expressed in terms of a relative value x_i given by

$$x_i = \frac{s_i^{max} - s_i}{s_i^{max} - s_i^{min}} \in [0; 1]. \tag{3}$$

The relative overall finger spreading γ can be expressed as

$$\gamma = \frac{\sum x_i - \sum x_i^{min}}{\sum x_i^{max} - \sum x_i^{min}} = \frac{1}{3} \sum x_i \tag{4}$$

since $x_i^{min} = x^{min} = 0$ and $x_i^{max} = x^{max} = 1$. The angular value relative to the minimal spreading can be interpolated between the empirically determined minimal and maximal overall finger spreading angles (i.e. $\phi_{min}^{FF/LF} = -11°$ and $\phi_{max}^{FF/LF} = 60°$):

$$\phi^{FF/LF} = \gamma(\phi_{max}^{FF/LF} - \phi_{min}^{FF/LF}), \tag{5}$$

and be split up into the appropriate proportions $\phi_i, (i = 1 \ldots 3)$ corresponding to the three inter-finger sensors,

$$\phi_i = \frac{x_i}{\sum x_i} \phi^{FF/LF}. \tag{6}$$

Finally, the absolute joint angles Θ are computed starting with the outer fingers (FF and LF) in order to satisfy the constraint. On the basis of these values, the two inner fingers (MF and RF) can be set according to the ϕ_i proportioning. The relevant equations are

$$\Theta_{FF} = \Theta_{FF}^{min} + \gamma(\Theta_{FF}^{max} - \Theta_{FF}^{min}) \tag{7}$$
$$\Theta_{LF} = \Theta_{LF}^{min} + \gamma(\Theta_{LF}^{max} - \Theta_{LF}^{min}) \tag{8}$$
$$\Theta_{MF} = \Theta_{FF} - \phi_1 - \Theta_{MF}^{min} \tag{9}$$
$$\Theta_{RF} = \Theta_{LF} - \phi_3 - \Theta_{RF}^{min} \tag{10}$$

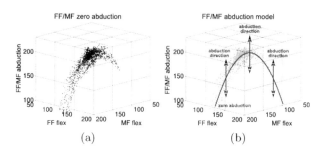

Fig. 4. The abduction mapping model of the fingers. **(a)** 'Zero abduction' sensor recordings from the forefinger (FF)/middle finger (MF) abduction sensor. Shown is the dependency of those recordings on the neighbouring FF/MF flexion sensors. **(b)** Model of the abduction mapping: the FF/MF flexion sensors dependency of the zero abduction sensor value shown in (a) is modelled as a two-dimensional paraboloid-like surface (shown here in red as a as 1D parabola). The 'abduction axis' (blue) is however constant and parallel to the axis of the abduction sensor.

3.3   The Abduction Sensor Dependency

Another intricate difficulty arises from the positioning of the spread sensor strips on top of the glove. Whereas the bend sensors are well suited for the flexion joints, since they can be incorporated into the glove in a flat position, the abduction sensor strips are placed on their edge on top of the glove [see Figure 1 (b)]. While this enables the measurement of finger spreading, the spread sensor values are also strongly dependent on the relative flexion of the neighbouring fingers [see Figure 1 (c)].

In order to compensate for this, correlations between abduction and corresponding neighbouring flexion sensors were evaluated. Figure 4 (a) shows the dependency of the FF/MF abduction sensor readings on its neighbouring flexion sensors. Depicted are different relative finger flexions for no finger spreading. The resulting data cloud resembles a noisy paraboloid-like surface, where the quadratic shape depends on the difference between the readings of the two flexion sensors. In terms of finger postures, this means that the abduction sensor value is maximal (indicating no spreading) when the neighbouring fingers are flexed equally and this decreases quadratically with an increasing difference between the two finger flexions.

In order to incorporate these observations into the sensor-to-joint mapping, the previously fixed maximal sensor values s_i^{max} are substituted in Equation (3) by dynamic zero-abduction values $s_i^{zero}(\cdot)$. These are adapted according to the sensor readings of the corresponding neighbouring flexion joints. This modification slightly changes the conceptual way of handling the abduction sensors. In the previous section we performed a linearly interpolation between minimal and maximal abduction, where minimal abduction corresponds to a finger crossing and thus a negative abduction. We now modify this so that the interpolation

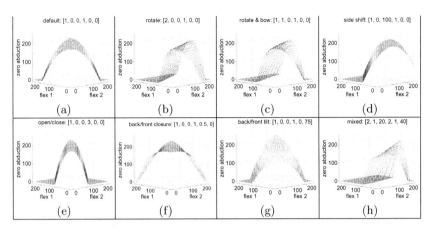

Fig. 5. Visualisation of the model parameters. **(a)** default configuration $\boldsymbol{\lambda} = [\lambda_1, \lambda_2, \lambda_3, \lambda_4, \lambda_5, \lambda_6] = [1, 0, 0, 1, 0, 0]$. The zero-abduction surface has parabolic form and is symmetric in the both flex joints (flex 1, flex2). **(b)** λ_1: rotation of the isosurface. **(c)** λ_2: similar to b), but rotation depends on the value of flex2, realising a bow form in addition to the rotation. **(d)** λ_3: left/right shift. **(e)** λ_4: open/close the parabolic form. **(f)** λ_5: change of parabolic form from front to back. **(g)** λ_6: tilt of the isosurface from front to back. **(h)** an example using all parameters at the same time.

is carried out only in the positive abduction range between the dynamic zero-abduction and maximal abduction. Negative abductions corresponding to finger crossings result in negative coefficients x_i in Equation (3) and therefore yield extrapolations in the positive abduction range. This modification results in no significant changes in the mapping results, but enables the incorporation of the dynamic zero-abduction values.

To calculate the dynamic zero-abduction values, a parametrisable model can be defined that includes the quadratic dependency on the flexion and can be fitted to the varying specific characteristics of the different abduction sensors. The final model depends on a height parameter h, the two neighbouring flexion sensor readings $s_{l(i)}$ and $s_{r(i)}$ (where $l(i)$ is the flexion sensor to the left of the abduction sensor i and $r(i)$ is the flexion sensor to the right of the abduction sensor i), and finally a parameter vector $\boldsymbol{\lambda} = (\lambda_1, \ldots, \lambda_6)$. It is denoted as follows:

$$s_i^{zero}\left(s_{l(i)}, s_{r(i)}; h, \boldsymbol{\lambda}\right) = h(1 - c \cdot \Delta^2) - d \tag{11}$$

where

$$\Delta = \frac{s_{l(i)} - s_{l(i)}^{min} - \lambda_3}{s_{l(i)}^{max} - s_{l(i)}^{min}} - a \cdot \frac{s_{r(i)} - s_{r(i)}^{min}}{s_{r(i)}^{max} - s_{r(i)}^{min}}, \tag{12}$$

$$a = \lambda_1 + \lambda_2 \left(1 - \frac{s_{r(i)}^{max} - s_{r(i)}}{s_{r(i)}^{max} - s_{r(i)}^{min}}\right), \tag{13}$$

$$c = \lambda_4 - \lambda_5 \left(\frac{s_{l(i)}^{max} - s_{l(i)}}{s_{l(i)}^{max} - s_{l(i)}^{min}} + \frac{s_{r(i)}^{max} - s_{r(i)}}{s_{r(i)}^{max} - s_{r(i)}^{min}} \right) , \tag{14}$$

$$d = \lambda_6 \cdot \frac{s_{l(i)}^{max} - s_{l(i)}}{s_{l(i)}^{max} - s_{l(i)}^{min}}. \tag{15}$$

Figure 5 visualises the effects of the model parameters $\lambda_1, \ldots, \lambda_6$ in comparison to the *default* shape [see Figure 5 (a)]. The parameters allow for rotating (λ_1) [see Figure 5 (b)] bending (λ_2) [see Figure 5 (c)], and shifting (λ_3) [see Figure 5 (d)] the parabolic-like surface. They also allow modifition of the width (λ_4) [see Figure 5 (e)], the back/front closure (λ_5) [see Figure 5 (f) and the back/front tilt of the shape (λ_6) [see Figure 5 (g)] of the surface. Figure 5 (h) shows an example in which all parameters are used at the same time. The height parameter h, used to determine the height of the surface, can be set as an additional parameter or coupled with the maximal abduction sensor reading s_i^{max}.

A least squares approach can be used to optimise the model parameters. In practice, however, due to rather noisy data samples, the resulting zero-abduction-surfaces tended towards overfitted solutions with poor generalisation abilities. In addition, the specific characteristics of the mapping problem means that it is preferable to overestimate the true zero abduction value than to underestimate it. Underestimating favours the mapping on negative finger abductions and therefore, in terms of the resulting hand posture, exaggerated finger crossings. Such crossings look unnatural and can easily cause undesirable finger collisions when actuating the corresponding hand postures on a real robot.

While such tendency towards overestimation can be incorporated in the least squares optimisation by modifying the corresponding loss function in an adequate manner, it introduces new (fairly non-robust) meta-parameters in the model. As the surface and the sample data are naturally embedded in three-dimensional space and therefore allow for an easy visualisation and the model parameters directly correspond to specific surface characteristics, one straightforward alternative to an automatic optimisation method is a visually guided manual optimisation of the parameters. Since this evaluation has to be done only once for each abduction sensor of the glove, it does not restrict the practical use of the model.

Figure 6 depicts the recorded finger abduction data and the resulting manually optimised zero-abduction surfaces for the three finger abduction sensors for the CyberGlove. The strategy of favouring an overestimation of the true zero-abduction value is clearly visible in Figure 6 (c), where data recordings and model surfaces are overlaid. Here, the surfaces represent an upper bound rather than a regression of the recorded data. Since the parameters $\boldsymbol{\lambda}$ of the dynamic zero-abduction model depend mostly on the glove and not on the user who wears it, this step need only be performed once for each glove.

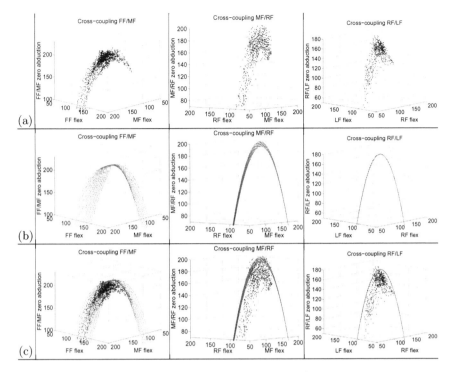

Fig. 6. Recorded finger abduction data and extracted models. **(a)** abduction sensor readings for zero-abduction depending on the flexion of the neighbouring fingers. left: forefinger (FF) and middle finger (MF), centre: middle finger (MF) and ring finger (RF) and right: ring finger (RF) and little finger (LF). **(b)** the corresponding zero-abduction models after manual optimisation of the presented parameters. **(c)** recorded data with overlaid model.

4 Evaluation of the Mapping

The calibration, which has to be performed every time the glove is used, therefore reduces to the simple problem of recording the minimal and maximal readings of the bend sensors of the glove. This can be done by moving the hand to its natural joint limits while wearing the glove. Figure 7 shows demonstrated hand postures and the corresponding mapping results. The figures illustrate that the mapping successfully provides a high degree of visual fidelity for the resulting hand postures. Figures 7 (a-b) illustrate that simple hand postures which do not involve finger abductions yield faithful mappings. Figures 7 (c-d) correspond to situations in which the dynamic zero-abduction model successfully avoids the spreading of the fingers (the abduction sensor between the forefinger and the middle finger in (c) and the middle finger and the ring finger in (d) is fully bent). Figures 7 (e-f) demonstrate the behaviour of the additional constraint for the finger abduction sensors, which had to be included in the mapping in order to overcome the under-specified sensor-to-joint mapping . Whereas the mapping

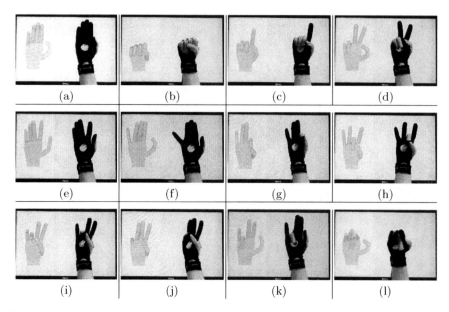

Fig. 7. Exemplary hand posture mappings illustrating a high degree of visual fidelity

is still adequate in case (e), only spreading the little finger as shown in (f) results in deviations from the demonstrated posture. Figures 7 (g-j) illustrate the performance of the mapping for the cases where the four fingertips and thumb tip touch each other. Whereas such contacts can be realised for the forefinger (g) and the middle finger (h), the same result is not achieved for the ring finger (i) and the little finger (j). Note that this shortcoming does not result from the mapping itself, but rather from the glove design and the missing flexibility of the hand model's palm: Figure 7 (j) reveals that the little finger of the demonstrator's hand is moved towards the thumb by extensively arching the hand palm. This movement is not possible in the hand model and also not sufficiently measured by the provided palm arch sensor in the glove. Figure 7 (k) depicts a hand posture which involves two finger abduction sensors and is an example of the successful combination of two dynamic zero-abduction models. Finally, Figure 7 (l) demonstrates that the mapping can also successfully cope with finger crossings. We have recently quantified the performance of the Cyberglove against two other approaches, a direct mapping and an inverse kinematics appraoch, using a sophisticated Vicon system and found that for the tested scenario the Cyberglove performed at least as well as the direct mapping approach, but not as well as the inverse kinematic approach. See [9] for more details.

5   Conclusion

We have presented a novel dataglove mapping technique which overcomes design issues in the Cyberglove. A solution was found for the cross coupled dependency of the thumb abduction and roll sensors, the under-specified abduction sensors for the four fingers, and finally the co-dependency of the finger abduction and flexion sensors. Our technique allows robust calibration of the cyberglove by simply moving the worn glove to extreme positions allowed by the human hand and has been successfully used in robot manipulation tasks.

References

1. Chang, L., Pollard, N., Mitchell, T., Xing, E.: Feature Selection for Grasp Recognition from Optical Markers. In: Proc. Int. Conf on Intelligent Robots and Systems, IROS (2007)
2. Chou, T.-S., Gadd, A., Knott, D.: Hand-Eye: A Vision-Based Approach to Data Glove Calibration. In: Proc. Human Interface Technologies (2000)
3. Fischer, M., van der Smagt, P., Hirzinger, G.: Learning techniques in a dataglove based telemanipulation system for the dlr hand. In: ICRA (1998)
4. Griffin, W., Findley, R., Turner, M., Cutkosky, M.: Calibration and Mapping of a Human Hand for Dexterous Telemanipulation. In: Proc. ASME Int. Mechanical Engineering Congress & Exposition (IMECE), Haptic Interfaces for Virtual Environments and Teleoperator Systems Symposium (2000)
5. Hollister, A., Buford, W.L., Myers, L.M., Giurintano, D.J., Novick, A.: The axes of rotation of the thumb carpometacarpal joint. Journal of Orthopaedic Research 10(3), 454–460 (1992)
6. Hollister, A., Giurintano, D.J., Buford, W.L., Myers, L.M., Novick, A.: The axes of rotation of the thumb interphalangeal and metacarpophalangeal joints. Clinical Orthopaedics & Related Research (320), 188–193 (November 1995)
7. Kahlesz, F., Zachmann, G., Klein, R.: Visual-fidelity dataglove calibration. In: Proc. Computer Graphics International, CGI (2004)
8. Maycock, J., Donrbusch, D., Elbrechter, C., Haschke, R., Schack, T., Ritter, H.: Approaching manual intelligence. In: KI-Künstliche Intelligenz - Issue Cognition for Technical Systems, pp. 1–8 (2010)
9. Maycock, J., Steffen, J., Haschke, R., Ritter, H.: Robust tracking of human hand postures for robot teaching. In: IEEE/RSJ International Conference on Intelligent Robots and Systems, IROS (2011)
10. Steffen, J.: Structured Manifolds for Motion Production and Segmentation - A Structured Kernel Regression Approach. Phd thesis, Neuroinformatics Group, Faculty of Technology, Bielefeld University, Bielefeld, Germany (2010)
11. Steffen, J., Elbrechter, C., Haschke, R., Ritter, H.J.: Bio-inspired motion strategies for a bimanual manipulation task. In: Humanoids (2010)
12. Supuk, T., Kodek, T., Bajd, T.: Estimation of hand preshaping during human grasping. Medical Engineering & Physics 27(9), 790–797 (2005)
13. Turner, M.: Programming Dexterous Manipulation by Demonstration. PhD Thesis, Stanford University, Department of Mechanical Engineering, Stanford, USA (2001)

Software/Hardware Issues
in Modelling Insect Brain Architecture

Paolo Arena[1], Luca Patané[1], Pietro Savio Termini[1],
Alessandra Vitanza[1], and Roland Strauss[2]

[1] Dipartimento di Ingegneria Elettrica, Elettronica e Informatica,
University of Catania, Italy
{parena,lpatane}@diees.unict.it
[2] Inst. f. Zool. III Neurobiology, University of Mainz, Germany
rstrauss@uni-mainz.de

Abstract. The concept of cognitive abilities is commonly associated
to humans and animals like mammals, birds and others. Nevertheless,
in the last years several research groups have intensified the studies on
insects that posses a much simpler brain structure even if they are able
to show interesting memory and learning capabilities. In this paper a
survey on some key results obtained in a joint research activity among
Engineers and Neurogeneticians is reported. They were focussed toward
the design and implementation of a model of the insect brain inspired by
the *Drosophila melanogaster*. Particular attention was paid to the main
neural centers the Mushroom Bodies and the Central Complex. Moreover
a Software/Hardware framework, where the model could be tested and
evaluated by using both simulated and real robots, is described. This
research activity aims at introducing an insect brain to act as a controller
for very smart and sophisticated insectoid body structures, to give rise
to a new generation of novel embodied intelligent machines.

Keywords: Insect brain, Drosophila melanogaster, hybrid robot,
dynamic simulation.

1 Introduction

In the bio-inspired robotics field, robots can be used to reproduce animal behavior in order to study their interaction with the environment. Robots help
to improve the understanding of animal behavior and animals help to create
efficient and robust robotic systems. The study of animal brains leads to new
control systems that could allow robots to be able to orient themselves in complex
environments, to take decisions, to accomplish dangerous missions, in order to
become completely autonomous. Robotic implementation of biological systems
could also lead to the introduction of new models for basic sciences, in particular when investigating the emergent properties of models. Several attempts are
present in literature related to algorithms or bio-inspired networks able to mimic
the functionalities of parts of the brain. A lot of work has been done in several

S. Jeschke, H. Liu, and D. Schilberg (Eds.): ICIRA 2011, Part II, LNAI 7102, pp. 46–55, 2011.
© Springer-Verlag Berlin Heidelberg 2011

animal species belonging to mammals, mollusks and insects [1]. Looking into the insect world different research groups around the world are trying to design models which are able to reproduce interesting behaviors shown by insects: cooperation mechanisms in ants [2], navigation strategies in bees [3], looming reflex in locusts [4], homing mechanisms in crickets [5], central pattern generator and obstacle climbing in cockroaches [6,7], reflex-based locomotion control in the stick insect [8], just to cite some examples. It is evident that the effort is focused on specific peculiarities associated with the different insect species that can be also useful for robotic applications. Nevertheless, a more challenging task consists of trying to model the main functionalities of an insect brain, looking from an higher level, trying to identify the mechanisms involved in the sensing-perception-action loop. The proposed work is focused on the development of an insect brain computational model mainly focused on the *Drosophila melanogaster*, the fruit fly. The insect brain architecture, structured in functional blocks, has been developed in a complete software/hardware framework in order to evaluate the capabilities of this bio-inspired control system on both simulated and real robotic platforms. In order to develop an useful and suitable architecture, the proposed framework is flexible and robust and presents a structure suitable to decouple simulations from control algorithms. The functional separation helps to isolate the application itself from graphic interfaces and the underlying hardware. The main aim is to develop an extensible and general purpose architecture. The insect brain model has been evaluated in scenarios strictly linked to the neurobiological experiments to make a direct comparison. Moreover the available data on wild type flies and mutant brain-defective flies allows to identify the main role of each neural assembly in performing specific tasks like visual orientation, olfactory learning, adaptive termination of behaviours and others. Finally the main guidelines used for the definition of evaluation criteria and the creation of benchmarking scenarios where the system performance can be evaluated, are also reported.

2   Insect Brain Model

In the last years, biological experiments unraveled details of the Drosophila brain, with particular emphasis to Mushroom Bodies (MBs) and Central Complex (CX), and a number of functional blocks, explaining the main functionalities of such centers. Starting from these results a new computationally-oriented model of the insect brain, specifically focused on the *Drosophila melanogaster* has been designed and implemented [14,15].

In the insect brain scheme, reported in Fig.1, it is possible to distinguish four main sensorial pathways; the olfactory and the visual pathways allow to perceive the environment, whereas gustation and nociception are indispensable to obtain information about the goodness or badness of the current situation. In particular the gustatory sensory modality, placed in the front legs of the fly, is reproduced in robotic experiments through signals coming from light sensors placed in the ventral part of the robots, facing with the ground. This modality is used in experiments like the adaptive termination of behaviours. Nociceptory signals, used for punishment, are reproduced through sound signals (or through the ventrally placed light sensors) and applied in such experiments as visual/odour learning. These sensorial pathways are linked together to make the system able to perform anticipatory actions to improve efficiency in finding rewards and to avoid dangerous situations. In the actual structure, learning is attained using mechanisms based on classical as well as operant conditioning. Olfactory and visual inputs, due to their complexity, are considered as pre-processed at the sensory level. Olfaction, has been studied at the aim to derive the corresponding MB neural models. Regarding the olfactory sensors, since the artificial ones are still too slow and difficult to be efficiently characterized, they were substituted by sound sensors, which are more reliable and able to provide both unconditioned and conditioned inputs to the neural processing network. Soon after the visual pre-processing stage we can find the Central Complex neuropil model, containing all its main components:

PB -   The Protocerebral Bridge (PB), which, in our model, performs its three main functions (Object Detection, Distance Estimation and Object Position extraction), as drawn by the biological experiments and neuro-anatomical evidence [12,13];

FB -   the Fan-shaped Body (FB), which performs two main functions: feature extraction (color, orientation, size, center of gravity, wideness, height) and feature evaluation/learning (the robot collects features and is able to associate those features to punishment or neutral situations.

EB -   the Ellipsoid Body (EB), where the robot spatial and the newly discovered decision making memory is formed and contained.

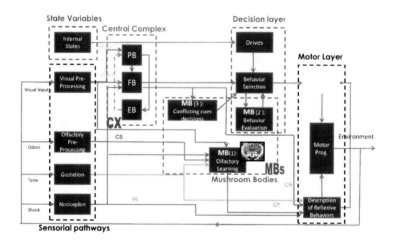

Fig. 1. Block diagram of the insect brain model

The other fundamental neuropil of the insect brain is constituted by the Mushroom Bodies (MBs). MBs were found to influence many different aspect of the insect brain plasticity. The main function of MBs is olfactory learning: this was implemented in our architecture through a hebbian or STDP based learning scheme in spiking networks. The other function experimentally found in MBs is behaviour evaluation, mainly acting at the decision level. For this reason this MB functionality, here called MB2 (Fig. 1) is included into the decision layer and implemented as a separate block with respect to the olfactory learning block. Another addressed function is decision making: this function was discovered working with MB defective flies which were unable to make a sharp choice among two different contradictory visual features (color and shape) in front of the fading of the preferred one (color). This is a function that, involving visual learning, cannot be ascribed to the conventional functionality of MBs (olfactory representation and leaning). So this function was modeled as a separated block (MB3) and placed at the decision layer (Fig.1). Moreover, from the block-size perspective, direct connections among FB and MB cannot be directly drawn for the lack of experimental evidence in the fly. So it is hypothesized that particular visual information, like color saturation reaches the MBs indirectly through other brain parts (like for example the Lateral Horn) and gives it the possibility to concurrently act on the Behaviour Selection block at the level of decision making.

A series of internal states are monitored through a set of virtual proprioceptive sensors; these internal states undergo a continuous interaction with the ongoing external state of the agent, recorded through the exteroceptive sensors. Internal states are chosen according to the applications prepared, discussed within each experimental scenario. An internal state (like hunger or "need for charging", need to sleep, etc.) is supposed to be directly related to drives which are typically reference control signals for the following Behaviour Selection Network (BSN) block (like desired battery level, zero home distance, etc.). In order to satisfy its drives, the robot has to choose a precise behaviour from a pre-defined set of available behaviours, each one oriented to satisfy one or several contemporary drives. Up to this stage, the BSN is implemented through a spiking network with dynamic synapses, leaving opened the possibility to learn other behaviours better satisfying the strongest drive. This functionality within the BSN takes place at the highest layer in the insect brain architecture. Till now, there are not yet specific experiments that can demonstrate the existence of such a network in the Drosophila brain; therefore the hypothesized artificial BSN was maintained to represent the highest level control functionality. The BSN was endowed, at this stage, with auto-excitatory synapses to avoid a continuous switching among the selected behaviours.

The other block residing at the decision layer is Behavior Evaluation. Experiments on the MB less flies show that this function is ascribed to MBs, even if apparently separated by the common MB functionality. So also this block was modeled separately with respect to the main MB block and so called MB2,

as also mentioned above. This block evaluates the capability of the selected behaviour to satisfy the active drive, represented by a given setpoint to be reached.
As soon as a given behaviour is initiated (behaviour initiation is ascribed as a
specific CX role) the MB2 block starts an increasing inhibitory function on the
ongoing behaviour in order to completely inhibit this one if the drive is not
satisfied within a certain time window. In this case another behaviour wins the
competition and is selected.

The Motor layer contains the following blocks: The Description of Reflexive
Behaviours describes the fixed actions that allow the robot to take the right
direction in the case of punishment. Here additional functions are included, considering the fact that a fly, repetitively punished, can reach a "no-motion state":
i.e. the insect is frozen for a certain amount of time.

The Description of Behavior block describes the available behaviours that the
robot can follow. The type and number of the possible behaviours the robot can
exhibit depends on the robot applications. As an example implemented is the
targeting behaviour. This behaviour, when selected in the BSN, causes a series of
actions focussed at moving the robot towards the visual target that elicited that
behaviour, while maintaining it at the center of the visual scene. In the proposed
model a hierarchical procedure is used to solve possible conflicts between learned
behaviours and reflexive ones, in fact the reflexive block inhibits the activity of
other potential behaviours. However other conflict resolution strategies can be
used including a feedback into the behaviour learning loop.

The Motor Programs block contains all the possible elementary actions the
robot can perform. They are supposed, up to now, to be pre-programmed unless a wide space for hosting learning strategies exists, which is currently under
investigation. This block is strictly dependent on the robotic architecture to be
used. It contains a series of control signals for the wheels/legs in order to realize
the desired advancement, steering or rotation. In particular, dealing with legged
robots, the central Pattern Generator paradigm was taken into account. This approach was recently accompanied to some powerful theoretical conditions which
a-priori guarantee global exponential convergence to any imposed gait that the
structure is asked to show [9].

3   Software/Hardware Framework

In a modular architecture the mechanisms used by each module to access to the
shared computational resources are extremely important together with the communication rules. Modularity and functional separation, together with reusabil-
ity and robustness, are the most basic software design principles that can be
ensured in software applications. The aim of modularity is to encapsulate all
the physical and logical characteristics of the main entities to decouple specific
implementations, defining a set of access functions. For this reason, it is possible
to divide our structure in specific parts, in order to decouple its functionalities.
The Architecture, named **RealSim for Cognitive Systems (RS4CS)**, can be
structured as reported in Fig. 2 where five main elements have been identified:

The *Graphical User Interface (GUI)* provides tools to display real-time data while allowing the user to control robot and execute algorithms. It is directly connected to the *Algorithm module* in order to obtain data to show and to convey external commands during executions. Interconnected with the Algorithm module there are other two important parts of the architecture, the *Algorithm libraries*, useful to obtain specific and peculiar functionalities related to Algorithm implementations and the *Log Handler* dedicated to log fundamental information to create historical traces. Finally, *Robot Hierarchy* part gives an abstract view of robots, decoupled from specific implementations.

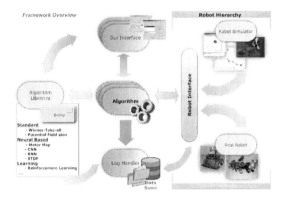

Fig. 2. Overview of the interactions between components in the software architecture for cognitive systems

An overview about already existing robotic simulation environments can be found in [17] where the novelty of the proposed framework are also underlined.

4   Robotic Platforms and Experiments

The software/hardware RS4CS framework implemented and evaluated, transparently uses, as a final actor, either a robot (wheeled, legged or hybrid) simulated in a detailed dynamical simulator (included within the simulation environment), or a real robot roving on a real environment. From the hardware point of view, mainly two robotic structures were used to test the architecture performance, one wheeled robot, the Rover, and one hybrid robot, the Tribot [10,11]. The latter appears in two different versions, adopting two different sensor configurations. Tribot I hosts contact, distance, sound, inertial and low-level light sensors; the visual architecture used here is the Surveyor SRV-1 Blackfin color camera, endowed with a series of image processing routines. Tribot II, hosts the new tiny version of the Eye-Ris visual processor [20], adopted for real time visual motion-based segmentation and classification, considered as a pre-processing functionality hosted in the insect optic lobe. From there, signals are sent to the CX block and the remainder of the insect brain model, hosted in the remote PC station. The Rover was equipped with contact, distance, sound and two different visual sensors: a classical camera and the Eye-Ris platform in a panoramic configuration, useful for implementing a stand alone, autonomously working model of the CX, where the orientation strategy is demonstrated in action [19]. For the testing of the motor layer in legged machines, also the MiniHex, a 12 dof autonomous walking minirobot was used [21]. The robot is able to communicate their whole sensory status to a host PC via a wireless communication. The proposed insect brain architecture was tested against the corresponding experiments already performed in the various worldwide laboratories on the fly. In particular the architecture was tested in experiments involving visual orientation, visual learning, visual detour against distractor, adaptive termination of behaviors, decision making in front of contradictory cues and others. Moreover, when experimental data are available, also robot experiments mimicking the damaged behaviours met in mutant flies were reproduced; more details about the experiments are reported in [16,18]. A series of different robotic platforms, as shown in Fig. 3, has been used to formalize robotic experiments in accordance to the neurobiological set-up used for insects in order to test the capabilities of the insect brain model.

Fig. 3. Robotic platforms used to evaluate the insect brain model

5   Definition of Scenarios

When a Cognitive architecture is designed and developed, one of the most important aspects to be considered is the definition of evaluation criteria and the creation of scenarios where the system performance can be evaluated. One of the most relevant attempts in this direction, can be found in the Darpa Project named BICA (Biologically Inspired Cognitive Architectures) that began in 2005 with the aim to create the next generation of Cognitive Architecture models of human artificial intelligence.Among the activities of the BICA, a core set of functions typical of a two-year-old human child was depicted with particular attention to cognitive, perceptual, and motor skills. These include behavioral tasks related to search, navigation, manipulation, memory, language, and three pathways to procedural knowledge: instruction, demonstration, and reinforcement/exploration [22].

From these experiences it is evident how several difficulties can be encountered when testing scenarios for cognitive architectures have to be designed. To facilitate the problem, we considered the formalization of scenarios like an integration process that involves several different elements that take part in the definition process. Due to the complexity of the problem, four different design principles have been considered.

Bottom-Up. A bottom-up process can be followed starting from the information about the basic behaviours of the robotic platforms taken into account. Each structure due to its mechanical peculiarities allows the definition of different basic behaviours that can be used in a scenario to solve a given task (e.g. the hybrid robot Tribot thanks to the frontal manipulator is able to move objects just pushing or carry them).

Top-down. The top-down approach is based on the formalization of scenarios that should be of interest for the robotic field. The idea is to include real life scenarios where the cognitive architecture can be evaluated considering the impact in solving open problems of interest for people producing an impact in the society (e.g. Rescue robots helping in post-disaster scenarios).

Biologically-driven. The validation of the insect brain model passes through tests and experiments that can show the similarity between the robot behaviour and the Drosophila. Starting from the experiments reported in literature, the elementary blocks that constitute the insect-inspired cognitive architecture are evaluated and compared with the biological data. The biologically-driven scenario definition is important to confirm the hypotheses formulated during the cognitive architecture design phase. Moreover, new experiments can be defined to be performed with wild-type and mutant flies to extract new data to be compared with the robot simulations and experiments to identify the part of the insect brain involved in these memory mechanisms.

Robot oriented. Finally the definition of scenarios can be considered following a robot-driven approach. Starting from the capabilities of the insect brain architecture, it is possible to extend the structure to solve tasks that are far beyond the drosophila capabilities. The relevant blocks of the architecture can be improved, in a simple way, expanding the memory available or duplicating elementary blocks. Following this design flow, the complexity of the scenarios and the insect brain computational model can grow up in parallel on the basis of the real fly's abilities to create a more powerful agent.

This is in line with the biological evidence that, for example bees brain can be considered as a grown model of the fly brain, where essentially the same areas can be identified (MB, CX, etc). This enables the enhanced capabilities of the bees (eg. labyrinth solving, social behaviour emergence, etc) with respect to the fly.

Among the proposed strategies for the design and assessment of robotic experiments, the biologically-driven and the robot-oriented approaches have been considered the most promising due to the direct links to the neurobiological results and to the possibility to further extend the robot capabilities slightly improving the insect brain blocks controlling the robot behaviour. The considered scenarios include situations of increasing complexity to show the acquisition of cognitive capabilities like multisensory integration, contradictory cues resolution, efficient information storage and retrieval. Those capabilities can be tested starting from classical exploration and foraging tasks, going up to tasks involving motivation, based on reward functions. The neural structures responsible for these behaviors have been very recently enriched with new substructures inspired by very recent discoveries in the insect counterparts. This gave the opportunity to design and simulate new networks that, via processes that can be described via reaction-diffusion dynamics, are able to lead to the emergence of complex behaviors like attention and expectation, which can be considered the basis of a cognitive behavior, i.e. the capability of planning ahead [23].

The experiments can be tailored to the sensory-motor loop available in each robotic structure. The scenarios envisaged will have to emphasize the model capabilities, using the robots as test beds.

6   Conclusion

In this paper some key results of a recent research activity among Neurogeneticians and Engineers to model an insect brain architecture are briefly presented. A block size model of an insect brain computational structure has been reported, outlining the main blocks and their specific roles and enhancing some emerging capabilities related to reaction-diffusion aspects, which open the way to a further refinement of the overall structure. A complete software/hardware framework has been developed in order to evaluate the insect brain model and performing experiments directly linked to the neurobiological experimental set-up. The developed architecture can be easily interfaced with both dynamic simulation environments and robotic platforms by using a communication interface layer in a client-server based topology.

Acknowledgments. The authors acknowledge the support of the European Commission under the projects FP7-ICT-2007-1 216227 SPARK II and FP7-ICT-2009-6 270182 EMICAB.

References

1. Webb, B., Consi, T.R.: Biorobotics: methods and applications. AAAI Press/MIT Press, Menlo Park (2001)
2. Dorigo, M., Stutzle, T.: Ant Colony Optimization. MIT Press (2004)
3. Srinivasan, M.V., et al.: Honeybee Navigation: Nature and Calibration of the Odometer. Science 287, 851 (2000)
4. Rind, F., Santer, R., Blanchard, J., Verschure, P.: Sensors and sensing in biology and engineering, springerwiennewyork ed. Barth, Humphrey, Secomb, ch. Locust's looming detectors for robot sensors (2003)
5. Webb, B., Scutt, T.: A simple latency dependent spiking neuron model of cricket phonotaxis. Biological Cybernetics 82(3), 247–269 (2000)

6. Arena, P., Fortuna, L., Frasca, M., Patané, L., Pavone, M.: Realization of a CNN-driven cockroach-inspired robot. In: Proc. of ISCAS (2006)
7. Watson, J., Ritzmann, R., Zill, S., Pollack, A.: Control of obstacle climbing in the cockroach, Blaberus discoidalis, I. Kinematics. J. Comp. Physiol. A 188, 39–53 (2002)
8. Cruse, H., Kindermann, T., Schumm, M., Dean, J., Schmitz, J.: Walknet a biologically inspired network to control six-legged walking. Neural Networks 11, 1435–1447 (1998)
9. Arena, E., Arena, P., Patané, L.: Efficient hexapodal locomotion control based on flow-invariant subspaces. In: Proc. of World Congress of IFAC, Milan, Italy (2011)
10. Arena, P., Patané, L., Pollino, M., Ventura, C.: Tribot: a new prototype of bio-inspired hybrid robot. In: Proc. of IEEE/RSJ International Conference on Intelligent RObots and Systems, St. Louis, Missouri, USA (2009)
11. Arena, P., De Fiore, S., Patané, L., Pollino, M., Ventura, C.: Stdp-based behavior learning on the TriBot robot. In: Proc. of SPIE, vol. 7365 (2009)
12. Triphan, T., Poeck, B., Neuser, K., Strauss, R.: Visual targeting of motor actions in climbing. Drosophila, Curr. Biol. 20, 663–668 (2010)
13. Joger, H., Kauf, C., Prochazka, U., Strauss, R.: The protocerebral bridge holds a representation for object positions – orientation studies in ocelliless and wild-type flies with partially occluded eyes. In: Proc. 33nd Goettingen Neurobiology Conference (2011)
14. Arena, P., Patané, L., Termini, P.S.: An insect brain computational model inspired by Drosophila melanogaster: Simulation results. In: Proc. of IJCNN, Barcelona, Spain (2010)
15. Arena, P., Berg, C., Patané, L., Strauss, R., Termini, P.S.: An insect brain computational model inspired by Drosophila melanogaster: Architecture description. In: Proc. of IJCNN, Barcelona, Spain (2010)
16. Arena, P., Patané, L., Termini, P.S.: Decision making processes in the fruit fly: a computational model. In: Proc. of 21th Italian Workshop on Neural Networks, Vietri sul Mare, Salerno, Italy (2011)
17. Arena, P., Cosentino, M., Patané, L., Vitanza, A.: SPARKRS4CS: a software/hardware framework for cognitive architectures. In: Proc. of SPIE Microtechnologies, Prague (2011)
18. Arena, P., De Fiore, S., Patané, L., Termini, P.S., Strauss, R.: Visual learning in Drosophila: application on a roving robot and comparisons. In: Proc. of SPIE Microtechnologies, Prague (2011)
19. Arena, P., De Fiore, S., Patané, L., Alba, L., Strauss, R.: Drosophila-inspired visual orientation model on the Eye-Ris platform: experiments on a roving robot. In: Proc. of SPIE Microtechnologies, Prague (2011)
20. Rodriguez-Vazquez, A., et al.: The Eye-RIS CMOS Vision System. In: Analog Circuit Design, pp. 15–32. Springer, Heidelberg (2007)
21. Arena, P., Fortuna, L., Frasca, M., Patané, L., Pollino, M.: An autonomous mini-hexapod robot controlled through a CNN-based CPG VLSI chip. In: Proc. of CNNA, Istanbul, Turkey, pp. 401–406 (2006)
22. Mueller, S.T., Jones, M., Minnery, S.: The BICA Cognitive Decathlon: A Test Suite for Biologically-Inspired Cognitive Agents (2007)
23. Arena, P., Patané, L., Termini, P.S.: An insect brain inspired neural model for object representation and expectation. In: International Joint Conference on Neural Networks, San Jose, California (2011)

Higher Brain Centers
for Intelligent Motor Control in Insects

Roland Strauss, Tammo Krause, Christian Berg, and Bianca Zäpf

Johannes Gutenberg-Universität Mainz, Institut für Zoologie III – Neurobiologie,
Col.-Kleinmann Weg 2,
55099 Mainz, Germany
rstrauss@uni-mainz.de

Abstract. The higher control of orientation, walking and gap climbing behavior in the fruit fly *Drosophila* is studied by neurogenetic means. An insect brain model is presented for the control of object approaches. The model comprises learning abilities of flies at two different time scales. A short-term orientation memory allows for the continued approach of objects that disappeared from sight. Flies can come back to the still invisible object even after a detour to a distracter object. A long-term memory allows for the storage of experience with particular types of objects in order to trigger avoidance behavior in the future instead of the default approach behavior. Moreover, we provide evidence that the highly adaptive and successful locomotion of flies relies also on short-term integrators, motor learning, body size representation and adaptive termination of behavior.

Keywords: Insect walking, insect motor control, insect orientation behavior, Drosophila neurogenetics, insect brain model.

1 Introduction

When comparing the performance of current, autonomously roving robots with the agility and maneuverability of insects one cannot help but notice the superiority of the time-tested biological systems. We study the walking, climbing and orientation behavior of the fruit fly *Drosophila melanogaster* in order to transfer control principles and algorithms from the biological model to technical systems. *Drosophila* flies can be classically conditioned with positive and negative reinforcers and they show operant learning. Plasticity of the nervous system is found at many time scales from seconds to potentially life long learning. Learning improves search and orientation behavior and locomotion as such. *Drosophila* offers unique non-invasive neurogenetic methods for the analysis of its nervous system since the fly serves as model organism for the geneticist since more than 100 years. The genome is fully sequenced since the year 2000.

The Walking Behavior of the Fly. Flies can walk on almost any substrate and at any orientation to the gravity vector thanks to two different attachment organs at the tips of the legs - claws for porous materials and adhesive pads called pulvilli for smooth

S. Jeschke, H. Liu, and D. Schilberg (Eds.): ICIRA 2011, Part II, LNAI 7102, pp. 56–64, 2011.

surfaces. Flies walk with up to 16 steps per second with every leg and can cover their own body length of 2.6mm with every step [1]. The standard coordination is the tripod gait which deviates towards a tetrapod coordination at the slower walking end. Excellent vision allows for optomotor compensation, color vision of objects, binocular vision within a range of less than 3mm and distance estimation by using parallax motion.

The Climbing Behavior of the Fly. Flies can climb over chiasms in the walkway of up to 1.6 times their own body length by a distinct climbing behavior [2]. Before they engage in this elegant behavior they have already measured the gap width visually. Only at gaps of about surmountable widths they lean out into the gap. The hind legs get closer and closer to the proximal edge. The middle legs, which have their foot holds at the proximal vertical wall, lift up the body into a horizontal position and the front legs stretch out as far as possible in order to reach the distal edge. If they succeed, a bridge is formed and the middle legs are released and placed on the distal vertical wall of the gap. Next, the hind legs are released and the body swings over to the distal side. The fly walks up and over the edge and continues walking at the distal horizontal surface. The whole attempt takes less than a second and needs to be studied with high speed cameras. At insurmountable gaps, the flies turn without a trial.

Genetic Manipulation of the Nervous System Using the GAL4/UAS System [3]. GAL4 is a transcription factor taken from the yeast genome. It does not naturally occur in the *Drosophila* genome but can be introduced at (almost) random positions with the help of a transposable element (P-element). Depending on the insertion position this P-element might come under the control of the regulatory region of a *Drosophila* gene. Then, GAL4 will be expressed in the same temporal (development-tal) and spatial (neuron type) pattern as the respective *Drosophila* gene. By itself, GAL4 has no meaning in a *Drosophila* cell nor, on a first approximation, does it hurt the cell. *Drosophila* labs all over the world have created thousands of GAL4 lines and have kept the ones with interesting expression patterns. The so called driver lines can be ordered from stock centers.

The natural docking sequence of GAL4 in the yeast genome is UAS (upstream activating sequence) and upon docking of GAL4 the yeast gene behind UAS is transcribed. Genes taken from any organism in the world can be cloned behind UAS, the construct be packed in a P-element and jumped into the *Drosophila* genome. Those lines are called the effector lines. For instance, green fluorescent protein (GFP) is taken from jelly fish and UAS-GFP used to visualize the expression patterns of GAL4 lines (review [4]).

A classical genetic cross between a GAL4 or driver line and a UAS or effector line leads to the expression of the effector gene in the temporal and spatial pattern determined by the GAL4 line in the nervous system of the offspring. An important effector for the functional analysis of the fly nervous system is the light chain of tetanus toxin. The genetic information is taken from a bacterium; the toxin silences neurons by blocking the exocytosis of neurotransmitters at the chemical synapses [5].

But sets of neurons can also be repaired in an otherwise mutant background. Partial rescue is a convenient approach for mapping memory functions in the brain [6]. Plasticity is restored by expressing the wild-type form of a learning gene in a set of neurons, which is determined by a GAL4 expression pattern, whereas the rest of the nervous system stays impaired in a mutant state for learning and memory.

2   Learning and Memory in the Central Complex for Approaching Objects

The central complex is a mirror-symmetrical, unpaired structure situated between and connecting the two protocerebral hemispheres of insect brains. It is composed of four neuropilar regions (Fig. 1). The large fan-shaped body has an anterior concavity in which the perfectly toroid-shaped ellipsoid body resides. A pair of noduli is found ventrally to the fan-shaped body and a protocerebral bridge posterior-dorsally to the fan-shaped body [7]. The four neuropils are connected by many projection systems which come in homologous sets of eight neurons. The fan-shaped body is subdivided in eight fans in the latero-lateral direction, the bridge is a linear array of 16 glomeruli and the ellipsoid body has 16 segments.

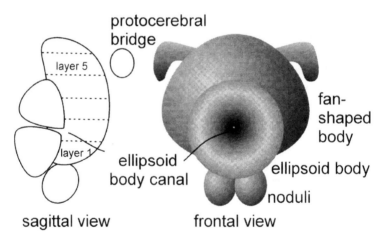

Fig. 1. Schematic representation of the central complex of *Drosophila melanogaster*. It is comprised of four neuropilar regions which are interconnected by many projection systems. The diameter of the fan-shaped body is about 100μm.

2.1   Experimental Evidence

Several learning functions in conjunction with orientation behavior have been assigned to the central complex as outcome of neurogenetic analyses. Flies can learn to avoid visual objects that have been previously negatively reinforced by a heat beam. The study was carried out at a flight simulator in which the stationary flying fly can steer a cylindrical visual panorama by its yaw torque. Two pairs of objects are presented alternatingly under four times 90°. Flight towards one type of objects is negatively reinforced by a heat beam, approach flights to the other pair are left unpunished. The flies learn to avoid the reinforced object and continue to avoid the punished objects after the heat has been turned off. The same type of experiment, when carried out on learning defective mutant flies, yields heat avoidance but no aftereffect after the heat has been turned off. Liu et al. [8] restored the learning function in learning mutants in just one of the six layers of the fan-shaped body and found a memory for the features of visual objects. Plasticity in layer 1 is needed to store and/or recall contour orientation whereas plasticity in layer 5 is needed to store/recall the elevation of objects in the panorama (Fig. 1).

Another important memory function of the ellipsoid body has been unraveled in walking flies. The animals can continue the approach of an attractive visual object for several seconds even after the object has been removed from their environment [9]. Later we could show that flies can come back to their previous, still invisible target even after a detour to a briefly presented visual distracter [10]. In contrast, mutant flies with a distorted ellipsoid body are lost in this situation and start random search behavior. Neurogenetic manipulation of the ring neurons in the ellipsoid body allowed us to firmly map this short-term orientation memory in the ellipsoid body. Three of the four groups of concentric ring neurons are necessary and the plasticity of two of the four systems is sufficient to bring about the orientation memory. We are currently unraveling the underlying biochemistry of the memory.

Where does the pertinent visual information come from? Accumulating evidence points to the protocerebral bridge as the entry point of visual object information. Partial rescue experiments of protocerebral bridge defective mutant flies restored the ability to walk straight towards objects [11] and to visually target the contra-lateral side in climbing experiments [12]. This led to the conclusion that the protocerebral bridge holds a representation of the azimuth angle of visual objects. Moreover, we have shown that the bridge influences step length differentially on the two sides of the body and most probably through the horizontal fiber system. This projection system connects the glomeruli of the bridge of one side with the contra-lateral accessory area of the central complex called ventral lobes. These lobes, in turn, are the starting point of descending projections to the motor centers in the thoracic nervous system.

2.2   The Central Complex Model

The central complex model for the control of object approaches uses known projection systems to explain, and reproduce in robots, the outcome of the above experiments [13]. The preprocessed information on the azimuth position of objects is conveyed to the protocerebral bridge (Fig. 2A). By means of the horizontal fiber system the information is used to enhance the step size contra-laterally to the eye on which the image of the most salient object falls. Without stimulation by the bridge the ipsi-lateral side will show just a basic step size. (This step size has been experimentally determined in protocerebral-bridge defective mutants [14] [15]). In effect, the fly will turn towards the object. It will continue to turn until the image of the object falls onto the binocular range of the compound eyes (Fig. 2B). In the model the binocular range is represented by the innermost glomeruli of the bridge. The step size is enhanced on both sides of the body and the fly will accelerate. As an exception and matter of fact of the anatomy of the horizontal fiber system the outermost glomeruli 8 on each side are connected ipsi-laterally. In the model they represent the rear visual field. In accord with the model, flies indeed turn away from objects that appear in their rear visual field.

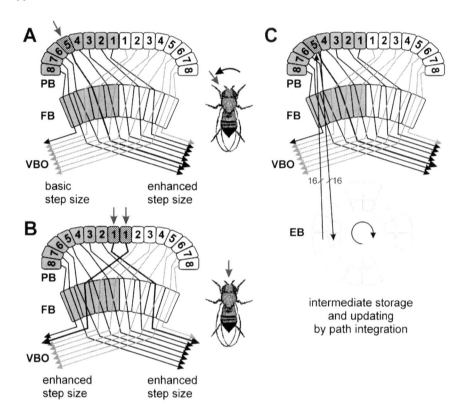

Fig. 2. Functional central complex model of object approach. **A.** The azimuth angle of a target is represented on the protocerebral bridge (PB) ipsi-laterally to the eye seeing it. By virtue of the horizontal fiber system of projection neurons from the PB through the fan-shaped body (FB) to the ventral bodies (VBO) step sizes are enhanced contra-laterally to the representation on the PB. **B.** The fly will turn until the object is seen by the binocular ranges of both eyes which are represented by the innermost glomeruli of the PB. Both body sides will enhance their step lengths. **C.** All the information entering the PB is copied to the ellipsoid body (EB; for clarity only one of the 16 glomeruli-to-segment connections is shown). If the target disappears from sight, the EB will feed information back to the PB which is updated by path integration. Its concentric ring structure seems ideal for translating body centered into world centered coordinates.

On its way from the bridge to the ventral lobes the horizontal fiber system passes through the fan-shaped body (and has synapses there). Our model assumes that the fan-shaped body acts like a look-up table for previous experience with the particular target object. The default state of the fly will be 'approach', but if previous negative experience is stored in the fan-shaped body, the step-length enhancement can be switched there from the contra-lateral to the ipsi-lateral body side and the fly will turn away from the object.

In our model (Fig. 2C) the ellipsoid body receives copies of all the visual input to the bridge via described 1-to-1 connections from glomeruli to segments [7]. If acute visual information stops, for instance due to transient occlusion, the ellipsoid body will replace the acute visual input to the bridge by input updated by path integration. The ellipsoid body consists of an inner and an outer concentric ring. This architecture would be ideally suited to represent body centered and world centered coordinates, respectively. In that way the ellipsoid body is able to bridge short times without sighting of the target object until after several seconds the typical errors of path integration are getting too large. The central complex model has been successfully implemented on wheeled roving robots.

3   Intelligent Motor Control beyond the Current Model

This chapter summarizes further achievements in motor control found in the fruit fly *Drosophila*. These recent findings of our lab are not yet integrated in the above central complex model because the relevant neuronal projection systems are not yet identified. Some of these control functions are based on the action of other brain regions like the mushroom bodies of the insect brain. Evidence accumulates that these known centers for olfactory learning and memory are critically involved as well in certain visual tasks and some non-olfactory learning functions.

3.1   An Integrator for the Orientation in Gradients

The orientation behavior of flies in noisy gradients is significantly more stable than predicted for chemotactic behavior. Integration of information straightens the paths, assists in finding the global optimum rather than a local one in a noisy gradient and helps to disambiguate decisions between targets of almost identical salience. Integration in neurobiological terms means plasticity and the need for plasticity can be mapped in the *Drosophila* nervous system using the GAL4/UAS system. Our first results point to the central complex as the seat of the integrator.

3.2   Motor Learning

Gap climbing flies improve their success rate and their speed of action when they perform at least 50 successful transitions within a few hours. A short-term memory can open out into a long-term, probably life-long memory. Analyses with high-speed motion pictures show, that many parameters of the climbing behavior improve a little bit rather than pointing to one big improvement in a single variable. A biologically meaningful modeling of motor learning is complex, as a trial-to-trial storage of the constituting parameters like single leg actions and probably even individual joint actions seems necessary in order to be able to find the relevant differences between an unsuccessful and a successful approach.

3.3   A Representation of Body Size in the Brain

Intact *Drosophila* flies limit their climbing efforts to approximately surmountable gaps [2]. Small flies systematically try to overcome only smaller chasms in the walkway whereas larger individuals try to surmount also wider gaps. The initiation of a climbing attempt depends on the own body size in relation to the width of the chasm, which is visually estimated. Body size critically depends on the food and temperature conditions during the larval stages and is not just genetically determined. Therefore, body size has to be learned after hatching. Indeed, the decisions of learning defective mutant flies are independent of their individual body size. They try to overcome chasms which are clearly insurmountable (Fig. 3). We rescued the climbing adaption in a learning mutant background by expressing the wild-type form of a learning gene in parts of the nervous system with the help of various GAL4-lines. We could localize the function in the central complex. Furthermore, we analyzed when and how wild-type flies learn their body size. Flies, which had been raised in constant darkness until the experiment showed significantly more climbing attempts at insurmountable gaps than their siblings which were raised under normal dark-light cycles. We conclude that the own body size is learned with the help of visual experience.

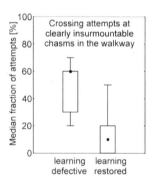

Fig. 3. Median fraction of crossing attempts at a clearly insurmountable gap of 5mm width. Boxes denote 25%-/75%-quartiles and whiskers the entire range of the distribution. Learning defective flies try hard where flies with restored learning function mostly turn back without futile attempts.

3.4   Termination of Inappropriate Behavior

A robot just programmed to approach an object will do so - regardless of unforeseen obstacles. A fly that encounters an unforeseen obstacle will terminate the approach behavior and start another type of behavior. Giving up or continuing a once chosen behavior requires delicate balancing. Brains that give up too easily will create inconsistent, erratic behavior. Brains, on the other hand, that insist on inappropriate behavior will waist time and energy. Flies with ablated or genetically silenced mushroom bodies show prolonged approaches and inappropriate continuation of chosen behavior that became ill-adapted. We try to integrate this careful balance in an extended model of locomotor control for roving robots.

3.5   Conclusion

The fruit fly *Drosophila* proves to be an excellent role model for future autonomous mobile systems with artificial cognitive control. Flies improve their performance in motor tasks by storing information gained by exercising. We found signs of a body representation in *Drosophila* used for determining chances before engaging in a given task. For uninterrupted orientation flies are able to bridge lacking sensory information by stored information and path integration. They are clearly not directly driven by sensory input like chemotactic bacteria are. Rather, sensory information is stored, compared with previous experience and used dependent on the current needs of the insect. Last not least flies can not just determine appropriate behavior but also give up on ongoing behavior that turns out to be non-productive.

Acknowledgments. This work is kindly supported by the EU project EMICAB (FP7-ICT, No. 270182) and by the German Science Foundation under STR590/2-4.

References

1. Strauss, R., Heisenberg, M.: Coordination of legs during straight walking and turning in *Drosophila melanogaster*. J. Comp. Physiol. A 167(3), 403–412 (1990)
2. Pick, S., Strauss, R.: Goal-driven behavioral adaptations in gap-climbing *Drosophila*. Curr. Biol. 15, 1473–1478 (2005)
3. Brand, A.H., Perrimon, N.: Targeted gene expression as a means of altering cell fates and generating dominant phenotypes. Development 118(2), 401–415 (1993)
4. Brand, A.H.: GFP in *Drosophila*. Trends Genet. 11(8), 324–325 (1995)
5. Sweeney, S.T., Broadie, K., Keane, J., Niemann, H., O'Kane, C.J.: Targeted expression of tetanus toxin light chain in *Drosophila* specifically eliminates synaptic transmission and causes behavioral defects. Neuron 14(2), 341–351 (1995)
6. Zars, T., Fischer, M., Schulz, R., Heisenberg, M.: Localization of a short-term memory in *Drosophila*. Science 288(5466), 672–675 (2000)
7. Hanesch, U., Fischbach, K.F., Heisenberg, M.: Neuronal architecture of the central complex in *Drosophila melanogaster*. Cell Tissue Res. 257(2), 343–366 (1989)
8. Liu, G., Seiler, H., Wen, A., Zars, T., Ito, K., Wolf, R., Heisenberg, M., Liu, L.: Distinct memory traces for two visual features in the *Drosophila* brain. Nature 439(7076), 551–556 (2006)
9. Strauss, R., Pichler, J.: Persistence of orientation toward a temporarily invisible landmark in *Drosophila melanogaster*. J. Comp. Physiol. A 182(4), 411–423 (1998)
10. Neuser, K., Triphan, T., Mronz, M., Poeck, B., Strauss, R.: Analysis of a spatial orientation memory in *Drosophila*. Nature 453, 1244–1247 (2008)
11. Poeck, B., Triphan, T., Neuser, K., Strauss, R.: Locomotor control by the central complex in *Drosophila* – an analysis of the *tay bridge* mutant. Dev. Neurobiol. 68, 1046–1058 (2008)

12. Triphan, T., Poeck, B., Neuser, K., Strauss, R.: Visual targeting of motor actions in climbing *Drosophila*. Curr. Biol. 20, 663–668 (2010)
13. Strauss, R., Berg, C.: The central control of oriented locomotion in insects - towards a neurobiological model. In: WCCI 2010 IEEE World Congress on Computational Intelligence, Barcelona, Spain, July 18-23, pp. 3919–3926 (2010)
14. Strauss, R., Hanesch, U., Kinkelin, M., Wolf, R., Heisenberg, M.: *No-bridge* of *Drosophila melanogaster*: portrait of a structural brain mutant of the central complex. J. Neurogenet. 8(3), 125–155 (1992)
15. Strauss, R.: The central complex and the genetic dissection of locomotor behaviour. Curr. Opin. Neurobiol. 12(6), 633–638 (2002)

An Insect-Inspired, Decentralized Memory
for Robot Navigation

Holk Cruse[1] and Rüdiger Wehner[2]

[1] Biological Cybernetics, and Center for Excellence CITEC,
University of Bielefeld, Bielefeld, Germany
[2] Brain Research Institute, University of Zürich, Winterthurerstrasse 190, CH-8057 Zürich,
Switzerland, and Biocenter, University of Würzburg, Germany
holk.cruse@uni-bielefeld.de, rwehner@zool.unizh.ch

Abstract. Navigation in animals is often discussed to require a 'cognitive map'. Here we propose an artificial neural system that consists of a network allowing for both path integration and landmark guidance. This network is able to describe experiments with desert ants and honey bees, the latter eventually interpreted as to show the existence of a cognitive map. In contrast, our network represents a decentralized system containing procedural memory elements and a motivation network, but no "central control room" or "global neural workspace". Its output can directly be used to control the forward movement of a robot.

Keywords: navigation, landmark guidance, path integration, cognitive map neural network.

1   Introduction

Since the early 1990s, a still ongoing discussion concerns the question whether a decentralized controller suffices to produce intelligent behaviour or whether - and under which conditions - a "cognitive" controller is required. An intensely debated paradigm concerns animal navigation and specifically the question whether a so-called cognitive map is used by animals or not.

Tolman [1] has defined the term 'cognitive map' in an only loosely way: "... the incoming impulses are usually worked over and elaborated in the central control room into a tentative, cognitive-like map of the environment. And it is this tentative map, indicating routes and paths and environmental relationships, which finally determines what responses, if any, the animal will finally release." ([1], p.192). Recently, Menzel and his coworkers have defined a 'cognitive map' as a system in which "spatial relations between environmental features [are] coherently represented" ([2], p. 3045) - as "a common spatial memory of geometric organisation (a map) ... as in other animals and humans" ([3], p. 429). Correspondingly, cognitive scientists nowadays often use the term 'global neural workspace' (see [4] for a review). Functionally, this term describes a supposed mechanism by which different elements stored separately in memory can deliberately be connected in various ways, for example to allow for

S. Jeschke, H. Liu, and D. Schilberg (Eds.): ICIRA 2011, Part II, LNAI 7102, pp. 65–74, 2011.
© Springer-Verlag Berlin Heidelberg 2011

the invention of new behaviours. Applied to the problem of navigation, this means that different memory elements, for example vectors representing the locations of two food sites, having been learned separately, may be used for common computation. In contrast, in a decentralized or, as it is often called, reactive system such a combination of separately stored vectors for computation is not possible. In such a reactive system, a memory content can only be used within the context in which it has been learned making the system faster but less flexible. (For an example how a reactive system can be transformed to constitute a cognitive system see [5]).

In the present account we design an architecture that allows us to test whether a distributed network based on the main experimental results obtained in the study of desert ant navigation is able to simulate the behavioural performances of ants and bees. A positive result would question statements of earlier authors [2, 3, 6] and would provide a non-cognitive solution for navigational problems.

The basic experimental results on which the simulation is based are the following (for references see the reviews [7-10]). Desert ants are extremely skillful long-distance navigators, which during their foraging journeys ('outbound trip') can leave their underground colonies for distances of more than ten thousand times their body length, and then return to their point of departure ('inbound trip'), an often inconspicuous hole in the desert ground, with amazing accuracy. Concerning the basic mechanism, path integration (PI) [11-15] we just assume that the animal possesses a PI vector memory, in which the nest-to-food vector is stored ('reference vector'), and that at any one time during an inbound and outbound trip the animal compares the state of its 'current vector' with the reference vector. If the former matches the latter, the path integrator has acquired its zero-state, and the animal has reached the goal. As any PI system is prone to cumulative errors, a 'zero-vector ant' that has not arrived exactly at the goal performs systematic search movements that are centred about the point at which the PI had reached its zero state (Area-concentrated search [16-19]). There is, in addition, landmark guidance [10,20,21] to further aid the localization of the (usually inconspicuous) nest entrance. Experimental results indicate that one or several 'snapshots' of the landmark scene at the home site are taken and memorized. Later this snapshot view, or an individual signpost within this view, is used to guide the animal from any place near the home site to the nest entrance. We will call this landmark a 'home landmark'. Correspondingly, landmark views can be acquired at the food source ('food landmarks'). In addition to landmarks at the nest and food sites, landmarks distributed in the area between these two sites may be used for navigation. Any such landmark view can be associated with a specific walking direction termed 'local vector'. As these landmarks are visited by the animals en route, they will be called 'route landmarks'.

Ants are able to learn and store (i) more than one reference vector pointing to more than one food site and (ii) several landmark-defined positions within their foraging terrain, and (iii) more than one landmark-defined route. If a familiar landmark is recognized, ants follow the corresponding (landmark-associated) local vector rather than their PI vector. Landmarks are stored and retrieved only in specific contexts. One of the most important (internal, motivational) contexts is whether the ant is on its 'outbound' or 'inbound' trip, i.e., whether it walks from home to food or from food to home, respectively.

2   The Model

To simulate basic properties of ant navigation during foraging the following network
has been implemented (Fig. 1). The net consists of three main parts: (i) a system being
responsible for path integration (PI) as depicted at the left hand side of Fig.
1, (ii) a
recurrent network controlling different motivations (Fig. 1, upper right, in red), and
(iii) a bank of procedural memories (horizontal row of blue boxes in the center of
Fig. 1). Each of these procedural elements receives sensory input, indicated by the
short bar at the upper left of each box (e.g., visual input concerning a specific
landmark), and input from the motivation network. As outputs these memory elements
provide vectors determining a walking direction (relative to an absolute external
reference system defined by a compass). The path integrator system represents a
procedure, too, containing memory elements (Fig. 1, blue boxes, upper left) and
providing a corresponding output vector. All these sensorimotor, or procedural,
memories are independent of each other. Their output values undergo a weighted
summation. The weights are dynamically determined by a lateral inhibition network
that, based on the vector lengths, determines a confidence or salience value for each
memory element. To keep the simulation as simple as possible, learning processes as
such are not simulated, but memories may be switched off or on by hand to simulate
different learning states. To study the behaviour of an agent controlled by this network
we apply an environment containing a nest (home) and two food sources (A and B). In
the experiments presented in Fig. 2, there are 12 route landmarks distributed over the
space between home and the two food sources (Further experiments including different
landmarks as well as more details concerning the model are presented in [22]).

In the following the different parts of the network will be described in more detail.
Let us begin with the path integrator. As detailed models are available (e.g., [23,24],
for a comprehensive review of types of model, see [25,26]), this part is simulated here
in an abstracted form only. The path integrator (not shown in Fig. 1) provides the
'current vector' (Fig. 1, left, Curr. Vect.). If a food source is detected, the actual
current vector is stored as a long term memory (e.g. Mem A, Fig. 1, upper left) and is
termed 'reference vector'. If the food source is rich enough, so that further visits are
intended, this vector might (and can be, by bees and ants) stored as a long term
memory element.

The stored reference vector can be used to later control visits of this food source by
subtracting the current vector from the reference vector (Fig. 1, upper left, circle
containing a subtraction symbol: Mem() – Curr. Vect.). The difference provides
angles describing the walking direction (defined relative to an absolute direction
given by a compass) and the remaining distance to the goal. The same system
controlling these 'outbound' walks can be used to control the walks from food back to
home ('inbound' walks), when the goal vector refers to the home site, i.e., has zero
length. The output of this system is represented in Fig. 1 by box PI. Before further
computation, the output vector of this box is normalized to show a length of 1.

Motivation network: To use this system for navigation, at least one basic decision must be made. Is the agent in inbound mode or in outbound mode? A further decision is necessary if the agent has learned the position of two different food sources, A and B. Which food source should be selected? On a higher level, the agent may furthermore have the ability to choose between foraging behaviour and any other type of behaviour. To take a simple example, we use as a second behaviour 'stay', i.e. stay in the nest. All these decisions are formed by a recurrent neural network (Fig. 1, red; units connected by double headed arrows or inhibitory connections), the units of which are called 'motivation' units here. A motivation unit can adopt a value between 0 and 1. The connections between these units (for technical details see [22, 27, 28]) are designed in a way that the three pairs (inbound – outbound), (forage – stay) and (sourceA – sourceB) are connected by mutually inhibitory weights (Fig. 1, dashed red lines). Only one unit of each pair can be active after the net has relaxed to a stable state. If unit forage is active, either unit sourceA or sourceB is active. The output of these units determines which memory content can be used by the vector navigation system (see input to boxes MemA and MemB in Fig. 1). The decision between units sourceA and sourceB may be a random decision or may be determined by other contents of the agent's memory. Correspondingly, a decision between inbound and outbound is made by sensory input to the corresponding units. For example, if food has been found, this stimulus activates unit 'inbound' (not depicted in Fig. 1). The motivation unit for 'outbound' controls the output of the memory elements (MemA, MemB). If outbound is switched off, their output will be zero. Thus, path integration depends on two motivations, sourceA or sourceB, and inbound or outbound, as is the case for the procedural memories that will be described next.

Route landmarks: After having learned the global vectors (MemA, MemB) pointing to the corresponding food sources, the agent may in addition learn specific route landmarks situated anywhere in the landscape between home and food sites. As mentioned in the Introduction, ants can learn 'local vectors' associated with each landmark or sets of landmarks. When having perceived a learned landmark, the animal follows a specific angle (relative to an absolute direction given by a compass). In the simulation the walking direction is simply provided as soon as the agent enters the catchment area.

For the simulations shown in Fig. 2 we assume that the agent has learned three route landmarks walking from home to food source A and three other route landmarks for the way back from A to home. Similarly, it has learned three further route landmarks on the way from home to source B (outbound) and three more route landmarks from B to home (inbound). The three long term memory elements belonging to one trip are graphically packed into one box, leading to four such boxes (see Fig. 1). To simplify the drawing, only one output vector is depicted. Note that no information is stored that concerns the spatial/temporal order according to which the landmarks may be visited.

A given landmark memory is only active if (i) the appropriate motivation unit (inbound or outbound) and (ii) the motivation unit concerning the actual goal (sourceA, sourceB) are active (see two motivation inputs for each box in Fig. 1).

How to deal with the output values provided by the procedural memories? Each procedure provides an output vector, consisting of an angle (Fig. 1, dashed arrows) and a vector length (Fig. 1, solid arrows). The vector of a route landmark vector is set to a length of 1 when the landmark was perceived. However, when the walk continues, some kind of 'forgetting' takes place. After 15 steps, the vector length of this route landmark decreases to zero.

Home and food landmarks: As mentioned, ants have been shown to use also landmarks that define particular places such as the home or a food site (for specific imulations see [29-31]). In our simulation we assume that there are three such procedures stored, that when stimulated provide an angle leading the agent to the corresponding goal, i.e., to either food source A, food source B, or home (Fig. 1: fLMA, fLMB and hLM, respectively) being stored in the form of a 'snapshot'. As for the landmark vectors explained above, the food memories and home memories are controlled by double motivational input (as depicted in Fig. 1).

Area concentrated search: Furthermore, a network consisting of elements ASCon and ASCoff, as well as a random generator (rand.gen) and a nonlinear function f(d) (see Fig. 1), that will not be detailed here (see however [22]), is able to control area concentrated search (ACS).

Finally we must implement ways of how to combine the outputs of the different procedures: To accomplish this task the angular output values of the active procedural memories are subject to a weighted summation. The weights, or 'salience values', are determined in the following way. The vector lengths (but not the angle values) provided by the procedures are given to a one-layered feedforward lateral inhibition network. This network is shown by the boxes "Lat. Inhibition" in Fig. 1. Lateral inhibition has the effect that there will be one winner while all other output values are zero or nearly zero when there is a large difference between the competitors. If the difference between two strong competitors is small, there will be no winner but only some kind of minor decrease of both salience values. However, the weights of the Lateral Inhibition network itself are chosen sufficiently strong to guarantee that in the simulation, with one exception noted below, there will always be one winner. In our Lateral Inhibition network, the connections between the units are basically symmetric using fixed inhibitory weights of b = -0.4. There are however two exceptions from complete symmetry. First, within the landmark procedures, there are inhibitory influences from the food- and home elements to those representing the route landmarks, but there are no influences in the opposite direction. This structure has the effect that information gained from landmarks signalling food or home will be weighted stronger than information signalling route landmarks. Second, the connections between the path integrator and the random walk procedure are separated from those of the landmark procedures (indicated by the separation of the two boxes "Lat. Inhibition" in Fig. 1). In the former case, there are situations were both vector lengths may show similar values leading to a mixed contribution of the random generator output and the path integrator output.

70   H. Cruse and R. Wehner

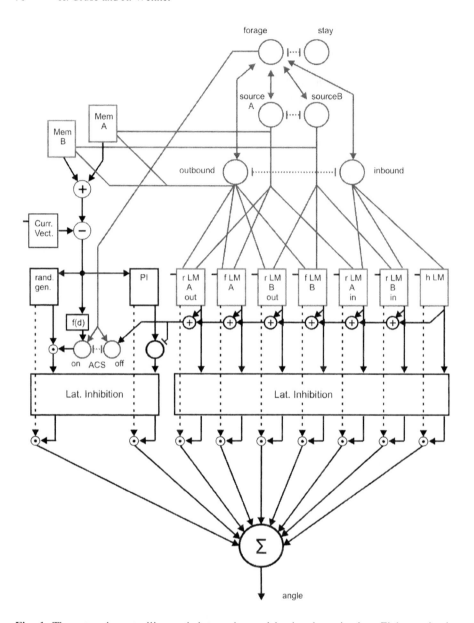

Fig. 1. The network controlling path integration and landmark navigation. Eight motivation units (red), a bank of memory elements shown in blue, (Mem A, Mem B) and seven further elements (two food landmark elements, fLMA, fLMB, one home landmark element, hLM, and four combined route landmark elements, rLMAout, rLMBout, rLMAin, rLMBin, lower right). The path integrator is schematically depicted at lower left (Curr. Vect, PI). Box rand.gen. and the motivation units ACS on, off control "area-concentrated search" walks. For further details see text.

How are the salience values used that are produced by the Lateral Inhibition network? As indicated in Fig. 1, each procedure has two output values, the vector length (full arrows), and the angle, represented as a vector with normalized length (dashed arrows). The vector is now multiplied by the salience value and then all these vectors are simply summed up (depicted by the unit marked by $\sum$ in Fig. 1). Therefore, the salience values weight the contribution of the different procedures. Summing up the weighted vectors and finally using the angle of the resulting vector would in principle correspond to calculation of the weighted mean of all angles. However, as mentioned above, there is always only one procedure exhibiting a salience value much higher than those of the other procedures. In particular, the salience of the PI element is zero whenever any landmark memory is active. This is guaranteed by the inhibitory influence mentioned above in the context of the area concentrated search. As explained earlier the network only provides an angle determining the walking direction which can directly be applied to a network controlling six-legged walking, as for example Walknet [32]. The length of the motor output vector, corresponding to velocity, is not controlled by the network but assumed to be a fixed value of ten length units in the simulation.

3   Results

Using this network, several experiments have been simulated using the environment depicted in Fig. 2. Here we will only report on one experiment that illustrates the ability of finding new shortcuts. Using shortcuts has often been used as an argument supporting the application of a cognitive map. In this experiment the ant has learned to visit two food sites (food A and food B) by running from the nest site independently to either food A or food B. Now let us assume that the ant has once arrived at site A but does not find food there (because the reward has been removed by the experimenter). Would it then run directly to site B? As illustrated in Fig. 2, the agent leaves home walking to food source A, because motivation unit sourceA is highly activated. Starting from home (yellow circle) to food source A, the agent is first controlled by path integration and thus follows a straight line which points from home to site A. As the agent reaches the catchment area of the first route landmark (red circle), the corresponding memory element takes over control. We have chosen the direction and the length of the local vectors in such a way that the agent will normally meet another landmark. The second landmark will then guide the agent to the third one. The last landmark provides an angle leading to the food source.

However, as the agent having arrived at site A is unsuccessful there (no food is provided), the value of the motivation unit sourceA is decreased (the input for stimulus 'food' is not shown in Fig. 1). Due to the properties of the motivation net – the motivation unit 'forage' is still running – motivation unit sourceB is activated. Consequently, the agent is immediately heading towards food source B (Fig. 2). This section of its path is controlled by path integration, as the agent does not meet any landmark. (If the agent had met an outbound route landmark associated with food source B, this landmark element would have guided the agent to site B). After the agent has arrived at food site B and has been rewarded there, the inbound motivation unit gets activated and the outbound motivation unit shut off. The agent would now move back towards home (Fig. 2, blue squares) – exactly as a real ant does ([8] and B. Voegeli, M. Knaden and R. Wehner, unpublished results). As the local vector to the first inbound route landmark is too short, path integration takes over.

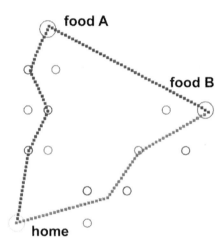

Fig. 2. Walk from home to food source A. As there is no food, the agent performs a short cut to food source B. After having found food, it returns to home using one route landmark. The catchment areas of the landmark elements home, and the two food sources A and B are shown by circles coloured in yellow and green, respectively. Catchment areas of route landmarks are shown in red or blue for outbound and inbound landmarks, respectively. Outbound walk is depicted by red squares, inbound walk by blue squares. For further explanations see text.

To avoid possible misunderstandings let us recall that except for the current vector within the PI system, our network does not have the ability to subtract two vectors stored in any of the memory elements (for example two food vectors). If this were possible, the behavior of the agent could be explained as resulting from a subtraction (B-A), because the resulting vector describes the route taken by the agent. Actually, however, only the memory of vector B is used. This is possible because the effect produced by vector A is given in the form of the already performed movement from the nest to site A. With its current vector numerically corresponding to vector A, the agent now continues to walk until its current vector state equals that of its reference vector, i.e. vector B, and when this has been accomplished has arrived at site B. Steering along the novel route A-to-B has been governed completely by the ant's path integrator. Once food has been picked up at site B, the ant reverses the sign of its reference vector, which in our model is realized by switching off the output of memory element B, and walks directly home to the starting point.

4   Discussion

Taken together, our network is able to "allow[s] the bee to perform novel shortcuts and to choose between two potential goals, the hive and the feeder" (Menzel et al. [2], p. 3044). However, contrary to the authors' conclusion, the spatial behaviour observed in the bees does not necessarily mean that a 'cognitive map' is in charge, which Menzel and his coworkers define as a "central integrator state" [33].

In our network, which to the best of our knowledge is the first approach to include path integration and landmark guidance, there is no information exchange between the different memory elements. Each memory element only has access to its "private" data. In other words, there is no cognitive map implemented in the sense defined in the Introduction. Nevertheless, the system allows for novel shortcuts - a behavioural property that is often used as a strong hint for the existence of a cognitive map - as well as other navigation behaviours observed in desert ants and honey bees [22]. As a next step this network will be tested on a physical robot.

Acknowledgments. This work has been supported by the Center of Excellence 'Cognitive Interaction Technology' (EXC 277), the EC project EMICAB # FP7 – 270182 (H.C.) and by the Humboldt Foundation (R.W.).

References

1. Tolman, E.C.: Cognitive maps in rats and men. Psychol. Rev. 55, 189–208 (1948)
2. Menzel, R., Greggers, U., Smith, A., Berger, S., Brandt, R., Brunke, S., Bundrock, G., Hülse, S., Plümpe, T., Schaupp, F., Schüttler, E., Stach, S., Stindt, J., Stollhoff, N., Watzl, S.: Honey bees navigate according to a map-like spatial memory. Proc. Natl. Acad. Sci. USA. 102, 3040–3045 (2005)
3. Menzel, R., Brembs, B., Giufra, M.: Cognition in invertebrates. In: Kaas, J.H. (ed.) Evolution of Nervous Systems. Evolution of nervous systems in invertebrates, vol. 2, pp. 403–442. Academic Press, New York (2007)
4. Cleeremans, A.: Computational correlates of consciousness. Progress in Brain Research 150, 81–98 (2005)
5. Cruse, H., Schilling, M.: Getting cognitive. In: Bläsing, B., Puttke, M., Schack, T. (eds.) The Neurocognition of Dance, pp. 53–74. Psychology Press, London (2010)
6. Gould, J.L.: The locale map of honey bees: do insects have cognitive maps? Science 232, 861–863 (1986)
7. Wehner, R.: Desert ant navigation: how miniature brains solve complex tasks. Karl von Frisch Lecture. J. Comp. Physiol. A 189, 579–588 (2003)
8. Wehner, R.: The desert ant's navigational toolkit: procedural rather than positional knowledge. J. Inst. Navigation 55, 101–114 (2008)
9. Ronacher, B.: Path integration as the basic navigation mechanism of the desert ant Cataglyphis fortis (Hymenoptera: Formicidae). Myrm. News 11, 53–62 (2008)
10. Cheng, K., Narendra, A., Sommer, S., Wehner, R.: Traveling in clutter: navigation in the central Australian desert ant Melophorus bagoti. Behav. Processes 80, 261–268 (2009)
11. Wehner, R., Labhart, T.: Polarization vision. In: Warrant, E., Nilsson, D.E. (eds.) Invertebrate Vision, pp. 291–348. Cambridge University Press, Cambridge (2006)

12. Müller, M., Wehner, R.: Wind and sky as compass cues in desert ant navigation. Naturwissenschaften 94, 589–594 (2007)
13. Wittlinger, M., Wehner, R., Wolf, H.: The ant odometer: stepping on stilts and stumps. Science 312, 1965–1967 (2007)
14. Wehner, R., Srinivasan, M.V.: Path integration in insects. In: Jeffery, K.J. (ed.) The Neurobiology of Spatial Behaviour, pp. 9–30. Oxford University Press, Oxford (2003)
15. Sommer, S., Wehner, R.: The ant's estimation of distance travelled: experiments with desert ants, Cataglyphis fortis. J. Comp. Physiol. A 190, 1–6 (2004)
16. Wehner, R., Srinivasan, M.V.: Searching behaviour of desert ants, genus Cataglyphis (Formicidae, Hymenoptera). J. Comp. Physiol. 142, 315–338 (1981)
17. Müller, M., Wehner, R.: The hidden spiral: systematic search and path integration in desert ants, Cataglyphis fortis. J. Comp. Physiol. A 175, 525–530 (1994)
18. Merkle, T., Knaden, M., Wehner, R.: Uncertainty about nest position influences systematic search in desert ants. J. Exp. Biol. 209, 3545–3549 (2006)
19. Merkle, T., Wehner, R.: Desert ants use foraging distance to adapt the nest search to the uncertainty of the path integrator. Behav. Ecol. 21, 349–355 (2010)
20. Wehner, R., Michel, B., Antonsen, P.: Visual navigation in insects: coupling egocentric and geocentric information. J. Exp. Biol. 199, 129–140 (1996)
21. Sommer, S., von Beeren, C., Wehner, R.: Multiroute memories in desert ants. Proc. Natl. Acad. Sci. USA 105, 317–322 (2008)
22. Cruse, H., Wehner, R.: No Need for a Cognitive Map: Decentralized Memory for Insect Navigation. PLoS Comput. Biol. 7(3), e1002009 (2011)
23. Hartmann, G., Wehner, R.: The ant's path integration system: a neural architecture. Biol. Cybern. 73, 483–497 (1995)
24. Haferlach, T., Wessnitzer, J., Mangan, M., Webb, B.: Evolving a neural model of insect path integration. Adapt. Behav. 15, 273–287 (2007)
25. Vickerstaff, R.J., Cheung, A.: Which coordinate system for modelling path integration? J. Theor. Biol. 263, 242–261 (2010)
26. Cheung, A., Vickerstaff, R.: Finding the Way with a Noisy Brain. PLoS Comput. Biol. 6, e1000992 (2010)
27. Kühn, S., Beyn, W.-J., Cruse, H.: Modelling Memory Functions with recurrent neural networks consisting of input compensation units. I. Static situations. Biol. Cybern. 96, 455–470 (2007)
28. Makarov, V.A., Song, Y., Velarde, M.G., Hübner, D., Cruse, H.: Elements for a general memory structure: Properties of recurrent neural networks used to form situation models. Biol. Cybern. 98, 371–395 (2008)
29. Lambrinos, D., Möller, R., Labhart, T., Pfeifer, R., Wehner, R.: A mobile robot employing insect strategies for navigation. Robot Auton. Syst. 30, 39–64 (2000)
30. Möller, R., Vardy, A.: Local visual homing by matched-filter descent in image distances. Biol. Cybern. 95, 413–430 (2006)
31. Basten, K., Mallot, H.A.: Simulated visual homing in desert ant natural environments: efficiency of skyline cues. Biol. Cybern. 102, 413–425 (2010)
32. Dürr, V., Schmitz, J., Cruse, H.: Behaviour-based modelling of hexapod locomotion: Linking biology and technical application. Arthropod Struct. Develop. 33, 237–250 (2004)
33. Menzel, R., Giurfa, M.: Cognitive architecture of a mini-brain: the honeybee. Trends Cogn. Sci. 5, 62–71 (2001)

Models of Visually Guided Routes in Ants: Embodiment Simplifies Route Acquisition

Bart Baddeley*, Paul Graham, Andrew Philippides, and Philip Husbands

Centre for Computational Neuroscience and Robotics
University of Sussex
Brighton, UK
bartbaddeley@googlemail.com

Abstract. It is known that ants learn long visually-guided routes through complex terrain. However, the mechanisms by which visual information is first learnt and then used to control a route direction are not well understood. In this paper we investigate whether a simple approach, involving scanning the environment and moving in the direction that appears most familiar, can provide a model of visually guided route learning in ants. The specific embodiment of an ant's visual system means that movement and viewing direction are tightly coupled, a familiar view specifies a familiar direction of viewing and thus a familiar movement to make. We show the feasibility of our approach as a model of ant-like route acquisition by learning non-trivial routes through a simulated environment firstly using the complete set of views experienced during learning and secondly using an approximation to the distribution of these views.

Keywords: Insect Navigation, Route Learning, View-Based Homing, Restricted Boltzmann Machine, Generative Models, Autonomous Robotics.

1 Introduction

Individual ant foragers show remarkable navigational performance, rapidly learning long idiosyncratic routes through cluttered environments [2]. While the initial stages of route acquisition are underpinned by the ants' path integration system, as ants become more familiar with a given route, so the use of visually mediated navigational strategies comes to the fore [20,4,21,6]. Behavioural studies of visual navigation have revealed how insects combine simple strategies to produce robust behaviour. This has established insect navigation as a model system for investigating the sensory, cognitive and behavioural strategies that enable animals to perform complex behaviours in the real world.

Here we take a synthetic approach to test whether ant-like navigational behaviour can be captured by a simple embodied strategy of scanning the world for familiar views.

---

* Corresponding author.

S. Jeschke, H. Liu, and D. Schilberg (Eds.): ICIRA 2011, Part II, LNAI 7102, pp. 75–84, 2011.
© Springer-Verlag Berlin Heidelberg 2011

1.1   Background

The most common model of insect navigation is view-based homing. Behavioural experiments with ants [20,6] and bees [1] have shown that individuals store 2D retinotopic views of the world as seen from their goal location. Subsequent search for that goal location can be driven by a comparison of their current view of the world and the view stored at the goal [8]. Computational studies have shown that this tactic is successful within a catchment area centred on the goal, the size of which depends on the depth structure of the world [23,18]. Because this can be an efficient and economical mechanism, it is not a great leap to imagine that navigation over larger scales, i.e. along routes, could be achieved by internalising a series of stored views linked together as a sequence. Route behaviour in this framework would entail homing from one stored view to another. However, attempts to model route navigation using linked view-based homing have shown it to be a non-trivial problem which requires the agent to both robustly determine at which point a waypoint should be set during route construction, and decide when a waypoint has been reached during navigation [7,16,17]. Moreover, if we think of the ant as an embodied visual sensory system, these complex mechanisms might not be necessary. Ants can only translate in one direction relative to their viewing direction, namely forward. This tight coupling of sensation and action allows us to reframe the problem of navigation in terms of a search for the views that are associated with a route. By visually scanning the environment and moving in the direction that is most similar to the views encountered during learning an ant or robot should be able to reliably retrace a given route. Indeed, recent studies of ants suggest that route-guidance could be performed using simpler procedural rules whereby the heading governing a path segment becomes associated with an appropriate visually identified location [3,11]. Moreover, both desert ants and wood ants have been seen to perform types of scanning behaviour that would support this behaviour [[9]; PG personal observation].

1.2   Overview of Our Approach

In order to test the feasability of our scanning approach we simulate an environment consisting of a series of grass tussocks with an occasional large tree such as is typical of the natural environment of the Australian desert ant *Melophorus bagoti*. Our simulated ant views the world as a series of skylines at a resolution of 4°/pixel. Training paths are generated in this environment by combining a Gaussian directional bias with a function that discourages the paths from passing through the grass tussocks. This is a challenging environment to navigate within due to the similarity of views in different parts of the world and due to the lack of large scale objects that can be seen from all points along a given route.

In a first set of experiments we look at what happens if we assume a perfect memory system that is able to store the entire set of views along a route. Our training routes consist of approximately 1000 views along a route and behaviour

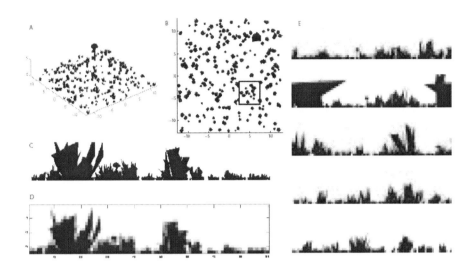

Fig. 1. The simulation environment. A,B) two views of the simulated environment used in our experiments. In B the box indicates the region from which the five example views that are shown in E are taken, the actual positions are indicated by the asterisks inside the box. C) Typical ant's perspective of the world. D) Low resolution representation of the view shown in C as used in our experiments. E) example views taken every 1 metre in our simulated world along a typical route used for learning, note how variable the views are and also how insignificant the large tree is from the perspective of an ant.

is driven by finding the best match in terms of the sum squared difference in pixel values between any of these views and the views experienced by scanning the world in all forward directions, relative to the current heading, in steps of 1°. The direction associated with this minimum determines the direction of movement and a small step is taken in this direction. Starting at the begining of the route this process is iterated a fixed number of steps or until the goal location is reached.

In a second set of experiments we attempt to learn a compact representation of the distribution of views experienced along the route by training a Restricted Boltzmann Machine (RBM) [13] on the set of training views. Once the RBM has been trained we can use the free energy associated with a given view as an approximation to the probability of that view being part of the training set. Behaviour is now driven by scanning the world and searching for the viewing direction that has the lowest free energy under the RBM, i.e. is most likely to be part of the training route.

2 Detailed Methods

A Restricted Boltzmann Machine (RBM) is a two-layered network consisting of stochastic binary neuron-like elements that can be used to model probability distributions over binary vectors. The data is represented by the *visible* units whereas the *hidden* units represent the unknown or hidden causes. Each visible unit is symmetrically connected to all hidden units however there are no visible-visible or hidden-hidden connections. This restriction to the standard Boltzmann Machine greatly simplifies learning and inference since it results in conditional independence of the visible units given the states of the hidden units and similarly conditional independence of the hidden units given the states of the visible units. A joint configuration (v,h) of the visible and hidden units has an *energy* given by:

$$E(v,h) = - \sum_{i \in visible} a_i v_i - \sum_{i \in hidden} b_i h_i - \sum_{i,j} v_i h_j w_{ij} \tag{1}$$

where v_i and h_j are the binary states of the visible unit i and hidden unit j, a_i and b_j are thier biases and w_{ij} is the weight between them. Through this energy function the probability of a given configuration is given by:

$$P(v,h) = \frac{e^{-E(v,h)}}{Z} \tag{2}$$

where Z is a normalization constant or "partition function" given by:

$$Z = \sum_{v,h} e^{-E(v,h)} \tag{3}$$

Thus, the probability assigned to a single data point, **v**, is found by summing over all possible hidden vectors.

$$P(v) = \sum_h P(v,h) = \frac{\sum_h e^{-E(v,h)}}{Z} \tag{4}$$

Following a maximum likelihood principle, training an RBM consists of increasing the probability that the network assigns to the observed data by adjustment of the weights and biases. This is achieved by decreasing the energy of the observed data and increasing the energy of unobserved configurations, especially those that have a low energy and thus contribute strongly to the partition function Z. In practice, it is usual to perform gradient ascent with respect to the weights and biases on the data log-likelihood $log P(v)$:

$$log P(v) = \phi^+ - \phi^- \tag{5}$$

where

$$\phi^+ = log \sum_h e^{-E(v,h)} \tag{6}$$

and

$$\phi^- = log Z = log \sum_{v,h} e^{-E(v,h)} \tag{7}$$

Thus,

$$\frac{\partial logP(v)}{\partial w_{ij}} = \frac{\partial \phi^+}{\partial w_{ij}} - \frac{\partial \phi^-}{\partial w_{ij}} \qquad (8)$$

The two gradients can be estimated through sampling,

$$\frac{\partial \phi^+}{\partial w_{ij}} = \langle v_i h_j \rangle_{data} \qquad (9)$$

and

$$\frac{\partial \phi^-}{\partial w_{ij}} = \langle v_i h_j \rangle_{model} \qquad (10)$$

where the angle brackets denote expectations over the distribution specified by the subscript.

Due to the conditional independence properties of RBMs it is straightforward to generate unbiased samples of $\langle v_i h_j \rangle_{data}$. Given a training datum, $\mathbf{v}$, an unbiased sample from the data distribution can be obtained by setting the binary state, h_j, of each hidden unit to one with a probaility given by:

$$P(h_j = 1|v) = \sigma(b_j + \sum_i v_i w_{ij}) \qquad (11)$$

where $\sigma(x)$ is the logistic function given by $1/(1 + exp(-x))$. Generating unbiased samples of $\langle v_i h_j \rangle_{model}$ is less straightforward. Because the visible units are conditionally independent given the states of the hidden units we can generate an unbiased sample of the state of a visible unit, *given the states of the hidden units.*

$$P(v_i = 1|h) = \sigma(a_i + \sum_j h_j w_{ij}) \qquad (12)$$

This allows alternating Gibbs sampling to be used to generate samples from the model distribution by repeatedly updating in parallel the states of all hidden units using equation 11 followed by updating of all of the visible units in parallel using equation 12. The drawback with this approach is that it is necessary to perform very many iterations of alternating Gibbs sampling (a so-called burn in period) before unbiased samples from the model distribution can be generated. There are a number of different approaches to training a RBM which differ mainly in how they finesse generating samples from the model. In the current work we employ an approach called Fast Persistent Contrastive Divergence to train a RBM with 1360 visible units and 500 hidden units, details of the training procedure can be found in [14] and [19].

Having trained a RBM, the probability of a visible datum is found by summing over all possible configurations of the hidden units.

$$P(v) = \sum_h P(v, h) = \sum_h \frac{e^{-E(v,h)}}{Z} \qquad (13)$$

This compuation is intractable for large h. We can however calculate the probability of a visible datum up to a normalisation constant by using an alternative formulation for the probabilty of a datum expressed in terms of the free energy. The free energy of a visible datum is given by:

$$\mathcal{F}(v) = -\log \sum_h e^{-E(v,h)} \qquad (14)$$

Which allows us to write

$$P(v) = \frac{e^{-\mathcal{F}(v)}}{Z} \, where \, Z = \sum_x e^{-\mathcal{F}(v)} \qquad (15)$$

For a RBM the free energy has an analytic form given by

$$\mathcal{F}(v) = -a'v - \sum_i \log(1 + e^{(b_i + W_i v)}) \qquad (16)$$

Since we wish to compare the relative probabilities of different views the normalisation constants cancel. This allows us to directly compare the free energies associated with each of the views in a scan to determine which view is most probable under the trained model.

3   Results

We start by showing how a system with perfect memory performs when employing our suggested scanning routine and show that the resultant routes exhibit features we observe in the routes of ants. If there is no noise in the system then recapitulating a route is straightforward since the simulated ant will never deviate from the desired route. More interesting is the behaviour when noise is added to the output of the scanning routine and when we look at what happens when we move away from the original learned route. Figure 2 A shows the original training route, the box in the middle of the figure indicates the region that is shown in greater detail in figures C and D. Figure 2 B shows performance over five runs when Gaussian noise with a standard deviation of 0.5 radians is added to the directional output. Despite the noise causing the simulated ant to deviate from its learned route performance is still robust. Figure 2 C shows the result of scanning the world from a dense grid of positions across the environment. At each position the best match in terms of the sum squared difference in pixel values is found to one of the views stored in memory. This minimum is represented using a pseudocolour plot with light colours indicating good matches and dark colours indicating no good match to any of the views stored in memory. Figure 2 D shows the directional output in terms of a pseudocolour plot and a quiver plot. We see a very distinct "route corridor" within which there is a close match to at least one view in memory. This is interesting since we also observe such "route corridors" in behavioural experiments with ants. Outside of their habitual routes ants become lost and initiate search routines that persist until such time as they happen upon their original route. Once they stumble across their normal route they continue along the route as if they had not been lost. We also see that the routes are one way which is also something we see with ants'

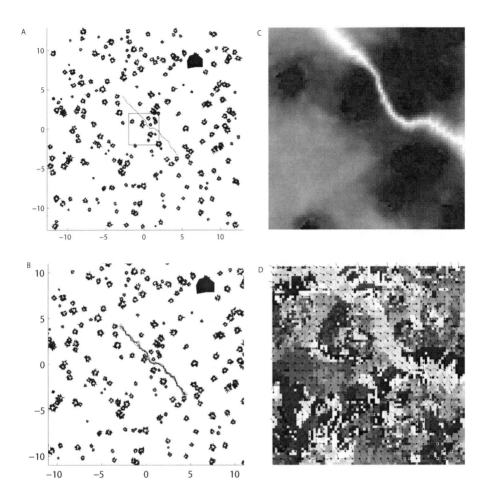

Fig. 2. A) The original training route, the box in the middle of the figure indicates the region that is shown in greater detail in C and D. B) Performance over five runs when Gaussian noise with a standard deviation of 0.5 radians is added to the directional output. C) The result of scanning the world from a dense grid of positions across the environment. At each position the best match in terms of the sum squared difference in pixel values is found to one of the views stored in memory. This minimum is represented using a pseudocolour plot with light colours indicating good matches and dark colours indicating no good match to any of the views stored in memory. D) Directional output represented as both a pseudocolour plot and a quiver plot for the zoomed in section.

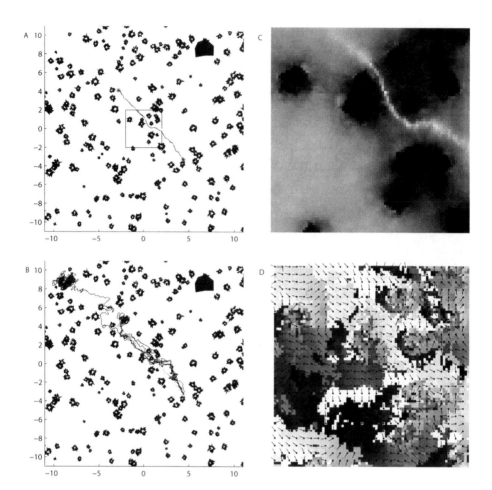

Fig. 3. A) The original training route, and the output of the RBM based navigation algorithm in the absence of noise, the box in the middle of the figure indicates the region that is shown in greater detail in C and D. B) Performance over five runs when Gaussian noise with a standard deviation of 0.5 radians is added to the directional output. Note the increased variability compared to the previous result. C) The result of scanning the world from a dense grid of positions across the environment. At each position the best match in terms of the sum squared difference in pixel values is found to one of the views stored in memory. This minimum is represented using a pseudocolour plot with light colours indicating good matches and dark colours indicating no good match to any of the views stored in memory. D) Directional output represented as both a pseudocolour plot and a quiver plot for the zoomed in section.

routes, that is knowing how to get from A to B does not allow the route from B to A to be followed. Figure 2 D shows a quiver plot indicating the direction that would be taken at any of a grid of points in the environment, again indicating the "route corridor" within which sensible actions are taken.

In a second set of experiments we replace the perfect memory system with a RBM and learn the same route that was used in the first experiment. Despite the learnt paths being more variable than in the previous experiment the overall performance is remarkably similar. This is despite the fact that the distribution of views has only been approximated by the RBM. We see a similar "route corridor" and partial robustness to noise. This suggests that it is possible to learn a compact representation to the set of views that are experienced during learning and that this approximation is sufficient to drive behaviour when used in conjunction with a scanning routine.

4   Summary

Our main goal was to show that by considering the tight coupling of sensation and action that is present in ants and some robots we were able to reframe the problem of route navigation in terms of a search for familiar views. Our subsequent goal was to demonstrate that routes can be represented holistically thus allowing route recapitulation to be described as a recognition problem. We implemented this approach in a simulated environment and learnt a series of non-trivial routes through visually cluttered environments. Our results indicate that it is possible to implement a holistic, view-based homing strategy for acquiring ant-like routes. Crucially, there is no need to break the route up into a series of discrete waypoints, instead learning occurs continuously. This avoids the problem of determining what should trigger the learning of a new view or waypoint and leads to a simpler mechanism. Moreover, we suggest this approach provides a powerful platform for investigating efficient encoding of route guidance information and how this depends on the visual ecology within which an agent navigates.

Acknowledgments. This work was supported by BBSRC grant BBF0100521 and EPSRC grant EP/I031758/1.

References

1. Cartwright, B.A., Collett, T.S.: Landmark learning in bees. Journal of Comparative Physiology A: Neuroethology, Sensory, Neural, and Behavioral Physiology 151(4), 521–543 (1983)
2. Cheng, K., Narendra, A., Sommer, S., Wehner, R.: Travelling in clutter: Navigation in Central Australian desert ant Melophorus bagoti. Behavioural Processes 80(3), 261–268 (2009)
3. Collett, M., Collett, T.S., Bisch, S., Wehner, R.: Local and global vectors in desert ant navigation. Nature 394, 269–272 (1998)
4. Collett, T.S., Dillmann, E., Giger, A., Wehner, R.: Visual landmarks and route following in desert ants. Journal of Comparative Physiology A: Neuroethology, Sensory, Neural, and Behavioral Physiology 170(4), 435–442 (1992)

5. Collett, T.S., Graham, P., Harris, R.A.: Novel landmark-guided routes in ants. Journal of Exp. Biol. 210(12), 2025–2032 (2007)
6. Durier, V., Graham, P., Collett, T.S.: Snapshot memories and landmark guidance in wood ants. Current Biology 13(18), 1614–1618 (2003)
7. Franz, M.O., Schölkopf, B., Georg, P., Mallot, H.A., Bülthoff, H.H.: Learning View Graphs for Robot Navigation. Autonomous Robots 5, 111–125 (1998)
8. Franz, M.O., Schölkopf, B., Mallot, H.A., Bülthoff, H.H.: Where did I take that snapshot? Scene-based Homing by Image Matching. Biological Cybernetics 79, 191–202 (1998)
9. Graham, P., Collett, T.S.: View-based navigation in insects: how wood ants (Formica rufa L.) look at and are guided by extended landmarks. J. Exp. Biol. 205(16), 2499–2509 (2002)
10. Graham, P., Collett, T.S.: Bi-directional route learning in wood ants. J. Exp. Biol. 209(18), 3677–3684 (2006)
11. Graham, P., Cheng, K.: Ants use the panoramic skyline as a visual cue during navigation. Current Biology 19(20), R935–R937 (2009)
12. Graham, P., Philippides, A., Baddeley, B.: Animal Cognition: Multi-modal Interactions in Ant Learning. Current Biology 20, R639–R640(2010)
13. Hinton, G.: Training Products of Experts by Minimizing Contrastive Divergence. Neural Computation 14, 1771–1800 (2002)
14. Hinton, G.: A Practical Guide to Training Restricted Boltzmann Machines. University of Toronto Technical Report 2010-003 (2010)
15. Kohler, M., Wehner, R.: Idiosyncratic route-based memories in desert ants, Melophorus bagoti: How do they interact with path-integration vectors? Neurobiology of Learning and Memory 83(1), 1–12 (2005)
16. Smith, L., Philippides, A., Graham, P., Baddeley, B., Husbands, P.: Linked Local Navigation for Visual Route Guidance. Adaptive Behavior - Animals, Animats, Software Agents, Robots, Adaptive Systems 15(3), 257–271 (2007)
17. Smith, L., Philippides, A., Graham, P., Husbands, P.: Linked Local Visual Navigation and Robustness to Motor Noise and Route Displacement. In: Asada, M., Hallam, J.C.T., Meyer, J.-A., Tani, J. (eds.) SAB 2008. LNCS (LNAI), vol. 5040, pp. 179–188. Springer, Heidelberg (2008)
18. Stürzl, W., Zeil, J.: Depth, contrast and view-based homing in outdoor scenes. Biological Cybernetics 96, 519–531 (2007)
19. Tieleman, T., Hinton, G.: Using Fast Weights to Improve Persistent Contrastive Divergence. In: Proceedings of the 26th International Conference on Machine Learning, Montreal, Canada (2009)
20. Wehner, R., Raber, F.: Visual spatial memory in desert ants, Cataglyphis bicolor (Hymenoptera: Formicidae). Cellular and Molecular Life Sciences (CMLS) 35(12), 1569–1571 (1979)
21. Wehner, R.: Visual navigation in insects: coupling of egocentric and geocentric information. Journal of Experimental Biology 199(1), 129–140 (1996)
22. Wehner, R., Boyer, M., Loertscher, F., Sommer, S., Menzi, U.: Ant Navigation: One-Way routes Rather Than Maps. Current Biology 16(1), 75–79 (2006)
23. Zeil, J., Hofmann, M.I., Chahl, J.S.: Catchment areas of panoramic snapshots in outdoor scenes. Journal of the Optical Society of America A 20(3), 450–469 (2003)

Robust Object Tracking
for Resource-Limited Hardware Systems

Xiaoqin Zhang[1,2], Li Zhao[1], Shengyong Chen[3], and Lixin Gao[1]

[1] College of Mathematics & Information Science, Wenzhou University, China
[2] Zhejiang Provincial Key Laboratory of Information Network Technology, China
xqzhang@wzu.edu.cn
[3] College of Computer Science, Zhejiang University of Technology, China
csy@zjut.edu.cn

Abstract. Resource-limited hardware systems often generate LFR (low frame rate) videos in many real-world robot vision applications. Most existing approaches treat LFR video tracking as an abrupt motion tracking problem. However, in LFR video tracking applications, LFR not only causes abrupt motions, and also large appearance changes of objects because the objects' poses and illumination may undergo large changes from one frame to the next. This adds extra difficulties to LFR video tracking. In this paper, we propose a robust and general tracking system for LFR videos. The tracking system consists of four major parts: dominant color-spatial based object representation, cross bin-ratio based similarity measure, annealed PSO (particle swarm optimization) based searching, integral image of model parameters. The first two parts are combined to provide a good solution to the appearance changes, and the abrupt motion is effectively captured by the annealed PSO based searching. Moreover, an integral image of model parameters is constructed, which provides a look-up table for evaluation, and this greatly reduces the computational load. Experimental results demonstrate that the proposed tracking system can effectively tackle the difficulties caused by LFR.

Keywords: Low frame rate, visual tracking, particle swarm optimization.

1   Introduction

In many real-world robot vision applications, such as embedded visual systems, the available resource is limited. Therefore, the LFR (low frame rate) videos are produced in the following two ways: 1) LFR videos may be produced when image frames are missed because of hardware delay in the image acquisition system or the limitation of transmission bandwidth; 2) the frame rate of the data streams may be down-sampled because of limitations in the storage or the processing power of the CPU.

The frame rate for LFR video is usually less than ten per one second, resulting in large appearance changes and abrupt motion in successive image frames. However, most traditional tracking algorithms are based on the state continuity hypothesis, in which it is assumed that the changes in object motion and appearance in successive image frames is small. In particle filter [1], motion prediction is based on the tracking results in the previous frame. For the iterative optimization based tracking algorithms, such as KLT (Kanade-Lucas-Tomasi) [2], template matching algorithm [3] and mean

S. Jeschke, H. Liu, and D. Schilberg (Eds.): ICIRA 2011, Part II, LNAI 7102, pp. 85–94, 2011.

shift [4], the initialization of optimization is also the tracking results in the previous frame. So the above classical tracking algorithms do not yield satisfactory results in the tracking applications of LFR video.

Tracking in LFR videos has been much less investigated than tracking in full frame rate videos. Porikli et al. [5,6] extend mean shift algorithm to multi-kernel mean shift algorithm, and apply it to the motion map which is obtained from background subtraction, in order to overcome the abrupt motion caused by LFR video. A cascade particle filter which integrates conventional tracking and detection is proposed by Li et al. [7] for LFR video tracking. In this approach, observers learned from different ranges of samples are adopted to detect the moving object. This approach requires complex observes and time-consuming off-line training, and the detectors only show efficiency in a face tracking case. In [8], the object motion is detected from background subtraction, and then four features, namely phase cross correlation, average intensity difference, velocity difference, and angle difference are combined for matching between consecutive image frames. Zhang et al. [9] adopt region based image difference to estimate the object motion. The predicted motion is used to guide the particle propagation. In summary, all the above work consider that LFR is equivalent to abrupt motion. However, in practice, LFR not only causes the abrupt motion, but also the large appearance changes of the object because the object pose and illumination may undergo large changes in the LFR video. As a result, we must take both the abrupt motion and the appearance changes of the object into consideration.

In order to design a robust tracking system for the LFR video, we start from the following three aspects: 1) object representation, 2) matching criterion, 3) searching method, and design a robust and general tracking system for LFR video. In addition, our algorithm is not limited to face tracking or pedestrian tracking which needs a trained detector to help the tracking. The main contributions of our work are:

1. The object is represented through dominant color-spatial distribution of the object region. This representation is more robust and discriminative than color histogram based representation.
2. A cross bin-ratio based similarity measure is used to evaluate the difference between the dominant color of the object template and the dominant color of the candidate region.
3. In order to handle the abrupt motions caused by LFR video, we propose an annealed PSO (particle swarm optimization) method. This mechanism realizes the robust searching for the abrupt motions.
4. In order to accelerate evaluation process in PSO iterations, we calculate a integral image of model parameters which establishes a parameter-particle look-up table. In this way, the computational complex remains the same to different iteration numbers.

This paper is organized as follows. The overview of our tracking system is given in Section 2. The dominant color-spatial based object representation is shown in Section 3. The cross bin-ratio based similarity measure is introduced in Section 4. The annealed PSO searching method and integral image of model parameters are presented in Section 5 and Section 6 respectively. Experimental results are shown in Section 7, and Section 8 is devoted to conclusion.

2   Overview of Tracking System

An overview of the proposed tracking system for LFR video is systematically presented in Fig. 1. There are four major components in the proposed tracking system: 1) dominant color-spatial based object representation, 2) cross bin-ratio based similarity measure, 3) integral image of model parameters, 4) annealed pso based searching process. We will give a detailed description of each component in the following sections.

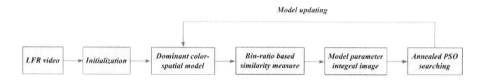

Fig. 1. The flow chart of the proposed tracking system

3   Dominant Color-Spatial Based Object Representation

In our work, the major color modes inside the object region are firstly obtained by dominant-set based clustering algorithm, and then the spatial distribution of each color mode is extracted to enhance the discriminative ability of the color model.

3.1   Dominant Color Mode Extraction

Given an image region, we first convert the *RGB* color space to the *rgI* space using the following formulations:

$$r = R/(R + G + B), \ g = G/(R + G + B), \ I = (R + G + B)/3$$

Then we define the pixel-pairwise graph, where the weight $w_{i,j}$ on the edge connected by the node i and node j is calculated in the following way:

$$w_{i,j} = ||f_i - f_j||^2 \tag{1}$$

where $f_i = (r, g, I)$ is the intensity value of pixel i in the *rgI* color space, and the weight of the arc depends on the Euclidean distance between the corresponding pixels.

Then, we apply the dominant set based clustering algorithm [10] to the constructed pixel-pairwise graph, and gradually obtain the dominant color modes $C = \{c_l\}_{l=1}^k$. The clustering process ends, when the left pixels are less than a predefined threshold. In this way, the main color modes are captured and the noisy image pixels are filtered out.

3.2   Spatial Layout of the Dominant Color

The above dominant color based representation captures the color distribution in the image region of interest. However, the spatial layout of pixels falling into the same color mode is ignored. In order to overcome this problem, we extract the spatial layout of the lth color mode using the spatial mean μ_l and the covariance Σ_l in the following way:

$$\mu_l = \frac{\sum_i p_i \delta(L(f_i) - l)}{\sum_i \delta(L(f_i) - l)} \tag{2}$$

$$\Sigma_l = \frac{\sum_i (p_i - \mu_l)(p_i - \mu_l)^T \delta(L(f_i) - l)}{\sum_i \delta(L(f_i) - l)} \tag{3}$$

where p_i is the position of the pixel i, and δ is the Kronecker function such that $\delta(L(f_i) - l) = 1$ if $L(f_i) = l$ and $\delta(L(f_i) - l) = 0$ otherwise.

As a result, the interested image region can be represented by $R = \{w_l, u_l, \mu_l, \Sigma_l\}_{l=1}^k$, where w_l is the weight of the lth dominant color mode and is calculated as follows:

$$w_l = \frac{\sum_i \delta(L(f_i) - l)}{\sum_{l=1}^k \sum_i \delta(L(f_i) - l)} \tag{4}$$

4   Similarity Measure for Matching

4.1   Cross Bin-Ratio Based Color Similarity Measure

For a k-bin histogram $U = \{u_l\}_{l=1}^k$, a ratio matrix A_r is defined to capture the cross bin relationship. Each element in the matrix is (u_i/u_j) which measure the relation between bin u_i and u_j. The whole ratio matrix is written as follows:

$$A_r = \left(\frac{u_i}{u_j}\right)_{i,j} = \begin{bmatrix} \frac{u_1}{u_1} & \frac{u_2}{u_1} & \cdots & \frac{u_k}{u_1} \\ \frac{u_1}{u_2} & \frac{u_2}{u_2} & \cdots & \frac{u_k}{u_2} \\ \cdots & \cdots & \cdots & \cdots \\ \frac{u_1}{u_k} & \frac{u_2}{u_k} & \cdots & \frac{u_k}{u_k} \end{bmatrix} \tag{5}$$

With the definition of the ratio matrix, we compare the vth bin between two histogram U^T and U^C using the similarity M_v, which is defined as the sum of squared difference between the lth rows of the corresponding ratio matrices of U^T and U^C:

$$M_v(U^T, U^C) = \sum_{l=1}^k \left(\frac{u_l^T}{u_v^T} - \frac{u_l^C}{u_v^C}\right)^2 / \left(\frac{1}{u_v^T} + \frac{1}{u_v^C}\right)^2 \tag{6}$$

where $\frac{1}{u_v^T} + \frac{1}{u_v^C}$ is normalization term to avoid the instability problem when u_v^T and u_v^C close to zero.

We simplify M_v using the $\mathbb{L}_2$ normalization $\sum_{l=1}^k u_l^2 = 1$ and formulate the cross bin-ratio dissimilarity M between histogram U^T and U^C as follows:

$$M(U^T, U^C) = \sum_{v=1}^k M_v(U^T, U^C) = \sum_{v=1}^k \left(1 - \frac{u_v^T u_v^C}{(u_v^T + u_v^C)^2}\|U^T + U^C\|_2^2\right) \tag{7}$$

4.2   Spatial Similarity Measure

In this part, we extract the spatial layout information of each dominant color mode, and introduce a spatial similarity measure to enhance the robustness of the color based similarity measure.

For the template image and a candidate region, the spatial mean and covariance of each color mode are computed as in Equ. (2)(3) accordingly: $\{\mu_l^T, \Sigma_l^T\}_{l=1}^k$, $\{\mu_l^C, \Sigma_l^C\}_{l=1}^k$. Together with the weight of the corresponding color mode, the spatial similarity measure is formulated as follows:

$$S(U^T, U^C) = \sum_{l=1}^k w_l \exp\{-\frac{1}{2}(\mu_l^T - \mu_l^C)^T (\Sigma_l^T + \Sigma_l^C)^{-1}(\mu_l^T - \mu_l^C)\} \qquad (8)$$

5   Swarm Intelligence Based Searching Method

The abrupt motions in LFR image sequences cause sample impoverishment problem when they are tracked using a particle filter. In this section, we propose a swarm intelligence based searching method–annealed particle swarm optimization to overcome the sample impoverishment problem.

5.1   Annealed Particle Swarm Optimization

Iteration Process. Particle swarm optimization [11,12], is a population-based stochastic optimization technique, which is inspired by the social behavior of bird flocking. In detail, a PSO algorithm is initialized with a group of random particles $\{x^{i,0}\}_{i=1}^N$ (N is the number of particles). Each particle $x^{i,0}$ has a corresponding fitness value $f(x^{i,0})$ and a relevant velocity $v^{i,0}$, which is a function of the best state found by that particle (p^i, for individual best), and of the best state found so far among all particles (g, for global best). Given these two best values, the particle updates its velocity and state with the following equations in the nth iteration,

$$v^{i,n+1} = w^n v^{i,n} + \varphi_1 u_1(p^i - x^{i,n}) + \varphi_2 u_2(g - x^{i,n}) \qquad (9)$$

$$x^{i,n+1} = x^{i,n} + v^{i,n+1} \qquad (10)$$

where w^n is the inertial weight, the φ_1, φ_2 are acceleration constants, and $u_1, u_2 \in (0,1)$ are uniformly distributed random numbers. The inertial weight w^n is usually a monotonically decreasing function of the iteration number n. For example, given a user-specified maximum weight w_{max}, a minimum weight w_{min} and the initialization of $w^0 = w_{max}$, one way to update w^n is as follows:

$$w^{n+1} = w^n - dw, \quad dw = (w_{max} - w_{min})/T \qquad (11)$$

where T is the maximum iteration number.

In order to reduce the number of parameters in the above PSO iteration process, we adopt an annealed Gaussian version of PSO algorithm[13,14], in which the iteration process is modified as follows:

$$v^{i,n+1} = |r_1|(p^i - x^{i,n}) + |r_2|(g - x^{i,n}) + \epsilon \qquad (12)$$

$$x^{i,n+1} = x^{i,n} + v^{i,n+1} \tag{13}$$

where $|r_1|$ and $|r_2|$ are the absolute values of the independent samples from the Gaussian probability distribution $\mathcal{N}(0,1)$, and ϵ is a zero-mean Gaussian perturbation noise which prevents the particles from becoming trapped in local optima. The covariance matrix of ϵ is changed in an adaptive simulated annealing way [15]:

$$\Sigma_\epsilon = \Sigma e^{-cn} \tag{14}$$

where Σ is the covariance matrix of the predefined transition distribution, c is an annealing constant, and n is the iteration number. The elements in Σ_ϵ decrease rapidly as the iteration number n increases which enables a fast convergence rate.

Then the fitness value of each particle is evaluated using the observation model $p(o^{i,n+1}|x^{i,n+1})$ as follows.

$$f(x^{i,n+1}) = p(o^{i,n+1}|x^{i,n+1}) \tag{15}$$

Here, the observation model $p(o^{i,n+1}|x^{i,n+1})$ reflects the similarity between the candidate image of state $x^{i,n+1}$ and the template model:

$$p(o^{i,n+1}|x^{i,n+1}) = \exp\{\frac{1}{2\sigma_1^2}(1 - S(U^T, U^C))\} * \exp\{\frac{1}{2\sigma_2^2}M(U^T, U^C)\} \tag{16}$$

where σ_1^2, σ_2^2 are the observation variance parameters which balance the influence of spatial distance and cross bin-ratio similarity.

After the fitness value of each particle $f(x^{i,n})$ is evaluated, the individual best and the global best of particles are updated in the following equations:

$$p^i = \begin{cases} x^{i,n+1}, & \text{if } f(x^{i,n+1}) > f(p^i) \\ p^i, & \text{else} \end{cases} \tag{17}$$

$$g = \arg\max_{p^i} f(p^i) \tag{18}$$

In analogy with the foraging behavior of the bird flocks, here the optimal state of $f(\cdot)$ corresponds to food, and the particles in state space correspond to birds.

As a result, the particles interact locally with one another and with their environment in analogy with the 'cognitive' and 'social' aspects of animal populations, and eventually cluster in the regions where the local optima of $f(\cdot)$ are located. In Equ. (12), the three terms on the right hand side represent *cognitive effect*, *social effect* and noisy part respectively, where *cognitive effect* refers to the evolution of the particle according to its own observations, and *social effect* refers to the evolution of the particle according to the cooperation between all particles.

6   Integral Image of Model Parameters

When evaluating the the fitness value of each particle in the PSO iteration process, we need to calculate the similarity between the candidate image region and the object template. The candidate image regions corresponding to the set of particles may have many overlapped areas, and the image pixels inside the overlapping region will be calculated repeatedly, and thus involves large and unnecessary computational load.

In order to avoid the unnecessary computation, we first construct a 5D vector for each pixel $\mathcal{F}_i = \{L(i), (p_i)_x, (p_i)_y, (p_i)_x^2, (p_i)_y^2\}$, where $L(i)$ is the color mode which the pixel i belongs to, and $(p_i)_x, (p_i)_y$ are, respectively, the x and y coordinate values of the pixel i, and then calculate the rectangle features of the 5D image as in [16]. In detail, the process is as follows:

- Estimate the probable candidate region R: for LFR video, it is difficult to estimate the abrupt motion. In our work, we introduce a variable r_t^{max} which represent the absolute value of the maximum velocity in the second up to time t, and then the probable candidate region R for time $t + 1$ is set to the image area covered by $[g_t - 1.2r_t^{max}, g_t + 1.2r_t^{max}]$, where g_t represent the tracking result of the object state at time t. Here, the probable candidate region is heuristically selected by utilizing the motion information in the previous tracking process, and thus provides a reasonable limitation to the moving of particles and a certain capability to absorb their acceleration.
- Cluster the pixels in the R via the assignment algorithm [17], and then record the 5D vector of each pixel.
- Calculate the rectangle feature of the 5D image, and then build the integral image for lth color mode. For the position i of the integral image, its corresponding value is

$$\mathcal{F}_i^* = \sum_{k \in R, p_k \leq p_i} \mathcal{F}_i$$

Similar to [16], given a rectangle, the parameters of the spatial-dominant color model can be easily obtained by four table lookup operations. All the evaluation process for each pixel is calculated only once.

Table 1. Frame rate number of the experimental data

Experimental data	Sequence 1	Sequence 2	Sequence 3
Down-sampling rate	3	5	3
Frame rate	5	3	5

7   Experimental Results

In the implementation, the object state is represented as $x_t = \{c_x, c_y, w, h\}$, which correspond to the center coordinate and size of the tracking window. To validate the effectiveness of the proposed tracking system, we test it from the following aspects: different object representations, different similarity measures, different searching methods. Finally, we will give a computational complexity analysis of the strategy described in Section 6. The frame rate numbers of the video sequences employed in the experiment are shown in Table 1.

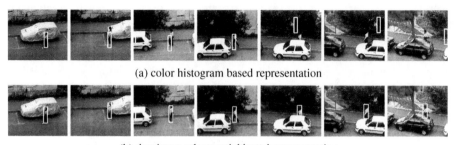

(a) color histogram based representation

(b) dominant color-spatial based representation

Fig. 2. Tracking performances of sequence 1 for frame #1,34,70,100,127,154,205

7.1   Different Object Representations

To show the influence of the object representation on the tracking performance, we conduct an experimental comparison between the dominant color-spatial based representation and the color histogram based representation.

As shown in Fig. 2, for the color histogram based object representation, its tracking window starts to offset the object position at frame 70 when the illumination changes and the track is completely lost when the object is partially occluded by the car. The reason is two-fold: first, the color histogram is sensitive to illumination changes; and second, the color histogram is not robust enough to the partial occlusion because the relative positions of the object pixels are ignored. In contrast, the dominant color-spatial based representation overcomes the above two limitations by using the dominant color modes and extracting their spatial information. As a result, the object is tracked successfully throughout the video sequence.

7.2   Different Similarity Measure

In this part, a experimental comparison between the cross bin-ratio based similarity measure and the histogram intersection based similarity measure is carried out to demonstrate the effectiveness of the cross bin-ratio based similarity measure.

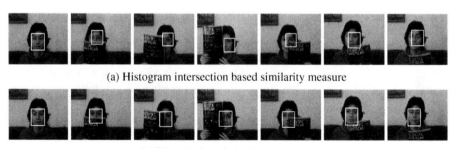

(a) Histogram intersection based similarity measure

(b) Bin-ratio based similarity measure

Fig. 3. Tracking performances of sequence 2 for frame #2,37,87,122,172,237,242

We test these two similarity measures on a video sequence with partial occlusion. As shown in Fig. 3, for the histogram intersection based similarity measure, the occluded pixels are discarded, since these pixels can not provide positive information for matching, leading to inaccurate localization. while the proposed similarity measure in Equ. (6) has a *'cross'* essence that the similarity between corresponding color bins is a summation of the ratio of all other color bins, and this effect can alleviate the bad influence of the occluded pixels, and achieve a more accurate localization.

7.3 Different Searching Methods

To provide experimental validation to the analysis in Section 5, we compare the annealed PSO based searching method with the particle filtering based searching method.

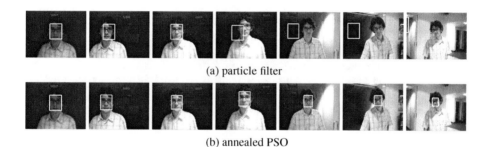

(a) particle filter

(b) annealed PSO

Fig. 4. Tracking performances of sequence 3 for frame #1,16,28,31,82,109,136

As shown in Fig. 4, the particle filtering based searching method fails to track the object, because it can not catch the rapid motion of the object. In annealed PSO based searching method, the particles evolve according to individual and environmental information in the search space, and thus never lose track of the object even under abrupt motion. Meanwhile, the random perturbations of the particles ensure that the search does not become trapped in local optimal and the annealing factor enables a much faster convergence rate.

8 Conclusion

This paper has proposed a tracking system for LFR videos. This system includes a new appearance model and a new search method. In the appearance model, the object is represented by the dominant color-spatial modes and a cross bin-ratio based similarity measure is used for matching. The space of object motions is searched by the annealed PSO based search method, and the model parameters are obtained from a look-up table which is constructed using an integral image. Experimental results demonstrate the effectiveness of the tracking system.

Acknowledgment. This work is supported by NSFC (Grant No. 61100147, 61074123), open project of State Key Laboratory of Industrial Control Technology (ICT1120),

Zhejiang Provincial Top Key Discipline of Information Processing and Automation Technology, and the open project of Zhejiang Provincial Key Laboratory of Information Network Technology.

References

1. Isard, M., Blake, A.: Condensation: conditional density propagation for visual tracking. International Journal of Computer Vision 29(1), 5–28 (1998)
2. Tomasi, C., Kanade, T.: Detection and tracking of point features. Technical Report CMU-CS-91-132 (1991)
3. Hager, G.D., Hager, P.N.: Efficient region tracking with parametric models of geometry and illumination. IEEE Trans. on Pattern Analysis and Machine Intelligence 20(10), 1025–1039 (1998)
4. Comaniciu, D., Ramesh, V., Meer, P.: Kernel-based object tracking. IEEE Trans. on Pattern Analysis and Machine Intelligence 25(5), 234–240 (2003)
5. Porikli, F., Tuzel, O.: Object tracking in low-frame-rate video. SPIE Image and Video Communications and Processing 5685, 72–79 (2005)
6. Porikli, F., Tuzel, O.: Object tracking in low-frame-rate video. US Patent Application Publication, US20060222205A1 (2006)
7. Li, Y., Ai, H., Yamashita, T., Lao, S., Kawade, M.: Tracking in Low Frame Rate Video: A cascade Particle Filter with Discriminative Observers of Different Lifespan. IEEE Trans. on Pattern Analysis and Machine Intelligence 30(10), 1728–1740 (2008)
8. Carrano, C.J.: Ultra-scale vehicle tracking in low spatial resolution and low frame-rate overhead video. In: Proceedings of SPIE, vol. 7445 (2009)
9. Zhang, T., Fei, S., Lu, H., Li, X.: Modified Particle Filter for Object Tracking in Low Frame Rate Video. In: Proceeding of IEEE Conference on Decision and Control, pp. 2552–2557 (2009)
10. Pavan, M., Pelillo, M.: A new graph-theoretic approach to clustering and segmentation. In: Proceeding of IEEE Conference on Computer Vision and Pattern Recognition, vol. 1, pp. 3895–3900 (2003)
11. Kennedy, J., Eberhart, R.: Particle swarm optimization. In: Proceeding of IEEE Conference on Neural Networks, pp. 1942–1948 (1995)
12. Zhang, X., Hu, W., Maybank, S., Li, X., Zhu, M.: Sequential Particle Swarm Optimization for Visual Tracking. In: Proceeding of IEEE Conference on Computer Vision and Pattern Recognition, pp. 1–8 (2008)
13. Zhang, X., Hu, W., Maybank, S.: A Smarter Particle Filter. In: Proceeding of Asian Conference on Computer Vision, pp. 236–246 (2010)
14. Zhang, X., Hu, W., Qu, W., Maybank, S.: Multiple Object Tracking Via Species-Based Particle Swarm Optimization. IEEE Trans. on Circuits and Systems For Video Technology 20(11), 1590–1602 (2010)
15. Ingber, L.: Simulated Annealing: Practice Versus Theory. Journal of Mathematical and Computer Modeling 18(11), 29–57 (1993)
16. Viola, P., Jones, M.: Robust Real-Time Face Detection. International Journal of Computer Vision 52(2), 137–154 (2004)
17. Pavan, M., Pelillo, M.: Efficient Out-of-Sample Extension of Dominant-Set Clusters. In: Proceeding of Advances in Neural Information Processing Systems, vol. 17, pp. 1057–1064 (2005)

Adaptive Rank Transform for Stereo Matching

Ge Zhao[1,2], Yingkui Du[1], and Yandong Tang[1]

[1] State Key Laboratory of Robotics, Shenyang Institute of Automation,
Chinese Academy of Sciences
[2] Graduate University of the Chinese Academy of Sciences, Beijing, P.R. China
{zhaoge,dyk,ytang}@sia.cn

Abstract. Window selection is the main challenge for local stereo matching methods based on the rank transform and it involves two aspects : the rank window selection and the match window selection. Most recent methods only focus on how to select the match window but pay little attention to the selection of the rank window. In this paper, we propose a novel matching method based on adaptive rank transform. Differing with the existing rank-based matching methods, the proposed method can deal with the rank and match window selection at the same time. The experimental results are evaluated on the Middlebury dataset as well as real images, showing that our method performs better than the recent rank-based stereo matching methods.

Keywords: stereo matching, rank transform, window selection.

1 Introduction

Stereo matching [1] is the process of finding corresponding pixels between the left and right input images. It is widely used in many vision applications such as 3-D reconstruction. There are mainly two types of stereo matching algorithms which are global and local methods. Global methods [2,3,4,5] model the stereo matching problem as an energy minimization process. These methods usually have high matching accuracy and robustness but requires long running time and complex parameter tuning. In contrast, local stereo methods [6,7,8] are generally fast and easy to implement but less accurate than the global methods. To improve the matching accuracy, local methods commonly gather the information from all pixels in a window which is centered at the pixel under consideration and this window is called match window. Both the local and global methods face some common problems, which are the brightness differences, certain types of noise and radiometric distortions. One solution to these problems is to pre-process the stereo pair prior to matching. The rank transform [9] is one kind of these pre-processing methods, in which the intensity of the rank window center is replaced by the number of pixels in the rank window whose intensity value is more than the center pixel. Fig.1 gives an concrete example of the original rank transform and Fig.2 gives the basic flow of stereo matching algorithms based on the rank transform.

S. Jeschke, H. Liu, and D. Schilberg (Eds.): ICIRA 2011, Part II, LNAI 7102, pp. 95–104, 2011.

$$
\begin{array}{ccc}
100 & 6 & 9 \\
35 & 60 & 115 \\
58 & 11 & 33
\end{array}
\Rightarrow
\begin{array}{ccc}
1 & 0 & 0 \\
0 & x & 1 \\
0 & 0 & 0
\end{array}
\Rightarrow Rank = 2
$$

Fig. 1. An example of the original rank transform

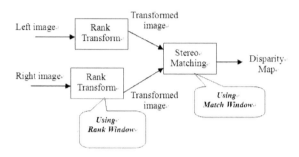

Fig. 2. Basic flow of rank-based stereo matching method

There are mainly two problems of stereo matching methods using the original rank transform or extensions of the original rank transform [10,11,12]. The first problem is the selection of the match window and this problem is well studied. For example, Zheng Gu and Xianyu Su [13] recently proposed a new stereo matching method using the rank transform. They assign adaptive weight to each pixel in a fixed match window according to the spatial proximity to the center of the match window. Kun Wang [14] also proposed a novel stereo matching algorithm using rank transform and he based his match window selection on edge detection. The second problem is the selection of an appropriate rank window for each pixel. However, until now, most rank-based methods pay little attention to this problem. In this paper, we are the first to deal with the rank and match window selection simultaneously.

The outline of this paper is as follows: in section 2, we propose the adaptive rank transform; in section 3, we propose a new way to construct self-adaptive match window based on adaptive rank windows; in section 4 we test our approaches with both benchmark and real stereo pairs and compare them with some recent matching methods; finally conclusion is summarized in section 5.

2   Adaptive Rank Transform

2.1   The Motivation Behind Adaptive Rank Transform

In stereo matching, window selection is a hard problem. In theory, the window should adapt to the local image structure which means only including the neighboring pixels from the similar depth of the scene with the pixel under consideration [15]. However, the 3D depth information is usually unknown beforehand and can only be estimated from the images. A common assumption is that pixels with similar intensities within a considered area are likely from the same depth in the scene. Based on this assumption, the requirement for the optimal window is that the window should avoid covering areas with big intensity variance such as object boundaries which often correspond to different depth in the scene. To satisfy this requirement, the rank window should be able to adapt its shape and size at different locations so object boundaries such as edges and corners can be preserved in the transformed images. However, until now, almost all recent extensions of the rank transform still use the square rank window, as a result, the fixed square window often blur object boundaries in the transformed image. Therefore, in this section, we propose a novel extension of rank transform that can adapt the shape and size of the rank window automatically.

2.2   Adaptive Rank Window

The key idea of the proposed method is to dynamically construct two 1-D rank windows which are perpendicular to each other. As shown in Fig.3, for every pixel $p=(x_p,y_p)$, there are two 1-D rank windows meeting at it. We refer the horizontal one as *horizontal window* and the vertical one as *vertical window*. Instead of fixing the size of these two windows, we adaptively extend the horizontal window leftwards and rightwards and the vertical window upwards and downwards to include as many pixels with similar intensities as possible. We use a quadruple $\left\{ h_p^+ \quad h_p^- \quad v_p^+ \quad v_p^- \right\}$ to demarcate the boundaries of the two windows. Taking h_p^- for example, it is the number of pixels between p and the leftmost pixel of the horizontal window. Using the above quadruple, the horizontal window $H(p)$ and the vertical window $V(p)$ are expressed as follows :

$$H(p) = \left\{ (x, y) \mid x \in \left[x_p - h_p^-, x_p + h_p^+ \right], y = y_p \right\} \tag{1}$$

$$V(p) = \left\{ (x, y) \mid x = x_p, y \in \left[y_p - v_p^-, y_p + v_p^+ \right] \right\} \tag{2}$$

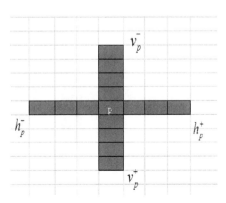

Fig. 3. The proposed rank window

We present a simple but effective approach based on intensity similarity to adaptively decide the quadruple for each pixel. Our strategy is as follows:

a) Apply a 3×3 median filter to filter the input image
b) Starting from the origin pixel p, then move by one pixel in all four directions *(up,down,left,right)* to reach four new image locations and associate the four image locations to the four directions.
c) Compare the intensity differences of four image locations with the origin respectively and if the intensity difference for any location is above the preset threshold τ, the associated direction is prohibited from further movement.
d) Choose the unprohibited direction which yields the minimum intensity difference.
e) Further move by one pixel in the chosen direction and associate the new image location to this direction.
f) Iterate steps (c) to (e) until all directions become prohibited from movement.
g) We use the distances between the four final image locations and the origin p to determine the quadruple.

Our strategy is basically a sequential search starting from the pixel under consideration for the optimal windows by maximizing the number of pixels with similar intensity.

2.3   New Transform Rules

The old rank transform rules [9] are originally designed to apply to the square window so they can not be applied directly to the adaptive rank window. Therefore, in this part, we will propose new rules particularly tailored to the adaptive rank window. Inspired by the work of Yoon and Kweon [6], we will assign exponential weight to each pixel in the rank window according to its distance to the window center. The new rules are described in Fig.4:

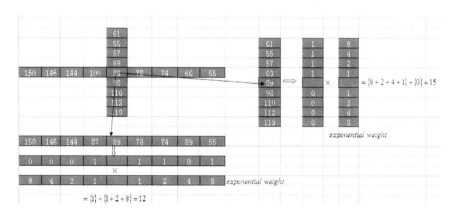

Fig. 4. New rank transform rules with window size 9 pixels, 8 bits considered

In Fig.4, the weight distribution started from the left and right neighbors of center pixel (2^0) to the ends of left and right side ($2^{\text{ceiling }(N/2)\text{-}2}$, e.g. $N=9$, $2^{\text{ceiling }(9/2)\text{-}2}=3$) . Letting weights decrease exponentially from the center is actually a common practice for adaptive-weight approaches. Our new rules can be mathematically expressed by (3)-(6):

$$s(x) \quad = \quad \begin{cases} 1 & x < 0 \\ 0 & x \geq 0 \end{cases} \tag{3}$$

$$r_h(N_h,C_h) = \sum_{n=1}^{C_h-1} s(I(n)-I(C_h)) \times 2^{(C_h-n-1)} + \sum_{n=C_h+1}^{N_h} s(I(n)-I(C_h)) \times 2^{(n-C_h-1)} \tag{4}$$

$$r_v(N_v,C_v) = \sum_{n=1}^{C_v-1} s(I(n)-I(C_v)) \times 2^{(C_v-n-1)} + \sum_{n=C_v+1}^{N_v} s(I(n)-I(C_v)) \times 2^{(n-C_v-1)} \tag{5}$$

$$r(c) = \sqrt{r_h^2 + r_v^2} \tag{6}$$

Where N_h and N_v are lengths of the horizontal and vertical window in pixel, $C_h = \left\lceil \dfrac{N_h}{2} \right\rceil$, $C_v = \left\lceil \dfrac{N_v}{2} \right\rceil$ are the locations of the center pixel c on the horizontal and vertical window respectively. $I(n)$ indicates intensity at arbitrary location n. r_h is the rank transform result for the horizontal window and r_v is the rank transform result for the vertical window. $r(c)$ is the final result for center pixel c. For example, in Fig.4, $r_h = 12$ and $r_v = 15$ the final rank transform result $r(c) = \sqrt{12^2 + 15^2}$.

2.4   Comparison between Adaptive and Original Rank Transform

Fig. 5 and Fig. 6 illustrate the differences between adaptive rank transform and original rank transform intuitively. In Fig. 5, we can see object boundaries are much sharper because the proposed method can adapt its window shape and size at boundary regions. In Fig. 6 we can see object boundaries are quite blurry because the original rank transform uses a fixed square rank window which often overlaps depth boundaries.

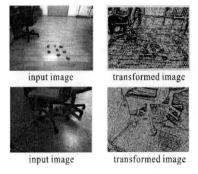

input image   transformed image

input image   transformed image

Fig. 5. The performance of adaptive rank transform

(a)   (b)

(c)   (d)

Fig. 6. The performance of original rank transform. (a),(c) the input images (b), (d) the rank transformed images.

3   Obtaining the Match Window from Multiple Rank Windows

After prepocessing the input images by the adaptive rank transform, the remaining job is to compute the pixel correspondence between two transformed images. To find the correspondence for a given pixel, local stereo matching algorithms commonly collect the information from all its neighbor pixels within a match window. This match window should also avoid covering depth boundaries while including as many pixels as possible for disambiguation [15]. Since the adaptive rank window is exactly designed to stretch in the direction of the same depth, we can easily assemble multiple adaptive rank windows together to obtain the match window.

Fig. 7 gives an visual example of the proposed method.We can see the proposed match window can adapt to local image structures accurately. Fig.8 shows the match window construction process. As illustrated in Fig.8, let p be a pixel to be matched, by using its horizontal window $H(p)$ and vertical window $V(p)$, we can easily construct its match window $U(p)$ (area inside blue lines). More specifically, let q be any pixel on $V(p)$, $U(p)$ is actually assembled by collecting **all** horizontal windows $H(q)$, which is expressed by formula 7 as follows:

$$U(p) = \bigcup_{q \in V(p)} H(q) \qquad (7)$$

Note that in section 2.2 because the quadruple has already been pre-computed for every pixel q, we can directly retrieve its horizontal window $H(q)$ here. Actually, $H(q)$ provides a connected set of pixels in the neighborhood of the pixel p. Similarly, $U(p)$ can also be constructed from multiple vertical windows, using $H(p)$ as the main axis.

Fig. 7. An example of the proposed match window

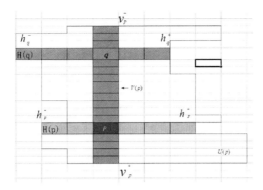

Fig. 8. The two rank windows $H(p)$ and $V(p)$ and the final match window $U(p)$

4   Experiments

In this section, we incorporate the adaptive rank transform and the adaptive match window into the Middlebury framework of local stereo matching [1] to evaluate their performance on the Middlebury dataset as well as intensity images. The Middlebury website provides test stereo pairs as well as an online evaluation system to evaluate performances of various stereo methods [16]. In our experiment, we deliberately add Gaussian noise ($\mu=0,\sigma=0.05$) to the Middlebury dataset in order to verify the robustness of our method. In addition, intensity images with brightness differences are also used in our experiment. We run another two algorithms across the same test images to compare with our proposed method. One of them is proposed by Yoon [6] , which is regarded as the best among the area-based local methods. The other is proposed by Zheng [14] and it is claimed to be the best-performing algorithm based on the rank transform so far.

Table 1 summarized the quantitative evaluation results using the Middlebury online evaluation system. Numbers in the table indicates the average percent of bad pixels. Fig.9 shows disparity maps and Fig.10 demonstrates corresponding bad pixel maps. Bad pixel maps are visualized quality indicators of disparity maps which are obtained by comparing disparity maps with ground truth and blackening image locations where absolute disparity errors are more than 2 pixels. From Fig.10, we can see that our method yields less bad pixels than the other two methods.

Table 1. Middlebury evaluation results

Algorithm	Tsukuba			Venus			Teddy			Cones		
	nonocc	all	disc	nonocc	all	disc	nonocc	all	disc	nonocc	all	disc
Our method	1.88	3.03	4.74	0.68	1.56	5.40	6.01	14.12	15.85	6.78	14.57	11.99
Zheng's Method[14]	2.38	3.22	6.35	0.75	1.89	8.86	7.22	14.10	18.68	7.32	14.82	13.22
Yoon's method [6]	2.90	3.96	7.33	0.88	1.87	9.09	8.36	15.02	20.35	7.09	13.24	15.86
Zabih's Method [14]	4.54	5.42	9.15	1.12	2.35	12.50	12.80	18.60	24.30	9.64	15.33	21.72

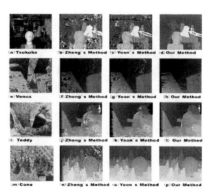

Fig. 9. Disparity Maps for noisy Middlebury stereo pairs

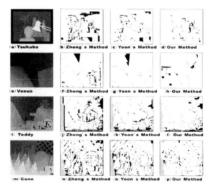

Fig. 10. Bad pixel maps for noisy stereo pairs

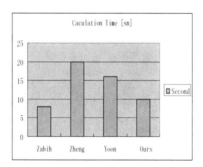

Fig. 11. Time consumed in calculations of the algorithms by a PC

Fig.11 are corresponding running time. From Fig.11 we can see our method is slower than the original method proposed by Zabih [9] but faster than Zheng's method and Yoon's method. Fig.12 shows the experimental results for intensity images and we can see that edges are more accurately recovered in our disparity maps (Fig.12 (e) and Fig.12 (j)) despite the brightness differences between two input images. More specifically, we can see the leg of the desk is blurred in Yoon's disparity map (Fig.12 (c)) and a piece of the desk surface is missing in Zheng's disparity map (Fig.12 (d)) but both the desk and the leg are accurately recovered in our disparity map (Fig.12 (e)). Besides, we can also see that the door knobs are much sharper in our disparity map (Fig.12 (j)) than those in Yoon's (Fig.12(h)) and Zheng's (Fig.12(i)) disparity maps.

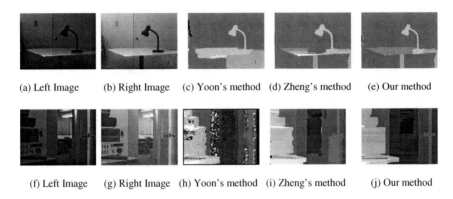

(a) Left Image   (b) Right Image   (c) Yoon's method   (d) Zheng's method   (e) Our method

(f) Left Image   (g) Right Image   (h) Yoon's method   (i) Zheng's method   (j) Our method

Fig. 12. Disparity maps for stereo pairs with brightness differences

One important application of disparity maps is 3D reconstruction.Now, we convert our disparity maps shown in Fig.12(e) and Fig.12 (j) to 3D models. The results are shown in Fig.13 and we can see depth surfaces of the 3D scene are successfully reconstructed by using our disparity maps.

Fig. 13. Corresponding 3D reconstruction results

5   Conclusion

In this paper, we propose an adaptive rank transform which is an image pre-processing method for enabling more accurate pixel correspondence computation. This new rank transform can adapt the shape and size of the rank window to the image local structure. Moreover, a new type of adaptive match window is further proposed by assembling multiple adaptive rank windows together. The results of experiments show that the proposed methods are effective and robust.

Acknowledgements. This work was supported by Natural Science Foundation of China (No. 60805046 and 60835004).

References

1. Scharstein, D., Szeliski, R.: A taxonomy and evaluation of dense two-frame stereo correspondence algorithms. International Journal of Computer Vision 47(1), 7–42 (2002)
2. Yang, Q.X., Ahuja, N.: A constant-space belief propagation algorithm for stereo matching. In: IEEE Conference on Computer Vision and Pattern Recognition, vol. 1, pp. 1458–1465. IEEE Press, San Francisco (2010)
3. Cheng, L., Selzer, J.: Region-Tree based stereo using dynamic programming optimization. In: IEEE Conference on Computer Vision and Pattern Recognition, vol. 1, pp. 2378–2385. IEEE Press, New York (2006)
4. Srivastava, S., Seong, J.H.: Stereo matching using hierarchical belief propagation along ambiguity gradient. In: IEEE International Conference on Image Processing, vol. 36(2), pp. 2085–2088. IEEE Press, Cairo (2009)
5. Vanetti, M., Gallo, I., Elisabeta, B.: Dense two-frame stereo correspondence by self-orgnazing neural network. In: Internation Conference on Image Analysis and Processing, vol. 2, pp. 456–489 (2009)
6. Yoon, K.J., Kweon, I.J.: Adaptive support-weight approach for correspondence search. IEEE Transaction on Pattern Analysis and Machine Intelligence 28(4), 650–656 (2006)
7. Guie, L., Yang, X.R., Qi, X.: Fast stereo matching algorithm using adaptive window. In: International Symposiums on Information Processing, pp. 25–30. IEEE Press, New York (2008)
8. Zhang, Z., Zhang, M.: Fast stereo matching algorithm based on adaptive window. In: International Conference on Audio Language and Image Processing, pp. 138–143 (2010)
9. Zabih, R., Woodfill, L.J.: Non-Parametric Local Transforms for Computing Visual Correspondence. In: Eklundh, J.-O. (ed.) ECCV 1994. LNCS, vol. 801, pp. 151–158. Springer, Heidelberg (1994)
10. Banks, J., Bennamoun, M.: Reliability analysis of the rank transform for stereo matching. IEEE Transactions on Systems, Man, and Cybernetics 31(6), 870–880 (2001)
11. Hirschmuller, H., Scharstein, D.: Evaluation of stereo matching costs on images with radiometric differences. IEEE Transactions on Pattern Analysis and Machine Intelligence 31(9), 1582–1599 (2009)
12. Ambrosch, K., Humenberger, M.: Extending two non-parametric transforms for FPGA based stereo matching using bayer filtered cameras. In: Computer Vision and Pattern Recognition Workshops, vol. 1, pp. 1–8. IEEE Press, Anchorage (2008)
13. Wang, K.: Adaptive stereo matching algorithm based on edge detection. In: IEEE International Conference on Image Processing, vol. 1, pp. 1345–1348. IEEE Press, Singapore (2004)
14. Zheng, G., Su, X.Y., Liu, Y.K.: Local stereo matching with adaptive support weight, rank transform and diaparity calibration. Pattern Recognition Letters 29(1), 1230–1235 (2008)
15. Veksler, O.: Stereo Matching by compact windows via minimum radio cycle. In: International Conference on Computer Vision, vol. 1, pp. 540–547 (2001)
16. Scharstein, D., Szeliski, R.: Middlebury Stereo Vision Page (2008), http://vision.middlebury.edu/stereo/

Real Time Vision Based Multi-person Tracking for Mobile Robotics and Intelligent Vehicles

Dennis Mitzel, Georgios Floros, Patrick Sudowe,
Benito van der Zander, and Bastian Leibe

UMIC Research Centre, RWTH Aachen University, Germany

Abstract. In this paper, we present a real-time vision-based multi-person tracking system working in crowded urban environments. Our approach combines stereo visual odometry estimation, HOG pedestrian detection, and multi-hypothesis tracking-by-detection to a robust tracking framework that runs on a single laptop with a CUDA-enabled graphics card. Through shifting the expensive computations to the GPU and making extensive use of scene geometry constraints we could build up a mobile system that runs with 10Hz. We experimentally demonstrate on several challenging sequences that our approach achieves competitive tracking performance.

1 Introduction

The recent research progress made towards the solution of important computer vision problems enables the development of mobile robotic systems that possess visual scene understanding capabilities. In this paper, we propose a framework for visual scene understanding from a mobile platform focusing on multi-person tracking in urban environments. The scenario on which we apply our system poses a number of challenges ranging from difficult lighting conditions and motion blur to occlusions caused by the moving objects. In order to produce robust results in such highly dynamic environments an integration of state-of-the-art computer vision components has to be carried out. The proposed system comprises a combination of a stereo visual odometry (VO) estimation module, a pedestrian detection module and a tracking-by-detection module. The careful implementation of each of the components making use of parallel computing capabilities that modern graphics cards provide, together with their careful combination in a common uncertainty handling framework enable our system to robustly track multiple persons at interactive frame rates.

In detail, our work makes the following contributions: 1) We present a tracking -by-detection system running in real-time 2) As part of this system, we present an efficient pedestrian detector which performs at very high frame-rates (26 Hz on a laptop with Core2Quad 1.86 GHz and GTX 285M), exploiting scene geometry information in a parallel implementation on a graphics card. 3) We combine the tracking by detection framework with a VO component which estimates the pose of our camera system at every frame, and thus enables our system to be mobile. Therefore, the system that we propose can serve as a demonstration of the

S. Jeschke, H. Liu, and D. Schilberg (Eds.): ICIRA 2011, Part II, LNAI 7102, pp. 105–115, 2011.
© Springer-Verlag Berlin Heidelberg 2011

vision capabilities that are already possible now for mobile robotics since the whole pipeline can be executed on a single, GPU-enabled laptop.

The paper is structured as follows. After discussing related work in the following section, Section 3 presents the overview of our system and the interplay between the different modules. In Section 4 our system is presented in detail, focusing on the realization of each of the modules. Finally, Section 5 evaluates the quantitative and qualitative performance on a number of challenging video sequences.

2   Related Work

The development of powerful object detectors [3] pushed the progress for robust multi-person tracking approaches in challenging crowded scenarios [17], [6], [5]. However for fulfilling the real-time constraint of robotic applications, many approaches follow a simple strategy of extracting ROIs based on motion [4], texture content [15] and stereo depth [8] in order to reduce the image area which should be scanned by the detector. This strategy however risks losing object detections if the corresponding regions are missed due to failures in the ROI extraction process. Furthermore, this strategy requires time consuming preprocessing steps, such as stereo depth or optical flow estimation.

In detail, two new approaches were proposed addressing the problem of real-time pedestrian detection from a moving vehicle. Firstly, [2] use a structure classifier to extract candidate ROIs on which the pedestrian detector is applied, resulting in a run-time of 10Hz. However, the system fails to handle crowded scenes in an urban environment and thus exhibits poor performance in such situations. Secondly, [1] presented a stereo-based pedestrian detection and tracking system that runs at 5Hz from a moving vehicle. Although their framework works at acceptable error rates in semi-urban datasets, the lack of any occlusion handling mechanism causes this system to underperform in cluttered urban datasets. Our framework outperforms both approaches as shown in Sec. 5, still running at 10Hz.

3   System Overview

Fig. 1 shows a system-level overview of our proposed tracking system that consists of three major parts: Visual Odometry, Object Detection and Tracking module. From the output of the stereo camera setup we first compute the stereo camera pose based on the VO approach by [13]. The method is adapted in such a way that a feedback loop from the detector provides the areas in the image with potential objects. These areas are excluded before computing and tracking feature points in the VO module resulting in increased robustness for busy scene scenarios. On the other side the output of the VO and a ground plane are utilized in the detector implementation for constraining the search window to a narrow corridor (ROI) for each scale. This allows us to run the detector on the GPU with more than 26Hz. The detected pedestrians are fed into the tracking

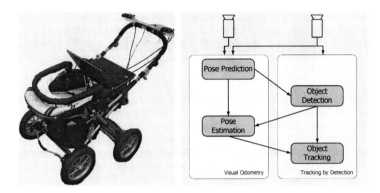

Fig. 1. Platform and System Overview: (left) Mobile platform used for our experiments, equipped with a stereo camera setup and a powerful laptop for processing the data. (right) System overview showing the interactions between the individual components.

module where the bounding boxes are converted to ground plane coordinates and are associated into trajectories employing Extended Kalman Filters (EKFs) and an appearance model. The detector is the most computationally expensive part of our framework. The VO module is optimized for multi-core processors and runs with approx. 12Hz. The tracking module is the cheapest part running with more than 20Hz.

For presenting our real-time multi-person tracking approach we built up a mobile platform equipped with two synchronized cameras that are mounted on a child stroller (Fig.1). The data are processed on a single laptop with a CUDA-enabled graphics card (Nvidia GTX 285M), an Intel Core i7 1.86 GHz processor and 8 GB RAM. Quantitative and qualitative results achieved with this mobile platform are presented in Sec. 5.

4   System Realization

In this section we will present the realization of the individual components of our system.

4.1   Visual Odometry

The VO module of our framework is responsible for computing the motion of the camera based solely on video input. As illustrated in Fig. 2, the front-end of our VO estimator is based on local feature extraction and tracking. Camera pose estimates can then be estimated from feature tracks using a RANSAC-based hypothesize-and-test framework. In the final stage, the camera pose estimates are fed into a Kalman Filter based tracker which predicts the pose of the camera in the next frame and the scheme is iterated.

Feature Extraction. For each frame, we correct the radial distortion and rectify the images in order to allow efficient feature matching along the same

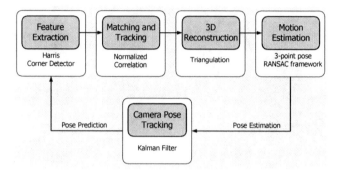

Fig. 2. Visual Odometry framework

scanline. Harris corners [9] are then extracted from each of the images. Our decision for this type of features is justified by their response stability and repeatability with regard to several image transformations as reported in [12]. To increase the stability of our algorithm we take two precautions. Firstly, following the approach of [13], we divide the image into a 10 by 10 grid and extract a maximum of 30 features in each of the 100 buckets. Secondly, we do not accept features that are localized on pixels corresponding to moving objects (as in [5]) by discarding all the Harris corners which lie inside the bounding boxes extracted from the pedestrian detector described in Sec. 4.2.

Feature Matching and Tracking.   For each of the extracted features, we create a descriptor in the form of an 11 x 11 pixel patch centered on the feature. The feature descriptors are then matched using normalized cross correlation. Features are matched between the left and the right image of the current frame, as well as the corresponding left and right image of the previous frame. Two features form a valid pair only if they mutually match with each other. The matches from the current frame are then triangulated to form the corresponding points in the 3D space. Matching between consecutive frames is mainly guided by the Kalman filter prediction of the camera pose.

Motion Estimation.   We follow the approach of [14] to compute the pose of the stereo head from triples of reconstructed landmarks (3-point pose). In particular, we use a RANSAC hypothesize-and-test framework to evaluate each of the hypotheses for the camera pose. The landmarks are grouped into triples and each of these triples gives a hypothesis for the camera pose. These hypotheses are then tested for all the other landmarks and are evaluated using the backprojection error as a scoring function and the best is selected.

Camera Pose Tracking.   In the final stage of our VO pipeline, we employ a Kalman filter with a constant-velocity motion model to track the pose of the stereo system, as suggested by [5]. The constant-velocity Kalman tracker extrapolates the camera path in cases where the majority of the scene pixels are occupied by moving objects and thus limits the effect of outliers.

Fig. 3. Ground plane corridor at scales $\sigma = 1.75$ (left) and $\sigma = 0.65$ (middle) with two valid detections inside. Valid detections upper border is located between the green lines, respectively the lower borders are between the red lines. This allows for some variation in detection window size. (right) The modules of the detection framework with individual computational time consumption.

Table 1. Run-time performance of our `cudaHOG` and `groundHOG` detector evaluated on a desktop (Core2Quad Q9550, GTX280) and a laptop (Core2Quad 1.86 GHz GTX 285M)

| | CPU-HOG | GPU-HOG ||
		cudaHOG	groundHOG
Desktop	7-10s	44ms	18ms
Laptop	7-10s	139ms	38ms

4.2   Object Detection

For pedestrian detection, we employ an efficient GPU implementation of a popular object detection algorithm named *Histograms of Oriented Gradients* [3]. In the following we provide some details of the detection framework. Our *CUDA*-based implementation [16] of the *HOG* algorithm achieves the same detection accuracy as the original implementation by Dalal [3], while reducing the run-time on a 640×480 image to around $20 - 30ms$. This enables our detector to be used in time critical applications. The *HOG* detector encodes the content of a *window* within the image as a feature vector, the so called *HOG descriptor*. Subsequently, a binary classifier, in our case a *linear Support Vector Machine*, determines whether the target object is found or not. This process is repeated for the entire image by effectively sliding the window over the image. In order to find objects of different sizes, the image is rescaled and the process is repeated again. Due to the design of the individual binary decisions, a final non-maximum suppression step is required to merge multiple detections regarding the same object in the scene. The *CUDA* implementation splits the detection algorithm into three *kernels*. These are subroutines that run highly parallel directly on the GPU. We use individual kernels to compute *gradients*, the *HOG blocks*, and finally to perform the SVM evaluation for each window (Fig. 3).

In common street scenarios, pedestrians can be expected to occur only in a small region of the image, practically speaking on the ground plane in the scene. To exploit this fact in our implementation, we use the scene geometry to constrain the search region to a narrow corridor on the ground plane for each scale, as shown in Fig. 3. This allows us to reduce the search region dramatically. Fig. 3 (middle) shows that the search region for smaller pedestrians is less than a third of the overall image area. Hence, by exploiting the ground plane constraint we can avoid computation of two thirds of the features. As the feature computation is a computationally expensive step, this yields a considerable speedup. At the same time invalid detections (false positives), where pedestrians are "floating" in the air are less likely, which leads to increased detection precision.

Computational Performance. In Tab. 1, we present the run-time performance of our `cudaHOG` and `groundHOG` pedestrian detectors on a desktop (Core2 Quad Q9550, GTX280) and our laptop (Core2Quad 1.86 GHz GTX 285M) computer. Through the geometrical constraints employed for `groundHOG`, we can reduce the run-time compared to `cudaHOG` nearly by a factor of three. This is one of the optimization steps that allow us to run the whole tracking system on a laptop at around 10Hz.

Ground Plane Estimation. The ground plane can be automatically estimated from stereo depth by employing the v-disparity approach [10]. Stereo depth-maps are obtained using the method of Geiger et. al. [7] which runs at 8-10Hz on a single processor core, which is sufficient for use in a real-time system.

4.3   Tracking

As tracking module, we employ an extended version of the robust multi-hypothesis tracking framework presented in [11]. In brief, the basic approach works as follows. Using the current camera position from SfM and the ground plane estimate, the detector output is transformed to 3D world coordinates (Fig. 4, left). These detections are connected to generate an over-complete set of competing trajectory hypotheses, by starting new trajectories in each frame from the new detections and extending the existing trajectories (see Fig. 4). For obtaining the final hypothesis set which best explains the current scene, we apply model selection in every frame.

Trajectory Estimation. For robust detection association, we employ an appearance model and a dynamic model for each hypothesis. As a hypothesis appearance model, we choose an $8 \times 8 \times 8$-bin color histogram in RGB space which is computed for each detection over an ellipse fitted inside the detection box. The pixel values are weighted with a Gaussian kernel, favoring pixels closer to the center. For describing the motion of a pedestrian, we employ an EKF assuming a constant-velocity motion model such that the state vector is defined as

$$s_t = [x_t, y_t, \theta_t, v_t], \tag{1}$$

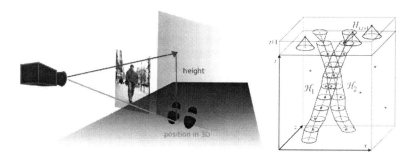

Fig. 4. (left) Computation of the 3D position and the height given the detection box and the scene geometry. (right) An example of trajectories generation by employing EKF. The blue hypothesis is one which was started in the new frame (with a high uncertainty represented by the size of the ellipse) and propagated backwards through previous frames. The red one is a hypothesis which was extended in the current frame.

where (x_t, y_t) is the position of the detection in 3D world space on the ground plane, θ_t the orientation of a pedestrian, and v_t the speed. The derived motion model which is the prediction function for the EKF is defined as follows:

$$f_{t+1}(x_t, y_t, \theta_t, v_t) = \begin{bmatrix} x_t + \delta_t \cdot v_t \cdot \cos(\theta_t) \\ y_t + \delta_t \cdot v_t \cdot \sin(\theta_t) \\ \theta_t + n_\theta \\ v_t + n_v \end{bmatrix}, \qquad (2)$$

n_θ and n_v are the noise components for orientation and speed, respectively. In contrast to [5], we propose to determine the unobservable variables, namely the orientation θ and velocity v, based on the prediction and the current observation achieving higher robustness:

$$z_t(x_t, y_t, \theta_t, v_t) = \begin{bmatrix} x_t^o \\ y_t^o \\ \mathrm{atan}\left(\dfrac{y_t^o - (y_t^p - \delta_t \cdot v_t^p \cdot \sin(\theta_t^p))}{x_t^o - (x_t^p - \delta_t \cdot v_t^p \cdot \cos(\theta_t^p))} \right) \\ \dfrac{1}{\delta_t} \cdot \sqrt{\begin{array}{l}(x_t^o + (x_t^p - \delta_t \cdot v_t^p \cdot \sin(\theta_t^p)))^2 + \\ + (y_t^o + (y_t^p - \delta_t \cdot v_t^p \cdot \cos(\theta_t^p)))^2\end{array}} \end{bmatrix}, \qquad (3)$$

where the indices o and p indicate the observed and predicted data.

The observation uncertainty C_{3D} for each 3D point is computed using error back-propagation, assuming a covariance $C_{2D} = [\sigma_x\, 0;\, 0\, \sigma_y]$ on pixel measurements:

$$C_{3D} = (F^{c1} C_{2D}^{-1} F^{c1} + F^{c2} C_{2D}^{-1} F^{c2})^{-1}, \qquad (4)$$

where F^{c1} and F^{c2} are the Jacobians of the projection matrix of the individual cameras. The uncertainty increases the further the 3D point is away from the camera position.

In each frame, when new pedestrian detections become available, the already existing trajectories are extended by predicting a new position and finding a possible observation that is inside the predicted uncertainty. For verifying the appearance similarity between the hypothesis and the observation, we employ the Bhattacharyya coefficient between the color histograms. When a new observation is added to the trajectory hypothesis, the appearance model of the hypothesis is adapted as $A_i = (1 - \alpha)h_o + \alpha h_i$, with h_i the color histogram of the hypothesis and h_o the color histogram of the observation. The weight α is the Kalman Filter uncertainty multiplied by the Bhattacharya distance.

In addition to the extension of existing trajectories, new trajectory hypotheses are created by starting from new detections and trying to extend these backwards in time through past detections in previous frames. Here we look up to 100 frames into the past. Due to the fact that a new detection is used for extension and also for generating new trajectories, each detection may end up in several competing trajectory hypotheses.

Final Hypothesis Selection. The result of the trajectory hypotheses generation is an overcomplete set of trajectories. The score of each trajectory hypothesis is composed of the likelihood of the associated detections under the motion and appearance model. For obtaining the final hypotheses set which best represents the scene, we prune the overcomplete set using model selection in a Minimum Description Length framework, as presented in [11].

Assigning Person Identities. As the model selection process selects the hypothesis independently, we require a method for assigning consistent person IDs to the chosen trajectories. In the case where a trajectory is selected which was extended, the assignment of IDs is simple. In the other case, we match the selected trajectory against the list of active tracks based on the number of occupied observations. If the overlap is larger than 90%, the ID of the active track is assigned, otherwise a new track ID is created and assigned.

5   Experimental Results

Datasets. In order to evaluate our approach, we run it on two challenging sequences captured in Zurich and provided generously by the authors of [5]. Both sequences, BAHNHOF and SUNNY DAY, were captured from a stereo rig mounted on a child stroller, similar to our setup, and can be downloaded from http://www.vision.ee.ethz.ch/~aess/dataset/. The BAHNHOF sequence was acquired on a crowded sidewalk during a clouded day and contains 999 frames with 5193 annotated pedestrians. The SUNNY DAY sequence was captured similarly to the BAHNHOF sequence on a crowded side walk but during a sunny day and contains also 999 frames from which 354 are annotated. In addition, the authors of [5] provided us with ground-truth structure-from-motion localization and ground plane estimates. The stereo depth maps were computed using the approach from [7] and are used for verifying the position on the ground plane of a detected object.

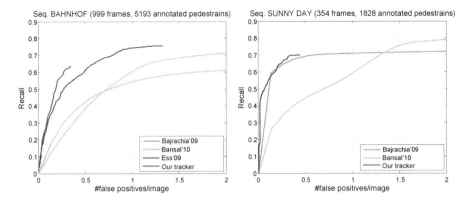

Fig. 5. (left) Quantitative tracking performance of our approach compared to the baselines from [5,1,2] on the **BAHNHOF** sequence. (right) Quantitative tracking performance on the **SUNNY DAY** sequence. The results show that our approach can reach state-of-the-art performance.

Fig. 6. Results from our tracking setup on our dataset and on the **BAHNHOF** sequence

Quantitative Performance. For validating the performance of our approach quantitatively, we employ the evaluation criteria proposed by [5]. The quality is measured by the intersection-over-union between tracked objects and given annotations where matches with an overlap grater than 0.5 are treated as correct. In Fig. 5 we show the performance in terms of recall vs. false positives per image (ffpi) for both sequences. As can been seen, our approach achieves state-of-the-art performance on both sequences. In particular, it clearly outperforms the approaches [1] and [2].

Qualitative Performance. Fig. 6 presents some results from our real time tracker showing that our system can track most of the visible pedestrians correctly in the presence of short time occlusions.

6   Conclusion

We have presented a robust system for multi-person tracking in urban environments. Our system builds on the framework presented by [5] extending and optimizing it towards real-time performance. In particular, we have systematically optimized a sliding window object detector employing geometrical constraints for reducing the search space. Furthermore, we have implemented and parallelized a visual odometry method which robustly estimates the camera pose using feedback from the object detector. Finally, we have extended a multi-hypothesis tracker with regard to speed, without losing accuracy in tracking performance. As our experimental results show our system runs in real time, reaching state-of-the-art performance.

Acknowledgments. This project has been funded, in parts, by the EU project EUROPA (ICT-2008-231888) and the cluster of excellence UMIC (DFG EXC 89).

References

1. Bajracharya, M., Moghaddam, B., Howard, A., Brennan, S., Matthies, L.: Results from a real-time stereo-based pedestrian detection system on a moving vehicle. In: ICRA 2009 (2009)
2. Bansal, M., Jung, S.H., Matei, B., Eledath, J., Sawhney, H.S.: A real-time pedestrian detection system based on structure and appearance classification. In: ICRA 2010 (2010)
3. Dalal, N., Triggs, B.: Histograms of oriented gradients for human detection. In: CVPR 2005 (2005)
4. Enzweiler, M., Kanter, P., Gavrila, D.: Monocular Pedestrian Recognition Using Motion Parallax. In: IVS (2008)
5. Ess, A., Leibe, B., Schindler, K., Van Gool, L.: Robust Multi-Person Tracking from a Mobile Platform. PAMI 31(10), 1831–1846 (2009)
6. Gavrila, D., Munder, S.: Multi-Cue Pedestrian Detection and Tracking from a Moving Vehicle. IJCV 73(1), 41–59 (2007)

7. Geiger, A., Roser, M., Urtasun, R.: Efficient Large-Scale Stereo Matching. In: Kimmel, R., Klette, R., Sugimoto, A. (eds.) ACCV 2010, Part I. LNCS, vol. 6492, pp. 25–38. Springer, Heidelberg (2011)
8. Geronimo, D., Sappa, A., Ponsa, D., Lopez, A.: 2D-3D-based On-Board Pedestrian Detection System. CVIU 114(5), 583–595 (2010)
9. Harris, C., Stephens, M.: A combined corner and edge detector. In: Alvey Vision Conference, AVC 1988 (1988)
10. Labayrade, R., Aubert, D., Tarel, J.: Real time obstacle detection in stereovision on non flat road geometry through v-disparity representation. In: IVS (2002)
11. Leibe, B., Schindler, K., Van Gool, L.: Coupled Object Detection and Tracking from Static Cameras and Moving Vehicles. PAMI 30(10), 1683–1698 (2008)
12. Mikolajczyk, K., Schmid, C.: Scale & affine invariant interest point detectors. IJCV 60(1), 63–86 (2004)
13. Nistér, D., Naroditsky, O., Bergen, J.: Visual odometry. In: CVPR 2004 (2004)
14. Nistér, D., Stewénius, H.: A minimal solution to the generalised 3-point pose problem. Journal of Mathematical Imaging and Vision 27(1), 67–79 (2007)
15. Shashua, A., Gdalyahu, Y., Hayon, G.: Pedestrian Detection for Driving Assistance Systems: Single-Frame Classification and System Level Performance. In: IVS (2004)
16. Sudowe, P., Leibe, B.: Efficient Use of Geometric Constraints for Sliding-Window Object Detection in Video ICVS (2011),
    http://www.mmp.rwth-aachen.de/projects/groundhog
17. Wu, B., Nevatia, R.: Detection and Tracking of Multiple, Partially Occluded Humans by Bayesian Combination of Edgelet Part Detectors. IJCV 75(2) (2007)

A Method for Wandering Trajectory Detection in Video Monitor

Ruohong Huan[1], Zhehu Wang[1], Xiaomei Tang[1], and Yun Pan[2]

[1] College of Computer Science and Technology, Zhejiang University of Technology, 310023 Hangzhou, China
[2] Department of Information Science and Electronic Engineering, Zhejiang University, 310027 Hangzhou, China
huanrh@zjut.edu.cn

Abstract. For video monitor system, wandering trajectory detection of moving targets is one of key problems needed to be solved, as it is an effective method to discover wandering behavior and prevent the potential harmful behavior. In view of the weakness of the existing algorithms, a method for wandering trajectory detection based on angle is proposed in this paper. In this method, wandering trajectory curves are divided into three kinds, which are closed curve, spiral curve and S curve. The occurring of wandering can be analyzed and judged through the angle of trajectory changing. The experimental results demonstrate that the method can detect the wandering trajectory accurately in video sequences, without any training samples. So, the method can improve the real-time performance of the monitor system.

Keywords: Wandering trajectory detection, Video monitor, Angle.

1 Introduction

Video monitor is an important component of the security systems, and it has become one of the main ways to improve safety, because it is intuitive, easy and effective [1~4]. Wandering trajectory detection is one of the important functions of video monitor, and it plays a significant role in monitoring the behavior of the moving target. For example, if the wandering objects appear close to some valuable objects such as a car, they are likely to steal something or do something unlawful. Also, if the moving objects appear near a river or a railway and hold on wandering, they may be inclined to do something dangerous to the public safety or their own safety. Therefore, wandering trajectory detection is an effective method to discover wandering behavior and prevent the potential harmful behavior.

At present, the methods proposed for wandering trajectory detection are few. Reference [5] describes two kinds of wandering trajectory which are closed curve and spiral curve. These two kinds of wandering trajectory are judged with different methods. If the points are evenly distributed in each quadrant of the rectangular coordinate system, the trajectory is judged as a spiral curve. To judge closed curve, first connect

S. Jeschke, H. Liu, and D. Schilberg (Eds.): ICIRA 2011, Part II, LNAI 7102, pp. 116–124, 2011.
© Springer-Verlag Berlin Heidelberg 2011

every two continuous trajectory points. Then calculate each cross point of two segments which is nonadjacent and judge whether this point is in this two segments. If so, it can be proved that these two segments cross and this trajectory can be judged as a closed curve. Although this method has good results, it is only suitable for two special kinds of wandering trajectory. If the wandering trajectory is beside those two kinds, it won't be detected. Even for those two kinds of trajectory, the methods for detection are different, which results in complexity for the detection system. An algorithm of getting the trajectory feature based on sub-trajectory is proposed in reference [6]. The space location and time series information of the trajectory segment is gotten by sub-trajectory in this algorithm. The local movement of the target is extracted and learned to obtain the distribution model of the sub-trajectory. The trajectory is rebuilt by the distribution model of sub-trajectory. Thus, the features of trajectory can be extracted. A large number of trajectory samples are needed in this algorithm. The complexity of time and space is large. Therefore, the algorithm is only suitable for trajectory detection in some particular scenes such as car trajectory detection in crossroads etc. And it is not always fit for people behavior trajectory detection.

In view of the above analyzed problems, a method for wandering trajectory detection based on angle is proposed in this paper. In our method, wandering trajectory curves are divided into three kinds, which are closed curve, spiral curve and S curve. A general algorithm is used for trajectory detection, and the occurring of wandering trajectory can be analyzed and judged through the angle of trajectory changing. The method does not require any training samples, which improves the real-time performance.

2　Algorithm Description

The main idea of wandering trajectory detection based on angle can be described as follows. The occurring of wandering trajectory can be analyzed and judged through the angle of trajectory changing. We divide the wandering trajectory curves into three kinds, which are closed curve, spiral curve and S curve, as shown in Fig. 1. We consider

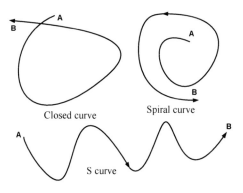

Fig. 1. Three kinds of wandering trajectory

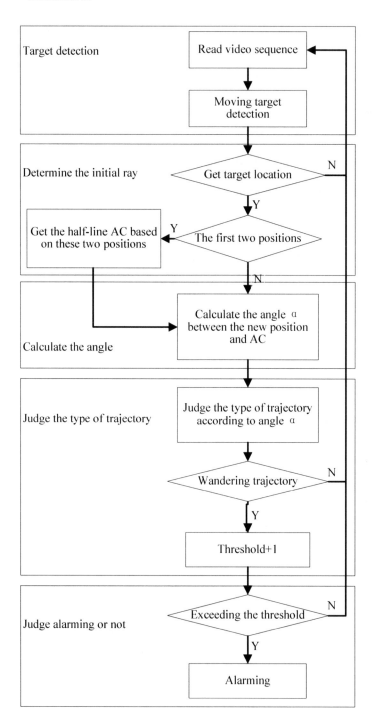

Fig. 2. Process of wandering trajectory detection based on angle in video monitor

various types of wandering trajectory curve can be formed by these three curves just referring to the idea in reference [5]. As the analysis above, reference [5] describes two kinds of wandering trajectory (closed curve and spiral curve), and considers other types of wandering trajectory curves all can be formed by these two curves. But two kinds of basis wandering trajectory are not comprehensive to cover all situations. So, in our method, S curve is to be added to the basis wandering trajectory, as it is a very common wandering trajectory in practice. The method of wandering trajectory detection based on angle is composed of five main steps. Its process is shown in Fig. 2.

2.1   Target Detection

Many classical methods, such as frame difference and background subtraction, can be used to detect the moving targets for each captured video sequence. Background subtraction is used in this paper to detect the moving targets. The principle of background subtraction [7, 8] is to subtract the background image from the current image to get the moving target areas. The algorithm is simple and easy to implement, and a complete feature data can be provided.

2.2   Determine the Initial Half-Line

After a moving target is detected, the positions A and C of the moving target should be determined in the initial frames. Suppose A is the start position of the moving target in the first frame, and C is the position of the moving target after a number of frames (10 frames in this paper). These two points are connected to generate the initial half-line AC . The process is shown in Fig. 3.

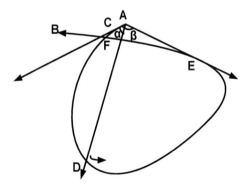

Fig. 3. Process of Half-line generation (Principle diagram of closed curve judgment)

2.3   Calculate the Angle

Suppose D is the next pass point of the moving target after the position C (see Fig. 3). The position A is still used as a start point, then the angle α between AD and AC can be calculated. Define the coordinate origin of the video sequence, and suppose $A(x_1,y_1)$, $C(x_2,y_2)$ and $D(x_3,y_3)$ as the coordinates of A, C and D. The angle α can be calculated as:

$$\cos\alpha = \frac{\overline{AC}\cdot\overline{AD}}{|AC||AD|} = \frac{(x_2-x_1,y_2-y_1)\cdot(x_3-x_1,y_3-y_1)}{\sqrt{(x_2-x_1)^2+(y_2-y_1)^2}\cdot\sqrt{(x_3-x_1)^2+(y_3-y_1)^2}} \tag{1}$$

2.4   Judge the Type of Trajectory

The type of the trajectory can be judged through the change of the angle α. Also, whether a wandering trajectory is occurring or not is needed to be judged. Set a wandering threshold with the initial value 0. The process for judgment is described as follows:

A. If the value of angle α becomes larger until it reaches a critical value. Then the angle α becomes smaller until it equals to $0°$. The moving target will cross with the original trajectory. This trajectory can be judged as a closed curve at this moment. The principle of closed curve judgment is shown in Fig. 3. Add 1 to the wandering threshold, and set the position D as a new start point. Next trajectory can be judged in the same way.

B. If the value of angle α becomes larger always until it equals to $180°$. At this moment, the moving target is arriving at E position. The point A, C and E are in the same line. This trajectory can be judged as a spiral curve. The principle of spiral curve judgment is shown in Fig. 4. Then add 1 to the wandering threshold, and set the position D as a new start point. Next trajectory can be judged in the same way.

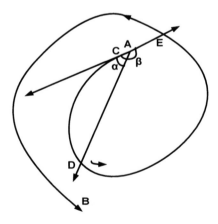

Fig. 4. Principle diagram of spiral curve judgment

C. If the value of angle α becomes larger until it reaches a critical value. Then the angle α becomes smaller until it reaches another critical value, and again the value of the angle α becomes larger. Moreover, the change range of the angle α is $0° < \alpha < 180°$ in the whole process. This trajectory can be judged as an S curve according to the cycle. The principle of S curve judgment is shown in Fig. 5. Then add 1 to the wandering threshold, and set the position D as a new start point. Next trajectory can be judged in the same way.

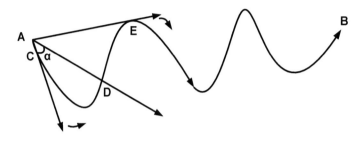

Fig. 5. Principle diagram of S curve judgment

2.5   Judge Alarming or Not

If the wandering threshold is beyond the setting value, the wandering alarm is triggered. Otherwise, return to the first step and re-capture the video sequences.

3   Experimental Results and Analysis

The method for wandering trajectory detection based on angle in video monitor are achieved and analyzed with C++ and OpenCV environment. The video sequences which captured in the campus are used as the experimental data. This paper only considers whether the algorithm is effective in the ideal environment, so the background of the video is a simple lawn and without any complex factors. And there is only one pedestrian in the video. The format of this video is AVI with XVID encoded. The frame rate is 25fps and the resolution is 352×288. The wandering trajectory detection results of the experiments are shown in Fig. 6, Fig. 7 and Fig. 8.

Fig. 6 shows the experimental results of the wandering trajectory as closed curve. Firstly, the position which is shown in figure (a) is set as the start point. When the target moves to the position which is shown in figure (b), the initial half-line AC can be determined. Then the angle α between each point and the half-line AC can be calculated. The angle α becomes larger until the target moves to the position shown in figure (g). Then, the angle α becomes smaller until it reaches $0°$, which is shown in figure (i). Therefore, this trajectory can be judged as a closed curve, and the warning message will be displayed on the monitor.

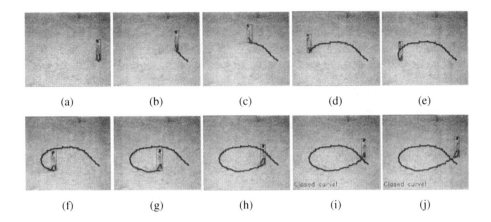

Fig. 6. The experimental results of closed curve

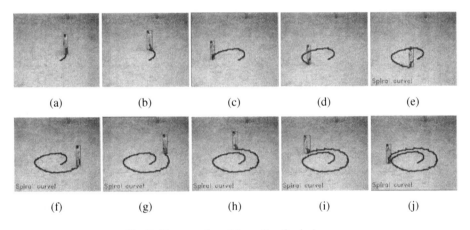

Fig. 7. The experimental results of spiral curve

Fig. 7 is the experimental results of the wandering trajectory as spiral curve. First, determine the initial half-line AC and calculate the angle α using the same method as above. The angle α becomes larger always before the target moves to the position shown in figure (d), and then the angle α reaches $180°$ in figure (e). The moving target and the initial half-line are in the same line. Therefore, this trajectory can be judged as a spiral curve, and the warning message will be displayed on the monitor. Make the position shown in figure (e) as a new start point. With the same method, when the target moves to the position shown in figure (j), the trajectory can be judged as a new spiral curve.

Fig. 8 is the experimental results of the wandering trajectory as S curve. First, determine the initial half-line AC and calculate the angle α using the same method as above. The angle α becomes larger always before the target moves to the position shown in figure (d). Then the angle α becomes smaller until the target moves to the position shown in figure (g), and then the angle α becomes larger again. The change range of the angle α is always $0° < \alpha < 180°$ in the whole process. Therefore, this trajectory can be judged as an S curve, and the warning message will be displayed on the monitor.

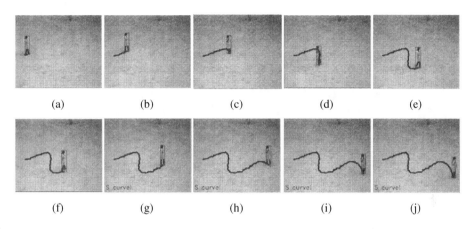

(a)   (b)   (c)   (d)   (e)

(f)   (g)   (h)   (i)   (j)

Fig. 8. The experimental results of S curve

We compare our method with some similar methods in reference [5] and reference [6] to prove the advantages of our method. Some measurements are used for evaluation, such as whether training samples are required in the algorithm, whether the algorithm can be real-time executed and how many kinds of trajectory the algorithm contains. The comparisons are given in Table 1. From the table 1, we conclude that our method does not require any training samples which can improve the real-time performance and describes three kinds of wandering trajectory which are more comprehensive.

Table 1. The comparison between this method and other similar methods

	The method in this paper	The method in reference [5]	The method in reference [6]
Training samples	Not required	Not required	Required
Execution	Real-time	Real-time	Not real-time
Kinds of trajectory	3	2	Unlimited

4   Conclusion

A method for wandering trajectory detection based on angle in video monitor is proposed in this paper. The experimental results prove that several common kinds of wandering trajectory can be judged by this method with a general algorithm, and the wandering trajectory can be detected accurately. The most important thing is that none of training samples is required in our method, which ensures the real-time performance of the monitor system.

Acknowledgments. The work reported in this paper was funded by research grants from the surface industry project of science and technology department of Zhejiang province. (Grant No. 2009C31002).

References

1. Collins, R., et al.: A system for video surveillance and monitoring: VSAM final report. Carnegie Mellon University: Technical Report CMU (2000)
2. Remagnino, P., Tan, T., Baker, K.: Multi-agent visual surveillance of dynamic scenes. Image and Vision Computing 16(8), 529–532 (1998)
3. Collision, P.A.: The application of camera based traffic monitoring systems. In: IEEE Seminar on CCTV and Road Surveillance, pp. 8/1–8/6 (1999)
4. Remagnino, P., Tan, T., Baker, K.: Agent orientated annotation in model based visual surveillance. In: Proc IEEE International Conference on Computer Vision, Bombay, India, pp. 857–862 (1998)
5. Zhang, Y., Liu, Z.: Irregular behavior recognition based on treading track. In: Proceedings of International Conference on Wavelet Analysis and Pattern Recognition, Beijing, China, vol. 3, pp. 1322–1326 (2007)
6. Qu, L.: Research on activity analysis and semantic retrieval in distributed intelligent visual surveillance system. The PhD thesis of Zhejiang University, 7 (2008)
7. McKenna, S., et al.: Tracking groups of people. Computer Vision and Image Understanding 80(1), 42–56 (2000)
8. Haritaoglu, I., Harwood, D., Davis, L.: W4: real-time surveillance of people and their activities. IEEE Trans. Pattern Analysis and Machine Intelligence 22(8), 809–830 (2000)

The Design
of a Vision-Based Motion Performance System

Cheng Ren, Shuai Ye, and Xin Wang[*]

College of Computer Science and Technology, Zhejiang University of Technology,
310023 Hangzhou, China
xinw@zjut.edu.cn

Abstract. This paper presents the structure of our real time vision-based motion performance system. The system requires user to wear markers with a certain color. Several novel algorithms in the system are introduced including algorithms for feature detection and feature tracking under occlusion. Feature Detection takes advantages of four properties of markers to avoid the interference from non-markers regions. Besides, we propose a simple but effective method to track these features and handle occlusion by estimating velocity of missing features based on prior, smoothness and fitness term. These algorithms are to ensure the accuracy and low computation cost of reconstruction of 3D points of the markers. At run time, the system automatically scans, identifies, tracks and finally reconstructs the markers to 3D points. We test the ability of our system by having user perform walking, running and jumping.

Keywords: Motion Performance, Feature Detection, Feature Tracking under Occlusion, Velocity Estimation, 3D Points Reconstruction.

1   Introduction

Video is the main source for human motion analysis and reconstruction. The ability of extracting useful information of human motion depends on several techniques including feature detection, feature tracking and human skeleton reconstruction. Any of them is a challenging issue in the area of computer vision. This paper presents architecture of a vision-based real time motion performance system. This system allows user to wear some markers with a certain color in front of a pair of stereo cameras and captures the 3D locations of the markers from the video sequence. The motion performance system consists of four parts (1) Initialization; (2) Feature detection; (3) Feature tracking; (4) 3D point construction and display. Each of these parts includes some novel algorithms which serve to reconstruct features of human motion accurately and efficiently. The main function of initialization is to obtain information of background of the image captured by camera and to correlate identified markers with corresponding body parts. Feature detection is to identify the

---

[*] Corresponding author.

S. Jeschke, H. Liu, and D. Schilberg (Eds.): ICIRA 2011, Part I, LNAI 7102, pp. 125–134, 2011.

markers on the user's body regardless of interference imposed by background and non-marker area of user's body. Feature tracking follows the path of motion of every identified marker. Under some circumstance where occlusion might occur, our tracking algorithm is able to reconstruct missing markers to some extent. The transformation from 2D to 3D is done by 3D reconstruction module. 3D information is then regarded as input to synthesis a detailed skeleton.

2   Related Work

Since our system mainly employs several vision algorithms including feature detection, feature tracking and 3D reconstruction, a brief overview about previous research on these issues is presented.

The work of feature detection in motion performance system mainly includes figure-background segmentation and feature extraction. There are several commonly implemented figure-background segmentation algorithms. The easiest way to model the background is with grayscale/color image B taken in absence of moving objects. Also, many authors model each background pixel with a probability density function learned over a set of training frames [1].

In this context, tracking is defined as establishing a correspondence between two successive frames. In [2], Tao, Sawhney and Kumar have proposed a method for tracking objects under occlusions by using temporal or spatial constrains on motion and appearance of the tracking objects in a dynamic layer representation. Authors from [3] have improved the method proposed in [2]. They use multiple occluding background layers and explicitly inferring the depth of foreground layers.

Human motion performance system reconstructs 3D motion information from 2D image sequence. Motion performance system can be divided into two categories: system based on top-down and bottom-up approaches [4]-[8]. Top-down approaches match human body model with images to obtain human pose parameters. With human body model, body geometrical structure and prior knowledge about motion model could be used to overcome difficulties in spatial position reconstruction. Bottom-up approaches do not use human body models. On the contrary, tracking of features and analysis are employed to acquire motion information.

3   System Overview

The motion performance system consists of four modules:

1. Initialization
2. Feature detection
3. Feature tracking
4. 3D points reconstruction and display

Each of these modules includes a certain robust and effective vision algorithms which help to reconstruct features both accurately and efficiently. The detail description of these four modules is as follows.

3.1   Initialization

Initialization lays the foundation for the later parts of the system. Initialization mainly includes two parts: (1) Establish background model (2) Scan all the markers on the body and determine which part of body these markers represent.

(1) Modeling of Background
Before reconstruction of human motion, the system records a series of images where no user is present, and then establishes background model by computing the mean values of every pixel value of these images and the mean deviations of these pixel values. Since the cost of the computation is large, it is should be done off-line.

(2) Scanning of Markers on Human Body
The goal of latter part is to relate markers to the corresponding human body parts so that human skeleton can be reconstructed. All of the body parts are stored in an array in a predetermined order. User is required to make a desirable pose according to that order. System would automatically detect markers and rearrange these markers so that these markers match that order. The scanning employs technique of feature detection, which would be introduced in the following part.

The experimental result of marker scanning is shown in Fig. 1.

Fig. 1. The result of marker scanning

In the figure above, ls, rs, lh, rh, lf, rf stand for left shoulder, right shoulder, left hand, right hand, left foot, right foot respectively.

3.2   Feature Detection

The goal of feature detection is to identify markers on the user's body accurately. Some interference parts whose color is similar to the markers including background regions and user's body might cause difficulty in detecting desirable markers. Traditional marker detection algorithm is improved in our application to ensure that all the markers are captured and no other region is mistaken as markers. Traditional methods dealing with marker detection problems mainly use color as the key to detect markers. If markers are green, for example, then pixels whose RGB values are within the range of green are regarded as where markers are located. However, some constraints in the real environment prevent traditional ways from achieving a satisfactory result including complex background, change in marker color due to change of lightening, or some regions of human body. Our method could effectively overcome such constrains and detect features accurately. The main difference between traditional ones and our method is that ours takes advantage of some other properties of markers in addition to color to filter the noisy regions in the image. These properties of marker are (1) area (2) shape (3) brightness (4) the distance a marker moved in the image. The detail about our algorithms is presented as follows:

First, we employ background subtraction [9] to remove background pixels with the model established in initialization module of the system. Then image is transformed to binary one, and white regions are marked by bounding rectangles (Fig. 2).

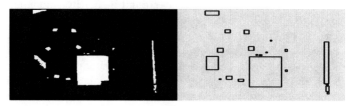

Fig. 2. The output of binarization (left image). White regions are marked by bounding rectangles (right image).

It should be noted that threshold for binarization in our method is set much lower. There are two reasons for lowering threshold: The first one is that it is to ensure that all of the suspicious regions in the image can be included. The second is to take into account the change in RGB value of markers caused by lightening. We lower the threshold so that all of the variation in RGB value of markers could be considered. However, the negative consequence brought about by lowering threshold is that many non-marker regions would also be included. To remove these regions, four properties of the real markers mentioned above are employed. We design four filters based on these four properties.

First, area filter demands that the area of bounding rectangles should be within a certain range. They could not neither be too small or too large. Then shape filter chooses the bounding rectangles of proper aspect ratios. Also, brightness filter selects appropriate blobs according to the amount of white pixels within the region of bounding rectangles. The rectangles contained more white pixels would be preferred. Distance filter relies on the fact that the distance a marker moved in the image is limited. Therefore, in order to identify the features in the current frame, algorithm only searches within the range close to the identified features of previous frame while others outside the range are excluded. Since bounding rectangles of ornaments or some other objects in the similar color to the markers contain less white pixels and might be outside the range of movement of features (for instance, necklace or earring), they could be removed by means of distance filter.

The experimental results of our feature detection are shown below:

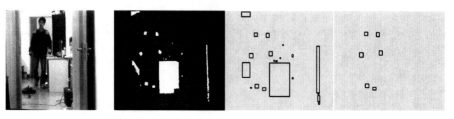

Fig. 3. The output of every step in feature detection algorithm

As illustrated in Fig. 3, the second image is the result of binarization of second one. The third is the image before filter, which might be the result of the feature detection algorithms considering color only. The forth image is the image after processing. It can be shown that all six markers are extracted.

3.3   Feature Tracking

In this section, we present a simple but effective way to track features for reconstructing use. Our tracking algorithm is as follows:

We denote the set of features in previous frame as A, that of current frame as B.

1. Distance between all of the markers in set A and markers in set B is computed. Then the distance and two ends of the edge are stored in an array named "edge";
2. Sort edge according to the distance from large to small.
3. Examine each element in the array to check whether the two ends of the marker have been matched, if not, they are labeled as matched and treated as the same features.

Above algorithm performs relatively well when frame rate of camera is higher because with high frame rate camera, the distance of the same feature between two consequent frames is small.

Another problem in feature tracking is occlusion. Much works on tracking under occlusion have been done [10]. In the system, we utilize a novel algorithm to reconstruct missing features under occlusion. We find that occlusion oftentimes prevents markers been seen by both cameras (Fig. 4). Under this circumstance, our approach takes advantage of the knowledge of corresponding feature in the other image in which the feature is not occluded.

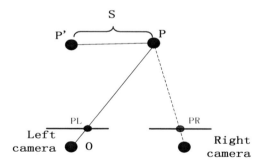

Fig. 4. Point P is occluded in the right image, while the corresponding point in the left image PL is not occluded

After calibration and rectification of cameras, images captured by stereo cameras are row aligned [11]. If spatial point P cannot seen by the right camera due to occlusion, the goal of our algorithm is to determine the location of P. As seen in Fig. 4, P is located on the line oP_l. Therefore, tracking algorithm can search the point along the line only. If the spatial distance between the feature of last frame and that of current frame S is determined, we could compute current spatial location of P by computing the intersection of the line p'p and oPL(Fig. 4), where p' is the point of the previous frame.

Moreover, if the velocity of the point's movement could be estimated, we could also be able to compute the distance between the point of last frame and that of the current frame. How the velocity of points' movement is estimated can be formulated as such problem: Given the previous h velocity values: $v_{t-h}, v_{t-h+1}, ..., v_{t-2}, v_{t-1}$, current velocity v_t should be determined. To calculate v_t, we assume that previous h velocities fit a kinematics function f:

$$v = f(t).\tag{1}$$

There could be numbers of candidate functions, and we choose the desirable function according to three evaluation terms – prior term, smoothness term, and fitness term.

The prior term estimates the posterior probability of a function f. More specifically, the prior term evaluates when function is given, the probability of occurrence of history data based on this function. Bayes' theorem provides a way to calculate the probability $P(h|D)$ [12] in the following way:

$$E_{prior} = \frac{P(D|h)P(h)}{P(D)}.\tag{2}$$

where h is a certain possible model. D is the history data. We define the set of possible models as H. $P(h)$ is the probability where h is selected among H. $P(D)$ is the prior probability that D will be observed. Since $P(h)$ can be assumed as a constant value and $P(D)$ is also a constant independent of h, the term $P(D|h)$ is only considered to find the most probable hypothesis [12].

$$E_{prior} = P(D|h).\tag{3}$$

In our problems, $v_{t-h}, v_{t-h+1}, ..., v_{t-2}, v_{t-1}$ is treated as D, and the every candidate function is h.

Smoothness term measures the smoothness of v_t produced by the function if v_t were placed after v_{t-2}, v_{t-1} [13]. We assume that the velocity at time t depends on only the velocities at time t-1, t-2. And the smoothness term is

$$E_{smoothness} = |v_t - 2v_{t-1} + v_{t-2}|^2.\tag{4}$$

The fitness term evaluates how well a function matches the history data. The fitness term is

$$E_{fitness} = \sum_{i=1}^{h} |v_i - f(t_i)|^2.\tag{5}$$

where v_i is the velocity of real history data and $f(t_i)$ is the simulation value computed by f.

We combine the three terms together as an indicator to evaluate the function f:

$$E = aE_{prior} - (bE_{smoothness} + cE_{fitness}).$$ (6)

Where a, b, c are weights of these three terms. Function f which maximizes E will be selected as the desirable one to estimate v_t. Then the distance can be computed by dividing v_t by frame rate.

The result of our tracking algorithm is shown below:

Fig. 5. The result of tracking algorithm

Left image in Fig. 5 is the first frame of a video sequence, and right one is the 50th frames. The result demonstrates that the tracking algorithm works well in the application.

3.4   3D Point Reconstruction and Display

Feature detection and tracking lay down the preparation for the 3D point reconstruction. Reconstruction algorithm the system uses is based on the theory of epipolar geometry [14]. After rectification of image pair, a correspondence between markers using epipolar geometry is established. Corresponding markers lie on a single epipolar line [14]. Given a point correspondence between the two cameras, depth of point Z is computed by finding the intersection of rays cast from the 2D markers in both cameras:

$$Z = \frac{fT}{xl - xr}.$$ (7)

Where f is the focal length, T is the length of translation vector between two cameras. xl and xr are the x-axle position of the points which stands for the same spatial point on a pair of images captured by stereo camera. The parameter f and T is obtained by camera calibration. Then how to calculate Z relies on how to compute xl and xr. Theoretically, after image rectification, corresponding points lie on the line parallel to x-axle. Therefore, it is easy to locate the xr on the right image if xl is already known.

However, because of the hardware limitation, for example, unsynchrony in capturing images by stereo camera, it becomes less possible to obtain such perfect result especially when markers are moving. In order to locate the x-axle value of corresponding point, we apply tracking algorithm to both images. Thus, system could locate corresponding point pair by identifying the pair of points who share the same tag in tracking despite real world limitations. The result image of locating corresponding points is shown in Fig. 6.

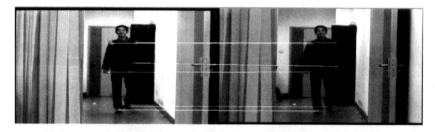

Fig. 6. Result of corresponding points match

As we can see, lines connect points are not absolutely parallel to x-axle, but by means of above technique, system could match corresponding points accurately. Then, we could get the depth of a point based on formula (7). To examine the accuracy of reconstruction, we use the 3D locations computed by motion performance system as the input of animation synthesis system. The experiment results are presented in the next section.

4   Experiments and Analysis

To demonstrate the effectiveness of our motion performance system, we conduct experiments by having user controlling six markers perform three kinds of behavior: walking, running and jumping. The output of our system is regarded as input of animation synthesis system which performs the reconstruction of full body skeleton from low-dimensional signals.

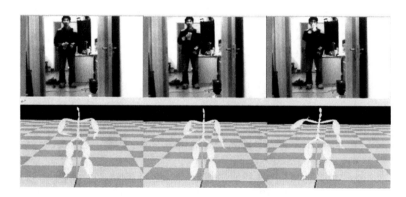

Fig. 7. User with six markers drinking and the corresponding animations

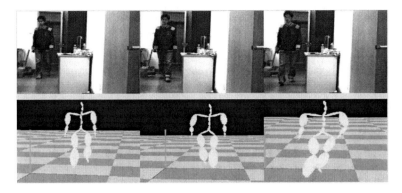

Fig. 8. User with six markers walking and the corresponding animations

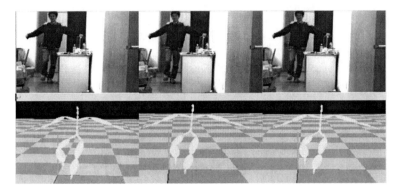

Fig. 9. User with six markers standing on one single foot and the corresponding animations

As seen by the figures, background imposes tremendous interference because behind the user is a red cabinet which has the similar color to the markers on the right part of the user's body. And some markers are blocked to some extent in some images, but the reconstruction results show that the outputs of motion performance system are reliable. Besides, average executing time cost of reconstruction of per frame is about 40ms. Therefore, our system can be running without obvious latency.

5   Conclusion

We have presented the detail on the architecture of a motion performance system that reconstructs the markers of users to the 3D points. The system includes four modules: Initialization, Feature Detection, Feature Tracking and 3D Point Reconstruction and Display. We propose some novel algorithms employed in each of these modules to ensure the reconstruction accuracy and efficiency. Our experiments show that the system could reconstruct the 3D location of markers both effectively and efficiently.

Acknowledgements. This work was supported by Natural Science Foundation of Zhejiang Province (Y1110882), and the Science and Technology Department of Zhejiang Province (Y200907765).

References

1. Wren, C., Azarbayejani, A., Darrell, T., Pentland, A.: Pfinder: Real-time Tracking of the Human Body. IEEE Trans. PAMI 19(17), 780–785 (1997)
2. Tao, H., Sawhney, H.S., Kumar, R.: Object Tracking with Bayesian Estimation of Dynamic Layer Representations. IEEE Transaction on Pattern and Machine Intell. 24(1), 75–89 (2002)
3. Wu, B., Nevatia, R.: Tracking of Multiple, Partially Occluded Humans based on Static Body Part Detection. In: Proc. of Comp. Vis. and Patt. Recogn., vol. 1, pp. 951–958 (2006)
4. Moeslund, T.B., Granum, E.: A Survey of Computer Vision-based Human Motion Capture. Computer Vision and Image Understanding 81(3), 231–268 (2001)
5. Chen, S.Y., Li, Y.F.: Determination of Stripe Edge Blurring for Depth Sensing. IEEE Sensors Journal 11(2), 389–390 (2011)
6. Chen, S.Y., Li, Y.F., Zhang, J.W.: Vision Processing for Real-time 3D Data Acquisition Based on Coded Structured Light. IEEE Transactions on Image Processing. 17(2), 167–176 (2008)
7. Chen, S.Y., Tong., H., et al.: Improved Generalized Belief Propagation for Vision Processing. Mathematical Problems in Engineering 2011, Article ID 416963 (2011), doi:10.1155/2011/416963
8. Chen, S.Y., Li, Y.F., Guan, Q., Xiao, G.: Real-time three-dimensional surface measurement by color encoded light projection. Applied Physics Letters 89(11), 111108 (2006)
9. Benezeth, Y., Jodoin, P.M., Emile, B., Laurent, H., Rosenberger, C.: Review and Evaluation of Commonly-implemented Background Subtraction Algorithms. In: 19th International Conference on Pattern Recognition, pp. 1–4 (2008)
10. Zhang., Z., Piccardi, M.: A Review of Tracking Methods under Occlusions. In: MVA 2007 IAPR Conference on Machine Vision Applications, vol. 30(30), pp. 146–149 (2007)
11. Bradski., G., Kaehler, A.: Learning openCV, p. 416. O'Reilly Media (2008)
12. Mitchell, T.M.: Machine Learning, pp. 156–157. McGraw-Hill (1997)
13. Chai, J., Hodgins, J.K.: Performance Animation from Low-dimensional Control Signals. In: SIGGRAPH 2005 (2005)
14. Hartley., R., Zisserman, A.: Multiple View Geometry in Computer Vision. Cambridge University Press (2000)

Window Function
for EEG Power Density Estimation
and Its Application in SSVEP Based BCIs

Gan Huang, Jianjun Meng, Dingguo Zhang, and Xiangyang Zhu

State Key Laboratory of Mechanical System and Vibration
Shanghai Jiao Tong University
Shanghai, China, 200240
huanggan1982@gmail.com
http://www.robot.sjtu.edu.cn

Abstract. A high quality power density estimation for certain frequency components in a short time is of key importance in Steady-State Visual Evoked Potentials (SSVEP) based Brain Computer Interface (BCI). In this paper, the effect of the window functions in SSVEP based BCIs is discussed. EEG signal is a typical color noise with a high energy of the low frequency component. The main findings are that (1) The spectral leakage for EEG signals has some regular patterns. An obvious oscillation with the corresponding frequency can be observed. The amplitude of the oscillation decreases with the growth of the frequency. A short analysis is also given for the leakage. (2) The leakage from the low frequency component can be effectively suppressed by the using of some windows, such as Hamming, Hann and triangle window; (3) By removing the influence of the leakage from the low frequency component with high pass filter, the classification results are mainly determined by the width of the main lobe. The rectangle window would have a better accuracy than Hamming, Hann and triangle window. Some windows constructed with a narrower main lobe width have a potential use in SSVEP based BCIs.

Keywords: SSVEP, EEG, Lowpass Filter, STFT.

1 Introduction

Brain Computer Interface (BCI), which has been developed fast in recent years, provides human beings direct ways to communicate with computer by intent alone. This new communication way is hoped to help the patients with sever neuromuscular disorders, such as late-stage amyotrophic lateral sclerosis, severe cerebral palsy, head trauma, and spinal injuries in the daily life. Several electrophysiological sources can be used for BCI control, including Event-Related Synchronization/Desynchronization (ERS/ERD), Steady-State Visual Evoked Potentials (SSVEP), Slow Cortical Potentials (SCP), P300 evoked potentials and μ and β rhythms [1]. Encouraged by the advantage of less training time [2–4], shorter response time [5] and higher information transfer rates [2, 6], SSVEP

S. Jeschke, H. Liu, and D. Schilberg (Eds.): ICIRA 2011, Part II, LNAI 7102, pp. 135–144, 2011.

based BCIs are more suitable to be developed in real time controlling. In recent years, SSVEP based BCIs used in cursor control [7], prosthetic control [8] and Functional Electrical Stimulation (FES) [9] have been reported. Some combination BCIs, based on SSVEP and other sources, have also been developed [10].

SSVEP is a continuous steady brain response for a repetitive stimulus with a certain frequency. It is mainly observed in visual and parietal cortical area. Occasionally, a smaller response is also observed in the mid-frontal region [11]. In SSVEP based BCIs, visual stimulus with different frequencies are simultaneously presented to the user. Each visual stimulus is associated with a command in an output (active) device. The user selected command can be detected as a larger maximum of the same frequency (and its harmonics) is found in the brain activity. Hence, the high quality power density estimation for certain frequency components in a short time is of key importance in SSVEP based BCIs.

In most SSVEP based BCIs, Fourier-related transforms are used widely in power density estimation[3, 5, 6, 8]. To estimate the power density at certain frequency ω of the signal in the vicinity of time t, Short-Time Fourier Transform (STFT) is used in this work. STFT is a Fourier-related transform used to determine the amplitude and phase-frequency distributions of local sections of a signal as it changes over time. In the continuous-time case, the STFT of signal $x(t)$ is written as

$$\mathrm{STFT}_x(t, \omega) = \int_{-\infty}^{\infty} x(\tau) w(\tau, t) e^{-j2\pi\omega\tau} d\tau,$$

where $w(s, t)$ is the window function which is nonzero for only a short period of time $s \in [t - L/2, t + L/2]$, L is the size of the window. The power density estimation of frequency ω at time t is

$$P_\omega(t) = \frac{1}{L} |\mathrm{STFT}_x(t, \omega)|^2 = \frac{1}{L} \left| \int_{-\infty}^{\infty} x(\tau) w(\tau, t) e^{-j2\pi\omega\tau} d\tau \right|^2.$$

Because of the signal truncation in STFT, the spectral leakage problem will occur. It appears as if some energy has "leaked" out from the true frequency of the signal into adjacent frequencies. To help reduce the spectral leakage, the window functions are used. The rectangular window with a narrow main lobe has excellent resolution characteristics for comparable strength signals with similar frequencies, but it is a poor choice for noise suppression. Flat top window have low side lobe peak, which does not provide well a frequency resolution but can measure the strength of a signal accurately at any frequency. Between the extremes, some moderate windows, such as Hamming, Hann and triangle windows, are used commonly as a tradeoff among narrow main lobe (corresponding to high frequency resolution), low side lobe peak and rapidly fall-off side lobes (corresponding to noise suppression). In the application of SSVEP based BCI, to get the transient response of the subjects and also as the simplest window, rectangular window have been widely used [3, 5, 6, 8, 9, 12]. Some other windows, like Hamming [7] and Gaussian windows [13], are also used in their applications.

In this paper, we study the effect of window function on power density estimation of EEG signals. In the following, the experiment is introduced in Section 2. The characteristic of EEG signals is introduced in Section 3. The spectral leakage problem and the use of window function are also discussed. In Section 4, we apply these methods in the SSVEP based BCI system to test the use of window function. Section 5 is the conclusion.

2   Experiment Setting

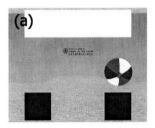 

Fig. 1. (a) A screenshot during the experiment. The rectangles in the left, up and right of the screen flick with the frequencies 5, 8.33 and 12.5Hz. During the experiment, the subjects would watch the corresponding flicking bar as the color ball indicated. (b) The experimental environment. The subjects were seated in a comfortable armchair in an electrically shielded room with the light on. 6 channel signals from occipital area were recorded for analysis.

2.1   Subjects

Six subjects, aged from 22-28 years, participated in the experiment. All participants were seated in a comfortable armchair in an electrically shielded room and viewed a 19 inches LCD display at a distance of 1m (Fig. 1(b)). The light is always on during the experiment. The subjects were instructed to keep still and try to avoid blinking during the experiment, but a habitually blinking was still observed from subject LJW and SXZ.

2.2   EEG Recording

EEG signals were recorded using a SynAmps system (Neuroscan, USA). Signals from channel P3, Pz, P4, O1, Oz and O2 were recorded for analysis (Fs=1000samples/s, 0.05-200Hz). The grounding electrode was mounted on the forehead and reference electrodes between position Cz and CPz according to the system of electrode placement described in [14]. The electrodes were placed according to the extended 10/20-system.

2.3   Experimental Paradigms

As shown in Fig. 1(a), the experiment was set up in a virtual room, and three flicking bars with their frequencies 5, 8.33 and 12.5Hz was placed in the left, up and right of the screen. The monitor was with the refresh rate 75Hz. The experiment consisted of 3 sections with 90 seconds per section. In each section, a color ball appeared in the left, right or front of the screen, which would be changed randomly every 5 seconds. The subjects were asked to watch the corresponding flicking bar.

3   EEG Signal and Window Function

The signal displayed in Fig.2 is a typical EEG signal at channel Oz with 6 seconds length without visual stimulus. The spectral characteristics are shown in the subfigure. The energy of the low frequency components is much higher than others. It can be treated as a color noise.

Fig. 3(a) shows the power density function $P_\omega(t)$ of the signal in Fig.2 at certain frequencies (ω =8Hz, 10Hz, 12Hz, 14Hz and 16Hz), in which the rectangle window is used with the window size $L = 1s$ for $t \in [0.5, 5.5]$. Due to the high energy of the low frequency components, the spectral leakage problem in the power density estimation is serious. Unlike the power density estimation of white noise, the leakage in the EEG like color noise has some regular patterns. As shown Fig. 3(a), an obvious oscillation is observed in the power density estimation of all the frequency compontents. The oscillation of $P_\omega(t)$ at frequency $\omega = 16$Hz is faster but smaller than it at frequency $\omega = 10$Hz and $\omega = 8$Hz. Taking FFT on $P_\omega(t)$, Fig.3(b) shows the Power Spectrum Density (PSD) of $P_\omega(t)$, denoted by $\text{PSD}_{P_\omega}(\Omega)$. It is clear that the oscillation frequency of $P_\omega(t)$ is related to its frequency ω. The amplitude of the oscillation decreases with the growth of ω. Lower frequencies will make a larger oscillation.

The following analysis will make us understand the oscillation. Let the signal $x(t) = \sin(2\pi\omega_0 t)$ to be used to present the low frequency component with ω_0 close to 0. The rectangle windows is represented as

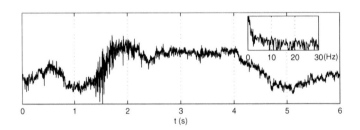

Fig. 2. Typical EEG signals with 6 seconds length without visual stimulus. The subfigure is the frequency spectrum for 0 to 30 Hz. It can be seened as a color noise with the high energy of low frequency components.

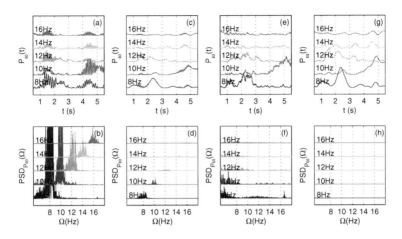

Fig. 3. A comparison of the effect of the window function and high pass filter in the power spectral density estimation of the real EEG signals. The figures in the left show the time-frequency property $P_w(t)$ of the signal, and the right figures are the corresponding power spectrum density of $P_w(t)$, $\text{PSD}_{P_w}(\Omega)$. In fig. (a) and (b), the rectangular window is used without high pass filter. In fig. (c) and (d), the hamming window is used with no high pass filter. In fig. (e) and (f), the rectangular window is used with the 4-order butterworth high pass filter with the cutoff frequency 2Hz. In fig. (g) and (h), the hamming window is used with the 4-order butterworth high pass filter with the cutoff frequency 2Hz. The window size $L = 1.0s$.

$$w(s,t) = \begin{cases} 1 & s \in [t - L/2, t + L/2], \\ 0 & else. \end{cases}$$

The Fourier transformation for $x(t)$ and $w(s,t)$ is

$$\mathcal{F}_x(t,\omega) = X(\omega) = \tfrac{1}{2}j[\delta(\omega + \omega_0) - \delta(\omega - \omega_0)],$$
$$\mathcal{F}_w(t,\omega) = W(t,\omega) = \tfrac{1}{2j\pi\omega}e^{-j2\pi\omega t}[e^{j\pi\omega l} - e^{-j\pi\omega l}] = \tfrac{1}{\pi\omega}e^{-j2\pi\omega t}\sin(\pi\omega l),$$

where $\mathcal{F}_x(t,\omega)$ keeps unchanged with time t, and the amplitude of $\mathcal{F}_x(t,\omega)$ is a periodic function of t with the frequency ω. The STFT of the signal $x(t)$ can be expressed as

$$\begin{aligned}
&\text{STFT}_x(t,\omega) \\
&= \mathcal{F}_{x \cdot w}(t,\omega) \\
&= X(t,\omega) * W(t,\omega) \\
&= \int_{-\infty}^{+\infty} X(\tau)W(t,\omega - \tau)d\tau \\
&= \tfrac{1}{2}j \int_{-\infty}^{+\infty} [\delta(\tau + \omega_0) - \delta(\tau - \omega_0)]W(t,\omega - \tau)d\tau \\
&= \tfrac{1}{2}j[W(t,\omega + \omega_0) - W(t,\omega - \omega_0)]
\end{aligned}$$

Considering the expression of $W(t,\omega + \omega_0)$ and $W(t,\omega - \omega_0)$, the leakage from the low frequency component $x(t)$ at frequency ω behaves as an oscillation at the frequencies $\omega + \omega_0$ and $\omega - \omega_0$. If ω_0 is close to 0, the oscillation frequencies will be close to the frequency ω. The oscillation amplitude is larger as ω near $\pm\omega_0$, and decreases with ω getting away from $\pm\omega_0$. If the energy of frequency ω_0 is much larger than the other frequencies' energy, the oscillation will be observed. This coincides with the power density estimation result in Fig. 3(a).

In STFT, all the data points outside the window are truncated and therefore assumed to be zero, which leads to the spectral leakage problem in the power density estimation. The leakage is unavoidable with the use of window function. But some window functions with low level of the side lobes can reduce the leakage. As shown in Fig. 3(c) and (d), the use of hamming window can make the oscillation weaken but never fade away.

Due to the oscillation caused by the high energy of the low frequency component, high pass filters provide a directly way to solve this problem. In Fig. 3(e) and (f), a 4-order butterworth high pass filter with the cutoff frequency 2Hz is applied before the power density estimation. The curves $P_\omega(t)$ in Fig. 3(e) are not smoother than those in Fig. 3(c). But the oscillation related to the frequency ω is suppressed effectively, while the oscillation in other frequencies still exists.

The combination of high pass filter and hamming window can make the estimation curves even more smooth in Fig. 3(g). Its power spectral density $\mathrm{PSD}_{P_\omega}(\Omega)$ in Fig. 3(h) shows that the oscillation with both frequency ω and the other frequencies are effectively suppressed.

4   Application in SSVEP

Table 1. The classification accuracies with different window functions before and after high pass filter in six subjects. Four type of window functions are compared, which is rectangle, Hamming, Hann and triangle window. The high pass filter here is the 4-order butterworth high pass filter with the cutoff frequency 2Hz. The maximum value of the accuracy among the four windows is marked in bold.

subject	no filter				high pass filter			
	rectangle	hamming	hann	triangle	rectangle	hamming	hann	triangle
HPH	71.78	**80.00**	**80.00**	**80.00**	**80.37**	79.70	80.00	79.70
HG	86.59	88.74	88.37	**89.11**	**92.44**	88.89	88.22	89.11
LJW	77.19	88.52	87.70	**89.56**	**90.89**	88.81	87.70	89.41
PLZ	**99.56**	99.19	99.19	99.19	**99.33**	99.19	99.19	99.19
SXZ	48.15	**69.48**	69.26	69.33	**77.04**	71.93	69.33	71.56
YL	91.93	92.89	91.93	**93.19**	**93.85**	92.74	91.93	93.11
mean	78.98	86.47	86.07	**86.73**	**88.99**	86.88	86.06	87.01

4.1   Method

In this section, the effects of several window functions the power spectral density estimation are compared before and after and high pass filters in the application of SSVEP. As mentioned in Section 2.3, subjects are asked to focus on the targeted flicking bars, which will change every 5 seconds. From $t \in [1.5, 4]$, the power spectral density has been estimated in steps of 0.1 second (25 samples per 5 seconds). Hence there are 1350 samples in three classes for each subject. For each sample, the value of $|\text{STFT}_x(t, \omega)|$ is calculated with 6 electrodes (P3, Pz, P4, O1, Oz and O2) at the characteristic frequencies and their harmonics (ω = 5, 8.33, 12.5 and 10, 16.67, 25Hz). Linear Discriminant Analysis (LDA) is used for classification [15, 16]. The accuracy rates are given by 3 fold cross validation (two sections are used to train, the remained section is retained as the validation data for testing).

4.2   Result

In Tab.1, the accuracy rates are compared with the four window functions (rectangle, Hamming, Hann and triangle windows) before and after the high pass filter. The window size $L = 1.0s$. The best classification result among the four windows is marked in bold. The high pass filter used is the 4-order butterworth high pass filter with the cutoff frequency 2Hz. Without high pass filter, the results with Hamming, Hann and triangle window are similar and better than those with rectangle window. After high pass filter, a 10% improvement is achieved for rectangle window in average. An extreme growth happens on subject SXZ, in which the high pass filter makes an approximate 30% increasement with rectangle window. In contrast, the results for other windows hold on or increase a little. Hence, the best accuracies for all subjects come from rectangle window. Some windows provide smoother power density estimations, such as hamming window shown in Fig. 3(g), fail to get a better accuracy after high pass filter, which does not meet our expectations.

In the following, we extend our test on more window functions and different window sizes. 17 window functions with their main lobe width and side lobe peaks are listed in Tab. 2 in descending order of the main lobe width. The first 16 window function are natively implemented in matlab. The last window "anti-flattopwin" is constructed by $1 - 0.7 \times \text{window}(@\text{flattopwin}, N)$, which has narrower main lobe but higher side lobe than rectangle window. N is the number of sampling points, which is related with the window size L and sampling rate Fs. Fig. 4 shows the average accuracies of six subjects with different main lobe width of the 17 windows for different window sizes (L=0.5, 1.0, 1.5 and 2.0s). The accuracies before and after high pass filter are correspondingly marked by blue star and red circle. The recognition rates increase for all windows with the growth of window size. For the windows with the -3dB main lobe width($\times 2\pi/N$) greater than 1, the accuracies before and after high pass filter are similar and decrease as the growth of the main lobe width. It indicates that if the side lobe below certain level, the spectral leakage from low frequency component have

Table 2. The 17 window function used in Fig. 4 with their -3dB main lobe width and side lobe peak. The "anti-flattopwin" is constructed by us with narrower main lobe width than rectangle windows.

window	-3dB main lobe width ($\times 2\pi/N$)	side lobe peak (dB)
flattopwin	3.72	-96.00
blackmanharris	1.90	-98.97
nuttallwin	1.87	-98.86
chebwin	1.84	-100.00
parzenwin	1.82	-53.05
bohmanwin	1.70	-46.00
blackman	1.64	-96.31
hann	1.44	-31.47
barthannwin	1.40	-35.88
gausswin	1.37	-43.30
hamming	1.30	-44.20
bartlett	1.27	-26.52
triang	1.27	-26.52
tukeywin	1.15	-15.12
kaiser ($\beta = 2$)	0.99	-18.45
rectwin	0.88	-13.26
anti-flattopwin	0.81	-7.72

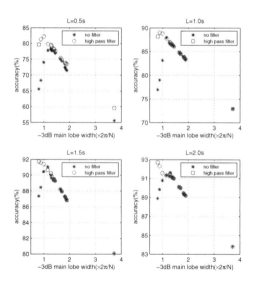

Fig. 4. The average classify results of the six subjects by using 17 window functions of different main lobe width. The results before and after high pass filters are marked by blue stars and red circles. The window size $L = 0.5, 1.0, 1.5, 2.0s$ in the subfigures from (a) to (d).

been suppressed effectively and a smaller side lobe would not help to improve the classication results any more. However the increasing of the main lobe width makes the windows' frequency domain resolution weaken, which leads to the decreasing of the accuracies. For the last three windows (kaiser, rectwin, anti-flattopwin) in Tab. 2, all of them have narrower main lobe width with larger side lobe. The spectral leakage from low frequency component is large enough for these windows to influence the classication results. The accuracies are improved greatly after high pass filter. The better accuracy is achieved by is a tradeoff with frequency domain resolution and spectral leakage. For shorter window size, such as $L = 0.5s$ in Fig. 4(a), a window with smaller side lobe is preferred. While a longer window size ($L = 1.5, 2.0s$ in Fig. 4(c) and (d)) could make the window with narrower main lobe improve their classication results. Some windows with narrower main lobes, like "anti-flattopwin", have their uses.

Remark1: In the comparison above, the "anti-flattopwin" has been constructed with a narrower main lobe than rectangle window. In fact, we can construct a series of windows in the following forms $1 - \alpha \times w(s,t)$ where $\alpha \in (0,1]$, w can be chosen from the first 15 windows listed in Tab. 2. As α grows from 0 to 1, these "anti" type windows have narrower main lobe but a higher side lobe. Take "anti-tukeywin" window with $\alpha = 1$ for example, -3dB main lobe width is $0.58(\times 2\pi/N)$, however the peak of the side lobe -0.62dB is real large, which is close to the main lobe.

Remark2: It's worth noting that although the side lobe peak of tukey window is larger than kaiser window, it is decayed much faster. Hence tukey window has less been influenced by high pass filter than kaiser window. The speed for the side lobes fall-off is not listed in Tab. 2, because for some windows, like "nuttallwin", "blackmanharris", "flattopwin" the peaks of the side lobes is not monotonically decreasing.

5 Conclusion

In this paper, we discussed the use of the window function in the application of SSVEP based BCIs. An ideal window function should have a narrow main lobe and low side lobes. In the noisy circumstances, the lower side lobes could reduce the impact of spectral leakage to the accuracy. And the narrower main lobe could provide a higher frequency domain solution, which leads to a better transient response. However, it is impossible for a window to satisfy both parties. The choice of the windows is to determine the quality of the signals. The windows with high frequency domain solution could be used to improve the classification results if the Signal to Noise Ratio (SNR) has been improved by some methods, such as high pass filter used here.

Acknowledgment. This work is supported by National High Technology Research and Development Program of China (No. 2009AA04Z212), National Natural Science Foundation of China (No.51075265), and Science Technology Commission of Shanghai Municipality (No.09JC1408400).

References

1. Wolpaw, J.R., Birbaumer, N., McFarland, D.J., Pfurtscheller, G., Vaughan, T.M.: Brain-computer interfaces for communication and control. Clinical Neurophysiology 113(6), 767–791 (2002)
2. Garcia, G.: High frequency SSVEPs for BCI applications, In: Computer-Human Interaction (2008)
3. Lin, Z., Zhang, C., Wu, W., Gao, X.: Frequency recognition based on canonical correlation analysis for SSVEP-based BCIs. IEEE Transactions on Biomedical Engineering 54(6), 1172–1176 (2007)
4. Wu, Z., Yao, D.: Frequency detection with stability coefficient for steady-state visual evoked potential (SSVEP)-based BCIs. Journal of Neural Engineering 5, 36 (2008)
5. Pfurtscheller, G., Solis-Escalante, T., Ortner, R., Linortner, P.: Self-Paced Operation of an SSVEP-Based Orthosis With and Without an Imagery-Based" Brain Switch": A Feasibility Study Towards a Hybrid BCI. IEEE Transactions on Neural Systems and Rehabilitation Engineering: a Publication of the IEEE Engineering in Medicine and Biology Society 18(4), 409–414 (2010)
6. Cheng, M., Gao, X., Gao, S., Xu, D.: Design and implementation of a brain-computer interface with high transfer rates. IEEE Transactions on Biomedical Engineering 49(10), 1181–1186 (2002)
7. Trejo, L.J., Rosipal, R., Matthews, B.: Brain–computer interfaces for 1-D and 2-D cursor control: designs using volitional control of the EEG spectrum or steady-state visual evoked potentials. IEEE Transactions on Neural Systems and Rehabilitation Engineering 14(2), 225 (2006)
8. Muller-Putz, G.R., Pfurtscheller, G.: Control of an electrical prosthesis with an SSVEP-based BCI. IEEE Transactions on Biomedical Engineering 55(1), 361–364 (2008)
9. Gollee, H., Volosyak, I., McLachlan, A., Hunt, K., Graser, A.: An SSVEP based brain-computer interface for the control of functional electrical stimulation. IEEE Transactions on Bio-Medical Engineering 57(8), 1847–1855 (2010)
10. Edlinger, G., Groenegress, C., Prückl, R., Guger, C., Slater, M.: Goal orientated Brain-Computer interfaces for Control: a virtual smart home application study. BMC Neuroscience 11(suppl. 1), 134 (2010)
11. Burkitt, G.R., Silberstein, R.B., Cadusch, P.J., Wood, A.W.: Steady-state visual evoked potentials and travelling waves. Clinical Neurophysiology 111(2), 246–258 (2000)
12. Friman, O., Volosyak, I., Graser, A.: Multiple channel detection of steady-state visual evoked potentials for brain-computer interfaces. IEEE Transactions on Biomedical Engineering 54(4), 742–750 (2007)
13. Cui, J., Wong, W.: The adaptive chirplet transform and visual evoked potentials. IEEE Transactions on Biomedical Engineering 53(7), 1378–1384 (2006)
14. Chatrian, G.E., Lettich, E., Nelson, Ten, P.L.: percent electrode system for topographic studies of spontaneous and evoked EEG activity. Am J. EEG Technol. 25, 83–92 (1985)
15. Krzanowski, W.J.: Principles of multivariate analysis: a user's perspective. Oxford University Press, USA (2000)
16. Seber, G.A.F.: Multivariate Observations (1984)

Efficient Multi-resolution Plane Segmentation
of 3D Point Clouds

Bastian Oehler[1], Joerg Stueckler[2], Jochen Welle[1], Dirk Schulz[1], and Sven Behnke[2]

[1] Research Group Unmanned Systems, Fraunhofer-Institute for Communication,
Information Processing and Ergonomics (FKIE), 53343 Wachtberg, Germany
[2] Computer Science Institute VI, Autonomous Intelligent Systems (AIS),
University of Bonn, 53012 Bonn, Germany

Abstract. We present an efficient multi-resolution approach to segment a 3D point cloud into planar components. In order to gain efficiency, we process large point clouds iteratively from coarse to fine 3D resolutions: At each resolution, we rapidly extract surface normals to describe surface elements (surfels). We group surfels that cannot be associated with planes from coarser resolutions into co-planar clusters with the Hough transform. We then extract connected components on these clusters and determine a best plane fit through RANSAC. Finally, we merge plane segments and refine the segmentation on the finest resolution. In experiments, we demonstrate the efficiency and quality of our method and compare it to other state-of-the-art approaches.

Keywords: Plane segmentation, multi-resolution, RANSAC, Hough transform.

1 Introduction

Depth sensors such as 3D laser range finders or the Microsoft Kinect provide dense 3D measurements that typically consist of millions of points. In robotics applications like object manipulation or teleoperation, it is often crucial to interpret this massive amount of data in real-time. In this paper, we propose efficient means to segment 3D point clouds into planar segments (see Fig. 1). In structured environments, the planar segmentation gives a compact representation of scene content. It can also be used to generate object hypotheses by focussing on point clusters not explained by the main planes.

We gain the efficiency required for the processing of large point clouds by adopting a coarse-to-fine strategy: We extract surface elements (surfels, described by location, extent, and surface normal) on multiple resolutions, starting from the coarsest one. On each resolution, we associate the surfels with planar segments that have been found on coarser resolutions. New planes are created from the remaining unassociated surfels by first grouping them into co-planar clusters with the Hough transform. We split each cluster into a set of connected components. For each connected component, we apply RANSAC to determine a best plane fit and to reject outliers robustly. In a final processing step, we merge plane segments and refine the segmentation on the finest resolution.

The use of a coarse-to-fine strategy has several advantages over a segmentation on a single resolution. Firstly, large plane segments can be detected from only few surfels

S. Jeschke, H. Liu, and D. Schilberg (Eds.): ICIRA 2011, Part II, LNAI 7102, pp. 145–156, 2011.

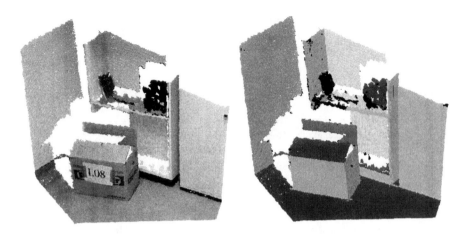

Fig. 1. Example scene and its planar segmentation

which renders our method very efficient. Furthermore, our approach handles variability in the extent of plane segments more robustly, since it uses as much context as possible to decide for co-planarity.

We organize this paper as follows: After a brief discussion of related work in Sec. 2, we detail our approach to plane segmentation in Sec. 3. Finally, we evaluate our method in experiments in Sec. 4.

2   Related Work

The robotics and computer graphics communities have developed a rich set of approaches for segmenting a scene into geometric shape primitives. Many of these approaches also extract plane segments. We identify three main lines of research: approaches based on Random Sample Consensus (RANSAC, [1]), methods using the Hough transform, and algorithms that perform region growing on depth images.

RANSAC [1] is a method to robustly fit a model into a set of data points that may contain even a large number of outliers. It randomly selects a minimal set of data points for estimating the model parameters. From the random samples, it chooses the one that is best supported by the complete set of points. As of its general formulation, RANSAC can be easily applied to fit any kind of geometric shape primitive. However, the basic RANSAC approach assumes that only one model can be fit to the data. Schnabel et al. [10] propose to extend basic RANSAC through multi-resolution and locality heuristics. Instead of uniformly drawing samples for the minimal sample set from the complete point cloud, they sample from a local normal distribution in 3D Cartesian space. Furthermore, they randomly select a sampling scale in an octree representation of the point cloud. By such means, they achieve an efficient and robust method. Gotardo et al. [3] extract planar surfaces with a modified RANSAC approach. They first extract an edge map from the depth gradient image and determine connected components in the edge map. Then they apply RANSAC to robustly fit planar segments into the connected components.

The Hough transform [6] is an alternative approach to estimate model parameters from a set of measurements. In contrast to RANSAC, its formulation is sound when the measured points support multiple instances of the model with different parametrizations (such as different planes in a scene). It transforms the given measurements from the original space (e. g., $\mathbb{R}^3$ for point clouds) into a set of possible parameter vectors in the parameter space of the model. Each original point votes for a manifold in parameter space. Vote clusters in the parameter space then represent the model fits. The Hough transform is computationally demanding when extracting geometric shape primitives from 3D point clouds, because such models contain multiple parameters which corresponds to a high-dimensional Hough space. Consequently, in a naive implementation a single point in 3D must vote for a high-dimensional manifold in parameter space. The quality of the model fit strongly depends on the clustering method in parameter space. Using histograms, for example, the quality is affected by the discretization of the histogram. Vosselman et al. [12] propose an efficient variant of the Hough transform for extracting shape primitives. They estimate model parameters from surfels (points with local surface normals) and divide model fitting into several stages. In a first stage, they apply the Hough transform to find parallel surfels. Secondly, they find co-planar surfels in parallel surfels with a similar distance to the origin of the coordinate frame. In our approach, we improve this method in efficiency and accuracy by applying a coarse-to-fine strategy and combining the Hough transform with efficient RANSAC.

Both, the Hough transform and RANSAC, are global methods that ignore point neighborhood. Some methods have been proposed that exploit the neighborhood information in dense depth images. In [7] or [2], region-growing and region-merging techniques are applied to extract planar segments. Taylor et al. [11] use a split-and-merge approach. Finally, Harati et al. [4] extract edges from bearing-angle images to find connected components. Our approach is not restricted to point clouds for which an image-like point neighborhood is known. It can be readily applied to point clouds that have been registered from multiple views. We consider the neighborhood of points, since we process surface normals in local neighborhoods on multiple resolutions. In addition, we reestablish the neighborhood of surfels by finding connected components in co-planar surfels.

3   Efficient Multi-resolution Segmentation into Planar Segments

We combine the Hough transform with RANSAC to robustly extract plane segments from 3D point clouds (s. Fig. 2). In order to improve efficiency, we use a coarse-to-fine strategy: We extract local surface normals at multiple resolutions to describe surface elements (surfels). We implemented a highly efficient method for multi-resolution normal estimation using octrees. At each resolution, we determine which surfels can already be explained by planes that have been found on coarser resolutions. On the remaining surfels, we apply the Hough transform to pre-segment the scene into co-planar surfels. In order to improve accuracy and robustness, we fit plane segments on connected components using RANSAC. On the finest resolution, we merge co-planar connected plane segments and distribute the remaining points.

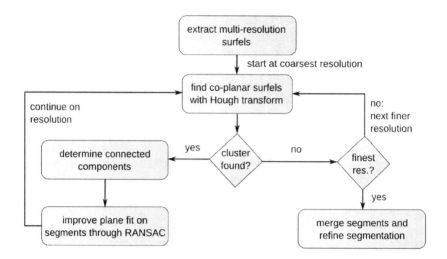

Fig. 2. Overview over our coarse-to-fine planar segmentation approach. See text for details.

3.1 Efficient Normal Estimation through Multiple Resolutions

We represent the point cloud with an octree. An octree consists of branching nodes and leaf nodes that each cover a 3D volume. The root of the tree spans the complete 3D volume of interest. Each branching node divides its volume into eight equally sized cubes (called octants) at its center position. For each of its octants, the node contains a child that is either a branching node itself or a leaf in the tree.

The octree can naturally be used to regularly sample the point cloud at sampling resolutions that correspond to the volume sizes of the nodes in the various depths of the tree. For a sampling depth d, we determine all nodes at the sampling depth or all leaf nodes at coarser resolutions. Furthermore, the octree allows to efficiently calculate integral values in the volume of nodes: In each node, we maintain the integral over the values of points that lie within the volume of the node. During the construction of the tree, we distribute the value of a point to all nodes that the point visits while it is recursively passed from the root to its final leaf node.

We exploit this property to efficiently calculate the mean and sample covariance of points in each node. For the mean $\boldsymbol{\mu} = \frac{1}{N}\sum_i \boldsymbol{p}_i$, we simply maintain the number of points N and the sum of 3D point coordinates $\sum_i \boldsymbol{p}_i$. The sample covariance can be obtained by the computational formula of variance

$$Cov(\boldsymbol{p}) = E\left[\boldsymbol{pp}^T\right] - (E\left[\boldsymbol{p}\right])(E\left[\boldsymbol{p}\right])^T = \frac{1}{N}\sum_i \boldsymbol{p}_i\boldsymbol{p}_i^T - \boldsymbol{\mu}\boldsymbol{\mu}^T.$$

Thus, it suffices to additionally maintain the sum of squared 3D point coordinates $\sum_i \boldsymbol{p}_i\boldsymbol{p}_i^T$ in each node.

Once the octree has been constructed, we estimate surface normals at every resolution by finding the eigenvector to the smallest eigenvalue λ_0 of the sample covariance ($\lambda_0 \leq \lambda_1 \leq \lambda_2$). Fig. 3 shows example normals extracted on two resolutions with our method.

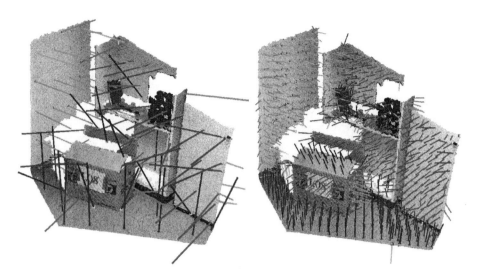

Fig. 3. Normals on a coarse (left) and a fine (right) resolution estimated with our fast normal estimation method. The normals are color-coded for direction (best viewed in color). The length of the normals indicates the space discretization.

We require a minimum number of points to support the normal estimate. We further evaluate the quality of the normals by considering the eigenvalues of the covariance matrix. The curvature

$$\gamma := \frac{\lambda_0}{\lambda_0 + \lambda_1 + \lambda_2} \tag{1}$$

is small, when the points are mainly distributed in a plane. The relation λ_1 / λ_2 is close to one, when the points are equally distributed in both directions in the plane. Thresholding these indicators rejects normal estimates on ridges and at plane borders. Finally, we require the largest eigenvalue λ_2 to be large in relation to the volume length of the node, such that the points fully spread the volume size.

3.2   Pre-segmentation in Hough-Space

We find clusters of co-planar surfels on a single resolution with the Hough transform. Similar to Vosselman et al. [12], we use a fast two-stage approach.

In the first stage, each surfel votes for planes with corresponding normals in an orientation histogram. We discretize the orientation histogram approximately equidistant in inclination and azimuth angles following the approach by Rabbani [8]. The curvature γ in Eq. (1) provides a measure of uncertainty in the normal estimates. We use this curvature to distribute the normal orientation of surfel k with a weight w_j to a range of bins j with similar orientations in the histogram, i. e.,

$$w_j = N_k \cdot \left(1 - \frac{\gamma_k}{\gamma_{\max}}\right) \cdot \left(|\langle \boldsymbol{n}_k, \boldsymbol{n}_j \rangle| - \cos(\alpha)\right) / \cos(\alpha),$$

Fig. 4. Clusters found by the Hough transform on two consecutive resolutions (grey: not yet segmented, blue: previously segmented)

where N_k is the number of points in the surfel, $\gamma_{\max}$ is the threshold on the normal curvature, n_k and n_j are the normal of the surfel and the histogram bin, respectively, and $\alpha < 90°$ is the angular influence range of the normal. We detect local maxima in the orientation histogram in order to find clusters of parallel surfels.

In the second stage, we determine co-planar surfels from the clusters of parallel surfels. Each surfel votes for the distance of a plane to the origin of the coordinate frame (e. g., the view point). Similar to the orientation histogram, we distribute votes onto neighboring bins with a linear decay. We find clusters of co-planar surfels again at the maxima of the distance histogram. Figure 4 shows results of this pre-segmentation step in our example scene. To make this process efficient, we keep the resolution of the histograms coarse and postpone an accurate estimate of the model parameters to later processing stages. The resolution of the distance histograms is increased with the resolution of the surfels, however.

3.3 Segmentation into Connected Components

The Hough transform does not consider the spatial connectivity of surfels. We therefore extract connected components from the sets of co-planar surfels. Fig. 5 illustrates this with an example. We overlay a grid over the plane that corresponds to the Hough-space maximum of the surfels. The resolution of the grid is chosen according to the resolution of the surfels. We project each surfel position into the grid and mark occupied grid cells. Region-growing yields connected components which we discard when the component is not supported by a minimum number of surfels (set to 3 in our implementation).

3.4 Accurate Segmentation through RANSAC

We further improve the plane fit to the connected components of co-planar surfels. The plane estimate by the Hough transform is only a rough estimate of the true underlying plane due to the coarse resolution of the orientation and distance histograms. We therefore apply RANSAC directly to the points represented by the surfels. An example of the outlier detection is visualized in Fig. 6.

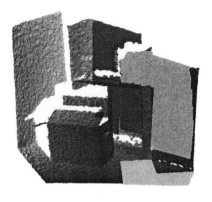 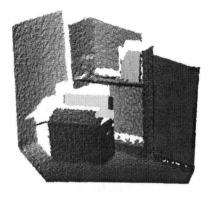

Fig. 5. Segmentation of the clusters from Fig. 4 into connected components. In the left image, the green segment is split into two components. The left component is not supported by sufficient surfels and is discarded. In the right image, the segmentation is only shown for the red cluster from Fig. 4, which is split into two planar segments (yellow and cyan). The rightmost part is discarded for low support.

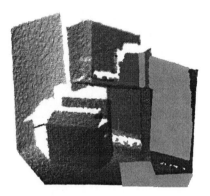 

Fig. 6. RANSAC refinement on connected components (green: inliers, red: outliers)

RANSAC estimates plane parameters from a random set of three point samples. Within a fixed number of iterations, we determine the plane estimate that is best supported by all points of the surfels. Points are accepted as inliers to the plane fit when their distance to the plane is below some threshold. We adapt this threshold to the resolution of the surfels. We only accept plane fits that are supported by a large fraction of the surfel points. We also require the extracted plane to be similar to the initial fit determined by the Hough transform. When the plane fit is accepted, we redetermine the connected component of the segment.

3.5 Coarse-to-Fine Segmentation

In the previous sections we detailed how we segment planes on a single resolution. We propose however to segment a scene with a coarse-to-fine strategy. By this, large plane segments can be detected efficiently from only few surfels. Furthermore, our approach inherently adapts to the extent of planes in the scene. It uses as much context as possible to decide for co-planarity.

We process the scene from coarse to fine resolutions. We transit to the next finer resolution, when no more plane segments are found on a resolution. In order to improve the segmentation of the already found plane segments, we redistribute the surfels on the finer resolution onto the segments. We test, if the surfel orientation and position fits well to each plane segment, and if it lies within or at the border of its connected component.

Eventually, we also adapt the connected components. For this purpose, we increase the sampling rate of the occupancy map according to the new resolution. We project the surfels into the plane segment and mark the corresponding cells occupied. However, we keep the coarser occupancy decisions from previous layers. Note, that while plane segments may expand during this process, segments that grow together are not merged. We merge co-planar connected segments in a final processing step.

3.6 Post-Processing

After all resolutions have been processed, we improve the segmentation on the finest resolution. First, we merge connected co-planar plane segments. We then distribute the nodes onto the plane segments without using normal information. For each node, we determine a list of plane segment candidates with small distance towards the mean of the points within the node's volume. In addition, the node needs to fall within the connected component or at the borders of each candidate.

We further examine nodes that could not be assigned uniquely to plane segments and distribute the points in the node's volume individually. We pick the best two plane segment candidates s_1, s_2 according to distance and compute the equidistal plane through the intersecting line of s_1 and s_2 with normal direction

$$ n_{cut} = \left(\frac{n_{s_1} + n_{s_2}}{2} \right) \times (n_{s_1} \times n_{s_2}). $$

When the center of gravities of the plane segments lie on distinct sides of this plane, we distribute the points on either side of the equidistal plane accordingly. Otherwise, we simply associate the points to the closest plane.

4 Experiments

We evaluate our approach on Kinect depth images and 3D laser scans as well as on range images from the popular SegComp ABW image dataset [5][1]. The SegComp dataset allows for an objective evaluation of our approach in the context of planar range image segmentation. We compare our approach with results published in [3].

The 30 ABW test images have a resolution of 512×512 pixels. The dataset also provides ground truth segmentation in conjunction with an evaluation tool. Table 1 shows the results of our approach on the SegComp ABW test images at 80% tolerance for the overlap with the ground truth. While our approach is not specifically designed for range images, its segmentation quality as well as plane fit accuracy lies in the upper range of

---

[1] Available at http://marathon.csee.usf.edu/seg-comp/SegComp.html

Table 1. Comparison with other segmentation approaches (from [3]) on the SegComp ABW dataset at 80% overlap tolerance. The ground truth images contain 15.2 regions on average.

approach	correct	error	overseg.	underseg.	missed	noise	time (sec)
USF	12.7 (83.5%)	1.6°	0.2	0.1	2.1	1.2	-
WSU	9.7 (63.8%)	1.6°	0.5	0.2	4.5	2.2	-
UB	12.8 (84.2%)	1.3°	0.5	0.1	1.7	2.1	-
UE	13.4 (88.1%)	1.6°	0.4	0.2	1.1	0.8	-
OU	9.8 (64.4%)	-	0.2	0.4	4.4	3.2	-
PPU	6.8 (44.7%)	-	0.1	2.1	3.4	2.0	-
UA	4.9 (32.2%)	-	0.3	2.2	3.6	3.2	-
UFPR	13.0 (85.5%)	1.5°	0.5	0.1	1.6	1.4	-
RansacOnly	6.6 (43.4%)	2.4°	1.9	0.2	6.2	7.8	13.2
HoughOnly	4.4 (28.9%)	3.1°	0.2	0.4	9.7	3.0	3.163
singleRes16	5.6 (36.8%)	1.4°	0.0	0.5	8.6	1.1	0.555
singleRes8	10.0 (65.8%)	1.5°	0.2	0.3	4.4	1.2	0.655
singleRes4	7.2 (47.4%)	1.2°	1.1	0.1	6.8	7.0	1.001
ours	11.1 (73.0%)	1.4°	0.2	0.7	2.2	0.8	1.824

Fig. 7. Two segmented scenes from the SegComp ABW dataset

results on this dataset. Note, that the best segmentation results have been obtained with methods that exploit the connectivity information encoded in the image structure. This also restricts these methods to the processing of single-view range images. Furthermore, the range images contain strong systematic noise in the form of depth discretization effects, which are difficult to handle for small segments composed of only few points.

In order to assess the contribution of the individual stages of our algorithm, we performed tests with several variants. The method RansacOnly uses a greedy method to detect planes (implemented with the Point Cloud Library, PCL [9]). It iteratively finds the best supported plane fit for the not yet attributed points without using normal information. It only achieves average performance and its run-time strongly depends on the complexity of the scene. HoughOnly is based on our multi-resolution approach but does not perform RANSAC to refine the initial Hough segmentation. It is thus similar to the approach by Vosselman et al. [12]. The HoughOnly method segments the scenes with less accuracy compared to our complete approach. This is attributed to discretization

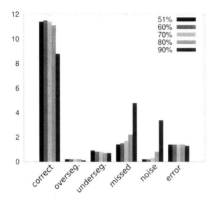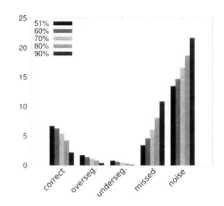

Fig. 8. Results of our approach on the SegComp ABW (left) and our Kinect (right) dataset for various overlap tolerances. The ground truth contains 15.2 and 12.8 regions on avg., respectively.

effects introduced by the accumulator histograms in the Hough transform. In our method, the subsequent RANSAC step filters outliers from the Hough planes and renders the approach robust and accurate. For the methods singleRes16, singleRes8, and singleRes4 we restrict our method to operate on single resolutions (16 cm, 8 cm, 4 cm). The results demonstrate that our multi-resolution approach is important to capture all scales of planes in a scene.

Fig. 8 (left) shows results of our approach on the SegComp ABW test images for different overlap tolerances. It can be seen that the errors in our approach are in large parts due to missed plane segments. As of the high noise, some points may not be assigned to planes or boundaries may not be resolved correctly. Since our method does not consider image neighborhood, it is difficult to achieve 90% overlap. Fig. 7 shows two exemplary segmentations for the ABW dataset. In the left image our algorithm missed multiple planar segments. We attribute some of the misses to the discretization by the octree. This issue could be solved by reprocessing the unsegmented parts in a different discretization.

We also evaluate our approach on depth images of indoor scenes obtained with a Microsoft Kinect camera (s. Fig. 10). Our approach requires ca. 2.06 sec on 640×480 images. In QQVGA resolution (160×120), we are able to process single images in about 106 msec, which allows for real-time applications. We generated a segmentation dataset[2] of 30 images with manually annotated ground truth and evaluate segmentation quality with the SegComp evaluation tool. From Fig. 8 (right) we see that our approach correctly segments 54.9% but only misses 24.2% of the planes at an overlap tolerance of 51%. Despite the strong noise of the sensor due to the discretization of the disparity measurements, our approach is able to segment the major planes in the scene. Note that non-planar segments have been annotated as noise in the ground truth. We therefore neglect the noise in the evaluation. Furthermore, for the manual annotation itself it is not possible to achieve perfect overlap with the actual segments in the scene. Since no ground truth of the relative angle between surfaces is available, we do not assess the angular error on this dataset.

---

[2] Available at http://www.ais.uni-bonn.de/download/segmentation/kinect.html

Fig. 9. Indoor scene acquired with a 3D laser mounted on a manipulator (black: unsegmented)

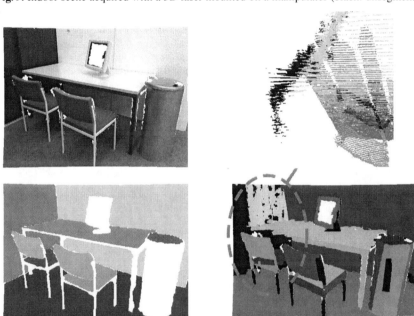

Fig. 10. Example Kinect scene (top left), close-view on segmented points in the upper left image corner (top right), ground truth (bottom left), and resulting segmentation (bottom right). White: invalid/unknown, black: unsegmented.

In addition to Kinect depth images, we tested our approach on indoor scenes acquired with a laser scanner that is swept with the end-effector of a manipulator (s. Fig. 9). Our approach finds the major plane segments in the building structure. It also finds planar segments in cluttered regions where the sampling density is sufficient.

5 Conclusion and Future Work

In this paper we proposed an efficient method for extracting planar segments from 3D point clouds. We combine the Hough transform with robust RANSAC to fit planes on multiple resolutions. By using a coarse-to-fine strategy, we make efficient use of the available data. It allows to consider the largest possible context to make decisions of co-planarity. This also makes our approach data efficient.

In experiments, we demonstrate the robustness and the run-time efficiency of our approach. We compare our method to state-of-the-art approaches using the SegComp database. Our experiments show that we process 3D point clouds of 3D lasers and depth sensors such as the Kinect at high framerates with good quality.

In future work, we will extract further types of geometric shape primitives such as cylinders and spheres. We also plan to tune our approach to the sequential processing of depth images from high framerate sensors such as the Kinect.

Acknowledgments. This research has been partially funded by the FP7 ICT-2007.2.2 project ECHORD (grant agreement 231143) experiment ActReMa.

References

1. Fischler, M.A., Bolles, R.C.: Random sample consensus: a paradigm for model fitting with applications to image analysis and automated cartography. Commun. of the ACM (1981)
2. Fitzgibbon, A.W., Eggert, D.W., Fisher, R.B.: High-level model acquisition from range images. Computer-Aided Design 29(4), 321–330 (1997)
3. Gotardo, P., Bellon, O., Silva, L.: Range image segmentation by surface extraction using an improved robust estimator. In: Proc. of the Int. Conf. on Computer Vision and Pattern Recognition, CVPR (2003)
4. Harati, A., Gächter, S., Siegwart, R.: Fast range image segmentation for indoor 3D-SLAM. In: 6th IFAC Symposium on Intelligent Autonomous Vehicles (2007)
5. Hoover, A., Jean-Baptiste, G., Jiang, X., Flynn, P.J., Bunke, H., Goldgof, D.B., Bowyer, K., Eggert, D.W., Fitzgibbon, A., Fisher, R.B.: An experimental comparison of range image segmentation algorithms. IEEE Trans. on Pattern Analysis and Machine Intelligence 18(7), 673–689 (1996)
6. Hough, P.: Method and means for recognizing complex patterns. U.S. Patent 3.069.654 (1962)
7. Jiang, X., Bunke, H.: Fast segmentation of range images into planar regions by scan line grouping. Machine Vision Applications 7, 115–122 (1994)
8. Rabbani, T.: Automatic reconstruction of industrial installations using point clouds and images. Ph.D. thesis, TU Delft (2006)
9. Rusu, R.B., Cousins, S.: 3D is here: Point cloud library (PCL). In: Proc. of the Int. Conf. on Robotics and Automation (ICRA), Shanghai, China (2011)
10. Schnabel, R., Wahl, R., Klein, R.: Efficient RANSAC for point-cloud shape detection. Computer Graphics Forum 26(2), 214–226 (2007)
11. Taylor, R.W., Savini, M., Reeves, A.P.: Fast segmentation of range imagery into planar regions. Computer Vision, Graphics, and Image Processing 45(1), 42–60 (1989)
12. Vosselman, G., Gorte, B.G.H., Sithole, G., Rabbani, T.: Recognising structure in laser scanner point clouds. In: ISPRS - Laser-Scanners for Forest and Landscape Assessment (2004)

3D Body Pose Estimation Using an Adaptive Person Model for Articulated ICP

David Droeschel and Sven Behnke

Autonomous Intelligent Systems Group, Computer Science Institute VI
University of Bonn, Bonn, Germany
droeschel@ais.uni-bonn.de, behnke@cs.uni-bonn.de

Abstract. The perception of persons is an important capability of today's robots that work closely together with humans. An operator may use, for example, gestures to refer to an object in the environment. In order to perceive such gestures, the robot has to estimate the body pose of the operator.

We focus on the marker-less motion capture of a human body by means of an *Iterative Closest Point* (ICP) algorithm for articulated structures. An articulated upper body model is aligned with the depth measurements of an RGB-D camera. Due to the variability of the human body, we propose an adaptive body model that is aligned within the sensor data and iteratively adjusted to the person's body dimensions. Additionally, we preserve consistency with respect to self-collisions. Besides that, we use an inverse data assignment, that is particularly utile for articulated models.

Experiments with measurements of a Microsoft Kinect camera show the advantage of the approach compared to the standard articulated ICP algorithm in terms of the *root mean squared* (RMS) error and the number of iterations the algorithm needs to converge. In addition, we show that our consistency checks enable to recover from situations where the standard algorithm fails.

Keywords: Human-Robot Interaction, Marker-less motion capture, Articulated ICP.

1 Introduction

Today's robots need to operate in environments closely together with humans. For example, in household environments a *domestic service robot* has to interact with people, navigate around them or deliver objects to a user. Interacting with a user hereby could mean that the user refers to an object in the environment by pointing to it, rather than verbally describing it [8]. Pointing to an object is a way of communication where humans use their whole body as a medium. Therefore, the robot has to perceive the human's body pose , i. e., the individual joint angles and the location and orientation of the body parts, in order to detect a motion as a gesture, to determine the pointing direction, and map it to a target in the environment.

We focus on marker-less estimation of such body poses by means of an Iterative Closest Point (ICP) approach to fit a human body model in 3D point measurements from a depth camera. Hence, a precise and complete model of a human body is necessary.

S. Jeschke, H. Liu, and D. Schilberg (Eds.): ICIRA 2011, Part II, LNAI 7102, pp. 157–167, 2011.

The human body is an articulated object that is highly variable in its size and shape. It consists of a skeleton with many degrees of freedom covered with tissue and skin. In addition, the human body is usually covered in clothes that obfuscate its shape. Due to the variability in the human body shape, a static model is disadvantageous. Hence, a person-dependent model has to be adapted from a generic model.

In contrast to previous work, our approach leverages the advantage of an adaptive body model that is aligned within the measured 3D points and iteratively adjusted to the person's body dimensions. Besides that, we use an inverse data assignment that is particularly utile for articulated models. Our approach is based on depth images from a RGB-D camera [16] that provides depth and color information at high frame rates.

The remainder of this paper is organized as follows: After a brief review of related work, we describe the structure of the body model (Section 3.1) as well as the basic idea of articulated ICP (Section 3.2). Section 4 describes our extensions to the articulated ICP algorithm that enables an adaptive body model. Finally, we evaluate our extensions and compare the adaptive body model to the static body model.

2 Related Work

Perceiving humans has been studied in many research areas since decades. The vast majority of this work employs information from one or more color cameras to estimate the human body pose as surveyed by Moeslund et al. [17]. However, recently affordable depth cameras became available, which fosters research on depth-based approaches to human body pose estimation. Furthermore, these approaches do not suffer from varying lighting conditions.

Ganapathi et al. [10] investigate marker-less human pose tracking from monocular depth images. They combine an accurate generative model with a discriminative model that provides data-driven evidence about body part locations. The generative model applies a local model-based search that exploits the kinematic chain of a body model. The discriminative model utilizes a set of trained patch classifiers to detect body parts and is used for initialization and reinitialization if the local search loses track of the body, e. g., due to fast movements. The detection and localization algorithm has been published by Plagemann et al. [22]. They propose an interest point detector based on identifying geodesic extrema in point clusters that coincide with salient points of the body.

Several recent approaches focus on the extension of a well-established 3D registration method, the *Iterative Closest Point* (ICP) algorithm [4], to articulated models by fitting a static (non-adaptive) cylindrical human body model into 3D measurements. Demirdjian et al. [6], for example, estimate the pose of individual body parts using the ICP algorithm in 3D point clouds generated by dense stereo. Thereby, the poses for individual body parts are estimated independently and kinematic constraints are enforced after registration. These constraints are implemented by a support vector machine (SVM) classifier that is trained on data from a motion capture system.

Ogawara et al. [19] estimate the human body pose from an occupied volume from multiple video streams. They use a deformable skin model with joint structure consisting of Bézier surfaces, as proposed in [15]. The idea is inspired by Kehl et al. [11] who use an extension of the ICP formulation to deformable objects [20] and an M-estimator, a generalized form of the least squares method, to minimize the ICP error function [23]. In contrast, Ziegler et al. [24] formulate the problem of tracking a body pose as state estimation problem, modeling the joint angles as a state vector in an unscented Kalman filter (UKF). Their approach is related to the ICP algorithm since they determine point correspondences by spatial neighborhood and iteratively refine their estimation of the joint angles.

The work by Mündermann et al. [18] and their more recent work [5] generalize the ICP algorithm to articulated models by jointly minimizing the distance from the registered data points to the model surface using a Levenberg-Marquardt minimization scheme. To overcome the variations in the human body, they propose to match a person against a database of articulated models [1]. A specific articulation model is chosen from the database that correlates in height and volume. Such a body model consists of a set of triangle meshes.

Pellegrini et al. [21] propose to divide the articulated body into parts that can be aligned rigidly using a closed-form solution. Therefore, the articulation structure is split into two branches and a single joint angle is adapted. Knoop et al. [14] also apply the ICP to each body part individually.

Azad et al. [3] use a particle filter to estimate the pose of a upper body model from a stereo camera. Their body model consists of fixed-sized cones connected by ball (shoulder) or hinge (elbow) joints. The head is directly connected to the abdomen, omitting a neck. By means of image-based cues, like edges or color they update the particle set. In [2], the authors extend their work by a 3D hand/head tracking as a separate cue for the particle filter. Kim et al. [12] combine the ICP algorithm with a particle filter. The human body is modeled by a set of cylinders and a sphere for the head. Each body part consists of a set of 3D points that model the surface of it. In [13], the same authors propose heuristics to speed up the assignment of correspondences.

All of the mentioned approaches employ a person model that is static during alignment. In contrast, we adapt a generic person model to a person-specific body model to account for the variability in the person's dimensions.

3   Basic Algorithm

3.1   Human Body Model

We model the human body as an directed acyclic graph. The rigid body parts $b_1, b_2, ...b_B$ are the vertices of the graph. Starting from the pelvis, which is the root node of the graph, body parts are connected to other body parts by edges j_i representing the joints. Each body part b_i is modeled by a cylinder with parameters l_i (length) and r_i (radius) and a transformation $\mathbf{T}_i$ that defines the orientation and translation to its parent. In case of the root node b_r, $\mathbf{T}_r$ describes the transformation of the complete body model to the coordinate system origin. In addition, every part has a set of points $\mathbf{m}_1^{b_i}, .., \mathbf{m}_L^{b_i}$ assigned to it that model the cylindrical surface, based on l_i and r_i.

3.2   Articulated Iterative Closest Point Algorithm

The general formulation of the ICP algorithm [4] aims at finding a rigid transformation between a model point set M and a scene point set D. For a set of N corresponding point pairs a transformation T that minimizes

$$E(\mathbf{T}) = \sum_{i=1}^{N} ||\mathbf{m}_i - \mathbf{T}d_i||^2 , \tag{1}$$

is determined by performing an iterative least squares minimization scheme. The solution can be determined by several closed-form algorithms. In the articulated case, Equation 1 is extended to

$$E(\mathbf{T}_1...\mathbf{T}_B) = \sum_{j=1}^{B} \sum_{i=1}^{L} \left|\left|\mathbf{T}_j m_i^{b_j} - d_i\right|\right|^2 . \tag{2}$$

Similar to [21], we split the complete body chain in two subsets at joint j_s and align them with a rigid transformation with respect to j_s which can be solved in closed-form. The splitting joint j_s is chosen successively and varied in every iteration. In case of j_s being the joint assigned to the root node, the entire model is aligned in the data.

4   Proposed Extensions

4.1   Data Segmentation

We apply Euclidean clustering in the 3D point cloud to segment the input data and reduce the number of possible correspondences. Neighboring points are assigned to the same point cluster if the Euclidean distance between them does not exceed a threshold τ_d. The distance threshold needs to be chosen appropriately to take the sensor's accuracy in distance measurements into account. For our setup we use a threshold $\tau_d = 5$ cm. We exclude clusters with less than $\tau_n = 500$ points from further processing. The person model is aligned to each remaining cluster with a standard ICP run, i.e., $j_s = j_r$, with j_r being the root joint. After convergence the point cluster that minimizes Eq. 2 is assumed to be the point cluster that corresponds to the person and remaining clusters are removed from the point cloud.

4.2   Data Assignment

An important step in the ICP algorithm is the data assignment where point correspondences between the model point set and the scene point set are established. A common way is to determine the nearest neighbor d_k for every model point m_i in the scene point set. This can also be conveyed to articulated structures and correspondences are determined for every body part individually. However, this assignment is disadvantageous for scene points that are close to more than one body part, e.g., points close to a joint.

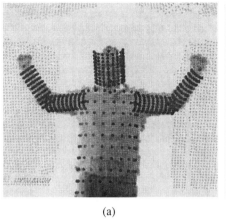 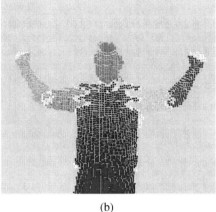

(a)   (b)

Fig. 1. (a) Exemplary scene with aligned body model. (b) Resulting scene points after segmentation with color coded assignment to body parts. Points that are rejected due to distance ratio or absolute distance from any body part are colored white.

In contrast, we use an inverse data assignment where every scene point is assigned to its closest body part. We reject ambiguous correspondences that cannot be clearly assigned to one body part using the distance ratio between closest and the second-closest body part. For our setup, we reject all assignments in which the distance ratio exceeds 0.8. Moreover, we reject points that are too far away from any body part. Fig. 1 shows the resulting assignment for an exemplary scene.

4.3 Model Adaption

After assigning correspondences and before estimating the joint angle, we adapt the model for each body part based on the surface of the assigned points. Assigned points hereby means the correspondences from the previous step. Similar to the splitting joint j_s, we choose the body part that is adapted successively and vary it in every iteration.

By means of a RANSAC [9] estimator, a cylindrical model is fitted into the data points corresponding to a body part. Randomly, data points are selected and the best cylindrical model in terms of the overall number of inliers is calculated, where inliers are points that are closer than 5 cm to the cylinder model. Since the quality of the fitted cylindrical model increases with the number of inliers, a model estimation with less than 100 inliers is neglected. Fig. 2 shows the calculated inliers for an exemplary scene and body part (upper arm). The resulting cylinder is described by vector $\hat{d}$ and radius $\hat{r}$, where $\hat{d}$ corresponds to the direction of the cylinder in the coordinate origin. In order to get the length l of a cylinder, the inliers are transformed by the inverse of $\hat{d}$ to align with the x-axis.

Since the measurements are subject to noise and the assignment of data points can be inaccurate, especially in the first iterations, the model parameters p (i.e., radius r and length l) are filtered over time. Parameter p_k at time step k is calculated by

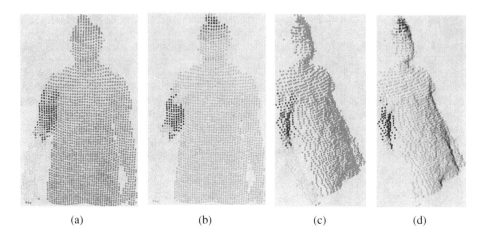

(a)	(b)	(c)	(d)

Fig. 2. (a+c) Data assignment for the upper arm (violet) and forearm (yellow) from two different perspectives. (b+d) The resulting inliers (red) for a the estimated cylindrical upper arm model.

$$p_k = c\hat{p}_k + (c - 1)p_{k-1}. \tag{3}$$

We trust a new estimation of the model parameter $\hat{p}_k$ at time step k with $c = 0.1$. From the resulting model parameters a new set of model points $\mathbf{m}_1^{b_i}, .., \mathbf{m}_L^{b_i}$ for the body part b_i is generated that replaces the previous model points.

In case of a wrong assignment or an insufficient cylindrical fit as well as for initialization, we use a prior for the radius and length of every body part. It prevents from growing or shrinking to abnormal dimensions. For instance, in our system a forearm has a minimum radius of 5 cm and a maximum radius of 15 cm.

4.4   Self-collision Checking

After each ICP iteration, the current state of the model is checked for consistency with respect to self-collisions. A self-collision of a body part is detected by calculating the distance to every body part in the articulation chain except its direct parent and children (i. e. neighboring nodes in the graph). Thus, we allow neighboring body parts to collide with each other, e. g., the forearm can collide with the upper arm but not with the abdomen. In case of a self-collision, the transformation of the current iteration is inverted and applied to the selected joint j_s.

4.5   Model Initialization

For a good alignment of the model in the first data frames a proper initialization of the articulation structure is necessary. In order to do so, a body segmentation step as proposed in [7] can be used. In this approach, body features such as shoulder, elbow and hand are extracted from a point cluster, based on geodesic distances and geometric priors. The resulting body features can be used to initialize the joint states of the model.

Fig. 3. Each column shows one frame from the test data set. The first row shows the raw sensor measurements. The second row shows the adapted body model (red points).

5   Experiments

We evaluate our approach with measurements of a Microsoft Kinect camera [16]. For the following experiments, we use a down-sampled depth image with QQVGA resolution (160 × 120). The average runtime of our current implementation on the down-sampled depth image is 112 ms on a 2.4 GHz single core of a Core2Duo laptop computer. The runtime depends on the number of iterations that are necessary to converge. In general, the number of iterations decreases after an initial model alignment and a frame rate of 8 Hz can be achieved. We focus on an upper body model, since the camera has a field-of-view of 58° × 45°. An adult person with typical European body proportions stands in front of the camera in two meter distance.

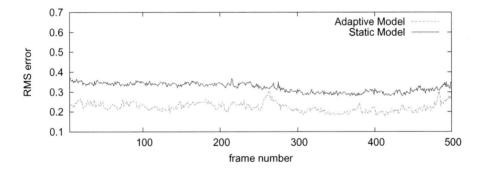

Fig. 4. RMS error for each data frame after convergence. The adaptive model (green dashed) is compared to the static model (red).

In a first experiment, we compare the *root mean squared* (RMS) error of the aligned body model with and without model adaption. The data set consists of 500 data frames of a person performing four different body poses. Fig. 3 shows the four body poses with the adapted body model. After convergence of the ICP algorithm, the RMS error of a model configuration is calculated by Equation 2 for every data frame. Fig. 4 shows the RMS error of the entire data set for the adaptive and the fixed body model. It can be observed that the adaptive model is better aligned with the data. Besides that, using an adaptive model reduces the necessary number of iterations to converge, as shown in Fig. 5.

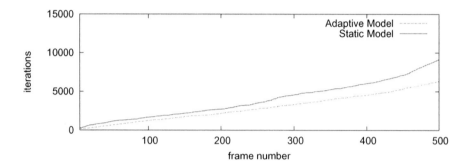

Fig. 5. Number of iterations that are necessary to converge, cumulated up to every frame, for the test data set

In a second experiment, we demonstrate the effect of self-collision prevention. Here, the test person relaxes his arms and keeps them close to his body. Without self-collision checking, body parts of the articulated model may collide with each other, e. g., the forearm with the abdomen. This could result in wrong correspondences, e. g., points from the abdomen could be assigned as correspondences for the forearm. With self-collision checks, a minimal distance between body parts is maintained that prevents from these wrong assignments. Fig. 6 shows frames from the dataset with and without self-collision checks.

The third experiment, shown in Fig. 7, demonstrates how the algorithm aligns the body model when using an incorrect initialization. Here, the angle of the shoulder joint differs between test person and body model and the cylinder dimensions of the body parts are initialized too large (Fig. 7, top left). After 72 iterations (Fig. 7, bottom right), the body model is correctly aligned and the parameters of the model are properly adapted.

6   Conclusions

We propose an extension to the ICP algorithm for articulated models. Due to the variability in the human body shape, we use an adaptive body model that is aligned to 3D point measurements and iteratively adjusted to the person's body dimensions, in contrast to previous approaches, that rely on the correctness of a static model. Besides that, we use an inverse data assignment, that is particularly utile for articulated models. Our approach is based on depth measurements of a RGB-D camera. In experiments,

Fig. 6. Self-collision prevention. Without self-collision prevention (top row) false correspondences are assigned which results in a wrong alignment of the forearm. With enabled self-collision prevention (bottom row) the model can be aligned correctly.

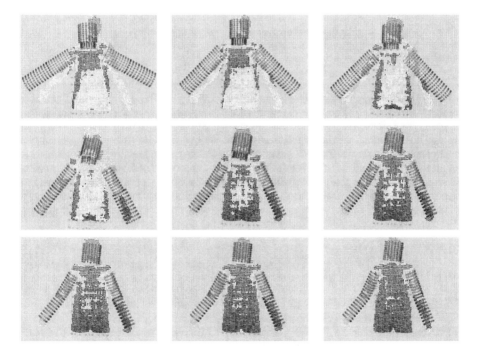

Fig. 7. The alignment of the model at different iterations for the same data frame. Even with an incorrect initialized model, the algorithm converges after 72 iterations.

we compare our approach to the standard articulated ICP algorithm with a static body model. The evaluation shows that an adaptive model aligns better with the data in terms of the RMS error.

We also implement a self-collision check and demonstrate its utility in an experiment. Furthermore, we show how an incorrect model initialization still results in a correct aligned body model.

Up to now, our system only relies on the depth measurements of the camera. However, in some situations, the color images might be beneficial. It is a matter of future work to integrate color information into the algorithm. Besides that, the extracted body pose can be used to interpret, e.g., pointing gestures and an intended pointing target. To do so, the system described in [7] will be adapted to the described body pose estimation. Another possibility for future work is a GPU-based implementation to benefit from the full resolution of the camera and achieve real-time performance.

Acknowledgment. This work has been supported partially by grant BE 2556/2-3 of German Research Foundation (DFG).

References

1. Anguelov, D., Srinivasan, P., Koller, D., Thrun, S., Rodgers, J., Davis, J.: SCAPE: Shape completion and animation of people. In: Proc. of the 32nd International Conference on Computer Graphics and Interactive Techniques (SIGGRAPH), Los Angeles, California (2005)
2. Azad, P., Asfour, T., Dillmann, R.: Robust real-time stereo-based markerless human motion capture. In: IEEE/RAS International Conference on Humanoid Robots (Humanoids), pp. 700–707 (2008)
3. Azad, P., Ude, A., Asfour, T., Dillmann, R.: Stereo-based markerless human motion capture for humanoid robot systems. In: Proceedings of the IEEE International Conference on Robotics and Automation (ICRA), pp. 3951–3956 (2007)
4. Besl, P.J., McKay, N.D.: A method for registration of 3-D shapes. IEEE Transactions on Pattern Analysis and Machine Intelligence 14, 239–256 (1992)
5. Corazza, S., Mündermann, L., Gambaretto, E., Ferrigno, G., Andriacchi, T.P.: Markerless motion capture through visual hull, articulated ICP and subject specific model generation. International Journal of Computer Vision 87, 156–169 (2010)
6. Demirdjian, D., Ko, T., Darrell, T.: Constraining human body tracking. In: Proceedings of the IEEE International Conference on Computer Vision, p. 1071. IEEE Computer Society, Washington, DC (2003)
7. Droeschel, D., Stückler, J., Behnke, S.: Learning to interpret pointing gestures with a time-of-flight camera. In: Proceedings of the 6th International Conference on Human-Robot Interaction (HRI), pp. 481–488. ACM, New York (2011)
8. Droeschel, D., Stückler, J., Holz, D., Behnke, S.: Towards Joint Attention for a Domestic Service Robot – Person Awareness and Gesture Recognition using Time-of-Flight Cameras. In: Proceedings of the IEEE International Conference on Robotics and Automation (ICRA), Shanghai, China, pp. 1205–1210 (2011)
9. Fischler, M.A., Bolles, R.C.: Random sample consensus: a paradigm for model fitting with applications to image analysis and automated cartography. Communications of the ACM 24, 381–395 (1981)

10. Ganapathi, V., Plagemann, C., Thrun, S., Koller, D.: Real Time Motion Capture Using a Single Time-of-Flight Camera. In: Proceedings of the IEEE Conference on Computer Vision and Pattern Recognition (CVPR), San Francisco, CA, USA (2010)
11. Kehl, R., Bray, M., Van Gool, L.: Full body tracking from multiple views using stochastic sampling. In: Proceedings of the 2005 IEEE Computer Society Conference on Computer Vision and Pattern Recognition (CVPR), Washington, DC, USA, pp. 129–136 (2005)
12. Kim, D., Kim, D.: A novel fitting algorithm using the ICP and the particle filters for robust 3d human body motion tracking. In: Proceeding of the 1st ACM Workshop on Vision Networks for Behavior Analysis. VNBA, pp. 69–76. ACM, New York (2008)
13. Kim, D., Kim, D.: A fast ICP algorithm for 3-D human body motion tracking. IEEE Signal Processing Letters 17(4), 402–405 (2010)
14. Knoop, S., Vacek, S., Dillmann, R.: Modeling joint constraints for an articulated 3D human body model with artificial correspondences in ICP. In: Proceedings of the IEEE-RAS International Conference on Humanoid Robots (Humanoids), pp. 74–79 (2005)
15. Komatsu, K.: Human skin model capable of natural shape variation. The Visual Computer 3, 265–271 (1988)
16. Microsoft (2010), http://www.xbox.com/en-US/kinect
17. Moeslund, T.B., Hilton, A., Krüger, V.: A survey of advances in vision-based human motion capture and analysis. Computer Vision and Image Understanding 104, 90–126 (2006)
18. Mündermann, L., Corazza, S., Andriacchi, T.: Accurately measuring human movement using articulated ICP with soft-joint constraints and a repository of articulated models. In: Proc. of the IEEE Conference on Computer Vision and Pattern Recognition, CVPR (2007)
19. Ogawara, K., Li, X., Ikeuchi, K.: Marker-less human motion estimation using articulated deformable model. In: Proceedings of the IEEE International Conference on Robotics and Automation (ICRA), pp. 46–51 (2007)
20. Ogawara, K., Takamatsu, J., Hashimoto, K., Ikeuchi, K.: Grasp recognition using a 3D articulated model and infrared images. In: Proceedings of the IEEE/RSJ International Conference on Intelligent Robots and Systems (IROS), pp. 1590–1595 (2003)
21. Pellegrini, S., Schindler, K., Nardi, D.: A generalization of the ICP algorithm for articulated bodies. In: British Machine Vision Conference, BMVC (2008)
22. Plagemann, C., Ganapathi, V., Koller, D., Thrun, S.: Realtime identification and localization of body parts from depth images. In: Proceedings of the IEEE International Conference on Robotics and Automation (ICRA), Anchorage, Alaska, USA (2010)
23. Wheeler, M.D., Ikeuchi, K.: Sensor modeling, probabilistic hypothesis generation, and robust localization for object recognition. IEEE Transactions on Pattern Analysis and Machine Intelligence 17, 252–265 (1995)
24. Ziegler, J., Nickel, K., Stiefelhagen, R.: Tracking of the articulated upper body on multi-view stereo image sequences. In: Proceedings of the IEEE Conference on Computer Vision and Pattern Recognition (CVPR), Washington, DC, USA, pp. 774–781 (2006)

Artificial Cognition
in Autonomous Assembly Planning Systems

Christian Buescher[1], Marcel Mayer[2], Daniel Schilberg[1], and Sabina Jeschke[1]

[1] RWTH Aachen University
Institute of Information Management in Mechanical Engineering
Dennewartstr. 27, 52068 Aachen, Germany
{Christian.Buescher,Daniel.Schilberg,Sabina.Jeschke}
@ima-zlw-ifu.rwth-aachen.de
[2] RWTH Aachen University
Chair and Institute of Industrial Engineering and Ergonomics
Bergdriesch 27, 52056 Aachen, Germany
m.mayer@iaw.rwth-aachen.de

Abstract. Cognition is of great interest in several scientific disciplines. The issue is to transfer human cognitive capabilities to technical systems and so generate artificial cognition. But while robots are learning to communicate or behave socially only a few examples for applications in production engineering and especially in assembly planning exist. In this field cognitive systems can achieve a technological advance by means of self-optimization and the associated autonomous adaption of the system's behavior to external goal states. In this paper cognitive technical systems and their software architectures in general are discussed as well as several assembly planning systems. A precise autonomous assembly planning system and its implementation of cognitive capabilities is presented in detail.

Keywords: Cognition, Self-Optimization, Cognitive Technical Systems, Assembly Planning Systems.

1   Introduction

Nowadays, due to shortening product life-cycles and changing customer demands manufacturing and assembly systems should be flexible to quickly react to changes in products and their variants. Highly automated manufacturing systems therefore tend to be neither efficient enough for small lot production nor flexible enough to handle products to be manufactured in a large number of variants. To increase flexibility *"future manufacturing systems should focus on the integration of the human operator … due to his or her extraordinary problem solving abilities, creativity and sensorimotor skills"* [1]. Based on simulated cognitive functions, technical systems shall not only be able to (semi-) autonomously derive manufacturing planning, adapt to changing supply conditions and to learn from experience but also to simulate goal-directed human behavior and therefore significantly increase the systems flexibility. These

S. Jeschke, H. Liu, and D. Schilberg (Eds.): ICIRA 2011, Part II, LNAI 7102, pp. 168–178, 2011.

systems offer the possibility to generate effective, efficient and finally self-optimizing joint cognitive systems [2].

In this paper, cognitive technical systems (CTS) and their software architectures as skeletal structure for artificial cognition are presented. Following a definition of the terms *cognition* and *self-optimization* several architectures and approaches are discussed. The focus is on cognitive assembly planning systems. Within the Cluster of Excellence "Integrative production technology for high-wage countries" at RWTH Aachen University, basics for a sustainable production-scientific strategy and theory, as well as for the necessary technological approaches are developed[1]. In the research field "Self-optimizing Production Systems", the project "Cognitive Planning and Control System for Production" develops and implements such a cognitive assembly planning system which is presented in section 4. Furthermore, the way of realization of cognitive capabilities in this technical system is shown.

2   Definitions

2.1   Cognition

The term *cognition* is defined inconsistent and in a predominant human-centered perspective in literature. Within the field of psychology several definitions are applied. A popular definition is the one of Matlin [3], who describes cognition in this context as acquisition, storage, transformation and use of knowledge. Thereby the term knowledge is to be understood as an aggregation of information which is related to a human. Strohner [4] extends the term to technical systems and defines cognition as "... *any kind of information processing by the central nervous system of a human or an appropriate information processing in artificial systems...*". With regard to technical systems cognitive capabilities which are necessary to build up the processes aforementioned are (1) perception, (2) reasoning, (3) remembering, (4) planning, (5) decision making, (6) learning and (7) action [5], [6].

Perception presents the process of including sensory data and its processing and aggregation to information. It is realized by a continuous observation of the system itself and the environment and can also involve the integration of results from different modalities into a single assessment [6]. **Reasoning** describes the transaction of augmentation of knowledge from already present knowledge and the assumption about the environment involved through inductive and deductive reasoning. **Remembering** is the ability to encode and store the results of cognitive processing in memory and to retrieve or access them at a later point in time [7]. **Planning** usually refers to cognitive activities within the human's respectively agent's head. A plan is generated which is than represented as a set of actions [8]. Thus planning is the basis for **decision making** in which a decision is derived matching the goal state which furthermore generates an adequate behavior.

[1] The authors would like to thank the German Research Foundation DFG for supporting the research on human-robot cooperation within the Cluster of Excellence "Integrative Production Technology for High-Wage Countries" at RWTH Aachen University.

An important cognitive capability is the process of **learning**. Out of the experiences and the sensory information new behavior patterns and knowledge can be derived. This augmentation of knowledge differs from that through reasoning, where tacit knowledge is made aware while the process of learning generates entirely new knowledge [3]. Finally, **action** comprises the realization of the capabilities aforementioned by actively manipulating the environment.

The impact on cognitive technical system and its structure and implementation is explained in section 3.

2.2   Self-optimization

The term *self-optimization* is defined in a convincing way by the Collaborative Research Centre 614 „Self-optimizing concepts and structures in mechanical engineering" (CRC 614) at the University of Paderborn, Germany [9]:

"Self-optimization describes the ability of a technical system to endogenously adapt its objective regarding changing influences and thus an autonomous adaption of the system's behavior in accordance with the objective. The behavior adaption may be implemented by changing the parameters or the structure of the system. Thus self-optimization goes considerably beyond the familiar rule-based and adaptive control strategies; Self-optimization facilitates systems with inherent "intelligence" that are able to take action and react autonomously and flexibly to changing operating conditions."

The process of self-optimization can be divided into three distinct steps [10]:

1. **Analyzing the current situation:** The current situation contains the system's state and the relevant information from the environment as well as stored information from previous observations. These pieces of information can also be picked up by communication with other systems (human or technical). This step includes the analysis of the achievement of the objectives given by the operator or other technical systems.
2. **Determining the system's objectives:** During the determination, new system's objectives can be created by generation, adjustment or selection. Selection results from a predetermined quantity of prioritized objectives, whereas adjustment means an incremental transformation of existing objectives or rather their relative weighting. Generation describes the creation of absolute new objectives.
3. **Adapting the system's behavior:** An adaption of the system's behavior is required because of the modified system of objectives. This is done by adjusting single parameters of the system or the whole structure. Finally, the loop of self-optimization is closed by this step.

The whole process is executed by the cooperation of all units of the system which perform the mentioned steps recurrent. Self-optimizing systems do not compulsory require cognitive capabilities up to a certain degree. Contrary, technical systems with cognitive capabilities are not necessarily self-optimizing. However, a technical system which fulfills the aforementioned definition of self-optimization completely has to possess cognitive capabilities in the narrow sense of the word especially regarding learning. This is highlighted by the fact that a self-optimizing system has to react "autonomously and flexible" to unforeseen changes [10].

3 State of the Art

3.1 Software Architectures for Cognitive Technical Systems

The integration of the above mentioned cognitive capabilities into a technical system is a promising approach to increase flexibility and adaptability of such a system. These cognitive technical systems have a specific architecture and are provided with artificial sensors and actuators to act in a physical world [2]. In the field of autonomous robots, several architectures are proposed as a basis for these systems with cognitive behavior [11], [12]. The software architectures concentrate on the combination of a deliberative part for the actual planning process (planning layer) with a reactive part for the direct control (operation layer). Herein, the three-layer-architecture, shown in Fig. 1, with a cognitive, an associative and a reactive control layer is classified as a widespread approach [13], [14].

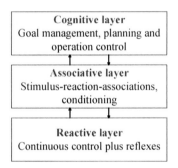

Fig. 1. Three-Layer-Architecture according to Paetzold [14]

The upper layer presents the **cognitive operator**. At this point, the system provides knowledge about itself and its environment to improve the own behavior. This is achieved by the use of various methods like planning and learning behavior, model-oriented optimization procedures or the application of knowledge-based systems. The **associative layer** in the middle supervises and controls the system. Here, the transferred modified behavior patterns from the cognitive layer are implemented by modifying the control in the reactive layer. A large part of auxiliary functions (like sequence control, monitoring and emergency procedures as well as adaption routines to improve the system behavior) are located in this layer. The **reactive layer** contains the control-oriented components of the information processing and manipulates the system behavior by connecting sensors and actuators to reach the required dynamics.

The architecture of cognitive technical systems often resort to modifications of architectural patterns like the presented layer model to implement the required system.

However, the final architecture is adapted to the specific application to achieve the optimal performance of the system [15]. Therefore, the architecture is extended in many cases with a presentation layer on top of the other layers to guarantee a safe and clear human-machine interaction [15], [16].

Advanced approaches of cognitive technical systems can be found in the field of autonomous vehicles and unmanned aerial vehicles (UAV) [17], [18], [19]. Within this field, especially the different architectures of the winning teams of the DARPA Grand Challenge, a competition for driverless vehicles funded by the Defense Advanced Research Projects Agency, the most prominent research organization of the United States Department of Defense, have to be referenced. Those regularly point out the current state of research [19]. Most of these architectures are based on the so called relaxed layered system, in which every layer can utilize the services of all layers located below. Hence, the flexibility and performance of the system rises with complete information in all layers [19].

Another CTS is developed within the collaborative research center 614. The Operateur-Controller-Modul (OCM) is designed to control a mechatronical system in the field of traffic engineering, in this case a drive and braking system as well as a spring and tilting system [10]. This architecture uses the layer model as well, while the cognitive capabilities are focused to enforce a self-optimization.

3.2   Cognitive Technical Systems in Production Engineering

For a few years cognitive technical systems are being explored in the field of production engineering but these systems are not yet ready to use in practice [8]. In addition to various research efforts like [20] and [21] within the mentioned Cluster of Excellence at RWTH Aachen University and CRC 614, the Cluster of Excellence "Cognition in Technical Systems" (CoTeSys) at Technical University of Munich studies cognitive and self-optimizing (technical) systems with the vision of a cognitive factory [22].

Within this cluster, different approaches to implement cognitive capabilities in technical systems are being developed to improve primarily safe human-machine-interaction and -cooperation. The so called Cognitive Safety Controller (CSC) supervises the interaction between human operators and several robots inside of a production system [23]. Again, the architecture of this controller is based on the relaxed layered system. Instead, the objective of the project "Adaptive Cognitive Interaction in Production Environments" (ACIPE) consists in the implementation of an assistive system to autonomously plan a production process [2]. Additional details are presented in section 3.3.

Further general analyses about cognitive technical systems are related to [18] and, particularly in the field of production engineering, to [8] and [23].

3.3   Assembly Planning Systems

Assembly planning systems described in the literature do not relate cognitive technical systems. Therefore, the current state of technology of assembly planning systems is illustrated as part of assembly systems in general to be able to classify the explanations in the section below. Assembly planning systems are the main basis for the automated realization of assembly tasks. They plan the sequence of an assembly assumed that one or more production units or human workers are available. Every single action presents a work step which is executed by the robot or the worker.

At this point, the cognitive capability of planning from the field of artificial intelligence (AI) is of great interest. Numerous applicable approaches do exist for planning tasks in different applications. Hoffmann generated the so called Fast-Forward-Planer (FF) to derive action sequences for specified deterministic problems [24], while other planners are able to deal with uncertainty [25]. However, all these planners are based on a symbolic logical representation. For the application of an assembly planning which is dependent on an appropriate representation of geometrical relations between states and the corresponding transformations this becomes very extensive even for simple tasks. Because of the generic characteristic, these planners collapse to calculate assembly sequences within an acceptable time.

Other planners were developed in particular for assembly planning. They directly operate with geometrical information and data to generate assembly sequences. A widespread approach is the "Archimedes" method, which uses the Assembly-by-Disassembly strategy in conjunction with an AND-/OR-graph to demount an assembly into its single parts [26]. A further development of this is the planning strategy developed by Thomas [27], which uses solely the geometrical data of the assembly and the single parts and which reaches a higher degree of autonomy at that point. Despite this fact, these approaches are not able to deal with uncertainty, concerning the sequence of the delivered single parts.

The assembly planner mentioned in section 3.2, is developed by Zaeh and Wiesbeck within the project ACIPE of the CoTeSys cluster [2]. It computes the action sequence autonomously as far as possible, then presenting the result to the human operator. The planner is designed to support manual assembly, while the decision making for executing the sequence is still task of the worker and therefore not implemented in the system [16]. This planner works on a geometrical representation using a state graph. After generating the graph with the methods mentioned above, the current state of the system is matched to the graph after each manipulation and the optimal sequence is derived by a search algorithm [2]. Related approaches are presented in [28] and [29].

As described in this section, existing assembly planning systems nowadays possess only single cognitive capabilities like perception, action and especially planning, but they are neither cognitive at all nor self-optimizing. In the following, research activities are presented which try to close this gap.

4 The Project "Cognitive Planning and Control System for Production"

4.1 Objectives and Approach

The overall objective of the project "Cognitive Planning and Control System for Production" is to develop design methodologies for self-optimizing production with the use of cognitive control units that refer, for instance, to single machine controllers as well as to the organizational setup. Hence, a production system based on this reduces the work of planning in advance of an assembly and is capable of optimizing itself during the running process.

The basis of the system developed in this project is the software architecture shown in Fig. 2. The skeletal structure consists of the planning, coordination and reactive layer following the three-layer-architecture. This is supplemented by the presentation layer and a logging module to ensure that the operator is provided with situation-relevant information in order to be able to monitor the system as well as to perform a targeted system operation and to deliver a goal state. The knowledge module contains the knowledge base which comprises the domain knowledge that is necessary for the system with regard to the performance of the assembly tasks [30]. This architecture is connected with the technical layer, representing a robot cell. A detailed description of this architecture can be found in [15].

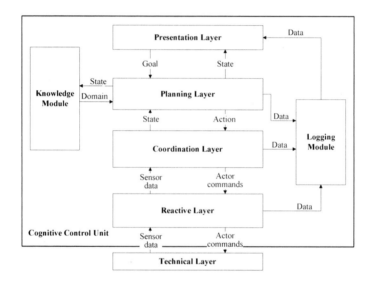

Fig. 2. Software architecture of the cognitive technical system

An important cross section component of the system is the cognitive control unit (CCU), which plans and controls the assembly of a product solely described by its CAD data. The requirements for this planning component are to allow fast reaction times during assembly and a detailed generation of all possibilities to assemble the product from its single parts, which requires a large number of computations. There-fore, a hybrid approach has been designed which combines cognitive and therefore reactive capabilities with the functions of the assembly planning system as developed by Thomas [27] and extended by Zaeh [2] (see Fig. 3). Another hybrid planning approach for self-optimizing systems can be found in [31], which distinguishes a discrete preplanning and a continuous online planning.

The offline planner of the CCU autonomously generates a state graph with all possible solutions to assemble a product prior to the actual assembly process and stores all information in the knowledge base. The online planner receives the current state of the system during the assembly and generates a set of optimal sequences which is analyzed by the subcomponent cognitive control. At this point, in contrast to Zaeh, the system itself reaches a decision and sends the command to the robot cell. The detailed procedure of the CCU is explained in [32]. By means of this approach, it is possible to react to unforeseen changes – in the constraints of the generated plan – concerning the environment, to increase the flexibility of assembly systems and to decrease the planning effort previously.

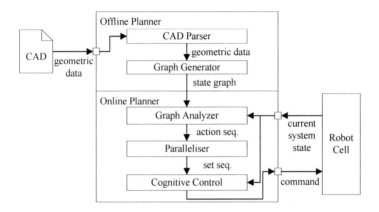

Fig. 3. Hybrid Planner of the CCU

4.2 Cognitive Capabilities of the CCU

Based on the explanations from section 4.1, the linkage between the components of the software architecture and the CCU on the one hand and the listed cognitive capabilities on the other hand is shown. In the following, the seven capabilities aforementioned and their methods or concepts of realization are illustrated:

- **Perception** is located in the lower layers of the architecture. While vision modules, which are part of the technical layer, collect the data from the environment, the reactive and coordination layer aggregate the information to a system state and transmit it to the planner [33].
- **Reasoning** is a process which takes place in the knowledge module. Using the Web Ontology Language (OWL) as a means of representation in the knowledge base, structured storage of all information is allowed as well as an efficient access later on [30].
- **Remembering** is exactly this process of using the knowledge for planning or similar activities. This capability is provided by a knowledge compiler within the knowledge module [30].
- **Planning** is the main aspect of this system. It is performed by the planning layer more precisely by the CCU. This capability is implemented by means of graphical analysis in the graph generator and by classical search algorithms in this case the A* search algorithm in the graph analyzer [32].

- **Decision making** is the task of the cognitive control component. This component is based on Soar, a cognitive framework for decision finding, that aims on modeling the human decision process [6]. An overview of Soar and other existing cognitive frameworks is given in [6]. In addition to these general aspects, specific human behavior pattern concerning assembly processes can be implemented to support decision making [34].
- **Learning** is included in Soar as a learning mechanism called "chunking", which can store new rules in production memory [6]. Concepts are being developed beyond that for example to lead back information of the assembly operation to the graph generation. This kind of 'reinforcement learning' allows improving the planning performance by learning from previous mistakes or failures.
- **Action** is, on the one hand, the direct realization of a command by a robot and its actuators. Therefore, the command is transformed into several control commands by the coordination and reactive layer. On the other hand, the human operator can be asked to perform a work step. This is delivered by the human-machine interface in the presentation layer in an appropriate way [34].

To reach the performance of an automated assembly system concerning the execution speed all processes of a cognitive technical system described above have to be real-time capable. This is as well as the learning component subject of current research. As described before, the system contains several cognitive capabilities but still not being self-optimizing in terms of the named definition.

5   Conclusion and Outlook

By defining the terms *cognition* and *self-optimization* with respect to technical systems it was shown that both are not synonymous but cause each other in a certain way. A sophisticated self-optimizing system requires several cognitive capabilities in particular decision-making and learning. The implementation happens using a special category of architectures which usually base on the three-layer-model in combination with the relaxed layered system. Different cognitive technical systems from diverse scientific disciplines were presented with a focus on production engineering and assembly planning. The specifications of those architectures are tailored to the particular needs of the application.

Using the example of the project "Cognitive Planning and Control System for Production" the implementation of cognitive capabilities within one precise software architecture was presented. This autonomous assembly planning system is advanced but does not contain all required cognitive capabilities in a sufficient way. Especially the learning component has to be improved on the way to self-optimization.

The explanations have shown that the transfer of human cognitive capabilities to technical systems is yet not done sufficiently. On the one hand single components and methods to perform cognitive capabilities require further research as well as the integration of those components in a suitable architecture. As a result, the possibilities of an extend use of cognitive technical systems within production technology are immense. By means of a cooperation of several cognitive systems, the realization of self-optimizing production systems can be put forward. This approach has to be proved by industrial use cases while the current situation is fundamental research.

References

1. Schlick, C., Reuth, R., Luczak, H.: A Comparative Simulation Study of Work Processes in Autonomous Production Cells. Human Factors and Ergonomics in Manufacturing, West Sussex 12(1), 31–54 (2002)
2. Zaeh, M.F., Wiesbeck, M.: A Model for Adaptively Generating Assembly Instructions Using State-based Graphs. In: The 41st CIRP Conference on Manufacturing Systems, Tokyo, Japan (2008)
3. Matlin, M.W.: Cognition, 7th edn. John Wiley & Sons, Hoboken (2008)
4. Strohner, H.: Kognitive Systeme – Eine Einführung in die Kognitionswissenschaft. Westdeutscher Verlag, Opladen (1995)
5. Zimbardo, P., Gerrig, R.: Psychology and Life. Pearson, Boston (2005)
6. Langley, P., Laird, J.E., Rogers, S.: Cognitive architectures: Research issues and challenges. Journal of Cognitive Systems Research 10(2), 141–160 (2009)
7. Strube, G.: Modelling Motivation and Action Control in Cognitive Sytems. In: Schmid, U., Krems, J.F., Wysocki, F. (eds.) Mind Modelling: A Cognitive Science Approach to Reasoning, Learning and Discovery, Papst, Lengerich, pp. 89–108 (1998)
8. Bannat, A., Bautze, T., Beetz, M., Blume, J., Diepold, K., Ertelt, C., Geiger, F., Gmeiner, T., Gyger, T., Knoll, A., Lau, C., Lenz, C., Ostgathe, M., Reinhart, G., Roesel, W., Ruehr, T., Schuboe, A., Shea, K., Stork, I., Stork, S., Tekouo, W., Wallhoff, F., Wiesbeck, M., Zaeh, M.F.: Artificial Cognition in Production Systems. IEEE Transactions on Automation Science and Engineering 8(1), 148–174 (2011)
9. Collaborative Research Centre 614, Self -optimizing concepts and structures in mechanical engineering (CRC 614) (March 23, 2011),
   http://www.sfb614.de/en/sfb614/research-program/
10. Frank, U., Giese, H., Klein, F., Oberschelp, O., Schmidt, A., Schulz, B., Vöcking, H., Witting, K.: Selbstoptimierende Systeme des Maschinenbaus - Definitionen und Konzepte. Bonifatius GmbH (2004)
11. Gat, E.: On Three-Layer Architectures. In: Kortenkamp, D., Bonnasso, R., Murphy, R. (eds.) Artificial Intelligence and Mobile Robots, pp. 195–211 (1998)
12. Karim, S., Sonenberg, L., Tan, A.-H.: A Hybrid Architecture Combining Reactive Plan Execution and Reactive Learning. In: Yang, Q., Webb, G. (eds.) PRICAI 2006. LNCS (LNAI), vol. 4099, pp. 200–211. Springer, Heidelberg (2006)
13. Russell, S.J., Norvig, P.: Artificial Intelligence: A Modern Approach. Pearson Education (2003)
14. Paetzold, K.: On the importance of a functional description for the development of cognitive technical systems. In: International Design Conference 2006, Dubrovnik (2006)
15. Hauck, E., Gramatke, A., Henning, K.: A Software Architecture for Cognitive Technical Systems for an Assembly Task in a Production Environment. In: Rodic, A. (ed.) Automation and Control, Theory and Practice, pp. 13–28. In-Tech, Vukovar (2010)
16. Stork, S., Schuboe, A.: Human cognition in manual assembly: Theories and applications. Advanced Engineering Informatics 24, 320–328 (2010)
17. Putzer, H.J.: Ein uniformer Architekturansatz für Kognitive Systeme und seine Umsetzung in ein operatives Framework. Verlag Dr. Köster, Berlin (2004)
18. Onken, R., Schulte, A.: System-Ergonomic Design of Cognitive Automation. Springer, Berlin (2010)
19. Thrun, S., Montemerlo, N., Dahlkamp, H., Stavens, D., Aron, A., Diebel, J., Fong, P., Gale, J., Halpenny, M., Hoffmann, G., et al.: Stanley: The Robot That Won the DARPA Grand Challenge. In: The 2005 DARPA Grand Challenge, Springer Tracts in Advanced Robotics, vol. 36, pp. 1–43 (2007)

20. Loosen, P., Schmitt, R., Brecher, C., Müller, R., Funck, M., Gatej, A., Morasch, V., Pavim, A., Pyschny, N.: Self-optimizing assembly of laser systems. Production Engineering Research and Development 5(4), 443–451 (2011)
21. Müller, R., Esser, M., Janssen, M., Vette, M., Corves, B., Huesing, M., Riedel, M.: Reconfigurable handling system. Production Engineering Research and Development 5(4), 453–461 (2011)
22. Cluster of Excellence Cognition in Technical Systems(CoTeSys) (March 23, 2011), http://www.cotesys.de/about.html
23. Kain, S., Ding, H., Schiller, F., Stursberg, O.: Controller Architecture for Safe Cognitive Technical Systems. In: Saglietti, F., Oster, N. (eds.) SAFECOMP 2007. LNCS, vol. 4680, pp. 518–531. Springer, Heidelberg (2007)
24. Hoffmann, J.: FF: The Fast-Forward Planning System. The AI Magazine 22 (2001)
25. Hoffmann, J., Brafman, R.: Contingent Planning via Heuristic Forward Search with Implicit Belief States. In: Proceedings of the 15th International Conference on Automated Planning and Scheduling, Monterey, CA, USA (2005)
26. Kaufman, S., Wilson, R., Jones, R., Calton, T., Ames, A.: The Archimedes 2 mechanical assembly planning system. In: Proceedings of the IEEE International Conference on Robotics and Automation, vol. 4, pp. 3361–3368 (1996)
27. Thomas, U., Molkenstruck, S., Iser, R., Wahl, F.M.: Multi Sensor Fusion in Robot Assembly Using Particle Filters. In: Proceedings of the IEEE International Conference on Robotics and Automation (ICRA), pp. 3837–3843 (2007)
28. Medellín, H., Corney, J., Ritchie, J.M., Lim, T.: Automatic Generation of Robot and Manual Assembly Plans Using Octrees. Assembly Automation 30(2), 173–183 (2010)
29. Biswal, B.B., Mishra, D., Dash, P., Choudhury, B.B.: An overview and comparison of four sequence generating methods for robotic assembly. International Journal of Manufacturing Technology and Management 20(1-4), 169–196 (2010)
30. Hauck, E., Ewert, D., Schilberg, D., Jeschke, S.: Design of a Knowledge Module Embedded in a Framework for a Cognitive System Using the Example of Assembly Tasks. In: Proceedings of the 3rd International Conference on Applied Human Factors and Ergonomics. Hrsg. v. CRC Press / Taylor & Francis, Ltd., Miami (2010)
31. Gausemeier, J., Rammig, F.J., Schäfer, W. (eds.): Selbstoptimierende Systeme des Maschinenbaus: Definitionen, Anwendungen, Konzepte. Westfalia, Paderborn (2009)
32. Ewert, D., Thelen, S., Kunze, R., Mayer, M., Schilberg, D., Jeschke, S.: A Graph Based Hybrid Approach of Offline Pre-planning and Online Re-planning for Efficient Assembly under Realtime Constraints. In: Liu, H., Ding, H., Xiong, Z., Zhu, X. (eds.) ICIRA 2010, Part II. LNCS (LNAI), vol. 6425, pp. 44–55. Springer, Heidelberg (2010)
33. Kempf, T., Herfs, W., Brecher, C.: SOAR-based Sequence Control for a Flexible Assembly Cell. In: Proceedings of the 2009 IEEE Conference on Emerging Technologies and Factory Automation, Palma de Mallorca (2009)
34. Mayer, M., Schlick, C., Ewert, D., Behnen, D., Kuz, S., Odenthal, B., Kausch, B.: Automation of robotic assembly processes on the basis of an architecture of human cognition. Production Engineering Research and Development 5(4), 423–431 (2011)

Self-optimization as an Enabler
for Flexible and Reconfigurable Assembly Systems

Rainer Müller[1], Christian Brecher[2], Burkhard Corves[3], Martin Esser[1],
Martin Riedel[3], Sebastian Haag[2], and Matthias Vette[1]

[1] Laboratory for Machine Tools and Production Engineering (WZL), Chair of Assembly
Systems, RWTH Aachen University, Steinbachstraße 19, 52074 Aachen, Germany
{R.Mueller,M.Esser,M.Vette}@wzl.rwth-aachen.de
[2] Fraunhofer Institute for Production Technology (IPT),
Steinbachstraße 17, 52074 Aachen, Germany
{Christian.Brecher,Sebastian.Haag}@ipt.fraunhofer.de
[3] Department of Mechanism Theory and Dynamics of Machines (IGM), RWTH Aachen
University, Eilfschornsteinstraße 18, 52062 Aachen, Germany
{corves,riedel}@igm.rwth-aachen.de

Abstract. In the face of continuously increasing cost pressure, a wide range of
product versions and shorter innovation cycles, the demand for more versatile
assembly and handling systems is steadily growing. Co-operating robots
represent a suitable approach for this purpose. However, reconfiguring a multi-
device robot cell usually involves a certain programming effort and unfavorable
down times. By integrating self-optimizing functions, the complex task of
reconfiguration is substantially simplified in order to make economic use not
only of the referenced co-operating robotic systems. Therefore, several self-
optimizing functions for different stages of production have been developed and
applied to various production tasks. The implemented functions comprise self-
optimizing planning and commissioning as well as a self-optimizing joining
process. Based on the experience gained from these examples, the self-
optimizing functions will be similarly applicable to various cases with relatively
small additional effort.

Keywords: Self-optimization, Reconfiguration, Integrative Production.

1   Introduction

General conditions for manufacturing companies have changed fundamentally in
recent years. Growing globalization, fast technological developments and changing
resource conditions are responsible for growing complexity and dynamics within
companies and in the industrial environment [1, 2]. Further shortening of product life
cycles, lasting growth of the quantity of product variants and the constantly increasing
pressure to reduce production costs are some of the results [3].

Especially in high-wage countries, it will no longer be sufficient to design products
that can only be manufactured cheaply in mass production and are therefore capable
of being the price leader in the market or, in the other extreme case, customized

S. Jeschke, H. Liu, and D. Schilberg (Eds.): ICIRA 2011, Part II, LNAI 7102, pp. 179–188, 2011.
© Springer-Verlag Berlin Heidelberg 2011

products that are tailored to the clients' needs and solely follow a differentiation strategy. Ever shorter product life cycles, a growing number of product variants and a lack of skilled workers in combination with increasing wage costs force companies to no longer follow only one strategy. Instead of a firm commitment to either differentiation or price leadership, the advantages of both strategies have to be combined in order to offer customized products at competitive prices. However, this is not easily possible for the strategy of differentiation generally being associated with higher production costs and the strategy of price leadership not claiming to provide custom-tailored products. Thus, a conflict arises between the two contrary strategies, which initially are not compatible, i.e. the benefits derived from one strategy may only be achieved at the expense of the opposite strategy [3]. With regard to the referenced conflict between customized production on one hand and cost reduction by automation on the other hand, flexible assembly systems represent a promising solution for high-wage countries.

An example for a product featuring many variants and complex assembly processes are small laser systems. The technological development of opto-mechanical products is driven by changing customer demands and an on-going trend towards miniaturization. These circumstances put high demands on high precision manufacturing and assembly. Especially precision assembly is characterized by a significant amount of manual or semi-automated procedures. This results in high costs and subsequently in a competitive disadvantage for high wage countries. Hence, there is a strong demand for automation in this sector. To increase the automation in assembly, the layout of a marking laser was changed. While conventional lasers are built with concentric lenses, a miniaturized laser system has been developed using planar lenses. So, all its optical components can be assembled automatically from above. Because of the low volumes and many variants, a flexible assembly system is needed [4, 5].

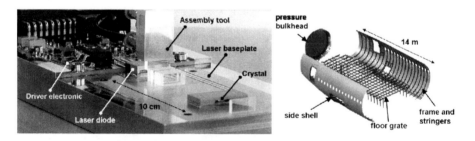

Fig. 1. Laser system and Airbus A350 XWB sections 16/18 [4, 6]

In another dimensional range, the handling of large components, that partially do not have an inherent stability, is another important task within various industrial sectors. Such components are deployed in aeronautical engineering, train wagon building and in shipbuilding. Considering aircraft structure assembly, ever larger shell elements from carbon fibre reinforced polymer (CFRP) have to be handled within the fuselage manufacturing. Especially for these CFRP components, it has to be taken into consideration that during the handling only restricted forces may be applied to the component. Furthermore, high accuracy and a large workspace are required [7]. Usually a single handling unit is not capable of moving the components in a way that only acceptable forces have an influence on them. So far, large jigs have to be used, which often cause high costs in combination with low versatility. The situation is further aggravated by the fact that individual structural elements of the airplane differ considerably in form, size and weight. Therefore, it is not possible to deploy universally applicable jigs. [7]

To eliminate the usual boundaries of single handling systems, such as work space limitations and a restricted range of parts and applications, the main goal is to increase adaptability by means of a highly reconfigurable and versatile system. The wide operational spectrum and the adaptability of the assembly system to changing requirements are achieved through a multi-level reconfigurability. [8]

The required flexibility for automated assembling of varying products is in some cases achieved by robotic systems [9]. Adequate assembly cells can, in particular, be realized through the use of co-operating robots. These robots can be set up for different tasks by retooling and reprogramming. Inflexible supporting devices for the handling of large components can be avoided by using multiple robot systems [10].

Furthermore, movements for joining and active alignment processes can be automated by means of in-line metrology and supplementary sensors located on the robot arms. However, highly flexible robot systems in combination with additional sensors and measurement instrumentation require increased planning, programming and commissioning efforts.

But planning, programming and commissioning of such systems is very complex and time consuming. Therefore, the planning and programming effort must be minimized and the start-up phase has to be as short as possible in order to allow efficient automated production [11].

Against this background, several self-optimizing functions are currently being developed at the RWTH Aachen University within the scope of the Cluster of Excellence "Integrative Production Technology for High-Wage Countries". These functions support the user in planning and commissioning as well as in implementing complex assembly processes and allow cost-effective production of products in small quantities and many variants. The product examples shown serve as example applications for the developed strategies.

2   Self-optimizing Functions for Assembly Systems

Especially in assembly technology, the ability to react to changing conditions is of major interest. Self-optimizing functions can be useful in many different stages of production, such as planning, programming and commissioning of production systems.

"Self-optimization of a technical system is the endogenous adaption of objectives as reaction to changing influences and the resulting autonomous adjustment of parameters or structure and consequently of the system's behavior: Thus self-optimization substantially goes beyond the well-known control and adaptation strategies; Self-optimization enables systems to act with inherent "intelligence", to react independently and flexibly to changing operation conditions." [12].

The process of self-optimization can be divided into three major steps:

- During the **analysis of the actual situation**, the actual system state is determined. Not only the system's internal states but also other conditions claimed by an operator or a higher-level control can be detected.
- The **determination of the system's objectives** is based on testing the current system's state in terms of its capability to fulfill the given task. If the current system is not able to perform this task, the system's objectives will be changed in order to fulfill the task.
- In the last phase, the **system's behavior is adjusted** according to the system objectives. The adaptation of the system's behavior can consist of changing several parameters or even include a structural adjustment, for which the whole system needs to be reconfigured.

In the following, three examples for self-optimizing planning, self-optimizing commissioning and self-optimizing joining processes are introduced, illustrated by a reconfigurable assembly system for large aircraft components and the assembly of a marking laser.

2.1   Grasp Planning and Configuration

For co-operating robots, there are a large number of possible configurations. It is not only further increased by the gripping and tool points, but also the robot's base positions are crucial. This important advantage over conventional "rigid" systems may only be used efficiently and economically if both the reconfiguration itself and the planning of an optimal configuration can be performed quickly and easily. Besides the accessibility of the gripping points along the trajectory, stiffness and accuracy as well as forces and torques for the component and the handling devices are considered as optimization criteria.

Several self-optimization tools have been developed to automatically define the system's additional degrees of freedom and to suggest a possible configuration according to the task. The procedure is shown in figure 2. Thus, the assembly system can be perfectly adapted to the new task without running time-consuming tests.

Starting point for the analysis of the current situation is the component. In addition to the description of the trajectory path and the working space, the degrees of freedom such as possible gripping points on the component or available grippers and handling devices have to be defined for optimization. Then the current configuration is determined and set as the starting point for the optimization process to achieve the lowest possible refitting effort. To finally select a solution, various quality criteria such as stiffness, driving torque and accuracy are defined.

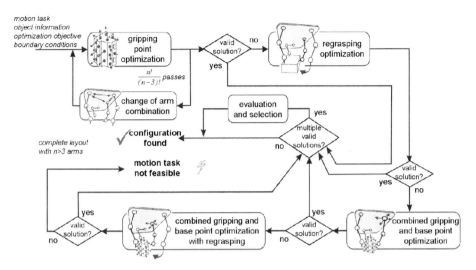

Fig. 2. Grasp planning and configuration

Subsequently, the system's objective is determined by proposing a configuration and a gripping point layout. First, the given potential gripping points are checked. This step is important, as a specification of only 9 points per surface of a cubic workpiece would generate 148.824 possible combinations (Fig. 3). For the pre-selection, the points are examined regarding the gripping process. Afterwards, it has to be verified whether the points are located within the range of the handling devices during the entire movement and if the joints of the manipulators remain within the allowed range.

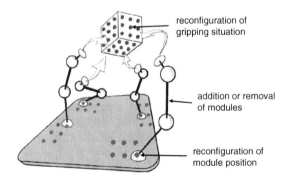

Fig. 3. Multi-level reconfigurability of the handling system

In the second step, the suitability of the combinations is tested. For this purpose, the kinetostatic and dynamic values are calculated at discrete points along the path. If one gripping point combination meets all performance requirements, it passes on for final selection. From this final pool of combinations, the solution which best meets the selected characteristics will be selected. If no combination meets the performance requirements, the handling modules can be repositioned in order to provide a variety of new combinations. The base point positioning is similar to the gripping point optimization. Again, the first step is to eliminate points that are beyond the reach of the manipulators. Then it is tested that during the movement the normal angle of the remaining points will not fall below the determined limits. A deficiency would render the module unable to handle the components in this area. Finally, kinetostatic and dynamic values for discrete points are calculated again. If there still is no valid solution, the system will be expanded by installing additional handling modules. In this case the handling object will be passed from one module to the next.

Finally, the assembly system is configured according to the elaborated proposal. In case of a simple gripping point reconfiguration, only the programs of the handling devices and the model of the assembly system have to be adapted. In a complete configuration change, the handling devices are moved or modules are, respectively, added or removed.

To validate this self-optimizing planning function, it has been applied to a reconfigurable assembly system. First, the kinematics had to be adapted for a further optimization process. Then, the necessary framework conditions such as path points and optimization criteria were entered via a graphical user interface. The optimization result was a possible system configuration permitting the component to be moved as necessary.

2.2   Quick Automated Commissioning of Assembly Systems after Reconfiguration

After a suitable gripping point and base point configuration has been found, the system has to be reconfigured. In order to minimize the set-up effort, handling modules are only roughly positioned within the assembly system. Afterwards, the simulation model of the assembly system is adapted to the system's behavior by means of self-optimizing commissioning functions. This helps avoiding a complex alignment procedure for each module.

To analyze the actual situation, the relevant parameters describing the process modules are identified. The handling devices can, for instance, execute a test movement, which is observed by a global measurement system. From the measured data, the base points of the handling modules can be derived. To match the real movements of the handling modules with the planned movements, the calculation model of the assembly system has to be adapted by matching the parameter values with the identified parameters (Fig. 4).

In addition to the handling modules, the positions of further devices and the component itself have to be identified and the model has to be adjusted. Especially for handling a component with several co-operating modules, it is important to exactly determine the gripping conditions of each module. Therefore, a method has been developed to identify a robot's gripping points by means of a test movement of the handling object. Then, the parameters can be adjusted according to this identification.

Using the exemplary reconfigurable assembly system, the method has been validated. With the help of a laser tracker, the world coordinate system of the assembly system and the base coordinate systems of the robots were determined. The world coordinate system has been identified by probing distinctive shapes of the system. Subsequently, the origins of the base coordinate systems could be discovered. A comparison to the nominal model revealed that the robots were displaced by several millimeters and rotated by a few degrees from their desired positions.

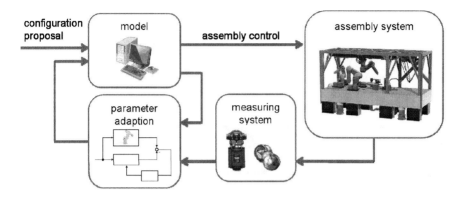

Fig. 4. System identification for model-driven assembly systems

In order to work with a laser tracker, the gripper had been equipped with a reflector that allowed determining the exact gripping point in the world coordinate system by a simple test movement.

In a further step, the system is enabled to perform a structural change. In case of intolerable inaccuracies of the handling system, the system can switch to an operating mode in which the component is continuously monitored, for example by a global measurement system. The deviations can then be determined from the measurement results and are considered correction values in the component path calculation. Through the fixed transformation from the reference coordinate system to the gripping points of the component, the handling modules directly obtain the corrected target positions. Thus, the component moves according to the specification. Through the additional global measurement system, the control structure of the entire handling system is expanded by a position controller for the component.

By means of in-line measurement, the position of the robot can be monitored during critical processes in order to compensate the position errors that are not modeled.

With the help of the presented approach it is possible to reduce the deviation between simulation and reality in order to transfer offline created programs to the real system without the necessity of complex adjustments. This allows a noticeable shortening of the start-up time after a changeover and therefore a more economical automated assembly of small series.

2.3 Planar Alignment for a Bonding Process

Another self-optimizing function was developed for a joining process. During the joining operation, process forces may occur that can damage components, devices and even robots. These process forces arise, for example, from large component tolerances which lead to geometric dimensions deviating from the desired contour. One result may be that the respective component touches another component earlier or later than expected, depending on its actual size.

Another major factor is the positioning accuracy in combination with the robot's kinematics. Contrary to gantry robots, position errors of a vertical articulated-arm robot always cause a change in the orientation. Depending on the specific reason for the position deviation, the error may vary over the entire working area so that no constant off-set can be used. Especially for small batches, not every joining process can be programmed by "Teaching" the compensation of these errors. Thus, a self-optimizing function for planar component placement has been developed and validated using the example of the laser assembly system. The quality of the laser mainly depends on the surface-to-surface alignment of the optical component onto the base plate. Therefore, the self-optimizing assembly makes use of a force/torque sensor attached between the robot's tool center point and its gripper.

The analysis of the forces and torques measured in combination with the knowledge of the tool's geometry and the component gripped allow the identification of the contact formation [13]. The contact formation can be regarded as the analysis of the actual situation.

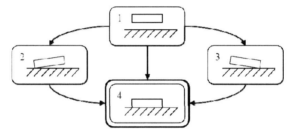

Fig. 5. Possible contact formation

The external objective requires a surface-to-surface alignment of the two components to be bonded. The knowledge of the current state allows determining the internal system objectives that will lead to the achievement of the external objective. In this case, a robot motion will be commanded that will improve the contact formation towards a surface-to-surface alignment (Fig. 5). The destination of the motion can be interpreted as the new internal objective and the underlying motion control as the adjusted system behaviour.

By means of sensor-guided positioning, the programming effort for the robot is tremendously reduced and the components may be joined automatically.

3   Summary and Outlook

Self-optimization forms the basis for an efficient and economic use of flexible and reconfigurable assembly systems. The presented examples illustrate how self-optimizing functions can be used for planning and commissioning of assembly systems as well as for the assembly process itself. The process of self-optimization generally comprises three major steps: After determining the actual system state, the system objectives are adapted and the system behavior is appropriately adjusted.

Self-optimizing functions do not only simplify the process of finding, comparing and choosing suitable system configurations. They also facilitate the compensation of inaccuracies in positioning devices or creating a model of an assembly cell. By means of adequate measurement equipment, self-optimization even enables permanent automated adjustments of system parameters during ongoing operations.

In the second phase of the Cluster of Excellence, a toolbox of general self-optimizing functions will be developed. It will be based on the functions introduced above, universally applicable and adjusted to the needs of various other assembly systems.

Another research area for self-optimization within the scope of multi-robot systems is automated path planning. Due to frequently changing conditions, such as a modified work space, a new configuration or a new assembly task, it is important to develop an automated collision-free path planning to put the system back into operation without time-consuming planning and programming effort. Especially when multiple robots are working closely together and corresponding programs are not firmly linked with each other, functions for motion optimization are needed to coordinate movements of the individual handling devices.

The described activities are supported by the German Research Foundation (DFG) within the scope of the Cluster of Excellence "Integrative Production Technology for High-Wage Countries" at the RWTH Aachen University.

References

[1] Nyhuis, P.: Wandlungsfähige Produktionssysteme. Heute die Industrie von morgen gestalten. PZH Produktionstechnisches Zentrum, Garbsen (2008)

[2] Möller, N.: Bestimmung der Wirtschaftlichkeit wandlungsfähiger Produktionssysteme. Forschungsbericht IWB, Band 212 (2008)

[3] Brecher, C.: Integrative Production Technology for High-Wage Countries. Springer, Heidelberg (2011)

[4] Schmitt, R., Pavim, A., Brecher, C., Pyschny, N.: Flexibel automatisierte Montage von Festkörperlasern. Auf dem Weg zur flexiblen Montage mittels kooperierender Roboter und Sensorfusion. Wt Werkstattstechnik Online 98(11/12), 955–960 (2008)

[5] Brecher, C., Pyschny, N., Loosen, P., Funck, M., Dolkemeyer, J., Morasch, V., Schmitt, R., Pavim, A.: Self-optimizing flexible assembly systems. In: Klöpper, B., Dangelmaier, W. (eds.) Self-x in Engineering. Workshop on Self-X in Mechatronics and Other Engineering Applications, Paderborn, Münster, MV-Wissenschaft (September 2009)

[6] Premium AEROTEC GmbH, http://www.premium-aerotec.com/Binaries/Binary5687/A350-Grafik_work_packages_DE.jpg (accessed August 2011)

[7] Millar, A., Kihlman, H.: Reconfigurable Flexible Tooling for Aerospace Wing Assembly. In: Proceedings of the SAE 2009 AeroTech Congress & Exhibition, Seattle, USA (November 2009)

[8] Helgosson, P., Ossbahr, G., Tommlinson, D.: Modular and Configurable Steel Structure for Assembly Fixtures. In: Proceedings of the SAE 2010 Aerospace Manufacturing and Automated Fastening Conference & Exhibition, Wichita, KS, USA (September 2010)

188   R. Müller et al.

[9] DeVlieg, R., Feikert, E.: One-Up Assembly with Robots. In: Proceedings of the Aerospace Manufacturing and Automated Fastening Conference & Exhibition, North Charleston, SC, USA (September 2008)

[10] Feldmann, K., Ziegler, C., Michl, M.: Bewegungssteuerung für kooperierende Industrieroboter in der Montageautomatisierung. Wt Werkstattstechnik Online 97(9), 713 (2007)

[11] Thomas, U., Wahl, F.: A system for automatic planning, evaluation and execution of assembly sequences for industrial robots. In: Proceedings of the 2001 IEEE/RSJ International Conference on Intelligent Robots and Systems, Maui, Hawaii, USA, pp. 1458–1464 (October 2001)

[12] SFB614 – Sonderforschungsbereich 614: Selbstoptimierende Systeme des Maschinenbaus – Finanzierungsantrag. Universität Paderborn, Paderborn (2004)

[13] Skubic, M., Volz, R.A.: Identifying Single-Ended Contact Formations from Force Sensor Patterns. IEEE Transactions on Robotics and Automation 16(5), 597–603 (2000)

Flexible Assembly Robotics
for Self-optimizing Production

Sebastian Haag, Nicolas Pyschny, and Christian Brecher

Fraunhofer-Institute for Production Technology IPT, Steinbachstraße 17,
52074 Aachen, Germany
{sebastian.haag,nicolas.pyschny,christian.brecher}
@ipt.fraunhofer.de

Abstract. This paper provides an overview of the research results on self-optimizing production systems. Self-optimization strategies developed for assembly systems will be presented focusing on the enhancement of flexibility of assembly processes through a holistic approach regarding product-process-interdependencies. Key elements of the research like automation-friendly product and process design as well as highly-flexible automation equipment and control will be pointed out. This paper then draws a conclusion from that work and derives future research topics for making self-optimizing assembly systems a technology ready to be transferred to industry. The authors identified cooperation technologies, sensor-integration and sensor-guidance as well as meta-level task specification as relevant enablers for self-optimization in assembly systems as they further increase flexibility, autonomy, and cognition – the pre-requisites for self-optimization. Concept approaches will be described.

Keywords: self-optimization, assembly, cooperating robots, sensor-guidance.

1 Introduction

Today, production systems are confronted with the polylemma of production – a topic addressed by the Cluster of Excellence "Integrative Production Technology for High-Wage Countries" at the RWTH Aachen University[1]. A production strategy has to decide whether to gain and to maintain market share either through mass production or through individualization of products. Therefore, a decision has to be made about the organization of production between value-orientation focusing on the avoidance of waste of any kind and planning-orientation focusing on the avoidance of mistakes. Self-optimization is an approach addressing both axes of the polylemma enabling batch-size independent cost efficient production paired with a reduction of planning efforts (Fig. 1).

A self-optimizing system is able to adapt its behavior autonomously through change of structure or through parameter adaption in order to fulfill variable and self-chosen internal set points (system objectives) meeting external demands. Thus, self-optimization goes beyond classical adaptive control limited to parameter adaption.

---

[1] See: http://www.production-research.de

S. Jeschke, H. Liu, and D. Schilberg (Eds.): ICIRA 2011, Part II, LNAI 7102, pp. 189–198, 2011.
© Springer-Verlag Berlin Heidelberg 2011

A self-optimizing system is additionally able to adapt its behavior through change of structure in order to fulfill the system objectives [9]. There are three types of actions in self-optimizing systems: analysis of the current situation, determination of objectives, and adaption of system behavior. Pre-requisites of self-optimizing production systems are flexibility, cognition in the sense of reasoning about information collected and making rational decisions [3] as well as autonomy.

The research presented here transfers the definitions in [9] to assembly systems confronted with highly-dynamic external demands [2]. The main difference between mechatronic systems as described in [9] and assembly systems is that mechatronic systems can be designed systematically by merely splitting and mapping motion functions to a hierarchy resulting in a system architecture including an agent-like control as proposed in [17]. Production systems have a more complex set of objective functions than mechatronic systems and it is not as straight forward to obtain a hierarchy of objective functions which can be used to layout the complete system.

This paper has a wider understanding of self-optimization than merely regarding mechatronic systems and technical control loops. A more holistic view of production systems is strived for within the Cluster of Excellence considering organizational and management issues as well as the influence of product design on the performance of assembly. However, this paper mainly focuses on the illustration of technical issues of implementing self-optimizing assembly systems.

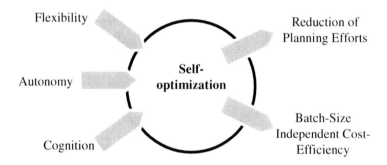

Fig. 1. Pre-requisites of self-optimization and its benefits

This paper gives an overview of the results from almost five years of research on self-optimizing micro-assembly systems and it introduces novel concepts for robotic assembly systems incorporating advanced self-optimizing functionality using robot cooperation and optimization strategies from research domains like artificial intelligence and operations research. These concepts will be addressed in future research activities.

2   Self-optimizing Assembly Systems

The overall challenge of implementing self-optimizing production systems is to efficiently find the globally ideal operating point. Under dynamically changing environmental conditions there may be contradicting objectives for different elements of a production system. The research presented in this paper focused on the assembly of micro-optical products such as miniature laser systems showing a strong interdependency between product design and assembly process. A summary of research results will be given in this section before outlining the vision of future work in the subsequent sections.

2.1   Research Results

Enablers for self-optimizing system behavior are flexibility, cognition, and autonomy. The term *flexibility* stands for the capability of a production system to produce many product variants without changing the structure of the system [6]. The research presented has increased flexibility in many ways on the part of the production system as well as on the product and process design.

The novel concept of a robot-based micro-assembly cell combined with the utilization of tool change systems for high-precision tools as well as the development of a micro-manipulator for precision tasks requiring six degrees of freedom were contributions to flexibility on the part of the production system [3]. Another research focus regarding flexibility was set on the product design for automated assembly including the geometric design of optical components as well as joining technologies. Fig. 2 shows a scene from an alignment procedure by the precision manipulator attached to a conventional robot. The planar design of the laser is clearly visible in the picture. The design shows similarities to the surface mounting technology (SMT) in electronics. The planar base plate allows efficient positioning and alignment of the optical components. A major benefit of planar alignment is the reduction of degrees of freedom needed for the alignment of lenses from six to three.

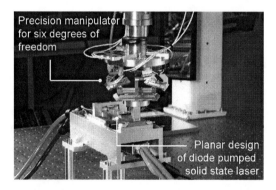

Fig. 2. Alignment of laser resonator with precision manipulator

The alignment of micro-optical components is crucial for the quality of a laser. Blind positioning of the components fails because the precision requirements are higher than tolerance chains can guarantee. The effort it would take to precisely characterize each optical component for using this information to assemble the laser would be too high from an economical point of view [3]. Therefore, function-oriented assembly strategies were developed optimizing component positions according to online-measurements such as image processing or output power analysis. Self-optimization in form of function-oriented assembly reduces planning efforts remarkably.

The joining of micro-optical components is a challenging task. For optimal support of the alignment strategies solder-based joining techniques have been developed [3]. Observing the resistance of the solder allows self-controlled stop of the soldering process reducing planning and control efforts.

Cognition is required for information processing and deriving decisions from information. The research on control architectures for self-optimization in production systems resulted in a multi-agent system with agents representing hardware units on a low level and dedicated agents for planning and fault resolution on higher levels. Agents are able to exchange information among each other and to interact by common semantics. Based on a world model and on perception of the environment agents are able to (re-) act. The autonomy of agents can be increased through planning algorithms based on world models and on knowledge bases.

Autonomy of a production system means that the system is able to react to unforeseen situations without the need of external instructions [18], [22]. Autonomy is best supported by the use of sensors because the system can analyze parts of the environment trying to find a solution for the current situation.

For overcoming failure states during the assembly process an expert system was implemented to serve as a knowledge base for an agent resolving such failure states [3]. The expert system is able to learn rules that will allow the resolution of the failure state in most cases. Naturally, the success rate of an expert system is limited to the amount of knowledge taught [20].

2.2   Intermediate Conclusion

The work in the research area of self-optimizing production systems has led to fundamental methodologies and hardware/ software implementations building a solid basis for ongoing research. In most cases, self-optimization is carried out locally and therefore only reaches local maxima regarding the optimal operating point. Future work needs to address methodologies considering a wider spectrum of production system levels requiring information exchange between different entities and different layers. Crucial for such inter-level communication is a common understanding of information exchanged. That includes specifications of which information content needs to be communicated and how it will be communicated.

The existing concepts for flexible and autonomous self-optimizing production systems need to be enhanced by more enablers for self-optimization. Key-enablers identified are the cooperation of robots increasing the flexibility of a multi-robot cell tremendously and sensor-integration increasing autonomy and robustness of assembly processes.

Much research effort has been put into planning and optimization algorithms in different research areas like artificial intelligence, operations research, and soft-computing. The utilization of such powerful algorithms would boost the cognitive capabilities of systems as well as their autonomy. Many of such algorithms require discrete input values in order to process the information. This circumstance makes it essential to provide interfaces for discrete information retrieval from continuous systems.

Another obligation of future work is the transfer of concepts towards an industrial level. Such claims are formulated in the Strategic Research Agenda 2020 (SRA) by the European Robotics Technology Platform[2] [21]. Thus, the implementation of self-optimizing concepts will take place on commercial hardware. Portability of the solutions to different hardware platforms is one measure of success.

3   Research Roadmap

The results accomplished demonstrate the feasibility and the benefit of self-optimization in complex and demanding assembly tasks. Future work needs to generalize the results and put effort in practical aspects which really allow the application of self-optimization in industrial environments. This section presents roadmaps of future work in the domain of self-optimization. Important milestones from the roadmaps will be explained in more detail and concept approaches will be outlined.

3.1   Enablers for Flexibility

Intense research has been put in the increase of flexibility in order to enable self-optimization. The Flexibility-Roadmap (Fig. 3) shows the milestones to more flexibility in production systems.

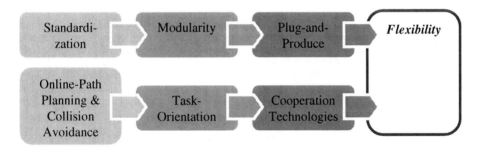

Fig. 3. Flexibility-Roadmap

Cooperation technologies including robot-robot cooperation and man-machine collaboration as well as *plug-and-produce* capabilities are technological issues that need to be adopted for self-optimization.

Plug-and-Produce Functionality. *Plug-and-produce* is a term used in analogy to the term plug-and-play known from consumer applications such as USB-devices. The

---

[2] See: http://www.robotics-platform.eu

vision is to be able to dynamically add new equipment to the production system without reconfiguration effort. Plug-and-produce functionality is a catalyzer for flexibility and mutability. Such functionality requires standardized mechanical and electrical interfaces as well as interfaces for energy and information exchange including communication protocols. Based on those standards a modular architecture has to be established. [5] provides methodologies of modularization from the automotive industry. [6] defines a generic terminology for modeling plug-and-produce systems. Based on these basic definitions an agent platform is outlined in [7].

The existing theoretical concepts need to be validated in the context of self-optimization and then be transferred to an industrial level. It will be necessary to define clear and quantifiable interfaces, behavior descriptions, and a middleware capable of handling the communication. This step will boost the efficiency of future research projects and has the potential to find its way to commercialization.

Cooperation Technologies. The cooperation of automation equipment such as robots but also between human workers and robots is a very powerful strategy to increase flexibility of a system [14]. The complexity of task specification rises due to increased degrees of freedom and synchronization requirements. The technology of human-machine-interaction is dominated by safety issues.

Firstly, cooperation allows the execution of more complex tasks due to an increase of degrees of freedom. Secondly, it can contribute to efficiency by avoiding changing fixation poses of work pieces. Thirdly, in macro-assembly cooperation allows the automated handling of large work pieces [4]. Fourthly, cooperation allows the handling of heavy goods through load sharing. Fifthly, cooperating robots can be used in cooperative tasks as well as in single robot tasks. Cooperation technologies mainly enhance structural and functional flexibility. The integration of human workers that are able to directly interact with robots in an intuitive manner additionally enhances flexibility aspects as well as cognition and autonomy.

The examples show the potential of cooperation technologies. The challenges that arise are highly complex and mission critical. The efficiency of robot programming can be increased drastically through task-orientation requiring automated path planning and collision avoidance. That holds also for multi-robot applications. The integration of sensors and a transfer to sensor-guided applications requires active collision avoidance strategies and online path modification capabilities.

Collision avoidance strategies have been outlined e.g. in [19]. Even on computing devices today, the amount of geometric calculations are a challenge for hard real-time systems. A practical issue is the lack of commercial open robot control architectures which prevents online-path modification. Many robot manufacturers offer external motion control only to research labs. A task of future activities is to establish such interfaces in commercial applications which again will require practical safety solutions.

3.2   Enablers for Cognition

The Cognition-Roadmap (Fig. 4) is a crucial element on the way towards self-optimizing systems. Flexibility builds a basis for self-optimization increasing the degrees of freedom regarding decision making and possible paths to a solution. Autonomy directly depends on cognitive capabilities. Cognition is the element implementing the planning and optimizing features.

The main task in enhancing cognition capabilities of a production system is to provide information interfaces and models for planning and optimization algorithms. Such algorithms have been subject to intensive research in the areas of artificial intelligence, operations research, and soft-computing.

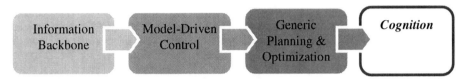

Fig. 4. Cognition-Roadmap

The Cognition-Roadmap (Fig. 4) shows the main tasks of making available planning and optimization algorithms from other research disciplines. A core element to be developed is the information backbone collecting and providing data throughout the production process. Model-driven control tracks the real world events and exchanges information with the information backbone. The model serves as a knowledge base for planning and optimization algorithms.

Generic Planning and Optimization. Searching the global optimum of a production system requires a common knowledge and fact base. Knowledge and fact data needs to be collected for subsequent analysis. In complex industrial use cases the monitoring of production performance data and its comparison to management actions are a practical way to achieve steady improvement in a control loop manner. The approach proposed in this paper specifically considers the feedback of key performance indicators from production to product design stage closing a self-optimizing loop spanning over several company departments. Feedback is carried out by storing process data in a database allowing analysis like data mining techniques.

Planning and optimization algorithms benefit from a wide and deep information base. An information backbone makes that information available. In order to achieve self-optimization based on structural and functional flexibility it is not sufficient to store only facts in a database. Reconfiguration of hardware and control requires meta-data about the collected facts for navigation through the knowledge-base so that planning and optimization algorithms can adapt themselves to the changes.

An architecture of an information backbone that is suitable for the requirements of self-optimization needs to be developed. That includes data structures and meta-data definitions and meta-data search strategies.

Cognitive systems need to have some kind of understanding of their environment in order to be able to react to external events in a rational way. Such an understanding is achieved through world models representing relevant properties and dependencies of the environment. Modeling is a major development step in engineering. Today, a second engineering step is necessary deriving source code from the models. In model-driven control that extra step is not needed because the model is interpreted directly.

First results from model-driven control were produced in the Cluster of Excellence regarding manufacturing execution. Model-driven control closely links the modeling step with the online information collection. Information updates directly lead to model changes and thus influence the execution of subsequent tasks.

3.3   Enablers for Autonomy

The proposed roadmap concerning autonomy is shown in Fig. 5. Autonomy reduces the need of communication in order to make decisions. Autonomous systems therefore need to be equipped with sensors for environmental perception. Through compliant behavior an autonomous system can better adjust to tolerances increasing the robustness of a system. Online-reaction to events require planning capabilities which depend on a kind of world model which is fed with information collected online. Cognition as one enabler of autonomy was subject to the previous section.

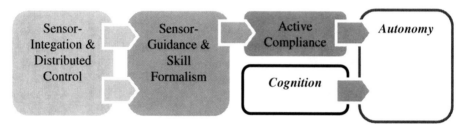

Fig. 5. Autonomy-Roadmap

Active Compliance. The integration of sensors allows a technical system (partial) perception of the environment. Potentially, sensor data can be integrated into motion control loops as known from impedance/ admittance control where force-torque feedback is used for robot motion control [11], [12], [13]. Such technology can be used to make a rigid robot arm a compliant device inducing useful characteristics for classical assembly tasks like the peg-in-hole problem.

The integration of sensors makes a system more complex. In order to maintain structural flexibility it is a logical consequence to introduce distributed and decentralized control architectures. In distributed control a control loop is closed via a network e.g. a field bus. In decentralized control, local control loops are established and hardly require communication with other system entities.

Architectures for distributed and decentralized control based on commercial hardware need to be developed and validated in the context of self-optimization. In order to provide application programming interfaces for sensor-guided tasks an intuitive way such as the skill formalism and supporting development tools need to be established.

Control theory is a domain of expert knowledge. It is a very powerful tool for implementing intelligent systems. Making pieces of control theory available to non-experts and in order to increase re-use of implementation efforts is the intention of the skill formalism. This paper refers to a *skill* as the combination of a skill primitive and device specifications. Early work on skills can be found in [10] and [16]. Establishing skills would drastically simplify the implementation of sensor-guided tasks.

Skill primitives as proposed in [8], [15], and [23] define closed-loop sub-tasks and they can be linked in a network similar to a finite state machine describing complex tasks. Skill primitives do not take into account the physical capabilities of the executing system as the naming lets assume. Such capabilities depend on the hardware in each specific case. E.g. a stop condition must not be defined as a force measurement that exceeds the valid range for the force sensor used. For this reason this paper proposes a fusion of skill primitives with facts from the device fact sheet. This approach allows validation of automation tasks taking physical capabilities into account.

Skill primitive templates can be stored as parameterizable structures. They allow intuitive and hardware-independent task-specification. In a second step concrete hardware allocation can take place. The allocation can be validated against the fact sheets.

Skills do not yet exist for cooperative tasks. It is desirable to transfer the skill formalism to cooperative tasks because the benefits of sensor-guided execution hold for cooperating robots as well. The increased complexity problem still exists because more manipulators and sensors are involved and need to be coordinated. Efficiency can only be achieved when robot programs can be generated automatically to a large extend from a task-oriented or another intuitive description. The approach of hybrid programming where a template of the task is generated offline and then filled with concrete parameters online [1] would be applicable for the skill formalism.

4   Conclusion

The research on self-optimizing assembly systems has shown promising results regarding the improvement of the performance of production mainly through reduction of planning efforts. Research so far could only prove the improvement of the local operating point by demonstrating representative and relevant processes of laser assembly. Successfully, it was shown that automated assembly of low-volume laser products is possible in principle by incorporating means of self-optimization. More work is needed in order to push production systems an their business organizations towards a global maximum of efficiency.

Such work aims at the enablers of the pre-requisites of self-optimization flexibility, cognition, and autonomy. Major milestones proposed are the introduction of standards for plug-and-produce systems, the skill formalism for compliant and cooperative tasks, and a model-driven control based on an information backbone allowing the use of planning and optimization algorithms from other research disciplines.

References

1. Brecher, C.: Werkzeugmaschinen 4. Automatisierung von Maschinen und Anlagen. Springer, Heidelberg (2006)
2. Brecher, C., Schapp, L.: Montagetechnik und -organisation. Strategien und Trends. Apprimus Verlag, Aachen (2009)
3. Brecher, C., Pyschny, N., Loosen, P., Funck, M., Morasch, V., Schmitt, R., Pavim, A.: Self-optimising flexible assembly systems. In: Workshop on Self-X in Mechatronics and Other Engineering Applications, Paderborn, pp. 23–38 (2009)

4. Bruhm, H.: Untersuchungen zur Handhabung großer Objekte durch Roboter mit kraftschlüssig kooperierenden Armen. Düsseldorf: VDI-Verl. (VDI-Reihe 8, 280) (1992)
5. Eversheim, W., Schernikau, J., Goemann, D.: Module und Systeme: Die Kunst liegt in der Strukturierung. VDI-Z 138(11/12), 44–48 (1996)
6. Feldmann, K., Weber, M., Wolf, W.: Design of a theoretical holistic system model as base of construction kits for building Plug&Produce-able modular production systems. Production Engineering 1(3), 329–336 (2007)
7. Feldmann, K., Wolf, W., Weber, M.: Design of a formal model for the specification of agent platforms based on Plug&Produce-able production systems. Production Engineering 1(3), 321–328 (2007)
8. Finkemeyer, B.: Robotersteuerungsarchitektur auf der Basis von Aktionsprimitiven. Aachen: Shaker (Fortschritte in der Robotik, 8) (2004)
9. Gausemeier, J., Rammig, F.J., Adelt, P.: Selbstoptimierende Systeme des Maschinenbaus. Definitionen, Anwendungen, Konzepte. Paderborn: Heinz Nixdorf Inst. (HNI-Verlagsschriftenreihe, 234) (2009)
10. Hasegawa, T., Suehiro, T., Takase, K.: A model-based manipulation system with skill-based execution. IEEE Trans. on Robotics and Automation 8(5), 535–544 (1992)
11. Hogan, N.: Impedance Control: An approach to manipulation. Part 1 - Theory. Journal of Dynamic Systems, Measurement, and Control 107(1), 1–7 (1985)
12. Hogan, N.: Impedance Control: An approach to manipulation. Part 2 - Implementation. Journal of Dynamic Systems, Measurement, and Control 107(1), 8–16 (1985)
13. Hogan, N.: Impedance Control: An approach to manipulation. Part 3 - Applications. Journal of Dynamic Systems, Measurement, and Control 107(1), 17–24 (1985)
14. Kurth, J.: Flexible Produktionssysteme durch kooperierende Roboter. Werkstatttechnik Online 95(3), 81–84 (2005)
15. Mosemann, H.: Beiträge zur Planung, Dekomposition und Ausführung von automatisch generierten Roboteraufgaben. Aachen: Shaker (Fortschritte in der Robotik, 6) (2000)
16. Nakamura, A., Ogasawara, T., Suehiro, T., Tsukune, H.: Skill-based backprojection for fine motion planning. In: IEEE Int. Conf. Intell. Robots Syst., pp. 526–533 (1996)
17. Naumann, R.: Modellierung und Verarbeitung vernetzter intelligenter machatronischer Systeme. Düsseldorf: VDI-Verl. (Fortschritt-Berichte VDI-Reihe 20, 318) (2000)
18. Pfeifer, T., Schmitt, R.: Autonome Produktionszellen. Komplexe Produktionsprozesse flexibel automatisieren. Springer (VDI-Buch), Berlin (2006)
19. Roßmann, J.: Echtzeitfähige, kollisionsvermeidende Bahnplanung für Mehrrobotersysteme. Universität Dortmund, Dortmund (1993)
20. Russell, S.J., Norvig, P.: Artificial intelligence. A modern approach. Prentice Hall series in artificial intelligence. Prentice Hall, NJ (2003)
21. Robotic Visions to 2020 and beyond. The strategic research agenda for robotics in Europe 07/2009. European Robotics Technology Platform (2009)
22. Scholz-Reiter, B., Freitag, M.: Autonomous Processes in Assembly Systems. Annals of the CIRP 56(2), 712–729 (2007)
23. Thomas, U.: Automatisierte Programmierung von Robotern für Montageaufgaben. Aachen: Shaker (Fortschritte in der Robotik, 13) (2008)

Meta-modeling for Manufacturing Processes

Thomas Auerbach[7], Marion Beckers[1], Guido Buchholz[1], Urs Eppelt[5],
Yves-Simon Gloy[3], Peter Fritz[6], Toufik Al Khawli[5], Stephan Kratz[7], Juliane Lose[6],
Thomas Molitor[8], Axel Reßmann[2], Ulrich Thombansen[4], Dražen Veselovac[7],
Konrad Willms[1], Thomas Gries[3], Walter Michaeli[2], Christian Hopmann[2],
Uwe Reisgen[1], Robert Schmitt[6], and Fritz Klocke[7]

[1] Welding and Joining Institute (ISF)
[2] Institute of Plastics Processing (IKV)
[3] Institut für Textiltechnik (ITA)
[4] Chair of Laser Technology (LLT)
[5] Department Nonlinear Dynamics of Laser Processing (NLD)
[6] Chair of Metrology and Quality Management (WZL-MQ)
[7] Chair of Manufacturing Technology (WZL-TF)
RWTH Aachen University
t.auerbach@wzl.rwth-aachen.de
[8] Fraunhofer Institute for Laser Technology (ILT)

Abstract. Meta-modeling for manufacturing processes describes a procedure to create reduced numeric surrogates that describe cause-effect relationships between setting parameters as input and product quality variables as output for manufacturing processes. Within this method, expert knowledge, empiric data and physical process models are transformed such that machine readable, reduced models describe the behavior of the process with sufficient precision. Three phases comprising definition, generation of data and creation of the model are suggested and used iteratively to improve the model until a required model quality is reached. In manufacturing systems, such models allow the generation of starting values for setting parameters based on the manufacturing task and the requested product quality. In-process, such reduced models can be used to determine the operating point and to search for alternative setting parameters in order to optimize the objectives of the manufacturing process, the product quality. This opens up the path to self-optimization of manufacturing processes. The method is explained exemplarily at the gas metal arc welding process.

Keywords: meta-modeling, process model, manufacturing processes.

1 Introduction

Today, the manufacturing industry in high-wage countries is more than ever challenged to economically manufacture high-quality products that are innovative and technologically demanding. Furthermore, the increasing use of versatile modular assemblies in manufacturing leads to an increase in variants in combination with a decrease in lot size. The depicted challenges are not limited to particular industries or manufacturing processes and therefore require a generic solution.

S. Jeschke, H. Liu, and D. Schilberg (Eds.): ICIRA 2011, Part II, LNAI 7102, pp. 199–209, 2011.
© Springer-Verlag Berlin Heidelberg 2011

The manufacturing industry tries to compensate these problems by employing sophisticated investment-intensive planning and specialized production systems [1]. Still, setting parameters for manufacturing processes are mostly based on empirical data, which are often not suitable for operating a manufacturing system at the technological limit. In many cases, deviations in properties of the base material or wear of tools lead to prolonged set-up procedures or premature deviation in product quality.

A new approach for manufacturing processes to reduce the described dilemma is the Model-Based Self-Optimization (MBSO). This approach is currently researched by the project "Technology Enablers for Embedding Cognition and Self-optimization into Production Systems" within the Cluster of Excellence "Integrative Production Technology for High-Wage Countries" which is funded by the German Research Foundation. The primary objective is to establish a new generation of manufacturing processes which autonomously operate at their technological limits by integrating self-optimization techniques.

A necessary precondition for the implementation of MBSO is the transfer of process knowledge into machine readable form. For the majority of the manufacturing processes, the cause-effect relationship between setting parameters as input and product quality as output is not completely described or even unknown. In the case of multidimensional and non-linear dependencies, finding optimal setting parameters by manual experimentation is cost intensive and time consuming. In cases, where the manufacturing process's behavior is described in detail by a physical process model, the model's complexity prevents its use for self-optimization due to a required computational effort that exceeds the time scale in which process control is executed. Because of these facts, it is necessary to develop a method for the generation of reduced process models. In this context, such models are called *meta-models for manufacturing processes*.

The presented method results from research on manufacturing processes that differ in technical properties and physical principles. It is the applicability to five axis milling, gas metal arc welding, injection molding, laser cutting and weaving which supports the transferability to other manufacturing processes. The method is explained exemplarily on the robot based gas metal arc welding process. Its use in MBSO for process control together with new findings in dynamic path planning for robot control [2], [3] opens up new operating domains that are oriented towards product quality while operating autonomously. At some points, additional examples from other processes are added to point out the diverse alternatives that are covered by the presented meta-modeling method for manufacturing processes.

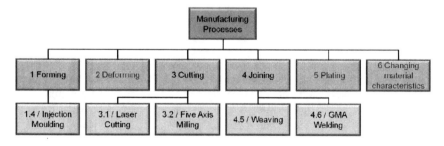

Fig. 1. Classification of manufacturing processes according to DIN 8580 [4]

2   Meta-modeling – Definition of Process-Independent Method

Meta-models provide the capability to enable the realization of self-optimizing production systems if physical, analytical process models are either unknown or if the computation of solutions requires too much time with respect to the production environment. In the context of this research, meta-models are used as surrogate models [5] and defined as *mathematical representations of functional relations between multivariate input and output parameters by means of approximation and interpolation.*

This makes meta-models for manufacturing processes a numeric description for process behavior. Their use enables generation of starting values for setting parameters or adaption of such values in-process with respect to the current operating point. Furthermore, meta-models offer a potential to improve and refine process knowledge by displaying process parameter dependencies and individual sensitivities. This also allows revealing inconsistencies or deviations between theory and experiment [6]. A general disadvantage of approximation methods is that discontinuities within the process are not invariably well reproduced by a meta-model. Therefore, despite all possible automation, human expertise is needed to select adequate model classes and structures as well as to evaluate the model quality with a focus on critical regions in the process domain.

The process-independent method for the creation of meta-models for manufacturing processes contains a set of steps and tools that are shown in Fig. 2. The method which has been validated against five different manufacturing processes will be explained exemplarily for the gas metal arc welding (GMAW) process.

2.1   Definition of Process Properties and Model Requirements (B1)

The creation of a meta-model for a manufacturing process starts with the compilation of relevant process parameters and the field of application. The efficiency of the model creation process is determined by the amount and precision of data on process parameters and model requirements evolving from the field of application.

For the GMAW process, the model is used in set-up for an offline generation of starting values for setting parameters as well as in-process for an online adaption of these values. Currently, the application is focused on a thin-metal-sheet range of up to four millimeters of mild steel (S235JR) and its typical weld preparation. Within the set-up procedure, a self-optimization system is to be realized to autonomously provide parameters for different applications according to the quality requirements based on DIN EN ISO 5817. The aim is to produce first-time-right at reduced set-up time and reduced rejects. The created model maps the setting parameters to the product quality (PQ) which is defined by the weld geometry. The ensuing requirements for the meta-model are an adequate precision in the calculation of the PQ. In-process, an online self-optimization procedure is to be realized for the GMAW process that adapts the setting parameters when disturbances occur that negatively influence the resulting weld geometry, thus PQ. Therefore, it is necessary to create a model which describes the cause-effect relationships between controllable setting parameters, the influences that lead to disturbances and the weld geometry. Further requirements to the model

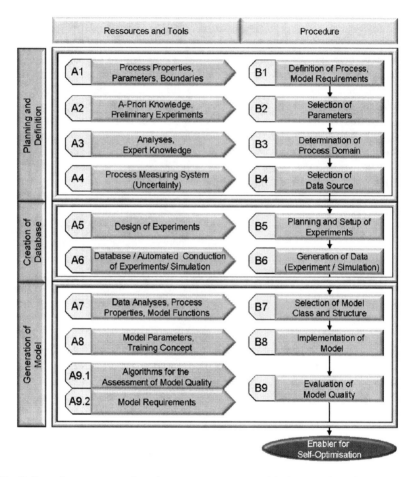

Fig. 2. Procedure, resources & tools to generate meta-models for manufacturing processes

are the portability of the model to a processing unit which is integrated into an actuator system of the welding system in a combination with a reduced complexity of the model in order to minimize the computation time.

2.2　Selection of Parameters (B2)

The product quality (PQ) of a work piece is determined by a large number of process parameters. Parameters that have a significant influence on PQ must be identified prior to entering the modeling procedure. Techniques such as mind-mapping provide a systematic approach to collect arbitrary information from engineering teams and experts in order to explore, analyze and extract modeling relevant parameters and requirements.

The GMAW process holds many possibilities of varying the setting parameters. The advantage of this flexibility is its ability to handle a large amount of different applications. However, the high degree of flexibility goes hand in hand with a high complexity of the modeling process if all possible parameter combinations are taken into account. In the first iteration of the modeling procedure, expert knowledge is used to reduce the number of parameters which leads to a pre-selection of the following ones: welding speed, wire feed speed, pulse time, pulse frequency, pulse voltage, base current and contact tube distance. Besides, the parameter gap width is identified and included as being the one which is mostly responsible for causing deviations of the weld geometry. In a second iteration, from executing a sensitivity analysis, the parameter set is reduced by pulse frequency and pulse voltage and hence the model is reduced in its complexity. This is important in regard to a reduction of computation time that is required to adapt a parameter set online. As measurable units for the PQ, the geometry values weld height, weld width, root height, root width and penetration depth (in case that the root height equals zero) have been used.

In the injection molding process, apart from setting parameters, also process variables like the cavity pressure must be controlled [7]. But to predict the prospective cavity pressure value, the recent history of these values is needed [8], [9]. Furthermore, the time variance of the process causes the addition of time into the selection of parameters. This results not only in augmented model requirements (like the involvement of time variance in computations on models) but also in adaptations regarding subsequent modeling steps.

2.3   Determination of Process Domain (B3)

After selecting the parameters that are to be included in the model, the process domain is defined as a preparation for the creation of the database. This requires an estimation of the setting parameters' value ranges.

Based on expert knowledge, exemplary welds are conducted and analyzed to identify those value ranges in which the desired PQ is achieved. This is done by laser scanning the resulting weld geometries as well as analyzing their cross sections. After that, the resulting ranges are extended to also cover a domain where a deficient PQ is produced, if no optimization would take place. The final value ranges that are taken into account for the first iteration with 2 mm thick metal-sheets are given in Table 1. The column Cardinality contains the number of discrete values that can be assigned to a corresponding parameter.

Table 1. Defining Parameter Ranges for the GMAW process modeling

Parameter	Interval	Step Width	Cardinality
Welding Speed	30-90 cm/min	5	13
Wire Feed Speed	3-8 m/min	0,1	51
Pulse Voltage	25-35 V	1	11
Frequency	50-100 Hz	1	51
Base Current	20-50 A	1	31
Pulse Time	1,5-2,5 ms	0,1	11
Contact Tube Distance	8-12 mm	1	5
Gap Width	0-1,5 mm	0,1	16

2.4   Selection of Data Source (B4)

On the basis of the analyzed parameter space, suitable measurands and sensors are selected to collect the significant parameter values that are required to create the model, if the data is derived from experiments. Since the collected data is directly used as sampling points for the approximation, it influences the prediction quality of the final model.

To record the measurands with adequate accuracy, the data sources must be selected carefully. Criteria for this choice are for example a sensor's signal-to-noise-ratio or the required resolution of the measurement. To a great extent, the applied sensors should be robust against process related disturbances, like mechanical and thermal loads [10], varying characteristics of optical components, electromagnetic effects that are able to falsify the desired observation.

If the data is generated by simulation, which is the case for the GMAW process, this step only deals with the boundary conditions of the simulation, which will be presented in detail in the section Generation of Data.

An example of varying process conditions can be found in the 5-axis milling operation of filigree parts, where instable process behavior is influencing the machined surface's quality. Therefore, regarding this process the analysis of process vibrations and disturbances is of major interest [11]. Prerequisite for the detection of these process variables are sensor solutions that provide high resonance frequencies and low signal-to-noise-ratios [12]. A combination of two accelerometers positioned at the machine table and spindle housing as well as one eddy current sensor facing the tool deliver the required information for this milling process.

In the weaving process, the warp tension is a representative process measurand to evaluate the PQ. To measure the dynamic warp tension during weaving, a new strain gauge based sensor system with a measurement frequency of 5 kHz is developed. In addition, research is being carried out to monitor the PQ online such as fabric basis weight [13].

2.5   Design and Setup of Experiment (B5)

Besides the data quality itself, a meta-model's accuracy significantly depends on the density and distribution of the training data. It is recommended to employ Design of Experiments (DoE) methods to acquire statistically optimized data sets with suitable sampling points.

For the GMAW process, as shown in Table 1, the execution of a full factorial design has a total of $13 \times 51 \times 11 \times 51 \times 31 \times 11 \times 5 \times 16 > 10.146 \times 10^9$ combinations, which cannot be executed efficiently. Data quantities greater than 2000 are only partly manageable due to the required computation time and storage space. Therefore, a homogeneous distribution of the selected combinations out of the whole parameter space is a prerequisite to achieve conclusive results. The method used for the creation of uniform distributions was thereby the *Latinized Centroidal Voronoi Tesselation* [14], a combination of *Latin Hypercube Sampling* [15] and *Centroidal Voronoi Tessel*ation [16]. With this method, 2000 combinations are distributed within the parameter space determined by Table 1, which can now be used as setting parameters for the following experiments and simulations. By analyzing the influence of distribution and data quantity, it could be shown for the GMAW process, that the homogeneous distribution of the sampling points for values of the parameter combinations is far more important for the quality of the trained meta-model than their number.

2.6   Generation of Data (B6)

After the selection of parameters, intervals and sampling points, the corresponding PQ-related data is generated. This is done by carrying out experiments and simulations.

For the GMAW process, a simulation tool called SimWeld has been developed at the Welding and Joining Institute of the RWTH Aachen (ISF). SimWeld performs numerical calculations of the welding geometry depending on given setting parameters as well as on static parameters like base and wire material, power source and shielding gas. Using SimWeld and executing an additional batch processing, the previously mentioned 2000 simulations with different parameter combinations are executed and correlated with the corresponding output parameters weld height, weld width, root height root width and penetration depth.

Contrary to the data acquisition via simulation, the acquisition by means of conducting experiments is the most time-consuming activity within the modeling procedure. Hence, automated solutions for the execution of experiments are needed to handle this part of the modeling procedure efficiently. Exemplarily, a test rig to automatically execute a statistically planned experiment (DoE) is developed to analyze the milling operations [17]. This system automatically generates the required process data, whereas a generic structure allows an easy adaptation of the experimental design and the autonomous execution of specific cutting operations, assigning new cutting parameters to each machining run.

Data pairs of input and output parameters for the welding process are plotted in the left picture of figure 3. This data provides the basis for the subsequent modeling steps which are described in the following sections. A visualization of the final model is displayed in the right image of figure 3.

2.7   Selection of Model Class and Structure (B7)

Restrictions regarding the applied functions or methods for the future model can be made that improve the approximation of the theoretical process model. Modeling methods are for example symbolic regression [18], linear least square regression [19] or artificial neural networks (ANN) [20]. Used base functions can vary from polynomials to radial base functions [21] including linear combinations of arbitrary functions (under the precondition, that the functions are supported by the chosen modeling method). The choice of the modeling method and functions influences the behavior of the model regarding approximation and interpolation.

The selection of a suitable modeling method and suitable functions is supported by expert knowledge about the presumable behavior of the considered process parameter. This helps both, the overfitting and the creation of too generalized models. Several programs for the creation of models exist, but most of them limit the possibilities of the user's choice of model class and structure. Within the GMAW process, two programs with minor restrictions were used and compared to each other for process modeling. An evaluation of their applicability is given in the next section.

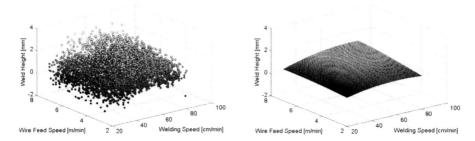

Fig. 3. GMAW process data. Left: point plot displaying results from experiment and simulation. Right: 3D surface plot visualizing the process model.

2.8   Implementation of Model (B8)

In this step, the meta-model is created using the generated data. For this, several commercial and non-commercial tools such as SNNS [22], DesParO [5], or SUMO [23] are available. Although partly restricted in the selection of approximation methods and underlying model functions, these tools allow a parameterization of the used functions. Thus, inter alia the degree of freedom (e.g. in polynomials) or the number of iteration steps for training an ANN is determined, so that the above mentioned problems are avoided. It has to be emphasized, that all steps of iteration have to be accompanied by a step of model evaluation to ensure that the modification does not cause a decrease in model quality.

To generate a model of the GMAW process, DesParO has been tested in a first iteration. This tool operates on radial basis functions (RBF) with a very fast algorithm, allowing the creation of models with high complexity in short time. In order to test different models against each other, also the Matlab-based toolbox SUMO has been used. SUMO offers a high flexibility in choosing different types of methods and functions, so that different combinations can be evaluated. Finally, the modeling process generated the parameterization of a polynomial that suits the requirements of the manufacturing process. This reduced process model provides excellent portability to subsystems with low computing resources. One exemplary 3D-surface plot of a generated model is visualized in the right image of figure 3.

2.9   Evaluation of Model Quality (B9)

Meta-modeling as described in the paper is used to create numeric surrogate models which describe the cause-effect relationships of manufacturing processes. As such, their ability to predict processing results from setting parameters has to be evaluated prior to application.

A general approach to determine the error of a model is the comparison to ground-truth data [24], [25] which can be done by cross validation. Herein, techniques such as holdout, random sub-sampling, k-fold and leave-one-out use different sub-sampling ratios and test run operations to determine a measure for the overall error of a model [26]. Different models can be compared with respect to model quality to track the development procedure by calculating the coefficient of determination (R^2) as this measure is invariant to parameter scaling. For the GMAW process models, k-fold cross-validation was used to compare the models which were based on different functions against each other and to evaluate the influence of modifications in the parameterization.

Consideration of the local error of a surrogate model is especially important for manufacturing processes that operate at technological or physical limits. Such limits inherently are connected to instabilities or even discontinuities and therefore require a precise description of the parameter dependencies. Fig. 4 shows the result of a leave-one-out cross validation which allows the calculation of a local error for the prediction of the Weber number for the laser cutting process. It can be seen, that in this case, the model's prediction of the Weber number in the vicinity of the operating point cutting speed v_s = 0.14 m/sec and focus position d_f = -2 mm is associated with an error that is twice the absolute value. This renders the model unusable in this region while the error in the rest of the process domain is within bounds.

Modifications of the model setup can reduce such errors. In using ANN's, special attention has to be taken on the number of neurons that are used for setting up the network, for the application of RBF the amount of smoothening may be used to avoid substantial local errors. The effort that is required to yield a functional model can be kept at a minimum by selecting the appropriate steps in the modeling procedure for the next iteration. However, within this work, methods for the automatic selection of the best path have not been researched yet. Iteration and therefore model improvement still relies on decisions by an experienced expert.

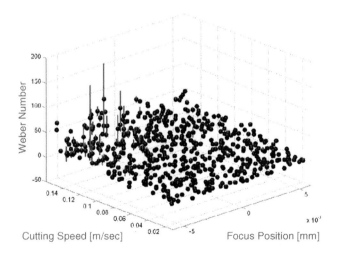

Fig. 4. Local error plot of the parameter Weber number in laser cutting

3   Conclusion

In this paper, a process-independent method for the creation of meta-models for manufacturing processes is introduced. The method results from research on five processes with different physical cause-effect relationships. This broad basis supports transferability to other manufacturing tasks. The procedure contains three sections, one for planning and definition of process model properties and requirements, one for the generation of base data which describe the process and one for the generation of the numeric surrogate model, the meta-model. In particular, the need to evaluate the model quality and improve the model iteratively has been emphasised.

Meta-modeling for manufacturing processes is capable of reducing the complexity of process models to obtain a machine readable and transparent representation of the behavior of a manufacturing process which is oriented towards a set of quality related objectives, the product quality (PQ). This makes meta-models an appropriate method for the creation of numeric models that allow the prediction of PQ based on setting parameters. Further work regarding the modeling procedure comprises the processing of the local error to address areas with instabilities separately and the inclusion of dynamic process behavior into the model. For the refinement of models, indicators have to be developed which suggest suitable re-entry points for iterating the design process.

Acknowledgements. The authors would like to thank the German Research Foundation DFG for the support of the depicted research within the Cluster of Excellence "Integrative Production Technology for High-Wage Countries".

References

1. Schuh, G., Klocke, F., Brecher, C., Schmidt, R.: Excellence in Production. Apprimus Verlag, Aachen (2007)
2. LaValle, S., Kuffner, J.: Radomized Kinodynamic Planning. The International Journal of Robotics Research 25(5), 378–400 (2001)
3. Kim, C., Tsujino, H., Sugano, S.: Rapid Short-Time Path Planning for Phase Space. Journal of Robotics and Mechatronics 23(2), 271–280 (2011)
4. N.N.: DIN EN 8580: Fertigungsverfahren – Begriffe, Einteilung (2003)
5. Stork, A., Thole, C.A., Klimenko, S., Nikitin, I., Nikitina, L., Astakhov, Y.: Simulated Reality in Automotive Design. In: International Conference on Cyberworlds, pp. 23–27 (2007)
6. Schüttler, J., Lose, J., Schmitt, R., Schulz, W.: Exploring Process Domain Boundaries of Complex Production Processes using a Metamodeling Approach. In: 12th CIRP Conference on Modeling of Machining Operations, Donostia-San Sebastián - Spain, Hrsg.: Arrazola, P. Conference on Modeling of Machining Operations, Mondragon, May 7-8, vol. 2, II, pp. 835–841 (2009)
7. Michaeli, W., Schreiber, A.: Der Weg zum geregelten Prozess. SwissPlastics 32(11), S.21–S.26 (2010)
8. Schultz, J.: Eine Strategie zur Gewinnung Neuronaler Modelle für nichtlineare, dynamische Systeme. In: VDI (Hrsg.): VDI-Berichte 1282, GMA-Kongress 1996, Mess- und Automatisierungstechnik. VDI-Verlag, Düsseldorf (1996)

9. He, X., Asada, H.: A New Method for Identifying Orders of Input-Output Models for Nonlinear Dynamic Systems. In: Proceedings of the American Control Conference, San Francisco, USA (1993)
10. Witt, S.: Integrierte Simulation von Maschine, Werkstück und spanendem Fertigungsprozess. Dissertation, RWTH Aachen University, pp. 40–41 (2007)
11. Insperger, T., Mann, B.P., Stépán, G., Bayly, P.V.: Stability of up-milling and down-milling part 1: Alternative analytical methods. International Journal of Machine Tools & Manufacture (43), 25–34 (2002)
12. Klocke, F., Kratz, S., Veselovac, D., Mtz. de Aramaiona, P., Arrazola, P.: Investigation on force sensor dynamics and their measurement characteristics. In: ASME International Mechanical Engineering Congress and Exposition, Boston (2008)
13. Gloy, Y.-S., Muschong, C., Gries, T.: Prediction of process- and product-quality of the weaving process. In: Abstract Book / AUTEX 2010: 10th World Textile Conference, p. 91. Technologija, Vilnius (2010)
14. Reisgen, U., Beckers, M., Willms, K., Buchholz, G.: Einsatz und Vorgehensweise bei der Ersatzmodellierung beim Impulslichtbogenschweißverfahren. DVS-Berichte 268, S.79–S.84 (2010)
15. Lin, D.: A construction method for orthogonal Latin hypercube designs. Biometrika 93(2), 279–288 (2006)
16. Romero, V., Burkardt, J., Gunzburger, M., Peterson, J.: Comparison of pure and "Latinized" centroidal Voronoi tessellation against various other statistical sampling methods. Journal of Reliability Engineering and system Safety 91(10-11), 1266–1280 (2006)
17. Klocke, F., Veselovac, D., Auerbach, T., Kamps, S.: Kennwertgenerator für die automatisierte Versuchsdurchführung von Zerspanversuchen. In: Virtuelle Instrumente in der Praxis-Begleitband zum 15. VIP-Kongress 2010, Hrsg.: Jamal, R.; Heinze, R., Hüthig Heidelberg, S. 75–S81 (2010) ISBN 978-3-8007-3235-7
18. Esparcia-Alcázar, A.I., Ekárt, A., Silva, S., Dignum, S., Uyar, A.Ş.: EuroGP 2010. LNCS, vol. 6021. Springer, Heidelberg (2010)
19. Draper, N.R., Smith, H.: Applied Regression Analysis. Wiley Series in Probability and Statistics (1998) ISBN 978-0-471-17082-2
20. Rojas, R.: Neural Networks. Springer, Heidelberg (1996)
21. Jurecka, F.: Robust Design Optimization Based on Metamodeling Techniques. Dissertation, Technische Universität München (2007)
22. Zell, A., Mache, N., Sommer, T., Korb, T.: Design of the SNNS Neural Network Simulator. In: Österreichische Artificial Intelligence Tagung, pp. 93–102 (1991)
23. Gorissen, D.: Grid-Enabled Adaptive Surrogate Modeling for Computer Aided Engineering, PhD Thesis, Ghent University (2010)
24. Wolberg, G.: Recent Advances in Image Morphing. In: Proceedings Computer Graphics International, pp. 64–71 (1996)
25. Efron, B., Gong, G.: A Leasurly Look at the Bootstrap, the Jackknife, and Cross-Validation. American Statistican 37(1), 36–48 (1983)

Control Architecture for Human Friendly Robots Based on Interacting with Human

Hiroyuki Masuta[1], Eriko Hiwada[2], and Naoyuki Kubota[2]

[1] 3-27-1 Rokkakubashi, Kanagawa-ku, Yokohama-shi,
Kanagawa-ken, 221-8686, Japan
[2] 6-6 Asahigaoka, Hino-shi, Tokyo, 191-0065, Japan
masuta-hiroyuki@kanagawa-u.ac.jp,
hiwada-eriko@sd.tmu.ac.jp, kubota@tmu.ac.jp

Abstract. This paper discusses a control architecture for human friendly robot. Recently, robot middleware is developed for intelligent robot software platform. The robot system can be constructed by making the program of each functional module and connecting each other module. However, software architecture for connecting various modules is not provided now, therefore general versatility of a software module is deteriorated. In particular, a human friendly robot is very complicated relationship between software modules, because it should consider various situations such as human interaction, communication and safety. Therefore, we propose a control software architecture for a human friendly robot. We verify that availability of our proposal through experiments of clearing a table. Moreover, we add some intelligent modules on the proposed architecture to discuss availability of our proposed software architecture.

Keywords: Human friendly robot, 3D-range camera, Software architecture.

1   Introduction

Recently, intelligent robots are expected to work in both known and unknown environments, moving, essentially, from the factory to the home and office[1]. In such environments, robots must have advanced intelligent functions. To realize intelligent robots, we should bring together all of intelligent functions. In recent years, intelligent robot software platform such as OpenRTM-aist and Robot Operating System is developed to collaborate with the various intelligent software[2][3].

We are developing an intelligent software module using OpenRTM-aist. By OpenRTM-aist the robot system can be constructed by making the program of each functional module and connecting each other module. Therefore, various modules developed by other university and company can connect easily. A software architecture is very important to define the interface between input and output for collaborating with other organizations[4]. However, a software architecture for connecting various modules is not provided now. Therefore general versatility of a software module is deteriorated because division of an intelligent module is difficult by the difference of hardware or algorithms[6]. In particular, a human friendly robot is very

S. Jeschke, H. Liu, and D. Schilberg (Eds.): ICIRA 2011, Part II, LNAI 7102, pp. 210–219, 2011.
© Springer-Verlag Berlin Heidelberg 2011

complicated relationship between software modules, because it should consider various situations such as human interaction, communication and safety.

In previous research, a robot control is often divided into the sense, plan and action[7]. However, it is difficult to divide general modules because a general module corresponding to general environment with human is very complicated and inseparable as represented by frame problem. On the other hand, behavior based architecture is proposed by R.Brooks[8]. A behavior based architecture divides a function based on behavior such as a collision avoidance, target following and so on. However, a behavior module lacks versatility because a behavior module that includes from inputs to output depends on hardware specification. Therefore, a high functionality module lacks versatility. On the other hand, a high versatility module is very simple and small size but a total system is needed a lot of modules.

Therefore, a control software architecture for human friendly robot is needed suitable module size and function. We propose a multi-layered control software architecture based on Human Performance Models for a human friendly robot[9]. We verify that availability of our proposal through experiments of clearing a table. Moreover, we add some intelligent modules on the proposed architecture to discuss availability of our proposed software architecture.

This paper is organized as follows: Section 2 explains our intelligent human friendly robot system for table clearing, Section 3 explains control software architecture for human friendly robot, Section 4 explains an experiment of clearing a table and adds the other intelligent module on the proposed architecture. Finally, Section 5 concludes this paper.

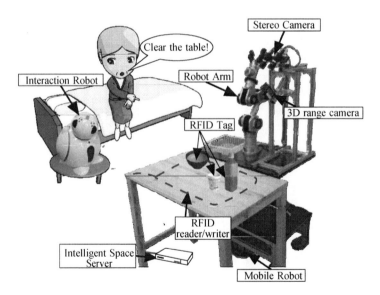

Fig. 1. The human friendly robot system overview

2   Intelligent Human Friendly Robot System

Fig.1 shows an overview of our intelligent human friendly robot system for clearing a table. The intelligent human friendly robot system consists of a service robot, an interaction robot, and an intelligent space server. The interaction robot recognizes human orders from hand gestures and spoken commands by using stereo vision system and voice recognition system [5]. The intelligent space server manages information on table objects, such as dish type, size and color by using RFID system[10]. The service robot that has a robot arm and a mobile robot pick up a dish based on vision information by stereo vision or 3D camera. The robot arm "Katana" is small and lightweight, similar in size to a human arm. Katana has 5 degree-of-freedom (5DOF) structure and 6 motors, including a gripper. We installed a 3D range camera and stereo vision system beside the robot arm like Fig.1. The stereo vision made by Toshiba can recognize dish position and posture from ellipse shape of dishes[11]. The 3D range camera can measure 3-dimensional distance up to 7.5 [m] [12], and outputs luminance and distance data to recognize illegal dish position and posture. The resolution of 3D range camera is in spatial quarter common intermediate format (QCIF 176*144 pixels).

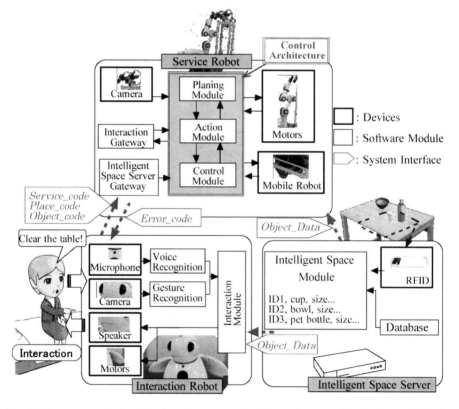

Fig. 2. The communication interface between each robot and servers for the human friendly robot system

We apply Robot Technology Middleware(RTM) to develop the robot system. Fig.2 shows the communication interface between robots and servers. The service robot receives human orders such as service order (Service_code), cleaning place (Place_code) and specified object (Object_code) from the interaction robot, and receives object information such as ID, diameter, height and so on from the intelligent space server. On the other hand, the service robot outputs request information for human support (Request_code) if encounter an unexpected situation, then the interaction robot interacts with human based on request information. The robot system can be constructed by connecting robots and servers easily using RTM.

3   Control Software Architecture for the Service Robot

This section explains control architecture for a service robot based on collaborating with other robot or server. Fig.3 shows the overview of our proposed control software architecture. The control software architecture is made by hardware dependency in lower level, and common architecture in higher level.

Generally, a specification of sensor and actuator is different. If sensor information is inputted directly, a sensor input interface has to change every update of sensors. Therefore, the role of hardware dependency is a translation of each input information into common interface and a translation of control command into actuator command. Sensor module at Fig.3 integrates various input information. In our robot, the service robot gets dish information (ID, name, position, posture) from different two vision systems, and dish property (ID, name, diameter, height, weight) from the intelligent space server. The sensor module in hardware dependency integrates a dish information and outputs perceptual information (ID, name, position, posture, diameter, height, weight, check parameters). If sensor information is lost, sensor module fills a lost information with general knowledge. Similarly, input interface of actuator module is general information such as hand position. Actuator module translates to actuator command including local loops such as current local loop control of motors. In this way, a higher level module doesn't need consideration of sensor or actuator devices.

Common architecture is constructed by 3 modules that are global planning module, robot action module and model base control module based on Human Performance Models. First, the highest layer is a global planning module (GPM) that makes a procedure for clearing of dishes based on perceptual information. GPM has some rules for table clearing such as descending order of near side, dish size and so on, and selects a suitable rule on a facing situation. Of course, GPM can install a learning algorithm such as AI, mining model and so on. Outputs of GPM are an action order command and an current target dish information. Moreover, GPM makes a plan of pause or changing procedure based on information of movement range of a robot if developers don't have specific control skill for a robot, because input information don't depend on devices. Second, the middle layer is a robot action module (RAM) that makes a procedure for robot behavior. RAM has some action sub modules such as searching a target dish (Search), making a posture for taking a dish (Approach), grasping a dish (Grasp), moving to a tray (Remove), putting on a tray (Release) and

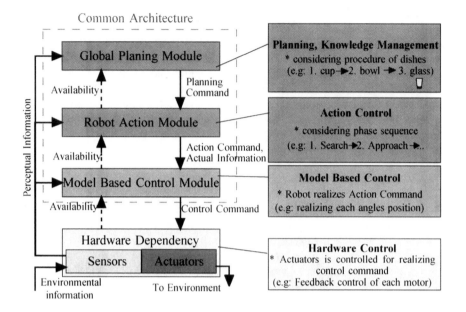

Fig. 3. Control Architecture for a service robot based on human interaction

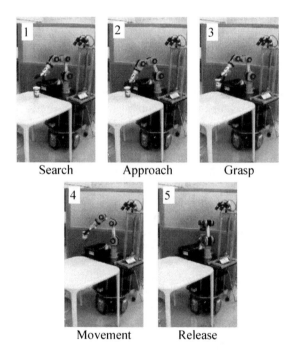

Fig. 4. The snapshots of robot action sub modules

returning to initialize position (Break). Fig.4 shows snapshots of robot action sub modules. RAM makes an action sequence using action sub modules for a clearing task. Outputs of RAM are a hand position, a hand posture and a switching parameter for gripper. Moreover, an action learning algorithm can be applied for each refined sub action. Third, the lowest layer is a model based control module (MCM) that control a robot based on model-based control. Specially, MCM compensate for hand position or posture.

As noted above, our proposed architecture is divided in small sub modules. Therefore, robot action can change flexibly in performing tasks with human interaction. For example, when a person orders "stop", RAM performs "Break" sub module after finishing current action sub module. However, if a robot has a dish, RAM performs "Break" sub module after finishing all action sub module.

4   Experimental Result of a Control Software Architecture

4.1   The Experiment for Clearing Table

Fig.5 shows an experimental condition. There are three dishes small bowl, big bowl and paper cup on the table without setting properly. First, she says "katazukete (meaning: clean up)" with pointing at the table to the interaction robot. Then, the service robot starts on a clearing task automatically. On the way, she says "dame (meaning: wait)" to want to wait the cleaning. After pausing the service robot, she says "donburi (meaning: big bowl)" to want to start clearing from big bowl. Then, the service robot restarts a clearing task based on human order.

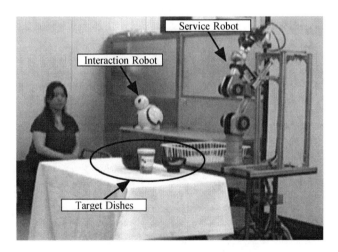

Fig. 5. The experimental condition for clearing dishes on the table

Fig.6 shows an experimental result on a dish clearing task. First, the service robot recognizes human orders in sensor module, then moves to a target table. GPM makes a plan for procedure of clearing dishes depending on a dish position by stereo vision system. In this case, we apply a rule for beginning as a nearest dish from the robot arm. Therefore, the first target dish is a small bowl. Then, RAM makes a plan that is action set for clearing a small bowl, after that the service robot is moved by MBM and actuator module. However a person says "dame" when the approach module in RAM is running. RAM changes a plan to run the break module after finishing the approach module. Next, a person says "donburi" then GPM makes a plan for beginning from the big bowl. So the service robot can clear all of dishes on the table. In this way, our proposed software architecture has flexibility for the situation that includes human interaction.

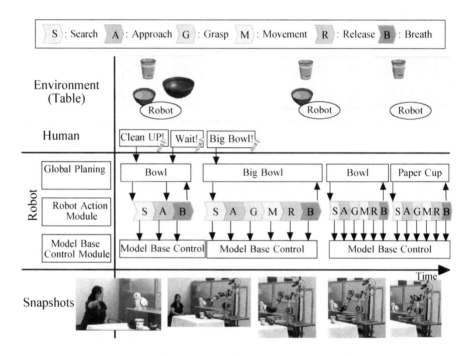

Fig. 6. Experimental result of a clearing task on the table

(a) The case of fallen paper cup   (b)The case of a ball of paper

Fig. 7. Snapshots of unknown object recognition (left: the robot condition, right: recognition result of 3D range camera image)

4.2   The Addition of a New Function to the Software Architecture

Here, we add the new perceptual sub module that is developed by our previous research to recognize an unknown object such as fallen cup and paper into a ball, using 3D range camera[13][14]. This paper simply explains the perceptual sub module, but spares the details for recognition of unknown objects. The perceptual sub module is proposed to pick up only necessary information using a three-dimensional (3D) range camera based on perceiving-acting cycle concept in ecological psychology[15][16]. To realize a perceptual sub module, we apply the surface detection method [17], the retinal model [18][19] and the spiking-neural network [20]. As an effect, Fig.7 shows snapshots that are result of unknown object recognition. This perceptual sub module can detect a dish position, posture and rough size. The perceptual sub module is installed to a sensor module in hardware dependency. The inputs of perceptual sub module is distance image from 3D range sensor, and the output is a dish position, posture and size that interface is about as same as stereo vision system. The perceptual sub module can't recognize dish name and ID, but the sensor module complements the missing information by general knowledge. Therefore, the service robot can perform a dish clearing task without software update of GPM, RAM and MBM. Fig.8 shows snapshots of experimental results that are grasp unknown objects. In this way, the proposed architecture has been shown to be effective for adding new function sub modules.

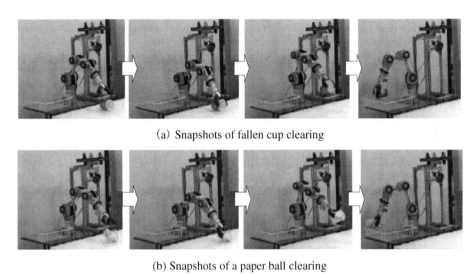

(a) Snapshots of fallen cup clearing

(b) Snapshots of a paper ball clearing

Fig. 8. The experimental results for unknown object

5   Conclusion

We have proposed the control software architecture for human friendly robots. The software architecture is required to be effective for not only connecting various intelligent modules easily, but also adding a new function easily. This paper, we verified the software architecture in table clearing task using human friendly robot system. As experimental results, our proposed software architecture has flexibility for the situation that includes human interaction and has been shown to be effective for adding new function sub modules.

We are going to verify our proposal that apply to other robot system.

References

[1] Mitsunaga, N., Miyashita, Z., Shinozawa, K., Miyashita, T., Ishiguro, H., Hagita, N.: What makes people accept a robot in a social environment. In: International Conference on Intelligent Robots and Systems, pp. 3336–3343 (2008)

[2] OpenRTM-aist, http://www.openrtm.org/

[3] Willow Garage, http://www.willowgarage.com/

[4] Andres, I., Diego, C.A., Francisco, J.O., Juan, F.P., Pedro, P.S., Barbara, A.: Design of Service Robots. IEEE Robotics & Automation Magazine 16(1), 24–33 (2009)

[5] Sato, E., Yamaguchi, T., Harashima, F.: Natural Interface Using Pointing Behavior for Human-Robot Gestural Interaction. IEEE Transactions on Industrial Electronics 54(2), 1105–1112 (2007)

[6] Garcia, J.G., Ortega, J.G., Garcia, A.S., Martinez, S.S.: Robotic Software Architecture for Multisensor Fusion System. IEEE Transactions on Industrial Electronics 56 (3), 766–777 (2009)

[7] Russell, S.J., Norving, P.: Artificial Intelligence. Prentice-Hall, Inc. (1995)

[8] Brooks, R.: A Robust Layered Control System for a Mobile Robot. IEEE Journal of Robotics and Automation 2(1), 14–23 (1986)

[9] Rasmussen, J.: Skills, Rules, and Knowledges; Signals, Signs, and Symbols, and Other Distinctions in Human Performance Models. IEEE Transaction on Systems, Man, and Cybernetics 13, 257–266 (1983)

[10] Chong, N.Y., Hongu, H., Ohba, K., Hirai, S., Tanie, K.: Knowledge Distributed Robot Control Framework. In: Proc. Int. Conf. on Control, Automation, and Systems, pp. 22–25 (2003)

[11] Nishiyama, M.: Robot Vision Technology for Target Recognition. Toshiba Review 64(1), 40–43 (2009)

[12] Oggier, T., Lehmann, M., Kaufmannn, R., Schweizer, M., Richter, M.: P., Metzler, Lang, G., Lustenberger, F., Blanc, N.,: An all-solid-state optical range camera for 3D-real-time imaging with sub-centimeter depth-resolution (SwissRanger). In: Proceedings of SPIE, vol. 5249, pp. 634–545 (2003)

[13] Masuta, H., Kubota, N.: An Integrated Perceptual System of Different Perceptual Elements for an Intelligent Robot. Journal of Advanced Computational Intelligence and Intelligent Informatics 14(7), 770–775 (2010)

[14] Masuta, H., Kubota, N.: Perceptual System using Spiking Neural Network for an Intelligent Robot. In: 2010 IEEE International Conference on Systems, Man and Cybernetics, pp. 3405–3412 (2010)

[15] Gibson, J.J.: The ecological approach to visual perception. Lawrence Erlbaum Associates, Hillsdale (1979)

[16] Lee, D.N.: Guiding movement by coupling taus. Ecological Psychology 10(3-4), 221–250 (1998)

[17] Overby, J., Bodum, L., Kjems, E., Ilsoe, P.: Automatic 3D building reconstruction from airborne laser scanning and cadastral data using Hough transform. International Archives of Photogrammetry, Remote Sensing and Spatial Information Sciences 34, 296–301 (2004)

[18] Masuta, H., Kubota, N.: The Intelligent Control based on Perceiving-Acting Cycle by using 3D-range camera. In: 2009 IEEE International Conference on Systems, Man, and Cybernetics (2009)

[19] Curcio, C.A., Sloan, K.R., Kalina, R.E.: Human photoreceptor topography. Journal of Comparative Neurology 292, 497–523 (1960)

[20] Maass, W., Bishop, C.M.: Pulsed Neural Networks. The MIT Press (1999)

Multi-modal Communication Interface
for Elderly People in Informationally Structured Space

Rikako Komatsu, Dalai Tang, Takenori Obo, and Naoyuki Kubota

Department of System Design, Tokyo Metropolitan University, Tokyo, Japan
{komatsu-rikako,tang,oobo-takenori}@sd.tmu.ac.jp,
kubota@tmu.ac.jp

Abstract. This paper proposes a universal remote controller using iPhone for elderly people. First, we discuss system configuration of universal remote controllers for elderly people in informationally structured space. The developed system is composed of database management server PC, physical robot partners, environmental systems, and human interface systems. Next, we explain human interface of universal remote controllers using accelerometer and compass. Finally, we discuss the usability of the developed universal remote controller through experimental results.

Keywords: Remote Control, Multi-modal Human Interface, Universal Design, Sensor Network.

1 Introduction

Recently, home appliances such as audio players, televisions, air-conditioners, lights, and fans, have been controlled by individual infrared remote controller. As a result, there are many remote controllers in a house. It is troublesome for elderly people to use many remote controllers in a living room, because each remote controller has the different layout and functions of buttons. Furthermore, elderly people sometimes forget to turn home appliances off. Therefore, the monitoring of environmental states inside the house is helpful for them. On the other hand, various types of personal data assistant (PDA) devices, personal organizers, and smart phones have been developed to access the personal information and Internet information until now [1]. Such a device can be used to control home appliances. However, the device is unfamiliar to elderly people, and it takes much time to choose the menu of the target home appliance from the candidates, as the number of home appliances increases in a house.

In our study, we have proposed the concept of informationally structured space [2-4] (Fig.1). The environment surrounding people should have a structured platform for gathering, storing, transforming, and providing information. The structuralization of informationally structured space realizes the quick update and access of valuable and useful information for users. Furthermore, we should consider the accessibility to required information, especially, human interface is very important to use devices [5,6].

S. Jeschke, H. Liu, and D. Schilberg (Eds.): ICIRA 2011, Part II, LNAI 7102, pp. 220–228, 2011.
© Springer-Verlag Berlin Heidelberg 2011

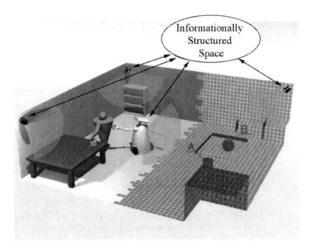

Fig. 1. Informationally Structured Space

In the previous researches, many universal remote controllers are proposed [7,8]. Most of the previous researches focus on the interface design of the remote controllers. However, the usability varies considerably from person to person because physical and cognitive abilities of elderly people are different from one person to another. The concept of multi-modal communication interface is one of the solutions to realize human interface suitable to the physical and cognitive abilities. Furthermore, the usability can be affected by individual taste and habits in daily life. It is difficult for a remote controller to detect human behaviors based on the taste and habits. Therefore, sensor network and portable sensing devices should be applied to observe and understand the human behaviors.

In this paper, we propose a universal remote controller of home appliances in the informationally structured space. We applied Apple iPhone [9] for remote controller of home appliance, because iPhone can provide the multi-modal communication interface to the user [10,11]. The iPhone can estimate the posture and direction of the device itself by the internal compass and accelerometer. Furthermore, the proposed system can get the environment information by using sensor networks [2,3].

This paper is organized as follows. Section 2 shows the proposed system for elderly people, and Section 3 shows the proposed universal remote controller for home appliances. Section 4 shows experimental results of the proposed method, and Section 5 summarizes the paper, and discusses the usability of the universal remote controller.

2   Monitoring System for Elderly People

Fig. 2 shows the system architecture in our system for monitoring and supporting elderly people. The developed system is divided into four main components; (1) database management server PC, (2) physical robot partners [12-16], (3) environmental systems, and (4) human interface systems. The environmental system is based on a wireless sensor network composed of sensors equipped with wall, floor, ceiling, furniture, and home appliances. These sensors measure the environmental data and human motions. The measured data are transmitted to the database server PC, and then feature extraction is performed. Each robot partner can receive the environmental information from the database server PC and serves to the person as a partner. For example, the robot partner informs the person of the time to take medicines, and call for family when elderly people fall down. Furthermore, the user interface system is used for the access to the environmental information through the developed universal remote controller, iPhone. The controller can't only provide the information, but also control the home appliances such as air-conditioner, TV, and lights.

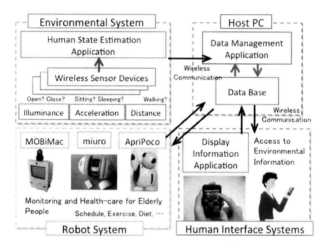

Fig. 2. System architecture in the developed system for monitoring and supporting elderly people

3   Universal Remote Controller

In our research, we developed a universal remote controller by using iPhone. The developed universal remote controller is used for the multi-modal communication interface to control home appliances. In this section, we explain the specification of the universal remote controller and the proposed system.

3.1   Problem of Usability

As previously explained, it isn't easy for elderly people to use many remote controllers. There are three main reasons of the problem.

The first reason is size and color of the buttons and the characters of remote controller. Physical abilities of elderly people are declining with aging [17]. Especially, the loss of visual acuity is remarkable. Therefore, many elderly people are not satisfied with the performance of remote controllers, and they claim that "The character around the button is too small", "The button is small", "The button is too near the button ", and others.

The second reason is complicatedness of the usage. Various functions are installed in the home appliances now. As a result, the number of buttons of remote controller increases and the operation methods are various. Furthermore, because the memory of some elderly people is gradually declining, they cannot easily remember how to use them [18,19].

The third reason is to provide the information of the home appliances by the character. The information is displayed on the small monitor. Therefore, some elderly people cannot read them and understand the state of home appliances because of the loss of visual acuity.

In the following, we explain the proposed universal remote controller in order to solve the three problems.

3.2   Input Interface

Multimodal interface is one of the iPhone's features. The iPhone has a multi-touch display, and some sensors, microphone, accelerometer, digital compass, and so on. Therefore, the iPhone can provide various interfaces by using the input devices. In our study, we developed two types of interfaces for selecting the home appliances and turning on or off them.

First, we developed the button operation and the direction operation when a home appliance is selected. The button operation is a way to select a home appliance that the user touches the button to select them. The direction operation is a way that the home appliance is automatically changed if the user points the iPhone at a home appliance. The iPhone has a wireless communication function. Therefore, the iPhone can get the position of the person and the home appliance communicating with the environmental system. And the home appliance can be detected by compass and accelerometer in the iPhone (Fig. 3,4).

Next, we developed the button operation and the shake operation when a home appliance is turned on or off. The button operation is a way to select a home appliance that the user touches the on/off button. The shake operation is a way for that the user can turn on or off them when the user shakes the iPhone.

In our study, we developed four types of CUI modes combined with these operation methods. But, on the CUI mode combined with the direction operation and the shake operation, it is an operation problem that the selected home appliance is changed when the user shake the iPhone. Therefore, on the mode, waiting time is applied for the decision of the selected home appliance.

3.3   Information Visualization

Fig. 4 shows two modes of touch interface based on character-based user interface (CUI) and graphical user interface (GUI).

(a) CUI mode   (b) GUI mode

Fig. 3. Universal remote controller for home appliance

Fig. 4. Information display modes in the universal remote controller

In the CUI mode, the menu of controller is composed of the home appliance name, on/off button, and manual operation button for the home appliance. If a person turns the iPhone to a home appliance, the menu of home appliance is automatically changed. The color and size of fonts and buttons are designed according to the results of questionnaire (see Fig. 4 (a)). If a home appliance is turned on, the menu is changed from the combination of "turn on" and "turned out" to that of "turned on" and "turn out". In general, the switch for power supply is only one in a standard remote controller, but elderly people sometimes push the button twice owing to the shaking of a finger. Therefore, we divide the switch for power supply into two buttons.

Furthermore, in the GUI mode, the user can directly touch a home appliance in the simulator to turn on/off its corresponding home appliance. If the home appliance is turned on, its color in the simulator is brightened. In this way, the user can easily understand the state of home appliance in the GUI mode. However, it is difficult to adjust the state of home appliances, e.g., the temperature of air, and the channel and volume of TV in the GUI mode. Therefore, we intend to incorporate the small menu for the adjustment of home appliances in the GUI mode like augmented reality environments as a future work.

4   Experimental Result

In this section, we show the usability evaluation results of the proposed universal remote controller in term of screen design and handling ability. In the experiment, we conducted experiments to ten healthy people between the age of 22 and 26. They put on special goggles and gloves designed to simulate not cognitive, but perceptual capacity of the elderly [20,21]. The goggle is used to simulate elderly people's view. The user's view becomes narrowed, cloudy, and yellowed. The gloves are used to simulate the decrease in the sensory function of the finger. Because the gloves are made of slippery materials, it is difficult for the user to hold something with the hands.

First, we had a questionnaire of the color and the size of the characters on the buttons. We prepared three colors of the characters (red, blue, and green), and two colors of the buttons (black and yellow). And we prepared five types of the size of the character (24 points, 36 points, 48 points, 60 points, and 72 points).

Next, we had a questionnaire of the handling ability. We prepared four kinds of CUI modes (CUI-A, CUI-B, CUI-C, CUI-D). Table 1 shows the specification of each CUI mode.

Table 1. Specification of CUI mode

CUI	A	B	C	D
Selecte	Button	Direction	Button	Direction
Turn on/off	Button	Button	Shake	Shake
Screen switching	Vertically and Horizontally	Vertically and Horizontally	Vertically only	Vertically only

4.1 Evaluation Result of Screen Design

Fig. 5 shows the questionnaire results of the color and the size of the characters on the buttons.

First, Fig. 5(a) shows the questionnaire result of the colors combinations that the user felt user-friendly. In this questionnaire, the user could select two combinations. As the result, it shows that the two combinations are remarkable. One is the combination of yellow character and blue button, another one is the combination of black character and green button. On the other hand, the combination of black character and blue button was regard as the worst one by the users. It is difficult for elderly people to recognize the difference of black and blue because of age-related yellowed view.

Next, Fig. 5 (b) shows the questionnaire result of the characters size. It was evaluated by 5-point scale from 1 to 5 (1: very difficult to read, 5: very easy to read). According to the result, on average, the point of 72pt character is 4.7, the point of 60pt character is 4.4, the point of 48pt character is 4.0, the point of 36pt is 3.3, and the point of 24pt character is 1.8 points. As a result, the character sizes over 36pt are easy to read for elderly people.

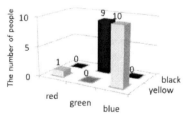

(a) The questionnaire result of the colors combinations

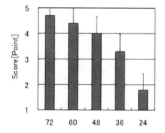

(b) The questionnaire result of the characters size (average of score).

Fig. 5. The questionnaire results of the color and the size of the characters on the buttons

4.2   Evaluation Result on Handling Ability

Fig. 6 shows the questionnaire results on human handling ability. The proposed universal remote controller has three types of operation methods, button operation, directional operation, and shake operation. Fig. 6 (a) shows the comparative result of the button operation, the directional operation, and the shake operation. The results were evaluated by 5-point scale from 1 to 5 (1: very difficult to use, 5: very easy to use). It shows that the button operation is the most user-friendly. Moreover, Fig. 6 (b)

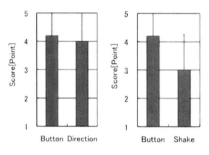
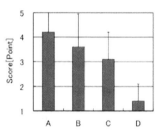

(a) The comparative result of the button operation, the directional operation, and the shake operation

(b) The comparative result of CUI modes

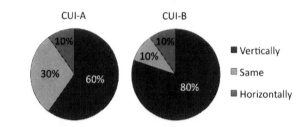

(c) The comparative result of CUI modes

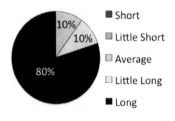
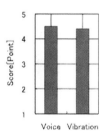

(d) Each user's feeling for the waiting time operation in CUI-D

(e) The comparative result of the guide by the voice and the vibration

Fig. 6. The questionnaire results of human handling ability

shows the comparative result of each CUI mode. According to the result, CUI-A is the most user-friendly mode, and conversely, CUI-D is the worst one. Fig. 6 (c) shows the comparative result of the horizontally screen and the vertically screen. It shows that the vertically screen is the most user-friendly. This is attributed to the fact that the users are accustomed to the vertically one because most of remote controllers are vertically. But, on CUI-A, some user who use the remote controller by two-hand selected the horizontally screen. Fig. 6 (d) shows the result of waiting time on CUI-D. In the experiment, the waiting time is 3 seconds. According to the result, most of the users felt that the time is very long. Fig. 6 (e) shows the comparative result of the operation guide by the voice and the vibration. The results were evaluated by 5-point scale from 1 to 5 (1: very unnecessary, 5: very necessary). It shows that both of the guides are very effective for the users.

5   Summary

We developed a universal remote controller for elderly people. Specifically we designed the interface in term of screen design and handling ability suitable to physical capacity of the elderly people. Furthermore, in the experiment, we evaluated usability of the developed interfaces by using four CUI modes.

In the future work, we should expand the function of the universal remote controller, and also evaluate the usability of GUI mode. On the functionality expansion, we would like to introduce learning function suitable to a history of individual operation. Furthermore, we will evaluate the usability of universal remote controller based on not only physical function but also cognitive function of elderly people.

Acknowledgments. This research was (partially) supported by Japan Science and Technology Agency, JST, under Strategic Promotion of Innovative Research and Development Program.

References

1. Zimmermann, G., Vanderheiden, G., Gilman, A.: Universal Remote Console – Prototyping for the Alternate Interface Access Standard. In: 7th ERCIM International Workshop on User Interfaces for All, pp. 524–531 (2002)
2. Kubota, N., Tang, D., Obo, T., Wakisaka, S.: Localization of Human Based on Fuzzy Spiking Neural Network in Informationally Structured Space. In: Proc. of 2010 IEEE World Congress on Computational Intelligence, pp. 2209–2214 (2010)
3. Kubota, N., Obo, T., Lee, B.H.: Localization of Human in Informationally Structured Space Based on Sensor Networks. In: Proc. of IEEE World Congress on Computational Intelligence 2010, pp. 2215–2221 (2010)
4. Kubota, N., Yorita, A.: Topological Environment Reconstruction in Informationally Structured Space for Pocket Robot Partners. In: Proc. of 2009 IEEE International Symposium on Computational Intelligence in Robotics and Automation (2009)
5. Card, S.K., Moran, T.P., Newell, A.: The Psychology of Human-Computer Interaction. Lawrence Erlbaum Associates (1983)

6. Norman, D.A.: The Design of Everyday Things. Basic Books (1988)
7. Kiyokawa, K., Yamamoto, S., Shibata, N., Yasumoto, K., Ito, M.: UbiREMOTE: Framework for Remotely Controlling Networked Appliances through Interaction with 3D Virtual Space. In: Proc. of ACM Multimedia Systems 2010, pp. 271–280 (2010)
8. Yasumura, M., Yoshida, R., Yoshida, M.: Prototyping and Evaluation of New Remote Controls for People with Visual Impairment. In: Miesenberger, K., Klaus, J., Zagler, W.L., Karshmer, A.I. (eds.) ICCHP 2006. LNCS, vol. 4061, pp. 461–468. Springer, Heidelberg (2006)
9. Apple Inc., http://www.apple.com/jp/iphone/
10. Kubota, N., Wakisaka, S., Yorita, A.: Tele-operation of Robot Partners through iPod touch. In: Proc. of 4th International Symposium on Computational Intelligence and Intelligent Informatics (2009)
11. Kubota, N., Sotobayashi, H., Obo, T.: Human Interaction and Behavior Understanding Based on Sensor Network with iPhone for Rehabilitation. In: Proc. of International Workshop on Advanced Computational Intelligence and Intelligent Informatics (2009)
12. Kubota, N., Nishida, K.: Perceptual Control Based on Prediction for Natural Communication of A Partner Robot. IEEE Transactions on Industrial Electronics 54(2), 866–877 (2007)
13. Kubota, N., Tomoda, K.: Behavior Coordination of A Partner Robot based on Imitation. In: Proc. of 2nd International Conference on Autonomous Robots and Agents, pp. 164–169 (2004)
14. Kubota, N.: Computational Intelligence for Structured Learning of A Partner Robot Based on Imitation. Information Science (171), 403–429 (2005)
15. Kubota, N., Nishida, K.: Development of Internal Models for Communication of A Partner Robot Based on Computational Intelligence. In: Proc. of 6th International Symposium on Advanced Intelligent Systems, pp. 577–582 (2005)
16. Kubota, N., Tomioka, Y., Abe, M.: Temporal coding in spiking neural network for gestures recognition of a partner robot. In: Proc. Joint 3rd Int. Conf. on Soft Computing and Intelligent Systems and 7th International Symposium on Advanced Intelligent Systems, pp. 737–742 (2006)
17. Okajima, K.: Color perception of the elderly - basic researches and applications. In: Proc AIC 2003 Bangkok, Color Communication and Management, pp. 413–416 (2003)
18. Small, S.A., Stern, Y., Tang, M., Mayeux, R.: Selective decline in memory function among healthy elderly. Neurology 52(7), 1392–1396 (1999)
19. Scott, A., Small, M.D.: Age-related memory decline - current concepts and future directions. Arch. Neurol. 58(3), 360–364 (2001)
20. Suzuki, T., Qiang, Y., Sakuragawa, S., Tamura, H., Okajima, K.: Age-related changes of reaction time and p300 for low- contrast color stimuli: effects of yellowing of the aging human lens. Journal of Physiological Anthropology 25(2), 179–187 (2006)
21. Suzuki, T., Yi, Q., Sakuragawa, S., Tamura, H., Okajima, K.: Comparison of response speed to color stimuli between elderly and young adults with and without filter simulating an aged human lens. In: Proc AIC 2003 Bangkok, Color Communication and Management, pp. 442–446 (2003)

Motion Control Strategies for Humanoids Based on Ergonomics

Christian Schlette and Jürgen Rossmann

Institute for Man-Machine Interaction, RWTH Aachen University,
Ahornstr. 55, 52074 Aachen, Germany
{schlette,rossmann}@mmi.rwth-aachen.de
http://www.mmi.rwth-aachen.de

Abstract. Due to the body analogy and their ability to communicate also via body language, humanoid robots are discussed as being mostly fit for applications in service robotics. An essential precondition of their deployment in human environments is the generation and control of human-like and thus predictable motions. This contribution introduces new motion control strategies which are based on the "Rapid Upper Limb Assessment" (RULA), a method for the analysis of ergonomic conditions at manual workplaces. We have previously adapted RULA to work with the Virtual Human, a simulated anthropomorphic multiagent system for the analysis of human motions and manipulations. Enabled by the control framework behind the Virtual Human, we here transfer RULA to humanoids in general and propose it as a well-defined and transparent heuristic for the control of human-like motions.

Keywords: Service robotics, Motion control, Multiagent systems.

1 Introduction

The main application of motion control strategies for humanoids is in fields where humanoids operate in human environments and/or in direct interaction with human co-workers. In such applications, it is necessary to generate predictable motions so human co-workers are able to assess and foresee the intention and consequences of movements. It is often mentioned as an advantage of humanoids in human environments, that based on the body analogy, the motions of humanoids are intuitively understood and body language opens a very direct level of communication [1] [2] [3]. Several approaches already use body language as a tool to bring internal states of humanoids to the surface [4] [5] [6].

In comparison to such developments, the motion control strategies presented here are aiming at the control of body language based on a well-defined and transparent heuristic to bias motions towards human-like postures and movements. Particularly layered and prioritized whole-body control frameworks for anthropomorphic kinematics such as the approaches of Khatib et al [7], Kajita et al [8] as well as our own approach at the Institute for Man-Machine Interaction (MMI) [9] can benefit from the new motion control strategies based on ergonomics.

S. Jeschke, H. Liu, and D. Schilberg (Eds.): ICIRA 2011, Part II, LNAI 7102, pp. 229–240, 2011.
© Springer-Verlag Berlin Heidelberg 2011

In 1993, McAtamney and Corlett published a method for the fast and easy evaluation of ergonomic conditions at manual workplaces called "Rapid Upper Limb Assessment" (RULA) [10]. Based on data compiled from the examination of work-related upper limb disorders, RULA introduces a scoring system which investigators can carry out for a selection of possibly critical work postures in order to assess the resulting stresses and strains. Investigators roughly estimate the postures of the limbs in terms of relative angles and positions and combine the estimations in a calculation of an overall score for a given work posture.

Together with the team around "Justin", the development of a humanoid platform at the German Aerospace Center [11], we have already investigated the application of RULA to support *motion planning* for humanoids [12]. Here, we concentrate on strategies for *motion control* based on the control framework for anthropomorphic multiagent systems which we have previously developed to simulate the Virtual Human [13]. In this contribution, we will briefly explain the control framework that is also the basis of applying ergonomics for humanoids (Sect. 2). We will then describe in detail how RULA works (Sect. 3) and how we adapt RULA to be calculated from animations of anthropomorphic multiagent systems (Sect. 4). Finally, we will propose how RULA can be extended and applied to control human-like motions of humanoids (see Sect. 5) and close this contribution with a discussion of the results (see Sect. 6).

2   Simulating Anthropomorphic Multiagent Systems

For the simulation and analysis of manual workplaces in virtual production systems, we implemented a simulation model of the Virtual Human (see Fig. 1) based on a control framework for anthropomorphic multiagent systems (aMAS). Here, the aMAS enable the transfer of ergonomics from the Virtual Human to humanoids by providing structures and algorithms to control and analyze anthropomorphic kinematics based on the same general approach.

Fig. 1. The concept of the Virtual Human

2.1   Modeling Anthropomorphic Kinematics as Kinematic Trees

The simulation environment at the MMI is organized around an all-purpose database, which extends the general idea of a scene graph [14] [15], a hierarchy to structure and access the information for the simulation and visualization of complex 3d scenarios. In this database, *nodes* can be typified and structured in a tree hierarchy to meet the requirements of various applications and simulation goals. *Extensions* can be attached to any node, containing additional functionalities and parameters for nodes in a modular way.

To model kinematics, nodes representing the links are enhanced with joint definitions that define their spatial arrangement and degrees of freedom. We support simple rotary and prismatic joints as well as more complex definitions such as universal joints and joints directly defined via their Denavit-Hartenberg parameters. As no restrictions apply where frames and joint definitions can be used in the scene graph, the resulting kinematics generally have the form of *kinematic trees*.

The framework for aMAS is based on the control and coordination of the motions of selected *kinematic paths* within the trees. The definition of kinematic paths starts with attaching a so-called *kinematic root* extension to the root node of the kinematic tree, which acts as the central access point for controllers to interact with the kinematic path it defines. To select individual joints from a kinematic tree to belong to a kinematic path definition, the user attaches so-called *kinematic mapping* extensions to the joints between the nodes representing the links of the kinematic. The mapping extensions then register automatically with their supervising root extension as elements of the kinematic path. The mapping mechanism is hardly restricted and a kinematic tree can have several root extensions that define different paths but partly include the same joints.

2.2   Controlling Anthropomorphic Kinematics as Multiagent Systems

As a typical instance of anthropomorphic kinematics, the Virtual Human is modeled as a set of individual kinematic paths for the limbs and the trunk that are coupled to form the kinematic tree of the human body. The system is then controlled as an *anthropomorphic multiagent system*, which – at a glance – can be seen as a human-like coupling of conventional robots representing the individual limbs and the trunk. Each of the individual kinematic paths representing the limbs and the trunk is controlled by a *control agent*. With respect to the advanced requirements of human kinematics the agents are combined to work as a multiagent system. On the supervising level of the multiagent system, an additional *coordination agent* monitors and coordinates the motions and other actions of the individual agents.

Initially, the control agents react independently on incoming requests. In their reactions, they only care about the kinematic paths they are assigned to control, without any deeper considerations of the system of kinematic couplings in which they operate. Of course, although the control agents act locally in the first place, the control of the limbs in an anthropomorphic compound can not be carried out independently. Due to the fact that the limbs are coupled to the common trunk, another layer of control has to act on these couplings globally. In order to accomplish human-like motions of the whole kinematic tree in our control framework, the anthropomorphic coordination agent observes motion generation and motion control from the perspective of the multiagent system based on so-called *multiple redundancies* [9] [13].

3   Processing RULA

Following the original RULA article, several authors designed worksheets for the easy compilation of RULA scores directly at workplaces [17] [16]. The "process-ing" of RULA described in these worksheets is also the basis of our algorithm to calculate RULA scores for anthropomorphic multiagent systems. The origi-nal processing of RULA as it is carried out for single, presumably critical work postures, yields in a score

$$S_{rula} \in \{1, 2, 3, 4, 5, 6, 7\} \ , \tag{1}$$

where a lower score stands for an ergonomically better posture. Textual interpre-tations are associated with the scores as a help for investigators to appropriately act upon the result, ranging from *Acceptable* ($S_{rula} = 1$) to *Investigate further and change immediately* ($S_{rula} = 7$). Calculation of S_{rula} consists of eights steps for assessing relevant subscores and finally the summary score:

1. Evaluation of the *upper arm position* as the angle α_u between the elbow and the midcoronal plane of the body. The angle is mapped to an intermediate score S_u. The investigator makes adjustments to S_u to account for ($\tilde{S}_{u_1}$) if the shoulder is raised, ($\tilde{S}_{u_2}$) if the arm is lifted to the side or ($\tilde{S}_{u_3}$) if the arm is supported, $S_u := f(\alpha_u, \tilde{S}_{u_1}, \tilde{S}_{u_2}, \tilde{S}_{u_3})$.
2. Evaluation of the *lower arm position*. The investigator estimates the angle α_l between the lower arm and the upper arm in order to determine an intermediate score S_l. Modificators are applied to incorporate ($\tilde{S}_{l_1}$) if the arm is crossing the midsagittal plane or ($\tilde{S}_{l_2}$) if the arm is working out to the side of the body, $S_l := f(\alpha_l, \tilde{S}_{l_1}, \tilde{S}_{l_2})$.
3. Evaluation of the *wrist position* to gain an intermediate score S_w from the flexion/extension angle α_w of the wrist. The investigator makes adjustments to the wrist score to account for ($\tilde{S}_{w_1}$) if the wrist is bent from the midline and ($\tilde{S}_{w_2}$) if the wrist is twisted, $S_w := f(\alpha_w, \tilde{S}_{w_1}, \tilde{S}_{w_2})$.
4. Based on a table, the *arm posture score* S_A is calculated from the intermedi-ate scores S_u, S_l and S_w. The investigator can make additional adjustments to S_A to take into account ($\tilde{S}_{A_1}$) the loads the arm is lifting and ($\tilde{S}_{A_2}$) if the arm posture is straining the muscles, e.g. in case of repetitive movements, $S_A := f(S_u, S_l, S_w, \tilde{S}_{A_1}, \tilde{S}_{A_2})$.
5. Evaluation of the *neck position* as the angle α_n between the head and the midcoronal plane of the body. The angle is mapped to an intermediate score S_n. Modificators are applied to incorporate ($\tilde{S}_{n_1}$) if the neck is twisted or ($\tilde{S}_{n_2}$) if the neck is side-bending, $S_n := f(\alpha_n, \tilde{S}_{n_1}, \tilde{S}_{n_2})$.

6. Evaluation of the *trunk position* to identify an intermediate score S_t from the angle α_t the trunk is bent from the midcoronal plane. The investigator makes adjustments to the trunk score to consider $(\tilde{S}_{t_1})$ if the trunk is twisted, $(\tilde{S}_{t_2})$ if the trunk is side-bending and $(\tilde{S}_{t_3})$ the support of legs and feet, $S_t := f(\alpha_t, \tilde{S}_{t_1}, \tilde{S}_{t_2}, \tilde{S}_{t_3})$.

7. A *body posture score* S_B is calculated from the intermediate scores S_n and S_t with the help of a table. The investigator can make additional adjustments to S_B to take into account $(\tilde{S}_{B_1})$ the loads and forces acting on the body and $(\tilde{S}_{B_2})$ if the body posture is straining the muscles, e.g. in case of repetitive movements, $S_B := f(S_n, S_t, \tilde{S}_{B_1}, \tilde{S}_{B_2})$.

8. Finally, indexed by arm posture score S_A and body posture score S_B, the investigator looks up the summary RULA score S_{rula} from a last table, $S_{rula} := f(S_A, S_B)$.

4 Connecting RULA to Anthropomorphic Kinematics

RULA was developed to evaluate postures of human arms and the human trunk. Here, it is interpreted as an abstract algorithm for the evaluation of anthropomorphic kinematics – kinematics very closely related to the human body, such as the Virtual Human (see Fig. 2), but also more open forms, such as humanoids and other robotic systems with human features. In order to continuously calculate RULA for aMAS, we developed several modifications, extending RULA beyond the scope of the worksheets.

Fig. 2. The default posture, yielding a RULA score "Acceptable (1)"

4.1 RULA Only Considers one Arm at a Time, in Its Original Form It Is Not Assessed for Both Arms at Once

Also it is possible to symmetrically calculate left and right arm posture scores, $S_{A^{left}}$ and $S_{A^{right}}$, both based on subscores $S_u, ..., S_A$, the table to determine S_{rula} from S_A and S_B only works with one arm. To solve this problem, we introduce an alternative arm posture score S'_A, which mixes the left and the right arm posture scores

$$S'_A := f\left(S_{A^{left}}, S_{A^{right}}\right) = \left\lceil \frac{S_{A^{left}} + S_{A^{right}}}{2} \right\rceil , \tag{2}$$

to serve as an adequate input for identifying a two-armed summary score

$$S_{rula2} := f\left(S'_A, S_B\right) . \tag{3}$$

The original RULA score S_{rula} depends on 5 angles and 16 modificators. The two-armed RULA score S_{rula2} now depends on 8 angles and 25 modificators.

4.2 RULA Is Only Assessed for Single Work Postures, in Its Original Form It Is Not Calculated Continuously

In order to extract scores from continuous animations of anthropomorphic kinematics, we process RULA quasi-continuously, for each time step of the animation. The angles and modificators, and hence also S_{rula2}, become functions of the time

$$S_{rula2}(t) := f\left(S'_A(t), S_B(t)\right) = f\left(\alpha_{[1..8]}(t), \tilde{S}_{[1..25]}(t)\right) . \tag{4}$$

Now, the algorithm to determine S_{rula2} for each time step of the animation is very straightforward

1. Left arm:
   (a) Identify angles α_u, α_l and α_w
   (b) Identify modificators $\tilde{S}_{u1,2,3}$, $\tilde{S}_{l1,2}$, $\tilde{S}_{w1,2}$ and $\tilde{S}_{A1,2}$
   (c) Look up left arm posture score $S_{A^{left}}$
2. Right arm:
   (a) Identify angles α_u, α_l and α_w
   (b) Identify modificators $\tilde{S}_{u1,2,3}$, $\tilde{S}_{l1,2}$, $\tilde{S}_{w1,2}$ and $\tilde{S}_{A1,2}$
   (c) Look up right arm posture score $S_{A^{right}}$
3. Calculate two-arm posture score S'_A
4. Neck, trunk and legs:
   (a) Identify angles α_n and α_t
   (b) Identify modificators $\tilde{S}_{n1,2}$, $\tilde{S}_{t1,2,3}$ and $\tilde{S}_{B1,2}$
   (c) Look up body posture score S_B
5. Look up two-armed RULA score S_{rula2} .

4.3 RULA Only Considers Postures Feasible for Humans, but Humanoids Are Typically Not Restricted to Human Joint Limits

Joint limits of humanoid robots can be far-ranging, beyond human possibilities of movement, or even intentionally left open to account for free-turning joints. To adapt our implementation of RULA to such open definitions of anthropomorphic kinematics as well, we decided to introduce a post-processing step, in which we calculate penalties in the range of RULA scores if kinematics operate beyond the scope of human joints. To prepare the penalties, we define *virtual joint limits* which provide additional, human-like joint limits. These joint limits are solely used for penalizing "unhuman" movements in RULA assessments without affecting the regular functions of the anthropomorphic kinematic in any way.

We currently support two penalty functions. If the joint values grow beyond the human-like limits, the *strict function* P_{strict} instantely yields a penalty of 7, and the *smooth function* P_{smooth} linearly increases the penalty up to a value of 7, starting at 0 (no penalty). The penalties are separately calculated for each of the arm kinematics and the trunk kinematic. In a variation of (3), the summary RULA scores with penalties are evaluated based on the maximum function

$$S_{rula2}^{strict} = f\left(\max\{S_A', P_{A_{strict}}'\}, \max\{S_B, P_{B_{strict}}\}\right) \tag{5}$$

$$S_{rula2}^{smooth} = f\left(\max\{S_A', P_{A_{smooth}}'\}, \max\{S_B, P_{B_{smooth}}\}\right), \tag{6}$$

where P_B is the body penalty and P_A' is the arm penalty for a two-handed system, similar to (2)

$$P_A' = \left\lceil \frac{P_{A^{left}} + P_{A^{right}}}{2} \right\rceil . \tag{7}$$

Of course, the joint limit penalties are an artificial extension to the original assessment, which never was necessary for the evaluation of human workers at manual workplaces and hence we distinguish between the three different calculations of RULA scores, $S_{rula2}(t)$, $S_{rula2}^{strict}(t)$ and $S_{rula2}^{smooth}(t)$ through all later stages of the evaluation of ergonomic conditions.

5   Motion Control Strategies from RULA

RULA also has the potential of being applied as a heuristic to form human-like motions. With the adaptions from Sect. 4, our control framework for anthropomorphic multiagent systems allows for transferring the calculation of RULA from the Virtual Human to humanoid robots, e.g. "Justin" of the German Aerospace Center [11] (see Fig. 3).

5.1   Interpretation of RULA Scores as "ergonomic stress"

From a robotics perspective, RULA is a function to compile scores expressing the "ergonomic stress" of anthropomorphic kinematics. The basic idea of the strategies presented here is to feed back the scores to motion control in order to react on it. Reducing the stresses will cause motion control to avoid unergonomic and thus unhuman (resp. nonhuman) postures. The minimum stress occurs with RULA at a relaxed default posture (see Fig. 2). Without additional input, anthropomorphic kinematics consequently reducing RULA stresses would assume a similar default posture. Two diverse factors contribute to maximum

Fig. 3. Calculation of RULA for the humanoid "Justin" (German Aerospace Center)

stresses. The first factor is coded in RULA itself – arm joints at extreme values, hand positions hardly in reach and unusual twists of the wrist quickly yield very bad scores. The second factor was introduced in Sect. 4.3 with opening our implementation of RULA to be adaptable to various anthropomorphic kinematics. For example, a kinematic description of an arm that allows the elbow to make several turns will produce regular RULA scores if operating in a range also possible for humans, but growing penalties will occur for joint configurations not realizable with the human arm. In terms of "ergonomic stress", the definition of penalties introduces artificial stress factors, which roughly drive kinematics into the RULA scheme, where more differentiated stresses are formulated.

5.2   Reduction of RULA Scores with Nullspace Motions

Because of the flexibility of the approach, motion control in the control agents (see Sect. 2.2) for aMAS is performed based on velocity kinematics and the Jacobian J,

$$\underline{\dot{q}} = \underline{J}^+ \underline{\dot{x}} + \underline{P}\underline{w} = \underline{J}^+ \underline{\dot{x}} + \left(\underline{I} - \underline{J}^+ \underline{J}\right) \underline{w} \qquad (8)$$

with $\underline{J}^+$ being the generalized pseudo-inverse to $\underline{J}$ and $\underline{P}$ being the orthogonal nullspace projection matrix. In order to consider RULA scores as a heuristic to form human-like motions for the arms, (8) can be implemented in the upper limb agents arm,

$$\underline{\dot{q}}_{des_{arm}} = \underline{\dot{q}}_{spec_{arm}} + \underline{\dot{q}}_{nsp_{arm}} \qquad (9)$$

$$= \underline{J}^+ \underline{\dot{x}}_{spec_{arm}} + \left(\underline{I} - \underline{J}^+ \underline{J}\right) \underline{w}_{rula} . \qquad (10)$$

For an arm, we calculate joint velocities $\underline{\dot{q}}_{spec_{arm}}$ to carry out a specified Cartesian motion $\underline{\dot{x}}_{spec_{arm}}$. Supposing the arm kinematic itself is redundant (as the human arm is with $7DOF$), we can superpose nullspace motions $\underline{\dot{q}}_{nsp_{arm}}$ without changing the specified Cartesian motion. The key to "RULA-aware" motion control is to find adequate vectors $\underline{w}_{rula}$ resp. adequate nullspace velocities that guide the arm kinematic in the direction of minimal stresses.

5.3 Inversion of RULA to Identify Favorable Joint Configurations

According to (4), the two-handed, continuous summary RULA score $S_{rula2}(t)$ is calculated from subscores which depend on angles and modificators. While the angles can be modified for better scores, most of the modificators are defined by the specified Cartesian motions, e.g. the hand crossing the midsagittal plane. Thus, we concentrate on finding joint configurations which produce favorable angles and deal with a modified summary RULA score $S_{rula2^{nsp}}(t)$, in which the angles $\alpha_{[1..8]}$ depend on the joint configuration but the modificators $\tilde{S}_{[1..25]}(t)$ are accepted as fixed values,

$$S_{rula2^{nsp}}(t) := f\left(\alpha_{[1..8]}(\underline{q}(t)), \tilde{S}_{[1..25]}(t)\right) . \tag{11}$$

To reduce the RULA score for a given configuration in (11), we look for an inversion of $\alpha_{[1..8]}(\underline{q}(t))$ in the sense that we want to calculate joint configurations from favorable angles. Motivated by the worksheets, it is possible to find such inversion for each of the individual functions $\alpha_i(\underline{q}(t))$, $i \in [1..8]$. Each inversion produces a distance vector in joint space $\Delta\underline{q}_i$ pointing from the current joint configuration $\underline{q}(t)$ to a configuration which would result in a more favorable angle α_i,

$$\Delta\underline{q}_i(\alpha_i(\underline{q}(t))), \; i \in [1..8] . \tag{12}$$

For example, α_u is evaluated as the angle between the elbow and the midcoronal plane of the body and thus depends on the joints of the shoulder (see Sect. 3). For a given configuration of the arm, the corresponding inversion produces a distance vector in joint space from the current configuration of the shoulder to a more relaxed configuration in terms of RULA. Since the functions $\alpha_i(\underline{q}(t))$ depend on only a few joint values each and do not fully depend on the same joint values, it is straightforward to compile a balanced summary distance vector $\Delta\underline{Q}$ from the results $\Delta\underline{q}_i$ of the individual inversions. Already measuring a distance rather than a configuration in joint space, we finally use $\Delta\underline{Q}$ to formulate the desired, "RULA-aware" nullspace velocity for (10), e.g. for a single arm,

$$\underline{\dot{q}}_{nsp_{arm}} := \frac{\Delta\underline{Q}}{\Delta t} . \tag{13}$$

Depending on the rank of the nullspace in a given time step Δt of motion control, the redundancy is then used to steer the kinematic towards joint configurations with reduced "ergonomic stress".

5.4 Results

We verified the motion control strategies with a simulation model of "Justin". Based on the modifications described in Sect. 4, the humanoid was rigged to be controlled as an aMAS, thus enabling the continuous calculation of RULA scores from its animation. The tests were carried out for the right arm of the humanoid only, ignoring the RULA scores for the left arm and the trunk in order to focus on the central effects of the strategies without interference from concurrent motions. Nonetheless, based on 4.1 the results are also applicable for two arms.

We commanded motions of the humanoid in the form of two sets of Cartesian targets for the right arm, each motion starting at the relaxed default position. For each time step (40ms) of the commanded motions, we calculated the RULA score of the unmodified and the "RULA-aware" solution according to (10).

The first set "WORKSPACE" of 100 Cartesian targets was a sampled over the whole workspace of the right arm, the RULA scores at the targets ranging from 1 to 7. As shown in Fig. 4, the motion control strategies yield a significant reduction of the overall RULA scores (Unmodified: $N = 595224$ samples, $\mu = 2,82$ population mean, $\sigma^2 = 1,72$ variance; RULA-aware: $N = 595224$ samples, $\mu = 2,50$ population mean, $\sigma^2 = 1,54$ variance). The reduction of "ergonomic stress" mainly shifted postures with score in the range 4..7 to better RULA scores. The second set "TABLE" contained 100 Cartesian targets

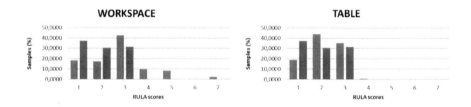

Fig. 4. Rel. frequencies of sampled RULA scores for sets "WORKSPACE" (left) and "TABLE" (right). Shown are "unmodified" (blue resp. left column) and "RULA-aware" (red resp. right column) results.

sampled from manipulations actions above a table in front of the right arm, the RULA scores at the targets ranging from 1 to 4. As shown in Fig. 4, for motions typical at manual workplaces, the strategies yield even more explicit reductions of the overall RULA scores (Unmodified: $N = 568922$ samples, $\mu = 2,18$ population mean, $\sigma^2 = 0,55$ variance; RULA-aware: $N = 568922$ samples, $\mu = 1,94$ population mean, $\sigma^2 = 0,69$ variance). Here, the reduction of "ergonomic stress" is able to produce about two times as many RULA scores 1.

6   Conclusion

The scoring system of the "Rapid Upper Limb Assessment" (RULA) proposes a fast and easy method to estimate the stresses and strains of single work postures of human workers. Based on our control framework to simulate and analyze anthropomorphic multiagent systems, we adapted RULA to be continuously calculated from motions not only of a simulation model of the Virtual Human, but also anthropomorphic kinematics in general. The basic idea of motion control strategies based on ergonomics as presented here is to interpret the RULA scores as "ergonomic stress" which motion control for humanoids needs to reduce in

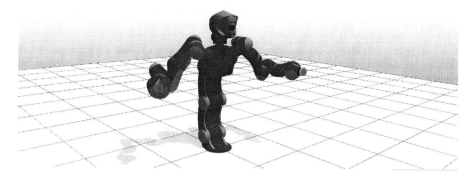

Fig. 5. Control of human-like motions by reducing "ergonomic stress". Shown are unmodified (solid) and "RULA-aware" (transparent, red) solutions without hand grippers.

order to avoid unergonomic and thus unhuman postures. Strategies are investigated for a single arm of a simulation model of "Justin", the development of a humanoid platform at the German Aerospace Center. The scoring system of RULA is inverted in order to produce velocity vectors in the direction of better scores and thus in the direction of reduced "ergonomic stress". Based on velocity kinematics and the Jacobian, the velocity vectors are superposed on the actual motion as nullspace motions. To test and verify the effect of the proposed strategies, such "RULA-aware" motions are compared to unmodified motions by calculating RULA scores for both solutions in each time step of the motion control. The results demonstrate that the proposed motion control strategies lead to significantly better RULA scores, which can be interpreted as yielding in relaxed, more human-like motions (see Fig. 5).

In conclusion, we regard the described motion control strategies for humanoids as a valid and effective approach to bias motions towards more human-like forms. The strategies are aiming at applications in the field of service robotics, where human-like and predictable motions are important to human co-workers. Single-handed as well as two-handed humanoids with or without actuated trunks can meaningfully be addressed with such "RULA-aware" means of motion control, since also the human-centered RULA can be carried out for one or two arms and calculating the trunk is optional, too. In comparison to other possible heuristics to form human-like motions, RULA is backed up by statistical ergonomics and thus offers a transparent definition already rooted in investigations of actions at manual workplaces.

References

1. Mutlu, B., Yamaoka, F., Kanda, T., Ishiguro, H., Hagita, N.: Nonverbal Leakage in Robots: Communication of Intentions through Seemingly Unintentional Behavior. In: Proceedings of the ACM/IEEE Conference on Human-Robot Interaction, DVD (2009)

2. Hegel, F., Lohse, M., Swadzba, A., Wachsmuth, S., Rohlfing, K., Wrede, B.: Classes of Applications for Social Robots: A User Study. In: Proceedings of the IEEE International Symposium on Robot and Human Interactive Communication, pp. 938–943 (2007)

3. Breazeal, C.: Designing Sociable Machines: Lessons Learned. In: Dautenhahn, K., Bond, A.H., Canamero, L., Edmonds, B. (eds.) Socially Intelligent Agents, vol, vol. 3, pp. 149–156. Springer, New York (2002)

4. Richardson, R., Devereux, D., Burt, J., Nutter, P.: Humanoid Upper Torso Complexity for Displaying Gestures. JHR 1(1), 25–32 (2008)

5. Osawa, H., Ohmura, R., Imai, M.: Embodiment of an Agent by Anthropomorphization of a Common Object. In: Proceedings of the IEEE/WIC/ACM International Conference on Web Intelligence and Intelligent Agent Technology, pp. 484–490 (2008)

6. Sugiyama, O., Kanda, T., Imai, M., Ishiguro, H., Hagita, N.: Three-Layered Draw-Attention Model for Humanoid Robots with Gestures and Verbal Cues. In: Proceedings of the IEEE/RSJ International Conference on Intelligent Robots and Systems, pp. 2423–2428 (2005)

7. Sentis, L., Khatib, O.: A Whole-Body Control Framework for Humanoids Operating in Human Environments. In: Proceedings of the IEEE International Conference on Robotics and Automation, pp. 2641–2648 (2006)

8. Neo, E.S., Yokoi, K., Kajita, S., Tanie, K.: Whole-Body Motion Generation Integrating Operator's Intention and Robot's Autonomy in Controlling Humanoid Robots. T-RO 23(4), 763–775 (2007)

9. Freund, E., Rossmann, J., Schlette, C.: Controlling Anthropomorphic Kinematics as Multi-Agent Systems. In: Proceedings of the IEEE/RSJ International Conference on Intelligent Robots and Systems, pp. 3662–3667 (2003)

10. McAtamney, L., Corlett, E.N.: RULA: A Survey Method for the Investigation of Work-Related Upper Limb Disorders. Appl. Ergo. 24(2), 91–99 (1993)

11. Borst, C., Wimbock, T., Schmidt, F., Fuchs, M., Brunner, B., Zacharias, F., Giordano, P.R., Konietschke, R., Sepp, W., Fuchs, S., Rink, C., Albu-Schaffer, A., Hirzinger, G.: Rollin' Justin - Mobile Platform with Variable Base. In: Proceedings of the IEEE International Conference on Robotics and Automation, pp. 1597–1598 (2009)

12. Zacharias, F., Schlette, C., Schmidt, F., Borst, C., Rossmann, J., Hirzinger, G.: Making Planned Paths Look More Human-Like in Humanoid Robot Manipulation Planning. Accepted for the IEEE International Conference on Robotics and Automation (2011)

13. Schlette, C., Rossmann, J.: Robotics enable the Simulation and Animation of the Virtual Human. In: Proceedings of the International Conference on Advanced Robotics, DVD (2009)

14. Eberly, D.H.: 3D Game Engine Design. A Practical Approach to Real-Time Computer Graphics. Elsevier, Oxford (2006)

15. Kuehne, B., Martz, P. (eds.): OpenSceneGraph Reference Manual. Blue Newt Software & Skew Matrix Software. Ann Arbor & Louisville (2007)

16. Osmond Group Limited: Rapid Upper Limb Assessment Worksheet, http://www.rula.co.uk

17. Hedge, A.: RULA Employee Assessment Worksheet, http://ergo.human.cornell.edu

Fuzzy Representations and Control
for Domestic Service Robots in Golog

Stefan Schiffer, Alexander Ferrein, and Gerhard Lakemeyer

Knowledge Based Systems Group
RWTH Aachen University, Aachen, Germany
{schiffer,ferrein,gerhard}@cs.rwth-aachen.de

Abstract. In the ROBOCUP@HOME domestic service robot competition, complex tasks such as "get the cup from the kitchen and bring it
to the living room" or "find me this and that object in the apartment"
have to be accomplished. At these competitions the robots may only
be instructed by natural language. As humans use qualitative concepts
such as "near" or "far", the robot needs to cope with them, too. For
our domestic robot, we use the robot programming and plan language
Readylog, our variant of Golog. In previous work we extended the action
language Golog, which was developed for the high-level control of agents
and robots, with fuzzy concepts and showed how to embed fuzzy controllers in Golog. In this paper, we demonstrate how these notions can be
fruitfully applied to two domestic service robotic scenarios. In the first
application, we demonstrate how qualitative fluents based on a fuzzy set
semantics can be deployed. In the second program, we show an example
of a fuzzy controller for a follow-a-person task.

1 Introduction

Classical applications for approaches to cognitive robotics and reasoning about
actions are delivery tasks, where the robot should deliver a letter or fetch a
cup of coffee. In these domains, it becomes obvious that solving such tasks
deploying reasoning and knowledge representation is superior to, say, reactive
approaches in terms of flexibility and expressiveness. An even more advanced application domain is ROBOCUP@HOME [13, 14]. As a distinguished league under
the roof of the RoboCup federation the robots have to fulfil complex tasks such
as *"Lost&Found"*, *"Fetch&Carry"*, or *"WhoIsWho"* in a domestic environment.
In the first tasks the robot has to remember and to detect objects, which are
hidden in an apartment, or has to fetch a cup of coffee from, say, the kitchen and
bring it to the sitting room, while in the latter the robot needs to find persons
and recognise their faces. The outstanding feature of these applications is that
they require integrated solutions for a number of sub-tasks such as safe navigation, localisation, object recognition, and high-level control (e.g. reasoning). A
particular complication is that the robot may only be instructed by means of
natural interaction, e.g. speech or gestures. Human-robot interaction is hence
largely based on natural language. For example, in the *Fetch&Carry* task it is
allowed to help the robot with hints like "The teddy is near the TV set".

S. Jeschke, H. Liu, and D. Schilberg (Eds.): ICIRA 2011, Part II, LNAI 7102, pp. 241–250, 2011.
© Springer-Verlag Berlin Heidelberg 2011

Humans make frequent use of qualitative concepts like *near* or *far*, as the example shows. It would be desirable that the robot could interpret these concepts and cope with them. When reasoning techniques are deployed to come up with a problem solution for these domestic tasks, also these mechanisms need to be able to cope with those qualitative concepts. But even as logic-based reasoning approaches make inherently use of qualitative concepts, the rest of the complex robot architecture does not. Hence, one needs to bridge the gap between the qualitative high-level control and the quantitative robot control system.

In this paper, we show how this gap can be bridged for domestic robot applications. We extended the logic-based high-level robot programming and plan language Readylog [4] with so-called *qualitative fluents* describing properties of the world based on fuzzy set theory [5] and integrated fuzzy control techniques into the robot control language [6]. This enables us (1) to map qualitative predicates to quantitative values based on a well-defined semantics, and (2) to combine fuzzy control and logic-based high-level control. In the sequel, we show how these concepts can be used beneficially to formulate compact solutions for tasks such as *Fetch&Carry*. While we only give a preliminary specification here, for our future work we aim at deploying these programs to our domestic robot platform, which participated successfully at RoboCup@Home competitions in the past.

The rest of this paper is organised as follows. In Section 2, we give a brief introduction to the robot programming and planning language Readylog and the situation calculus, which Readylog is based on. We recapitulate previous work on integrating fuzzy sets and fuzzy control structures into Golog in Section 3, before we show our qualitative domain description in Section 4. In particular, we define necessary qualitative predicates for the domestic service robotics domain and define fuzzy control structures to enable the robot to cope with qualitative predicates. We conclude with Section 5.

2   The Situation Calculus and Golog

The Situation Calculus [10] is a second order language with equality which allows for reasoning about actions and their effects. The world evolves from an initial situation due to primitive actions. Possible world histories are represented by sequences of actions. The situation calculus distinguishes three different sorts: *actions*, *situations*, and domain dependent *objects*. A special binary function symbol $do : action \times situation \rightarrow situation$ exists, with $do(a, s)$ denoting the situation which arises after performing action a in situation s. The constant S_0 denotes the initial situation, i.e. the situation where no actions have yet occurred. We abbreviate the expression $do(a_n, \ldots do(a_1, S_0) \ldots)$ with $do([a_1, \ldots, a_n], S_0)$.

The state the world is in is characterized by functions and relations with a situation as their last argument. They are called *functional* and *relational fluents*, respectively. The third sort of the situation calculus is the sort *action*. For each action one has to specify a *precondition axiom* stating under which conditions it is possible to perform the respective action and *effect axioms* formulating how the action changes the world in terms of the specified fluents. An action precondition axiom has the form $Poss(a(\boldsymbol{x}), s) \equiv \Phi(\boldsymbol{x}, s)$ where the binary predicate $Poss \subseteq action \times situation$ denotes when an action can be executed, and $\boldsymbol{x}$ stands for the arguments of action a. After having specified when it is physically possible to perform an action, it remains to state how the respective action changes the world. This is done by so-called successor state axioms [11].

READYLOG [4] is our variant of GOLOG [9] and also makes use of Reiter's BATs as described above. The aim of designing the language READYLOG was to create a GOLOG dialect which supports the programming of the high-level control of agents or robots in dynamic real-time domains such as domestic environments or robotic soccer. READYLOG borrows ideas from [9,8,3,7,1] and features the following constructs: (1) sequence $(a; b)$, (2) non-deterministic choice between actions $(a|b)$, (3) solve a Markov Decision Process (MDP) $(solve(p, h)$, p is a GOLOG program, h is the MDP's solution horizon), (4) test actions $(?(c))$, (5) event-interrupt $(waitFor(c))$, (6) conditionals $(if(c, a_1, a_2))$, (7) loops $(while(c, a_1))$, (8) condition-bounded execution $(withCtrl(c, a_1))$, (9) concurrent execution of programs $(pconc(p_1, p_2))$, (10) probabilistic actions $(prob(val_{prob}, a_1, a_2))$, (11) probabilistic (offline) projection $(pproj(c, a_1))$, and (12) procedures $(proc(name(parameters), body))$. The idea of GOLOG to combine planning with programming was accounted for in READYLOG by integrating decision-theoretic planning; only partially specified programs which leave certain decisions open, which then are taken by the controller based on an optimization theory, are needed.

A nice feature of GOLOG and READYLOG is that its semantics is based on the situation calculus. That means that both languages have a formal semantics and properties of programs can be proved formally. We refer the interested reader to [4] for the complete formal definition of the language. Golog languages come with run-time interpreters usually programmed in Prolog. Also, a READYLOG implementation is available in Prolog.

3   Qualitative Fluents and Fuzzy Controllers in Golog

In this section, we briefly go over our previous work on integrating fuzzy fluents and fuzzy controllers into Golog. For technical details we refer to [5,6].

3.1   Fuzzy Fluents

The essence of qualitative representations is to find appropriate equivalence classes for a number of quantitative values and to group them together in these qualitative classes. Fuzzy set theory seems appealing as it avoids sharp boundaries of the classes: a quantitative value can be, for instance, in two classes at the same time, the transition between two neighbouring classes can be designed as being smooth. This characteristic can avoid problems every roboticist already has experienced: sensor values oscillate between two categories resulting in awkward behaviour of the robot.

Our formalisation of fuzzy fluents is based on the idea to extend ordinary functional fluents with a degree of membership to a certain qualitative category.

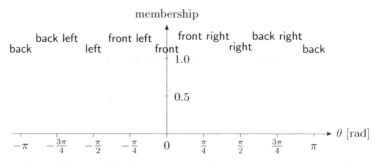

Fig. 1. Membership function for qualitative orientation at level 3

To use these fluents, one simply defines the different categories and membership values in the domain specification. An example for the orientation fluent is given in Fig. 1. What is further needed in order to do reasoning with these kinds of fluents, is a routine that restores a quantitative value from a qualitative category, that is, to *defuzzify* a category. In [5], we formalise a *centre-of-gravity defuzzifier* in the situation calculus. However, other defuzzifiers known from fuzzy set theory can easily be used as well.

For illustrating reasoning with qualitative positional information consider the following simple example. A robot is situated in a one dimensional room with a length of ten metric units. To keep things simple, we restrict ourselves to integer values for positions in the following. We have one single action called $gorel(d)$ denoting the relative movement of d units of the robot in its world. This action is always possible, i.e. $Poss(gorel(d), s) \equiv \top$. The action has impact on the fluent *pos* which denotes the absolute position of the robot in the world. The successor state axiom of *pos* is defined as

$$pos(do(a, s)) = y \equiv a = gorel(d) \land y = pos(s) + d \lor a \neq gorel(d) \land y = pos(s).$$

There is a table in the robot's world, its position is defined by the macro $pos_{table} = p \doteq p = 9$. In the initial situation, the robot is located at position 0, i.e. $pos(S_0) = 0$. We want to evaluate the robot's position and its distance to the table. Therefore we define a functional fluent $dist$ which returns the distance between the robot and the table:

$$dist(do(a, s)) = d \equiv \exists p_1.pos_{table} = p_1 \land \exists p_2.pos(do(a, s)) = p_2 \land d = p_1 - p_2.$$

We partition the distance in categories close, medium, and far, and introduce qualitative categories for the position of the robot as back, middle, and front. We give the (fuzzy) definition of those categories below, where we use (u_i, μ_i) as an abbreviation for $u = u_i \land \mu = \mu_i$. For instance, the fuzzy categories for the position of the robot in the world can be defined as

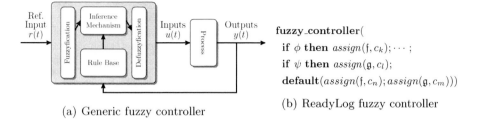

(a) Generic fuzzy controller

(b) ReadyLog fuzzy controller

fuzzy_controller(
    if ϕ **then** $assign(\mathfrak{f}, c_k); \cdots$;
    if ψ **then** $assign(\mathfrak{g}, c_l)$;
    default$(assign(\mathfrak{f}, c_n); assign(\mathfrak{g}, c_m)))$

Fig. 2. Generic architecture and ReadyLog statement for a fuzzy controller

$$\mathfrak{F}(position, u, \mu_u) \equiv$$
$$(position = \mathsf{back} \supset (0, 0.25) \vee (1, 0.75) \vee (2, 0.75) \vee (3, 0.25)) \vee$$
$$(position = \mathsf{middle} \supset (3, 0.25) \vee (4, 0.75) \vee (5, 0.75) \vee (6, 0.25)) \vee$$
$$(position = \mathsf{front} \supset (6, 0.25) \vee (7, 0.75) \vee (8, 0.75) \vee (9, 0.5)),$$

Similary, the orientation relation can be defined. Note that $\mathfrak{F}(c, u, \mu)$ is our first-order definition of a fuzzy set for a linguistic category c with μ_u being the membership value of the quantitative value u denoting to which degree u belongs to c (see [5] for the complete axiomatization).

The robot can move around in integer steps. Restricting to integers presupposes that we need to use an altered version $cog'(c)$ of the centre-of-gravity defuzzyfier formula: $cog'(c) \doteq \lfloor cog(c) \rfloor$.

Suppose now that the robot's control program contains the action gorel(far) mentioning the qualitative term far. At which position will the robot end up in situation $s = do(\mathsf{gorel(far)}, S_0)$? The qualitative category has to be handled in the successor state axiom. We need to apply the function $cog'(c)$ to the qualitative term which yields always a quantitative representative. The extended definition of the successor state axiom then looks as follows:

$$pos(do(a, s)) = y \equiv$$
$$a = \mathsf{gorel}(d) \wedge ((\exists d', c, u, \mu_u.\mathfrak{F}(c, u, \mu_u) \wedge c = d \wedge d' = cog'(d)) \vee$$
$$(\neg\exists c, u, \mu_u.\mathfrak{F}(c, u, \mu_u) \wedge d' = d)) \wedge \ y = pos(s) + d' \vee a \neq \mathsf{gorel}(d) \wedge y = pos(s).$$

Note that we rely on the completeness of the specification of the membership function here, so that if d is a linguistic term there always is an entry in the membership function for that d. Otherwise we could end up computing y as the sum of a real and category. Our formalization yields is$(pos(do(\mathsf{gorel(far)}, S_0)), \mathsf{front})$, i.e. the robot ends up in the front part of its world after executing gorel(far). Note that "is" denotes a predicate in our framework to query fuzzy fluent values. It will be also used in Algorithms 1 and 2.

3.2   Fuzzy Controller in Readylog

Fig. 2 shows a schematic fuzzy controller. The quantitative sensor values $y(t)$, together with some reference input $r(t)$, which describes the vital state of the system, need to be fuzzified, i.e. the membership to a certain class needs to be determined. The *Inference Mechanism* uses these fuzzified input values together with a rule base of fuzzy rules to select the appropriate control output. The output as such uses fuzzy categories and thus must be defuzzified to serve as an input $u(t)$ for the real world (the control output). The output of the real world process serves as the sensor input for the next control step.

To map this into Readylog, we introduce a statement **fuzzy_controller** which takes a rule base as input and returns the control output (cf. also [6]). We give the general form of this statement in Fig. 2(b).

A fuzzy rule base in Readylog is interpreted as follows. Each matching fuzzy rule will be replaced by its consequence, i.e. a special assignment statement, while non-matching ones contribute *nil*. The assignment statement $assign(\mathfrak{f}, c)$ used in the controller is a Readylog action which assigns the qualitative category c to the fuzzy fluent $\mathfrak{f}$. As defuzzifier, we use the centre-of-gravity (*cog*). Depending on the assigned output category, control actions can be sent to the actuators. The condition of a rule can be a complex formula over fuzzy fluents stating for example: *is the object close and very close?* Sometimes, it may happen that no given rule in a controller block matches at all, nevertheless some output would be required. We therefore define an additional statement **default**$(assign(\mathfrak{f}, c); \ldots)$, which is interpreted in case the control output was the *nil* action after evaluating the rule base. This gives the basic idea how a rule base is encoded in Readylog. We left out the formal definition of the construct. It can be found in [6].

4   Applications in a Domestic Service Robotics Domain

In this section we give two examples for using fuzzy fluents and fuzzy controllers in the domestic robot domain. We start with a brief description of the tasks. Before we show the example Readylog programs, we define the required distance and orientation relations.

4.1   A Domestic Service Robotics Domain (RoboCup@Home)

In the RoboCup@Home competition *service and assistive robot technology* that is highly relevant for future personal domestic applications should be demonstrated [12]. In the competition, the robots have to fulfil tasks such as:

- *FollowMe!*: the robot has to follow a human through the apartment;
- *Fetch&Carry*: a human names known objects and the robot needs to fetch them. The human may give hints such as: "The teddy is near the TV";
- *Walk'n'Talk*: in a guidance phase, a human instructor leads the robot around in an apartment and tells it certain landmarks such as "kitchen table", "TV set", or "fridge". In a second phase the robot is instructed to navigate to some of these just learnt places.

The rules of the RoboCup@Home competition state that a robot—to be successful in the competition—is to be endowed with a certain set of basic abilities, like navigation, person and object recognition, and manipulation. Furthermore, fast and easy calibration and setup is essential, as the ultimate goal is to have a robot up and running out of the box. Also, human-robot interaction has to be achieved in a natural way, i.e. interacting with the robot is allowed only using natural language (that is by speech) and gesture commands. As mentioned in the introduction, humans tend to make use of qualitative concepts such as *near* or *far*. With introducing suitable qualitative concepts, we bridge the gap between human and robot representations of domestic environments.

But not all parts of the solution of a domestic task require deliberation. For some decisions simple reactive controllers are sufficient. However, these reactive mechanisms also need to understand qualitative concepts. Here, we can make use of our embedding of fuzzy controllers in Readylog. In the next sections, we show some specification examples.

4.2   Qualitative Representations for Domestic Environments

One very important form of interaction between a human and a robot in the RoboCup@Home domain is to give the robot some hints where objects might be located. Based on Clementini, Felici, and Hernandez [2], we deploy qualitative representations for positional and directional information that can be used to instruct the robot. The position of a *primary object* is represented by a pair of distance and orientation relations with respect to a *reference object*. Both relations depend on a so-called *frame of reference* which accounts for several factors like the size of objects and different points of view.

In the domestic settings we can define different distance relations according to: (1) external references such as the maximal size of the apartment: *"The plant is at the far end of the corridor"*; (2) intrinsic references used in relating objects to each other such as room or table: *"The cup is on the table close to the plate"* vs. *"The teddy is close to the TV"*; and (3) an appropriate distance system. In our domestic environment we suggest to make finer distinctions in the neighbourhood of the reference object than in the periphery. Hence, we can distinguish the scales $dist\text{-}scale \in \{\text{apartment}, \text{room}, \text{object}(o)\}$, where object o refers to objects such as *table*, or *bookshelf*.

Hence, we must provide a procedure *analyseHint*, which takes a hint given by the human instructor and distills the position of the object, the frame of reference as well as the scale from that hint. For instance: (a) *"The plant is far on the left side of the corridor"*; the primary object is the plant, the point of view is the view point of the robot, the distance scale is set to the size of the corridor. (b) *"The cup is on the table close to the plate"*; the primary object is the cup, the reference object is the plate, the distance scale is set to the size of the table. No orientation relation is given. (c) *"The teddy is close to the TV"*; the primary object is the teddy, the reference object is the TV, the distance scale should be set to the size of the room where the TV is located. Again, no orientation relation is given.

With this procedure at hand, we can adopt our fuzzy fluents for the qualitative distance and orientation. The membership function for the orientation fluent was given in Fig. 1. We can define the membership function for distance in a similar way. In the next section, we give an idea of how these fluents can be used for programming the robot.

4.3   Qualitative Notions in High-level Programs

Now that we have proposed an initial modelling of qualitative representations of positional information in a domestic setting we show how we can make use of these representations within our existing high-level control mechanism. Algorithm 2 shows a slightly abstracted version of a Readylog control program for the *Fetch&Carry* task.

The procedure *fetch_and_carry* takes the object that should be fetched and a user hint as input. At first, the action *analyseHint* is executed. This is a complex action which involves natural language processing. From the user phrase, the frame of reference for orientation and distance as well as the distance scale is extracted (as pointed out in the previous section). The action's effect axioms are changing fluent values for the fluents describing the orientation's frame of reference, the distance system, the distance scale, the distance's frame of reference as well as the qualitative position of the reference object. The next statement in the program is a so-called *"pick"* statement (π) which is used to instantiate the free variables in the logical formula in the next test action (denoted by the "?"). The whole construct can be seen as an existential quantifier, and the effect is that the variables pos, for_θ, for_{dist} are bound. The next step is to call the search routine with these parameters. The search involves the activation of decision-theoretic planning (*solve*) at a position where the object is meant to be according to the user's hint. The position is defuzzified, taking the frame of reference information into account. That is, the position based on the distance scales and the quantitative orientations given the points of view etc. can now be calculated. The action *lookForObject* again is a complex action which actually tries to seek the object.

4.4   Domestic Golog Fuzzy Controllers

As detailed in Sect. 3.2 we integrated fuzzy controllers in Golog in [6]. If (a part of) a task does not require high-level decision making (decision-theoretic planning as used in the previous section), but can instead be solved with a reactive mechanism it may still be convenient to make use of the qualitative representations. One example in the domestic setting is the *"FollowMe!"* test. The control of the follow behaviour can be modelled quite straight-forwardly.

In the following we show a simple rule base that can be used to solve the *FollowMe!* task. The rule base for this test could look like Alg. 1. As we stated in Sect. 3, a rule base consists of a number of if-then rules where both, the antecedent and the consequence, mention fuzzy fluents. So, the first rule reads as follows: *"if the distance to the user is close and its speed is slow, then set the robot speed to slow"*, the second rule reads *"if the distance to the user is far and its speed is medium, then set the robot speed to fast"*, where user is the person

proc follow_me_rulebase
    fuzzy_controller(...;
        if is$_\star$(dist$_{user}$, close, speed$_{user}$, slow) **then** $assign$(speed$_{robot}$, slow);
        if is$_\star$(dist$_{user}$, far, speed$_{user}$, medium) **then** $assign$(speed$_{robot}$, fast);
        ...; **default**(speed$_{robot}$, medium))) ;/* **end fuzzy_controller** */
    applySpeed()
endproc

Algorithm 1. A fuzzy controller for the *"FollowMe!"* test

proc fetch_and_carry(*object*, *hint*)
    analyseHint(*hint*);
    $\pi(pos, for_\theta, for_{dist}).[ori\_type(for_\theta) \wedge dist\_system(for_{dist}) \wedge$
        $dist\_scale(for_{dist}) \wedge dist\_type(for_{dist}) \wedge object\_pos(pos)]?;$
    search(*object*, *pos*, for_θ, for_{dist})
endproc
proc search(*object*, *pos*, for_θ, for_{dist})
    solve(**while** ¬objectFound **do**
        pickBest(*search_pos* = defuzzify(*pos*, for_θ, for_{dist}));
        lookForObjectAt(*object*, *search_pos*);
      endwhile, H) /* *end solve with horizon H* */
    pickup_and_return(*object*);
endproc

Algorithm 2. A Readylog program for the *"Fetch&Carry"* test

to be followed. The $is_\star$ predicate is defined in [6] and denotes the conjunction of the fuzzy fluents $dist_{user}$ and $speed_{user}$. If neither condition applies, the default speed selection is set to medium. Finally, the $speed_{robot}$ fuzzy fluent has to be defuzzified, that is, a quantitative value is calculated for the qualitative class. Then, we can apply the quantitative speed to the robot motors.

By using a fuzzy controller with its simple concept of a set of rules we alleviate the specification of the control. We can use linguistic terms to describe the intended behaviour and leave the details on what values to send to the mid- and low-level modules to our automatic machinery.

5   Conclusions

In this paper, we presented an approach on how high-level robot controllers could deal with qualitative representations for domestic environments. For robot competitions such as RoboCup@Home this is useful, as the robot needs to be instructed by a human operator by natural language. Having qualitative representations in place allows for more human-like instructions as humans tend to use qualitative (spatial) representations such as *far* or *left-of*. In our previous work, we defined qualitative fluents in the situation calculus based on fuzzy sets. This allows us to define qualitative fluents in a well-founded way. Particularly, it gives a semantics to derive quantitative values from qualitative categories and vice versa. Further, we proposed a semantics for fuzzy controller in Golog. Both, the definition of fuzzy fluents and fuzzy controllers, allows us to write programs mentioning qualitative values in a straight-forward way.

For the RoboCup@Home tasks *Fetch&Carry* and *FollowMe!* we showed example implementations, how qualitative representations and fuzzy controllers could be beneficially deployed. While these programs only reflect first ideas of deploying fuzzy fluents and fuzzy controllers in domestic robot applications, we aim at implementing different controllers and programs making use of the fuzzy notions for our future work on our domestic robot platform.

References

1. Boutilier, C., Reiter, R., Soutchanski, M., Thrun, S.: Decision-theoretic, high-level agent programming in the situation calculus. In: Proc. 17th Nat'l Conf. on Artificial Intelligence (AAAI 2000), pp. 355–362 (2000)
2. Clementini, E., Felice, P.D., Hernandez, D.: Qualitative representation of positional information. Artificial Intelligence 95(2), 317–356 (1997)
3. De Giacomo, G., Lésperance, Y., Levesque, H.J.: ConGolog, A concurrent programming language based on situation calculus. Artificial Intelligence 121(1–2), 109–169 (2000)
4. Ferrein, A., Lakemeyer, G.: Logic-based robot control in highly dynamic domains. Robotics and Autonomous Systems, Special Issue on Semantic Knowledge in Robotics 56(11), 980–991 (2008)
5. Ferrein, A., Schiffer, S., Lakemeyer, G.: A Fuzzy Set Semantics for Qualitative Fluents in the Situation Calculus. In: Xiong, C.-H., Liu, H., Huang, Y., Xiong, Y.L. (eds.) ICIRA 2008. LNCS (LNAI), vol. 5314, pp. 498–509. Springer, Heidelberg (2008)
6. Ferrein, A., Schiffer, S., Lakemeyer, G.: Embedding fuzzy controllers into golog. In: Proc. IEEE Int'l Conf. on Fuzzy Systems (FUZZ IEEE 2009), pp. 894–899 (2009)
7. Grosskreutz, H.: Probabilistic projection and belief update in the pGOLOG framework. In: Proceedings of the 2nd Cognitive Robotics Workshop (CogRob 2000) at the 14th European Conference on Artificial Intelligence (ECAI 2000), pp. 34–41 (2000)
8. Grosskreutz, H., Lakemeyer, G.: cc-Golog – An Action Language with Continuous Change. Logic Journal of the IGPL 11(2), 179–221 (2003)
9. Levesque, H.J., Reiter, R., Lespérance, Y., Lin, F., Scherl, R.B.: Golog: A logic programming language for dynamic domains. J. Logic Program 31(1-3), 59–84 (1997)
10. McCarthy, J.: Situations, actions and causal laws. TR. Stanford University (1963)
11. Reiter, R.: Knowledge in Action. Logical Foundations for Specifying and Implementing Dynamical Systems. MIT Press (2001)
12. Wisspeintner, T., van der Zant, T., Iocchi, L., Schiffer, S.: Robocup@home: Scientific Competition and Benchmarking for Domestic Service Robots. Interaction Studies. Special Issue on Robots in the Wild 10(3), 392–426 (2009)
13. van der Zant, T., Wisspeintner, T.: RoboCup X: A Proposal for a New League Where Robocup Goes Real World. In: Bredenfeld, A., Jacoff, A., Noda, I., Takahashi, Y. (eds.) RoboCup 2005. LNCS (LNAI), vol. 4020, pp. 166–172. Springer, Heidelberg (2006)
14. van der Zant, T., Wisspeintner, T.: Robotic Soccer. In: RoboCup@Home: Creating and Benchmarking Tomorrows Service Robot Applications, pp. 521–528. I-Tech Education and Publishing (2007)

Minimum Jerk-Based Control
for a Three Dimensional Bipedal Robot

Amira Aloulou and Olfa Boubaker

National Institute of Applied Sciences and Technology, INSAT Centre Urbain Nord,
BP 676 - 1080 Tunis, Tunisia
olfa.boubaker@insat.rnu.tn

Abstract. In this paper, an optimized gait pattern generation is produced for a three dimensional bipedal robot using a Minimum Jerk criterion in the single support phase. Three approaches are introduced and compared in this framework. The Minimum Jerk based control approaches are the point-to-point, the Via-point and the shape function trajectory. Simulation results show that the point-to-point Minimum Jerk-based control cannot be satisfactory since the supposed swinging leg of the bipedal robot doesn´t lift off the ground. However, a bipedal stable human-like movement is guaranteed using both last approaches.

Keywords: Bipedal robot, Minimum Jerk criterion, Gait pattern generation.

1   Introduction

Present researches work to make humanoid robots more and more autonomous so they can assist human in social activities. In that context, one of the most important features required for a humanoid robot is its mobility and its ability to move like a human being. In this framework, gait pattern generation is the key problem of research dedicated to bipedal robots.

A typical walking cycle may include three phases [1]: the single support phase (SSP) that occurs when one limb is pivoted to the ground while the other is swinging in the air from the rear to the front. The impact phase (IP) occurs when the toe of the forward foot starts touching the ground. The double support phase (DSP) is the last stage of the walking cycle, when both limbs remain in contact with the ground. As soon as the third phase of the swing foot ends, the foot of the supporting leg goes into its own first stage of the swing motion.

Two categories of works dedicated to the bipedal walking pattern generation can be distinguished [2]. Studies assimilating robots as elementary models [3] and works considering the whole and complete robotic model using all morphological data including mass, location of center of mass and inertia of each link [4, 5].

For the first approach, the linear inverted pendulum model (LIPM) concept [6] is the mostly used concept in order to simplify the trajectory generation task. The LIPM method is founded on the supposition that during the SSP as the humanoid robot is

S. Jeschke, H. Liu, and D. Schilberg (Eds.): ICIRA 2011, Part II, LNAI 7102, pp. 251–262, 2011.
© Springer-Verlag Berlin Heidelberg 2011

supporting its body on one leg, its main dynamics can be modeled by an inverted pendulum joining up the center of mass of the whole robot to the supporting foot. Therefore, LIPM assumes that the humanoid robot consists of a point mass body and a massless telescopic leg. To achieve stable walking trajectories, many reference generation algorithms apply the Zero Moment Point (ZMP) Criterion to the LIPM [2,7,8] even if LIMP doesn't consider the dynamics of the swing leg. If the legs are heavy, the omission of the swing leg's dynamics can generate tracking problems and disturbances during the SSP. To attenuate these stability problems, some studies [9, 10] proposed a switching LIPM between a one-mass model during the double support phase and a two-mass model when the SSP occurs. In [11], a virtual LIPM called VLIPM is used to reach the desired center of gravity (COG) position and velocity without modifying the foot placement of the biped robot. The walking path generation based on the VLIPM consists on using a virtual supporting point (VSP) to compensate the margin between the virtual modified and desired foot placements.

For the second class of works relying on the accuracy of the robotic model, studies related to this approach can be classified into two groups. The first group focused on the generation of a simple reference trajectory and a trajectory tracking control [12]. The second group opted for the recourse to an objective function composed of one or more terms to minimize [13]. In most times, criterions to optimize in bipedal gait pattern generation are total time execution, advance velocity, torque or energy [14, 15].

On the other hand, the jerk defined as the third derivative of position or the time derivative of acceleration of the desired trajectory can be an attractive objective function to be minimized for generating bipedal robots pattern gait. It can be noted that the Minimum Jerk problem has barely and mainly been used to ensure optimal trajectories for arm manipulators [16, 17, 18, 19]. Only very few works using Minimum Jerk criterion were devoted to optimize humanoid motion, in particular those related to arm movements [20] or gait pattern generation [21]. Yet, it can be shown that Minimum Jerk trajectories are similar to human joint movements and have the capability to limit robot vibrations [18].

In this paper, an optimized gait pattern generation in single support phase is produced for a three dimensional bipedal robot using a Minimum Jerk criterion. Three approaches are introduced and compared in this framework. The paper is organized as follows: In the next section, the three dimensional bipedal will be presented and kinematic and dynamic models will be developed. Three approaches of the Minimum Jerk based control will be introduced and compared in section 3. Simulation results will be finally presented in section 4.

2   The Three dimensional Bipedal Robot

2.1   Morphology

The bipedal robot prototype [22] is composed of seven links associated to 12 DOF. Fig.1 and Table 1 show the involved rotations for each link.

Table 1. Rigid bodies and joints

Link description	Joint description	Degrees of Freedom
C1:Right foot	J1:Right ankle	$\xi_1=[0 \quad \theta_1 \quad \theta_2]$
C2:Right leg	J2:Right knee	$\xi_2=[0 \quad \theta_1 \quad \theta_3]$
C3:Right thigh	J3:Right hip	$\xi_3=[\theta_4 \quad \theta_5 \quad \theta_6]$
C4:Pelvis	J7:Passive joint	$\xi_4=[0 \quad 0 \quad 0]$
C5:Left thigh	J4:Left hip	$\xi_5=[\theta_7 \quad \theta_8 \quad \theta_9]$
C6:Le t leg	J5:Left knee	$\xi_6=[0 \quad \theta_{10} \quad \theta_{11}]$
C7:Left foot	J6:Left ankle	$\xi_7=[0 \quad \theta_{10} \quad \theta_{12}]$

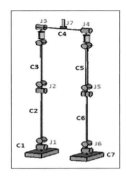

Fig. 1. The bipedal robot prototype

Each rigid body Ci of the humanoid robot is characterized by the following physical parameters:

- $m_i \in \Re$: Mass of the link C_i
- $i_i \in \Re$: Inertia about the center of mass of the link C_i
- $k_i \in \Re$: Proximal distance defined as the distance from the center of gravity to the connect joint of the previous link C_{i-1}
- $li \in \Re$: Distal distance defined as the distance from the center of gravity to the connect joint of the next link $Ci+1$

The kinematic and dynamic models will be elaborated in the three dimensional space, as a result the three dimensional parameters are:

- $M_i \in \Re^{3\times3}$: mass matrix of the link C_i given by:

$$M_i = \text{Diag} \begin{bmatrix} m_i & m_i & m_i \end{bmatrix}^T$$

- $I_i \in \Re^{3\times3}$: Inertia matrix about the center of mass of the link Ci described by:

$$I_i = \text{Diag} \begin{bmatrix} i_{ix} & i_{iy} & i_{iz} \end{bmatrix}^T$$

- K_i and $L_i \in \Re^{3\times3}$: Proximal and distal distance vectors of the link C_i given by:

$$K_i = [0\ 0\ k_i]^T \quad \text{and} \quad L_i = [0\ 0\ l_i]^T$$

All physical parameters involved in the kinematic and dynamic models are given by Table 2.

Table 2. Physical parameters

Link	Mass (Kg)	Inertia about centre of mass (Kg m^2)			Ki (m)	Li (m)
Right foot	1.015	0.001	0.001	0.002	0.034	0.034
Right leg	3.255	0.051	0.051	0.004	0.184	0.241
Right thigh	7.000	0.113	0.113	0.017	0.184	0.240
Pelvis	9.940	0.112	0.112	0.472	0.021	0.178
Left thigh	7.000	0.113	0.113	0.017	0.240	0.184
Left leg	3.255	0.051	0.051	0.004	0.241	0.184
Left foot	1.015	0.001	0.001	0.002	0.034	0.034

2.2   Kinematic Model

The robot kinematic model is then given by:

$$X_i = A_i (L_i - K_i) + X_{i-1} \ , \ \forall \, i \in [1, ... ,7] \,. \tag{1}$$

where $X_i \in \mathfrak{R}^{3 \times 1}$ is the Cartesian position of center of gravity of each link Ci, and $A_i \in \mathfrak{R}^{3 \times 3}$ is the transformation matrix from the body coordinate system to the inertial coordinate system [23].

2.3   Dynamic Model

For each link Ci, generalized motion equations for the rotation and the translation are used such as [22]:

$$I_i \dot{\omega}_i = f_i + F_i + F_{i+1} + G_i + G_{i+1} + \tau_i + \tau_{i+1} \,. \tag{2}$$

$$M_i \ddot{X}_i = M_i g + \Gamma_i - \Gamma_{i+1} \,. \tag{3}$$

where:

$\dot{\omega}_i \in \mathfrak{R}^{3 \times 1}$: Angular acceleration of the link Ci.

F_i and $F_{i+1} \in \mathfrak{R}^{3 \times 1}$: Torques due to the holonom force applied respectively to the proximal and distal articulation of the link Ci expressed in the body coordinate system.

G_i and $G_{i+1} \in \mathfrak{R}^{3 \times 1}$: Non-holonom torques applied respectively to the proximal and distal articulation of the link Ci expressed in the body coordinate system.

τ_i and $\tau_{i+1} \in \mathfrak{R}^{3 \times 1}$: Muscular torques applied respectively to the proximal and distal articulation of the link Ci expressed in the body coordinate system.

$\ddot{X}_i \in \mathfrak{R}^{3 \times 1}$: Linear acceleration of the link Ci.

Γ_i and $\Gamma_{i+1} \in \mathfrak{R}^{3 \times 1}$: Holonom forces applied respectively to the proximal and distal articulation of the link Ci expressed in the inertial coordinate system.

$f_i \in \mathfrak{R}^{3 \times 1}$: Intrinsic torque of the link Ci expressed in the body coordinates system (x_i, y_i, z_i) and relating angular velocity to the link inertia. It is described by:

$$f_i = f(W_i) = I_i W_i \times W_i \,. \tag{4}$$

Human body's balance of forces and torques reveals that humanoid limbs are subject to three kinds of forces: holonom, non holonom and muscular forces. Fig.2 shows the applied forces and torques to the humanoid lower body. Holonom forces and torques result of the interaction between limbs. They are described by:

$$F_i = \pm K_i \times A_i^T \Gamma_i. \tag{5}$$

$$F_{i+1} = \pm L_i \times A_i^T \Gamma_{i+1} \,. \tag{6}$$

A limb is also subject to a certain effort in order to remain aligned with the previous limb. This effort is resulting from non-holonom torques described by:

$$G_i = \pm A_i^T A_{i-1} R_i \Lambda_i \,. \tag{7}$$

$$G_{i+1} = \pm R_{i+1} \Lambda_{i+1} \,. \tag{8}$$

where:

$\Lambda_i \in \mathfrak{R}^{2\times 1}$: Non-holonom torque applied to the proximal articulation of the link Ci expressed in the body coordinate system of the previous link Ci-1.

$\Lambda_{i+1} \in \mathfrak{R}^{2\times 1}$: Non holonom torque applied to the distal articulation of the link Ci expressed in the body coordinate system.

R_i and $R_{i+1} \in \mathfrak{R}^{3\times 2}$: Matrix of mechanical relations between the bipedal rigid bodies that are subject to non-holonom forces.

Mechanic torques are described by:

$$\tau_i = \pm A_i^T A_{i-1} T_i . \tag{9}$$

$$\tau_{i+1} = \pm T_{i+1} . \tag{10}$$

where:

$T_i \in \mathfrak{R}^{3\times 1}$: torque applied to the proximal articulation of the link Ci expressed in the body coordinate system of the previous link Ci-1.

$T_{i+1} \in \mathfrak{R}^{3\times 1}$: torque applied to the distal articulation of the link Ci expressed in the body coordinate system.

The bipedal robotic model can be finally written as:

$$P_1 z_1 = P_2 + P_3 \Gamma + P_4 \Lambda + P_5 T . \tag{11}$$

Where z_1 is a state vector, Γ, Λ and T are the holonom, non-holonom and muscular forces and torque vectors respectively. P_1, P_2, P_3, P_4 and P_5 are matrices of appropriate dimensions including all morphological data of the bipedal robot and products between proximal/distal distances and Euler's transformation matrices.

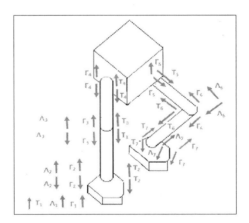

Fig. 2. Applied forces and torques

3   Minimum Jerk-Based Control

From (11), the general robotic dynamical model is obtained as following:

$$J(\theta)\ddot{\theta} + H(\theta, \dot{\theta}) + G(\theta) = D.\tau . \tag{12}$$

where $\theta = [\theta_1 \quad \cdots \quad \theta_{12}]^T, \dot{\theta} = [\dot{\theta}_1 \quad \cdots \quad \dot{\theta}_{12}]^T, \ddot{\theta} = [\ddot{\theta}_1 \quad \cdots \quad \ddot{\theta}_{12}]^T$ are the joints angular position, velocity and acceleration vectors, respectively. $J(\theta) \in \Re^{12 \times 12}$ is the inertia matrix, $H(\theta, \dot{\theta}) \in \Re^{12 \times 1}$ is the vector of the Coriolis and centripetal torques, $G(\theta) \in \Re^{12 \times 1}$ is the gravity vector. The matrix $D \in \Re^{12 \times 12}$ is a nonsingular input map matrix whereas $\tau \in \Re^{12 \times 1}$ is the control input vector. We impose to the robotic model (12) the following second order linear input-output behavior [22]:

$$\left(\ddot{\theta} - \ddot{\theta}_d(t)\right) + K_v\left(\dot{\theta} - \dot{\theta}_d(t)\right) + K_P\left(\theta - \theta_d(t)\right) = 0. \tag{13}$$

where $K_v \in \Re^{12*12}$ and $K_P \in \Re^{12*12}$ are two positive definite diagonal matrices chosen to guarantee global stability, desired performances and decoupling proprieties for the controlled system. If λ is the desired bandwidth, then to obtain a critically damped closed-loop performance, we must select:

$$K_v = \text{diag} [2\lambda] \quad \text{and} \quad K_p = \text{diag} [\lambda^2]. \tag{14}$$

The control law obtained from relations (12) and (13) is then described by:

$$\tau = D^{-1}\left(J(\theta)\left[\ddot{\theta}_d(t) - K_v\left(\dot{\theta} - \dot{\theta}_d(t)\right) - K_P(\theta - \theta_d(t))\right] + H(\theta, \dot{\theta}) + G(\theta)\right). \tag{15}$$

In the following, the desired trajectories $\ddot{\theta}_d(t)$, $\dot{\theta}_d(t)$ and $\theta_d(t)$ will be defined using the Minimum Jerk principle. Our objective is to minimize the quantity of jerk done by the bipedal robot so that the final trajectory is a smooth and graceful one.

The Minimum Jerk Principle

Many works have assumed that maximizing the smoothness of dynamical systems equals to minimizing the mean-square jerk [20]. The term jerk means a sudden and abrupt motion and is defined mathematically as the third time derivative of position of desired joint trajectory. The criterion function to be minimized is then:

$$C_J = \int_{t_i}^{t_f} 0.5\left(\dddot{\theta}_d\right)^2 dt \tag{16}$$

where C_J is the criterion function to be minimized, t is time, t_i is the time where the motion starts and t_f is the time where it ends. Even if not essential, some additional terms could be included in the criterion function to minimize a weighted sum of multiple criteria. In [17], for example, the objective function to be minimized is the integral of a weighted sum of squared jerk and the execution time.

In this paper, only the mean-square jerk will be considered. A fifth order polynomial trajectory will be generated for desired joint positions using the Minimum Jerk principle. Each desired joint position θ_i is described by:

$$\theta_{id}(t) = a_i . t^5 + b_i . t^4 + c_i . t^3 + d_i . t^2 + e_i . t + f_i . \tag{17}$$

where a_i, b_i, c_i, d_i, e_i and f_i are some constants to be determined for $i = 1, \ldots, 12$. The desired joint velocities and accelerations are then deduced as:

$$\dot{\theta}_{id}(t) = 5a_i . t^4 + 4b_i . t^3 + 3c_i . t^2 + 2d_i . t + e_i . \tag{18}$$

$$\ddot{\theta}_{id}(t) = 20a_i.t^3 + 12b_i.t^2 + 6c_i.t + 2d_i. \qquad (19)$$

Boundary conditions are given for i = 1,…,12 by:

$$\theta_{id}(t_i) = \alpha_i \qquad \dot{\theta}_{id}(t_i) = 0 \qquad \ddot{\theta}_{id}(t_i) = 0$$

$$\theta_{id}(t_f) = \beta_i \qquad \dot{\theta}_{id}(t_f) = 0 \qquad \ddot{\theta}_{id}(t_f) = 0$$

where α_i and β_i are joint positions at boundaries.

Minimum Jerk with the Point-to-Point Method

This methodology is based on very few data to provide in order to generate an expected trajectory. The algorithm needs only the expression of the function to minimize and two points' coordinates corresponding to the initial and final times [20]. For each angular position θ_i and its angular velocity and acceleration, we have:

$$
\begin{pmatrix} a_i \\ b_i \\ c_i \\ d_i \\ e_i \\ f_i \end{pmatrix}
=
\begin{pmatrix}
t_i^5 & t_i^4 & t_i^3 & t_i^2 & t_i & 1 \\
t_f^5 & t_f^4 & t_f^3 & t_f^2 & t_f & 1 \\
5t_i^4 & 4t_i^3 & 3t_i^2 & 2t_i & 1 & 0 \\
5t_f^4 & 4t_f^3 & 3t_f^2 & 2t_f & 1 & 0 \\
20t_i^3 & 12t_i^2 & 6t_i & 2 & 0 & 0 \\
20t_f^3 & 12t_f^2 & 6t_f & 2 & 0 & 0
\end{pmatrix}^{-1}
\begin{pmatrix} \alpha_i \\ \beta_i \\ 0 \\ 0 \\ 0 \\ 0 \end{pmatrix}. \qquad (20)
$$

Minimum Jerk with the via-Point Method

In the via-points method, the trajectory took by each angular position must be specified not only by indicating the initial and final positions but also by stating a certain number of intermediate desired positions [18, 20]. These positions should be characterized by the times at which they should be reached. As a consequence, the more there are intermediate positions provided, the more the trajectory imposed is precisely determined. The software implementation implies a multiple run of the algorithm executed between couple of intermediate positions.

Minimum Jerk with a Trajectory Shape

We suggest, here, replacing the fifth order polynomial joint desired trajectory (17) used in both point-to-point and via-points approaches by a whole function expression that must satisfy, in the Cartesian space, a general trajectory shape we aim to reach. As the bipedal robot foot must follow a trajectory similar to the one took by the human foot during the achievement of a walking step, we choose a semi-elliptic shape for the desired Cartesian trajectory described by:

$$X_{des} = \begin{bmatrix} a * \cos(\theta_{id}(t)) & b & c * \sin(\theta_{id}(t)) \end{bmatrix}^T. \qquad (21)$$

where a is the width of the step, b is the gap between the two biped legs and c the maximal height of the step.

4   Simulation Results

Simulation results are obtained solving the dynamical robotic model (12) for the initial position $X_i = [0 \quad 0.1 \quad 0]^T$ and final position $X_f = [0.3 \quad 0.1 \quad 0]^T$ using biped physical data given by table 2 for the control law (15). For a given Cartesian position of the swing foot, an inverse kinematic modeling algorithm has been implemented to provide the corresponding angular positions of the bipedal robot. Matrices K_v and K_P are given by (14) for which we choose a constant bandwidth $\lambda = 10$. Desired position, velocity and acceleration trajectories to be followed are respectively described by (17), (18) and (19). For each Minimum Jerk approach, the parameters a_i, b_i, c_i, d_i, e_i and f_i are differently computed.

Minimum Jerk with the Point-to-Point Method

The parameters a_i, b_i, c_i, d_i, e_i and f_i are computed using relation (20) for $t_i = 0s$ and $t_f = 3s$. In Fig.3 the supposed moving leg doesn't lift off the ground and just translates along the horizontal axis from the initial position to the final one.

Minimum Jerk with the via-Point Method

In this case, an intermediate desired position to be reached by the end-effector of the robot is considered. This leads to the building of a more complex numerical Minimum Jerk algorithm. Simulation results are shown by Fig.4 and Fig.5.

Minimum Jerk with a Trajectory Shape

In this case, the semi-elliptic shape (21) is imposed for the desired Cartesian trajectory where the width of the step, the gap between the two legs and the maximal height of step are respectively given by: $a = 0.15$; $b = 0.1$; $c = -0.1$.

Simulation results are shown by Fig.6. Table 3 gives a comparative study between the three Minimum Jerk approaches even if the point-to-point approach doesn't bring a satisfactory robot motion. The comparative criteria are the maximum velocity, the mean square energy, torque and jerk costs, defined respectively by:

$$C_\theta = \frac{1}{N}\sum_{i=1}^{N} 0.5(\,\theta^T\theta\,). \tag{22}$$

$$C_\tau = \frac{1}{N}\sum_{i=1}^{N} 0.5(\,\tau^T\tau\,). \tag{23}$$

$$C_J = \frac{1}{N}\sum_{i=1}^{N} 0.5(\,\ddot{\theta}^T\ddot{\theta}\,). \tag{24}$$

where N is the number of iterations of the integration algorithm of system (12).

One may think that the improvements provided by the via-point and trajectory shape approaches are due essentially to the initial choice of the desired trajectory. Consequently, this would imply that each method is solving a different jerk minimization problem. In fact, the differences noticed when moving from a methodology to another come from the addition of supplementary constraints and thus a more precise definition of the expected trajectory. Indeed, whatever approach is used, the optimization problem described by equation (16) remains the same and the desired joint positions θ_{id} follow equation (17). In the point-to-point case, the constraints of the optimization problem are the boundary conditions related to the initial and final desired Cartesian positions. The transition from the point-to-point methodology to the via-point one is then only accompanied by the addition of an intermediate desired position characterized by its own boundary condition. Finally, regarding the shape function trajectory, instead of imposing one or more desired Cartesian positions to reach, we impose a Cartesian trajectory function which depends on the different desired joint positions θ_{id}. The θ_{id}'s coefficients are defined and determined using the same way as for the two other approaches. It is therefore the choice of the method that conditions the resulting performances and not the choice of a given initial trajectory instead of another one.

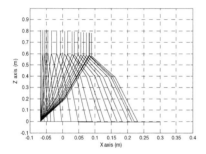 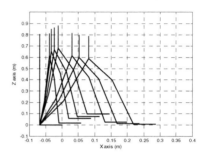

Fig. 3. Walking step: Point-to-point approach   **Fig. 4.** Walking step: Via-point approach

Table 3. Comparative study

Minimum Jerk approach	Maximum Velocity (rad.s^{-1})	Energy cost (N.m)^2	Torque cost (N.m^{-1})^2	Jerk cost (rad.s^{-3})^2
Point-to-point	0.1123	0.7640	2.9435	0.0134
Via-point	0.4094	0.6747	982.8087	2.9625
Shape trajectory	0.1933	4.4778	57.4493	0.4685

As noticed previously, the point-to-point approach leads to unacceptable simulation results. One may think that the foot translation is due to the gravity effect which tends to keep the foot in contact with the ground but in fact the dynamic model previously developed and exploited in simulations for the three approaches takes account of the gravity force. Furthermore, the via-point and trajectory shape methodologies provide satisfactory results in the joint space. Thus, Fig. 4 for the via-point approach and Fig. 5 and 6 for the shape trajectory approach show well that the foot of the moving leg does progressively lift off the ground before touching down again in a motion similar to the one performed by a human leg. Then, the translational movement in the point-to-point case may be explained by the fact that the minimizing criterion is applied using an initial and a final position with the same z coordinate set to zero. As the criterion aims at reducing the quantity of jerks done, translation is the displacement involving the lowest energy consumption. Indeed, Hogan asserted in [20] that the predicted trajectory was only depending on the initial and final positions of the body and it is invariant under translations and rotations.

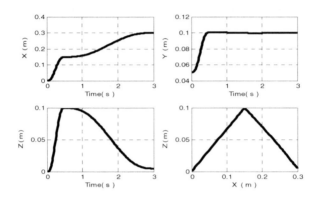

Fig. 5. Cartesian positions of the right leg via the via-point Minimum Jerk approach

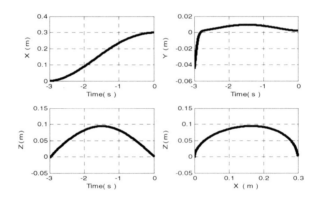

Fig. 6. Cartesian positions of the right leg via shape trajectory Minimum Jerk approach

As shown by Table 3, the point-to-point method involves very low values for both torque and jerk costs. Indeed, the trajectory obtained doesn´t follow a curving path and is a straight and smooth line. The via-point method ensures the faster dynamics and involves the less cost energy but it presents very high values for both the torque and jerk costs. Fig.5 shows well that the trajectory followed by the moving leg has a triangular shape. It represents a very abrupt motion thus involving a significant jerk and requiring high torque values in order to move the biped joints to the desired positions. Regarding the trajectory shape method, it presents the highest energy cost. This very significant energy consumption finds its origin in the complexity of the implemented algorithm and its heaviness of execution. Unlike the point-to-point and via-points cases where the constraints are expressed as boundary conditions of a certain but limited number of desired positions, the trajectory shape approach requires the replacement of the fifth order polynomial joint desired trajectory by a whole function expression that must satisfy, in the Cartesian space, a general trajectory shape we aim to reach. As a consequence, the optimization algorithm runs in every iteration of the main walking program and a desired position to be reached with its corresponding boundary conditions are generated during each iteration. When comparing the performances of the three approaches, the point-to-point Minimum Jerk-based control can be easily ruled out because the moving leg foot motion doesn't look like the human one especially that the foot does never lift off the ground. The via-point method ensures faster dynamics and involves less cost energy but our first interest in this study is to minimize the jerk and to produce a human-like gait pattern. In that context, the trajectory shape method appears to be the one leading to better results because a more human-like gait is guaranteed and lower torque and jerk costs are generated.

In order to compare our approach to the related works, we consider the paper [21], one of the rare works using minimum Jerk-based control to ensure a smooth motion for gait pattern generation. In [21], the technique applied consisted in the determination of the control inputs or torques required whereas in our work a desired trajectory ensuring a minimum jerk optimization was determined. In both cases, simulation results were satisfactory but in [21], only the point-to-point was considered, simulations were only provided in the joint space and the extension to the 3D- space was part of the further work.

5   Conclusion

To produce a humanlike gait pattern generation, three Minimum Jerk-based control approaches have been applied to a bipedal robot in the three dimensional space. Simulation results have shown that imposing a desired shape function trajectory to the bipedal foot in the Cartesian space provides better dynamical behavior and lower torque and jerk costs.

References

1. Vukobratovic, M., Borovac, B., Surla, D., Stokic, D.: Biped Locomotion: Dynamics, Stability, Control and Application. Springer, Heidelberg (1989)
2. Kajita, S., Kanehiro, F., Kaneko, K., Yokoi, K., Hirukawa, H.: The 3D Linear Inverted Pendulum Mode: A Simple Modeling for a Biped Walking Pattern Generation. In: IEEE International Conference on Intelligent Robots and Systems, vol. 1, pp. 239–246 (November 2001)
3. Sugihara, T., Nakamura, Y., Inoue, H.: Realtime Humanoid Motion Generation through ZMP Manipulation based on Inverted Pendulum Control. In: IEEE International Conference on Robotics and Automation, vol. 3, pp. 1404–1409 (May 2002)
4. Hirai, K., Hirose, M., Haikawa, Y., Takenaka, T.: The Development of Honda Humanoid Robot. In: IEEE International Conference on Robotics and Automation, vol. 2, pp. 1321–1326 (May 1998)
5. Huang, Q., Yokoi, K., Kajita, S., Kaneko, K., Arai, H., Koyachi, N., Tanie, K.: Planning Walking Patterns for a Biped Robot. IEEE Transactions on Robotics and Automation 17(3), 280–289 (2001)

6. Kajita, S., Tani, K.: Study of Dynamic Biped Locomotion on Rugged Terrain –Theory and Basic Experiment. In: IEEE International Conference on Advanced Robotics, vol. 1, pp. 741–746 (June 1991)

7. Erbatur, K., Kurt, O.: Natural ZMP Trajectories for Biped Robot Reference Generation. IEEE Transactions on Industrial Electronics 56(3), 835–845 (2009)

8. Kajita, S., Kahehiro, F., Kaneko, K., Fujiwara, K., Harada, K., Yokoi, K., Hirukawa, H.: Biped Walking Pattern Generation using Preview Control of the Zero-Moment-Point. In: IEEE International Conference on Robotics and Automation, vol. 2, pp. 1620–1626 (September 2003)

9. Park, J.H., Kim, K.D.: Biped Robot Walking using Gravity Compensated Inverted Pendulum Mode and Computed Torque Control. In: IEEE International Conference on Robotics and Automation, vol. 4, pp. 3528–3533 (May 1998)

10. Erbatur, K., Seven, U.: An Inverted Pendulum Based Approach to Biped Trajectory Generation with Swing Leg Dynamics. In: IEEE International Conference on Humanoid Robots, pp. 216–221 (November 2007)

11. Motoi, N., Suzuki, T., Ohnishi, K.: A Bipedal Locomotion Planning Based on Virtual Linear Inverted Pendulum Model. IEEE Transactions on Industrial Electronics 56(1), 54–61 (2009)

12. Tzafestas, S., Raibert, M., Tzafestas, C.: Robust Sliding-mode Control Applied to a 5-link Biped Robot. J. Intelligent and Robotic Systems. 15(1), 67–133 (1996)

13. Hurmuzlu, Y.: Dynamics of Bipedal Gait: Part I-Objective Functions and the Contact Event of a Planar Five-link Biped. J. Applied Mechanics. 60(2), 331–336 (1993)

14. Chevallereau, C., Aoustin, Y.: Optimal Reference Trajectories for Walking and Running of a Biped Robot. J.Robotica 19(5), 557–569 (2001)

15. Tlalolini, D., Chevallereau, C., Aoustin, Y.: Comparison of Different Gaits with Rotation of the Feet for a Planar Biped. J. Robotics and Autonomous Systems 57(4), 371–383 (2009)

16. Gasparetto, A., Zanotto, V.: A Technique for Time-jerk Optimal Planning of Robot Trajectories. J. Robotics and Computer-Integrated Manufacturing 24(3), 415–426 (2008)

17. Gasparetto, A., Zanotto, V.: Optimal Trajectory Planning for Industrial Robots. J. Advances in Engineering Software 41(4), 548–556 (2010)

18. Piazzi, A., Visioli, A.: Global Minimum-jerk Trajectory Planning of Robot Manipulators. IEEE Transactions on Industrial Electronics 47(1), 140–149 (2000)

19. Yang, J., Kim, J., Pitarch, E.P., Abdel-Malek, K.: Optimal Trajectory Planning for Redundant Manipulators Based on Minimum Jerk. In: International Conference on Design Engineering Technology and International Conference on Computers and Information in Engineering, pp. 1141–1150 (August 2008)

20. Hogan, N., Flash, T.: The Coordination of Arm Movements: An Experimentally Confirmed Mathematical Model. J. Neuroscience 5(7), 1688–1703 (1985)

21. Boonpratatong, A., Malisuwan, S., Degenaar, P., Veeraklaew, T.: A Minimum Jerk Design of Active Artificial Foot. In: Mechtronic and Embedded Systems and Applications, pp. 443–448 (October 2008)

22. Aloulou, A., Boubaker, O.: Control of a Step Walking Combined to Arms Swinging for a Three Dimensional Humanoid Prototype. J. Computer Science 6(8), 886–895 (2010)

23. Hemami, H.: A General Framework for Rigid Body Dynamics, Stability and Control. J. Dynamic Systems, Measurement, and Control 124(2), 241–252 (2002)

Development of a Smart Motion Control Card with an IEEE-1394 Interface

Guo-Ying Gu[1], LiMin Zhu[1], and Ying Feng[2]

[1] State Key Laboratory of Mechanical System and Vibration, School of Mechanical
Engineering, Shanghai Jiao Tong University, 200240, China
{guguoying,zhulm}@sjtu.edu.cn
[2] College of Automation Science and Engineering, South China University of
Technology, Guangzhou, Guangdong, 510641, China
zhdfengying@gmail.com

Abstract. IEEE 1394 is a high-efficiency communication network to
guarantee timely data transmission and perform excellent network interconnection. In this paper, an IEEE-1394-based smart motion control card
is presented, which is constructed by the hardware structure of the combination of a digital signal processor (DSP) and a field-programmable gate
array (FPGA). The former DSP module implements an IEEE-1394 controller, a servo controller and memory mapping for FPGA access, while
the FPGA module is utilized to achieve the logical functions containing quadrature-encoder-pulse (QEP) circuit, feedback count, direction
decoder, addressing mapping, DAC pre-processing circuit and I/O interface. For real-time communication, an ISA/IEEE-1394 interface board
for the host is designed and the Ardence Real-time Extension (RTX) is
adopted for deterministic control of Windows XP-based systems. As a
meaningful attempt, an experimental platform is established to evaluate
the communication performance of the IEEE-1394 interface. The experimental results show excellent real-time communication performance,
which demonstrates the feasible application of the IEEE 1394 interface
for distributed motion control systems.

Keywords: Smart motion control card, IEEE 1394, real-time communication.

1   Introduction

Along with the rapid evolution of robotic manufacturing systems, distributed
control systems are increasingly required in autonomous robots with lots of sensors and actuators [14,6,15]. Such a concept of distribution is found on the application of smart motion control cards with real-time communication technologies
for data exchanges. For example, a humanoid robot generally consists of more
than thirty DOFs to be actuated and requires multiple sensors to provide precise description of these actuators. It therefore attracts increasing attentions to
develop a smart motion control card with an efficient communication interface.

S. Jeschke, H. Liu, and D. Schilberg (Eds.): ICIRA 2011, Part II, LNAI 7102, pp. 263–274, 2011.
© Springer-Verlag Berlin Heidelberg 2011

With the development of microelectronics, information technology and VLSI, high-speed digital signal process (DSP) and Field Programmable Gate Array (FPGA) are widely applied to construct the hardware structure of the motion control card [12]. DSP, integrating a variety of sophisticated power electronics peripherals, has been adopted to implement multiple functions for motion control [13]. This application of DSP core not only simplifies the design process but also offers the capability of incorporating various extra features. FPGA with deterministic computation times through parallel architectures can create custom hardware logical circuits that can not be realized by DSP. FPGA is utilized in areas of motion control [3] to structure reconfigurable systems and to develop high-performance algorithms. These microprocessor-based motion control cards fill the flexibility, performance, power dissipation, and development cost gap.

Such a smart motion control card relies not only on the control hardware structure but also on the real-time communication techniques. Over the past decade, many different networked control techniques [7,8,9] such as control area network (CAN), Profibus, FIP, SERCOS and Ethernet have been proposed to realize the real-time communication for distributed motion control systems. The IEEE 1394 is a high-efficiency communication network to guarantee timely data transmission and perform excellent network interconnection as modern IEEE standard parallel buses but at a much lower cost. However, the discussions on the fusion of the IEEE-1394 interface with motion control cards are surprisingly spare [11,4] in the literature. Therefore, an IEEE-1394 interface is developed in this paper to satisfy the requirements of high-speed and real-time information exchanges in distributed motion control systems.

In this paper, a smart motion control card with the IEEE-1394 interface is presented. The developed motion control card adopts the hardware structure of the combination of DSP and FPGA. The former DSP module implements an IEEE-1394 controller, a servo controller and and memory mapping for FPGA access, while the FPGA module performs quadrature-encoder-pulse (QEP) circuit, feedback count, direction decoder, addressing mapping, DAC pre-processing circuit and I/O interface. A DAC interface is subsequently developed to convert digital signals to analog signals and to amplify the analog signals for servo drivers. For real-time communication, an ISA/IEEE-1394 interface board for the host computer is designed and the Ardence Real-time Extension (RTX) is adopted for deterministic control of Windows XP-based systems. As a meaningful attempt, we develop an experimental platform with the host computer and the smart motion control card to evaluate the communication performance of the developed IEEE-1394 interface. The experimental results show excellent real-time communication performance, which demonstrates the feasible application of the IEEE-1394 interface for distributed motion control systems.

2   Overview of IEEE 1394

IEEE 1394 (well-known as fireware) [1] was established in 1995 and amended three times as an industry standard data interface to standardize data structure and communication. As a high performance serial bus, IEEE 1394 defines a serial data transfer protocol with only three layers (including transaction layer, link layer and physical layer) and an interconnection system. Fig. 1 illustrates the structure of the IEEE 1394. The transaction layer implements the request-response protocol and provides minimum circuitry to interconnect with standard parallel buses, which is obligatory for an open platform. The link layer handles two types of basic protocol data unit (PDU) packet (guaranteed-data-delivery asynchronous and constant-rate-data transfer) transmission and reception responsibilities, plus an acknowledged datagram (a one-way data transfer with request confirmation) to the transaction layer for asynchronous subaction and the provision of cycle control for isochronous subaction respectively. The physical layer performs the initialization and arbitration services to assure that only one node at a time is sending data and to translate the serial bus electrical signals to those required by the link layer. A flexible bus management is also provided to offer connectivity between a wide range of devices, which assures easy set-up, maintenance, diagnostics and bus supervision without including a personal computer (PC) or other bus controller.

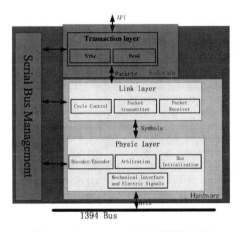

Fig. 1. Structure of the IEEE 1394

In applications, IEEE 1394 defines two bus categories: backplane and cable [1]. The cable bus mode, adopted in this paper, is a non-cyclic network with finite branches, consisting of bus bridges and nodes. The IEEE 1394 bus adopts memory mapped model, conforming to the ISO/IEC 13213 (ANSI/IEEE Std 1212), and control and status register (CSR) architecture with 64-bit fixed addressing. The high 16-bit addressing provides for up to 64K nodes in a system: 10-bit Bus_IDs allow up to 1,023 bus bridges; 6-bit $Node\_IDs$ accommodate up to 63 nodes for a single bridge. All data is sent along IEEE-1394 serial bus in serious four bytes (32-bit) words (called $quadlets$), which are encoded together with their clock signal onto two non-return to zero (NRZ) bus signals, using a technique known as Data-Strobe (DS) coding. This improves transmission reliability by ensure that only one of the two signals changes in each data bit period. The IEEE-1394 bus implements "plug and play" and adopts a "tree" topology to realize a peer to peer communication.

3   System Design

The developed smart motion control card in this work mainly consists of four parts: an IEEE-1394 interface, a DSP module, a FPGA module and a DAC interface. Fig. 2 shows the hardware structure of the developed card.

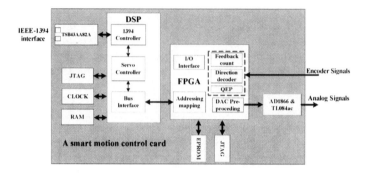

Fig. 2. The hardware structure of the smart motion control card

3.1   IEEE-1394 Interface

In this work, a commercia chip TSB43AA82A from Texas Instruments (TI) is used to construct the IEEE-1394 interface. Fig. 3 shows the schematic diagram of the IEEE-1394 interface. This selected chip is a stand-alone controller for IEEE-1394 communication within automotive and general industrial environments, which is compatible with IEEE 1394-1995 and IEEE 1394a standard and is integrated with PHY and link layer with two connectors. This chip provides all necessary control and status register (CFR) as well as three FIFOs for sending and receiving packets. In case of asynchronous transaction, *quadlets* are written to the asynchronous transmit FIFO (ATF) to transmit a packet depending on the type of the IEEE-1394 controller required through CFR. To read an incoming packet, *quadlets* are read from the asynchronous receive FIFO (ARF). This chip also implements arbitration, transaction manager, auto-response and other functions.

To achieve real-time communication, the cable bus mode is adopted in this work. Three phases should be done for the cable mode configuration:

  i) bus initialization;
  ii) tree identification;
  iii) self-identification.

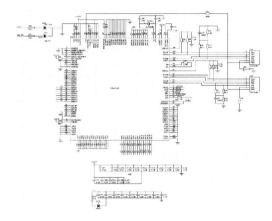

Fig. 3. External circuit of the IEEE 1394 interface

In order to achieve this configuration, an IEEE 1394 controller shall be embedded to set *ConfigRom* registers in TSB43AA82A, which will be clearly addressed in the DSP module.

3.2 DSP Module

The specific DSP chip chosen for the developed card is TMS320F2812 from TI, which provides maximum 150MIPS at 30MHz and lots of on-chip resources and is essentially split into three modules. The DSP module mainly implements three functions and the software program is coded in the common C/C++ language. The first one is an IEEE-1394 controller, which is used to set the configuration registers of the IEEE 1394-chip TSB43AA82A for proper communication. During the communication period, this controller performs the transaction-layer function of the IEEE 1394 bus. Fig. 4 shows configuration and operating process of the IEEE-1394 controller. The second one is FPGA configuration through memory mapping. Once finishing the configuration, the DSP can directly access the FPGA, which can be recognized as an I/O memory space of the DSP. The third one, discussed in this paragraph, is a servo controller, which contains position loop control and optional interpolation interface function.

The servo controller is designed to realize the high accuracy demand processing functions. Therefore, a great deal of effort is made to ensure the performance of closed-position-loop control. In this work, a proportional integral differential (PID) plus velocity and acceleration forward control algorithm is implemented on DSP. In particular, other advanced algorithms can easily be updated to improve performance through the interface function. In this work, a digital PID controller is used as follows

$$U_n = E_n K_p + (E_n - E_{n-1}) K_d + (\sum_n E_n) K_i + V_{ideal} K_{vff} + ACC_{ideal} K_{aff} + B \quad (1)$$

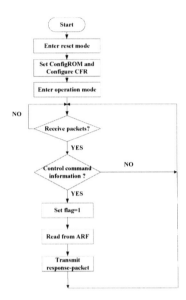

Fig. 4. The flow chart of the 1394 controller process

where $E_n = (P_{ideal})_n - (P_{actl})_n$; E_n is position error of the nth sample time; U_n is control variable of the nth sample time; $(P_{ideal})_n$ the ideal position of the nth sample time; $(P_{actl})_n$ is the actual position of the nth sample time; $(\sum_n E_n)$ is the cumulate position error of the last n sample times; V_{ideal} is the ideal velocity for velocity feedforward, ACC_{ideal} is the ideal acceleration for acceleration feedforward, K_{vff} and K_{aff} are the gains of velocity feedforward and acceleration feedforward, respectively; B is the static compensation; K_p, K_i and K_d are the proportional gain, integral gain, and derivative gain. It should be noted that saturation control is used to limit the output magnitude (maximum 16-bit integer 65536) and output static compensation is adopted to compensate external force influence of signal axis such as motor shaft and mechanical load. All the parameters in this control law can be updated by the host computer through the IEEE-1394 interface optimize the control performance.

In order to clearly describe the operation process, Fig. 5 shows the flow chart of the servo controller process. It should be noted that the period of the time interrupt is selected as 100 μs in this work.

3.3   FPGA Module

FPGA is a programmable micro-processor containing lots of logic components and interconnects, which can be programmed to perform the functions of basic logic gates and their combinations. In this paper, a FPGA chip EP2C35484 from ALTERA is utilized to achieve the logical functions, containing quadrature-encoder-pulse (QEP) circuit, feedback count, direction decoder, addressing

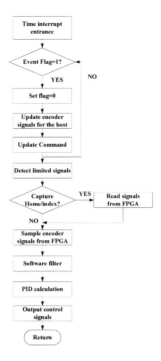

Fig. 5. The flow chart of the servo controller process

mapping, DAC pre-processing circuit, and I/O interface. The QEP circuit is designed to sample encoder signals (maximum 8MHz) and multiply four times to improve position accuracy of orientation. The direction decoder is applied to determine the rotary direction of the motors. The DAC pre-processing circuit realizes dividing frequency for the DAC interface. The DSP bus interface circuit provides signals communication between FPGA and DSP through the address mapping. The I/O interface implements interconnections with servo drivers and sensors. In order to determine an original point, a home/index-capture circuit is also designed to capture the home/index signal. Once this signal is captured, the circuit is toggled unless the sample data has been read.

The FPGA module is developed to improve control performance by replacing very time-consuming software process with cost-effective hardware solutions. The logic of all circuits is coded in Verilog language or GDF editor based on quartus tool from ALTERAL and burned in EPROM configuring FPGA once this system powers on.

3.4   DAC Interface

This interface is utilized to convert digital signals to analog signals for servo drivers. Two 16-bit dual-serial input and voltage output AD1866s are adopted to realize digital to analog convert. In order to amplify the analog signals, a four-channel amplifier TL084 with the capability of low-power consumption, high input impedance and low total harmonic distortion is used in this module. Fig. 6 shows the external circuit of the DAC interface.

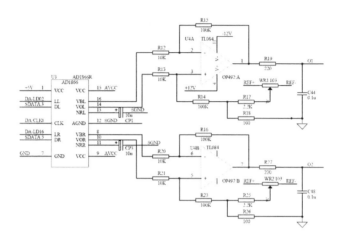

Fig. 6. External circuit of the DAC interface

4   Operation of Communication

With the use of the IEEE-1394 interface, the motion control card can receive the command data from the host computer and transfer the feedback data to the host real time. The following describes the operation process of the communication. First, the IEEE-1394 controller initializes the IEEE-1394 chip. Then, the IEEE-1394 controller waits until the command data enters the buffer of the IEEE-1394 chip through the IEEE-1394 bus. The IEEE-1394 chip will check the command before the data are received. If the data's ID number is same with the one of the motion control card, the IEEE-1394 controller will be triggered to read the received data. Then, the servo controller will update the command of the host. At the same time, real-time feedback data information will be updated for transferring back to the host.

To verify the performance of the IEEE-1394 interface, it is necessary to eval-uate the average latency of an asynchronous transaction during a predefined communication period [2]. In order to measure the average packet transfer time (latency) for an asynchronous transaction, timing constraint of the asynchronous transaction service is discussed firstly. As shown in Fig.7, a dynamic runtime structure of the asynchronous transaction is schematically illustrated. In case of a read or write asynchronous operation, the time latency includes require time (T_{req}), response time (T_{resp}), acknowledge time (T_{ack1} or T_{ack2}) and operation execution time (T_{exec}), which can be expressed as

$$T_{lant} = T_{req} + T_{ack1} + T_{exec} + T_{resp} + T_{ack2}. \qquad (2)$$

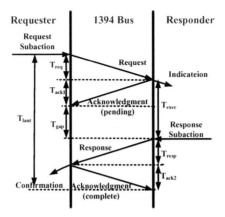

Fig. 7. Schematic runtime structure of the IEEE 1394 asynchronous transaction

5   Experimental Tests

To verify the efficiency of the developed IEEE-1394 interface, an experimental platform consisting of a smart motion control card, a host computer, an ISA/IEEE-1394 interface board and an IEEE-1394 bus is established. The ISA/IEEE-1394 interface board is designed for communication with the host computer. For the requirement of real-time communication, a real-time operating system (Windows XP+RTX) is adopted where RTX serving as the extension of Windows system's kernel modifies and extends the whole Hardware Abstraction Layer (HAL) to realize the independence kernel drive mode. The use of RTX gives developers deterministic control of Windows XP-based systems for real-time high-performance communication [10]. Fig. 8 shows the hardware cards used in this experimental platform. The smart motion control card consists of a DSP, a FPGA, an IEEE-1394 interface chip, a DAC, an operational amplifier and servo driver interfaces. The ISA/IEEE-1394 interface board contains an ISA interface circuit and an IEEE-1394 interface chip. The communication test is achieved by using an IEEE-1394 bus. The communication program of the host is written in the Visual C++ environment.

In this work, asynchronous transaction is adopted to provide guaranteed data delivery targeted for non-error-tolerant applications. Real-time performance of the IEEE-1394 interface is evaluated on commercial Ardence RTX software platform. According to the specifications of the IEEE-1394 chip TSB43AA82A [5], two basic block data packets are used to exchange data information between the host and the smart motion control card. Fig. 9 describes two types of data packet formats used in this work and the detailed field descriptions can be found in the specifications of TSB43AA82A [5]. It should be noted that three steps are necessary to finish an asynchronous data packet transmission [5]:

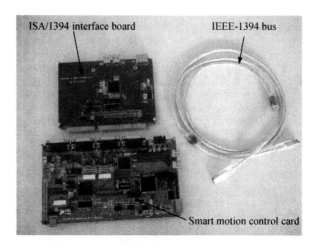

Fig. 8. Experimental system

i) Write first *quadlet* of the packet to asynchronous packet transmit FIFO (ATF) at the Write_First (70h) register which is a write only register providing the host with the capability to write the first *quadlet* of a transmit packet to the transmitting FIFO.

ii) Write any *quadlet* other than the first or the last quadlet to ATF at the Write_Continue (74h) register which is a write only register providing the host with the capability to write any *quadlet* other than the first or last of a transmit packet to the transmitting FIFO.

iii) Write last *quadlet* of the packet at the Write_Update (78h) register which is a write only register providing the host with the capability to write the last *quadlet* of a transmit packet to transmitting FIFO.

A-Generic transmit format of packet (block data)

0 1 2 3	4 5 6 7	8 9 10 11	12 13 14 15	16 17 18 19	20 21	22 23	24 25 26 27	28 29 30 31
Reserved				spd	tLabel		rt	tCode	prior
destination ID				destination offset_high				
destination offset_low								
data_length				extended_tCode				
block data								

B-Generic received format of packet (block data)

0 1 2 3	4 5 6 7	8 9 10 11	12 13 14 15	16 17 18 19	20 21 22 23	24 25 26 27	28 29 30 31
status	Reserved			spd	Reserved		ack
destination ID				tLabel	rt	tCode	prior
source ID				rCode	Reserved		
Reserved							
data_length				extended_tCode			
block data							

Fig. 9. Two types of the IEEE-1394 data packet format

Fig. 7 has shown a sequence diagram of asynchronous transaction event and the transaction time T_{lant} between the host the smart motion control card can be calculated by (2). As an illustration, a series of asynchronous read-transaction tests have been conducted. From more than 38 thousand sample data, the worst case execution time for different data payloads is listed in Table 1, which demonstrates the efficiency of the IEEE-1394 based smart motion control card and the developed ISA/1394 interface board.

Table 1. Worst case execution time for asynchronous read-transaction with different data payloads in the Windows XP+RTX enviroment

Data payload (Bytes)	4	16	32	64	128	256	512
$T_{lant}(\mu s)$	99.3	117	144.5	191.7	298.4	518.5	961.1

6   Conclusion

This paper presents a smart motion control card with the IEEE-1394 interface. The developed card adopts the hardware structure of the combination of both a DSP and a FPGA. The former DSP module implements an IEEE-1394 controller, a servo controller and memory mapping for FPGA access, while the FPGA performs quadruple rate circuit, direction decoder, addressing decoder, digital analog converter (DAC) pre-processing circuit, and input/output (I/O) interfaces. A DAC interface is then developed to convert digital signals to analog signals and amplify the analog signals for servo drivers. For real-time communication, an ISA/IEEE-1394 interface board for the host is designed and the Ardence RTX is utilized for deterministic control of Windows XP-based systems. As an illustration, a series of asynchronous read-transaction tests are done to verify the efficiency of the IEEE-1394-based smart motion control card, which demonstrates the feasible application of the IEEE 1394 interface for distributed motion control. In the future work, motion control performance tests will be conducted.

Acknowledgment. This work was partially supported by the National Natural Science Foundation of China under grant No. 91023047, the Science and Technology Commission of Shanghai Municipality under Grant No. 09520701700, and the "Shu Guang" project supported by Shanghai Municipal Education Commission and Shanghai Education Development Foundation under Grant No. 10SG17.

References

1. IEEE Standard for a High Performance Serial Bus (IEEE Std, IEEE 1394-1995, 1996)
2. Albert, A.: Comparison of event-triggered and time-triggered concepts with regard to distributed control systems. In: Embedded World, pp. 235–252 (2004)

3. Dubey, R., Agarwal, P., Vasantha, M.K.: Programmable logic devices for motion controla review. IEEE Transactions on Industrial Electronics 54(1), 559–566 (2007)
4. Gu, G.Y., Zhu, L.M., Xiong, Z.H., Ding, H.: Design of a distributed multi-axis motion control system using the IEEE-1394 bus. IEEE Transactions on Industrial Electronics 57(12), 4209–4218 (2010)
5. Inc., T.I.: Tsb43aa82 (isphynx ii) data manual (July 2001), www.ti.com
6. Kanehiro, F., Ishiwata, Y., Saito, H., Akachi, K.: Distributed control system of humanoid robots. In: Proceeding of the 2006 IEEE/RSJ International Conference on Intelligent Robots and Systems, pp. 2471–2477 (2006)
7. Li, T.J., Fujimoto, Y.: Control system with high-speed and real-time communication links. IEEE Transactions on Industrial Electronics 55(4), 1548–1557 (2008)
8. Lian, F.L., Moyne, J., Tilbury, D.: Network design consideration for distributed control systems. IEEE Transaction on Control Systems Technology 10(2), 297–307 (2002)
9. Lin, S.Y., Ho, C.Y., Tzou, Y.Y.: Distributed motion control using real-time network communication techniques. In: Proceedings of the 3rd International Power Electronics and Motion Control Conference, vol. 2, pp. 843–847 (2000)
10. Pu, D., Sheng, X., Zhang, W., Ding, H.: An application of real-time operating system in high speed and high precision motion control systems. In: Proceedings of the 3rd Annual IEEE Conference on Automation Science and Engineering, pp. 997–1001 (2007)
11. Sarker, M.O.F., Kim, C.H., Baek, S., You, B.J.: An IEEE-1394 based real-time robot control system for efficient controlling of humanoids. In: Proceedings of IEEE/RSJ International Conference on Intelligent Robots and Systems, pp. 9–15 (2006)
12. Shao, X., Sun, D., Mills, J.K.: A new motion control hardware architecture with FPGA-based IC design for robotic manipulators. In: Proceedings of IEEE International Conference on Robotics and Automation, pp. 3520–3525 (2006)
13. Shireen, W., Arefeen, M.S., Figoli, D.: Controlling multiple motors utilizing a single DSP controller. IEEE Transactions on Industrial Electronics 18(1), 124–130 (2003)
14. Yasuda, G.: Distributed autonomous control of modular robot systems using parallel programming. Journal of Materials Processing Technology 141(3), 357–364 (2003)
15. Yu, Z.G., Huang, Q., Li, J.X., Shi, Q., Chen, X.C., Li, K.J.: Distributed control system for a humanoid robot. In: Proceedings of the 2007 IEEE International Conference on Mechatronics and Automation, pp. 1166–1171 (2007)

Control System by Observer
for a Hyper-redundant Robot

Mircea Ivanescu[1], Nirvana Popescu[2], and Mihaela Florescu[1]

University of Craiova, 13 Cuza street, 200585, Romania
{ivanescu,mihaela}@robotics.ucv.ro
University "Politehnica" Bucharest, 313 Spl. Independentei, 060042, Romania
nirvana.popescu@cs.pub.ro

Abstract. The paper focuses on the control of a class of hyper-redundant arms with continuum elements, with boundary measuring and control. First, the dynamic model of the continuum arm is presented. The measuring systems are based on the film sensors that are placed at the terminal sub-regions of the arm. The observers are proposed in order to reconstruct the full state of the arm. A back-stepping method is used to design a boundary control algorithm. Numerical simulations of the arm motion toward an imposed position are presented. An experimental platform shows the effectiveness of the proposed methods.

Keywords: hyper-redundant arms, observer, control.

1 Introduction

The hyper-redundant arms are a class of manipulators that can reach any position and orientation in space. A special class of these robots is represented by the mechanical structures with continuum elements described by the distributed parameter model. The control of these systems is very complex and several researchers have tried to cater solutions. In [2, 3], Gravagne analyzed the kinematic models. Important results were obtained by Chirikjian and Burdick [4], which laid the foundations for the kinematical theory of hyper-redundant robots. Their results are based on a "backbone curve" that captures the robot's macroscopic geometric features. Mochiyama has also investigated the problem of controlling the shape of an HDOF rigid – link robot with two-degree-of-freedom joints using spatial curves [5]. In other papers [6, 7], several technological solutions for actuators used in hyper-redundant structures are presented and conventional control systems are introduced. In [8] control problem of a class that performs the grasping function by coiling is discussed. A frequency stability criterion for the grasping control problem is advanced in [9].

The development of feedback controllers and compensators for these models is a highly complex. The difficulty is determined by the complexity of the dynamic models expressed by partial differential equations and by the observability problems in distributed parameter systems. An essential part of designing feedback controllers for these models is represented by designing practical controllers that are

S. Jeschke, H. Liu, and D. Schilberg (Eds.): ICIRA 2011, Part II, LNAI 7102, pp. 275–286, 2011.
© Springer-Verlag Berlin Heidelberg 2011

implementable. Standard feedback control design presupposes full-state feedback with measurements of the entire state. Recent advances in distributed sensor technology, as Polyvinylidene Fluoride film sensors [10], assure the quality of position measuring in distributed systems. The observability problems are solved by an approach derived from the Luenberger observer type and the "back-stepping method" developed in [11].

In the current paper, the control problem of a class of hyper-redundant arms with continuum elements, with boundary measuring and control is developed.

The paper is structured as follows: section II presents technological and theoretical preliminaries, section III discusses the dynamic model, section IV presents the control by boundary observer, section V verifies the control laws by computer simulation and section VI is concerned with an experimental model.

2   Technological and Theoretical Preliminaries

The hyper-redundant technological models are complex structures that operate in 3D space, but the control laws of the elements can be inferred from the planar models. Admittedly, the model discussed in this paper is a 2D model.

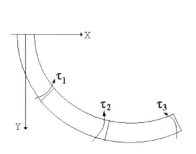
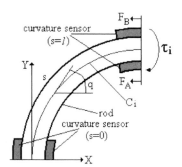

Fig. 1. A hyper-redundant arm   **Fig. 2.** A hyper-redundant segment

The technological model basis is presented in Fig.1. It consists of a number (N) of continuum segments, each segment having a layer structure that ensures the flexibility, the driving and position measuring (Fig.2).

The high flexibility is obtained by an elastic non-extensible backbone rod with distributed damping and negligible shear effects. The driving system consists of two antagonistic cable actuators that are connected at the end of each segment and determine the bending of the arm. The position measuring of the segment is obtained by an electro-active polymer curvature sensor that is placed on the surface at the terminal sub-regions of each segment. These sensors can measure the curvature on the boundary of the segment ($s = 0$ or $s = l$). The essence of the segment i is the backbone curve C_i. The length of each segment is l. The independent parameter s is related to the arc-length from origin of the curve C_i, $s \in \Omega$, $\Omega = [0, \ l]$. We denote by τ the equivalent moment at the end of the segment $(s = l)$ exercised by the cable forces F_A and F_B. The position of a point s on curve C_i is defined by the position vector $r = r(s)$, $s \in [0, \; l]$. For a dynamic motion, the time variable will be introduced, $r = r(s,t)$. The segment has the elastic modules E, the moment of inertia I, the bending stiffness EI, the linear mass density ρ and rotational inertial density I_ρ.

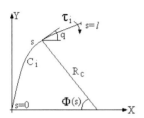
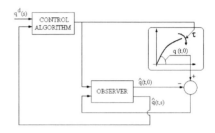

Fig. 3. The hyper-redundant arm parameters   **Fig. 4.** The control in Problem 1

3   Dynamic Model

The dynamic model of a segment can be derived from the Hamiltonian principle. Using the same procedure as in [3], it yields the partial differential equations of the arm segment,

$$I_\rho \ddot{q} + b_1 \dot{q} - EI q_{ss} + c_1 q = 0 \qquad (3.1)$$

with the initial and boundary conditions

$$\dot{q}(0,s) = 0, \quad EI q_s(t,l) = \tau, \quad q_s(t,0) = 0 \qquad (3.2)$$

where $q = q(t,s)$, $\dot{q}$, q_s, q_{ss} denote $\dfrac{\partial q(t,s)}{\partial t}$, $\dfrac{\partial q(t,s)}{\partial s}$, $\dfrac{\partial^2 q(t,s)}{\partial s^2}$, respectively, b_1 is the equivalent damping coefficient and c_1 characterizes the elastic behavior.

The equations (3.1), (3.2) can be rewritten as

$$\ddot{q} = a q_{ss} + b\dot{q} + cq \qquad (3.3)$$

$$q_s(t,0) = 0, \quad q_s(t,l) = d \cdot \tau, \quad \dot{q}(0,s) = 0, \quad s \in [0, \; l] \qquad (3.4)$$

where $a = \dfrac{EI}{I_\rho}$; $b = -\dfrac{b_1}{I_\rho}$; $c = -\dfrac{c_1}{I_\rho}$; $d = \dfrac{1}{EI}$.

The input of the system is represented by the moment τ applied at the boundary $s = l$ of the arm. The output is determined by the angle values measured by the sensor,

$$y(t) = q(0,t) \quad \text{or} \quad y(t) = q(l,t) \qquad (3.5)$$

4   Control by Boundary Observer

We shall analyze three cases: 1) the measurement system allows to measure the angle at the bottom end $(s = 0)$; 2) the measurement system allows to measure the angle at the upper end $(s = l)$; 3) the measurement system allows to measure the angle at $s = 0, s = l$. In all cases, a regional boundary observer is introduced in order to reconstruct the state in the domain and generate a full-state feedback.

4.1   Problem 1: $q(t,0)$ Is Available for Measurement (Fig.4)

The following observer is proposed

$$\ddot{\hat{q}} = a\hat{q}_{ss} + b\dot{\hat{q}} + c\hat{q} + k_1(s)\big(q(t,0) - \hat{q}(t,0)\big) \tag{4.1}$$

$$\hat{q}_s(t,0) = k_0\big(q(t,0) - \hat{q}(t,0)\big), \quad \hat{q}_s(t,l) = d \cdot \tau, \quad \dot{\hat{q}}(0,l) = 0 \tag{4.2}$$

where $\hat{q} = \hat{q}(t,s)$ is the observer state and $k_1(s)$, k_0 are a function and a constant, respectively, that define the observer parametres. The objective is to determine these parametres in order to reconstruct the state in the domain, i.e., to find $k_1(s)$ and k_0 such that $\hat{q}$ converges to q as time goes to infinity.

An error variable $\tilde{q}$ is introduced

$$\tilde{q} = q - \hat{q} \tag{4.3}$$

and the error system will be

$$\ddot{\tilde{q}} = a\tilde{q}_{ss} + b\dot{\tilde{q}} + c\tilde{q} - k_1(s)\tilde{q}(t,0) \tag{4.4}$$

$$\tilde{q}_s(t,0) = -k_0\tilde{q}(t,0), \quad \tilde{q}_s(t,l) = 0, \quad \dot{\tilde{q}}(0,l) = 0 \tag{4.7}$$

where $\lim_{t \to \infty} \tilde{q}(t,s) = 0$, $s \in [0, \ l]$.

We consider that the desired states of the arm motion are given by the curve C_d,

$$C_d : \big(q^d(s), \quad s \in [0, \ l]\big) \tag{4.6}$$

The control problem is to find the moment control law $\tau(t)$ in order to achieve the desired state.

Control algorithm 1. The closed loop control law of the arm (3.5) – (3.8) with the boundary observer (4.1), (4.2) is given by

$$\tau(t) = EI\left(-k(l,l)\big(\hat{q}(t,l) - q_d(l)\big) + q_s^d(l) - \int_0^l k_s(l,z)\big(\hat{q}(t,z) - q^d(z)\big)dz\right) \tag{4.7}$$

where $k(s,z)$ is the solution of the following partial differential equations,

$$-ak_{ss}(s,z)+ak_{zz}(s,z)+ck(s,z)=0 \tag{4.8}$$

$$k_{ss}(s,s)=\frac{c}{2a}(l-s) \tag{4.9}$$

with the boundary condition $k(l,z)=0$, $z\in[0,\ \ l]$, and the observer parameters are defined by the equations

$$k_0=-k(0,0),\ \ k_1(s)=-ak_z(s,0)-\int_0^s k_1(z)k(s,z)dz \tag{4.10}$$

Proof. See Appendix 1.

4.2   Problem 2: $q(t,l)$ Is Available for Measurement (Fig.5)

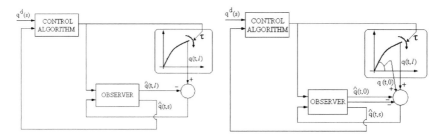

Fig. 5. The control in Problem 2   **Fig. 6.** The control in Problem 3

The observer will be

$$\ddot{\hat{q}}=a\hat{q}_{ss}+b\dot{\hat{q}}+c\hat{q}+k_1(s)\big(q(t,l)-\hat{q}(t,l)\big) \tag{4.11}$$

with the boundary conditions

$$\hat{q}_s(t,0)=\hat{q}_0,\ \ \hat{q}_s(t,l)=k_0\big(q(t,l)-\hat{q}(t,l)\big)+d\tau,\ \ \dot{\hat{q}}(0,0)=0 \tag{4.12}$$

The error system has the form

$$\ddot{\tilde{q}}=a\tilde{q}_{ss}+b\dot{\tilde{q}}+c\tilde{q}-k_1(s)\tilde{q}(t,l) \tag{4.13}$$

$$\tilde{q}_s(t,0)=-\hat{q}_0,\ \ \tilde{q}_s(t,l)=-k_0\tilde{q}(t,l),\ \ \dot{\tilde{q}}(0,0)=0 \tag{4.14}$$

Control algorithm 2. The closed loop control law of the arm (3.3), (3.4) with the boundary observer (4.10) – (4.12) is given by

$$\tau(t)=EI\Big(q_s^d(l)-k(l,l)\big(q^d(l)-\hat{q}(t,l)\big)\Big) \tag{4.15}$$

where $k(s,z)$ is the solution to the following equations

$$ak_{ss}(s,z)-ak_{zz}(s,z)+ck(s,z)=0 \tag{4.16}$$

$$k(s,s)=\frac{c}{2a}s \tag{4.17}$$

with the boundary conditions $k(0,z) = 0$, $z \in [0, \ l]$. The observer parameters are obtained by solving the following equations

$$k_0 = k(l,l), \quad k_1(s) = ak_s(s,l) + \int_s^l k_1(z) k(s,z) dz \tag{4.18}$$

Proof. See Appendix 2.

4.3   Problem 3: q(t,l) and q(t,0) Are Available for Measurement (Fig.6)

The following observer is proposed

$$\ddot{\hat{q}} = a\hat{q}_{ss} + b\dot{\hat{q}} + c\hat{q} + k_{10}(s)\big(q(t,0) - \hat{q}(t,0)\big) + k_{11}(s)\big(q(t,l) - \hat{q}(t,l)\big) \tag{4.19}$$

$$\hat{q}_s(t,0) = k_{00}\big(q(t,0) - \hat{q}(t,0)\big), \quad \hat{q}_s(t,l) = k_{01}\big(q(t,l) - \hat{q}(t,l)\big) + d \cdot \tau \tag{4.20}$$

$$\dot{\hat{q}}(0,0) = 0, \quad \dot{\hat{q}}(0,l) = 0 \tag{4.21}$$

where $\hat{q} = \hat{q}(t,s)$ is the observer state and $k_{10}(s)$, $k_{11}(s)$, k_{00}, k_{01} are the functions and the constants that define the observer parameters. The error system will be

$$\ddot{\tilde{q}} = a\tilde{q}_{ss} + b\dot{\tilde{q}} + c\tilde{q} - k_{10}(s)\tilde{q}(t,0) - k_{11}(s)\tilde{q}(t,l) \tag{4.22}$$

$$\tilde{q}_s(t,0) = -k_{00}\tilde{q}(t,0), \quad \tilde{q}_s(t,l) = -k_{01}\tilde{q}(t,l), \quad \dot{\tilde{q}}(0,0) = 0, \quad \dot{\tilde{q}}(0,l) = 0 \tag{4.23}$$

where $\lim\limits_{t \to \infty} \tilde{q}(t,s) = 0$, $s \in [0, \ l]$.

Control algorithm 3. The closed loop control law of the arm (3.3), (3.4) with the boundary observer (4.22), (4.23) is given by

$$\tau = -\frac{1}{d}\big(k^1(l,l) - k^0(l,l)\big)\big(q(t,l) - q^d(l)\big) \tag{4.24}$$

where $k^1(s,z)$, $k^0(s,z)$ are the solutions to the following partial differential equations,

$$ak_{ss}^1 - ak_{zz}^1 - ck^1 = 0, \quad ak_{ss}^0 - ak_{zz}^0 - ck^0 = 0 \tag{4.25}$$

$$\frac{d}{ds}k^1(s,s) = \frac{c}{4a}, \quad \frac{d}{ds}k^0(s,s) = -\frac{c}{4a} \tag{4.26}$$

with the boundary conditions

$$k^1(0,z) = 0, \ k^0(l,z) = 0, \ k_s^0(l,z) = 0, \ k_s^1(0,z) = 0, \ z \in [0,l] \tag{4.27}$$

and the observer parameters are defined by the equations

$$k_{01} = k^1(l,l) - k^0(l,l), \quad k_{00} = k^1(0,0) - k^0(0,0) \tag{4.28}$$

$$-k_{10}(s) + \int_s^l k^1(s,z)k_{10}(z)dz + \int_0^s k^0(s,z)k_{10}(z)dz - ak_z^0(s,0) = 0 \quad (4.29)$$

$$-k_{11}(s) + \int_s^l k^1(s,z)k_{11}(z)dz + \int_0^s k^0(s,z)k_{11}(z)dz + ak_z^1(s,l) = 0 \quad (4.30)$$

Proof. See Appendix 3.

5   Simulation

A hyper-redundant manipulator control with continuum segments is simulated. The parameters of the arm were selected as: bending stiffness $EI = 1$, rotational inertial density $I_\rho = 0.001 kg \cdot m^2$, damping ratio 0.35 and elastic coefficient 4.8. These constants are realistic for long thin backbone structures. The length of each segment is $l = 1$.

Problem 1. q(t, 0) is Available for Measurement. The observer parameters k_0, $k_1(s)$ are computed. First, a numerical solution for $k(s,z)$ is obtained by the integration of partial differential equation (4.8) with boundary conditions (4.9) and (4.10). The result is presented in Fig.7.

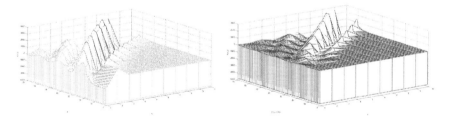

Fig. 7. $k(s,z)$ for the Problem 1   **Fig. 8.** k(s,z) in Problem 2

The parameter k_0 is obtained from (4.10) as $k_0 = -k(0,0) = 12.4$. The parameter k_1 is determined from the integral equation. The numerical solution is presented in the Table 1.

Table 1. Parameter $k_1(s)$ in Problem 1

S	0	0.2	0.4	0.6	0.8	1.0
$k_1(s)$	3.30	3.80	0.52	0.14	0.06	0.00

A desired trajectory defined as

$$q^d(s) = 0.05 \cdot \pi s^2, \quad s \in [0, \ 1] \tag{5.1}$$

is proposed and the control law (4.7) is used.

A MATLAB simulation of the observer arm system is implemented. The result is presented in Fig.9.

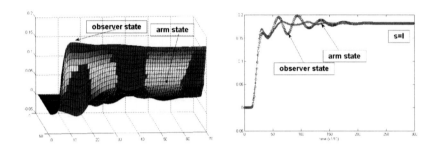

Fig. 9. The state trajectory in Problem 1   **Fig. 10.** The state trajectory for s = 1 (Problem 1)

In Fig.10 is shown the arm and observer state for the position s = 1. We can remark the convergence of the trajectories and the quality of motion.

Problem 2. q(t,l) Is Available for Measurement. The numerical solutions to k(s,z) is obtained from the equations (4.16), (4.17) with the specified boundary conditions. For example, the solution to k(s,z) is presented in Fig.8.

The observer parameters are obtained from (4.18), $k_0 = 0$ and k_1 is represented in Table 2.

Table 2.

s	0	0.2	0.4	0.8	1.0
k_1	4.83	8.64	2.15	-0.01	0.00

The same desired trajectory (5.1) is proposed and the same initial and boundary arm conditions, as for in Problem 1, are used.

The control law (4.24) is applied and a simulation in MATLAB of the global system, as presented in Fig.6, is implemented. The result, for the position s = 1, is shown in Fig.11.

Fig.10 and Fig.11 demonstrate the quality of motion for the both control problem. As expected, the performance of the control is the same as the target system (A.1.2), (A.1.3) [11].

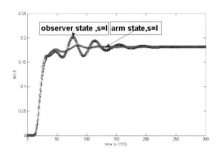
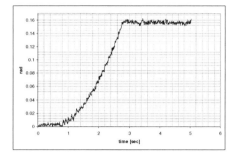

Fig. 11. The state trajectories, for s = l, in Problem 2   **Fig. 12.** The experimental trajectory $\left(s = l \right)$

6   Experimental Results

In order to verify the suitability of the control algorithm, a platform with a hyper-redundant arm has been employed for testing. The arm consists of three continuum segments with a flexible backbone rod. Three antagonistic cable actuators for each segment ensure the actuation system (Fig.13, Fig.14). The force in each cable is determined by the DC motors and a transmission system.

Fig. 13. A hyper-redundant arm platform **Fig. 14.** A sensor layer on the arm

A polymer thick film layer is placed on the upper level of the rod on each segment $\left(s = l = 0.3m \right)$. A sensor exhibits a decrease in resistance when an increase of the film curvature is used. A Wheatstone bridge system is used to measure the variation of the resistance. A Quancer-based platform is used for control and signal acquisition. A control law (4.24) with $q_d \left(s \right) = 0.05\pi \cdot s^2$ is implemented. The result is presented in Fig.12. We can remark the similitude between experimental and simulation results.

7   Conclusions

The paper addresses the control problem of a class of hyper-redundant arms with continuum elements. The observability problems of these models described by partial differential equations are analyzed. The measuring systems are based on the sensors placed on the boundary of the arm. Several observers are proposed for reconstructing the full state of the arm. A back-stepping technique is used in order to design a boundary control algorithm. The numerical simulations and an experimental platform illustrate the effectiveness of the method.

References

1. Hemami, A.: Design of light weight flexible robot arm. In: Robots 8 Conference Proceedings, Detroit, USA, pp. 1623–1640 (June 1984)
2. Gravagne, I.A., Walker, I.D.: On the kinematics of remotely - actuated continuum robots. In: Proc. 2000 IEEE Int. Conf. on Robotics and Automation, San Francisco, pp. 2544–2550 (April 2000)
3. Gravagne, I.A., Walker, I.D.: Kinematic Transformations for Remotely-Actuated Planar Continuum Robots. In: Proc. 2000 IEEE Int. Conf. on Rob. and Aut., San Francisco, pp. 19–26 (April 2000)
4. Chirikjian, G.S., Burdick, J.W.: An obstacle avoidance algorithm for hyper-redundant manipulators. In: Proc. IEEE Int. Conf. on Robotics and Automation, Cincinnati, Ohio, pp. 625–631 (May 1990)
5. Mochiyama, H., Kobayashi, H.: The shape Jacobian of a manipulator with hyper degrees of freedom. In: Proc. 1999 IEEE Int. Conf. on Robotics and Automation, Detroit, pp. 2837–2842 (May 1999)
6. Robinson, G., Davies, J.B.C.: Continuum robots – a state of the art. In: Proc. 1999 IEEE Int. Conf. on Rob and Aut, Detroit, Michigan, pp. 2849–2854 (May 1999)
7. Ivanescu, M., Stoian, V.: A variable structure controller for a tentacle manipulator. In: Proc. IEEE Int. Conf. on Robotics and Aut., Nagoya, pp. 3155–3160 (1995)
8. Ivanescu, M., Florescu, M.C., Popescu, N., Popescu, D.: Position and Force Control of the Grasping Function for a Hyperredundant Arm. In: Proc. of IEEE Int. Conf. on Rob. and Aut., Pasadena, California, pp. 2599–2604 (2008)
9. Ivanescu, M., Bizdoaca, N., Florescu, M., Popescu, N., Popescu, D.: Frequency Criteria for the Grasping Control of a Hyper-redundant Robot. In: Proc.of IEEE International Conference on Robotics and Automation, Anchorage, Alaska (ICRA 2010), May 3-8, pp. 1542–1549 (2010)
10. Miller, D.W., Collins, S.A., Peltzman, S.P.: Development of Spatially Convolving Sensors for Structural Control Applications. In: The 31st AIAA Structures, Structural Dynamic and Materials Conference, paper 90 – 1127 (1992)
11. Krstic, M., Smyshlyaev, A.: Boundary Control of PDEs: A Short Course on Backstepping Design. In: VCSB (2006)
12. Krstic, M.: Compensation of Infinite – Dimensional Actuator and sensor Dynamic. IEEE Control Systems 30(1), 22–41 (2010)
13. Camarillo, D., Milne, C.: Mechanics Modeling of Tendon – Driven Continuum Manipulators. IEEE Trans. On Robotics 24(6), 1262–1273 (2008)

Appendix 1

The control algorithm is derived by using the back-stepping method developed in [11]. The coordinate transformation

$$w(t,s) = \tilde{q}(t,s) - \int_0^s k(s,z)\tilde{q}(t,z)dz \qquad \text{(A.1.1.)}$$

transforms the error system (4.4), (4.5) into a stable $(b<0)$ target system

$$\ddot{w} = aw_{ss} + b\dot{w} \qquad \text{(A.1.2)}$$

$$w_s(t,0) = 0,\ w_s(t,l) = 0,\ \dot{w}(0,s) = 0,\ s \in [0,\ l] \qquad \text{(A.1.3)}$$

where
$$\lim_{t \to \infty} w(t,s) = 0,\ s \in [0,\ l] \qquad \text{(A.1.4)}$$

From (A.1.1), we have

$$\dot{w} = \dot{\tilde{q}} - \int_0^s k(s,z)\dot{\tilde{q}}(t,z)dz \qquad \text{(A.1.5)}$$

$$\ddot{w} = \ddot{\tilde{q}} - \int_0^s k(s,z)\left(a\tilde{q}_{ss} + b\dot{\tilde{q}} + c\tilde{q} - k_1(z)\tilde{q}(t,0)\right)dz \qquad \text{(A.1.6)}$$

$$w_{ss} = \tilde{q}_{ss} - \int_0^s k_{ss}(s,z)\tilde{q}(t,z)dz - k_s(s,s)\tilde{q}(t,s) -$$
$$\qquad\qquad\qquad\qquad\qquad\qquad\qquad\qquad\qquad\qquad\qquad \text{(A.1.7)}$$
$$- \frac{dk(s,s)}{ds}\cdot\tilde{q}(t,s) - k(s,s)\tilde{q}_s(t,s)$$

If we substitute (A.1.5), (A.1.8) in (A.1.2) and integrate by parts we get

$$\int_0^s \left(-ak_{zz}(s,z) + ak_{ss}(s,z) + ck(s,z)\right)\tilde{q}(t,z)dz +$$

$$+ \left(c + ak_z(s,s) + ak_s(s,s) + a\frac{dk(s,s)}{ds}\right)\tilde{q}(t,s) + \qquad \text{(A.1.8)}$$

$$+ \left(-ak_z(s,0) - k_1(s) - \int_0^s k_1(z)k(s,z)dz\right) = 0$$

If the left hand side is to be zero, the condition (4.13), (4.14) can be easily inferred.

From (A.1.5), the velocities at $t=0$, $s=l$ will be

$$\dot{w}(0,l) = \dot{\tilde{q}}(0,l) + \int_0^l k(l,z)\dot{\tilde{q}}(0,z)dz \qquad \text{(A.1.9)}$$

and by the boundary and initial conditions (3.4), (4.5), (A.1.3), we have

$$k(l,z) = 0,\ z \in [0,\ l] \qquad \text{(A.1.10)}$$

From (A.1.1), we get

$$w_s\left(t,s\right) = \tilde{q}_s\left(t,s\right) - \int_0^s k_s\left(s,z\right)\tilde{q}\left(t,z\right)dz - k\left(s,s\right)\tilde{q}\left(t,s\right) \tag{A.1.11}$$

and by using the boundary condition (4.5) $\left(s=0\right)$ this relation becomes

$$-k_0\tilde{q}\left(t,0\right) - k\left(0,0\right)\tilde{q}\left(t,0\right) = 0 \ \text{ or } \ k_0 = -k\left(0,0\right) \tag{A.1.12}$$

Also, if we consider that the desired position is defined by $q^d\left(s\right)$, $s \in \left[0, \ l\right]$ and if we use the boundary conditions (3.4), (A.1.3) in the relation (A.1.11), the control law (4.7) is easily obtained.

Appendix 2

The back-stepping transformation is chosen as [11, 12]

$$w\left(t,s\right) = \tilde{q}\left(t,s\right) - \int_s^l k\left(s,z\right)\tilde{q}\left(t,z\right)dz \tag{A.2.1}$$

with the target system defined by (A.1.2), (A.1.3). The procedure is the same as in Appendix 1.

Appendix 3

The coordinate transformation

$$w\left(t,s\right) = \tilde{q}\left(t,s\right) - \int_0^s k^0\left(s,z\right)\tilde{q}\left(t,z\right)dz - \int_s^l k^1\left(s,z\right)\tilde{q}\left(t,z\right)dz \tag{A.3.1}$$

transforms the error system (4.5), (4.6) into a stable $\left(b<0\right)$ target system defined by (A.1.2), (A.1.3). The procedure is the same as in Appendix 1.

Towards a Multi-peclet Number Pollution Monitoring Algorithm

John Oyekan, Dongbing Gu, and Huosheng Hu

University of Essex,
Wivenhoe Park, Colchester, Essex CO4 3SQ, United Kingdom
{jooyek,dgu,hhu}@essex.ac.uk
http://www.essex.ac.uk/csee/

Abstract. Environments can range from low peclet numbers in which diffusion is predominant to high peclet numbers in which turbulence and advection occur. Control algorithms deployed on robotic platforms to monitor spatiotemporal distributions are often very specific to a particular peclet number environment and suffer reduction in efficiency when used in another peclet number environment. This paper investigates this issue and proposes the development of a pollution monitoring controller that can be used in various environments possessing different peclet numbers. A diffusion based controller and a controller that uses velocity flow information present in the environment are used as candidates for investigation. Even though the diffusion based controller lacks the ability to find a pollution source in a high turbulent environment, it still possess a desirable characteristic that could be used to map a pollution plume in a seaport environment.

Keywords: Bio Inspired Controllers, Pollution Plume Characterization, Environmental Monitoring.

1 Introduction

Monitoring pollution levels in the natural environment as become a major priority for governments around the world due to the issue of global warming. This is especially true as rises in sea levels have been recorded in low level areas around the world. Global warming has also resulted in an increase in specie invasion of habitats not native to them because of rises in sea temperature and the extinction of wild life[1]. As a result of this, researchers in the mobile sensor field have been developing various techniques to monitor the environment. This includes developing algorithms that would enable a swarm of agents form the spatial distribution of a pollutant as in [2][3]. Also, algorithms have been developed that enable a single agent find a pollution source as in [4][5][6][7].

In the natural marine environment flow conditions can vary from one area to another depending on the topology of the environment and speed of flow of the water. These conditions can vary from very low peclet number in which diffusion is predominant (e.g reservoirs or man made lakes) to very high peclet numbers in which naturally occurring chemicals such as pheromone experience a combination of diffusion, advection and turbulent mixing with the water medium (e.g a river at high tide). In such turbulent environments, chemicals often undergo turbulent "tearing" from the main chemical

S. Jeschke, H. Liu, and D. Schilberg (Eds.): ICIRA 2011, Part II, LNAI 7102, pp. 287–296, 2011.

plume resulting in a patchy pollutant distribution. Organisms living in these different conditions have developed different schemes that enable them to deal with challenges posed by their environment. For example, in diffusion based environments, the bacteria has developed a gradient based scheme that enables it to find food sources while the male moth uses a zigzag casting procedure to fly cross wind in a turbulent windy environment to find a female moth for mating. Strategies used by these organisms and others have inspired various algorithms that have been deployed on robots to find and characterize pollution sources in the environment. For example, [8][9] used bacterial inspiration to develop controllers for spatial source quantity pollution source localisation in a diffusion based environment while [5][7] used inspiration from the moth to develop casting maneuvers to find sources in a turbulent environment.

However, these source localisation techniques are often restricted to one kind of environment and the technique either fails when used in another environment or reduces in efficiency. For example, the method used by [5][7] depends on the flow information in the environment to aid agents in moving upstream towards the pollution source. This method works very effectively when a velocity flow field is present but fails when there is no such information or no flow in the environment such as in a diffusion based environment. A diffusion based controller such as a bacteria controller does not rely on flow information but can only find its food sources reliably in a diffusion based environment. Having mentioned that, it has been observed that marine bacteria can find food sources in the ocean which is a high turbulent environment.

In this paper, we compare and investigate the advantages of both techniques and then investigate a controller that could work effectively in both environments. According to present knowledge, no pollution source seeking controller has taken into account working in two different conditions of low peclet and medium to high peclet number environments. The rest of this paper is organised as follows: in section 2, we discuss the controllers that would be investigated in this study, in section 3 the experimental setup is discussed while in we present experimental results in section 4 and then conclude with discussion and future work direction in section 5.

2   Technical Approach

2.1   Diffusion Based Controller

There has been various investigations into the development of controllers that can operate in diffusion like environments. For example, Mayhew et al used inspiration from a line minimization-based algorithm in [10] to develop a robust source-seeking hybrid controller. In their work, gradient information and exact coordinates of the vehicles (For vehicles in GPS denied environments) were not needed. In [11], Baronov et al developed a hybrid reactive control law that enables an agent to ascend or descend along a potential field. However, some researchers have looked towards nature and taken inspiration from the bacteria as in [8] and [9]. In [8], Marques et al compared a rule based bacteria controller with the silkworm algorithm amongst other algorithms while in [9], Dhariwal et al used a keller segel model of bacteria population as an inspiration to develop a source seeking controller.

In this work, the Berg and Brown model [12] is used because of its ease of analysis and ability to compare the behaviour of the bacteria algorithm driven robots with biological results. In addition, this model was chosen above models such as the one in [13] because it was deemed sufficient to implement a biased random walk. Furthermore, it gives the user the ability to control both the exploratory and exploitation behaviour of robotic agents through the tuning of its parameters.

The bacterium motion is governed by a series of tumbles and run phases. A run phase can be viewed as a straight line for simplicity purposes while the tumble phase can be viewed as reorienting itself to a randomly chosen direction. When the bacteria is moving towards a favorable food source, the run phase is increased in duration whilst if moving in an unfavourable direction, the tumble phase is increased. This was discovered and modelled by Berg and Brown according to the equations 1 to 3.

$$\tau = \tau_o exp(\alpha \frac{\overline{dP_b}}{dt}) \tag{1}$$

$$\frac{\overline{dP_b}}{dt} = \tau_m^{-1} \int_{-\infty}^{t} \frac{dP_b}{dt'} exp(\frac{(t'-t)}{\tau_m})dt', \tag{2}$$

$$\frac{dP_b}{dt} = \frac{k_d}{(k_d + C)^2} \frac{dC}{dt} \tag{3}$$

τ is the mean run time and τ_o is the mean run time in the absence of concentration gradients, α is a constant of the system based on the chemotaxis sensitivity factor of the bacteria, P_b is the fraction of the receptor bound at concentration C. In this work, C was the present reading taken by the Robotic agent. k_d is the dissociation constant of the the bacterial chemoreceptor. $\frac{dP_b}{dt}$ is the rate of change of P_b. $\frac{\overline{dP_b}}{dt}$ is the weighted rate of change of P_b, while τ_m is the time constant of the bacterial system. The above equations determine the time between tumbles and hence the length of the run phase between tumbles. During the tumble phase, the agent can randomly choose a range of angles in the uniform distribution $\sigma \varepsilon \{0..., 360\}$.

In addition to the above equations, we also use a "foraging equation" that controls the velocity of the agents. This equation enables agents to dwell longer in areas of high pollution concentration and lesser in areas of low pollution concentration. This equation is presented in equation 4 where β is the dynamic velocity that depends on the present reading of the pollution C, β_o is the standard velocity without any reading and v_k is a constant for tuning the dynamic velocity β.

$$\beta = \frac{\beta_o * v_k}{C} \tag{4}$$

The bacteria controller has previously discussed does not rely on flow information and needs only a pollution measuring sensor.

2.2   A Flow Information Controller

Most controllers that use flow information to navigate towards the source of a pollution are inspired by the moth behaviour. Examples include the spiral surge algorithm developed by Hayes et al in [5] and casting algorithms developed by Li et al in [7]. The spiral surge algorithm is suitable for high turbulent conditions in which there are patchy distributions of pollution. Nevertheless, the flow information controller that was chosen in this investigation was the one developed in [7] because of its performance in field trial tests. The passive strategy for maintaining contact with plume was chosen. The strategy relies on having a sensor that reads both the medium's flow information and a sensor for detecting pollution levels C. Whenever the pollution sensor detects a value above threshold v , the agent gets the flow information in its immediate vicinity and moves upstream.

As mentioned previously, chemicals in a turbulent environment often undergo "tearing" leading to a patchy distribution in addition to meandering in a non-uniform environment. As a result, of the patchiness of the plume, it is possible that the agent might not have any reading during its upstream travel for sometime even though it is on course towards the source of the plume.

In order to solve this, a constant κ is used. If the pollution sensor reading C at time t has been above the threshold v for the last κ seconds $t\epsilon[t - \kappa, t]$, then it is assumed that the agent is still in contact with the plume and upstream motion is continued. Every time an above threshold reading is obtained, a variable T_{LAST} is set to the current time t. Another variable called T_{LOST} is used to determine when the plume is lost and is calculated by using $T_{LOST} = T_{LAST} + \kappa$. When T_{LOST} is equal to $T_{LAST} + \kappa$, the agent tries to reacquire the plume by going at $90°$ to the present direction of the agent. This is carried out by using equations 5 and 6 where ζ_v is the commanded heading of the vehicle, ζ_u is given by equation 7 and ψ can be either -90 or $+90$ depending on equation 6. The agents uses equation 7 to go upstream and this is obtained by adding $180°$ to the instantaneous wind direction ζ_w.

$$\zeta_v(t) = \zeta_u(t) + sign(\psi) \tag{5}$$

$$\psi = \begin{cases} +90 & if \quad \zeta_v(T_{lost}) - \zeta_w(T_{lost}) > -180° \\ -90 & if \quad \zeta_v(T_{lost}) - \zeta_w(T_{lost}) < -180° \end{cases} \tag{6}$$

$$\zeta_u(t) = \zeta_w(t) + 180 \tag{7}$$

In this investigation, κ was set to 1000 ms and v set to 1. For more information on the flow controller and its pseudo code implementation, the reader is referred to [7].

3   Experimental Setup

In order to develop the plume used in these studies, an environment was constructed as shown in Figure 1. The environment had dimensions of 400 by 1000 with obstacles placed in it to generate its boundaries. Computational fluid dynamics simulation was then performed on this environment using OpenFoam computational fluid dynamics package. Flow vectors were obtained from the simulation carried out. The plume puffs were constructed from a Gaussian distribution of particles around a mean point μ that was advected from the plume source according to the flow field. The spread or standard deviation ω of the distribution of particles was increased according to the equation 8. Where k is a constant that can be tuned to the user's preference.

$$\omega_{t+1} = \omega_t + kt \tag{8}$$

In this way, the plume shown in Figure 1 was obtained. By multiplying the flow vectors with either a constant or random value, it is possible to control the x and y speeds of the plume resulting in either a defined plume with a predictable path or a meandering plume. In this case, the x and y speeds x_v and y_v were set to 14 times their scalar values. In Figure 1, it can be observed that the plume was more patchy towards the source. This is because the flow field energy was strong in the narrow space. However this energy dissipated after the area enlarged resulting in a less patchy section of the plume. This energy was slightly regained in the lower section of the simulated environment resulting in a patchy plume again.

The agents in our simulations were equipped with noiseless sensors that could read the concentration of particles by counting the number of particles in a 10 by 10 grid around their position.

Fig. 1. Test Environment

4   Results

Before investigating the possibility of developing a controller that could work in both a diffusion based environment and a medium to high peclet environment, we tested both schemes to see their performance in both scenarios.

4.1   Diffusion Based (Low Peclet Number) Environment

In this environment, the speeds for x and y directions, x_v and y_v, were set to zero so that the plume puffs were not advected. The source of the pollutant was placed at (x, y) = (200, 550) in the section of the environment as shown in Figure 2(a) where diffusion was most likely to occur as a result of low flow energy as discussed previously. 50 agents for each technique were placed at the same position at (x, y) = (70, 500) on the fringes of the generated pollution as shown in Figure 2(a) and allowed to run. The oval shaped agents are those running the flow controller method described in section 2.2 while the square agents are those running the bacteria method. An agent is assumed to have found the source if it was within 10 by 10 units of the source. It was discovered that none of the agents using the flow method discovered the source as a result of not having any flow information against which they could navigate. This can be seen more clearly by considering equation 7 in which once pollution is detected, the agent would always move in a $\zeta_w(t) + 180°$ direction. As there was no flow information, $\zeta_w(t)$ would be equal to zero resulting in the agents moving in the direction 180° away from the pollutant as seen in Figure 2(b). Since the flow controller method is deterministic and the pollutant is static in our experiments, all the 50 agents behaved deterministically resulting in all of them having the same final position as seen in Figure 2(b).However, 48 out of 50 of the agents using the bacteria controller however were able to find the source after 5 minutes of run time with an average of 2052 iterations.

In this experiment, the β_o for the bacteria controller was set to 64 with a velocity limit of 10 in order to enable the agents explore the environment aggressively while $\alpha = 500$ and $k_d = 10$ in order to achieve faster exploitation towards the source when in the pollutant. From previous experiments carried out in [14][15], it was observed that α was responsible for controlling the rate of descent or exploitation while k_d was responsible for controlling the level of chemical sensitivity of the agent. The higher k_d the more the agents stick to the pollutant particles. As a result, by using the parameter values as above, the agent stuck to the pollutant particles whilst achieving faster descent towards the source. For more information about tuning the bacteria controller, the reader is referred to [14][15].

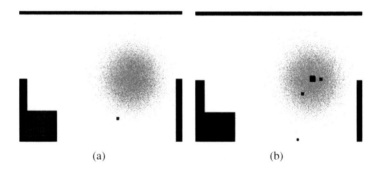

(a)   (b)

Fig. 2. Agent distribution initially (Oval shaped agents using the flow controller are under the square shaped agents using the bacteria controller) - Fig. (a) and after 8 minutes Fig. (b)

4.2   Medium to High Peclet Environment

The oval agents representing those using the flow controller method were placed in a well established plume as shown in Figure 3(a) with the blue square indicating the source. It was discovered that all the agents were able to find the plume source for this method with an average iteration of 230.

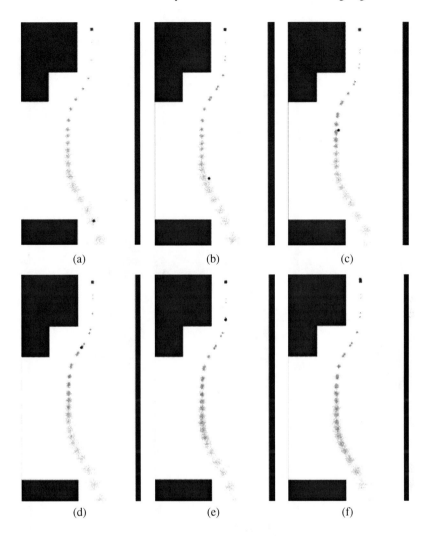

Fig. 3. Showing stages of the agents finding the source of the plume using the flow controller method

However, for the bacteria controller, the technique failed to follow the plume as is shown in Figure 4(a). The boundaries of the environment were deliberately not considered in this experiment for comparison purposes. Reliance on the gradient information makes the bacteria controller fail because it is not possible to get that information in such a turbulent environment. Nevertheless, it was discovered that if the straight runs were modified into circular casting motions by using a biological inspired step angle of $\sigma \in 59$ degrees $\pm$ rand() based on the S.putrefaciens tracking a falling algae, it is possible to obtain an emergent characteristic as shown in Figure 4(b) to 4(d).

This characteristic enabled some of the agents to find the source even though it took a larger number of iterations (over 5000) compared to the flow controller method whilst

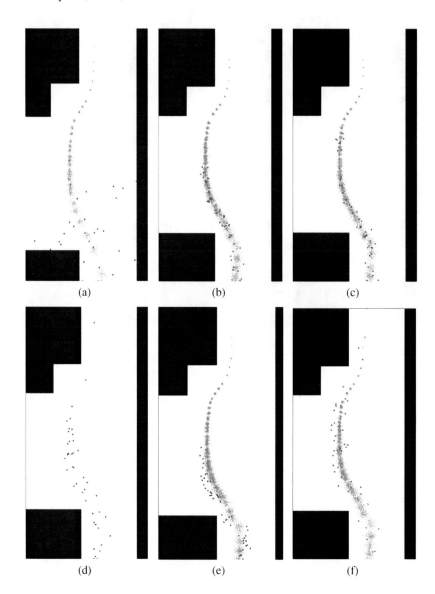

Fig. 4. Agent distributions for ordinary bacteria behaviour - Fig 4(a); modified bacteria behaviour - Fig 4(b) to 4(d); and for modified bacteria behaviour with negative gradient - Fig 4(e) to 4(f). Red was used for the square shaped agents so that it could stand out of the black boundary. Their size was also made smaller so that the forming of the shpae of the plume could be seen more clearly.

still forming the shape of the plume as shown in Figure 4(d). The plume in Figure 4(d) was deliberately left out to show that the agents followed the structure of the plume. This behaviour was obtained by using the bacteria parameters $k_d = 1000$, $\alpha = 500$, $\tau_o = 2$, $\beta_o = 6$ in order to achieve more exploitation when in the plume than exploration of the environment. Another emergent property that was discovered was that when an agent got to the source, the agent stopped moving. Stopping at the source was something not programmed into the agent's behaviour. This property could be as a result of the k_d parameter being saturated and could be used as a way of declaring the source of the plume.

By changing the sign in equation 3 to negative as in $-\frac{dC}{dt}$, it was possible to make the bacteria dwell on the outskirts of the plume as shown in Figure 4(e) and Figure 4(f). In this case, the agents were always pushed to the boundary of the plume whenever they come into contact with the plume. This behaviour could be used to contain the pollution plume whilst tracing its shape and moving to the source.

4.3   Combining Controllers

From the results of the experiments carried out above, the ordinary bacteria controller works well in a diffusion based environment while when a medium to high peclet number environment. However, after modifying its straight runs to circular motions, it is capable of finding the source of the pollution whilst characterizing or providing a visual map of the plume. On the other hand, the flow controller method only works in a medium to high peclet environment but its efficiency at finding the source of the plume is much better compared to the bacteria controller. As a result, we propose the following hybrid control law:when working in a low peclet environment, the bacteria controller should be used. However, when working in a high peclet environment, the user can either choose the bacteria controller with circular runs if the aim is plume characterization or the flow controller method if the aim is finding the source of the plume quickly.

5   Conclusion

In this work, we have compared the performances and characteristics of two different source seeking controllers- a flow based controller and a gradient based bacteria inspired controller. We have presented results that show that by modifying the bacteria controller's run phase from purely straight runs to circular runs, it is possible to use it to find the source of a plume in a medium peclet environment. However, its performance is not as good as the flow based controller. Nevertheless, this shows that the bacteria controller can work in both low and medium peclet number environments paving the way towards a multi peclet number source seeking controller. On the other hand, the flow based controller can only work in a medium peclet number environment where information about flow is present but not in a low peclet number environment where flow information is absent. In the future, we plan to mathematically investigate the characterization property of the bacteria inspired controller.

Acknowledgements. This research work is financially sponsored by European Union FP7 program, ICT-231646, SHOAL.

References

1. Stachowicz, J.J., Terwin, J.R., Whitlatch, R.B., Osman, R.W.: Linking climate change and biological invasions: Ocean warming facilitates nonindigenous species invasions. Proceedings of the National Academy of Sciences of the United States of America 99(24), 15497–15500 (2002)
2. Shucker, B., Murphey, T., Bennett, J.K.: An Approach to Switching Control Beyond Nearest Neighbor Rules. In: American Control Conference, p. 7 (2006)
3. Schwager, M., Mclurkin, J., Slotine, J.-j.E., Rus, D.: From Theory to Practice: Distributed Coverage Control Experiments with Groups of Robots. STAR, vol. 54(1), pp. 127–136 (2009)
4. Lochmatter, T., Heiniger, N., Martinoli, A., Systems, D.I.: Localizing an Odor Source and Avoiding Obstacles: Experiments in aWind Tunnel using Real Robots. In: 13th International Symposium on Olfaction and Electronic Nose, Brescis, Italy, vol. (C), p. 1137 (April 2009)
5. Hayes, T., Martinoli, A., Goodman, R.M.: Distributed odor source localization. IEEE Sensors Journal 2(3), 260–271
6. Pang, S., Farrell, J.A.: Chemical Plume Source Localization 36(5), 1068–1080 (October 2006)
7. Li, W., Farrell, J.A., Card, R.T.: Strategies for Tracking Fluid-Advected Odor Plumes. Adaptive Behavior (2001)
8. Marques, L., Nunes, U., Almeida, T.D.: Olfaction-based mobile robot navigation. Thin Solid Films 418(1), 51–58 (2002)
9. Dhariwal, A., Sukhatme, G.S., Requicha, A.A.G.: Bacterium-inspired robots for environmental monitoring. In: Proc. of IEEE Int. Conf. on Robotics and Automation, New Orleans, LA, pp. 1436–1443 (April 2004)
10. Mayhew, G., Sanfelice, R.G., Teel, A.R.: Robust source-seeking hybrid controllers for nonholonomic vehicles. In: American Control Conference, pp. 2722–2727 (2008)
11. Baronov, D., Baillieul, J.: Autonomous vehicle control for ascending/descending along a potential field with two applications. In: Proc. of the American Control Conference, pp. 678–683 (2008)
12. Brown, D.A., Berg, C.: Temporal stimulation of chemotaxis in Escherichia coli. Proc. Natil. Acad. Sci. U.S.A. 71, 1388 (1974)
13. Yi, T., Huang, Y., Simon, M., Doyle, J.: Robust perfect adaptation in bacterial chemotaxis through integral feedback control. Proc. Natl. Acad. Sci. 97(9), 4649–4653 (2000)
14. Oyekan, J., Hu, H., Gu, D.: Bio-Inspired Coverage of Invisible Hazardous Substances in the Environment. International Journal of Information Acquisition 7(3), 193 (2010)
15. Oyekan, J., Hu, H.: Bacteria Controller Implementation on a Physical Platform for Pollution Monitoring. In: Proc. of IEEE Int. Conf. on Robotics and Automation, Anchorage, Alaska, USA, May 3-8, pp. 3781–3786 (2010)

Self-balancing Controllable Robots in Education: A Practical Course for Bachelor Students

Paul Hänsch, John Schommer, and Stefan Kowalewski

Embedded Software Laboratory, RWTH Aachen,
Ahornstrae 55, 52074 Aachen, Germany
http://www.embedded.rwth-aachen.de

Abstract. We present a framework for a programming course for undergraduate computer science students. The technical motivation is to implement a two-wheeled self-balancing controllable robot. Advanced requirements make it a full-grown software project. The emphasis of this course is on one hand to teach basic concepts of software programming. The students work in groups of five and each student is assigned a role, which is typical for the software development process. On the other hand, the course is intended to give some basic hands-on experience in control theory.

Keywords: Java Programming, Software Engineering, Inverted Pendulum, Self-balancing, Robotics, Control.

1 Introduction

Embedded system design is one of the most important links between computer science and engineering science. As such, it is a vital part of the educational process to provide computer science students with an understanding of basic engineering principles. This includes both, a theoretical background covered in lectures, as well as an intuition of physics, which is best taught by practical experiments in suitable courses. In particular, the latter can be experienced by students in an early stage of their studies.

The technical motivation of our practical course is the implementation of an NXT-controlled, mobile inverted pendulum (robot) build from LEGOs, which can be steered via a Bluetooth remote control. More sophisticated features, such as collision avoidance, tracking the mobile pendulum on a computer screen and that kind are also in the scope of this course.

There are plenty different approaches that aim on balancing NXT-controlled robots. The first implementation is due to Steve Hassenplug and uses EOPDs (*electro-optical proximity detector*) to measure the distance to the ground. Another approach is to use a gyro sensor, and finally, there have been implementations using a gyro sensor in combination with an accelerometer. The last approach is inspired by the well known Segway Personal Transporter[1], which

---

[1] Segway Inc.™

S. Jeschke, H. Liu, and D. Schilberg (Eds.): ICIRA 2011, Part II, LNAI 7102, pp. 297–306, 2011.

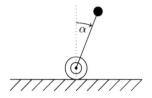

Fig. 1. The Inverted Pendulum Problem

includes a number of redundant gyroscopes and acceleration sensors in order to achieve a high level of safety.

The inverted pendulum, which is shown in Figure 1, is one of the most popular educational examples in control theory. For instance, a proportional controller is not capable of keeping it upright, whereas a PID controller suffices to do so. Therefore, the pendulum is appropriate to demonstrate the effects of the proportional, integral and derivative parameters of a PID controller. At the same time, most basic rules for parameter tuning can be applied to obtain working parameters. All this, however, assumes perfect information of the control variable, i.e. the angle of the pendulum. In practice, drift and noise of measured data can render a controller-design unusable. Thus, a much more complicated model of the plant would be necessary to apply model-based design successfully as demonstrated by Takashi Chikamasa[2]

To the best of our knowledge, there is no documentation of an implementation of a selfbalancing controllable robot with LEGO Mindstorms NXT and Java. As such, a part of our contribution is to state that it is basically possible and further the performance of the NXT together with leJOS is high enough to include more extra features.

The remainder of the paper is organized as follows: In the next section we describe the realization of the inverted pendulum from hardware to firmware level and summarize essential requirements that systems of the participants have to fulfill. The project is divided into two stages. Each group has to accomplish at least the first stage to get a certification. In the following section we describe the aims of the software project programming course, which includes the typical project roles the students have to claim and fill with life. After that, we briefly describe in Section 4 the design of a simple controller that is sufficient for keeping the robot upright. In the last section we give a brief evaluation.

2   Realization of the Inverted Pendulum

In this section we briefly summarize the characteristics and capabilities of the chosen platform. We also mention some popular alternatives to put the described course into a larger context.

---

[2] See http://www.mathworks.com/matlabcentral/fileexchange/19147

2.1   Hardware

In 1998 LEGO presented the LEGO Mindstorms RIS (Robotics Invention System), the first in a line of programmable robotics toys. It was built around the RCX, a brick whose core is an 8-bit Renesas H8/300 microcontroller with 32 Kbytes of RAM that stores the firmware and user programs. The brick provides three input ports to read sensor data and three output ports to control (and also read data from) electric motors.

In our lab exercise we use the successor, Mindstorms NXT, which was released in 2006[3]. The NXT brick features a 32-bit ARM7 microcontroller with 256 Kbytes FLASH, 64 Kbytes RAM. An 8-bit AVR microcontroller is handling the data transfer between the ARM7 and the four sensor ports. There are plenty different sensors available, provided by LEGO and third-party vendors, such as HiTechnic and Mindsensors. Besides, any I2C sensor is supported which allows for using custom-made sensors. The NXT has built-in Bluetooth support and thus can be controlled not only by a remote desktop computer, but also by smart phones and game pads.

2.2   Firmware

There is a variety of ways of programming the NXT-brick, each of which is based on a specific firmware that provides APIs to the developers and a toolchain for cross compiling and uploading the projects. The standard NXT-kit includes NXT-G, a graphical programming environment that enables the creation and downloading of programs to the NXT. Although it is a potential language, more ambitious goals should be pursued using one of the textual programming languages among which are assembly- and C-like languages and many more, as well as free and commercial ones. An overview can be found in the world wide web[4].

Another remarkable way of programming the NXT-brick is from within the MATLAB[5] environment as proposed in [2]. A similar toolkit is also available for LabView[6]. However, these approaches are suited for courses in practical engineering but they are not appropriate in our case where the focus is on state-of-the-art software engineering with a touch of embedded system design and a handful of control theory. Therefore, in our course we use the leJOS library [1], which provides the developers with a Java extending API including a Bluetooth implementation. As a Java derivative, leJOS is well documented and supported in the world wide web[7]. It allows a high level of abstraction and is best suited for the use with an up-to-date IDE such as Eclipse.

---

[3] The newest version, LEGO Mindstorms NXT 2.0, released in 2009, brings some minor improvements compared to the NXT.

[4] http://www.teamhassenplug.org/NXT/NXTSoftware.html

[5] © MathWorks.

[6] © National Instruments.

[7] On the leJOS project homepage at http://leJOS.sourceforge.net you will find tutorials, the leJOS API and also an active forum.

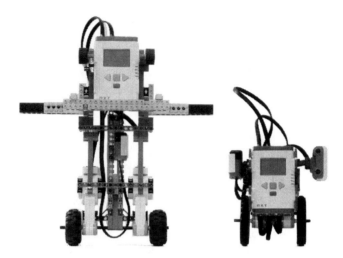

Fig. 2. Two different robots requiring different settings of the controller parameters to keep them upright and balancing

2.3   Essential Requirements

Back to the technical motivation of our course, the whole project consists in two stages. The goal of the first stage is to provide a framework that enables the user to control the robot via a remote desktop application. This project stage can be divided into the following subtasks:

1. Find a controller that is able to make the robot stay upright. In case the robot falls, the motors should automatically stop.
2. Create a GUI application that enables you to modify your controller parameters in (close to) real time from your computer via Bluetooth, monitor parameters that are of interest, such as the angle, the position, the maximum cycle time of the control loop and so forth.
3. Extend the existing controller and GUI such that your robot is able to move forward and backward, turn left and right.

In a second stage the students have to implement advanced features. The first feature that is to be implemented, is a system that manages several robots such that the user can, first, scan the environment for robots in range (which have to be registered Bluetooth devices on the computer which is running the application), choose one of the robots, connect to it, drive around with it, disconnect (the robot then has to stay at its current position and balance) and continue in the same way. Figure 3 shows a screen shot of an implementation including this feature. In the upper right panel you see the list of robots that are in range and can be connected to. The panel below can be used to steer the robot, however, it is much more convenient to use the keyboard. The panel in the middle is used to set the controller parameters (more details on these parameters will be given in Section 4). After pressing the upload-button, the parameters are committed to the NXT and one can immediately see how they change the behaviour of the robot. The remaining buttons in this panel allow to save and load controller setups and to choose a setup as the default setup for the currently connected robot. The panel on the right monitors all important variables of the robot (some of them, for instance *offset* and *offset base* depend on the controller design used). The second advanced feature that is to be implemented can be chosen by the

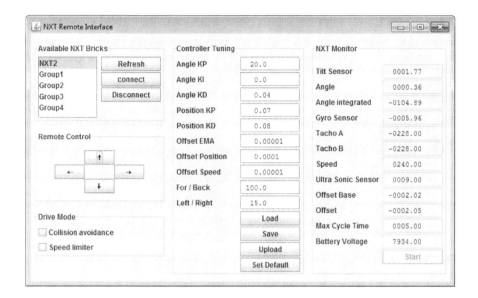

Fig. 3. Remote GUI application for managing several robots (top left panel), tuning and maintaining the controller paramters (middle panel) and watching specific variables (right panel)

students themselves. Appropriate ones, that can also be implemented with our platform are for instance

1. Collision avoidance and speed limiter.
2. Tracking system that plots a two-dimensional image of the trajectory of the robot.
3. Scanning the environment and producing a two-dimensional picture that represents the shape of the room.

In fact, Feature 1 can be found in the screen shot in Figure 3 where the user can choose whether he wants to drive safe or fast. It is nice to have the safe-driving-mode when letting other people drive the robot. For a competetive performance these safety features should be turned off, which, however, can make the robot fall in case of too abrasive maneuvers.

Feature 2 is to be realized as a dead reckoning system. It is of course subject to an error which highly depends on the characteristics of the floor. It further depends on the way the robot is moving and if, for instance, a compass sensor is used.

The visualization part of Feature 3 can be build upon Feature 2. The scanning itself can be done using ultra sonic sensors. Those provided by LEGO have a range of around 1.5 meters. The accuracy of the sensor output depends very much on the surface of the walls and also on the angle between sensor and wall. If the sensor is placed perpendicularly in front of the wall, the value is more accurate than if it is tilted.

3   Aims of the Software Project Programming Course

Apart from applying and broadening Java programming skills (see [3]), one of the major aims of this course is to make the students familiar with the typical roles in the software development process, including *project manager, requirement analyst, software architect, software engineer* and *software tester*. The students work in several groups in parallel with five students per group. Each group can be considered as one company and the course as a competition between the different groups.

We propose that each student has to sense the role of the software engineer and contribute a fair part to the overall programming work. Further, we introduce a role which is responsible for *version control*. In a nutshell, each student has to play the role of a software engineer and, additionally, two further roles.

In the remainder of this section we briefly recapitulate the responsibilities and specific tasks of each of the roles.

Project Management. Every software project needs some kind of release planning, where the question is answered of how the vision can be turned into a winning product. There exists a huge number of conventional or agile frameworks or processes, but always some kind of project management must be done to accomplish the technical goal of the project. Typically, in the release planning a time plan including stages and milestones of the project and the resources scheduling over time is specified. In every process at least one responsible person is chosen that ensures the progress. He or she records the release plan, broadcasts tasks to roles/resources and encourages the team to fulfill their roles. The process iterations and meetings are organized by this role. It is also responsible for updating the process plan due to delays, newly identified functionality or additonal constraints.

Requirement Analysis. One essential workpackage of every software project is the reqiurement analysis. The goal of this analsyis is a precise specification of the product requirements, which is needed in every kind of development process.

The specification consists of the functional and non-functional requirements the final software product shall fulfill. It also serves as a kind of contract between the customer and the development team, therefore any ambiguities should be avoided. Further, this document is very central in the whole development process, such that it often contains further constraints of the project and additional information like the project planning in a summarized version. The requirements analyst is responsible for the correctness of this document which includes to keep it up-to-date in every stage of the project.

Finally, note that in general profound knowledge of the hardware is needed in order to tell whether a specific requirement can theoretically be realized or not. Hence, in a group of only five students, the analyst is the one who has to get acquainted with the used platform in more detail.

Software Architecture. The architecture of the software that runs on the NXT has to meet one major requirement. The control loop has to be processed sufficiently fast. Time consuming tasks have to be identified and executed in separate threads. Luckily, the variables that are essential for the controller, i.e. the gyro sensor and the motor encoders can be read in almost no time (between 50 to 100 micro-seconds per reading). Other sensor data and in particular the communication via Bluetooth can take up to several milliseconds and hence should not be done inside the control loop. In our fully equipped prototype including at least three different threads, the control loop, which corresponds to one of the threads, is processed in less than ten milliseconds. This is sufficiently fast to make the robot pretty stable. If the control loop cycle time increases, the robot gets more and more bumpy until it finally gets completely unstable when the cycle time is approaching 25 milliseconds (this value of course is specific to our implementation and controller parameters).

The architecture of the desktop application is driven by the GUI-concept, which is, in turn, designed according to the results of the requirement analysis. Designing the logical backend of the application becomes challenging if one or more of the advanced features are implemented.

The software architects have to use the *Unified Modeling Language (UML)* to design essential features of their software product. A good introduction to UML is given for example in [4]. As such, *sequence diagrams* provide a way to describe the interaction between the robot and the GUI. *Activity diagrams* can for example be used to show how the interpretation of remote commands (for/back/left/right or whatever commands the students choose for their robot) is incorporated into the control loop. Regarding the GUI in figure 3, a *use case diagram* can for instance show how the user disconnects from a robot, scans for available NXTs and connects to one of these. Finally, *class diagrams* are used to give an overview of the implementation itself. The architects have to choose an appropriate tool for tool-supported diagram generation and evaluate it.

Software Testing. One of the most important but mostly ignored stages of the software development is the software quality assurance. Software as a product must be tested intensively to prevent systematic failures. A long time ago, developers and engineers identified that testing the project in early stages – that includes for instance planning and modeling of the project – is essential for its success and getting the product to market right in time. Several methodologies are developed and established in the software industry. One essential method is the establishment of unit tests. Such tests are or should in reality be written in early stages of the project, each time a new small software unit is planned and specified. Such tests ensure two things: First, errors are identified on detail level before the system integration starts, where finding errors is very hard. And second, this allows a smart way to run regression tests when changing details of software parts in late stages of the development process.

In our course one role is responsible for all the tests that need to be done on the growing software project. However, the focus lies on unit testing code fragments of the whole project. This is because unit tests are highly integrated in the Java/leJOS IDEs used in our courses, e.g. Eclipse.

Version Control. In a software project it is of course essential to have a proper *version control* system which enables a team to work on a software product in parallel, track the development of a product and possibly different branches of it.

The role responsible for version control has to decide for one system and has to set it up and integrate the existing project, if there is any. Further, a *manual* should be written which is intended for the other members of the group and should allow them to set up a project, integrate it with the version control and checkout a working copy. In the context of a development environment this is not trivial and it is definitely recommendable to have some expertise on the version control system used.

4   Simple Controller Design

In this section we briefly describe the realization of the control loop, which is the central technology for keeping the robot upright. At first, we explain the controller design for the case that only the gyro sensor is used. The output of the gyro sensor is the angular velocity $\omega(t)$ in degrees per second. When the sensor is at rest, however, the output is in general some constant non-zero value, called *offset*. This offset is to be subtracted from each sensor date in order to get the actual angular velocity.

Let us assume the tilt of the robot to be $\alpha = 0$ when the robot is in its steady state, i.e. standing perfectly still. The control objective is then to keep the current tilt $\alpha(t)$ at zero. Since the output of the gyro sensor is the angular velocity $\omega(t)$ we have

$$\alpha(t) = \alpha(0) + \int_0^t \omega(\tau)\mathrm{d}\tau.$$

We assume $\alpha(0) = 0$ which means that at time $t = 0$ the robot is—more or less—in its steady state. By numerical integration we obtain $\alpha(t)$. Even if the time steps between two successing readings of the gyro sensor are sufficiently small to get a good numerical integration, the value $\alpha(t)$ is definitely not reliable. This is because the offset depends on conditions such as the temperature and battery voltage. Consequently the offset tends to drift with time and the integrated value $\alpha(t)$ can—with increasing time—differ drastically from the actual current tilt of the robot. Thus, a PID controller that is based solely on the tilt and the gyro sensor, is doomed to fail. The calculation of the angle $\alpha(t)$ can be improved by, e.g., taking the influence of battery voltage and temperature into account; the NXT and the leJOS API provide the means to determine the battery voltage, the temperature could be measured using another sensor. It is also possible to use several gyro sensors and to take for instance their average value. The drift of the offset can be—to some extent—captured as follows. Under the assumption that the robot is balancing, and thus oscillating around its steady state, the offset should be equal to a long-term average of the gyro sensor values. A drifting offset can then be approximated by a *weighted moving average* or an *exponential moving average* of the gyro sensor values. All these remedies can improve the performance, but are not sufficient to make a reliably balancing robot.

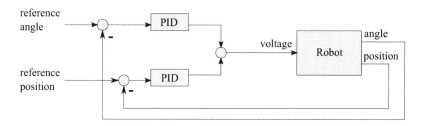

Fig. 4. Basic controller design, sufficient to make the robot balance

The simplest way to make the robot balance is to take the current position of the robot into account. Since the motors of the NXT provide a tachometer no further hardware is needed. In fact, it is sufficient to take one PID controller for the angle and another PID controller for the position as suggested by Figure 4. Changing the reference position, one can make the robot move for and back. Having a separate reference position for each of the wheels allows to make the robot turn left and right. However, even though the controller design from Figure 4 is sufficient to make the robot stand upright for a long time, it will most probably not stay at a certain position because the drifting offset will be leveled out by a drift of the position. A remedy to this problem is to modify the offset according to the drift of the position. Regarding the GUI in Figure 3 where you can see the monitored variables *offset base* and *offset* in the right panel, the first one is the initial offset (-2.02) and the latter (-2.05) is the current working offset where the positional error has been taken into account.

5   Evaluation and Summary

It is a good advice to have all necessary software[8] preinstalled and running. In our course the students decided to use their own laptops and installed all software that is necessary on their own. However, it turned out that diverse problems can arise, all of them solvable but more or less time-consuming.

In the world wide web one can find implementations of the balancing robot that make use of acceleration sensors. This is to avoid a drift of the angle which is unavoidable when using only the gyro sensor. Unfortunately, our evaluation of the acceleration sensor by HiTechnic and the leJOS firmware has shown that the access times are way too long to be placed in the control loop. However, the acceleration sensor can be used to compute the initial angle when the robot starts balancing and can be used to detect if the robot falls.

References

1. Bagnall, B.: Maximum lego nxt: Building robots with java brains (2009)
2. Behrens, A., Atorf, L., Schwann, R., Neumann, B., Schnitzler, R., Balle, J., Herold, T., Telle, A., Noll, T.G., Hameyer, K., Aach, T.: Matlab meets lego mindstorms – a freshman introduction course into practical engineering. IEEE Transactions on Education 53(2), 306–317 (2010)
3. Bloch, J.: Effective Java: A Programming Language Guide, 2nd edn. Addison-Wesley Longman (2008)
4. Miles, R., Hamilton, K.: Learning UML 2.0. O'Reilly (2007)

---

[8] Including Java 32-bit JDK, leJOS libraries, leJOS firmware, USB and Bluetooth driver, a development environment (Eclipse or Netbeans), version control system (e.g. SVN and Tortoise).

Intelligent Control Design in Robotics and Rehabilitation

Petko Kiriazov, Gergana Nikolova, and Ivanka Veneva

Institute of Mechanics, Bulgarian Academy of Sciences,
Acad. G. Bonchev Str. bl. 4, 1113 Sofia, Bulgaria
{kiriazov,gergana,veneva}@imbm.bas.bg

Abstract. For control purposes in robotics or rehabilitation, we may use properly simplified dynamic models with a reduced number of degrees of freedom. First, we define a set of variables that best characterize its dynamic performance in the required motion task. Second, driving forces/torques are properly assigned in order to achieve the required dynamic performance in an efficient way. The usual performance requirements are for positioning accuracy, movement execution time, and energy expenditure. We consider complex biomechatronic systems (BMS) like human with active orthosis or robotic arm that have to perform two main types of motion tasks: goal-directed movements and motion/posture stabilization. We propose new design concepts and criteria for BMS based on necessary and sufficient conditions for their robust controllability. Using simplified, yet realistic, models, we give several important examples in robotics and rehabilitation to illustrate the main features and advantages of our approach.

Keywords: rehabilitation robots, control, design, learning, optimization.

1 Introduction

Persons who suffer from functional impairment due to stroke, trauma, or neurological diseases often have not reached their full potential for recovery when they are discharged from hospital. This leads to high levels of patient dissatisfaction for not receiving adequate and sufficient training possibilities.

Several authors advocate the use of rehabilitation methods that include repetition of meaningful and engaging goal-directed movements in order to induce changes in the cerebral cortex that support motor recovery (brain plasticity) [1, 2]. It seems that the impact of rehabilitation technology on functional outcome could be optimised by offering more chances to the central nervous system (CNS) to experience "real" activity-related sensorimotor input during training. Efficiency means that goal-directed motion tasks are performed in a way that is as economic as possible for the human body and training for activities of daily living (ADL) is done with minimal patient and therapist time consumption.

Difficulties to study robotic or biomechatronic systems (BMS), like human with active orthosis or robotic arm, are mainly due to their complex dynamics and external disturbances. Along with the basic design requirement for strength/load capacity additional design criteria for BMS are needed to meet the continuously increasing

S. Jeschke, H. Liu, and D. Schilberg (Eds.): ICIRA 2011, Part II, LNAI 7102, pp. 307–316, 2011.

demands for faster response, improved precision and reduced energy consumption. As robots or BMS present functionally directed compositions of mutually influencing components: control, actuator, (bio-) mechanical, and sensor subsystems, it is indispensable to have a conceptual framework for their integrated structure-control design. Of primary importance is to define an appropriate, control-relevant structure of the input-output relations, i.e., numbers and locations of inputs and outputs and their interconnections. In practice, decentralized manner of control is adopted for its main advantages to the centralized one: simplicity, reliability and faster response.

The aim of this paper is to present a new conceptual framework and introduce modelling and control design concepts in robotics and rehabilitation of patients with various movement disorders. Our study is based on underlying principles of optimal control theory, movement neuroscience and controlled multi-segmental dynamics, [3]. For control purposes, we may use properly simplified dynamic models with a reduced number of degrees of freedom. It means that, with given motion task, we have to work with models that sufficiently well represent human kinematics, dynamics, and control functions. In order to be able to generate such models in a simple way, we can use a general 3D computer model of human body with 16 segments [4, 5].

To design and control such complex systems, appropriate nominal dynamic models are needed and they have to be easily and accurately identifiable, [8]. Nominal dynamic models can be derived considering the flexible in general BMS as compositions of rigid bodies connected by joints, springs, as well as damping and actuator forces. Using such a model, we can define the corresponding control transfer matrix (TM). Applying the theory in [6, 7, 9], relevant design criteria can be derived on the basis of necessary and sufficient conditions for robust decentralized controllability. The main feature of these criteria is that they enable a decomposition of the overall design task into a sequence of design solutions for the BMS components.

Using simplified, yet realistic, models, we give several important examples in robotics and rehabilitation to illustrate the main features and advantages of our approach.

2   Computer Modelling of Human Body or Humanoid Robots

In Fig. 1ab, we present a general 16-segment geometrical model of the human body and its computer generation. The analysis and control of human motion requires knowledge of its segment parameters - mass, volume, position of the centre of mass and principal moments of inertia. These parameters can be estimated by a methodology as described in [4, 5].

By properly combining the segments, we can represent human kinematics and the control functions for many important motion tasks. Then we are able to apply the multibody system approach [16] and find mathematical models that can be used for control optimization and to represent the corresponding human dynamic performance.

We will consider two types of motion tasks: posture stabilization by applying robust closed-loop controllers and point-to-point motion tasks where open loop control functions can be efficiently synthesized by iterative learning, described in the next section.

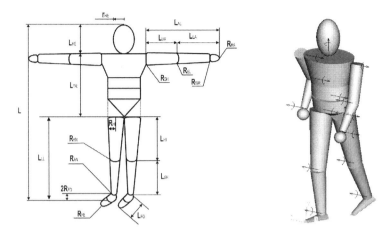

Fig. 1ab. Geometrical model of the human body and a 3D model generation using SolidWorksTM

3   Control Structure Design and Optimal Motor Learning

The usual performance criteria for goal-directed movements are: the positioning accuracy, the movement execution time and the energy consumption. Such movements can be generated by the corresponding muscles or by robotic orthoses (exoskeletons). The excitation signals naturally come from the brain and they may be processed via brain-computer interface (BCI) and/or EMG/FES devices.

Of primary importance in designing the movement control system is to properly define the control structure. It means to specify what are the most appropriate performance variables for a given motion task and which are the corresponding driving control functions. While defining the control structure for a reaching and standing-up task is not a big problem, a challenging issue is how to define it in the most complicated case of the 3-D bipedal walking.

Once the control structure is defined, the next main stage in the control design is how to learn and optimize the specific control functions with a given motion task. For simplicity, we could now have in mind only a single-joint movement. The main steps in our procedure for iterative motor control learning and optimization are as follows, [7]:

1. Choose a set of appropriate test control functions: The term "appropriate" concerns the structure, shape, and bounds of the test control functions. Simple linear-spline control functions of "bang-pause-bang" or "bang-slope-bang" shape can be used for a first-order optimization. Parameters, describing the test control functions, like switch times, slopes, or pause lengths, mostly influence the reached position and the performance criteria.
2. Define the most relevant pairs of control parameters and control outputs: It means that for each controlled output we have to assign a control input, which mostly

influences it. Regarding the controllability in multijoint tasks, the input-output pairs will be most relevant if couplings between these single-input single-output subsystems are to be as small as possible.

3. Solve shooting equations and perform control parameter optimization: With the above input-output pairing, the given goal-directed motion task is transformed into systems of learning parameter equations with respect to the switch times. They are solved applying natural bisection algorithms and this is the first level of our control synthesis procedure. At the next level, the rest of the control parameters are varied to optimize the movement execution time and the energy consumption.

Following the above approach, we can find satisfactory suboptimal solutions with minimum number of control parameters to be learnt. Existence of feasible solutions and convergence of the bisection algorithms are guaranteed, which ensures feasibility and efficiency of our control learning procedure.

4   Design of Optimal Stabilizing Controllers

Robots or BMS are in general highly non-linear dynamical systems due to dynamic couplings, friction, backlash, elasticity, actuator limits, and load change. The mechanical subsystem, though actually flexible, can be approximated by a composition of rigid bodies connected by joints, springs, dampers, and actuator forces, [5].

First, we have to define a set of variables q that best characterize the dynamic performance of the robot or BMS in the required motion task. Second, to enable them to fulfil the required motion tasks, control forces/torques u are to be properly assigned in order to achieve the required dynamic performance in an efficient way.

Applying the approach proposed in [16], the dynamic performance can be described by the following system of differential equations, [7]

$$\ddot{q} = M(q)^{-1}(Bu - C(q,\dot{q}) + g(q)). \tag{1}$$

where q is the vector of l generalized co-ordinates (e.g., links' rotation angles or joint angles), $M(q)$ is the inertia matrix, $C(q,\dot{q})$ is the vector of velocity forces, $g(q)$ stands for friction and gravitation forces, matrix B represents the control force u distribution, and $A = M^{-1}(q)B$ is the control transfer matrix (TM);

By feedforward control, we can compensate to some extent for the inertia, velocity, friction and gravitation forces. Then, the following reduced model for the error dynamics can be used for the purpose of feedback control

$$\ddot{e} = A(q)u + d. \tag{2}$$

where $e = q - q^{ref}$ and A is the control TM; vector d stands for uncompensated terms, as well as for measurement and environment noises.

As a measure of tracking precision, we take the absolute value of $s = \dot{e} + \lambda e$, $\lambda > 0$. We consider decentralized controllers, which means that, during motion, the stabilizing control force u_i of each actuator depends solely on the corresponding controlled output s_i.

A decentralized controller is robust against random disturbances d with known upper bounds $\bar{d}$ if it gets the local subsystem state $(\dot{q}, q)$ at each joint to track the desired state $(\dot{q}^{ref}, q^{ref})$ with maximum allowable absolute values $\bar{s}$ of errors s. A necessary and sufficient condition for a dynamic system (1) to be robustly controlled by a decentralized controller is that matrix A be generalized diagonal dominant (GDD), [6,9]. With A being GDD, the non-negative matrix theory [6] states that there always exists a positive vector $\bar{u}$ solving the following system of equations

$$A_{ii}\bar{u}_i - \sum_{j \neq i} |A_{ij}| \bar{u}_j = \bar{d}_i . \tag{3}$$

For the feedback stabilization, we can use sliding-mode controllers or other bounded-input controllers, and the magnitudes of the control functions are estimated from the optimal trade-off relations (3). To avoid chattering, the following continuous control functions of saturation type can be used

$$u_i(s_i) = \bar{u}_i \, \mathrm{sat}(s_i / \delta_i), i = 1,...,n . \tag{4}$$

where: $\mathrm{sat}(y) = y$ if $|y| < 1$; $\mathrm{sat}(y) = \mathrm{sgn}(y)$ if $|y| \geq 1$.

5   Case-Studies

We consider three important motion control tasks where full, but properly simplified, dynamics models have been used: standing-up motion, upward standing stabilization, and steps performing. Then we briefly present a real BMS: active ankle-foot orthosis.

5.1   Standing-Up Motion

The task is simulated by a full dynamic model of a three-link manipulator where a Hill model for the muscle activation is employed, [9]. We apply optimal control learning, as in Section 3, for the knee joint motion, and robust stabilizing controllers, as in Section 4, for the other two joint motions: at hip and ankle joints. Our generic control synthesis approach can be also applied in the case when the arms are (synergistically with legs) used to stand-up from an arm-chair.

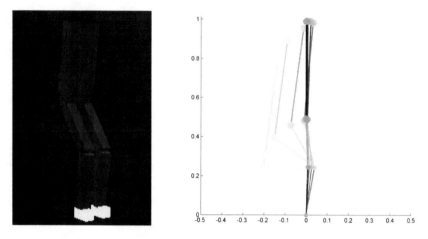

Fig. 2ab. Standing-up motion

5.2   Upward Standing Stabilization

The task to stabilize the vertical posture of human body is considered at least in [10, 11] (Fig.3a is adapted from these references), where the body is represented as a two-link system with joints at the ankle and the hip. According to our theory [15], any two-degree of freedom mechanical system can be robustly stabilized by decentralized controllers. Our numerical simulation of the robust stabilization of such a system applying optimal bounded PD controllers, as in Section 4, is presented in Fig. 3b.

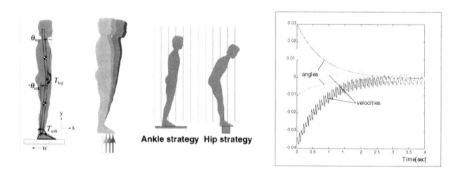

Fig. 3ab. On upward standing stabilization

5.3   Steps Performing

Human locomotion is such that, in different motion phases, one has to deal with different dynamics structures. In double support phases, we use two-degree of freedom dynamic model, and in the single support phase – four-degree-of-freedom dynamic model. Accordingly, the control system has to have different structures, with two and four control functions. A computer simulation for optimal control synthesis by learning (as in Section 3) for a planar biped [9] is depicted in Fig. 4a.

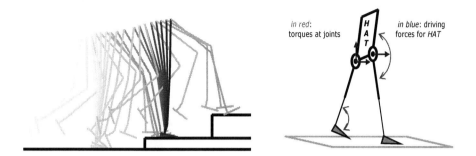

in red:
torques at joints

H
A
T

in blue: driving
forces for *HAT*

Fig. 4ab. On steps performing in 2D and 3D

Our pilot study on 3D human locomotion has been first presented in [3]. The main driving forces for the HAT (head-arms-trunk) system during pushing-off the left leg (or when landing it) can be seen in Fig. 4b.

Besides helping to determine the control structure in the double-support phase, Fig. 4b can be used to explain why it is better to apply more effort at the ankles than at the hip joints in cases when there are some neuromuscular lesions (pains) in the spine/pelvis. That conception has been verified in various clinical experiences [12].

5.4   On Designing Active Orthoses

We have designed a control system for ankle-foot orthosis (AFO) with one degree of freedom which foot segment is connected to the shank segment by a rotational joint. A direct drive actuator is attached laterally to the AFO, [17]. The control signals are received from two sensor arrays incorporated in the foot part of AFO and in the insole of the healthy leg which is basement of the control algorithm, *Fig.1*. A feedback with Proportional-Integral-Derivative (PID) control was used to estimate the trajectory of the foot and positioning the actuated foot segment of AFO when the foot rotates about the ankle, [18]. During each gait cycle a microcontroller estimates forward speed and modulates swing phase flexion and extension in order to assure automatic adaptation of the joint torque, [19]. The ankle foot orthoses device and the applied PID control discussed in this paper can be used in cases of the drop foot treatment and also for possible applications of this device in rehabilitation.

In designing control systems for orthoses with more than one degree of freedom, e.g. knee-ankle-foot orthosis, such rehabilitation devices have to be robust enough with respect to external disturbances as well as to disturbances due to joints' coupling. The power of the actuators and the gains of the controllers can be optimally determined following the proposed control design approach.

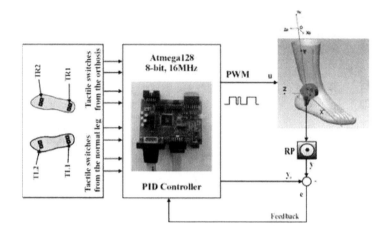

Fig. 5. Autonomous Control System with Active Ankle-Foot Orthoses

6   On Design Optimization of Biomechatronic Systems

Along with the basic design requirement for strength/load capacity additional design criteria for robots and BMS are needed to meet the continuously increasing demands for faster response, improved precision and reduced energy consumption.

Eqs(3) present optimal trade-off relations between the bounds of model uncertainties and the control force limits. The greater the determinant D of this system of linear equations, the less control forces are required to overcome the disturbances. In other words, D quantifies the capability of robots or BMS to be robustly controlled in a decentralized manner. For these reasons, D can be taken as a relevant integrated design index for the subsystems whose parameters enter the control TM.

The linearity of (3) makes it possible a decomposition of the overall design problem into design problems for the BMS's components: (1) mechanics, (2) actuators/sensors, and (3) controllers. This order will correspond to the hierarchy in a multi-level optimization procedure in which a series of design problems for these subsystems are to be solved.

Integrated Structure-Control Design Scheme

A. Mechanics
- design parameters: all inertial/geometrical data;
- design constraints: strength and GDD conditions;
- design objective: maximize D;

B. Actuators/Sensors
- design parameters: actuator masses and positions;
- design constraints: strength and GDD conditions;
- design objective: maximize D;

C. Controllers
- design parameters: control gains;
- design constraints: optimal trade-off relations (3);
- design objective: minimize the control effort;

The overall design problem for robots or BMS with decentralized control structure thus can be decomposed into a convergent sequence of design solutions for their subsystems.

7   Discussion

The proposed design optimization criteria for robots or BMS do not conflict with the basic design requirement for strength/load capacity. Moreover, they allow for a decomposition of the overall design problem into easy-to-solve design problems for their components. In this way, we can successively optimize the mechanical structure, the sizes and locations of the actuators, and at the final design stage, decentralized controllers with maximum degree of robustness can be designed. Thus the work of the different design teams can be coordinated and performed very efficiently.

In the light of the fast developments in rehabilitation technology, it will be very useful to offer engaging rehabilitation with optimal training possibilities. Active training approaches allow patients to take an active role in the rehabilitation process and a technology should be able to offer exercises that are close to what the patient prefers to train on [13]. This is especially stimulating when patients can exercise with some self-selected, well-defined and individually meaningful functional goals in mind. Personal goal setting in motion tasks encourages patient motivation, treatment adherence and self-regulation processes.

To summarize, we think that we have the necessary scientific basis to develop efficient robot design and rehabilitation methodologies. In general, it is reasonable that a rehabilitation technology should provide first of all as good as possible musculoskeletal rehabilitation. Then, our motion control principles and concepts can be used to develop efficient neurological rehabilitation.

References

1. Fisher, B.E., Sullivan, K.J.: Activity-dependent factors affecting post-stroke functional outcomes. Top Stroke Rehabil 8(3), 31–44 (2001)
2. Teasell, R., Bayona, N., Salter, K., et al.: Progress in clinical neurosciences: stroke recovery and rehabilitation. Can J. Neurol. Sci. 33(4), 357–364 (2006)
3. Kiriazov, P.: Control Strategy for Efficient Motion Rehabilitation. In: Proc. 2nd European Conference, Technically Assisted Rehabilitation, March 18-19, pp. 1–4 (2009), http://www.tar-conference.eu/tar-conference-archive/tar-2009-1; Proc. on CD ISSN 18624871
4. Nikolova, G., Toshev, Y.: Zlatov. N., Yordanov. Y., Humanoid robot based on 3D biomechanical model. In: Proceedings of the International Symposium on Robotics and Automation, Toluca, Mexico (2002)

5. Nikolova, G., Toshev, Y.: Estimation of male and female body segment parameters of the Bulgarian population using a 16-segmental mathematical model. Journal of Biomechanics 40(16), 3700–3707 (2007)
6. Lunze, J.: Feedback Control of Large-Scale Systems. Prentice-Hall, UK (1992)
7. Kiriazov, P.: Robust Decentralized Control of Mechanical Systems. In: van Campen, D. (ed.) Solid Mechanics and its Applications, vol. 52, pp. 175–182. Kluwer Acad. Publ. (1997)
8. Kiriazov, P.: Efficient Approach For Dynamic Parameter Identification and Control Design of Structronic Systems. In: Gabbert, U., Tzou, H. (eds.) Solid Mechanics and its Applications, vol. 89, pp. 323–330. Kluwer Publ. (2001)
9. Kiriazov, P.: Efficient Learning Control and Adaptation in Dynamic Locomotion. In: Proc. 3rd Int. Symp. Adaptive Motion in Animals and Machines, Ilmenau, Germany, pp.1–8 (2005) ISBN: 3932633997
10. http://biomt.kaist.ac.kr/research/index.php
11. Park, S., Horak, F.B., Kuo, A.D.: Postural feedback responses scale with biomechanicalconstraints in human standing. Exp. Brain Res. 154, 417–427 (2004)
12. Lewis, C.L., Ferris, D.P.: Walking with increased ankle push off decreases hip moments. Journal of Biomechanics 41(10), 2082–2089 (2008)
13. Timmermans, A., Seelen, H., Willmann, R., Kingma, H.: Technology-assisted training of arm-hand skills in stroke: concepts on reacquisition of motor control and therapist guidelines for rehabilitation technology design. J. NeuroEngineering and Rehabilitation 6, 1 (2009), http://www.jneuroengrehab.com/content/pdf/1743-0003-6-1.pdf
14. Kiriazov, P., Nikolova, G.S.: Motor control strategy for efficient neurorehabilitation. Neurorehabilitation 4(1-2), 3–6 (2010)
15. Kiriazov, P.: Optimal Robust Controllers for Multibody Systems. In: Ulbrich, H., Günthner, W. (eds.) Solid Mechanics and its Applications, vol. 130, pp. 183–192. Springer-Verlag GmbH, Heidelberg (2005)
16. Schiehlen, W. (ed.): Multibody Systems Handbook. Springer, Berlin (1990)
17. Veneva, I., Toshev, Y.: Control Algorithm For Ankle-Foot Orthosis and Applications. In: Proc. the 9th International Robotics Conference, Varna, Bulgaria, pp. 225–230 (2007)
18. Veneva, I., Boiadjiev, G.: Control System for Data Acquisition and Processing of Ankle-Foot Orthosis. In: Proceedings of the 9th IFAC Symposium on Robot Control, SYROCO 2009, Gifu, Japan, September 9-12, pp. 745–750 (2009)
19. Veneva, I.: Intelligent device for control of active ankle-foot orthosis. In: Proceedings of the 7th IASTED International Conference on Biomedical Engineering, BioMed 2010, Innsbruck, Austria, February 17-19, pp. 100–105. Acta Press (2010)

Behavior Based Approach for Robot Navigation and Chemical Anomaly Tracking

Sambit Bhattacharya[1], Bogdan Czejdo[1], Shubo Han[2], and Mohammad Siddique[1]

[1] Department of Mathematics and Computer Science
[2] Department of Physics and Chemistry
Fayetteville State University
Fayetteville, NC 28301, USA
{sbhattac,bczejdo,shan,msiddiqu}@uncfsu.edu

Abstract. We present a system for detecting chemical anomaly and to track the anomaly to its source. The chemical sensors are mounted on mobile robots. We describe navigating through medium and close proximity environments through a behavior-based approach, which can be represented through subsumption architecture approach. In this paradigm different robot behaviors compete for the actuators that make the robot act in the world. Further, these behaviors are driven by sensory data received through sensors and analyzed. In our case we support three competing behaviors that will be arbitrated: 1) navigation of indoor spaces through visual landmark recognition, 2) confined spaces navigation through close proximity sensors, and 3) airborne chemical and / or ground trail following.

Keywords: autonomous robot navigation, confined space navigation, computer vision, Hough transform, K-Means clustering, histogram difference measurement, state diagram methodology, chemical anomaly detection.

1   Introduction

Our goal is to build a system for detecting chemical anomaly and to track the anomaly to its source. In order to do this we will have to mount chemical sensors on mobile robots. We will also have to develop the capabilities of navigating through environments while tracking the anomaly to its source. The problem of robot navigation is an active area of research that has yielded a variety of experimental approaches, which can be broadly classified as indoor and outdoor navigation [2]. Indoor environments like corridors have regular geometric features that can be captured by the robot's camera and effectively analyzed to navigate the robot. In this paper we present our approach to solving the indoor navigation problem and the tracking of chemical anomaly to its source through a behavior based approach that can be represented through state diagrams [1, 9, 10. 11].

Chemical sensors analyze our environment, i.e. they detect which substances are present and in what quantity. Recent research in chemical sensors has tended to produce smaller sensory devices that take advantage of the processing power of computers

S. Jeschke, H. Liu, and D. Schilberg (Eds.): ICIRA 2011, Part II, LNAI 7102, pp. 317–327, 2011.

and can also be carried on board a mobile robot with embedded processors. On the other hand robotics research has mainly focused on creating artificial intelligence algorithms that take actions and manipulate objects in the world based on interpretations of sensory data arising from visual information [2] and to a lesser extent auditory information. These are the technical sensing organs, i.e. eyes and ears of robots. However biological sensing also includes smell and taste so chemical sensors which analyze the surrounding air, liquids and objects for chemical composition can be said to be the artificial noses and artificial tongues of robots.

There are primarily two types of chemical sensors, electrochemical and optical. In an electrochemical sensor, gas diffuses into the sensor resulting in an electrochemical reaction. This reaction results in an electric current that passes through an external circuit. This current after amplification and other signal processing produces the measurement for the amount of chemical detected. In the case of an optical chemical sensor, laser light is projected at an object. The light reflected by the object after absorption is then detected and the frequency spectrum of this detected light is analyzed to find the chemical composition of the object.

2   Subsumption Architecture for Robot Navigation and Chemical Anomaly Tracking

The diagram in Figure 1 summarizes our idea of working within the *behavior based paradigm of artificial intelligence and robotics* to create subsumption *architecture* for *behavior arbitration*. In this paradigm different robot behaviors compete for the actuators which make the robot act in the world. Further, these behaviors are driven by

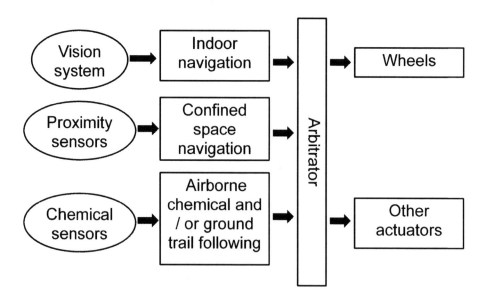

Fig. 1. Subsumption architecture for combining three different behaviors

sensory data received through sensors and analyzed. In our case we support at a minimum three competing behaviors that will be arbitrated: 1) navigation of indoor spaces through visual landmark recognition, 2) confined spaces navigation through close proximity sensors, and 3) airborne chemical and / or ground trail following which will rotate and steer the robot towards the source of a chemical.

3   Navigation Based on Computer Vision System

Our approach for robot navigation in an indoor environment uses a vision system with different components. The first component used is the Hough transform for detecting line segments. The second component uses histogram based difference calculation methods for discriminating between corridor features.

The Hough transform is widely used in computer vision for detecting regular geometric features such as line segments and circles in images. Our system uses an efficient version of the Hough transform known as the Progressive Probabilistic Hough Transform [4] for detecting naturally occurring lines in indoor images of corridors and hallways. Before applying the Hough Transform we perform Canny edge detection on the corridor images to obtain binary images where edge pixels are white and all other pixels are black.

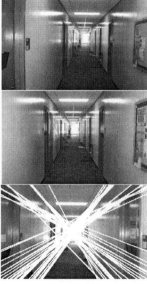

Fig. 2. The images are numbered with letters A to F in the left to right, top to bottom ordering. (A) and (B) are examples of corridor images with door on the left; (C) and (D) are examples of corridor images with wall on the left. (E) Shows image (A) processed with our Hough Transform program; the detected lines are colored white and superimposed on the original image. (F) Shows the result of clustering all lines in (E) into two major diagonal groups; the average line representing each group is shown; their point of intersection is the point of orientation for the robot when moving across the corridor.

The Hough line transform assumes that any point in a binary image could be part of some set of possible lines. As a result of applying the Hough Transform we detect almost all lines in the image along with a few false positives. Our next step is to reduce the set of lines to two major clusters which represent the direction of the corridor. In order to do that we first eliminate the approximately vertical and horizontal lines from the set. Next, we apply the K-Means algorithm [5] to cluster the lines into two groups as shown in the example in Figure 2 (E) and then we take the average representative line for each cluster (as shown in Figure 2 (F)). In the final step the intersection of these two representative lines yields the orientation point for the robot moving in the corridor.

In the course of indoor robot navigation a significant problem is recognition of major landmark objects [2] such as doors and wall surfaces between them. Landmarks are used in most aspects of navigation. If a robot finds a landmark in the world and that landmark appears on a map, then the robot is localized with respect to the map. If the robot plans a path consisting of segments, landmarks are needed so the robot can tell when it has completed a segment and another should begin.

Our system recognizes wall surfaces and doors through histogram based techniques. These recognition techniques create the trigger conditions that we describe later in our state diagram framework. Our problem is the following: sample the current camera image so that the program is able to decide whether the robot is currently beside a wall or a door. We solve this problem by analyzing the left and right most vertical slices of the image; then the program classifies the slice as "wall" or "door" based upon histogram difference measures. We have tested two widely used histogram difference measuring techniques, namely the Earth Mover's Distance (EMD) [3] and the statistical technique of calculating the correlation coefficient between two distributions.

Our measurement process compares new samples with stored representative histogram patterns for wall and door. Our program therefore uses these techniques to classify whether the robot is beside a door or wall. The Hough transform and histogram analysis can produce triggers reflecting the environment characteristics. Let us first discuss the environmental triggers based on histogram analysis. When the robot moves beside a door and the edge of the camera detects the door pattern then the trigger condition DoorPatternDetected becomes True otherwise the condition is False. Similarly, when the robot moves beside a wall and the edge of the camera detects wall pattern then the trigger condition WallPatternDetected becomes true.

The other triggers e.g. MiddleOfDoorDetected can be derived from these basic triggers. When the trigger WallPatternDetected changes from False to True a robot odometer is initialized and the trigger MiddleOfDoorDetected becomes False. When the value of that odometer is equal or greater than half of the width of the door, then the trigger MiddleOfDoorDetected becomes True.

Let us now discuss the environmental triggers based on Hough transform. The OrientationPointToLeft and OrientationPointToRight triggers are computed based on the algorithm for orientation point described in the previous section. The triggers are listed in Table 1 that includes the Obstacle trigger typical for infrared sensors.

Table 1. List of advanced visual sensor triggers

Trigger name	Based on
Obstacle	Infrared Sensor
DoorPatternDetected	Histogram Analysis
WallPatternDetected	Histogram Analysis
MiddleOfDoorDetected	Histogram Analysis and odometer
OrientationPointToLeft	Hough Transform
OrientationPointToRight	Hough Transform

We assume that the robot's environment is known in advance. Under this assumption the robot behavior can be modeled by a state diagram [6, 7, 8] that has different states depending on the location of the robot in the corridor.

Generally, the state diagram in addition to states has transitions consisting of triggers that cause the transition of the robot from one state to another, and actions, that are invoked during a transition. Triggers are expressed by Boolean conditions evaluated continuously to respond to changes in environment. To specify state diagrams we used the notation based on Universal Modeling Language (UML) [10, 11] where a state is indicated by a box and a transition is indicated by an arrow with a label. The first part of the transition label (before the slash) specifies the trigger and the part after the slash specifies the action to be invoked during the transition [1].

The typical simple mobile robot behavior includes states such as Moving Forward, Moving Backward, Stop, Turning Right, and Turning Left. Some of these simple states are also included in the state diagram in Figure 2. The most interesting, however are advanced states that are related to advanced image analysis.

Let us convert a specific corridor map into a state diagram for the movement of our robot until it reaches the goal. The state diagram is shown in Figure 3. In brief, the robot behavior in our specific example can be described as follows:

1. Initially the robot is in the START state and with no trigger, the transition to the BW 1 (where BW is abbreviation for Beside Wall) state takes place immediately. During the time of transition the forward command is executed. This built-in command engages the motors to move the robot forward.

2. The robot stays in the BW 1 state (and continues moving forward) until it detects a door pattern and the trigger condition DoorPatternDetected becomes True. Detecting the door pattern triggers the transition to the BD 1 (where BD is abbreviation for Beside Door) state while moving forward.

3. The robot stays in the BD 1 state until it detects a wall pattern and the trigger condition WallPatternDetected becomes True. Detecting the wall pattern triggers the transition to the BW 2 state.

5. The robot stays in the BW 2 state (and continues moving forward) until it detects an obstacle (which is the turning point of the corridor) and the trigger condition Obstacle becomes True. Detecting the obstacle initiates the turnLeft operation and

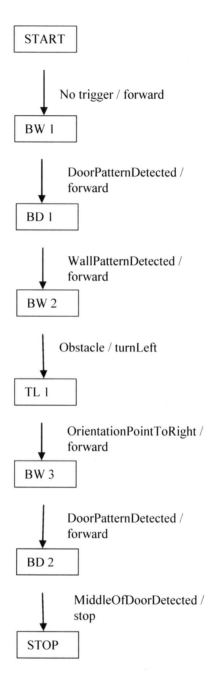

Fig. 3. State diagram representation of our specific autonomous navigation example

transition to the TL 1 (where TL is abbreviation for Turning Left) state. The turnLeft command engages the motors to start turning the robot counter clockwise. Similar to the forward command, the turnRight command causes the motors to be engaged until any new movement command deactivates the older settings.

6. The robot stays in TL 1 state (and continues turning) until the robot is aligned to the orientation point and the trigger condition OrientationPointToRight becomes True. OrientationPointToRight becoming True means that the direction the robot is facing just becomes aligned with the orientation point. This trigger causes the invocation of the forward command and transition to the BW 3 state.

7. The robot stays in the BW 3 state (and continues moving forward) until it detects door pattern and the trigger condition DoorPatternDetected becomes True. Detecting the door pattern triggers the transition to the BD 2 state while moving forward.

8. The robot stays in the BD 2 state (and continues moving forward) until it is in the middle of the door and the trigger condition MiddleOfDoorDetected becomes True. Detecting the middle of the door triggers the stop operation and transition to the STOP state. Arriving at this door was the goal of the robot.

4   Close Proximity Navigation

While navigating the robot may have to enter confined spaces in the environment. Identifying and defining such environmental triggers is crucial for proper robot behavior. The environmental triggers are based on proximity sensors.

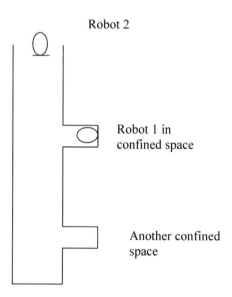

Fig. 4. Environment for medium and close proximity maneuvering of the robot

Let us assume an environment of the open corridor from the previous section with two openings leading to confined spaces as shown in Figure 4. The goal is to specify properly robot behavior to carefully enter the narrow opening without touching any of the enclosures. This behavior involves close proximity operations and close proximity triggers.

For the close proximity operations values generated by infrared or touch sensors are most often used. They allow to develop environmental triggers AllignedToLeft and AlignedToRight that makes the robot to direct itself to the middle of the confined space. Very important for the close proximity operations are combined environmental/ behavioral triggers. The SpeedToHigh trigger is an example of such trigger. Let us consider the maneuvering of robot in close proximity operations. We need to perform such maneuvering on a relatively high level of safety. The high level (the safest) is when we are sure that the distance to each landmark or object is larger than a safety threshold T. The safety threshold expresses some safety precautions related with a) delays related to algorithm processing, b) communication delays, c) the precision of adjustment of direction (turning), d) the precision of speed forward, and e) approximation of geometrical computations. In general, the safety threshold can have different values for different sensors e.g. the damage related with the hitting the left landmark can be much bigger than the damage related with the hitting the right landmark. The sample constraints with the safety threshold can be expressed for each of the sensors as follows: Dest - Eest > T

In our experiments we used three sensors: left, front and right. The constraint simply says that the estimated distance (taking into consideration the worst error) should be greater that an experimentally developed threshold value. If these constraints are satisfied the behavioural trigger SpeedToHigh is False. If the robot, however, moves too close to one of the container wall the behavioural trigger SpeedToHigh becomes True.

Let us look at an example of robot behavior in a confined space as shown in Figure 5 that describes the close proximity maneuvering.

Let us look at robot close proximity maneuvering as shown in Figure 5. The robot behavior can be described naturally by the states identifying the robot position in such close object environment: (a) start in front of confined spaceing station called shortly "Start", (b) turning to face the confined space called shortly "Turning to Face Confined Space", (c) entering the confined space called "Entering Confined space", and (d) within confined space called the same "Within Confined Space". The state diagram shown in Figure 5 includes also state called "Correcting Speed". This is an important state present at all close proximity maneuvers to avoid bumping into any object. Notice that correcting speed in the state diagram and in the corresponding computer program is controlled by using the basic feature of robotics systems that cancels any movement when the new request for the movement is issued.

Let us consider the maneuvering of robot to pass through the narrow opening of the confined space. If the constraint is not satisfied then the trigger SpeedToHigh becomes true and we proceed with decreasing the forward speed. Since the precision of estimation is dependent on forward speed, the decreasing the speed should result at some moment in satisfying the constraints. We may also proceed with the adjustment of direction (turning) if necessary.

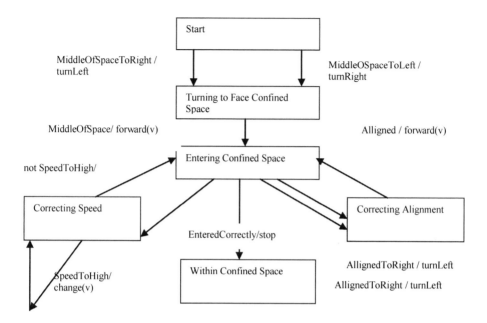

Fig. 5. Close proximity maneuvering of the robot

5   Chemical Sensors

A possible way to find the source of an odor / chemical plume is to estimate the local concentration gradient and move the robot in the direction of the gradient's increase. This can be done with a robot equipped with two or more physically separated sensing units where the robot heading is steered toward the direction in which the gradient increases. Here the two or more physically separated sensors are located on the same robot to provide spatially separated measurements of the amount of chemical. This is done because only with spatially separated sampling points can we estimate the gradient value and its direction. One other possibility is to use multiple robots to measure the gradients over large areas instead of a single robot. This will be necessary when the gradient measurement on the chassis of the same robot is low in accuracy i.e. readings at the spatially close sensors on the same chassis are very close in value.

The state diagrams can be constructed to specify how robots would follow the chemical gradient in order to detect the source of anomaly. For example the state diagram can reflect how the silk worm tracks a pheromone plume. Here the silk worm inspired robot starts to cross the wind in order to find traces of the target odor. After detecting the odor of interest, the robot implements an upwind surge, a series of sinusoidal movements limited by the plume boundaries (zigzag). If the robot loses contact with the plume it loops back trying to recover.

To ensure robustness of the previous tracking algorithm the chemical sensors have to be calibrated or baseline corrected. This is because chemical sensors are subject to variations due to changing environmental conditions like temperature and humidity.

Precise knowledge of the influence of factors like ambient temperature is needed and has to be used by the micro-controller on sensor nodes to perform automatic calibration. The calibration data needs to be recorded under these varying conditions and this database will be used for software based automatic calibration. Generally automatic baseline correction is easier to achieve than automatic self calibration. Analytical signals in many methods sit on a baseline in the form of peaks. Normally, the peak area contains the useful analytical information. The baseline varies only to a certain extent. The signal is extracted commonly by subtracting the baseline and subsequently integrating the peak. The baseline is determined by means of two successive measurements, one with and another without the sample. Subtraction of the baseline determined in this way usually result in error, since the conditions in both measurements can be different. We thus also perform only one measurement (with sample) and extract the most probable course of the baseline from the recorded graph. Different methods of approximating the baseline, e.g. by a straight line or a curved line as generated by spline interpolation, are possible. Since only mathematical functions of the measurement are used, our approximation procedures can be fully automated.

6   Conclusion

We presented a system for detecting chemical anomaly and to track the anomaly to its source. We described navigating through medium and close proximity environments through a behavior based approach which can be represented through subsumption architecture. We were able to determine the choice between the three competing behaviors: navigating indoor spaces, close proximity navigation and airborne chemical following.

Acknowledgement. We acknowledge the National Science Foundation (award id: 0959958), internal grants from the Graduate School of Fayetteville State University, and the Belk Foundation for supporting this research.

References

[1] Czejdo, B.D., Bhattacharya, S.: Programming robots with state diagrams. Journal of Computing Sciences in Colleges 24(5), 19–26 (2009)
[2] Desouza, G.N., Kak, A.C.: Vision for mobile robot navigation: a survey. IEEE Transactions on Pattern Analysis and Machine Intelligence 24(2), 237–267 (2002)
[3] Rubner, Y., Tomasi, C., Guibas, J.L.: The Earth Mover's Distance as a Metric for Image Retrieval. International Journal of Computer Vision 40(2), 99–121 (2000)
[4] Galamhos, C., Matas, J., Kittler, J.: Progressive probabilistic Hough transform for line detection. In: Conference on Computer Vision and Pattern Recognition, vol. 1, pp. 560–566. IEEE Computer Society (1999)
[5] Bradley, P.S., Fayyad, U.M.: Refining initial points for k-means clustering. In: Proc. of 15th International Conf. on Machine Learning, pp. 91–99 (1998)

[6] Baszun, M., Miescicki, J., Czejdo, B.: Multilevel modeling of iterative engineering design of remote robot system. In: Proceedings of The Second World Conference on Integrated Design and Process Technology, Austin (1996)

[7] Czejdo, B., Messa, K.: Generating Smalltalk code from graphical operations and rules. In: Proceedings of the IEEE Symposium on Visual Languages, Bergen, Norway (1993)

[8] Czejdo, B., Daszuk, W., Miescicki, J.: Concurrent software design based on constraints on state diagrams. In: Proceedings of The Third World Conference on Integrated Design & Process Technology, Berlin, Germany (1998)

[9] Embley, D., Kurtz, B., Woodfield, S.: Object-Oriented Systems Analysis – a model driven approach. Prentice Hall, New Jersey (1992)

[10] Harel, D.: On visual formalisms. Communications of the ACM 31(5), 514–530 (1988)

[11] Rumbaugh, J., Blaha, M., Premerlani, W., Eddy, F., Lorensen, W.: Object-Oriented Modeling and Design. Prentice Hall, New Jersey (1990)

Detection of Lounging People
with a Mobile Robot Companion

Michael Volkhardt, Steffen Müller, Christof Schröter, and Horst-Michael Groß[*]

Neuroinformatics and Cognitive Robotics Lab,
Ilmenau University of Technology, 98684 Ilmenau, Germany
michael.volkhardt@tu-ilmenau.de
http://www.tu-ilmenau.de/neurob

Abstract. This paper deals with the task of searching for people in home environments with a mobile robot. The robust estimation of the user's position is an important prerequisite for human robot interaction. While detecting people in an upright pose is mainly solved, most of the user's various poses in living environments are hard to detect. We present a visual approach for the detection of people resting at previously known seating places in arbitrary poses, e.g. lying on a sofa. The method utilizes color and gradient models of the environment and a color model of the user's appearance. Evaluation is done on real-world experiments with the robot searching for the user at different places.

Keywords: people detection, various poses, home environment.

1   Introduction

This work is part of the CompanionAble[1] project, which intends to develop a personal robot for assisting elderly people with mild cognitive impairments in their home. The goal of the project is to increase the independence of the user by means of a combination of a smart home and a mobile robot. Therefore, the system provides different services, like e.g. day-time management, and allows for video conferences with care-givers or friends. Furthermore, it recognizes emergency situations, like falls, and tries to prevent progression of the cognitive impairments by providing stimulation programs. To offer these service functionalities, the robot system provides several autonomous behaviors. First, observing the user in a non-intrusive way allows to facilitate services that require interaction or to react on critical situations. Second, the robot must seek for the user if a reminder has to be delivered or a video call comes in. A third behavior is following and approaching the user if interaction is desired. A prerequisite to these behaviors is the robust detection and tracking of the user in the apartment. In contrast to other interaction applications in public environments, people in

---

[*] This work has received funding from the European Communitys Seventh Framework Programme (FP7/2007-2013) under grant agreement no. 216487.

[1] www.companionable.net

S. Jeschke, H. Liu, and D. Schilberg (Eds.): ICIRA 2011, Part II, LNAI 7102, pp. 328–337, 2011.

home environments often do not face the robot in an up-right pose but sit on chairs or lie on sofas. Therefore, our system tries to detect the user independent of their pose at places, where he or she usually rests. In this work, we focus on a robot-only solution – not relying on any smart home sensors – to enable the robot to function autonomously in any home environment. The key idea is to learn the visual appearance of predefined resting places and the user beforehand and to compare the current visual impression to both of these models in the detection phase.

The remainder of this paper is organized as follows: Section 2 summarizes previous work carried out on the research topic. We present the innovation of detecting lounging people at places in detail in Sec. 3. Afterwards, Sect. 4 gives a description of the experiments carried out, while Sec. 5 summarizes our contribution and gives an outlook on future work.

2   Related Work

People detection and tracking are prominent and well-covered research areas, and impressive results have been accomplished in recent years. Considering the constrained hardware of mobile robots, two main fields for people detection have been established – range-finder-based and visual approaches. [1] employ Ada-Boost on laser range scans to combine multiple weak classifiers to a final strong classifier that distinguishes human legs from the environment. Visual approaches mainly focus on the face or the human body shape. The most prominent up-to-date face detection method also utilizes AdaBoost, which learns and applies a cascade of simple, but very efficient image region classifiers to detect faces [2].

Histograms of Oriented Gradients (HOG) have been established as the state-of-the-art method for upright people detection. The basic idea is to compute block-wise histograms of gradient orientations, resulting in robustness to slight spatial variation of object shape, color, and image contrast. The histograms inside a detection window are concatenated into a high-dimensional feature vector and classified by a linear Support Vector Machine [3]. Further extensions to the original HOG method focus on upper body detection [4] or use deformable sub-parts, which increase detection performance given partial occlusion [5]. Detection, segmentation and pose estimation of people in images is addressed by [6] who combine HOG features with the voting scheme of the Implicit Shape Model [7]. [8] augment the HOG features with color and texture information achieving impressive results on outdoor datasets. Unfortunately, the latter two approaches are far beyond real-time capabilities.

Plenty of research has been done to develop methods for people tracking on mobile robots in real-world applications. Most of these approaches focus on pedestrian tracking and single poses [3,7,9]. Yet, few approaches handle the detection and tracking of people in home environments, especially on mobile robots. Often smart home technologies, like static cameras with background subtraction methods [10] or infrared presence sensors, are applied, which facilitate the problem of detection [11,12]. On occasion, approaches working with mobile robots

(a) Place in Occupancy Map

(b) Projection to Camera Image

Fig. 1. Place definition. (a) Bounding box of place in the occupancy map. The robot is in its observation position (red circle). (b) Place's bounding box projected into the camera image.

process the data captured offline to apply computationally heavy detection methods [9]. The CompanionAble project aims to develop a mobile robot that is able to react on and interact with the user. Therefore, all those approaches employing background subtraction or a retro-perspective analysis are not applicable.

3   Detection of Lounging People at Places

Typical scenarios in a home environment include the user walking to another room, or the user sitting on a chair or lying on a sofa. The latter case occurs quite frequently, i.e. when the user is watching TV, reading newspaper, making phone calls, working or sleeping. Our previous system comprises a multi-modal, multi-cue tracking framework based on the Kalman Filter update regime similar to [13]. In this former work, we apply boosted laser-based leg detection [1], a face detector [2], motion detection [14], and two HOG people detectors [3,4]. The system is able to detect and track people in upright pose (mainly through legs and HOG) and frontal-view (mainly through face and upper-body HOG) in the surroundings of the robot. In the following, we go beyond the state-of-the-art by presenting a trained method for detecting people in difficult poses, that solely runs on a mobile robot in real-time. The system at first learns the appearance of places in the apartment where the user usually rests. Afterwards, the deviation of occupied places from the model and the similarity to a user model are used for detection.

3.1   Definition of Places

We define places as positions in the apartment where the user is usually encountered, i.e. chairs, sofas, working desk. Each place P is represented by a 3D box $\mathbf{b} = (x, y, z, d_x, d_y, d_z)$ with x, y, z being the center coordinates of the box and d_x, d_y, d_z denoting the width in each dimension. Figure 1 shows an exemplary place position in the world centered occupancy map used for navigation and the 2D-projection of the place box into the current camera image of the robot. Naturally, the content of the place-boxes looks completely different in the camera image, if observed from different positions. Since the system is learning the appearance of different places in the apartment, we need to restrict the pose from which the robot is observing them. Therefore, each place is assigned n observation poses $\mathbf{O} = (\mathbf{o}_1, \ldots, \mathbf{o}_n)$, where $\mathbf{o} = (x, y, \phi)$ with x, y representing the world coordinates of the robot's position and ϕ denoting the heading of the robot. The restriction of the observation position ensures that the variance of the place appearance is limited. Additionally, some kind of feature description model $\mathcal{M}$ of the place is added, where the nature of the description is variable. In this work, we use a contextual color histogram (Sec. 3.2) and a HOG description (Sec. 3.3). Thus, the full description of a place is given by $P = (\mathbf{b}, \mathbf{O}, \mathcal{M})$.

3.2   Color-Based User Detection

The color-based feature model comprises the appearance of each place in multi-modal histograms. Each place is observed from different, but predefined viewpoints given different illumination conditions, i.e. ambient day-light and electric lighting in the evening. Therefore, the color model must be learned for each day-time and observation angle, independently. Instead of storing the histograms for each context (day-time, view-point) in a vector, a more efficient way is using a set containing only the observed appearances and the corresponding context. The size of this set can be limited by merging similar entries and keeping only distinctive ones. Therefore, we use a multi-modal color model augmented by a discrete context distribution capturing the circumstances of the histogram's acquisition.

Multi-modal Contextual Color Model. The model is defined by $\mathcal{M} = \{\kappa_1, \ldots, \kappa_n\}$, where $\kappa_i = (H_i, C_i)$ represents a component in the model with H_i denoting a color histogram and C_i being a multi-dimensional discrete context distribution. The histogram is 3 dimensional in RGB color space with 8 bins in each dimension (tests with other color spaces like HSV and Lab showed no significant difference in performance). The context distribution captures arbitrary aspects of the origin of the histogram, like viewpoint and day-time, in separate dimensions. We set the maximum number n of components in $\mathcal{M}$ to nine. At the start of training, the model comprises zero components. At first a histogram is extracted from the box of the non-occupied place in the camera image and added as a new component to the model. Once the number of components exceeds n, the model must be pruned by merging similar components. This is done by first calculating the pairwise similarity s of all components:

$$s = \mathcal{BC}\left([H_i, C_i], [H_j, C_j]\right) ,\tag{1}$$

where $[H, C]$ is the concatenation of a histogram distribution and a context distribution and $\mathcal{BC}(p, q)$ denotes the Bhattacharyya coefficient of two distributions:

$$\mathcal{BC}(p, q) = \sum_{x \in X} \sqrt{p(x)q(x)} .\tag{2}$$

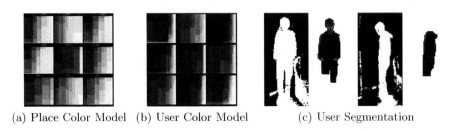

(a) Place Color Model   (b) User Color Model   (c) User Segmentation

Fig. 2. Color models. (a) Place model with 9 components. (b) User color model with 9 components. (c) Background subtraction output (binary image) and GrabCut refinement (color image) to learn color model of user. Left – shadow is removed very well. Right – parts of the person are removed.

The components with the highest similarity are merged by averaging the histogram and context distributions, respectively. The model $\mathcal{M}$ is learned for each place P in multiple teach runs including different day-times and illumination conditions. In the process of learning, the model maintains unique and distinctive representations of a place but merges similar descriptions. Figure 2(a) shows an exemplary color histogram of a place on the couch. Each bin in the 3 dimensional histogram is plotted as a 2D area with its corresponding mean color with the area size corresponding to the bin height. The state of the two dimensional context distribution, capturing point of view and day-time, is displayed in two small lines above each histogram. Red color indicates the probability of a state in the corresponding dimension. The histograms capture different lighting conditions, i.e. the couch normally appears in yellow-green (third column), bright given sunlight (second histogram in top row) or very dark at evening (histogram in the middle). Note that the model contains similar color histograms, but with different context distributions (first column).

Learning of the User Model. The color model of the user is similar to the aforementioned color model of places, but without the context distribution. Model learning is done by first creating a Gaussian Mixture background model [10], when the robot is standing still and no hypothesis is in front of the robot's camera (given by the tracker output). This background model is used for background subtraction once a hypothesis is visible in the image. To remove shadows and to refine the segmentation we apply the GrabCut algorithm [15]. The algorithm is automatically initialized with foreground pixels of the segmentation and background pixels in the bounding box of the person. Figure 2(b) shows an exemplary learned color model of the user capturing mostly blue clothing which appear green under artificial light. One problem is the consistent segmentation of the user in the image. Although the GrabCut algorithm produces satisfying segmentation (Fig. 2(c) left), from time to time background pixels are misclassified in the segmentation, or parts belonging to the person are left out (Fig. 2(c) right). Therefore, at the moment and as a kind of interim solution, we trigger the learning of the user model once per day when the robot is standing in front of a white wall. The user is then asked to walk in front of the robot's camera.

Recognition of the User. Once the place models and the user model have been trained, the system is able to detect the user in arbitrary poses at the learned places. For that purpose, the robot drives to the predefined observation positions and checks each place. By comparing the current appearance to the place and user model the system decides if the place is occupied by the user. Therefore, the robot first extracts the current color histogram H_c from the place's box in the camera image. Furthermore, a context distribution C_c is created including current day-time and view-angle. The system now calculates the similarity of the current observation histogram H_c to the color histogram H_l from the place model using the Bhattacharyya coefficient:

$$s = \mathcal{BC}(H_c, H_l) , \tag{3}$$

where H_l is the histogram of the best matching component κ_l in the place model with l selected by:

$$l = \arg\max_{i=1,\ldots,n} \left\{ \mathcal{BC}\left([H_c, C_c], [H_i, C_i]\right) \right\} . \tag{4}$$

Consequently, Eq. (3) is also used to calculate the similarity to the user model. Yet, a direct comparison of the complete histogram H_c to the user model's histograms would result in a very low match value, because the user usually only occupies a small region in the place's box and many background pixels are included in H_c. Therefore, the similarity to the user model is calculated by using a correlation window inside the place's bounding box and shifting it to find the highest similarity. To select the best matching component κ_l from the user model, Eq. 4 is applied again, but the context distribution is omitted and only the histograms are used.

If the user is present, this results in low similarity to the place model, because the appearance of the place is partially covered, and a high similarity to the user model, because the correlation window fits to the position of the user. If the user is not present, the results are vice versa. Proper decision criteria must be defined for both similarities to decide if a place is occupied. To this end, we trained a *single* linear Support Vector Machine (SVM) on data of multiple labeled runs with empty and occupied places [16]. The resulting SVM then decides for each place if the user is present given the similarities to both the place and user model. If the training data is diversified enough, the SVM is generally applicable to other scenarios without the need of retraining.

3.3 HOG-Based User Detection

Besides the color-based approach described in Sec. 3.2, we developed an illumination invariant gradient-based feature description model $\mathcal{M} = (\mathbf{H})$, where $\mathbf{H} = (\mathbf{d}_1^T, \ldots, \mathbf{d}_n^T)$ with $\mathbf{d}_i$ being a HOG feature descriptor. Recall from Sec. 3.1 that the definition of a place is $P = (\mathbf{b}, \mathbf{O}, \mathcal{M})$. Each bounding box $\mathbf{b}$ of the place in the image viewed from different observation position of $\mathbf{O} = (\mathbf{o}_1, \ldots, \mathbf{o}_n)$ is scaled to a fixed size of 64×128 pixels allowing to extract a $3,780$-dimensional

(a) Empty Place   (b) Occupied Place   (c) Place Examples   (d) Overlapping Places

Fig. 3. HOG descriptor and place examples. (a) HOG Descriptor of an empty place (b) HOG Descriptor of an occupied place. A linear SVM is trained on multiple views of both cases. (c) Examples of places given different illumination conditions. (c) Overlapping places induce confusions.

feature vector d_i using the standard HOG descriptor used for people detection [3]. We trained a separate linear SVM for *each* place on the same data as in Sec. 3.2. Therefore, the system learns to distinguish the HOG descriptors of an empty place, viewed from different positions, from the HOG descriptors of occupied places (Fig. 3). An explicit user model is not required in this case.

4   Experiments

In this section, the color-based and the HOG-based user detection are evaluated separately, because the training and estimation works differently for both approaches. The first method requires different illumination conditions to train robust empty place models and relies on a user model, while the latter needs to learn the gradient features of empty and occupied places without requiring an explicit user model.

4.1   Color-Based User Detection

We first learned the appearance of seven predefined (empty) places of the apartment in multiple training runs including three different lighting conditions – ambient day light, bright sunlight, and artificial light at evening. Furthermore, a user model was trained with the user wearing two different clothes, which he also weared in the test runs. In the test scenario the robot was placed on a starting position and was searching for the user, who was either lounging at one of the places or not in the apartment. Figure 3(c) visualizes some exemplary places occupied by the user. The robot checked each place for the user's presence and logged the similarities to the place and user models. A linear SVM was trained and tested via 5-fold cross validation on the collected data of similarities of all places. The ground truth of the user's presence was labeled manually. For evaluation, we calculated the probability of the test examples belonging to the two classes of the SVM model (user present and not). By varying the probability

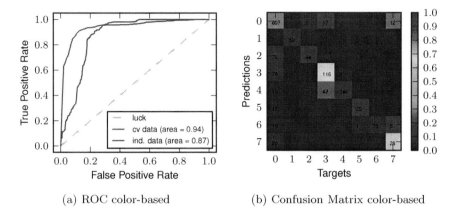

(a) ROC color-based   (b) Confusion Matrix color-based

Fig. 4. Evaluation of the color-based detection approach (Sec. 3.2). (a) ROC curves for cross-validation and independent data (b) Confusion Matrix of multiple independent test runs. Classes $1-7$ represent different places, class 0 denotes user was not present.

threshold that is required to assign an example to one class, an ROC curve can be plotted (Fig. 4(a)). The blue curve shows the ROC of the cross-validated data used for training and validation. The red curve was generated on data from multiple independent test runs not seen by the system before. The high true positive rate and a low false positive rate of the red curve indicate that the system is actually able to robustly detect the user on the places. Furthermore, we evaluated the detection performance of the color-based detection system on the independent data sets used to generate the red ROC curve. The trained SVM is used to decide if the user is present or the place is empty. Each place is considered as a class and classification rates are calculated. Since the robot checks different places for the user's presence, it can wrongly detect the user at a place different from the ground truth. Additionally, sometimes more than one place is visible in the robot's camera image (Fig 3(d)). Hence the detection of places can be confused. Therefore, for evaluation a confusion matrix is chosen (Fig. 4(b)). Class 0 is used to denote that the user is not present (accumulated over all places). The classes $1-7$ correspond to places in the hall, a desk, 2 couch positions, 2 chair positions and an arm chair, respectively. Detection rates for each class are given in the main diagonal of the matrix. The average classification rate is above 85% with the biggest outliers in classes 3 (couch) and 7 (arm-chair). When the user is resting on the couch, he occasionally occupies two places (class 3 and 4) due to overlapping boxes (Fig. 3(d)). If the user is sitting on the edge of the couch like in Fig. 3(b), this results in high similarities to the user model in both couch places leading to the realtive high confusions in class 3. In the case of class 7, direct sunlight caused the camera to overexpose and proper color extraction was hardly possible. Additionally, some false positive detections occured (non-0-predictions of class 0).

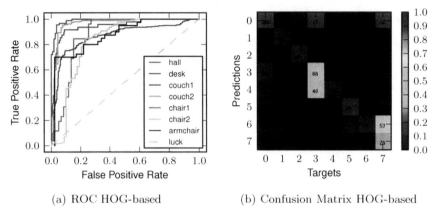

(a) ROC HOG-based   (b) Confusion Matrix HOG-based

Fig. 5. Evaluation of HOG-based detection (Sec. 3.3). (a) ROCs generated by SVMs for each individual place on the ind. data set. (b) Confusion Matrix generated by SVMs on ind. test runs. Classes $1 - 7$ represent places from (a), class 0 denotes user not present.

4.2   HOG-Based User Detection

The HOG-based detection method was evaluated by first training a separate 5-fold cross validated linear SVM for each place. The SVMs learned to distinguish the HOG features of an empty and occupied place. In contrast to the color-based SVM, the resulting classifiers are only effective on data similar to the training set and must be retrained in new environments. The datasets were the same as for the evaluation of the color-based approach. For clarity, we omit the ROC curves of the cross-validated data and only present the ROCs for each place on the independent data set (Fig. 5(a)). The curves substantiate that the HOG-based approach is also applicable to detect the user resting on places. The worst ROCs are given by the chair and arm-chair examples (classes $5, 6, 7$). This happens because the chairs got moved and turned a little during the experiments, disturbing the HOG descriptor. Figure 5(b) presents the confusion matrix that was generated on the aforementioned test runs by using the trained HOG-SVMs to classify the user's presence at each corresponding place. Similar to the color-based approach, the system confuses some examples of the couch place (class 3). Furthermore, the overexposure of the camera in the case of class 7 results in misclassification and the aforementioned moving of the chairs causes confusions with class 6. Compared to the results of the color-based approach in Fig. 4(b), the HOG-based approach produces slightly fewer false positives.

5   Conclusion and Future Works

We presented a method to detect lounging people independent of their resting pose at predefined places. The system either learns color histograms of the user and places in the apartment or builds up a gradient model for each place, beforehand. Then SVMs are trained to decide if a place is occupied by the user.

Afterwards, the system is able to detect the user in the given environment. Experiments on multiple independent test runs substantiate that the approach actually improves recognition performance in living environments by detecting the user in situations not captured by common detection and tracking systems on mobile robots. In future work, we intend to combine the advantages of the color-based and gradient-based approach. With the color-based approach being invariant to moved furniture to some degree and the HOG-based approach's advantage of illumination invariance, a proper combination of both methods shall be developed. Furthermore, the segmentation of the user should be improved to facilitate the recording of the user model for the color-based approach. Last but not least, the manual definition of places should be replaced by an interactive training guided by the user.

References

1. Arras, K.O., Mozos, Ó.M., Burgard, W.: Using Boosted Features for the Detection of People in 2D Range Data. In: Proc. IEEE ICRA, pp. 3402–3407 (2007)
2. Viola, P., Jones, M.: Robust Real-time Object Detection. International Journal of Computer Vision (2001)
3. Dalal, N., Triggs, B.: Histograms of Oriented Gradients for Human Detection. In: Conference on CVPR, pp. 886–893. IEEE Computer Society (2005)
4. Ferrari, V., Marin-Jimenez, M., Zisserman, A.: Progressive search space reduction for human pose estimation. In: Conference on CVPR, pp. 1–8 (2008)
5. Felzenszwalb, P.F., et al.: Object Detection with Discriminatively Trained Part Based Models. In: PAMI, pp. 1–20 (2009)
6. Bourdev, L., Maji, S., Brox, T., Malik, J.: Detecting People Using Mutually Consistent Poselet Activations. In: ECMR, pp. 168–181 (2010)
7. Leibe, B., et al.: Robust Object Detection with Interleaved Categorization and Segmentation. IJCV 1-3 77, 259–289 (2008)
8. Schwartz, W.R., Kembhavi, A., Harwood, D., Davis, L.S.: Human detection using partial least squares analysis. In: 2009 IEEE 12th ICCV, pp. 24–31 (2009)
9. Ess, A., Leibe, B., Schindler, K., van Gool, L.: A Mobile Vision System for Robust Multi-Person Tracking. In: IEEE Conf. on CVPR, pp. 30–37 (2008)
10. Stauffer, C., Grimson, W.E.L.: Adaptive Background Mixture Models for Real-Time Tracking. In: CVPR, pp. 2246–2253 (1999)
11. Han, T.X., Keller, J.M.: Activity Analysis, Summarization, and Visualization for Indoor Human Activity Monitoring. In: IEEE TCSVT, pp. 1489–1498 (2008)
12. Rusu, R.B., et al.: Human Action Recognition Using Global Point Feature Histograms and Action Shapes. Advanced Robotics 23(14), 1873–1908 (2009)
13. Müller, S., Schaffernicht, E., Scheidig, A., Böhme, H.-J., Gross, H.-M.: Are you still following me? In: Proc. ECMR, pp. 211–216 (2007)
14. Martin, C., et al.: Sensor Fusion using a Probabilistic Aggregation Scheme for People Detection and People Tracking. RAS 54(9), 721–728 (2006)
15. Rother, C., Vladimir, K., Blake, A.: Grabcut: Interactive foreground extraction using iterated graph cuts. ACM SIGGRAPH 2004 Papers, 309–314 (2004)
16. Chang, C.-C., Lin, C.-J.: LIBSVM: a library for support vector machines (2001), http://www.csie.ntu.edu.tw/~cjlin/libsvm

Autonomous Control for Human-Robot Interaction on Complex Rough Terrain

Mahmoud Mustafa and Alex Ramirez-Serrano

Department of Mechanical Engineering
Schulich School of Engineering, University of Calgary
Calgary, Canada
{mmmustaf,aramirez}@ucalgary.ca

Abstract. Cooperation control between human's and mobile manipulators has received big interest in the last few years. Mobile manipulators (MMs) have been suggested for various applications such as tasks involving hazardous environments, explosive handling, waste management, outdoor exploration and space operations. This paper describes a novel control algorithm for human-MM cooperation executing tasks in rough outdoor terrains. The proposed approach uses inexpensive common MM sensors such as wrist force/torque, IMU and joint/wheel encoders to achieve minimal human effort. The paper describes a control mechanism that enables ground mobile manipulators to execute complex tasks in cooperation with humans or other autonomous robots when working in unknown, dynamic heterogeneous outdoor rough terrains/environments. Simulation tests using a detailed SIMMECHANICS/ SIMULINK model of the employed MM are presented to illustrate and show the performance of the developed mechanisms.

Keywords: Mobile Manipulators, human robot interaction, intelligent fuzzy logic control, motion on rough terrains.

1 Introduction

A mobile manipulator (MM) is a robotic arm mounted on a (ground, aerial or underwater) mobile platform. The mobile platform (e.g., ground wheeled vehicle) increases the size of the manipulator's workspace, and as a result the increased degree of mobility enables better positioning of the manipulator in different configurations for efficient task execution [1]. Herein the proposed work in targeted for (wheeled and tracked) ground MMs but could potentially (with suitable changes) be applicable to other types of MMs including legged and aerial systems. Thus, in what follows when we refer to MMs we are specifically refereeing to wheeled and tracked MMs. Despite their degree of mobility and their potential uses the complex physical structure, the highly coupled dynamics between the mobile platform and the mounted robot arm, and the potential (common) nonholonomic dynamics of the mobile base are some of the aspects that increases the difficulties of the system design and control. In this regard, the aim of this paper is to present a recently developed control architecture that enables MMs cooperate and interact with humans in static and dynamic heterogeneous outdoor rough

S. Jeschke, H. Liu, and D. Schilberg (Eds.): ICIRA 2011, Part II, LNAI 7102, pp. 338–347, 2011.
© Springer-Verlag Berlin Heidelberg 2011

terrain environments where current cooperation mechanism fail to provide an effective solution for the handling of rigid objects in 3D space (i.e.,translates and rotate objects in cooperation). Flexible objects can potentially be handled with the same approach but significant research still needs to be performed before this is effectively possible. In this paper we focus our attention to cooperation control mechanisms between the robot and the human for handling a single object, where the MM (i.e., slave) grasps the object and a human (master) guides the task by applying an intentional force/torque to the MM's end-effector. These intentional forces are sensed by the robot's wrist via F/T sensor which are then used control the MM and minimize the efforts of the human to enable him/her to manipulate large/heavy objects easily. To achieve this, the goal is for the MM to takes all the effort, which in turn is distributed between the manipulator and the mobile base. Robot assistance in this kind of task is particularly useful when heavy or big complex loads must be handled in both smooth and rough terrain. The master role of the task is assigned to the actor having better perception capabilities (i.e., human). Thus, in this paper assume that the human is responsible for diverse tasks associated with perception such as collision avoidance. This assumption will be relaxed in the future work where the MM will also have the responsibility to avoid obstacles among other things. The result of this assumption is that the autonomous MM only has two main tasks: i) comply with the force(s) exerted by the human while driving the task, and ii) comply with the MM-rough terrain interaction via its own motion. In contrast to typical pure human-robot arm cooperation in structured environments a few references reporting human-MM cooperation applications have been reported [2-6]. Human mobile manipulator through intention recognition was reported in [7] where the MM is required to realize the master's intention in order to cooperate actively in the task execution. This is provided by an intention recognition process integrated in the cooperation module. The contribution of this approach is that the recognition process is applied on the frequency spectrum of the force-torque signal measured at the robot's gripper. Furthermore, previous works on intention recognition are mostly based on the monitoring of the human's motion [8, 9]. Coordinated task between a human and a MM in which the human takes an initiative of the task execution was reported in [10]. In [6] the task trajectory can be arbitrarily modified by the human. Similar to the work described in this paper two issues are resolved simultaneously: i) the coordination between locomotion and manipulation, and ii) the task execution itself (e.g., transporting an object). In [6] the force control scheme is integrated with the coordination algorithm. The force control part sustains the object while the coordination between the manipulator and the mobile platform is maintained at a position level such that the manipulator does not fully extend or retract. Computer simulations provided in [10] show the efficacy of the proposed approach. Without a priori knowledge about the trajectory of the object, the mobile manipulator is able to keep up with the motion of the object, hence the motion of human, while carrying objects. Human swarm mobile robot cooperation (e.g., handling of a single object by multiple mobile manipulators in cooperation with a human) has also been investigated by a number of researchers based on virtual 3D caster dynamics [11]. In this approaches authors have proposed decentralized motion control algorithms. In the reported control algorithms, the grasping point of the MM has been controlled as if it has a caster-like dynamics referred to as virtual 3D caster while assuming each MM could handle the complete object based on the intentional force(s)/moment(s) applied by the human. In addition, the coordinated motion control algorithm between the manipulator and the mobile base for each mobile manipulator has been taken into consideration. By using these motion control algorithms, the coordination among multiple mobile manipulators is realized without using the geometric relations among robots. From the published approaches for human-robot cooperation the existing methods are diverse. However, the existing literature only considers human-robot interaction within engineered environments (e.g., office buildings). Current approaches/mechanisms do not provide solutions to the human-MM cooperation on outdoor heterogeneous rough terrains. The human-MM interactive control algorithm presented in this paper seeks to fill this void. First we present the mathematical models used followed by the description of the proposed control mechanism.

2   Mobile Manipulator Modeling

2.1   Kinematics of the Wheeled Mobile Robot

The MM used in this work is composed of a rigid platform and assumed rigid wheels (i.e., tracks). This assumption is to neglect the complex terramechanics interactions between the wheels and the terrain. The two left wheels and the two right wheels are connected respectively with a synchronous belt forming a traditional track locomotion system. As a result the mobile platform can be simplified as a model of two wheels platform (Fig.1) where:

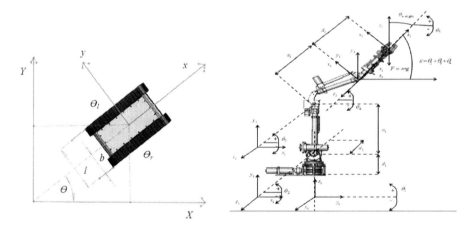

Fig. 1. Wheeled mobile robot model   **Fig. 2.** Kinematic Parameters of the robot Arm

l: The distance between the left and the right wheel and r: The wheel radius.

The configuration of the mobile robot is described by the following two vectors.

$$\theta = [\theta_r \quad \theta_l]^T, X_v = [X \quad Y \quad \theta_v]^T$$

$\dot{\theta}_l, \dot{\theta}_r$: Angular velocity of the left and the right wheel

θ: Absolute rotation angle (heading angle) of the MM,

x, y: Absolute position of the MM's center of mass,

v_l, v_r: left/right wheel linear velocity, respectively.

The vehicle linear velocity (v) and a angular velocity is ($\dot{\theta}$) obtained using Equations (1) and (2)

$$v = \frac{v_l + v_r}{2} = \frac{r(\dot{\theta}_l + \dot{\theta}_r)}{2} \tag{1}$$

$$\dot{\theta} = \frac{r}{l}[\dot{\theta}_r - \dot{\theta}_l] \tag{2}$$

As a result, the kinematics model of the vehicle's velocity v and the angular velocity $\dot{\theta}$ can be represented in a matrix form as:

$$\begin{bmatrix} v \\ \dot{\theta} \end{bmatrix} = \begin{bmatrix} r/2 & r/2 \\ r/l & -r/l \end{bmatrix} \begin{bmatrix} \dot{\theta}_r \\ \dot{\theta}_l \end{bmatrix} \tag{3}$$

2.2 Kinematic Modeling of the Robot Arm

Based on the typical coordinate transformation concept, the frame of reference fixed on the MM platform can be transformed to the base frame of reference of the manipulator by two translational and one rotation matrices. The frames of reference of the manipulator under consideration are shown in Fig.2. The transformation matrix between the manipulator's frames for the employed 5 DOF manipulator is obtained using the well known Denavit_Hartenberg method. As a result the final link transformation matrix with respect to the base of the manipulator is obtained as: $T_0^5 = T_0^1 * T_1^2 * T_2^3 * T_3^4 * T_4^5$

Therefore the forward kinematics of the manipulator is formulated as:

$$T_0^5 = \begin{bmatrix} n_x & o_x & a_x & p_x \\ n_y & o_y & a_y & p_y \\ n_z & o_z & a_z & p_z \\ 0 & 0 & 0 & 1 \end{bmatrix};$$

Where: $p_x = -d_2 s_1 + c_1(a_2 c_2 + a_3 c_{23} - d_5 s_{234})$;
$p_y = d_2 c_1 + s_1(a_2 c_2 + a_3 c_{23} - d_5 s_{234})$; $p_z = d_1 - a_2 s_2 - a_3 s_{23} - d_5 c_{234}$;
$n_x = c_1 c_{234} c_5 + s_1 s_5$; $n_y = s_1 c_{234} c_5 - c_1 s_5$; $n_z = -s_{234} c_5$;
$o_x = -c_1 c_{234} s_5 + s_1 c_5$; $o_y = -s_1 c_{234} s_5 - c_1 c_5$; $o_z = s_{234} s_5$;
$a_x = -c_1 s_{234}$; $a_y = -s_1 s_{234}$; $a_z = -c_{234}$

In the above expressions: $c_i = \cos(\theta_i)$; $s_i = \sin(\theta_i)$; $s_{23} = \sin(\theta_2 + \theta_3)$; $c_{23} = \cos(\theta_2 + \theta_3)$; $c_{234} = \cos(\theta_2 + \theta_3 + \theta_4)$; $s_{234} = \sin(\theta_2 + \theta_3 + \theta_4)$ and θ_i for $i=1$ to 5 are the joint angles of the manipulator.

As a result the linear velocity and angular Jacobians in matrix form can be written as:

$J_v = [J_{v1} \quad J_{v2} \quad J_{v3} \quad J_{v4} \quad J_{v5}]$

To find the manipulator's singularities the determinant of the jacobian is set to jacobian $Det(J) = 0$. Subsequently, the manipulability value of the arm, which is a critical parameter used in the proposed cooperation mechanism, can be calculated as: *Manipulability*= $Det(J) = (a_2 c_2 + a_3 c_{23})(a_3 a_2 s_3)$. In the proposed approach one of the important factors to achieve the cooperation on rough terrain is to model the F/T sensor by cooperating the motion of the robot as it moves on rough terrain. As a result the F/T values are a function of the robot's arm joint angles and the robot's roll, pitch and yaw measured by the Inertia Measurement Unit (IMU) sensor. The forces and moments sensed in a robot's wrist when the MM moves on rough terrain can be obtained using Equation (4):

$$J = \begin{bmatrix} -s_1(a_2c_2 + a_3c_{23}) & -a_2c_1s_2 - a_3c_1s_{23} & -a_3c_1s_{23} \\ c_1(a_2c_2 + a_3c_{23}) & -a_2s_1s_2 - a_3s_1s_{23} & -a_3s_1s_{23} \\ 0 & -a_2c_2 - a_3c_{23} & -a_3c_{23} \end{bmatrix}$$

$$\theta_{weight} = \frac{\pi}{2} - (\emptyset + \theta_2 + \theta_3 + \theta_4); F = mg = \sqrt{F_x^2 + F_y^2 + F_z^2} ; F_x = F \sin\theta_{weight}$$

$$F_y = F \cos\theta_{roll}; F_z = F \cos\theta_{weight} \tag{4}$$

$\emptyset$: The pitch angle of the vehicle, θ_{roll} : The roll angle of the vehicle

where m is the mass of the object been manipulated, g the local acceleration of gravity and F_x, F_y and F_z are the sensed forces along the x, y and z direction of the F/T sensor frame of reference, respectively. For ease of explanation, here we neglect the moments, which should be considered to fully determine the effect of the object as the MM rolls, pitches and yaws as it interacts with the terrain.

3   Control Architecture

In order to address the problems found in current human-MM cooperation mechanisms a new yet simple control approach is proposed herein. The approach combines well known techniques in an attempt to maximize their advantages while reducing their disadvantages. Figure 3 shows the schematic block diagram of the proposed human-MM's cooperation architecture. This architecture consists of 4 main blocks:

1. The MM's SIMMECHANICS modeling block,
2. The force torque sensor,
3. Mathematical modeling of the robot, and
4. The fuzzy logic controller.

In this architecture the human interacting with the MM provides the external forces and moments which the manipulator must follow. For this, we consider the human and the MM as a coupled system carrying an object (assumed to be rigid) in cooperation. The process starts by initializing the system (i.e., the sensed changes in the force torque sensor values should be equal to zero. This is achieved by avoiding any disturbance to the manipulator). Subsequently, during cooperation there will be changes sensed in the F/T values. According to the value of such changes, Δ(F/T), the robot computes its motion (i.e., joint angle velocities) to eliminate any changes in the F/T values (i.e., make Δ(F/T)=0 at all times). Herein, we refer to this approach as a velocity feedback. The goal is to eliminate (minimize) the human's effort in the accomplishment of the task. The motion of the mobile base is subject to nonholonomic kinematics constraints, which renders the control of MM very challenging, especially when robots work in non engineered environments. To achieve the cooperation between the human and the MM in outdoor environments we developed a new set of equations for the changing in forces and torques on the robot's arm wrist caused by the interaction of the MM on the rough terrain. All the forces and torques are a function of the roll, pitch and yaw angles of the vehicle which are computed using Equation (4). Figure (4) shows the detailed control algorithm represented in general form Fig. 3.

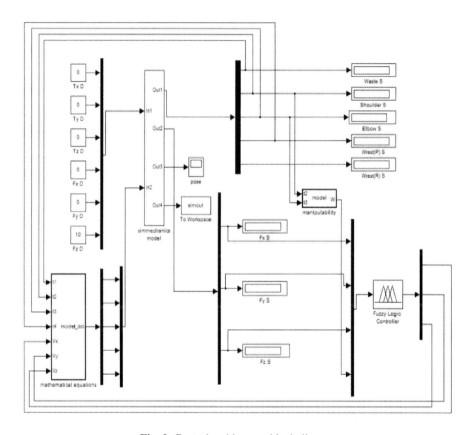

Fig. 3. Control architecture block diagram

The cooperation starts by initializing the robot. This includes placing the object to be manipulated on the robot's gripper and gathering all sensor data (at this point the robot holding the object by itself). Sensor data at initialization is considered the reference value. Once cooperation starts the initial sensor value, used as a reference, are update at all times according to the roll, pitch and yaw of the mobile base (Equation 4). The updated reference F/T values allow the cooperation to be based only on the human's intention and not on the terrain aspects.

4   Simulation and Results

The kinematics-dynamics simulation model of the robot was performed using SIMMECHANICS. The model comprises a set of connected blocks (i.e., body, joint, actuator, sensors, constraint and driver and initial conditions) (Fig. 5). These blocks were defined using special forms available in the modeling environment and all bocks included the real MM's properties such as mass, and moments of inertia. The controller was implemented in SIMULINK. Figure 6 shows the results of one test showing the performance of the controller. In this test the MM was placed on a rough terrain and pulled forward in a straight line (i.e., human was pulling the object being transported). Thus the end-effector was aimed at tracking sinusoidal trajectory Figure 6 shows the corresponding end-effector sensed forces (i.e., $\Delta(F/T)$ in the X, Y and Z direction of the F/T sensor's frame of reference.

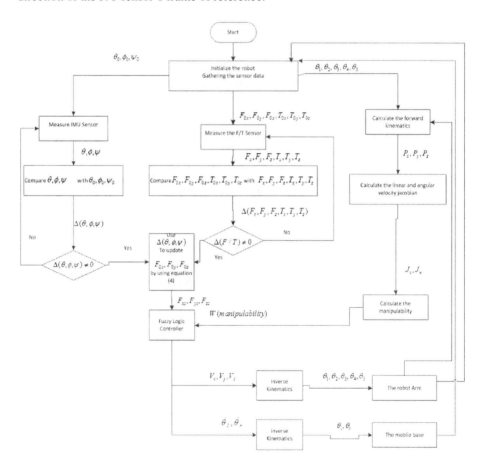

Fig. 4. Flowchart of the control algorithm

These forces include the human's intention as well as the forces induced on the MM by the terrain. According to the changes in F/T values the robot compensates this change by arm joint motion and mobile robot motion. Figure 7 shows the desired linear velocity of the MM to compensate the changes in the F/T values. In this case there are two types of cooperation. The first is the cooperation between a human and MM. The second is the cooperation between the arm and the mobile base to achieve the desired object's motion and minimize the human's effort in guiding the robot. Due to the change in roll, pitch and yaw angles of the mobile base were be a change in the wrist's F/T sensor values. Figure 8 shows the robot vehicle linear velocity and robot arm linear velocity. As seen in this figure, the end-effector converges (i.e., tracks) the desired motion accurately. The base also tracks the desired motion accurately with only small disturbances due to the oscillating motion of the end-effector. The vehicle is contributes to the motion in two dimensions (i.e., x and y velocities) while the arm contributes in 3D dimentions (i.e., x, y and z velocities). In this approach the manipulability is used to coordinate the motion between locomotion and manipulation of the mobile manipulator. The control mechanism measures the manipulability value and according to this change the control divides the desired velocity between the mobile base and the manipulator. Figure 9 shows the changes in the robot arm manipulability value. As can be seen when the manipulability value is maximum the robot's arm velocity is maximum and when the manipulability value is minimum the vehicle's velocity is maximum. During the cooperation between the human's and the MM the control mechanism calculates the manipulability value and divides it by the maximum manipulability value. Subsequently, the obtained value is multiplied by the total desired velocity to calculate the robot arm velocity. The rest of the desired object's velocity is achieved by the vehicle. Figure 10 shows the simulation results of the MM in 3D environment during the cooperation at 5, 10, 15 and 20 seconds of the cooperation task.

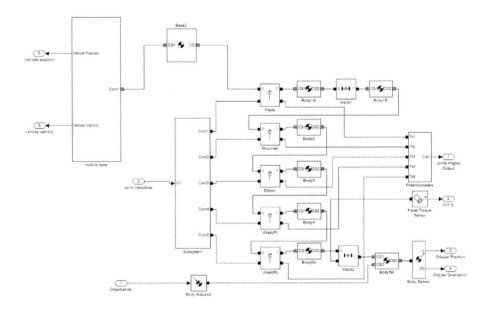

Fig. 5. Mobile Manipulator SIMMECHANIC model

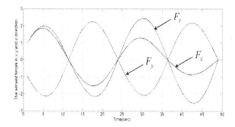

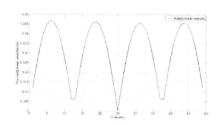

Fig. 6. The changes of forces at robot wrist   **Fig. 7.** The desired linear velocity of the MM

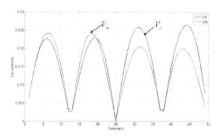

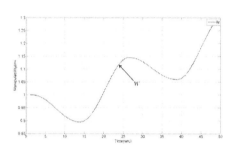

Fig. 8. The vehicle's and arm's linear velocities   **Fig. 9.** Changes of the arms manipulability

a) 5 seconds (w=0.96, V_m=0.023m/s)   b) 10 seconds (w=0.91, V_m=0.014m/s)

c) 15 seconds (w=0.90, V_m=0.015m/s)   d) 20 seconds (w=1.1, V_m=0.023m/s)

Fig. 10. Graphical time lapsed simulation results of MM

5   Conclusions

This research achieved a simple yet effective control strategy/algorithm with the corresponding software, which enables robots and humans to interact and perform tasks in cooperation on unknown rough terrains with a minimal human effort. This is achieved by enabling the robot's arm and the vehicle's wheels to cooperate (on top of the human-robot cooperation) to achieve the desired velocity that will accurately follow the human's intentions. The proposed system displays safe, easy to use, reliable and intelligent features, which has a number of potential benefits to society from a non-industrial point of view. In this research the cooperation between the MM and the master was not targeted to be performed at high speeds (fast navigation of robots in unknown rough terrains). As a result of the current work future work is needed to improve the control algorithms to achieve the human-robot cooperation with high speed navigation in unknown rough (potentially dynamic) terrains.

References

1. Sheng, L., Goldenberg, A.A.: Neural-network control of mobile manipulators. IEEE Transactions on Robotics 12(5), 1121–1133 (2001)
2. Jae, H.C.: Interactive force control of an operator-mobile manipulator coordination system. J. of Robotic Systems 19(4), 189–198 (2002)
3. Fujisawa, Y., et al.: Control of manipulator/vehicle system for man-robot cooperation based on human intention. In: IEEE Int. Workshop on Robot and Human Communication (1992)
4. Yamanaka, E., Ohnishi, K.: Cooperative motion control by human and mobile manipulator. In: 7th Int. Workshop on Advanced Motion Control (2002)
5. Yamanaka, E., Murakami, T., Ohnishi, K.: Motion control of mobile manipulator for human interaction. In: 28th Annual Conf. of the Industrial Electronics Society (2002)
6. Kristensen, S., Neumann, M., Horstmann, S., Lohnert, F., Stopp, A.: Tactile Man-Robot Interaction for an Industrial Service Robot. In: Hager, G.D., Christensen, H.I., Bunke, H., Klein, R. (eds.) Dagstuhl Seminar 2000. LNCS, vol. 2238, pp. 177–194. Springer, Heidelberg (2002)
7. Fernandez, V., et al.: Active human-mobile manipulator cooperation through intention recognition. In: IEEE Int. Conf. on Robotics and Automation (2001)
8. Hayakawa, Y., Ogata, Y.K.T., Sugano, S.: Extraction of Human Intention for Human Cooperating Systems. In: 9th Int. Conf. on Advanced Robotics, Tokyo, pp. 199–204 (1999)
9. Yamada, Y., et al.: Construction of a human/robot coexistence system based on a model of human will-intention and desire. In: IEEE Int. Conf. on Robotics and Automation (1999)
10. Yamamoto, Y., Eda, H., Xiaoping, Y.: Coordinated task execution of a human and a mobile manipulator. In: IEEE Int. Conf. on Robotics and Automation (1996)
11. Hirata, Y., et al.: Handling of a Single Object by Multiple Mobile Manipulators in Cooperation with Human Based on Virtual 3-D Caster Dynamics. JSME Int. J. Series C Mechanical Systems, Machine Elements and Manufacturing 48(4), 613–619 (2005)

A Modular Approach to Gesture Recognition for Interaction with a Domestic Service Robot

Stefan Schiffer, Tobias Baumgartner, and Gerhard Lakemeyer

Knowledge-Based Systems Group
RWTH Aachen University, Aachen, Germany
tobias.baumgartner@rwth-aachen.de,
{schiffer,gerhard}@cs.rwth-aachen.de

Abstract. In this paper, we propose a system for robust and flexible visual gesture recognition on a mobile robot for domestic service robotics applications. This adds a simple yet powerful mode of interaction, especially for the targeted user group of laymen and elderly or disabled people in home environments. Existing approaches often use a monolithic design, are computationally expensive, rely on previously learned (static) color models, or a specific initialization procedure to start gesture recognition. We propose a multi-step modular approach where we iteratively reduce the search space while retaining flexibility and extensibility. Building on a set of existing approaches, we integrate an on-line color calibration and adaptation mechanism for hand detection followed by feature-based posture recognition. Finally, after tracking the hand over time we adopt a simple yet effective gesture recognition method that does not require any training.

1 Introduction

In the development of domestic service robots easy and natural interaction is a vital property of a successful system. Intuitive control and interaction can, for example, be achieved with natural language. However, a huge part of meaning in communication is also transferred via non-verbal signals [1]. A very important mode of this non-verbal communication is using gestures. This is especially true in interaction with a domestic service robot, since controlling the robot often relates to entities in the world such as objects and places or directions. References to objects can conveniently be made by pointing gestures while other dynamic gestures can be used to indicate directions or commands.

Quite some approaches tend to pose undesirable requirements both, before the start of operation as well as within operation itself. For example, they may require a tedious calibration of hand colors or depend on initialization poses of the human. Also, some approaches are quite costly and demand high computational resources. We try to avoid these undesirable properties and aim for a flexible, modular, and robust system that is both easy to set up and easy to use while minimizing computational demands. We designed a modular architecture where gesture recognition is decomposed into sub-tasks orchestrated in a multi-step system. This enables a filter-and-refine like processing of the input where

S. Jeschke, H. Liu, and D. Schilberg (Eds.): ICIRA 2011, Part II, LNAI 7102, pp. 348–357, 2011.

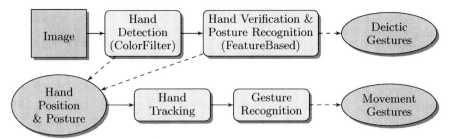

Fig. 1. Architectural overview of our approach

the single steps are as independent as possible to allow for an easy replacement of the particular method used for any of them. Further, the output of each step can already be used for specific purposes. That is, for example, pointing gestures can already be inferred from the position (and possibly the posture) of a hand and a face, while recognition of dynamic gestures additionally requires hand tracking to extract a trajectory. What is more, the overall computational demands are kept low because the amount of information to be processed gets reduced in each step.

2   A Multi-step Approach

The process of gesture recognition is subdivided into four main steps: *hand detection*, *posture recognition*, *hand tracking*, and finally *gesture recognition*. Hand detection is the task of finding the position of one or more hands in an image, where we follow a color-based approach. To increase robustness against false detections, we additionally apply a *hand verification* step. Posture recognition then is to determine the shape of the hand, that is to say the configuration of the fingers (e.g., a *fist* or an *open hand*) and the orientation of this posture. Both, hand verification and posture recognition are performed with a feature-based classification method. Binary classification is used to decide whether a candidate area actually contains a hand and a multi-class classification determines one of multiple possible postures. Hand tracking refers to recording the position of the hand (and its posture) over a sequence of images. Finally, gesture recognition is understood as identifying a specific dynamic movement of the hand from the trajectory formed over time. A graphical overview of our system's architecture is depicted in Figure 1.

Note that the intermediate steps yield useful information already. The hand detection and verification provide us with hand positions and posture recognition adds the posture of a hand detected. Specific commands such as a lifted open hand can already be processed, for example, as an indication of a *stop*-request or the user's request for attention. Taking an existing face detector as a secondary cue also allows for identifying pointing gestures when the posture is, say, a lifted index finger. We refer to gestures at this stage as *deictic gestures*. Also, by iteratively refining the information we can dismiss wrongly detected hands and attach additional information thus enabling increased performance of later steps.

3   Related Work

Hand Detection. A lot of the existing hand detection approaches are color-based, since skin-colored regions can quite easily be detected in an image [2,3]. There are two main issues with (such static) color-based hand detection, however. For one, not every skin-colored region in an image is in fact a hand. For another, in dynamic environments the values of skin color may vary over time, for example, because of changes in lighting conditions or due to obstructions like shadows or colored reflections. A combined way to tackle the problems mentioned above is to make use of the assumption that an image containing a hand also contains a face. This does not seem to be too restrictive given a human-robot interaction scenario. If a face is detected, a skin color can be extracted from that face and then be used for hand detection. Such an approach was already presented in [4]. We follow similar directions but apply some variations. We operate on the HSV color space which, according to [5], seems most appropriate for skin color detection. We then use a modified scheme to dynamically adapt the color values over time. Another way to detect hands is to use features instead of color. In [6] a sliding window is used and a classifier is applied on this window to decide on whether this window contains an object of interest (i.e. a hand) or not. It is an extension of a method presented for object detection in [7], namely a haarcascade, which is a cascade of haar-like visual features. The classifier is built using the AdaBoost method [8] for boosting. An alternative to classical boosting could be random forests [9], especially for multi-class classification as we will employ for posture recognition. Random forests have successfully been applied to face recognition for multiple identities on a mobile robot [10] already.

A method to recognize hand postures is followed in [11]. The idea is to bring the fingers of a hand in a meaningful relation by considering the hand's convex hull and counting the defects of this hull. However, this is only done for planar hands and it is not generally applicable in its current form. Triesch and v.d. Malsburg present a system for posture recognition using elastic graph matching [12]. Several points on a hand are used to build a graph which is compared to graphs trained on a set of postures before. Although both these methods seem appealing and could potentially be plugged into our modular architecture, we opt for a feature-based posture recognition following the approach in [6] to be able to exploit the similarities in hand verification and posture recognition.

Hand Tracking. Tracking can, for example, be realized with a method called "Flocks of Features" [13]. To track, the hand position is initialized by detecting one of a set of six trained postures. Then, features are chosen on this hand and followed with KLT feature tracking [14]. Another successful tracking mechanism is CAMSHIFT [15], a modification of the *mean shift* algorithm. The position of a fixed size window is iteratively computed. However, CAMSHIFT is color-based and it is thus subject to the drawbacks we mentioned earlier. That is why we follow the lines of [14] in tracking.

Gesture Recognition. There is a huge body of work on gesture recognition, a survey can be found in [16], for example. A lot of the approaches use statistical methods such as Hidden Markov Models (HMMs) which we think are computationally too demanding for our setting. Also, statistical methods usually rely on (often huge amounts of) training data which the recognition then depends on. Instead, we plan on extending a simple approach to gesture recognition described in [17]. It is especially intriguing since it does not require any form of training and does not depend on any external library or toolkit either.

4   Hand Detection and Posture Recognition

In this section we detail our approach to hand detection, hand verification, and posture recognition. First, we employ a color-based approach for hand detection. A *ColorFilter* selects those parts of the image that are skin-colored. The extracted parts are then forwarded to a *Hand Verification* step which decides whether these areas actually contain a hand or not. All detected and verified hands are subsequently processed by a multi-class classifier determining one of a set of specific postures for each hand. The result of this procedure, that is, the hands in an image and their (possibly undefined) postures are then available for any later module. This multi-step processing tries to reduce the search space with every step. The cheapest, color-based classification is done first. The false positive rate may be comparatively high here, though. However, the subsequent step filters out further false positives, now with a feature-based method which is computationally more costly, but only has to consider fewer candidates. Only those hands are processed in the posture classification that passed the first two steps. This way, we proceed with less effort than it would have taken to do the classification of the different postures on the complete image instead of on candidate regions only.

4.1   Hand Detection

The maybe most obvious feature of hands in an image is color. Skin color may easily be detected [2,3], but especially a static color model suffers from dynamic changes in the environment such as lighting, shadows, and inter-person skin color variations. Further, static color models typically require a training which has as many examples for skin color as possible. Any hand exhibiting a color that is not covered by the training set will not be detected by this color model. That is why we opt for a dynamically adapting skin color model with almost no prior information. Instead, we exploit the following assumption: If the robot is to interact with a person, this person is most likely facing the robot. So, similarly to [4], we first detect faces in the image to extract parameters for our color model from the face region. For one, the face detection module is active on our robot already, so no additional effort is required. For another, there are properly working face detection methods [18] readily available in OpenCV[1]. After a sufficiently reliable detection of a face in x subsequent images we compute expectation values σ_c and standard deviation μ_c for each of the HSV color space channels c, i.e., hue, saturation, and value. Pixels in the image with a value of v_c in color channel c are then classified according to the formula $\mid \sigma_c - v_c \mid \leq \alpha \cdot \mu_c$ where α is a positive real-valued factor allowing us to control the adaptivity.

[1] http://opencv.willowgarage.com/

Table 1. Results of Color Evaluation

Cover Percentage[2]		True positive	False positive	Mean iterations
Face	Image			
0.3	0.6	0.83	0.19	0.71
0.5	0.8	0.90	0.19	1.03
0.6	0.8	0.93	0.24	3.42
0.7	0.5	0.96	0.33	11.25
0.9	0.9	0.99	0.44	54.10

Additionally, we compute two control values for every image that help in determining when and how we need to adapt our model. The *image cover percentage* indicates how many percent of the image are classified to be skin-colored. Analogously, the *face cover percentage* tells us how many pixel of the face region were classified to be of skin color. If the *face cover percentage* is too low, this indicates that only few pixels were considered to be skin, which obviously is undesirable. In that case we have to increase α to make our skin color classifier more lenient. If, on the other hand, the *image cover percentage* is too high, too much of the overall image is considered to be skin. In that case we need to lower our α for the model to be more restrictive.

Evaluation. To determine appropriate values for the *image cover percentage* and *face cover percentage* we constructed a database of around 800 pictures of typical application scenario settings. To do so, we placed faces and hands with variations in lighting and brightness on indoor background images. Faces and corresponding hands were varied in size to mimic a user standing in front of the robot at distances of between two and three meters. For every combination of *image cover percentage* between $[0.5 \ldots 0.9]$ and *face cover percentage* between $[0.3 \ldots 0.9]$ in steps of 0.05 we computed the true positive and false negative rate as well as the number of iterations it took the color model to reach a fixed value as *mean iterations*. Selected results are listed in Table 1.[2]

The final ColorFilter then used a threshold of 0.5 for the *face cover percentage* and 0.8 for the *image cover percentage*. We chose to do so because at these values the true positive rate of 90% was reasonably high while the false positive rate of 19% was tolerable, especially since further false detections can still be sorted out in later steps. A mean number of 1.03 iterations also indicates that these values are quite stable and do not require too many adaptations. Combinations beneath the horizontal line after the values 0.6 and 0.8 have a very high number of iterations so that it would take too long to compute color models with these.

4.2   Hand Verification and Posture Recognition

Since the previous step, the color-based hand detection, results in a non-negligible amount of false positives, the next step is to verify the candidate regions. Also, we want to determine the posture of every hand verified. For both these tasks we choose a feature-based approach. A basic technique in feature-based detection is to use a so-called *sliding window*. A window of fixed size is slid over the image and

---

[2] Percentages are given as values between 0.0 for 0% and 1.0 for 100%, respectively.

Table 2. Results for *Haarcascade* trainings in overview

| | Training Images | | True | False | Stages | Training |
	Positive	Negative	Positive	Detections		Time
All Hands	1000	700	0.15	71.95	11	21h
All Upright	1000	1000	0.36	3.06	18	42h
Open Own	3000	2000	0.98	12.71	12	7h
Open Kumar	1000	700	0.93	2.37	14	9h
Fist	130	100	0.57	0.23	4	1h
Fist + Open	500 + 500	1000	0.28	0	19	41h
L	100	100	0.25	0	10	3h

for each position of the window a decision rule (i.e. a classifier) decides whether the window contains an object of interest or not. Since the classifier used with the sliding window can be a binary or a multi-class classifier and the window does not need to be slided over the whole image but can also be only slided over regions of interest (ROIs) we opt to use feature-based classification (with haar-like features) for both, the hand verification and the posture recognition.

Data Sets. A major question in building feature-based classifiers in general, and for binary classifiers for hand verification in particular, is the selection of an appropriate training set. In contrast to faces, the variations found with many different hand postures are considerably larger. To determine a good classifier for hand verification we trained and evaluated several haarcascades (using OpenCV) and random forests with different training sets compiled from collections available on the Internet, namely one with high resolution images of a single posture[3], a set with lower resolution images of ten different postures[4] and a collection by Ajay Kumar[5] used as training data for a touchless palmprint authentication [19]. Additionally, we constructed our own data set from hand images extracted from video sequences and placed on complex backgrounds. The video sequences were recorded by gesturing in front of our robot. We intend to make our data set publicly available soon. Negative examples were taken from a data set collected by Natoshi Seo.[6]

Evaluation. We conducted extensive evaluation series with both, classical haarcascades and random forests. Results from different trainings for haarcascades and random forests are given in Table 2 and Table 3, respectively. The evaluation suggests that training does not seem suitable to generate a single cascade capable of detecting arbitrary hands with any of the available training sets. An in-depth investigation revealed that the choice of haar-like features available to the classifier influences the recognition results. This finding is supported by results from [6], where instead of traditional haar-like features the authors use so-called *"four box"* features that are more fine-grained. Despite the unsatisfactory results for both, haarcascades and random forests, it is worth noting, that random forests have considerably lower training times while providing better results. Moreover, it is possible to extend our current implementation of random forests to use the

---

[3] http://www2.imm.dtu.dk/~aam/datasets/datasets.html
[4] http://www.idiap.ch/resources/gestures/
[5] http://www.comp.polyu.edu.hk/~csajaykr/IITD/Database_Palm.htm
[6] http://tutorial-haartraining.googlecode.com/svn/trunk/data/negatives/

Table 3. Results for *Random Forest* classifiers

	TP rate	FP rate	Samples	Trees	Time (h:m)
All hands, old feat.	0.73	0.25	2×190	10	0:36
All hands, 4 orient.,	0.79	0.25	5×200	3	0:20
5 classes	0.63	0.03	5×2000	20	16:02
Open	0.73	0.07	2×250	5	0:09
Fist	0.78	0.07	2×250	7	0:21
Open + Fist	0.77	0.21	2×250	9	0:12
Closed	0.60	0.12	2×1000	2	1:18
Victory	0.61	0.16	2×180	1	0:06
Classify Postures	0.19	-	5×150	5	0:31

"*four box*" features to improve on our results. Until we finish to do so, we make use of a haarcascade created by Daniel Baggio.[7] Evaluation on our test data yielded a true positive rate of 74% and a false negative rate of $9.1822 * 10^{-8}$, which corresponds to one false detection every six frames. Hence, in the current system it may happen, that the user has to repeat a gesture as a result of false detections.

Besides classifying between "hand" and "no hand" only, an additional dimension is to differentiate between several hand *postures*. As Tables 2 and 3 indicate, it is possible to train haarcascades as well as random forests to recognize specific single postures with true positive rates of up to 98% for haarcascades and at least 60% for random forests. Training times for random forests were considerably lower than for haarcascades. However, we did not succeed in building a single random forest classifier that was able to tell apart five different postures with a sufficiently high true positive rate. We hope to eventually achieve more accurate posture classification once we fully integrate the "*four box*" features used in the classifier from [6] into our random forest classifiers. Until then, we restrict ourselves to a few postures that we could train sufficiently accurate single classifiers for. Those classifiers can then be applied independently in parallel.

4.3 Deictic Gestures

As already mentioned, we can make use of the intermediate results after the hand detection and posture recognition steps already. These static gestures are referred to as *deictic gestures*. We trigger detection either when a specific posture (such as a pointing) is recognized or by means of an external trigger such as keywords like "*stop*" or "*there*" spotted by the speech recognition module running on the robot. As an additional cue to extract information from for pointing gestures we make use of the face detection module we used before already. We extract the face's position and compute a vector from the center of the face position to the center of the hand's position to identify a pointing target.

5   Tracking and Gesture Recognition

After the position of a hand has been determined, its trajectory has to be tracked over time to enable gesture recognition. *Tracking* and *Gesture Recognition* are thus closely connected.

---

[7] http://code.google.com/p/ehci/wiki/HandTracking

5.1   Hand Tracking

The general idea with tracking is that a hand's position will not change too rapidly from one image frame to the next. A naive method to track a hand is to detect all hands in the image and associate the closest hand in the subsequent frame. However, this presupposes a very reliable hand detection. A different technique is applied in [6], where hands with the same posture are tracked over time. The underlying assumption that the posture of the hand stays the same throughout a gesture does not seem to allow for too natural gestures, though.

In our system, we use a tracking scheme called "Flocks of Features" as proposed in [13]. Components to realize the tracking are readily available in OpenCV. After detecting a hand, features are computed and then tracked using KLT feature tracking [14]. In a test series of 20 "tries-to-escape" where the user erratically moved around the hand within the camera's field of view, the selected tracking scheme proved sufficiently robust. Hands were tracked over periods of between 1.5 and 34.98 seconds with an average of 18.48 seconds. This is sufficient for most gestures in a domestic setting.

5.2   Gesture Recognition

The final step in our system is to recognize a gesture from following the hand's position over time. First, the trajectory of the hand is recorded. Then, this trajectory is compared to a set of known gestures. Since we want to keep our system as free from training and as computationally inexpensive as possible, we opt to adapt a method introduced by Wobbrock et al. [17] initially designed for one-stroke hand-written gestures. It is fast to implement and still yields reliable results. The basic principle is to norm trajectories to a certain scheme and then to compare performed gestures to a set of known gestures by computing their individual points' distances.

The preparation of trajectories before the comparison to known gesture templates is as follows. Since pairwise comparing all points is too costly only points with the same index are compared. For this to work, the trajectories have to contain the same number of points, which is why every trajectory is filled to have equidistant points. Here we chose 128 as the number of points following results given in [17]. Afterwards, the trajectory is rotated to a standard orientation, i.e., an orientation of $0°$ between the first point and the centroid, to achieve rotational invariance. Then, the resulting point set is scaled to fit a box of 100×100 pixels. Preparation steps are shown in Figure 2.

Basic movements like "left to right" correspond to lines in a trajectory. Unfortunately, the detection of straight horizontal and vertical lines is problematic with the method from [17]. This is why we need to slightly modify the approach by applying a different scaling mechanism. If the ratio between width and height of the unscaled trajectory is below a certain threshold (empirically determined to be 0.3) we only scale the larger side of the box. This prevents the scaled line-trajectories from being too scattered to be recognizable. We adjust the gesture templates to compare with accordingly.

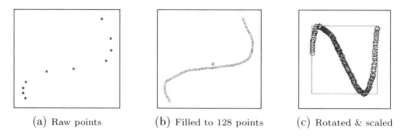

(a) Raw points   (b) Filled to 128 points   (c) Rotated & scaled

Fig. 2. Processing steps on a *Snake* trajectory for gesture recognition [17]

Evaluation. We conducted a separate mouse-based evaluation of the gesture recognition component to yield results independent from the hand detection itself. We recorded a total set of 314 gestures (one of *Line*, *Wave*, *Square*, *Circle*, and *Triangle*) where 85.67% were recognized correctly. More than 50% of the false detections were confusions between *Square* and *Circle* gestures. One reason could be imperfections in the mouse-based input. Preliminary findings in the analysis of human gestures suggest that humans perform gestures surprisingly precise. If we then assume the trajectories from human gestures to be more precise than the ones created artificially, these confusions might drop down already. Moreover, we additionally applied a corner detection on the trajectory to clear up these confusions. With this extension in effect we could raise the detection rate to above 92%.

6   Conclusion

In this paper, we proposed a modular system for visual gesture recognition for interaction with a domestic service robot. The processing pipeline is organized to reduce the amount of information to process at every step, starting with an inexpensive on-line adapting color-based method for hand detection, leaving only parts of the image to be processed by the more expensive feature-based posture recognition. The actual gesture recognition adopts a fast approach originally designed for hand-written gesture recognition that does not require any training. Results from intermediate processing steps can already be used for interaction, for example, to react on deictic pointing or stop gestures.

Although our system suffers from shortcomings in the hand verification and posture recognition steps yet, the overall performance is sufficient for it to be applicable in a domestic setting with some minor restrictions. While we successfully used the system at a recent major robotics competition already, each individual step can still be improved. These improvements, however, can be realized relatively easily due to the modular design. Likewise, anyone replicating the system can exchange any of the proposed components to his or her liking. Our next step is to fully integrate the *"four box"* features from [6] in our random forest implementation. Future work further includes the extension to work on 3D position information for hands and for gestures, respectively.

References

1. Engleberg, I.N., Wynn, D.R.: Working in Groups: Communication Principles and Strategies, 4th edn. Allyn & Bacon (2006)
2. Saxe, D., Foulds, R.: Toward robust skin identification in video images. In: Proc. 2nd Int'l Conf. on Automatic Face and Gesture Recognition, p. 379 (1996)
3. Jones, M., Rehg, J.: Statistical color models with application to skin detection. International Journal of Computer Vision 46, 81–96 (2002)
4. Francke, H., Ruiz-del-Solar, J., Verschae, R.: Real-Time Hand Gesture Detection and Recognition Using Boosted Classifiers and Active Learning. In: Mery, D., Rueda, L. (eds.) PSIVT 2007. LNCS, vol. 4872, pp. 533–547. Springer, Heidelberg (2007)
5. Zhu, X., Yang, J., Waibel, A.: Segmenting hands of arbitrary color. In: Proc. 4th Int'l Conf. on Automatic Face and Gesture Recognition, p. 446 (2000)
6. Kölsch, M., Turk, M.: Robust hand detection. In: Proc. of the 6th IEEE Int'l Conf. on Automatic Face and Gesture Recognition, pp. 614–619 (2004)
7. Viola, P.A., Jones, M.J.: Rapid object detection using a boosted cascade of simple features. In: Conf. on Computer Vision and Pattern Recognition (CVPR 2001), vol. I, pp. 511–518. IEEE Computer Society, Los Alamitos (2001)
8. Freund, Y., Schapire, R.E.: A decision-theoretic generalization of on-line learning and an application to boosting. J. Comput. System Sci. 55, 119–139 (1997)
9. Ho, T.K.: Random decision forests. In: Proc. of the 3rd Int'l Conf. on Document Analysis and Recognition (ICDAR 1995), vol. 1, pp. 278–282 (1995)
10. Belle, V., Deselaers, T., Schiffer, S.: Randomized trees for real-time one-step face detection and recognition. In: Proc. of the 19th Int'l Conf. on Pattern Recognition (ICPR 2008), pp. 1–4. IEEE Computer Society (2008)
11. Panin, G., Klose, S., Knoll, A.: Real-Time Articulated Hand Detection and Pose Estimation. In: Bebis, G., Boyle, R., Parvin, B., Koracin, D., Kuno, Y., Wang, J., Pajarola, R., Lindstrom, P., Hinkenjann, A., Encarnação, M.L., Silva, C.T., Coming, D. (eds.) ISVC 2009. LNCS, vol. 5876, pp. 1131–1140. Springer, Heidelberg (2009)
12. Triesch, J., von der Malsburg, C.: Robust classification of hand postures against complex backgrounds. In: Proc. of the 2nd Int'l Conf. on Automatic Face and Gesture Recognition (FG 1996), Washington, DC, USA, pp. 170–175 (1996)
13. Kölsch, M., Turk, M.: Fast 2d hand tracking with flocks of features and multi-cue integration. In: IEEE Workshop on Real-Time Vision for Human-Computer Interaction at Conf. on Computer Vision and Pattern Recognition, p. 158 (2004)
14. Shi, J., Tomasi, C.: Good features to track. In: IEEE Conference on Computer Vision and Pattern Recognition (CVPR 1994), pp. 593–600 (1994)
15. Bradski, G.R.: Computer vision face tracking for use in a perceptual user interface. Intel Technology Journal 1, 1–15 (1998)
16. Mitra, S., Acharya, T.: Gesture recognition: A survey. IEEE Transactions on Systems, Man, and Cybernetics (Part C) 37, 311–324 (2007)
17. Wobbrock, J.O., Wilson, A.D., Li, Y.: Gestures without libraries, toolkits or training: a $1 recognizer for user interface prototypes. In: Proc. of the 20th ACM Symposium on User Interface Software and Technology, pp. 159–168 (2007)
18. Viola, P.A., Jones, M.J.: Robust real-time face detection. International Journal of Computer Vision 57, 137–154 (2004)
19. Kumar, A.: Incorporating cohort information for reliable palmprint authentication. In: Proc. 6th Indian Conf. on Computer Vision, Graphics & Image Processing, pp. 583–590 (2008)

Safety System and Navigation
for Orthopaedic Robot (OTOROB)

Muralindran Mariappan*, Thayabaren Ganesan,
Vigneswaran Ramu, and Muhammad Iftikhar

Robotics & Bio-Medical Engineering Research Group (RoBiMed),
Universiti Malaysia Sabah, Jalan UMS, 88400, Kota Kinabalu, Sabah, Malaysia
murali.ums@gmail.com

Abstract. OTOROB is a telemedicine mobile robot for orthopaedic surgeons
that have remote presence capability to diagnose patients in remote area. As a
telemedicine robot that interacts with human being, it is required to have
extensive safety system. This paper presents a Fuzzy Logic based Danger
Monitoring System (DMS) and Fail-Safe and Auto Recovery System (FSARS)
that monitors the robot's operation. It is incorporated to the onboard flexible
robotic arm vision system and the robot's navigation system. It monitors the
robot surrounding and internal systems for danger or failures and takes
precaution measures to overcome it. The system is tested by a set of
experiments and found to be demonstrating an acceptable performance.

Keywords: Telemedicine, mobile robot, robotic arm, holonomic navigation,
fuzzy logic.

1 Introduction

Recent development and deployment of medical robotic has tremendously increased
the ease of medical procedures in various fields of medicine. The increasing rate of
patients being admitted to hospitals and healthcare centers are calling for a new type
of medical assistance [1]. Shortage of specialist or surgeon especially in third world
countries mainly in rural areas demand for new kind of telemedicine system that
enables the specialist to be telepresence[2]. The practice of telemedicine for medical
examinations means that people can undergo medical examinations at anytime and
anyplace [3]. In order to overcome the time distance boundaries between surgeon and
patient in rural areas, OTOROB (Orthopaedic Robot) robotic mobile platform was
developed.

Medical robots can be classified into non-contact and in-contact with patient robot.
OTELO system for echo-graphic diagnosis is fully integrated with end-to-end
communication between patient and expert through a six degree of freedom (DOF)
light robot with an ultra-sound probe [5]. ROBODOC which is a surgical CAD/CAM
robot system uses orthopedic implants in joint replacement surgery [4]. While non-
contact with patient robot refers to systems such as tele-monitoring robot such as RP-7.

---

* Corresponding author.

S. Jeschke, H. Liu, and D. Schilberg (Eds.): ICIRA 2011, Part II, LNAI 7102, pp. 358–367, 2011.
© Springer-Verlag Berlin Heidelberg 2011

Yet one of the most significant constrain in current medical robotics is the ability to obtain a flexible view of the patient or injuries, especially in orthopedic cases. Surgeons overwhelmingly rely on vision as their dominant source of feedback during surgery [4]. The da Vinci system for instance, improves the surgeon's eyes and hands by enabling them see and manipulate tissues inside the patient [6]. In order to overcome this constrain, OTOROB was developed with a Flexible Robotic Arm which holds a video camera as an end effector.

Robot navigation system is one of the most crucial parts of any mobile robot. Telemedicine mobile robot such as OTOROB requires a navigation system that is reliable and has a high degree of mobility in order for it to navigate through hospital environment. At the same time, it also requires extensive safety system to ensure it does not harm human beings or the robot itself. Holonomic navigation system is very famous among researchers that are developing mobile robots. Mariappan in [7] designed an optical tracking system for a holonomic mobile robot with four wheels. Tests show that it is very useful navigating on tight spots and difficult angles. L.Huang in [8] also developed a similar mobile robot using four omnidirectional wheels. Y.P.Hsu in [9] used obstacle sensors such as ultrasonic and laser range finder are incorporated to the robot to detect obstacles. For OTOROB, a four wheel diagonal holonomic wheel configuration similar to [9] is chosen for its ability to move in slightly uneven terrain. A combination of ultrasonic and infrared range finder sensors is incorporated to detect obstacles. Fuzzy Logic is used to process the inputs from all the navigation sensors and user inputs to decide the robot's movement. Figure 1 shows the designed and developed Orthopaedic Robot (OTOROB).

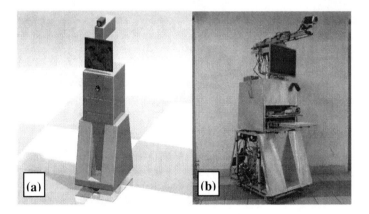

Fig. 1. Orthopaedic Robot (OTOROB) (a) 3D Design Model, (b) Developed Robot

In section 2 of this paper, the architecture of the safety system for OTOROB is explained. This section is divided into two parts to discuss in detail the safety of the flexible robotic arm and the navigation system. Section 3 presents the experimental result from testing the system and finally section 4 concludes this research.

2   Architecture

2.1   Flexible Robotic Arm Vision System Architecture

The OTOROB flexible arm is a mechanical telescopic arm with reach stroke of 80cm, which is crucial in obtaining full view of the patient. This feature together with 180 degrees of yaw and pitch motion of the video camera provides increased working envelope and proper coverage compare to present medical robots with static camera in the discipline of orthopedic. The flexible robotic arm in docked position (a), half extension (b) and full extension (c) figures are shown as Figure 2.

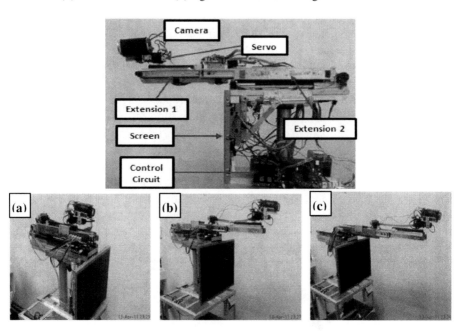

Fig. 2. Extending Flexible Robotic Arm Vision System

Development of the flexible arm is divided into three stages. The first stage involves hardware development; second stage involves software development while third stage is the implementation of fuzzy logic as Artificial Intelligence (AI). The articulation of the robotic arm is integrated with fuzzy logic in order to enhance the safety measures. Some medical ultrasound robots only permit movement of ultrasound probe through a pre-specified trajectory which limits flexibility due to safety [10]. Manual articulation by doctor is combined with fuzzy logic which includes Fail Safe & Auto-Recovery System (FSARS) and Obstacle Avoidance System (OAS) to provide more safer, stable and reliable system. Constant feedback from actuators (DC Quadrature Encoder Motors) and sensors (Ultrasonic Range Finder Array) monitor every motion of the mechanical arm which facilitates the implementation of AI. Several recent research works have been reported employing sophisticated fuzzy and neural technologies for motion control and trajectory tracking of robotic manipulators [11].

FSARS concept in flexible arm refers to two circumstances which are power failure and hardware (actuator) failure. This failure will interrupt flexible arm articulation and the OTOROB system does not permits the navigation mode due to safety reasons until the flexible arm is being docked. Trial runs and experiments show that power failure in flexible arm occurs due to three factors, which are: i) low battery voltage; ii) sudden power failure due to power cable disconnection or master power distributor malfunction; iii) over drawing of current by arm peripherals which is protected by fuse in power monitoring circuit. The FSARS scheme of flexible arm is as illustrated in the Figure 3.

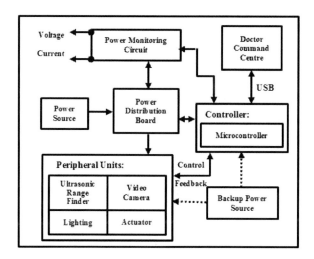

Fig. 3. OTOROB Flexible Robotic Arm FSARS scheme

The control, processing, and command execution of flexible arm is done through a dedicated microcontroller unit. The command executed by the remote doctor is processed by the controller unit and executed through the peripherals and simultaneously receives continuous feedbacks from the peripheral units and process the data then transmit to remote doctor. The incorporated fuzzy logic scheme of Fail Safe & Auto-Recovery interrupts the remote doctor's commands during the specified circumstances. If the procedure is paused for any reason, there are a number of error-recovery procedures available to permit the procedure to be resumed or restarted at one of several defined checkpoints [4]. A power monitoring circuit constantly monitors current usage and voltage level of the power distribution board which distribute power to controller unit and peripheral units.

In the case of low battery voltage, controller will send message to the remote doctor to indicate low battery level and eventually will trigger Fail Safe scheme if the battery level drains below the critical level. While in the case of current over drawing, any circuit breaking activity by dedicated fuses will trigger the Fail Safe scheme. At this point fuzzy logic will utilize a backup power source dedicated for the flexible arm to safely dock the arm back in position. The third scenario of sudden power down will immediately freeze remote doctor's control and will trigger the Fail Safe scheme to dock back the flexible arm into docking position by utilizing backup power source. All the fuzzy logic trigger inputs are monitored by the Fail Safe scheme and best solution accordance with the inputs is calculated and executed.

The Fail Safe scheme for hardware failure continuously monitors the feedbacks from the actuators and any negative or abnormal feedback will trigger the Fail Safe scheme to resolve any malfunction issues. The fuzzy logic will find alternate motion to dock the flexible arm back in place automatically. Any non-recoverable hardware malfunction or power failure will prohibit the flexible arm articulation, while recoverable hardware and software failures will trigger Auto-Recovery scheme. Auto-Recovery scheme will run a self-diagnose routine, and the flexible arm system will be refreshed so that it can be articulated by the remote doctor.

Obstacle Avoidance refers to the capability of flexible arm to respond against approaching objects in the course of collision with the flexible arm with the aid of peripheral units of sensors. An array of Ultrasonic Range Finders is integrated with flexible arm's mechanical structure frame at calculated angels and distance to provide lateral coverage surrounding the flexible arm. The coverage zone is divided into medium zone which covers from 8-20 inches and critical zone which covers from 1-8 inches. For instance, obstacle avoidance in SpiderBot-II, layers of force fields around an obstacle were created and the computing reaction is based on penetration into force layers [12]. Analog data from the sensor array is converted to detection distance and detection beyond the medium zone is ignored by the controller. The sensor coverage zone of flexible arm is as illustrated in Figure 4.

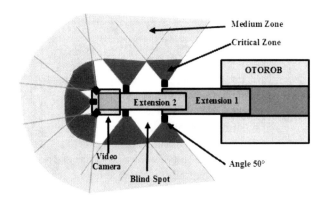

Fig. 4. Flexible Robotic Arm Vision Obstacle Avoidance System (Top View)

The sonar coverage area overlay enables to determine the position which is divided into certain regions in remote doctor's Graphical User Interface (GUI) that indicates any approaching obstacle at any particular region. The fuzzy logic implementation monitors the continuously sent data by sensor array and deduces the motion, projection and course of obstacle and thus the system warns the remote doctor. A message is sent to remote doctor's GUI regarding the approaching or static obstacle when detected in the medium zone. Any penetration of obstacle into critical zone will override remote doctor's command and Obstacle Avoidance scheme will be triggered to safely dock flexible arm without colliding with the approaching obstacle. If any obstacle approaching the blind spot is detected in the medium zone, the fuzzy logic will deduce the distance and speed of the obstacle to anticipate the penetration into blind spot and accordingly the Obstacle Avoidance scheme will be activated. Upon activation of the Obstacle Avoidance scheme, the flexible robotic arm navigates autonomously to maximize the distance between obstacle and robotic arm until a safe distance is reached.

2.2   Navigation System Architecture

OTOROB requires a safe and robust navigation system which will enable a user to control it from a remote location over the internet. In order to realize this, OTOROB is equipped with industrial standard equipment that is tested rigorously to meet the requirements. Microcontrollers are incorporated to the design as overall system controller and communication device. Figure 5 shows the block diagram of the system's architecture.

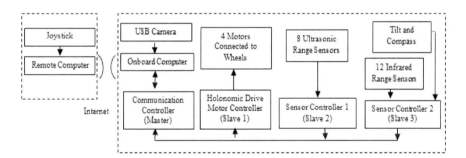

Fig. 5. Remote Navigation Architecture

Basically, the navigation system is divided into two parts which are remote user station and the robot itself. The computer in remote user station hosts the Graphical User Interface (GUI) that takes joystick data and transmits it to the robot over through internet. It also displays the navigation video and obstacle detection from the robot. On-board the robot, there is another computer which acts as the mediator to transmit robots data and navigation video feed to remote station and at the same time receive control signals from user.

SRF05 ultrasonic and Sharp GP2D120X / GP2Y0A21 infrared range finder sensors are used to detect objects or obstacles surrounding the robot. These sensors are placed such as in Figure 6 to give maximum coverage with minimum number of sensors. The robot's wheels are configured in a diagonal four wheel holonomic setting to give better manoeuvrability and ability to navigate in uneven terrain. Digital compass module is included to the system to show the robots orientation. ADXL335 accelerometer is used to obtain the tilt measurement of the robot to avoid it from collapsing due to unsafe inclination.

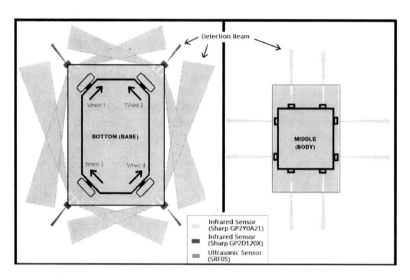

Fig. 6. Robot base and middle part sensor placement (Top view)

Since OTOROB is a telemedicine robot that physically interacts with human being, it is fitted safety features such as Danger Monitoring System (DMS), Fail Safe and Auto Recovery System (FSARS). In order to achieve this, it is equipped with a fuzzy logic based artificial intelligence system to process the data from all the sensors and user inputs as shown in Figure 7. DMS monitors the robot surrounding to identify potential danger to the robot and also to human being. When danger is detected, it will take precautions such as stopping the robot or giving warning to the user. Fail Safe monitors the operation of robot's internal system for signs of failure. When an anomaly is detected, it triggers the Auto Recovery to reset the hardware and try to reboot the system. If this fails, the fail safe system will move the robot to a safe location and turn off unnecessary system to safe power and request for a service. Failure includes internet connection lost, hardware failure, low battery and overlapping instructions from other systems of the robot. Figure 8 shows sensors placement on OTOROB's bottom and middle part

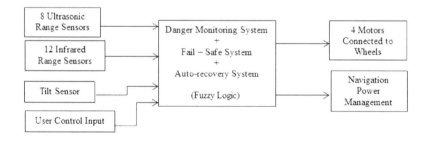

Fig. 7. Navigation System Artificial Intelligence

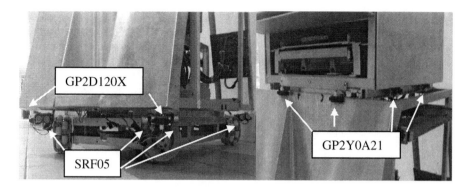

Fig. 8. Sensor placement on OTOROB's bottom and middle part

The DMS is set to monitor the distance of obstacles from the body of the robot. The obstacle distance is categorized in two regions. Obstacles are placed in first region if it is located between 1 meter and 0.5 meter from the robot meanwhile the second region covers distance below 0.5 meter. When an obstacle is detected within the first region, the maximum speed of the robot will be reduced to half and the user will be alerted by a displayed warning. This is to ensure that the user is aware of the obstacle and at the same time reducing the possibility of accidently hitting the obstacle. This is useful when navigating in narrow spaces and also detecting moving obstacles such as humans. If an obstacle is detected in the second region which is also called the critical region, the robot will stop moving in the direction of the obstacle even if the user insisted it. The user has to turn or reverse the robot to find another route. The system will provide a suggestive direction to the user but it is entirely up to the user to select the different route.

3   Experimental Results

3.1   Flexible Robotic Arm Vision System Experimental Results

The flexible robotic arm was developed and programmed to be manually controlled by the remote doctor and was integrated with fuzzy logic and implemented in Fail Safe & Auto-Recovery and Obstacle Avoidance. Tweaking the fuzzy logic with various inputs increases the ability of problem solving in the AI scheme. The utilization of fuzzy logic scheme in flexible arm docking procedure for Fail Safe & Auto-Recovery and Obstacle Avoidance was carried out with various inputs at various extension stroke lengths. The fuzzy logic is tuned to achieve the objective of Fail Safe & Auto-Recovery and Obstacle Avoidance through the various feedback protocols and sensors. Test results show that the fuzzy logic system was able to detect and avoid danger with an acceptable accuracy. Figure 9 shows the rule diagram for front side obstacle detection sensor of the Robotic Arm.

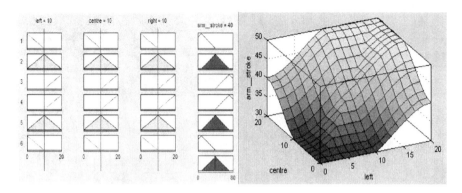

Fig. 9. Rule diagram and 3D surface plot for front side obstacle detection sensor of Robotic Arm

3.2   Navigation System Experimental Results

OTOROB's navigation system fuzzy logic system is tweaked to reach the desired output. Figure 10 shows the rule diagram and 3D plot for bottom front obstacle detection sensor of navigation system. The tweaked fuzzy logic system is tested on the robot and the result shows that it is able to detected danger and failures effectively. It was able to stop the robot and take necessary precautions when any danger is presented to the robot.

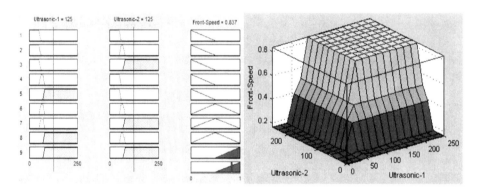

Fig. 10. Rule diagram and 3D surface plot for bottom front side obstacle detection sensor of Navigation System

To test the overall remote navigation system, a user at the remote station computer is connected to the robot. The person is provided with a set of directions that has several obstacles and narrow pathway. The user successfully navigated the robot to the destination on all tests without hitting any obstacles such as shown in Figure 11. The robot was able to go through narrow doorway and elevator. DMS and FSARS were able to detect dangers to the human beings nearby the robot and the robot itself and take preventive measures.

4 Conclusion

The development of flexible robotic arm has increased the working envelope of camera projection for better and clearer vision from remote doctor site. The holonomic navigation system provided a good platform for OTOROB. Tests show that the navigation and robotic arm system is very stable and robust in long run. When danger or failure is detected, the fuzzy logic was able to take precautions to avoid the danger or recover the system. The holonomic wheel configuration proved to be very suitable for OTOROB's application. The fuzzy logic scheme is executed in FSARS and DMS in order to enhance the safety of OTOROB.

References

1. Muralindran, M., Nagarajan, R., Goh, K.H.: AI Application for the PALMBOT Patient Position Tracking System. In: Malaysia- Japan International Symposium on Advance Technology 2007 (MJISAT), Kuala Lumpur, Malaysia, November 12-15 (2007)
2. Muralindran, M., Thayabaren, G., Iftikhar, M., Ramu, V., Brendan, K.: A design methodology of a flexible robotic arm vision system for OTOROB. In: 2010 International Conference on Mechanical and Electrical Technology (ICMET 2010), Singapore, September 10-12, pp. 161–164 (2010)
3. Suzuki, H., Kageyama, Y.: Development of Teleassist Biopsy System with Remotely Controlled Robot Arm. In: IEEE TENCON, pp. 1581–1583 (1999)
4. Taylor, R.H., Stoianovici, D.: Medical Robotics in Computer-Integrated Surgery. IEEE Transactions on Robotics and Automation 19(5), 765–781 (2003)
5. Cristina, C., Nikolaos, T., Triantafyllidis, A., Litos, G.C., Strintzis, M.G.: Mobile Tele-Echography: User Interface Design. IEEE Transactions on Information Technology in Biomedicine 9(1), 44–49 (2005)
6. Kazandides, P., Fichtinger, G., Hager, G.D., Okamura, A.M., Whitcomb, L.L.: Surgical and Interventional Robotics. IEEE Robotics & Automation Magazine, 122–128 (2008)
7. Muralindran, M., Wee, C.C., Kumarhesan, V., Weng, C.K.: A Navigation Methodology of an Holonomic Mobile Robot Using Optical Tracking Device (OTD). In: TENCON 2009 - 2009 IEEE Region 10 Conference, pp. 1–6 (2009)
8. Huang, L., Lim, Y., Lee, D., Teoh, C.E.L.: Design and analysis of a four-wheel omnidirectional mobile robot. In: 2nd International Conference of Autonomous Robots and Agents, pp. 425–428 (2004)
9. Hsu, Y.P., Tsai, C.C., Wang, Z.C., Feng, Y.J., Lin, H.H.: Hybrid navigation of a four-wheeled tour-guide robot. In: ICCAS-SICE, pp. 4353–4358. IEEE (2009)
10. Abolmaesumi, P., Salcudean, S.E., Zhu, W.H., Sirouspour, M.R., DiMaio, S.P.: Image-Guided Control of a Robot for Medical Ultrasound. IEEE Transactions on Robotics and Automation 18(1), 11–23 (2002)
11. Chatterjee, A., Chatterjee, R., Matsuno, F., Endo, T.: Augmented Stable Fuzzy Control for Flexible Robotic Arm Using LMI Approach and Neuro-Fuzzy State Space Modeling. IEEE Transactions on Industrial Electronics 55(3), 1256–1270 (2008)
12. Park, H., Yo-An, L., Pervez, A., Lee, B.C., Lee, S.G., Reha, J.: Teleoperation of a Multi-Purpose Robot over the Internet Using Augmented Reality. In: International Conference on Control, Automation and System 2007, COEX, Seoul, Korea, October 17-20, pp. 2456–2461 (2007)

Approaching a Person in a Socially Acceptable Manner Using a Fast Marching Planner

Jens Kessler, Christof Schroeter, and Horst-Michael Gross

Neuroinformatics and Cognitive Robotics Lab, Ilmenau University of Technology,
Gustav-Kirchhoff-Str. 2, 98683 Ilmenau, Germany
jens.kessler@tu-ilmenau.de
http://www.tu-ilmenau.de/neurob

Abstract. In real world scenarios for mobile robots, socially acceptable navigation is a key component to interact naturally with other persons. On the one hand this enables a robot to behave more human-like, and on the other hand it increases the acceptance of the user towards the robot as an interaction partner. As part of this research field, we present in this paper a strategy of approaching a person in a socially acceptable manner. Therefore, we use the theory of "personal space" and present a method of modeling this space to enable a mobile robot to approach a person from the front. We use a standard Dynamic Window Approach to control the robot motion and, since the personal space model could not be used directly, a Fast Marching planner is used to plan an optimal path to approach the person. Additionally, we give a proof of concept with first preliminary experiments.

Keywords: Social acceptable navigation, approaching strategy, fast marching method, dynamic window approach.

1 Introduction

In recent years, mobile robotics are developing towards fields of applications with direct interaction with persons. There are several prototypical systems that aim to help elderly people to improve cognitive abilities [1], to assist care givers in hospitals [2, 3], be an intelligent video-conferencing system [4], guide people in supermarkets and home improvement stores [5, 6] or simply improve the well-being by providing an easy-to-use communication platform. All these scenarios have to consider persons, interacting with the robot system. Psychologists and gerontologists showed in the 90s that technical devices are treated and observed as "social beings", for example cars, television and computers [7]. A robot system is recognized as a social being and has to behave like one. One important part of the robots behavior is the socially acceptable navigation. Navigation commonly includes tasks like mapping, motion control, obstacle avoidance, localization and path planning. Social acceptable navigation focuses on these tasks by keeping in mind that humans are within the operation area of the robot, and that an extra treatment of these humans is needed. The European Ambient Assisted

S. Jeschke, H. Liu, and D. Schilberg (Eds.): ICIRA 2011, Part II, LNAI 7102, pp. 368–377, 2011.

Living (AAL) association supports robotic projects to enable robotic technologies inside home environments. One of these projects is the ALIAS (Adaptable Ambient LIving ASsistant) project, we are contributing to. It has the goal of developing a mobile robot system to "interact with elderly users, monitor and provide cognitive assistance in daily life, and promote social inclusion by creating connections to people and events in the wider world" [8].

1.1 The ALIAS Robot and the Navigation System

The ALIAS project provides a variety of services, like auto-collecting and searching the web for specific events (concerts, sports events, news) that correspond to the users profile, a calendar function to remind the user on specific events, and, most important, a service to communicate by e-mail, social networks and voice- or video telephone, particularly adapted to the needs of the target group. All these tasks are provided by a mobile robot system (see Fig. 1).

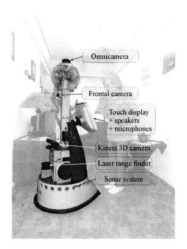

Fig. 1. The ALIAS robot, a SCITOS G5 platform from MetraLabs GmbH, with cameras, Kinect© 3D sensor and laser range finder. It interacts with the user by touch-display and speech output.

The benefit of a mobile system is the capability to move: the robot can be requested by the user and should autonomously drive to the user and approach him/her. In the home environment there are already some challenges that make navigation difficult, like narrow spaces, cluttered rooms and resting positions of the user, which are hard to detect. Navigation has to be smooth and exact, therefore our motion controlling system is based on the Dynamic Window Approach [9]. Based on this approach, we present here how to approach a person with known upper body pose while considering the "personal space" of the interaction partner. This provides a more natural, polite and unobtrusive approaching behavior of the robot. The personal space itself is not appropriate to use directly inside the DWA, so we need to apply a planning strategy to find an optimal approaching behavior.

2   State of the Art

Psychologists investigated the human-to-human interaction in public areas very carefully since the 70s of the last century. One of the foundations and most important publications is the work of Hall [10], who first introduced the concept of different spaces around a human being to support different modes of interaction. There is a space for non-interaction, public interaction, interactions with friends and also an intimate space for interaction with very close relatives.

Table 1. Psychological definition of the personal space. This space consists of 5 zones, each supporting different activities and different communication intentions.

zone	interval	example situation
close intimate	0.0m - 0.15m	lover or close friend touching
intimate zone	0.15m - 0.45m	lover or close friend talking
personal zone	0.45m - 1.2m	conversion between friends
social zone	1.2m - 3.6m	conversion to non-friend
public zone	from 3.6m	no private interaction

By formulating the theory that interaction is also coupled to spatial configurations between interaction partners, many investigations on this matter have taken place, and it could be shown that the configuration depends on many aspects like cultural background, age, sex, social status and person's character [11–13]. But is the personal space a valid description for human robot interaction? As Reeves and Nass [7] showed, complex technical devices are indeed seen as social beings and treated as such. So, we can assume that a robot with a person-like appearance is treated like a person. Additional proof is given by exhaustive experiments done within the COGNIRON project, where wizard of oz methods showed that a spatial configuration between robots and humans exists [14] and that this configuration also changes depending of the task of interaction (e.g. talking, handing over an object)[15], or such constraints like sex or experience with robots [16].However, non of these works tried to autonomously approach a person in a socially acceptable manner. But the wizard of oz experiments could find out useful spatial parameters to autonomously approach a person. Despite the thorough psychological background work, only few publications exist that describe an actual autonomous approaching behavior. Often a simple control policy is used, where a fuzzy controller [17], a PID controller [18, 19], or a similar technique is used to keep the robot at a certain distance to the person. The used distance thresholds or fuzzy-rules are always hand-crafted and set by the designer without sufficient psychological justification. Some can only approach a person from the front [18], since face detection is needed, and some simply do not consider the upper body orientation of the person and approach the person from any direction [17]. There are only a few works, more aware of the concept of personal space, which use this space to approach a person or drive around a person without intruding the person's personal zone. For example Pacchierotti [21] uses an elliptical region around a tracked person in a corridor to signal avoidance towards the person by changing the robot's driving lane in a corridor at an early stage of approaching, where collision avoidance would not have suggested such a driving behavior. The distance of the lane changing was tuned by hand and the distance threshold for driving by was determined by evaluating a questionnaire. A hand-made approaching scenario was also presented by Hoeller [23], where different approaching regions were defined, each with a different priority. At least one of these regions had to be free from obstacles and the region with the highest priority was the current target region. Hoeller uses expanding random trees[23] to plan the next motion step in an optimal fashion. The work of Svenstrup and Andersen [22] models the personal space explicitly and without the need of any thresholds, so they could create a dense representation of the personal space and approach a person by using a potential field method. Although their results do not consider any obstacles and could get stuck in local minima, they were the first with an actual mathematical model of the personal space. Other authors do not consider the personal space, but also have the need to approach a walking person from the front to catch customer attention [20]. The trajectory of the person is predicted, and a point on that trajectory is chosen as the goal, to give the robot enough time to turn towards that person and approach her from the front.

2.1   The Dynamic Window Approach

To move a robot, there must be decisions taken which action to be executed as next. Here, two parts are important. First, the robot has to know to which position it has to drive, and second, which trajectory it has to drive to reach a good position. As mentioned before, we use the Dynamic Window Approach [9] for motion planning and therefor can only support physical plausible paths towards the target. We can assume two things when decide upon the next action. First, we can measure the robots position and speed, and second we know the current obstacle situation. The Dynamic Window Approach's key idea is to select a rectangular region of rotation- and translation speeds around the current rotation- and translation speed, and decide which next speed pair is the best by evaluating different so called objectives. Each objective focuses on one aspect of navigation like avoiding obstacles, heading towards the target, drive at a certain speed and so on. The window's outer bounds are only based on physical constraints, like the robot's acceleration capabilities and maximum allowed speeds. The voting values of the objectives are summed up weighted, and the minimum vote of the current speed window is chosen to be the next valid action. Our goal is to design an objective for the DWA, which uses a personal space model to approach a person. The model of the personal space is described in the next section. After that section we show, how to include the model into the DWA.

3   Model of the Personal Space

As described in section 2, the model of the personal space is the key component to approach a person. Similar to the work of Dautenhahn [14], we also want the robot to approach a person from the front, but with a slight aberration from the direct front, since most user perceive such a behavior more comfortable. For this purpose, obviously we need the position and viewing direction of the person to calculate the configuration of the personal space model. The space configuration should enable the robot to drive around the person in a comfortable distance and turn towards the person when a "front position" is reached. Like in [22], we model the personal space with a sum of Gaussians. The space relative to the persons upper body direction is separated into two regions: a front-region, which is considered to be within $\pm 45°$ around the persons upper direction, and a back-region, which is the rest (see fig. 2).

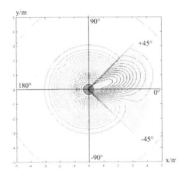

Fig. 2. Two regions of our personal space model. The front region is within an $\pm 45°$ interval (in red). The back region is the rest (in blue). Note, that the regions are not limited in radial extension, like it is done in the illustration.

In both areas we define a distance function to keep the robot out of the user's personal zone but within his/her social zone while approaching the person. The function is defined relative to the persons upper body direction.

$$a(x,y) = \frac{\alpha}{2\pi\sigma_1} \cdot e^{-\frac{x^2+y^2}{\sigma_1^2}} - \frac{\beta}{2\pi\sigma_2} \cdot e^{-\frac{x^2+y^2}{\sigma_2^2}} \tag{1}$$

The variables $\alpha, \beta, \sigma_1, \sigma_2$ describe a classical Difference of Gaussians function and are set in our case (see Fig. 2) to $\alpha = 0.6, \beta = 0.3, \sigma_1 = 2m, \sigma_2 = \sqrt{7}m$ to form a minimum cost region in a distance of 3.5 meters around the person. The front region is treated additionally with an "intrusion function" $i(x,y)$. This is also a Gaussian function and is simply added to $a(x,y)$.

$$i(x,y) = \frac{\gamma}{2\pi\sqrt{|\Sigma|}} \cdot e^{-x^T \Sigma^{-1} x} \tag{2}$$

$$\Sigma = \begin{bmatrix} \sigma_x^2 & 0.0 \\ 0.0 & \sigma_y^2 \end{bmatrix} \cdot \begin{bmatrix} \cos(\phi) & -\sin(\phi) \\ \sin(\phi) & \cos(\phi) \end{bmatrix}$$

Here the variables σ_x and σ_y define an elliptical region, that is rotated towards the needed approaching direction ϕ, as seen from the persons perspective. The vector x is simply a column vector $(x, y)^T$. The variables are set to $\gamma = -0.5$, $\sigma_x^2 = 2.9$ and $\sigma_y^2 = 1.1$. Only ϕ and σ_x need to be set at runtime to regulate the approaching distance and direction. All other parameters are constant and are chosen to reflect the properties of the personal space definition in [10]. So, the final definition of the personal space $p(x, y)$ relatively to the person coordinates $x = 0, y = 0$ and upper body pose towards the x-axis is defined as follows:

$$p(x, y) = \begin{cases} a(x,y) & \text{, if } \langle x, y \rangle \text{ in back-region} \\ a(x,y) + i(x,y) & \text{, if } \langle x, y \rangle \text{ in front-region} \end{cases} \tag{3}$$

To compute the personal space in the real world application each point $(\acute{x}, \acute{y})^T$ has to be transformed to the person-centered coordinate system $(x, y)^T$ presented here.

3.1 Planning with Fast Marching and the Dynamic Window Approach

Up to that point, we have shown how the personal space can be computed, if the upper body pose of a person is known. We also stated, that this space is used within the DWA. The basic idea of the DWA is to decide in a local situation, which next action is optimal. The local driving command is only valid for a certain Δt, than the next window configuration is evaluated. If the Dynamic Window uses the personal space directly, it is possible to predict for every speed pair V_{rot}, V_{trans} the trajectory within the interval Δt and simply evaluate the value of the personal space at this point, the robot has reached at that time. This is shown in Fig. 3. The minimal value leads to the most supported driving decision. By using the personal space directly, multiple driving decision lead to the same minimal value and a single local optimum can not be guaranteed.

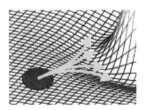

Fig. 3. No distinct speed decision is possible, when the personal space model is used directly. Here, several actions can lead toward the same minimal value.

3.2 Fast Marching and the Cost Function

To avoid situations, where no distinct decision is possible, path planning methods are used to create continuous decreasing functions to get to the optimum by

gradient descents. An excellent planning technique is the Fast Marching method
[24], which origins from the level set methods of single wave fronts and is applied
to path planning. The core idea is to code space as a physical medium, where
waves can travel with different speeds. For example in obstacles the speed is
nearly zero, while in free space the speed can be any feasible speed. By prop-
agating a wave front from the target to the robot, a function of the traveling
time of the wave for every point in space is constructed. The benefit is, that
also fuzzy values, that are not obstacles or free space, can be considered in this
simulation and deform the initial circular waveform. So all we have to do, is to
transform the personal space into a physical "speed-space". We know the minimum of $p(x, y)$ and use p_{min} to create a function that is non-negative. High
values of the personal space symbolize bad places to drive to, while low values
should be preferred. So we define the speed function $v(x, y)$ as follows:

$$v(x, y) = 1/\left(p(x, y) + p_{min} + \epsilon\right) \qquad (4)$$

The variable ϵ is used to prevent an infinite speed at the minimum point.

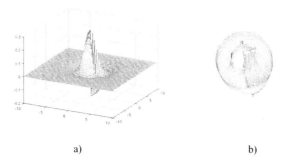

a)   b)

Fig. 4. From personal space to the planning function. The personal space function in
a) is transformed to create the continuously decreasing planning function b).

3.3 Extracting the Target Region

To navigate with the Dynamic Window, we use local occupancy maps to represent the surrounding obstacle situation around the robot. In this grid representation, we also have to rasterize the personal space values $p(\acute{x}, \acute{y})$ to merge
the costs of the personal space with the costs of obstacles to create an optimal
path. Each planning algorithm has to know the target, to which state the system
has to drive to. Since we have a rasterized personal space, we are able to easily
extract the minimum value $p_{min}(\acute{x}, \acute{y})$. The planning algorithm has to know the
target, to which state the robot has to drive to. This target is the origin of the
wave and each point $(\acute{x}, \acute{y})$ with $p(\acute{x}, \acute{y}) < p_{min} + \epsilon$ belongs to the target region.
Planning is complete when the traveling wave front hits the cell of the current
robot position, and now the values of the traveling function can be used directly
by the dynamic window to apply a gradient descent. When the robot reaches a
small region around the target region the approaching task is done.

4   Experiments

A problem on approaching a person is the estimation of the person's position and the associated measurement noise. We plan to detect the upper body pose by fusing two standard tracker methods, namely the leg-pair detector of [25] by using the laser range scanner and the OpenNI full body pose tracker by using the Kinect. To test the stability and robustness of the approach, we investigated three scenarios, two in narrow spaces and one in a large room of our lab. We use a simulator to avoid the problems of person detection and to control the (simulated) measurement noise of the person's and robot's pose. We could also proof in first test, that the approach is running well on the real robot, but here you have to face the challenging task of upper body pose estimation. To investigate the stability of the approaching behavior on a wider range of positions or sensor noise, the position of the person and the robot was chosen randomly to approach in a circle around a marked position. The robot and the person should face towards a given direction each. For each of the three locations, we define two person positions with different viewing angles and performed ten runs for each position. So we have a set of six trials with a sum of 60 single runs. The variance of the final robot position and the person's position are shown in table 2.

Table 2. Variance of the robot's final pose and variance of the wait position of the person

Person position		Robot final position
Scenario	σ_{pers} in meter/deg	σ_{rob}
1(I)	(0.4, 0.1)	(0.4, 0.1)
1(II)	(0.5, 0.1)	(0.4, 0.1)
2(I)	(0.2, 0.1)	(0.2, 0.2)
2(II)	(0.2, 0.2)	(0.3, 0.2)
3(I)	(0.1, 0.1)	(0.1, 0.1)
3(II)	(0.1, 0.2)	(0.1, 0.1)

From the experimental setup we get uncertainties of 0.1 to 0.5 meters in the person's resting position. The question to be answered in our experiments is, how the variance of the robot's target position will increase when approaching a person, by knowing the initial variance of the person's upper body pose. We also want to know, how the trajectories variate on the person's position noise. To do so, we record the trajectory of the robot and calculate the mean and standard deviation of the final robot position. The results are shown in table 2 and figure 5. The average distance from the person is 0.7 meters, the variance is within the same magnitude as the variance of the person's pose. So measurement noise is not amplified by this method. Figure 5 shows the path and the mean person position with variance of all six test cases. Scenario 2 shows, how the upper body pose heavily influences the trajectory of the robot. Scenarios 1 and 3 show, that in narrow spaces the trajectory has to follow the physical restrictions. The personal space has to be intruded, if there is no other chance.

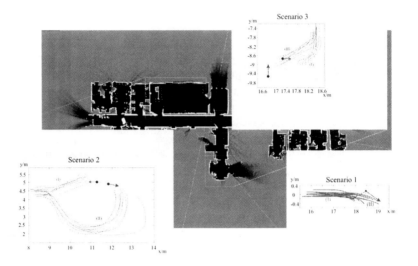

Fig. 5. Resulting trajectories of the three tested scenarios. Per scenario two different poses are evaluated by the user (I and II). The mean positions of the user are shown as black dots, the mean upper body poses as arrows. In each scenario the blue lines denote the robot's trajectories corresponding to the first person setup, while the red lines show trajectories of the second setup. All scenarios show, how the upper body pose influences the approaching trajectory. Scenario 2 also shows, that the social zone is respected if there is room to navigate.

5   Conclusions

In this paper we presented a method, working within the Dynamic Window Approach, to approach a person by considering his/her personal space. We could demonstrate, by using a planning strategy, that a stable and reliable solution could be achieved. Nevertheless the method of extracting the target region could be improved in future work. We also want to include obstacles into the personal space model, to improve planning quality and focus on the task of real time replanning, when the person changes his/her pose while the robot approaches.

Acknowledgment. This work was financed by the project AAL-2009-2-049 "Adaptable Ambient Living Assistant" (ALIAS) co-funded by the European Commission and the Federal Ministry of Education and Research (BMBF) in the Ambient Assisted Living (AAL) program.

References

1. Pastor, C., et al.: CompanionAble- Affective robotics for assisting elderly people. In: Conf. Proc. Assistive Technology From Adapted Equipment to Inclusive Environments: AAATE 2009, Florence, Italy, pp. 153–258 (2009)
2. Pollack, M.E., et al.: Pearl: A Mobile Robotic Assistant for the Elderly. In: AAAI Workshop on Automation as Eldercare (2002)

3. Weisshardt, F., et al.: Making High-Tech Service Robot Platforms Available. In: Joint International Conference of ISR/ROBOTIK 2010, pp. 1115–1120 (2010)
4. Schroeter, C., et al.: Autonomous Robot Cameraman - Observation Pose Optimization for a Mobile Service Robot in Indoor Living Space. In: ICRA, pp. 424–429 (2009)
5. Gross, H.-M., et al.: Toomas: Interactive shopping guide robots in everyday use - final implementation and experiences from long-term field trials. In: Proc. IROS, St. Louis, pp. 2005–2012 (2009)
6. Kanda, T., et al.: ShopBot: A Communication Robot in a Shopping Mall. IEEE Transactions on Robotics 26(5), 897–913 (2010)
7. Reeves, B., Nass, C.: The Media Equation: How People Treat Computers, Television, and New Medial Like Real People and Places. CSLI Press, Stanford (1996)
8. Walhoff, F., Bourginion, E.: ALIAS home page, http://www.aal-alias.eu/content/project-overview
9. Fox, D., et al.: The dynamic window approach to collision avoidance. IEEE Robotics and Automation 4(1), 23–33 (1997)
10. Hall, E.T.: The hidden dimension, NY, Doubleday (1966)
11. Gillespie, D.L., Leffler, A.: Theories of nonverbal behaviour: A critical review of proxemics research. Journal on Sociological Theory 1, 120–154 (1983)
12. Leffler, A., Conaty, J.C., et al.: The Effects of Status Differentiation on Nonverbal Behaviour. Social Psychology Quaterly 45, 153–161 (1982)
13. Smith, H.W.: Territorial Spacing on a beach revisited: A Cross-National Exploration. Social Psychology Quaterly 44, 132–137 (1981)
14. Dautenhahn, K., et al.: How I serve you? A Robot Companion Approaching a Seated Person in a Helping Context. In: Proc. HRI 2006, pp. 172–179 (2006)
15. Koay, K., et al.: Exploratory Study of a Robot Approaching a Person in the Context of Handing Over an Object. In: Proc. Association for the Advancement of Artifical Intelligence Spring Symposia (2007)
16. Takayama, L., Pantofaru, C.: Influences on Proxemic Behaviours in Human-Robot Interaction. In: Proc. IROS, pp. 5495–5502 (2009)
17. Hu, C., Ma, X., Dai, X.: Reliable Person Following Approach for Mobile Robot in Indoor Environment. In: Proc. 8th IEEE International Conf. on Machine Learning and Mechatronics, pp. 1815–1821 (2009)
18. Chen, Z., Birchfield, S.T.: Person Following with a Mobile Robot Using Binocular Feature-Based Tracking. In: Proc. IROS 2007, pp. 815–820 (2007)
19. Ma, X., Hu, C., Dai, X., Qian, K.: Sensor Integration for Person Tracking and Following with Mobile Robot. In: Proc. IROS 2008, pp. 3254–3259 (2008)
20. Satake, S., et al.: How to Approach Humans?- Strategies for Social Robots to Initiate Interaction. In: Proc. HRI 2009, pp. 109–116 (2009)
21. Pacchierotti, E., et al.: Evaluation of Passing Distance for Social Robots. In: RO-MAN 2006 (2006)
22. Svenstrup, M., et al.: Pose Estimation and Adaptive Robot Behaviour for Human-Robot Interaction. In: Proc. ICRA 2009, pp. 3571–3576 (2009)
23. Hoeller, F., et al.: Accompanying Persons with a Mobile Robot using Motion Prediction and Probabilistic Roadmaps. In: Proc. IROS 2007, pp. 1260–1265 (2007)
24. Sethian, J.A.: A Fast Marching Level Set Method for Monotonically Advancing Fronts. Proc. Nat. Acad. Sci. 93(4), 1591–1595 (1996)
25. Arras, K., Mozos, O.M., Burgard, W.: Using Boosted Features for the Detection of People in 2D Range Data. In: Proc. ICRA, pp. 3402–3407 (2007)

Stiffness Identification for Serial Robot Manipulator Based on Uncertainty Approach

Xiaoping Zhang[1], Wenyu Yang[1], Xuegang Cheng[2], and YuShan Chen[3]

[1] State Key Lab of Digital Manufacturing Equipment and Technology,
Huazhong University of Science and Technology, Wuhan, China, 430074
[2] Industrial Robot Research Centre Co. Ltd., Kunshan, China, 215347
[3] Huaheng Weld Co. Ltd., Kunshan, China, 215347
shoppinggre@hotmail.com, mewyang@mail.hust.edu.cn,
xg.cheng@huahengweld.com, tashan_0@163.com

Abstract. Stiffness of the robot manipulator plays a crucial role in improving welding accuracy. Due to the relatively low stiffness, the robot can hardly achieve the specified accuracy under the loading condition. Hence, identifying the joint stiffness and compensating the displacement in Cartesian space is an intuitive work to do in welding industry. Although substantial works had been done on stiffness modeling and identification, the uncertainties existed in transmission and manufacturing were neglected which may affect the manipulator's stiffness and accuracy to a certain extent, in practice. In this paper, we propose an uncertain approach to identify the stiffness of a welding manipulator KUKA-KR16. Firstly, the uncertainties of the D-H parameters are considered and simulated by Monte-Carlo method. Then, the Cartesian stiffness is identified through an experiment which is composed of API laser tracker and a cable pulley system with deadweights. Finally, combining the previous enhanced stiffness model, we obtain the distribution of the joint stiffness, based on which the compensation results are proved to be effective in Cartesian space.

Keywords: stiffness identification, stiffness modeling, D-H parameters, uncertainty, Monte-Carlo method, Nonlinear Least Square.

1 Introduction

Thanks to the flexibility and programmability of the robot manipulator, it has shown us a quite economic and environmental solution in welding industry during the last decade. However, due to the feature of low stiffness, robot can rarely reach the relative high accuracy when mounted with a 5kg welding suite to its end-effector. In order to compensate the translational error in Cartesian space, intuitively, sensor based feedback system [1], which records the deformation and adjusts position reference in the joint space and Cartesian space, is applied without considering its high cost. Another popular method is based on model prediction of the joint deformation and modification in terms of screw theory.

For model based methods, efforts have been made by many researchers for years. Mason and Salisbury [2] derived the conventional Cartesian stiffness model which is

S. Jeschke, H. Liu, and D. Schilberg (Eds.): ICIRA 2011, Part II, LNAI 7102, pp. 378–388, 2011.
© Springer-Verlag Berlin Heidelberg 2011

configuration dependant that the Jacobian matrix is irrelevant to the joint deformation and is valid only under the quasistatic situation without payload and. But, this classic model has been popularly used till recently [3] just for its simplicity and convenience for computation. It was lately updated by means of enhanced stiffness model from Kao *et al*. [4], [5], [6] and other researchers [7]. The complementary stiffness derived from enhanced stiffness model preserves the fundamental relationship between joint and Cartesian stiffness matrixes and makes the enhanced model more precisely than the conventional one, despite the contribution of this additional term to the Cartesian stiffness is small, relatively.

However, the factors that affect the Cartesian stiffness of the manipulator also include errors of the transmission and structural elements such as gearbox, motors and links which were all neglected by previous researchers for simplicity. Hence, in this paper, we provide a probability approach to randomly assign the unpredictable errors from each factor to simulate real Cartesian stiffness of manipulator based on Monte Carlo Method, which has been widely used in solving the nondeterministic model [8], [9]. And we reasonably assume that 1) the compliance in the joints play a major role for the robot Cartesian deformation, 2) the transmission and structure errors follow assigned normal distributions, respectively, 3) all links are assumed to be rigid bodies. 4) only serial manipulator is considered in our paper.

To note that the manipulator in our experimental system is KUKA KR16 whose maximum payload is 16kg. An extra flange fixture module is designed to be mounted on the end effector for loading and measuring, respectively.

2   Derivation of Enhanced Stiffness Model

KUKA KR16, which is the welding manipulator to be identified in this paper, is a 6-axis serial manipulator without prismatic joints. The schematic of KR16 and the coordinate frames which is based on Denavit-Hartenberg parameters are listed and depicted in Table 1 and Fig.1.

Table 1. D-H parameters for KUKA KR16

Link i	a_{i-1}(mm)	α_{i-1}(degree)	d_i(mm)	θ_i(degree)
1	0	180°	$d_1 = -675$	θ_1
2	$a_1 = 260$	90°	0	θ_2
3	$a_2 = 680$	0°	0	θ_3
4	$a_3 = 35$	−90°	$d_4 = -670$	θ_4
5	0	90°	0	θ_5
6	0	−90°	0	θ_6

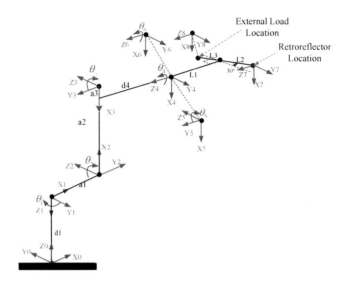

Fig. 1. Schematic representation of KUKA KR16 with D-H parameters

Once there is a small deformation $\Delta\Theta = [\Delta\theta_1, \Delta\theta_2, \Delta\theta_3, \Delta\theta_4, \Delta\theta_5, \Delta\theta_6]^T$ in the joint space, the displacement $\Delta X = [\Delta x, \Delta y, \Delta z, \Delta\alpha, \Delta\beta, \Delta\gamma]^T$ in Cartesian space is generated.

$$\Delta X = J \cdot \Delta\Theta \tag{1}$$

Where **J** is referred as the Jacobian matrix.

According to the D-H parameters, the transformation matrixes among all frames can be derived. And the ith column of **J** which represents the Cartesian twist of the end effector due to the deformation $\Delta\theta_i$ in the ith joint space, which is described as:

$$J^{i,ee} = \begin{bmatrix} z^i \\ z^i \times p^{i,ee} \end{bmatrix} \tag{2}$$

Where z^i is the unit vector along the rotation axis of joint i, $p^{i,ee}$ is the vector from the origin $\{i\}$ to the origin $\{ee\}$ viewed in Global frame or fixed frame $\{0\}$. Referred to the enhanced stiffness model in ref [7], the complete stiffness matrix of a serial manipulator in the Cartesian space is described as:

$$K_X = J^{-T} \cdot (K_\Theta - K_C) \cdot J^{-1} \tag{3}$$

Where $K_\Theta = diag(k_{\theta 1}, k_{\theta 2}, k_{\theta 3}, k_{\theta 4}, k_{\theta 5}, k_{\theta 6})$ is the joint stiffness matrix.

$K_C = \left[\dfrac{\partial J^T}{\partial\theta_1} \cdot f, \dfrac{\partial J^T}{\partial\theta_2} \cdot f, \dfrac{\partial J^T}{\partial\theta_3} \cdot f, \dfrac{\partial J^T}{\partial\theta_4} \cdot f, \dfrac{\partial J^T}{\partial\theta_5} \cdot f, \dfrac{\partial J^T}{\partial\theta_6} \cdot f \right]$ is called the complementary

stiffness matrix. f is the external load exerted at the origin of the end effector.

Referred to the [10], for rotation joint, the ith column of $\dfrac{\partial \mathbf{J}}{\partial \theta_j}$ can be derived as:

$$\frac{\partial \mathbf{J}^{i,ee}}{\partial \theta_j} = \begin{cases} \begin{bmatrix} \mathbf{z}^j \times & \mathbf{O}_{3\times3} \\ \mathbf{O}_{3\times3} & \mathbf{z}^j \times \end{bmatrix} \cdot \mathbf{J}^{i,ee} & j \le i \\[4mm] -\begin{bmatrix} \mathbf{O}_{3\times3} & \mathbf{z}^j \times \mathbf{p}^{j,ee} \\ \mathbf{O}_{3\times3} & \mathbf{O}_{3\times3} \end{bmatrix} \cdot \mathbf{J}^{i,ee} & j > i \end{cases} \tag{4}$$

In addition, for prismatic joint, the ith column of $\dfrac{\partial \mathbf{J}}{\partial \theta_j}$ can be derived as:

$$\frac{\partial \mathbf{J}^{i,ee}}{\partial \theta_j} = \begin{bmatrix} \mathbf{z}^i \\ \mathbf{O}_{3\times1} \end{bmatrix} \tag{5}$$

3   Estimating the Joint Stiffness

3.1   Identification of Joint Stiffness

Although the deformation of the end effector can be derived in terms of (3) as

$$\Delta \mathbf{X} = \mathbf{K}_X^{-1}(\mathbf{J}, \mathbf{K}_\Theta) \cdot \mathbf{f} \tag{6}$$

The model needs a slightly modification owing to the facts that deformation point is often different from the loading point with respect to different experiment setups. Then, the model can be rewrite as

$$\Delta \mathbf{X} = \mathbf{K}_X^{-1}(\mathbf{J}_f, \mathbf{J}_d, \mathbf{K}_\Theta) \cdot \mathbf{f} = \mathbf{J}_d \cdot (\mathbf{K}_\Theta - \mathbf{K}_C)^{-1} \cdot \mathbf{J}_f^T \cdot \mathbf{f} \tag{7}$$

Where $\mathbf{J}_f$ and $\mathbf{J}_d$ are the Jacobian matrixes relative to loading point and measure point in experiment.

Moreover, if only the translation displacement can be obtained, then (7) can be further rewrite as

$$\Delta \mathbf{X} = \mathbf{B}^T \cdot \mathbf{J}_d \cdot (\mathbf{K}_\Theta - \mathbf{K}_C)^{-1} \cdot \mathbf{J}_f^T \cdot \mathbf{f} \tag{8}$$

Where $\mathbf{B} = \begin{bmatrix} \mathbf{I}_{3\times3} & \mathbf{O}_{3\times3} \end{bmatrix}^T$ is referred as wrench base in ref [11].

Once measurement is done $r \times s \times t$ times, the joint stiffness $\mathbf{K}_\Theta$ can be solved by means of Nonlinear Square optimization method. The optimization model is described as below:

$$minimize \quad D = \sum_{k=1}^{r \times s \times t} \left(\Delta E_k \right)^T \left(\Delta E_k \right) \tag{9}$$

Where $\Delta E_k = (\Delta \mathbf{X}_m - \Delta \mathbf{X})_k$, $\Delta \mathbf{X}_m$ is the measured or real deformation in Cartesian space. r, s and t are the quantity of the configurations of manipulator, the directions of the loading forces and the magnitudes of the loading forces.

3.2   Simulating the Uncertainties of D-H Parameters

Previous researches often assumed that the D-H parameters are accurate for simplicity when predicting the joint stiffness. The uncertain effects to the Jacobian matrix, oriented from errors of D-H parameters, are existed, despite they are relatively small. Supposing θ_i is the joint variable of the ith joint, a_{i-1}, d_i, α_{i-1} are the structural parameters. Although θ_i is the nominal value read from the Teach Pendant Interface, the real value of $\hat{\theta}_i = \theta_i + \Delta\theta_i$ is decided by the resolution of the joint displacement transducer in which θ_i is recorded. In addition, due to the manufacturing error of the ith link, Δa_{i-1}, Δd_i, $\Delta \alpha_{i-1}$ are objectively existed that follow certain probability distributions, respectively. Then, the Jacobian matrix is uncertain without knowing the accurate values of D-H parameters so that the estimated joint stiffness and Cartesian stiffness are not precise, accordingly.

3.3   Probability Method of Estimating the Joint Stiffness

To simulate the uncertain errors of D-H parameters, Monte-Carlo Method (MCM) which is a technique for iteratively evaluating a deterministic model using sets of random numbers as inputs, is recommended. This method is often used when the model is complex, nonlinear, or impossible to compute an exact result with a deterministic algorithm. As we stated above, it is unfeasible of ignoring the uncertain D-H parameters as Δa_{i-1}, Δd_i, $\Delta \alpha_{i-1}$ and $\Delta\theta_i$. And the MCM can offer a good solution to simulate the joint stiffness and Cartesian stiffness of the manipulator.

According to the algorithm of the MCM, we describe the simulating process as follow:

a. Define Δa_{i-1}, Δd_i, $\Delta \alpha_{i-1}$ and $\Delta\theta_i$ as the uncertain inputs;
b. Randomly generate these inputs in terms of Normal distributions;
c. Perform the Nonlinear Least Square optimization computation, which is stated in previous section, using these inputs;
d. Gather the value of the joint stiffness $\mathbf{K}_\Theta$ from the individual computations into sets of results;
e. Evaluate the mean and variance of $\mathbf{K}_\Theta$;

To simulate the uncertain errors of D-H parameter in this paper, we refer to the KUKA KR16 technical data sheet and assume that Δa_{i-1}, Δd_i, $\Delta \alpha_{i-1}$ and $\Delta\theta_i$ follow normal distributions as $\Delta a_{i-1} \sim N(0, 2e-2)mm$, $\Delta d_i \sim N(0, 3e-2)mm$, $\Delta \alpha_{i-1} \sim N(0, 5e-3)°$ and $\Delta \theta_i \sim N(0, 1e-3)°$. We randomly assign 500 times to ensure these uncertain parameters are truly simulated that the standard errors are within set tolerances.

The flowchart of joint stiffness identification is described in Fig.2.

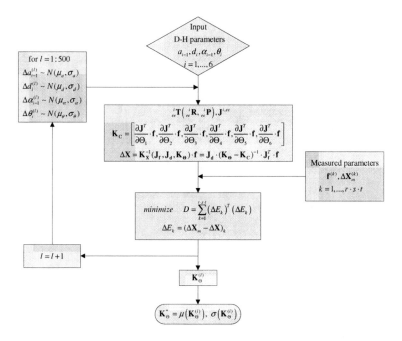

Fig. 2. Flowchart of Joint stiffness identification

After the MC simulation is done, the mean of $\mathbf{K_\theta}$ can be used as the real joint stiffness to compute the deformation in each joint space, according to which we can tune the joint angle to compensate the displacement in Cartesian space.

4   Experimental Setup and Results

The experimental setup to identify the Cartesian stiffness of the KUKA KR16 is shown in Fig.3. A flange module, fixed to the end effector, is designed for measuring displacement and loading force. The API laser retroreflector, which is located on one side of the flange module, is used to measure the displacement in Cartesian space. On the other side of the flange locates the ring, with which a cable pulley system is used to generate loading direction. The magnitude of the loading force varies in terms of three deadweights, which are 5kg, 10kg and 15kg, respectively.

There is no torque load exerted on the flange due to the string connection. The measure frame and the loading frame are not identical with the end effector frame. The position vector of the measuring point and the loading point are $[-31.6122, 54.754, -244.9166]^T \ mm$ and $[20, -34.641, -244.9166]^T \ mm$, with respect to the end effector frame.

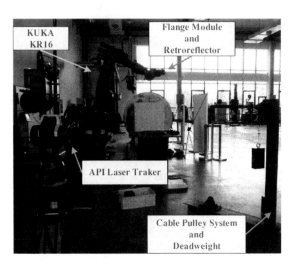

Fig. 3. Experimental setup

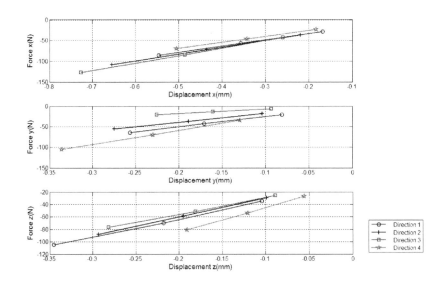

Fig. 4. Cartesian Force-Displacement curve for the configuration of $\theta_1 = 59.8939°$, $\theta_2 = -54.2445°$, $\theta_3 = 123.5570°$, $\theta_4 = -34.1249°$, $\theta_5 = -74.1946°$, $\theta_6 = 88.8684°$

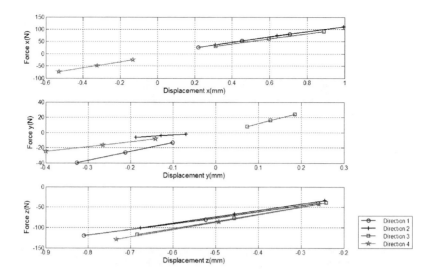

Fig. 5. Cartesian Force-Displacement curve for the configuration of $\theta_1 = 69.2364°$, $\theta_2 = 22.9257°$, $\theta_3 = -77.9818°$, $\theta_4 = 60.5127°$, $\theta_5 = 88.9091°$, $\theta_6 = -9.9742°$

In order to identify the joint stiffness, 6 different well-spaced configurations are commanded. In each configuration, 12 different forces are exerted by means of 4 kinds of directions and 3 kinds of deadweight. The displacement is measured 3 times, and the mean value is taken as the real one to eliminate the measurement noise. Two groups of force-displacement curves are depicted in Fig.4 and Fig.5 in which the Cartesian stiffness varies from the other one due to different configuration.

5   Prediction of Joint Stiffness and Results

According to the section 3.3, the uncertain D-H parameters are randomly assigned by Monte-Carlo method, iteratively. In each iteration, we apply the Nonlinear Least Square optimization method to solve the joint stiffness by means of 'trust-region-reflective' algorithm in Matlab Optimization toolbox. At the end of the iteration, the distribution of the joint stiffness is obtained which is described in Fig.6 and Fig.7.

The average joint stiffness, described in Fig.6 and Fig.7 as black star, is $[2.525578e8; 3.512531e8; 1.785034e8; 7.243868e7; 2.243008e7; 4.347826e6]^T \ N \cdot mm / rad$. The standard deviation of the joint stiffness, due to uncertain D-H parameters, is $[1.936511e4; 3.152256e4; 1.498928e4; 4.927197e4; 6.764628e3; 2.858827e4]^T$.

After that, we can use the average value as the real one to compensate the displacement in Cartesian space. The comparison between the displacement with and without compensation is depicted, selectively, in Fig.8 and Fig.9, where show some directions of the displacements are reduced 0.9mm after compensation. Considering the difficulties of measuring real D-H parameters without disassembly, the compensation results are more reliable than the one neglecting the existence of uncertainties.

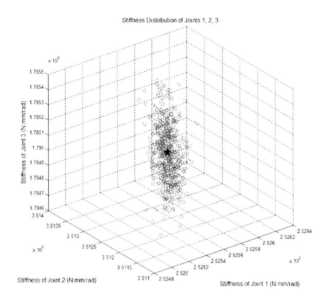

Fig. 6. Simulation of Joint stiffness of Joint1, 2, 3

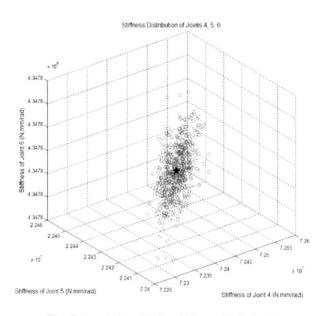

Fig. 7. Simulation of Joint stiffness of Joint4, 5, 6

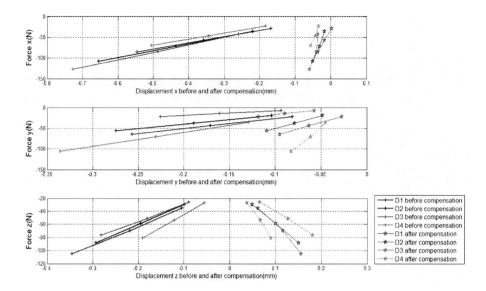

Fig. 8. Force-displacement curve before and after compensation at configuration $\theta_1 = 59.8939°$, $\theta_2 = -54.2445°$, $\theta_3 = 123.5570°$, $\theta_4 = -34.1249°$, $\theta_5 = -74.1946°$, $\theta_6 = 88.8684°$

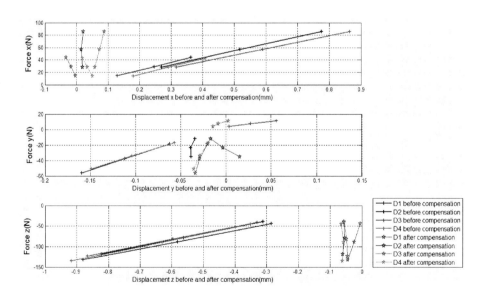

Fig. 9. Force-displacement curve before and after compensation at configuration $\theta_1 = 61.9107°$, $\theta_2 = -56.2108°$, $\theta_3 = 78.3659°$, $\theta_4 = 81.2759°$, $\theta_5 = 64.3615°$, $\theta_6 = -30.8931°$

6   Summary

In this paper, we provide an uncertainty approach of identifying the joint stiffness of KUKA KR16. In terms of Monte-Carlo method, the errors of the D-H parameters are randomly assigned according to corresponding distributions, firstly. Then, the experiment is designed, using the API laser tracker and the cable pulley system, to identify the Cartesian stiffness. After that, the distribution of the joint stiffness can be estimated by combining the classic enhanced stiffness model. Finally, the positional accuracy in Cartesian space is compensated through joint deformation by using the mean value of the simulated joint stiffness and the results are presented to be effective. The future works will be further concentrated on identifying the stiffness and compensating the positional accuracy of the welding robot manipulator, and the stiffness of the links will be considered.

Acknowledgments. This work was supported by the National Science and Technology Major Project '15kg spraying robot equipment' (No.2010zx04008-041) in CHINA. The authors would like to thank Wanchun Yan and Tao Wen for their kind help.

References

1. Oiwa, T.: Error compensation system for joints, links and machine frame of parallel kinematics machines. Int. J. Robotics Research 24(12), 1087–1102 (2005)
2. Mason, M.T., Salisbury, J.K.: Robot Hands and the Mechanics of Manipulation. MIT Press, Cambridge (1985)
3. Wang, J., Zhang, H., Fuhlbrigge, T.: Improving Machining Accuracy with Robot Deformation Compensation. In: The 2009 IEEE/RSJ International Conference on Intelligent Robots and Systems, St. Louis, USA (2009)
4. Chen, S.F., Kao, I.: Conservative congruence transformation for joint and Cartesian stiffness matrices of robotic hands and fingers. Int. J. Robot. Res. 19(9), 835–847 (2000)
5. Li, Y., Kao, I.: A review of modeling of soft-contact fingers and stiffness control for dextrous manipulation in robotics. In: Proc. IEEE Int. Conf. Robot. Autom., Seoul, Korea, pp. 3055–3060 (2001)
6. Li, Y., Chen, S.F., Kao, I.: Stiffness control and transformation for robotic systems with coordinate and noncoordinate bases. In: Proc. IEEE Int. Conf. Robot. Autom., Washington, DC, pp. 550–555 (2001)
7. Alici, G., Shirinzadeh, B.: Enhanced stiffness modeling, identification and characterization for robot manipulators. IEEE Trans. Robotics 21(4), 554–564 (2005)
8. Zheng, Y., Qian, W.H.: Coping with uncertainties in Force-closure analysis. International Journal of Robotics Research 24(4), 311–327 (2005)
9. Zhang, X., Yang, W., Li, M.: An Uncertainty Approach for Fixture Layout Optimization Using Monte Carlo Method. In: Liu, H., Ding, H., Xiong, Z., Zhu, X. (eds.) ICIRA 2010, Part II. LNCS (LNAI), vol. 6425, pp. 10–21. Springer, Heidelberg (2010)
10. Bruyninckx, H., De Schutter, J.: Kinematic models for rigid body interactions for compliant motion tasks in the presence of uncertainties. In: Proceedings of the IEEE International Conference on Robots and Automation, pp. 1007–1012 (1993)
11. Murray, R., Li, Z.X., Sastry, S.: A Mathematic Introduction to Robotic Manipulation. CRC Press (1994)

Serial Comanipulation in Beating Heart Surgery Using a LWPR-Model Based Predictive Force Control Approach

Juan Manuel Florez[1,2], Delphine Bellot,
Jérôme Szewczyk[1,2], and Guillaume Morel[1,2]

[1] Université Pierre et Marie Curie - Paris 6
Institut de Systèmes Intelligents et de Robotique
4 Place Jussieu, 75005, Paris, France
{florez,sz,morel}@isir.upmc.fr
[2] CNRS, UMR 7222, Paris, France

Abstract. Compensation of cardiac motion during robot-assisted surgical procedures is needed to ensure better quality stabilization. Serial Comanipulation to actively compensate physiological motion is one alternative to common used Teleoperation techniques. In this paper, a 1 DOF hand-held force controlled prototype is presented. The active part of the instrument moves in synchronism with the heart motion in order to guarantee that the contact is maintained thanks to the application of a controlled force, while the surgeon's hand is in charge to perform the surgical task.

It then focuses on a crucial control aspect: there is a lack of a parametric model describing the interaction between the surgical instrument and the heart that would provide enough precision for prediction. Namely, the robot low level controller and the beating heart are modeled thanks to a Locally Weighted Projection Regression (LWPR). The paper discusses how this technique can be used in the context of predictive force control and shows conclusive simulation results.

Keywords: Non Parametric Model Identification, Model Based Predictive Control, Force Control, Beating Heart Surgery, LWPR.

1 Introduction

In surgical applications such as epicardial lead placement for resynchronization therapy described in [15], a robotic tool could be suitable in order to allow maintaining contact with the heart surface for selection of implantation site through resynchronisation efficiency assessment before screwing the epicardial pacing lead. While the current clinical solution to deal with physiological motion compensation in cardiac surgery consists of canceling the heart motion thanks to passive mechanical stabilizers, robotics would allow to replace classical surgical instruments with more "intelligent" ones able to help the surgeon to overcome human limitations such as hand tremor and high frequency perturbations.

S. Jeschke, H. Liu, and D. Schilberg (Eds.): ICIRA 2011, Part II, LNAI 7102, pp. 389–400, 2011.
© Springer-Verlag Berlin Heidelberg 2011

Compensating for physiological motion can be achieved thanks to position control by maintaining a fixed relative distance between the moving organ and the surgical instrument [10], [4]. In these works, position is measured thanks to an external vision sensor, and visual servoing is exploited. Two approaches are used for the rejection of the physiological motion disturbance: iterative learning control (ILC, [4]) which has the disadvantage of rejecting only strictly periodic disturbances, and Model-Based Predictive Control (MPC), which has proven to provide great robustness during in vivo experiments [10]. Note that position MPC involving contacts between the robot and the heart has also been used for active stabilization in [1]. Here, the robot is in contact with the beating heart but the force in uncontrolled: rather, a visual servoing loop (*i.e.* a position controller) is used to cancel motion.

When interaction occurs, force control seems a logical solution to compensate for dynamic behaviour in the contact port. In this case, contrarily to [1], the goal is not to stabilize the heart thanks to motion cancellation, but to apply a controlled force to the beating heart while following its motion. This idea was for example developed in [5] using ILC, which has the advantage of not requiring a model of the contact interaction but, again, exhibits low robustness to irregularities. Predictive force control for beating heart surgery has been proposed in [7], but in this paper, a linear model is assumed for the interaction.

Similarly, in the context of serial comanipulation, *i.e.* where control of the instrument is shared between the surgeon and the robot, recent work [21] has shown good force disturbance rejection and precision improvement for intracardiac beating heart applications. However, this approach uses a parametric simplified linear model of the organ-instrument interactions which is inappropiate. Indeed, as outlined in [1], considering a Mass-Spring-Damper as an approximation of cardiac muscle dynamics is somewhat inaccurate: the non-linear time varying behavior of the stiffness, the mass and the damping parameters coming from electrical activity of the muscle, fluid motions and friction changes, are not taken into account. In the context of predictive control, these inaccuracies are expected to lead to poor performances.

Modeling the organ-instrument interaction dynamics in an accurate way is needed in order to allow the development of high performance predictive force control. Multiple modeling methods based on finite-element and complex differential equations provide accurate representation, [19], but they are too time consuming for a real time application. In this context, Machine learning methods are of interest because they include representation of time varying systems without the perfect periodicity constraint [11]. A good survey of the use these techniques is presented in [11] where the use of Gaussian Process is retained as well as in [13]. The main advantage of these *Black-Box* methods is that they allow an open loop identification scheme with no a priori knowledge of the dynamic system. But the need of continuous training to adapt the identified model of the local behavior of the organs calls for an incremental on-line learning algorithm such as LWPR [20].

This paper presents a first look at a 1 DOF demonstrator that will be tested in contact with a time varying mechanical impedance in the presence of unmodeled disturbances. To address the issue of performing a manipulation task while in contact with a moving surface having a non-linear time varying mass and stiffness, our approach is to include a LWPR based identification into a model-based predictive force control law in order to achieve good disturbance rejection.

The paper is organized as follows. Section 2 presents the comanipulation system of interest and compares it to the model used for the simulations, which is representative of the problems that have to be solved for the application. Section 3 describes the general structure of the controller, while the key component of the approach, which is the LWPR identification method is explained in Section 4. Simulation results are given in Section 5. The paper ends with conclusions and perspectives in Section 6.

2   A Hand-Held Instrument for Motion Compensation

In the teleoperation paradigm, surgeon manipulates a slave interface which transmits commands to the surgical master instrument. This separation allows the control law to filter hand tremor but makes force feedback difficult. But in comanipulation, control is shared between the surgeon and the robot, allowing the surgeon to intuitively perform his gesture with direct force feedback. From the control point of view this presents also a difficulty, because it is hard to distinguish the user's desired force from unwanted efforts (tremor or other perturbations). In [16], for example, an instrument is succesfully designed to sense its own motion, distinguish tremor from other components of motion, and deflect its own tip to perform active compensation of the tremor.

Analogously, in the considered system depicted in figure 1(a), in order to minimize forces applied on the tip, the active part of the instrument moves in synchronism with the heart motion aiming at guaranteeing that the contact is maintained thanks to the application of a controlled force. In surgical applications, force measurements are rarely collected on the end effector because of

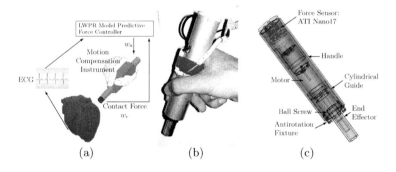

Fig. 1. (a) The Surgical System. Hand-held Surgical Instrument: (b) Prototype. (c) Design.

miniaturization and sterilization issues of strain gauge based sensors. Recently tip mounted optical force sensors have been included in surgical prototypes that overcome these limitations [21]. An equivalent solution was built in [8] that allows interaction force measurements with surgical target at the end effector. A second version is presented in this paper based on the same principle of placing a force sensor inside the instrument that allows measurements of the force applied at the tip (noted w_e) by means of a low friction transmission.

2.1   Model

The robot is modeled as depicted in figure 2(b), but can be simplified because of the low dry friction of the actuator+transmission set and the high stiffness of the sensor, as a mass m and damper b subjected to an actuation force w_a and environment contact force w_e, as depicted in figure 2(a). The varying damping $b(t)$ captures the effects of dynamics in the organ and viscous friction in the robot. Approximating the mechanical impedance of the environment as a spring with time varying stiffness $k_{org}(t)$ yields the system dynamics:

$$m\ddot{x} = w_a - (k_{org}(t)(x - x_{org}) + b\dot{x}(t))$$ (1)

Equation 1 makes explicit that the target motion x_{org} is a disturbance that interferes with the goal of w_e attaining w_d. The methodology presented in this paper allows to consider all the position and velocity terms as disturbances to force tracking even if they are poorly characterized and dependant on the robot's state. The controller designed in this paper is set to be insensitive to ignorance of the implicit properties of interaction. The simulations on this paper are aimed to identify in a non parametric way the tracking force transfer function in presence of an external force disturbance caused by the organ dynamics, *ergo* correlated with a biological signal.

It is necessary to add information to the model that will be learned by the identification algorithm. To add robustness to prediction, past control signals u are integrated into the input vector in Eq (2) as well as past ECG signals over a control horizon Nu.

$$x = [w_{t-Nu} \ldots w_t, u_{t-Nu-1} \ldots u_{t-1}, e_{t-Nu} \ldots e_t]^T$$ (2)

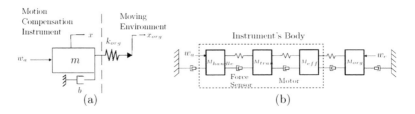

Fig. 2. Robot model in contact with an actively moving, compliant environment. (a) Simplified Model. (b) Complete Model.

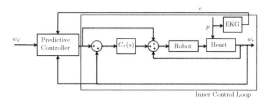

Fig. 3. Global Control scheme with predictive controller and PI force compensator. EKG provides a correlated measure of the disturbance.

An ECG contains records for the electrical activity of the heart which subsequently produces muscle contraction. In recent work presented in [2], fusion of these biological signals with motions measured on the surface of the heart was integrated into the algorithm to enhance predictive capacity of the control law. This signal is particularly interesting because the electrical excitation-mechanical contraction coupling of the heart has a lag of about 200ms that enables prediction of future heart activity [3].

In [21], spectral decomposition of the major axis motion trajectory was performed. The dominant motion components found were at 1.3, 2.6, and 5.2 Hz, with further components of decreasing amplitude at higher frequencies. This is consistent with the findings of previous tracking works by [14], [10] and [2]. For the cardiac simulations, it is then safe to assume that motion is essentially band limited to approximately 15Hz.

2.2   Modeling the Disturbance

The perturbation p is defined as the force exerted by the environment which prevents the instrument from attaining the calculated force. In the simplified model presented in figure 2(a), it is caused mainly by the effect of x_{org}. The transfer function of the disturbance will be defined as:

$$p(t)/x_{org}(t) = k_{org}(t) \qquad (3)$$

There is not much information in the literature about how k_{org} varies in time other than it is correlated with the ECG signal e. Nevertheless, x_{org} was tracked in [21].This seems coherent with the early tracking results of [12].This signal will be used in simulations in section 5. For simpler simulations, both k_{org} and x_{org} will be presumed to be a simple dephased sine function with the same frequency.

3   Model-Based Predictive Force Control

3.1   Error Feedback Force Control Scheme with Anticipation Term

A classical PI joint force control scheme that exploits an end-effector measurement with an anticipation term, as depicted in figure 3, is considered.

The following notations are used:

$C_\tau(s)$: the discrete PI force compensator for the inner loop
w_d : desired force
u : calculated control signal
w_e : measured force
p : physiological perturbation
e : measured ecg signal

In previous work, [22], the authors show that the inner loop alone is well suited for robotic surgery due to its stability and robustness to changes in nature and geometry of contacts but it is unable to finely reject periodic disturbances with large magnitude [5]. The outer predictive control loop is set to overcome this limitation.

3.2   General Idea of MPC

Model-Based Predictive Control can be described as depicted in figure 4. The model used is identified off-line with a training set of data. This model will provide predictions of behavior of the system as well as performance information. It will be updated online under precision criteria. A forgetting factor assures also that adaptation will match the expected time scale at which changes in target mapping occur. The following strategy characterizes the concept of predictive control [6]:

- Predictions over an horizon Np noted $w_p(t+k|t)$, for $k = 1...Np$, depend on the known values at instant t (past inputs and outputs) and on the future control signals $u(t+k|k)$, $k \in [0...Np-1]$ which is intended to be applied.
- Reference trajectory of desired force to be applied: $w_d(t+j|j)$ with $j \in [0...t_{final}]$ represent possible target forces required by the surgeon.
- Non linear MPC algorithms typically exploit the fact that consecutive optimal control problems are similar to each other. Future control signals $u(t+k|k)$, $k \in [0...Np-1]$ are calculated by minimization of a quadratic function of the errors between the predicted output signal and the reference trajectory. The optimization strategy used is based on an unconstrained multivariate function that applies Nelder-Mead direct search method.It is initialized by a suitably shifted guess from the previously computed optimal solution $u(t-1|t)$, saving considerable amounts of computation time.
- Since it is a receding horizon strategy, only the first element of the optimal control signal vector $u(t|t)$ is applied, and the process is repeated with updated values and a new horizon shifted in the future.

4   Identification of Interaction Forces with LWPR

The key issue in this identification scheme is that there is no interest on identifying separate behavior from the organ and from the robot. In comanipulation,

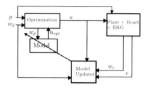

Fig. 4. Model-Based Prediction Controller Strategy

the goal is to compensate force disturbances that interfere with the surgical gesture. Because the robot is much stiffer than the heart, contact causes the tissue
to comply with the location of the robotic instrument tip. Thus identification
is performed assuming inner control loop in figure 3 as the *reference model*, as
opposed to using the *free response* of the system as used in other works using
parametric identification schemes [7], [9]. Nevertheless, the system is time varying so it needs incremental online training as well as adaptation because target
mapping depends on the surgeons will. LWPR is particularly suited for this kind
of regression problems.

4.1   LWPR

Locally weighted projection regression is a function approximator which provides accurate approximation in high dimensional spaces even in the presence
of redundant and irrelevant input dimensions [20]. At its core, it uses Gaussian
functions as depicted in figure 5(b):

$$\phi_i(x) = e^{-\frac{1}{2}(x-c_i)^T D_i (x-c_i)} \tag{4}$$

function $\phi_i(x)$ are called Receptive Fields (RFs). They span the input space in
regions delimited by the positive distance metric D_i with respect to the centers
c_i, to compute a prediction of the output function:

$$\hat{y}(x) = \frac{1}{\Phi(x)} \sum_{i=1}^{n_n} \phi_i(x)\hat{y}_i(x) \tag{5}$$

with $\Phi(x) = \sum_{i=1}^{n_n} \phi_i(x)$, n_n is the number of receptive fields and $\hat{y}_i(x)$ is the local
scalar output prediction with respect of each selected receptive field direction as
in equation (6):

$$\hat{y}_i(x) = \beta_i x \tag{6}$$

Weighted partial least squares (PLS) is employed to detect those directions and
the corresponding slopes β_i (see figure 5(d)).

Once a receptive field is considered trustworthy, *i.e.* has seen sufficient data
points, its distance metric D_i is optimized by using an incremental gradient
descent based on stochastic leave-one-out cross validation [20]. It is computed as
$D = M^T M$ where M is an uppertriangular matrix to ensure D to be positive.

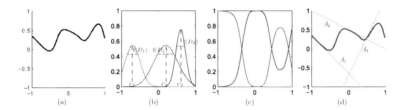

Fig. 5. LWPR approximates non-linear functions such as the one depicted in (a). The algorithm delimits the input space with receptive fields (b). These Gaussians are normalized (c) respectively to their capacity to approximate the non-linear function. The sum of the active linear models (with slopes β_i), weighted by their respective relative Gaussian results in an approximation of the non-linear function (d) [17].

M is adapted recursively and individually to regulate the size of the receptive fields with the update law:

$$M = M - \alpha \frac{\partial J}{\partial M} \qquad (7)$$

where α is the learning rate and J is a cost function. It includes a penalty term to prevent RFs to shrink indefinitely (see details in [18]).

4.2   Tuning LWPR for the Application

LWPR requires an intelligent input normalization, standard deviation in each direction of input space is not suitable. LWPR is adaptable to new "out of range" data sets but it needs to verify that the newly created RF is trustworthy before it is activated. This residual analysis is very suitable to prevent "outliers" from biasing the results. Nevertheless, the application's expected range of input data is not very well defined (it depends on desired efforts produced by the surgeon).

In order to have an approximate prediction even if a newly created RF has not seen enough points. A projection of "out of range" new input data onto the learned input range is proposed in [8].

Even if tunning of LWPR parameters was done following some guidelines provided by [20], some of them were finally tuned intuitively. Perhaps the most important is *init_D* the distance metric assigned initially to newly created local models, which has a great impact in performance and precision. After setting a batch set of training data for learning, the normalization input *norm_in* was chosen as the expected input range and updated as described in [8].Fitting the LWPR model with varying *init_D* starting with rather spherical RFs, provided some insight of performance. *Init_D* was finally set to 10 in order minimize least mean square error in long term.

5   Results

In order to assess, the optimal position of an epicardial lead, the surgeon places it and holds it until an evaluation through echocardiography with tissue-Doppler imaging is performed. This gesture can be modelled as pressing the instrument to the heart with a constant force step in presence of a perturbation. In [21], $8N$ was determined to be the tearing force for in vivo heart tissue using the a surgical anchor deployment instrument. Even though the required force to damage the tissue will vary according to its properties as well as the geometry of the instrument tip, this value will be accepted as a not tolerable limit. A $3N$ desired force step is chosen for simulation purposes (for safety the surgeon tries to maintain forces below this value of reference).

With the prototype presented in section 2 a good step response is attained but low robustness to force perturbations at the tip as shown in figure 6. This result confirms the need of a high level predictive controller.

Simulations have been performed to evaluate feasibility and performance of compensation algorithm with the Force Predictive Controller presented in the previous sections. As a means of performing identification, an output disturbance (a sine signal of $0.5N$ of amplitude and a frequency of $15Hz$) is applied to a Mass-Damper system compensated with a PI based inner-loop force controller. For simulation purposes m=200g (mass of the moving part of the instrument), b=500 (it depends on inner controler gains).

In figure 7, before the compensation algorithm is trigered, it is clear that disturbances are not rejected with the inner loop controller alone. This result is coherent with the result presented before in figure 6 and with the findings of related work: [5], [22]. This signal is used as learning dataset for LWPR identification. When the compensation algorithm is started the error between learning data forces and identified forces decreases due to adaptation of weigths in the learning algorithm, resulting in reduction of peak to peak errors. It should be noted that small time changes were applied to the perturbation signal in the form of linear function of the stiffness k_{org}, $p(t)$ is then defined as:

$$x_{org}(t) = A * sin(\omega t) \qquad (8)$$
$$k_{org}(t) = k_1 * t + k_0 \qquad (9)$$

This variation provoques increased peak to peak error. It is possible to cope with this problem by increasing the maximal number of the optimization iterations described in 3.2. High velocity changes were performed to evaluate robustness to target force variation. The algorithm adapted very efficiently to different frequency sine wave target forces with the same disturbance signal as before.

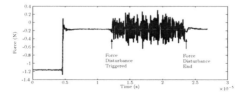

Fig. 6. Prototype step response and with manual disturbance

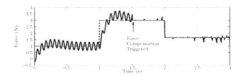

Fig. 7. Learning Dataset and response with sine disturbance (Amp=0.5N f=15Hz)

As shown in figure 8, closed loop foce gain decreases less than $0.2dB$ when a $20HZ$ sine wave is applied as desired force. It should be noted that in this case, the disturbance signal is dephased of $\pi/6$ rad.

Finally, the model identified previously (in figure 7), was used to compensate a disturbance signal with several frequency components, as described in section 2.2. Results are showed in figure 9, showing an RMS error reduction by 80% when compensation is trigered. Additionally to test for this approach's sensitivity to phase errors between the sine signal used for identification in 7 and the disturbance signal adopted, tests with several phase values $(2\pi/3, \pi/2, \pi/3, \pi/4, \pi/6)$ were performed with no influence on performance.

5.1   Discussion

Even though results are encouraging, it should be noted that with noisy signals, LWPR learning phase is more complex and results on more RFs creation and a decreased performance. A sine wave was used as an ECG signal for identification, since it is used by the regression algorithm to synchronise input and output data. The use of real ECG measurements should also have an impact in performance. Nevertheless, the results shown in figure 9 imply (although not formally proven) that the only a priori knowledge required for compensation through LWPR based MPC is the upper bandwidth limit of disturbance, if there is no or slow frequency changes. Since this will not necessarily be the case, it is expected a speedup decrease in the prediction phase resulting in higher errors. Also brutal changes in ECG wave complexes, for example in cases of asynchronous excitation syndromes, should have a negative effect in performance. In this case, a more radical model forgetting strategy should be evaluated in order to force LWPR receptive field updating.

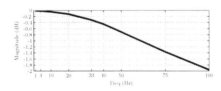

Fig. 8. Frequency response to sine target function

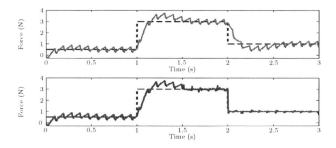

Fig. 9. Simulated Forces without compensation (top figure). Simulated Compensated Forces (bottom figure).

6 Overview and Conclusions

This paper addresses the issue of Serial Comanipulation in beating heart surgery. To avoid tearing of cardiac tissue, the instrument or the surgeon must be able to control the applied force in an accurate way.

A second prototype was presented to illustrate the problem of compensating time varying disturbances with a stiff instrument in contact with a compliant environment.

A Model-Based Predictive Force Control algorithm was presented. The particularity of the strategy is that the model was obtained through LWPR in a non parametric way. The strategy was tested in simulation using a periodic signal as ECG signal, to simplify regression resulting in lower errors.

The paper indicates that using LWPR models offers an attractive possibility for control design that results in a controller with a higher level of robustness due to online adaptability and insensitiveness to ignorance of the underlying properties of the interaction. It is necessary to stress that the presented control strategy represents only a feasibility test for this kind of identification process application for model predictive control and additional efforts are necessary before this approach will be applicable in practice.

Future work will focus on the validation of the proposed approach through the prototype presented in figure 1(a) and 1(b) in order to provide an experimental validation of the method.

References

[1] Bachta, W., Renaud, P., Laroche, E., Gangloff, J., Forgione, A.: Cardiolock: An Active Cardiac Stabilizer. In: Ayache, N., Ourselin, S., Maeder, A. (eds.) MICCAI 2007, Part I. LNCS, vol. 4791, pp. 78–85. Springer, Heidelberg (2007)

[2] Bebek, O., Cavusoglu, M.C.: Intelligent control algorithms for robotic-assisted beating heart surgery. IEEE Transactions on Robotics 23(3), 468–480 (2007)

[3] Berne, R., Levy, M.N., Koeppen, B.M., Stanton, A.: Physiology, 5th edn. Elsevier (2007)

[4] Busack, M., Morel, G., Bellot, D.: Breathing motion compensation for robot assisted laser osteotomy. In: ICRA 2010, pp. 4573–4578 (May 2010)

[5] Cagneau, B., Zemiti, N., Bellot, D., Morel, G.: Physiological motion compensation in robotized surgery using force feedback control. In: ICRA 2007, pp. 1881–1886 (April 2007)

[6] Camacho, E.F., Bordons, C.: Model Predictive Control. Advanced Textbooks in Control and Signal Processing, 2nd edn. Springer London Ltd., London (2004)

[7] Dominici, M., Poignet, P., Cortesão, R., Dombre, E., Tempier, O.: Compensation for 3d physiological motion in robotic-assisted surgery using a predictive force controller: experimental results. In: IROS 2009, pp. 2634–2639. IEEE Press, Piscataway (2009)

[8] Florez, J.M., Bellot, D., Morel, G.: Lwpr-model based predictive force control for serial comanipulation in beating heart surgery. In: 2011 IEEE/ASME International Conference on Advanced Intelligent Mechatronics, AIM (July 2011)

[9] Franke, T., Bebek, O., Cavusoglu, M.: Improved prediction of heart motion using an adaptive filter for robot assisted beating heart surgery. In: IROS 2007, pp. 509–515 (October 2007)

[10] Ginhoux, R., Gangloff, J., de Mathelin, M., Soler, L., Sanchez, M., Marescaux, J.: Active filtering of physiological motion in robotized surgery using predictive control. IEEE Transactions on Robotics 21(1), 67–79 (2005)

[11] Gregorčič, G., Lightbody, G.: Gaussian process approach for modelling of nonlinear systems. Eng. Appl. Artif. Intell. 22(4-5), 522–533 (2009)

[12] Fisher, V.J., Stuckey, J.H., Kavaler, F.: The potentiated contraction and ventricular "contractility". Bull. N Y Acad. Med., 592–601 (June 1965)

[13] Kocijan, J., Murray-Smith, R., Rasmussen, C.E., Girard, A.: Gaussian process model based predictive control. In: Proceedings of the 2004 American Control Conference, vol. 3, pp. 2214–2219 (June 2004)

[14] Nakamura, Y., Kishi, K., Kawakami, H.: Heartbeat synchronization for robotic cardiac surgery. In: ICRA 2001, vol. 2, pp. 2014–2019 (2001)

[15] Navia, J.L., Atik, F.A., Takagaki, M.: Robot-assisted epicardial lead placement. In: Gharagozloo, F., Najam, F. (eds.) Robotic Surgery, 1st edn., ch. 11, pp. 84–93. McGraw-Hill (2009)

[16] Riviere, C., Gangloff, J., de Mathelin, M.: Robotic compensation of biological motion to enhance surgical accuracy. Proceedings of the IEEE 94(9), 1705–1716 (2006)

[17] Salaun, C.: Apprentissage de modèles pour la commande de la mobilité interne en robotique. Ph.D. thesis, Université Pierre & Marie Curie - Paris VI (2010)

[18] Schaal, S., Atkeson, C.G., Vijayakumar, S.: Scalable techniques from nonparametric statistics for real time robot learning. Applied Intelligence 17(1), 49–60 (2002)

[19] Sermesant, M., Delingette, H., Ayache, N.: An electromechanical model of the heart for image analysis and simulation. IEEE Transactions on Medical Imaging 25(5), 612–625 (2006)

[20] Vijayakumar, S., D'Souza, A., Schaal, S.: Incremental online learning in high dimensions. Neural Computation 17, 2602–2634 (2005)

[21] Yuen, S.G., Yip, M.C., Vasilyev, N.V., Perrin, D.P., del Nido, P.J., Howe, R.D.: Robotic Force Stabilization for Beating Heart Intracardiac Surgery. In: Yang, G.-Z., Hawkes, D., Rueckert, D., Noble, A., Taylor, C. (eds.) MICCAI 2009. LNCS, vol. 5761, pp. 26–33. Springer, Heidelberg (2009)

[22] Zemiti, N., Morel, G., Cagneau, B., Bellot, D., Micaelli, A.: A passive formulation of force control for kinematically constrained manipulators. In: ICRA 2006, pp. 2238–2243 (May 2006)

Application of Wavelet Networks to Adaptive Control of Robotic Manipulators

Hamid Reza Karimi

Department of Engineering, Faculty of Engineering and Science,
University of Agder, N-4898 Grimstad, Norway
hamid.r.karimi@uia.no

Abstract. In this paper, a wavelet-based adaptive control is proposed for a class of robotic manipulators, which consist of nonlinearities for friction effects and uncertain terms as disturbances. The controller is calculated by using a mixed of feedback linearization technique, supervisory control and H_∞ control. In addition, the parameter adaptive laws of the wavelet network are developed using a Lyapunov-based design. It is also shown that both system tracking stability and convergence of the error estimation can be guaranteed in the closed-loop system. Simulation results on a three-link robot manipulator show the satisfactory performance of the proposed control schemes even in the presence of large modeling uncertainties and external disturbances.

Keywords: Wavelet networks, robotic manipulators, adaptive control.

1 Introduction

Wavelet theory has a profound impact on signal processing as it offers a rigorous mathematical approach to the treatment of multiresolution. The combination of soft computing and wavelet theory has lead to a number of new techniques: wavelet networks and fuzzy wavelet [2, 7, 25]. It has been applied in a wide range of engineering disciplines such as signal processing, control engineering, pattern recognition and computer graphics. In the literature, some of the attempts are made in solving surface integral equations, improving the finite difference time domain method, solving linear differential equations and nonlinear partial differential equations and modelling non-linear semiconductor devices [3, 6, 10-15, 21, 23, 24]. It has been shown that by employing the technique of feedback linearization and the theory of wavelet network, the robust adaptive control is designed based on Lyapunov method. The combination of wavelet theory and neural networks has lead to the development of wavelet networks. Wavelet networks are feed forward neural networks using wavelets as activation function. Wavelet networks have been used in classification and identification problems with some success. The strength of wavelet networks lies in their capabilities of catching essential features in "frequency-rich" signals. The origin of wavelet networks can be traced back to the work by [5] in which Gabor wavelets were used for image classification. Wavelet networks have become popular after the work by works

S. Jeschke, H. Liu, and D. Schilberg (Eds.): ICIRA 2011, Part II, LNAI 7102, pp. 401–411, 2011.
© Springer-Verlag Berlin Heidelberg 2011

[22, 26]. Recently, application of wavelet networks in identification and control design for a class of nonlinear dynamical systems has been investigated in [13].

On the other hand, robotic manipulators are non-linear models, if we take into account static frictions and dead zone will have non-linear models with unknown parameters. For systems that move at opposite directions and low speed (about zero), if we need high accuracy and performance, we have to consider static frictions and dead zone and if not, we will encounter a reduction in performance of system and even instability.

In the literature, there are some appreciable works related to utilizing different control techniques to the nonlinear robotic manipulators. These approaches often combine feedback linearization and optimal control techniques. It has been shown that how optimal control and adaptive control of robot motion may act in concert in the case of unknown or uncertain system parameters. Until now, often techniques that have been expressed need to exact model and exact value of model's parameters. However, in actual situations, the robot dynamics is rarely completely known, and it is thus difficult to express real robot dynamics in exact mathematical equations or to linearize the dynamics with respect to the operating point, see [4, 8, 9, 16, 17] and the references therein.

In this paper, a wavelet-based adaptive control is designed for a class of robotic manipulators. Model of robotic manipulators consists of some nonlinearity for friction effects and uncertain terms as disturbances. The controller is found by using the technique of feedback linearization, supervisory control and H_∞ control and the parameter adaptive laws of the wavelet network are developed using a Lyapunov-based design. It is also shown that both system tracking stability and error convergence of the estimation for nonlinear function can be guaranteed in the closed-loop system. Simulation results on a three-link robot manipulator show the satisfactory performance of the proposed control schemes even in the presence of large modeling uncertainties and external disturbances.

The paper is organized as follows. In Section 2 we will review some fundamentals of wavelet networks and mathematical notations. In Section 3 we give a wavelet-based adaptive control design for rigid robot systems. In Section 4, in order to demonstrate the validity of the proposed control method, a three-link robot controller is designed and simulated in the face of large uncertainties and external disturbances.

2   Wavelet Networks

The original objective of the wavelet theory is to construct orthogonal bases of $L_2(\Re)$. These bases are constituted by translation and dilation of the same function $\psi(.)$, namely wavelet function. It is preferable to take $\psi(.)$ localized and regular. The principles of wavelet construction are as follows [13, 26]:

1. $\phi(.)$ is a scaling function and the family $\phi(2^j x - k)$ for $0 \le k < 2^j$ constitutes an orthogonal basis of V_j,

2.   the function $\phi(x - k)$ are mutually orthogonal for k ranging over Z ,

3. the family $\psi(2^j x - k)$ for $0 \le k < 2^j$ constitutes an orthogonal basis of W_j.

4. the family $\{\phi(2^{j_0} x - k), \psi(2^j x - k)$ for $j \ge j_0\}$ forms an orthogonal basis of $L_2(\Re)$.

The wavelet subspaces W_j are defined as

$$W_j = \{\psi(2^j x - k), \quad 0 \le k < 2^j\} \tag{1}$$

which satisfy $W_j \cap W_i = 0$ for $\forall j \ne i$. For each $j \in Z$, let us consider the closed subspaces $V_j = \cdots \oplus W_{j-2} \oplus W_{j-1}$ of $L_2(\Re)$, where $\oplus$ denotes the direct sum, these nested subspaces have the following properties [13, 26]:

i. $\cdots \subset V_{-1} \subset V_0 \subset V_1 \subset \cdots$;

ii. $\text{close}_{L_2}(\bigcup_{j \in Z} V_j) = L_2(\Re)$;

iii. $\bigcap_{j \in Z} V_j = 0$;

iv. $V_{j+1} = V_j \oplus W_j \quad j \in Z$;

v. $f(x) \in V_j \leftrightarrow f(2x) \in V_{j+1} \quad j \in Z$.

If $\phi(.)$ and $\psi(.)$ are compactly supported, they give a local description, at different scales j, of the considered function. The wavelet series representation of the one-dimensional function $f(x)$ is given by

$$f(x) = \sum_{k \in Z} a_{j_0 k} \phi_{j_0 k} + \sum_{j \ge j_0} \sum_{k \in Z} b_{jk} \psi_{jk}(x) \tag{2}$$

where $\phi_{j_0 k}(x) = 2^{j_0/2} \phi(2^{j_0} x - k)$, $\psi_{jk}(x) = 2^{j/2} \psi(2^j x - k)$, and using the inner product property $<.,.>$, the wavelet coefficients $a_{j_0 k}$ and b_{jk} are obtained as

$$a_{j_0 k} = < f(x), \phi_{j_0 k}(x) >, \tag{3}$$

$$b_{jk} = < f(x), \psi_{jk}(x) >. \tag{4}$$

While the function $f(x)$ is unknown, the wavelet coefficients $a_{j_0 K}$ and b_{jk} cannot be calculated simply by (3) and (4), respectively. Since, it is not realistic to use an infinite number of wavelets to represent the function $f(x)$, we consider the following wavelet representation form of the function $f(x)$

$$\hat{f}(x) = \sum_{j=-M_1}^{M_2} \sum_{k=-N_1}^{N_2} b_{jk} \psi_{jk}(x) = \underline{\theta}^T \underline{\psi}(x) \tag{5}$$

for some positive integers M_1, N_1, M_2, N_2, vector $\underline{\theta} = (b_{M_1 N_1}, \ldots, b_{M_1 N_2}, \ldots, b_{M_2 N_1}, \ldots, b_{M_2 N_2})^T$ and vector $\underline{\psi}(x) = (\psi_{M_1 N_1}(x), \ldots, \psi_{M_1 N_2}(x), \ldots, \psi_{M_2 N_1}(x), \ldots, \psi_{M_2 N_2}(x))^T$.

If $\Xi_f(M_1, M_2, N_1, N_2) = f(x) - \hat{f}(x)$ is the Network Error (or approximation error), then it is easy to show that for arbitrary constant $\eta \geq 0$, there exist some constants M_1, N_1, M_2, N_2 such that $\|\Xi_f(M_1, M_2, N_1, N_2)\|_2 \leq \eta$ for all $x \in \Re$ [1]. This means that $f(x)$ can be approximated to any desired accuracy by a wavelet network $\hat{f}(x)$ with large enough M_1, N_1, M_2, N_2. The variable wavelet networks were introduced to achieve desired estimation accuracy and a suitable size network, and to adapt to variations of the characteristics and operating points in nonlinear systems [13, 26].

The wavelet series representation can be easily generalized to any dimension n. For the n-dimension case $\underline{x} = [x_1, x_2, \cdots, x_n]^T$, we introduce the wavelet function

$$\psi(\underline{x}) = \psi(x_1, x_2, \ldots, x_n) = \psi(x_1)\psi(x_2)\cdots\psi(x_n). \tag{6}$$

Now, we make a modification to replace the wavelet bases in (5) with (6). Then the modified wavelet network becomes

$$\hat{f}(\underline{x}) = \sum_{j=M_1}^{M_2}\sum_{k=N_1}^{N_2} b_{jk}\psi_{jk}(x) = \sum_{j=-M_1}^{M_2}\sum_{k=-N_1}^{N_2} b_{jk}\prod_{l=1}^{n}\psi_{jk}(x_l) = \underline{\theta}^T\underline{\psi}(\underline{x}) \tag{7}$$

where $\underline{\theta} = (b_{M_1N_1}, \ldots, b_{M_1N_2}, \ldots, b_{M_2N_1}, \ldots, b_{M_2N_2})^T$ and

$\underline{\psi}(\underline{x}) = (\psi_{M_1N_1}(\underline{x}), \ldots, \psi_{M_1N_2}(\underline{x}), \ldots, \psi_{M_2N_1}(\underline{x}), \ldots, \psi_{M_2N_2}(\underline{x}))^T$.

3   Robot Manipulators Dynamics

The dynamics of an n-link robot manipulator may be expressed in the Lagrange form [18]:

$$M(q)\ddot{q} + V_m(q,\dot{q})\dot{q} + F_V\dot{q} + f_c(\dot{q}) + g(q) + \tau_d(t) = \tau(t) \tag{8}$$

with $q(t) \in \Re^n$ joint variable, $M(q) \in \Re^{n \times n}$ inertia, $V_m(q, \dot{q}) \in \Re^{m \times n}$ Coriolis/centripetal forces, $g(q) \in \Re^n$ gravitational forces, $F_v \in \Re^{n \times n}$ diagonal matrix of viscous friction coefficients, $f_c(q) \in \Re^n$ Coulomb friction coefficients, and $\tau_d(t) \in \Re^n$ external disturbances. The bounded values of the external disturbances are given by $\|\tau_d(t)\| < b_d$. The external control torques to each joints are $\tau(t) \in \Re^n$. Given a desired trajectory $q_d(t) \in \Re^n$, the tracking error is

$$e(t) = q_d(t) - q(t) \tag{9}$$

and the instantaneous performance measure is defined as

$$r(t) = \dot{e}(t) + \Lambda e(t) \tag{10}$$

where Λ is the constant gain matrix or critic (not necessarily symmetric). The robot dynamics (8) may be written as

$$M(q)\dot{r}(t) = -V_m(q, \dot{q})r(t) + h(x) - \tau(t) + \tau_d(t) \tag{11}$$

where the robot nonlinear function is

$$h(x) = M(q)(\ddot{q}_d + \Lambda \dot{e}) + V_m(q,\dot{q})(\dot{q}_d + \Lambda e) + g(q) + F_v \dot{q} + f_c(\dot{q}) \tag{12}$$

where $\underline{x} = [e^T, \dot{e}^T, q_d^T, \dot{q}_d^T, \ddot{q}_d^T]^T$. This key function h(x) captures all the unknown dynamics of the robot arm. We employ an adaptive wavelet networks

$$\hat{h}(\underline{x}, \underline{\theta}_f) = \underline{\theta}_f^T \underline{\psi}_f(\underline{x}) \tag{13}$$

to approximate (or model) the nonlinear function h(x). The optimal weight vector $\underline{\theta}_f^*$ is quantities required only for analytical purposes. Typically $\underline{\theta}_f^*$ are chosen as

$$\underline{\theta}_f^* = \arg \min_{\underline{\theta}_f} \{ \max_{\underline{x}} |h(\underline{x}) - \underline{\theta}_f^T \underline{\psi}_f(\underline{x})| \}, \tag{14}$$

and the function h(.) which is valid for all $\underline{x} \in U_x$ has the following representation

$$h(\underline{x}) = \hat{h}(\underline{x}, \underline{\theta}_f^*) + \Xi_f(\underline{x}) = \underline{\theta}_f^{*T} \underline{\psi}_f(\underline{x}) + \Xi_f(\underline{x}) \tag{15}$$

By using definitions of (12)-(15), we rewrite (11) as

$$M(q)\dot{r}(t) = -V_m(q,\dot{q})r(t) + \underline{\theta}_f^{*T} \underline{\psi}_f(\underline{x}) + \Xi_f(\underline{x}) - \tau(t) + \tau_d(t)$$

Define the position error dynamics as

$$\dot{e}(t) = -\Lambda e(t) + r(t) \tag{16}$$

The following augmented system is obtained:

$$\dot{z}(t) = A(q,\dot{q})z(t) + B(q)(\underline{\theta}_f^{*T} \underline{\psi}_f(\underline{x}) + \Xi_f(\underline{x}) - \tau(t) + \tau_d(t)) \tag{17}$$

with

$$z(t) = \begin{bmatrix} e \\ r \end{bmatrix}, \quad A(q,\dot{q}) = \begin{bmatrix} -\Lambda & I \\ 0 & -M^{-1}V_m \end{bmatrix}, \quad B(q) = \begin{bmatrix} 0 \\ M^{-1} \end{bmatrix}.$$

Definition 1. The effect of $\tau_d(t)$, denoting the external disturbance, will be attenuated by the H_∞ control signal if the following H_∞ tracking performance holds

$$\int_0^T \underline{z}^T Q \underline{z} \, dt \leq \underline{z}^T(0)P\underline{z}(0) + \gamma^2 \int_0^T \tau_d^T \tau_d \, dt \qquad \forall \, 0 \leq T < \infty \tag{18}$$

where γ is a prescribed attenuation level, and P, Q are positive definite weighting matrixes.

4   Control Design

Consider the Lyapunov function

$$V = \underline{z}^T P \underline{z} + \frac{1}{2} \text{tr}(\tilde{\underline{\theta}}_f \, \tilde{\underline{\theta}}_f^T) \tag{19}$$

where matrix P is a positive definite matrix and $\tilde{\underline{\theta}}_f = \underline{\theta}_f - \underline{\theta}_f^*$. The first derivative of the Lyapunov function V with respect to time t is

$$\dot{V} = \underline{z}^T \left[\dot{P} + PA + A^T P \right] \underline{z} + 2\underline{z}^T P\underline{B} (\underline{\theta}_f^{*T} \underline{\psi}_f(\underline{x}) + \Xi_f(\underline{x}) - \tau(t) + \tau_d(t)) + \text{tr}(\dot{\tilde{\underline{\theta}}}_f \tilde{\underline{\theta}}_f^T) \quad (20)$$

Substituting [13, 19]

$$\tau(t) = \underline{\theta}_f^T \underline{\psi}_f(\underline{x}) + \tau^a + \tau^s \quad (21)$$

with

$$\tau^a = \frac{-1}{\beta^2} \underline{B}^T P\underline{z} \quad (22)$$

$$\tau^s = \mu_s \, \text{sgn}\,(\underline{z}^T P\underline{B})(h^U(\underline{x}) + \left| \hat{h}(\underline{x}, \underline{\theta}_f) \right|) \quad (23)$$

where

$$\mu_s = \begin{cases} 1 & \text{if } \|\underline{z}(t)\| \geq E \\ 0 & \text{if } \|\underline{z}(t)\| < E \end{cases}$$

into (20), we have:

$$\dot{V} = \underline{z}^T \left[\dot{P} + PA + A^T P + \frac{2}{\beta^2} P\underline{B}\underline{B}^T P \right] \underline{z}$$
$$+ 2\underline{z}^T P\underline{B} (\underline{\theta}_f^{*T} \underline{\psi}_f(\underline{x}) + \Xi_f(\underline{x}) - \underline{\theta}_f^T \underline{\psi}_f(\underline{x}) - \tau^s + \tau_d(t)) + \text{tr}(\dot{\tilde{\underline{\theta}}}_f \tilde{\underline{\theta}}_f^T) \quad (24)$$

By using (28), (35) and inequality $X^T Y + Y^T X \leq \gamma X^T X + \frac{1}{\gamma} Y^T Y$ for any matrices X and Y with appropriate dimensions and for any constant $\gamma > 0$, and the fact that $\dot{\tilde{\underline{\theta}}}_f = \dot{\underline{\theta}}_f$, we conclude:

$$\dot{V} \leq \underline{z}^T \left[\dot{P} + PA + A^T P + \frac{2}{\beta^2} P\underline{B}\underline{B}^T P + \frac{1}{\gamma^2} P\underline{B}\underline{B}^T P \right] \underline{z}$$
$$+ 2\underline{z}^T P\underline{B}(\Xi_f(\underline{x}) - \tilde{\underline{\theta}}_f^T \underline{\psi}_f(\underline{x}) - \tau^s) + \text{tr}(\dot{\underline{\theta}}_f \tilde{\underline{\theta}}_f^T) + \gamma^2 \tau_d^T(t)\tau_d(t) \quad (25)$$

Considering

$$\dot{P} + PA + A^T P + P\underline{B}(\frac{2}{\beta^2} + \frac{1}{\gamma^2})\underline{B}^T P + Q = 0 \quad (26)$$

and the adaptation law

$$\dot{\underline{\theta}}_f = \text{Proj}(\underline{\theta}_f, \underline{\Pi}_f) = \underline{\Pi}_f \quad (27)$$

with $\underline{\Pi}_f = 2\underline{z}^T P\underline{B}\,\underline{\psi}_f(\underline{x})$, we find:

$$\dot{V} \leq \begin{cases} -\underline{z}^T Q \underline{z} + \gamma^2 \tau_d^T(t)\tau_d(t) & \text{if } \|\underline{z}(t)\| \geq E \\ -\underline{z}^T Q \underline{z} + \gamma^2 \tau_d^T(t)\tau_d(t) + 2\left|\underline{z}^T P\underline{B}\right|(|h(\underline{x})| + |\hat{h}(\underline{x}, \underline{\theta}_f^*)|) & \text{if } \|\underline{z}(t)\| < E \end{cases} \quad (28)$$

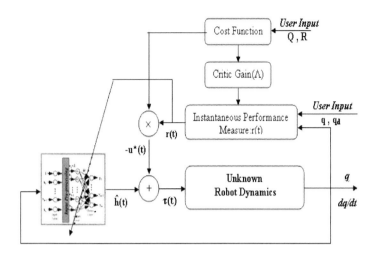

Fig. 1. Adaptive control design based on wavelet networks

By integrating both sides of (28) from 0 to T, we have:

$$V(T) + \int_0^T \underline{z}^T Q \underline{z} \, dt \le$$

$$\begin{cases} V(0) + \gamma^2 \int_0^T \tau_d^T(t)\tau_d(t) \, dt & \text{if } \|\underline{z}(t)\| \ge E \\ V(0) + \gamma^2 \int_0^T \tau_d^T(t)\tau_d(t) \, dt + 2\int_0^T \underline{z}^T P\underline{B} \left(|h(\underline{x})| + |\hat{h}(\underline{x}, \underline{\theta}_f^*)| \right) dt & \text{if } \|\underline{z}(t)\| < E \end{cases}$$

and after some simple manipulations on the inequality above, we conclude:

$$\lambda_{\min}(Q) \|\underline{e}(t)\|^2 \le \begin{cases} V(0) + \gamma^2 B_d^2 & \text{if } \|\underline{z}(t)\| \ge E \\ V(0) + \gamma^2 B_d^2 + 2\rho\|\underline{z}(t)\| & \text{if } \|\underline{z}(t)\| < E \end{cases} \tag{29}$$

where $\rho := \left\| |P\underline{B}| \left(|h(\underline{x})| + |\hat{h}(\underline{x}, \underline{\theta}_f^*)| \right) \right\|$. This demonstrates all states and signals involved of the closed loop system are bounded, furthermore, the H_∞ tracking performance can be achieved from the results above.

In summary, the block diagram in Fig. 1 shows the major components that embody the wavelet-based adaptive controller (21) with τ^a given by (22) and τ^s given by (23). Finally, we can guarantee that $\|\underline{z}(t)\| < E$ and the criteria of H_∞ tracking performance (18) will be satisfied.

5   Simulation Results

The dynamic equations for an n-link manipulator can be found in [20]. In this study we have simulated a three-link robot manipulator.

An external disturbance and frictions are

$$\tau(t) = [3 + \sin(2t) \quad 5 + \cos(t) \quad 2 + \sin(t)]^{T} \tag{30}$$

$$F_V \dot{q} + f_c(\dot{q}) = \text{diag}[2 \quad 2]\dot{q} + 1.5\,\text{sgn}(\dot{q}) \tag{31}$$

where $\text{sgn}(x)$ is a signum function. The weighting matrices in (18) are as follows:

$$Q_{11} = 10\,I \,, \, Q_{12} = -10\,I \,, \, Q_{21} = Q_{12}^{T} \,, \, Q_{22} = 30\,I \,.$$

Our target is that the manipulator moves in a predetermined path without error. With determinate path, by solving inverse kinematics, we obtain the desired joints trajectory. In this study, we want that robot moves on a crescent path wobbly, as $q(t) = [0.5\text{Sin}(0.1t), 1, 1.5]^{T}$.

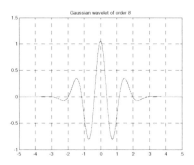

Fig. 2. Gaussian wavelet of order 8

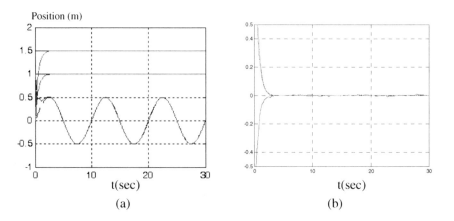

Fig. 3. Performance of adaptive control based on wavelet networks for system with uncertainties: (a) Tracking curve, (b) Tracking error

Fundamentally, the wavelet network can be characterized by

- Number of hidden neurons: 7*n+1, where 'n' is number of link of manipulator
- Hidden neuron activation functions: Gaussian wavelet of order 8 (Fig. 2)
- Output neuron activation functions: $\delta(x) = x$;
- Learning rate in the weight tuning law: F= diag [70 70], K=0.01;
- Network input: $x = \begin{bmatrix} 1 & q^T & \dot{q}^T & e^T & \dot{e}^T & r^T & q_d^T & \dot{q}_d^T \end{bmatrix}$;
- Inputs to hidden neurons: $p = x$.

The simulation results for wavelet-based neural network controllers with considering varieties of uncertainties for plant are shown in Fig. 3. The simulation results with assumption change system's parameters for wavelet-based controller are shown in Fig. 4. The results in Fig. 3 and Fig. 4 show the capability of the wavelet network for designing an adaptive controller for overcoming uncertainties; both structured and unstructured.

6   Conclusion

An adaptive control scheme was developed for a robotic manipulator using wavelet networks. It was shown that the entire closed-loop system behavior depends on the user specified performance indexes. The weighting matrices automatically generate the Lyapunov function for the stability of the overall system. In derivation of the computed torque controller, it has been assumed that nonlinearities in the robotic manipulator are completely known. However even with the knowledge about the nonlinearities, it is difficult to achieve the control objective in the presence of modeling uncertainties and frictional forces. Due to use of Gaussian wavelet function in neural network, an estimation of non-linear functions with presence uncertainties and friction forces have more accuracy and will improve performance of control system considerably because wavelet functions keep time and frequency domain properties. The proposed neural adaptive learning shows both robustness and adaptation to changing system dynamics.

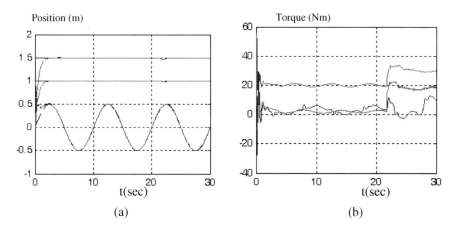

Fig. 4. Performance of adaptive control based on wavelet networks for system with inconstant parameters: (a) Tracking curve, (b) Controller output-$\tau(t)$

References

[1] Barron, A.R.: Universal approximation bounds for superposition of a sigmoidal function. IEEE Transactions on Information Theory 39(3), 930–945 (1993)

[2] Burrus, C.S., Gopinath, R.A., Guo, H.: Introduction to wavelets and wavelet transforms. Prentice Hall, Upper Saddle River (1998)

[3] Chen, C.F., Hsiao, C.H.: Haar wavelet method for solving lumped and distributed-parameter systems. IEE Proc. Control Theory Appl. 144(1), 87–94 (1997)

[4] Dawson, D., Grabbe, M., Lewis, F.L.: Optimal control of a modified computed-torque controller for a robot manipulator. International Journal of Robotics Automation 6(3), 161–165 (1991)

[5] Daugmann, J.: Complete Discrete 2-D Gabor Transforms By Neural Networks For Image Analysis And Compression. IEEE Trans. Acoust., Speech, Signal Proc. 36, 1169–1179 (1988)

[6] Hsiao, C.H., Wang, W.J.: State analysis and parameter estimation of bilinear systems via Haar wavelets. IEEE Transactions on Circuits and Systems I: Fundamental Theory and Applications 47(2), 246–250 (2000)

[7] Hunt, K.J., Sbarbaro, D., Zbikowski, R., Gawthrop, P.J.: Neural networks for control systems: a survey. Automatica 28(6), 1823–1836 (1992)

[8] Johansson, R.: Quadratic optimization of motion coordination and control. IEEE Transactions on Automatic Control 35(11), 1197–1208 (1990)

[9] Karami, A., Karimi, H.R., Maralani, P.J., Moshiri, B.: Intelligent optimal control of robotic manipulators using wavelets. International Journal of Wavelets, Multiresoloution and Image Processing 6(4), 575–592 (2008)

[10] Karimi, H.R.: A computational method to optimal control problem of time-varying state-delayed systems by Haar wavelets. International Journal of Computer Mathematics 83(2), 235–246 (2006)

[11] Karimi, H.R., Lohmann, B.: Haar wavelet-based robust optimal control for vibration reduction of vehicle engine-body system. Journal of Electrical Engineering (May 20, 2006) (online publication) (in press)

[12] Karimi, H.R., Lohmann, B., Maralani, P.J., Moshiri, B.: A computational method for parameter estimation of linear systems using Haar wavelets. International Journal of Computer Mathematics 81(9), 1121–1132 (2004)

[13] Karimi, H.R., Lohmann, B., Moshiri, B., Maralani, P.J.: Wavelet-based identification and control design for a class of non-linear systems. International Journal of Wavelets, Multiresoloution and Image Processing 4(1), 213–226 (2006)

[14] Karimi, H.R., Maralani, P.J., Moshiri, B., Lohmann, B.: Numerically efficient approximations to the optimal control of linear singularly perturbed systems based on Haar wavelets. International Journal of Computer Mathematics 82(4), 495–507 (2005)

[15] Karimi, H.R., Moshiri, B., Lohmann, B., Maralani, P.J.: Haar wavelet-based approach for optimal control of second-order linear systems in time domain. Journal of Dynamical and Control Systems 11(2), 237–252 (2005)

[16] Karimi, H.R., Yazdanpanah, M.J., Patel, R.V., Khorasani, K.: Modelling and control of linear two-time scale systems: applied to single-link flexible manipulator. Journal of Intelligent & Robotic Systems (June 8, 2006) (online publication) (in press)

[17] Kim, H.Y., Lewis, L.F., Dawson, D.M.: Intelligent optimal control of robotic manipulators using neural networks. Automatica 36(9), 1355–1364 (2000)

[18] Lewis, F.L., Abdallah, C.T., Dawson, D.M.: Control of robot manipulators. MacMillan, New York (1993)

[19] Lewis, F.L., Syrmos, V.L.: Optimal control. Wiley, New York (1995)
[20] Lewis, F.L., Yesildirek, A., Liu, K.: Neural net robot controller with guaranteed tracking performance. IEEE Transactions on Neural Networks 6(3), 703–715 (1995)
[21] Ohkita, M., Kobayashi, Y.: An application of rationalized Haar functions to solution of linear differential equations. IEEE Transactions on Circuit and Systems 9, 853–862 (1986)
[22] Pati, Y.C., Krishnaprasad, P.S.: Analysis and synthesis of feed forward neural networks using discrete affine wavelet transformations. IEEE Trans. Neural Networks 4, 73–85 (1992)
[23] Razzaghi, M., Ordokhani, Y.: A rationalized Haar functions method for nonlinear Fredholm-Hammerstein integral equations. International Journal of Computer Math. 79(3), 333–343 (2002)
[24] Tan, Y., Dang, X., Liang, F., Su, C.Y.: Dynamic wavelet neural network for nonlinear dynamic system identification. In: International Conference on Control Applications (2000)
[25] Thuillard, M.: A review of wavelet networks, wavenets, fuzzy wavenets and their applications. In: ESIT, Aachen, Germany, pp. 5–16 (2000)
[26] Zhang, Q., Benveniste, A.: Wavelet networks. IEEE Trans. Neural Networks 3, 889–898 (1992)

Development of a Deep Ocean Master-Slave Electric Manipulator Control System[*]

Xiong Shen, GuoHua Xu, Kun Yu, Guoyuan Tang, and Xiaolong Xu

Underwater Technology Laboratory, College of Navy and ship Science and Engineering,
Huazhong University of Science and Technology, Wuhan, 430074, China

Abstract. Underwater vehicles and manipulators play an important role in underwater tasks such as salvage, maintenance and so on. Underwater environment, especially deep Ocean is a hazard place for human to explore for its high water pressure. It is illustrated a development course of a deep ocean Master-slave manipulator for the demand of emergency oil exploration system. This paper describes a development of master-slave manipulator feedback control system. The underwater control system is based network and consisted of three embedded PC/104 computers which are used for servo control, task plan and target sensor respectively. The sensor control system and strategy of the master-slave manipulator control system are discussed in three parts include structure, modeling and experiment.Finally; establish the two-port network mode based scaling condition and analysis the stability of the overall manipulator control system .

Keywords: underwater electric manipulator, Master-slave, deep ocean, integration joints.

1   Introduction

The described manipulator is particularly applied for Emergency oil exploration system mounted on the ROV. The system will carry out precise operation include the oil equipment, installation, commissioning, monitoring, repair, emergency and other dangerous work.

Nowadays, two kinds of manipulator are applied in underwater manipulation. First kind is hydraulic manipulator. Such as the Work System Package of Naval Ocean Systems Center is a famous and typical remote underwater manipulation system. The system can exchange tools in the field not back to surface of water. There are several reasons for that electric manipulator isn't applied widely as hydraulic manipulator. The main technology difficulties include insulation of electric circuits, seal and pressure compensation. Except that, small output power is another reason. In recent decades, underwater vehicle-manipulator systems (UVMS) are extensively studied [1] [2].

---

[*] This work was funded by the China National 863 Program "deep-sea manipulator key technique" project (2006AA09Z203), State Commission of Science and Technology for National Defense Industry Project "micro underwater work tool" and National Science Foundation of China (Grant No. 50909046 and No. 51079061).

S. Jeschke, H. Liu, and D. Schilberg (Eds.): ICIRA 2011, Part II, LNAI 7102, pp. 412–419, 2011.
© Springer-Verlag Berlin Heidelberg 2011

For the particularly demand, the design of the underwater electric manipulator mounted on ROV should be faced to lightweight and precise operations in deep ocean.

The structure of the paper is given as following. In section 2, it is overview of the whole manipulator system Modular integration joints design is given in section 3. The sensor system and control system are introduced in section 4. Then we discuss experiment in section 5.

2   Manipulator System Overview

The whole manipulator system is consisted of an electric manipulator, an underwater control unit, a direct current power, a sensor system and a supervisor PC.

The manipulator is of three degree of freedoms (DoFs). They are shoulder revolving, shoulder rising/ down and elbow rising /down respectively. As illustrated in Fig.1, the mathematical descriptions of the kinematic chains for the manipulator were made based on the D-H parameters notation. The jaw of the manipulator has an open/close function. It can grasp cylinder object [3] [4].

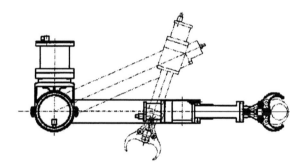

Fig. 1. The manipulator appearance

The manipulator is particularly applied for Emergency oil exploration system mounted on the ROV. In our design, the compensation device consists of a spring, a movable rubber piston and a chamber. Table 1 shows Parameters of the manipulator Joint.

Table 1. Parameters of the manipulator Joint

Motion	T(Nm)	m (Kg)	P(W)
yaw	41	4	85
yaw	200	6.7	250
yaw	600	4	85
roll	4	1.5	30

The chamber is in the axis of joint housing. If the environment pressure increases as manipulator work depth increases, the rubber piston moves to compensate the pressure error. The spring makes the inner pressure a little higher (but less than 0.1 MPA) than environment pressure. Increasing the joint's efficiency is another research problem. The motor's efficiency decreases after being filled with oil. Viscosity of oil and the shape of inner space are the main reasons. So the oil should be specially chosen. Appropriate hydraulic oil may have low density, small compress ratio in high pressure, nice insulation and chemical stability. Fig.2 shows the pressure compensation device and integrated joint [5].

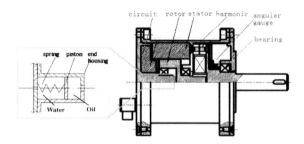

Fig. 2. Pressure compensation device and integrated joint

3   Hardware and Software of the Control System

3.1   Structure of Control System Hardware

The underwater control system is based network and consisted of three embedded PC/104 computers which are used for servo control, task plan and vision respectively. The A/D board, D/A board are of PC104 bus standards. Vxworks OS is used in the three embedded PC/104 computers. Like a hard disk, a Compact Flash card is the external memory of the embedded PC/104 computers. User's application program and the system operation system are stored in the Compact Flash card. Three embedded PC/104 computers communicate through User Datagram Protocol (UDP) multicast communication. Fig.3 shows its hardware structure.

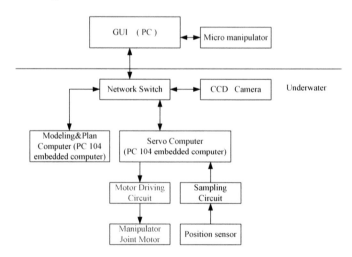

Fig. 3. Structure of control system hardware

3.2   Structure of Control System Software

The structure of control system software is hierarchical as shown in Fig 4. There are three layers: decision layer, function layer and execution layer. In remote control mode; the operator controls the manipulator through keyboard. The control commend is in the low control level such as joint angle. The 3D graphic model displays the states of the manipulator and the target. In automation mode, when repetition task need to be done, after offline simulation, the planed trajectory data is saved and can be used more than once. In autonomous mode, the target information is obtained from vision and ultra sonic sensor [6]. Once the target is in the range of sensors, the manipulator can work without operator's assistance.

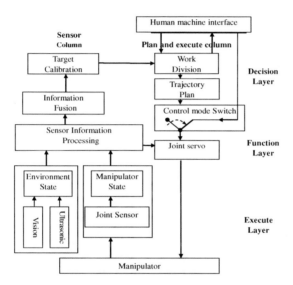

Fig. 4. Structure of control system software

4   Sensor System

The manipulator sensor system includes an underwater camera and a unique ultra-sonic probe array. Vision program is running in Vxworks OS in the embedded PC104 computer which is cable linked with the camera.

4.1   Ultra-Sonic Sensor

Ultrasound probe is the main important part of the ultra-sonic sensor. In our design, a unique three ultra-sonic probe array is designed. Kleeman, LeMay introduced multi-sonar system. Similar with them, our design is shown in Fig. 5. These three probes are arranged in a convex surface [7].

Fig. 5. Detection experiment

Wave beam angle of single probe is 11°, The advantage of the convex surface arrangement is that probe array can covers 30°. Furthermore, it can obtain a larger detectable angle, and detect both distance and approximate location of object.

4.2   Underwater Vision

SIFT was developed by Lowe for image feature generation in object recognition applications. The SIFT features are in-variant to image translation, scaling, rotation, and partially invariant to illumination changes and affine or 3D projection [8] [9]. A supervisor PC with a virtual 3D GUI is fiber linked to underwater control system. The target is a cylinder with artificial square in surface which is shown in Fig.6.

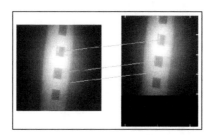

Fig. 6. Target recognition using SIFT

5   Experiments

5.1   Ultra-Sonic Underwater Experiment

In each work period, every probe emits 8us 500K Hz pulses and receives reflect wave once. The core unit (msp430) calculates the distance of target, and figures out its approximate location [10].The MSP430 communicate with plan embedded computer via RS232C asynchronous serial communication. Its baud rate is 11520bps.

Combined with the inner influence of the detection range, resolution, and the size of acoustic system. The frequency of the ultra-sonic is designed in 300 kHz or 500 kHz. Fig.7 shows the detection course of the ultra-sonic working.Fig.7 shows the signal communication style from ultra-sonic to the target.

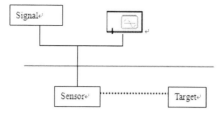

Fig. 7. Detection experiment of ultra-sonic

Compared results of the two ultra sensor underwater experiments as in Table 2,it show that it will reduce the blind detect area and weight without reducing the detection distance after boost the working frequency to 500kz.The manipulator works more facility.

Table 2. The underwater experiment result of ultra-sonic sensor in different frequency

probe frequency	echo wave/mv	Blind /mm	Blind /mm
300hz	412	30	16
500ha	315	60	40

In the constant working frequency, the probe fired equaled the number of the emission intensity. Wave emission may be beneficial to increase the number of echo intensity asked the echo will be influenced if it is in long launch. The result shows that the echo aptitude reaches saturation while the time of the emission.Fig.8 shows the experiment result while the launch cyclic wave is 40mm.T refers time while V refers echo wave.

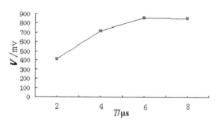

Fig. 8. Detection experiment of ultra-sonic

5.2   Grasp Experiment

(1) When the target is outside the detection area of the ultra-sonic sensor, move the targets within the region and observe he movement of the robot;
(2) Move the target to detection region of probe but outside the scope of the manipulator crawl. Move target and observe the movement of the robot;

(3) Move the target within crawl region. Then, move target and observe the movement of the robot;

The underwater experiment statement is operating in the huazhong university pool which size is 6m*8m*174m (depth*width*length).

Fig.9 shows the course of manipulator grasp in the system cooperation experiment.

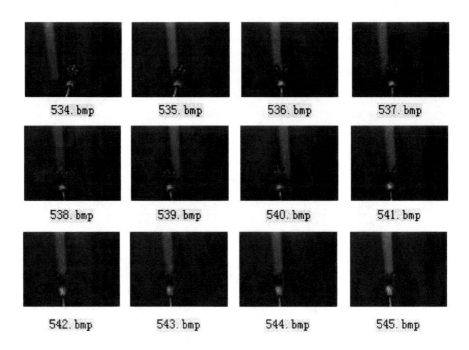

Fig. 9. Manipulator Auto grasp

Fig 10 shows the cooperation grasp experiment based multi sensor in the pool

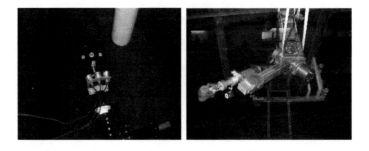

Fig. 10. Manipulator grasps experiment in the pool

6   Conclusion

In our laboratory, we have designed a deep ocean manipulator mounted in the ROV. Watertight test verifies the pressure compensation device. The underwater control system is based network. This manipulator can be remote controlled. It is equipped with a sensor system including a unique ultra-sonic probe array and an underwater camera. In future, there are some improvements left to be done. We want to study how to increase joint efficiency. Except that, the target cylinder is static and has artificial feature. Grasp unstructured objects in more complex environment will be studied.

References

1. Jiang, X.-s., Feng, X.-s., Wang, D.-t.: AUV. Science Press, Shenyang (2000)
2. Antonelli, G., Caccavale, F., Chiaverini, S., Villani, L.: Tracking control for underwater vehicle-manipulator systems with velocity estimation. IEEE Journal of Oceanic Engineering 3, 399–413 (2000)
3. Kleeman, L., Kuc, R.: Mobile Robot Sonar for Target Localization and Classification. The International Journal of Robotics Research 4, 295–318 (1995)
4. Denavit, J.S., Hartenberg, R.: A kinematic notation for lower-pair mechanisms based on matrices. Journal of Applied Mechanics, Transactions of the ASME (June 2005)
5. Shen, J.-h., Yang, Y.-q., Qu, X.-s.: MSP430 family of ultra-low power 16-bit single-chip Principle and Application. Tsinghua University Press, Peking (2004)
6. Xu, G.-h., Duan, G.-q., Jian, T.: A study on fuzzy self-rescue expert system of AUV. Shipbuilding of China 12, 38–41 (2004)
7. LeMay, J.B.L.J.: Error minimization and redundancy management for a three dimensional ultrasonic ranging system. In: Proc. of the IEEE/RJS International Conference on Intelligent Robots and Systems, vol. 2, pp. 165–183 (1992)
8. Saridis, D.R.: Toward the Realization of Intelligent. Controls Proceedings of the IEEE 67, 1115–1120 (2004)
9. Santos, C.H., Bittencourt, G., Guenther, R.: Motion Coordination for Underwater Vehicle Manipulator Systems using a Fuzzy Hybrid strategy. In: Proc. of IEEE/RSJ, Int. Conf. on Intelligent Robots and Systems, pp. 3018–3023 (2006)
10. Lowe, D.G.: Distinctive Image Features from Scale-Invariant Keypoints. International Journal of Computer Vision 60, 91–110 (2004)

Modelling of Flexible Link Manipulators

Clementina Mladenova

Institute of Mechanics, Bulgarian Academy of Sciences
Acad. G. Bonchev Str., Bl. 4, Sofia 1113, Bulgaria
`clem@imbm.bas.bg`

Abstract. The present work describes a method for generating the dynamic equations within the Hamiltonian formalism of flexible robots with open-chain linkage mechanisms. Rotations are presented through vectors as elements of a Lie group with a smart composition law. The exact treatment of the flexible robots leads to partial differential equations which describe the nature of the elasticity. In spite of the fact that examples for control laws obtained from such direct approach exist, the common practice is to work with finite–dimensional approximations. Both approaches are considered and some conclusions are made. An example of single-link flexible manipulator is given.

Keywords: Flexible manipulators, rotations, deformations, Hamiltonian equations, Ritz method, modelling.

1 Introduction

A considerable amount of research on developments in modelling, simulation and control of rigid and flexible robot manipulators has been carried out. For example, a lot of information in this area may be found in [2], [14], [15], [3], etc. and the references therein. At recent time attention is focused more towards flexible manipulators. Flexible dynamics (vibrations) has been the main research challenge in modelling and control of such systems and a lot of investigations concerning this problem are carried out. In this aspect this has led to using the theory of partially differential equations, or finite-dimensional ordinary differential equations. Numerical techniques using finite difference and finite element methods have been studied for dynamic characterization of flexible manipulators. Concerning control problems, an input/output description of the system is desired, which may be obtained through on-line estimations and adaptation mechanisms. Open-loop and closed-loop control strategies and their specific characters are considered in more details.

The purpose of this work is to present a method for generating the dynamic equations within the Hamiltonian formalism of flexible robots with open-chain linkage mechanisms. The author steps on his long experience in parameterizations of the rotation group in three-dimensional space and their using for modelling of rigid body mechanical systems (see [7] - [13]). The general transformation matrix associated with the elastic deformations is written using rotation

S. Jeschke, H. Liu, and D. Schilberg (Eds.): ICIRA 2011, Part II, LNAI 7102, pp. 420–429, 2011.
© Springer-Verlag Berlin Heidelberg 2011

vectors since such a parameterization of the SO(3) group is quite effective for many rotational degrees–of–freedom. The exact treatment of the flexible robots leads to partial differential equations which describe the nature of the elasticity. In spite of the fact that examples for control laws obtained from such direct approach exist, the common practice is to work with finite–dimensional approximations. Both approaches are considered and some conclusions are made.

2   Kinematic Equations

We consider open chains of N elastic members (links) interconnected by N rigid joints. The first link is connected by the first joint to a rigid base body (link 0). We assume that the deformation is essentially due to the flexure and that the flexure plane coincides with the rotation one. In this case two generalized coordinates can be associated to each link. The first ones θ_i denote the relative displacements between link $i - 1$ and link i, when the elastic deformation is neglected; that is the angle between the tangents in the joint to the two adjacent links (Fig.1).

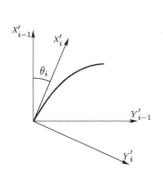

Fig. 1. Angle θ_i

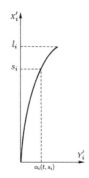

Fig. 2. Parameter α_i

The second ones α_i, which depend on time t and on the abscissa s_i on each link, characterize the shape of the neutral axis of the link i (Fig.2); $s_i \in [0, l_{f_i}]$, where l_{f_i} is such that the inextensibility condition holds, $\int_0^{l_{f_i}} \sqrt{1 + (\partial\alpha_i/\partial s_i)^2}ds_i = l_i$, and l_i is the length of the link i. With the link i a non-inertial frame (x_i', y_i', z_i') with the origin in the joint i is connected. The plane (x_i', y_i') coincides with the rotation one and x_i'- axis is tangent in the joint i to the flexed body (Fig.1). An inertial frame (x, y, z) is also defined, with origin at joint 1 and x-axis opposite to the gravity vector. In case of flexible arms, the transformation matrices are, in general, functions of the corresponding joint displacements and the elastic slopes. Further, a derivation for the kinematic equations of flexible robots is first presented. After that a general transformation matrix associated with the elastic deformation is introduced. Consequently, the possibilities of simplifying the expression of the matrix from the assumption that the

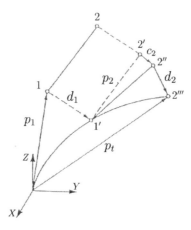

Fig. 3. Tip-point of a flexible robot

strain components and elastic slopes are small compared to unity are investigated. As it is shown in Fig. 3, the position vector for the tip-point of a flexible robot (point $2'''$) relative to the origin of the inertial frame is given by $P_t = P_1 + D_1 + (P_2 + C_2) + D_2$, or it can be written explicitly in terms of transformation matrices $P_t = \mathcal{R}_{01}\, p_1 + \mathcal{R}_{01}\, d_1 + \mathcal{R}_{01}\, \mathcal{R}_{11'}\, \mathcal{R}_{1'2}\, p_2 + \mathcal{R}_{01}\, \mathcal{R}_{11'}\, \mathcal{R}_{1'2}\, d_2$, in which $\mathcal{R}_{01}$ and $\mathcal{R}_{1'2}$ are the transformation matrices associated with the rigid-body motion, whereas $\mathcal{R}_{11'}$ is due to the elastic slopes of the end of the previous link. The vectors p_j and d_j ($j = 1, 2$) denote the vectors relative to the local coordinate systems. The system 0 is the inertial frame. By ignoring the elastic deformation, i.e., the rigid case, the terms d_1, d_2 and $\mathcal{R}_{11'}$ vanish, and we have $P_t = \mathcal{R}_{01}\, p_1 + \mathcal{R}_{01}\, \mathcal{R}_{12}\, p_2$. Following the routine execution of the matrix multiplication for expressing the coordinate transformation from the i-th link to the base coordinate system, and incorporating the additional transformation owing to deformation, the overall transformation matrix may be written as $\mathcal{R}_{0i} = \mathcal{R}_{01}\, \mathcal{R}_{11'}\, \mathcal{R}_{1'2}\, \mathcal{R}_{22'} \ldots \mathcal{R}_{(i-1)(i-1)'}\, \mathcal{R}_{(i-1)'i}$, where R_{mn} denotes the coordinate transformation from the system n to the system m. Note that $\mathcal{R}_{01} = \mathcal{R}_{00'}\, \mathcal{R}_{0'1} = \mathcal{R}_{0'1}$ since $\mathcal{R}_{00'}$ is identity matrix. The matrix $\mathcal{R}_{(i-1)'i}$ is a function of the corresponding joint angle associated with the rigid-body motion, while $\mathcal{R}_{ii'}$ depends on the elastic slopes of the previous link. Finally, the position vector of an arbitrary point on link i relative to the base frame can be written in a compact form as follows

$$P_i = \sum_{i=1}^{m} \mathcal{R}_{(i-1)i} h_i, \quad h_i = p_i + d_i \tag{1}$$

$$\mathcal{R}_{(i-1)i} = \mathcal{R}_{(i-1)(i-1)'}\, \mathcal{R}_{(i-1)'i}.$$

Further, we are going to find the general transformation matrix $\mathcal{R}_{ii'}$ associated with the deformation. Suppose the positions of points of the elastic body in the undeformed state are described by their projections on the axes of a system of Cartesian coordinates X, Y, Z. Let the deflection of the body points is given by the components u, v, w along the same axes. As a result of the deformation an arbitrary point M of the body will move to position M', and a point N infinitely near M will move to a position N'. The direction cosines of $M'N'$ in terms of direction cosines of MN is expressed as follows

$$
\mathcal{R} =
\begin{bmatrix}
\dfrac{1+\frac{\partial u}{\partial x}}{1+\Gamma_x} & \dfrac{\frac{\partial u}{\partial y}}{1+\Gamma_y} & \dfrac{\frac{\partial u}{\partial z}}{1+\Gamma_z} \\[3mm]
\dfrac{\frac{\partial v}{\partial x}}{1+\Gamma_x} & \dfrac{1+\frac{\partial v}{\partial y}}{1+\Gamma_y} & \dfrac{\frac{\partial v}{\partial z}}{1+\Gamma_z} \\[3mm]
\dfrac{\frac{\partial w}{\partial x}}{1+\Gamma_x} & \dfrac{\frac{\partial w}{\partial y}}{1+\Gamma_y} & \dfrac{1+\frac{\partial w}{\partial z}}{1+\Gamma_z}
\end{bmatrix}
\tag{2}
$$

in which

$$
\Gamma_x = \sqrt{1+2\,\epsilon_{xx}} - 1, \quad \Gamma_y = \sqrt{1+2\,\epsilon_{yy}} - 1, \quad \Gamma_z = \sqrt{1+2\,\epsilon_{zz}} - 1. \tag{3}
$$

We have to note that ϵ_{ij} is the deformation tensor and

$$
\epsilon_{ij} = \frac{1}{2}\left(\frac{\partial u_i}{\partial x_j} + \frac{\partial u_j}{\partial x_i}\right), \qquad i, j = 1, 2, 3. \tag{4}
$$

We use further the notation: $x_1 = x$, $x_2 = y$, $x_3 = z$; $u_1 = u$, $u_2 = v$, $u_3 = w$ and when $i = j = 1, 2, 3$ we have $\epsilon_{ij} = 2\epsilon_1, 2\epsilon_2, 2\epsilon_3$. So we have

$$
\epsilon_x = \frac{\partial u}{\partial x}, \qquad \epsilon_y = \frac{\partial v}{\partial y}, \qquad \epsilon_z = \frac{\partial w}{\partial z} \tag{5}
$$

$$
\gamma_{xy} = \frac{\partial u}{\partial y} + \frac{\partial v}{\partial x}, \qquad \gamma_{xz} = \frac{\partial u}{\partial z} + \frac{\partial w}{\partial x}, \qquad \gamma_{yz} = \frac{\partial v}{\partial z} + \frac{\partial w}{\partial y}. \tag{6}
$$

All components ϵ_x, $\epsilon_y, \ldots \gamma_{yz}$ are the components of deformation. The first three show the elongation along the axes, the second three - the flexion of the corresponding planes (for example γ_{xy} is the flexion between the planes xz and yz). By virtue of the assumption that the elongations ϵ_{xx}, ϵ_{yy}, ϵ_{zz} are negligible compared to unity, the rotation matrix (2) is reduced to

$$
\mathcal{R} =
\begin{bmatrix}
1+\frac{\partial u}{\partial x} & \frac{\partial u}{\partial y} & \frac{\partial u}{\partial z} \\[3mm]
\frac{\partial v}{\partial x} & 1+\frac{\partial v}{\partial y} & \frac{\partial v}{\partial z} \\[3mm]
\frac{\partial w}{\partial x} & \frac{\partial w}{\partial y} & 1+\frac{\partial w}{\partial z}
\end{bmatrix}. \tag{7}
$$

Let us now consider the case when not only the strain components, but also the angles of rotation (or elastic slopes) are small compared to unity. First of all, we may express the transformation matrix $\mathcal{R}$ in terms of vector-parameter

c (known also as Rodrigues or Gibbs vector) [1], [4], [5], [6], [7], [9]. The vector $c = (c_1,\, c_2\, c_3)$ is the vector-parameter which is parallel to the axis of rotation and $\mid c \mid = \tan(\alpha/2)$, α is the angle of rotation. The rotation matrix in vector-parameters seems like

$$\mathcal{R}(c) = \frac{1}{1+c^2} \begin{bmatrix} 1 + c_1^2 - c_2^2 - c_3^2 & 2\,(c_1\,c_2 - c_3) & 2\,(c_1\,c_3 + c_2) \\[6pt] 2\,(c_2\,c_1 + c_3) & 1 + c_2^2 - c_1^2 - c_3^2 & 2\,(c_2\,c_3 - c_1) \\[6pt] 2\,(c_3\,c_1 - c_2) & 2\,(c_3\,c_2 + c_1) & 1 + c_3^2 - c_1^2 - c_2^2 \end{bmatrix}. \tag{8}$$

The so defined vector-parameters form a Lie group with the following composition law

$$c = <c',c''> = \frac{c' + c'' + c' \times c''}{1 - c'\,c''} \tag{9}$$

$$\mathcal{R}(c) = \mathcal{R}(c')\mathcal{R}(c'') \quad \text{and} \quad \mathcal{R}(c)p = \mathcal{R}(c')\mathcal{R}(c'')p \quad \text{for any vector p.}$$

Here c'' is the first rotation. The symbol "$\times$" means cross product of vectors. Every component of c can take all values from $-\infty$ to $+\infty$ without any restrictions, which is a great advantage compared with the evident asymmetry in the Eulerian parameterization. Obviously, the vector $c \equiv 0$ corresponds to the identity matrix $\mathcal{R}(0) \equiv I$ and $-c$ produces the inverse rotation $\mathcal{R}(-c) \equiv \mathcal{R}^{-1}(c)$. From Eqs.(3) and (8) it may be seen that

$$\frac{\partial u}{\partial x} = \frac{c_1^2 - c_2^2 - c_3^2}{1 + c^2} \qquad \frac{\partial v}{\partial x} = \frac{2\,(c_2\,c_1 + c_3)}{1 + c^2} \qquad \frac{\partial w}{\partial x} = \frac{2\,(c_3\,c_1 - c_2)}{1 + c^2}$$

$$\frac{\partial u}{\partial y} = \frac{2\,(c_1\,c_2 - c_3)}{1 + c^2} \qquad \frac{\partial v}{\partial y} = \frac{c_2^2 - c_1^2 - c_3^2}{1 + c^2} \qquad \frac{\partial w}{\partial y} = \frac{2\,(c_3\,c_2 + c_1)}{1 + c^2} \tag{10}$$

$$\frac{\partial u}{\partial z} = \frac{2\,(c_1\,c_3 + c_2)}{1 + c^2} \qquad \frac{\partial v}{\partial z} = \frac{2\,(c_2\,c_3 - c_1)}{1 + c^2} \qquad \frac{\partial w}{\partial z} = \frac{c_3^2 - c_1^2 - c_2^2}{1 + c^2}.$$

After the additional assumption that the elastic slopes are small the matrix $\mathcal{R}$ looks like

$$\mathcal{R} = 2 \begin{bmatrix} 1 & -c_3 & c_2 \\ c_3 & 1 & -c_1 \\ -c_2 & c_1 & 1 \end{bmatrix}. \tag{11}$$

Let us rewrite Eq. (8) as

$$\mathcal{R} = 2 \begin{bmatrix} 1 + e_{xx} & \frac{1}{2}\,e_{xy} - \theta_z & \frac{1}{2}\,e_{zx} + \theta_y \\[6pt] \frac{1}{2}\,e_{xy} + \theta_z & 1 + e_{yy} & \frac{1}{2}\,e_{yz} - \theta_x \\[6pt] \frac{1}{2}\,e_{zx} - \theta_y & \frac{1}{2}\,e_{yz} + \theta_x & 1 + e_{zz} \end{bmatrix} \tag{12}$$

where

$$e_{xx} = \frac{\partial u}{\partial x}, \qquad e_{yy} = \frac{\partial v}{\partial y}, \qquad e_{zz} = \frac{\partial w}{\partial z}$$

$$e_{xy} = \frac{\partial u}{\partial y} + \frac{\partial v}{\partial x}, \quad e_{yz} = \frac{\partial v}{\partial z} + \frac{\partial w}{\partial y}, \quad e_{zx} = \frac{\partial u}{\partial z} + \frac{\partial w}{\partial x} \tag{13}$$

$$\theta_x = \frac{1}{2}\frac{\partial w}{\partial y} - \frac{\partial v}{\partial z}, \quad \theta_y = \frac{1}{2}\frac{\partial u}{\partial z} - \frac{\partial w}{\partial x}, \quad \theta_z = \frac{1}{2}\frac{\partial v}{\partial x} - \frac{\partial u}{\partial y}.$$

If all e_{ij} are set equal to zero, it follows from Eq. (12) that

$$\mathcal{R} = \begin{bmatrix} 1 & -\theta_z & \theta_y \\ \theta_z & 1 & -\theta_x \\ -\theta_y & \theta_x & 1 \end{bmatrix} \tag{14}$$

in which

$$\theta_x = \frac{\partial w}{\partial y} = -\frac{\partial v}{\partial z}, \quad \theta_y = \frac{\partial u}{\partial z} = -\frac{\partial w}{\partial x}, \quad \theta_z = \frac{\partial v}{\partial x} = -\frac{\partial u}{\partial y}. \tag{15}$$

It is seen that Eqs.(11) and (14) have the same form. Note that the Eqs. (8) and (13) are derived for general three-dimensional systems. In the case of flexible arms, however, attention is always limited to one-dimensional structure, that is beam- and rod- type systems in which is assumed that the physical properties are expressed with reference to a single dimension, the position along the elastic axis.

As is evident in the above examples, Eq.(11) or (14) is valid only if: (1) the strain components ϵ_{ij} and the elastic slopes c_i are small compared to unity, or: (2) all the parameters e_{ij} vanish. Otherwise, expression (2) for a general transformation matrix should be applied to retaining certain components that are significant.

3 Hamiltonian Equations of Motion

As we know the Lagrangian function is: $L = L(t, q_i, \dot{q}_i)$ and $t, q_i, \dot{q}_i$ are the Lagrangian coordinates. The The Hamiltonian coordinates are the quantities t, q_i, p_i as p_i are the generalized momenta. The Hamiltonian is introduced as the function $H(t, q_i, p_i)$ in the form $H = \sum_{i=1}^{n} p_i \dot{q}_i - L$ and the Hamiltonian's canonical equations are $2n$ ordinary first order differential equations of motions

$$\frac{\partial q_i}{\partial t} = \frac{\partial H}{\partial p_i}, \qquad \frac{\partial p_i}{\partial t} = -\frac{\partial H}{\partial q_i}, \qquad i = 1, 2, \ldots, n. \tag{16}$$

So, for our case denoting by x_i, y_i, z_i the parametric equations of the neutral line of link i referred to the inertial frame, the kinetic energy density is given by

$$T_i = \rho_i^* (\dot{x}_i^2 (\theta, \dot{\theta}, \alpha, \dot{\alpha}, s_i) + \dot{y}_i^2 (\theta, \dot{\theta}, \alpha, \dot{\alpha}, s_i)$$
$$+ \dot{z}_i^2 (\theta, \dot{\theta}, \alpha, \dot{\alpha}, s_i))/2 + \delta(s_i) I_{R_i} \dot{\theta}/2 \tag{17}$$

426   C. Mladenova

where: $\theta = [\theta_1, \theta_2, \ldots, \theta_N]^T$, $\alpha = [\alpha_1, \alpha_2, \ldots, \alpha_N]^T$, I_{R_i} represents the inertia of the ith actuator, $\delta(.)$ is the Dirac delta function and $\rho_i^* = \rho_i + \delta(l_{f_i} - s_i) M_{R_{i+1}}$ in which ρ_i is the link mass per unit length and $M_{R_{i+1}}$ is the mass of $(i+1)$th actuator. The payload is represented by $M_{R_{N+1}}$. The potential energy density consists of two terms. The gravitational one is $U_{R_i} = g \rho_i^* x_i (\theta, \alpha, s_i)$, where g is the gravity constant. The second term, due to flexure, is given by $U_{f_i} = E_i I_i (\partial^2 \alpha_i / \partial s_i^2)^2 / 2$, in which E_i is the Young's modulus and I_i is the moment of inertia of the body section. Then

$$L_i (\theta, \dot\theta, \alpha, \dot\alpha, \partial^2 \alpha_i / \partial s_i^2)^2, s_i) = T_i (\theta, \dot\theta, \alpha, \dot\alpha, s_i) - U_i(\theta, \alpha, \partial^2 \alpha_i / \partial s_i^2)^2, s_i).$$

where $U_i = U_{R_i} + U_{f_i}$, and $L = \sum_{i=1}^{N} \int_0^{t_{f_i}} L_i \, ds_i$. Let us introduce the further variables (momentum densities)

$$\pi_{\theta_j} = \sum_{i=1}^{n} \frac{\partial L_i}{\partial \dot\theta_j}, \qquad \pi_{\alpha_j} = \sum_{i=1}^{n} \frac{\partial L_i}{\partial \dot\alpha_j}, \qquad j = 1, \ldots, N. \tag{18}$$

As well known, the equations of motion can be derived by minimizing the action functional $S = \int_{t_i}^{t_f} L \, dt$ with respect to θ_i, α_i $i = 1, \ldots, N$, where t_i and t_f are the initial and final time of motion respectively. The solution of this minimization problem, that is trajectory followed by the robot, is given by the solution of the Hamiltonian differential equations.

$$-\dot\pi_{\theta_j} = \sum_{i=1}^{N} \frac{\partial H_i}{\partial \theta_j}, \qquad -\dot\pi_{\alpha_j} = \sum_{i=1}^{N} \left(\frac{\partial H_i}{\partial \alpha_j} + \frac{d^2}{d s_j^2} \frac{\partial H_i}{\partial(\partial^2 \alpha_j / \partial s_j^2)} \right)$$
$$\tag{19}$$
$$-\dot\theta_j = \sum_{i=1}^{N} \frac{\partial H_i}{\partial \pi_{\theta_j}}, \qquad -\dot\alpha_j = \sum_{i=1}^{N} \frac{\partial H_i}{\partial \pi_{\alpha_j}}, \qquad j = 1, \ldots, N$$

in which H_i is the Hamiltonian density associated to the ith link, defined as

$$H_i = \pi_{\theta_i} \dot\theta_i + \pi_{\alpha_i} \dot\alpha_i - L_i. \tag{20}$$

When a generalized force $u_i(t)$ is applied to the ith joint, the first of equations (19) must be modified as follows

$$-\dot\pi_{\theta_j} = \sum_{i=1}^{N} \frac{\partial H_i}{\partial \theta_j} - u_j \delta(s_i). \tag{21}$$

Because of the geometrical constraints the following boundary conditions have to be satisfied $\alpha_i(t, s_i) \big|_{s_i=0} = 0$, $\frac{\partial \alpha_i(t, s_i)}{\partial s_i} \big|_{s_i=0} = 0$. The dynamic model (19) consists of nonlinear partial differential equations that are scarcely useful from the control and/or simulation points of view. In order to obtain an approximate model with only ordinary differential equations the Ritz method may be applied ([15], ch.2). According this method we can expand each generalized coordinate

α_i in a function series $\alpha_i(t, s_i) = \sum_{k=0}^{\infty} \beta_{k,i}(t)\psi_k(s_i)$, where the functions $\psi_k \in C^2([x_i, x_f])$ In particular, if an approximate description is sufficient for analysis purposes, the expansion can be truncated $\alpha_i(t, s_i) \cong \sum_{k=0}^{n_i} \beta_{k,i}(t)\psi_k(s_i)$. In the static case a body subjected to gravity forces takes the shape represented by a fourth order parabola. Hence, in a first approximation we select a complete set of functions which ensures zero error, in the static case, if we set $n = 4$; namely $\{\psi_k(s_i)\} = \{s_i^k\}$. With this choice, owing to the boundary conditions, we must set $\beta_{0,i} = \beta_{1,i} = 0$. In this way the dependence of α_i on the spatial parameter s_i has been made known and then the integral (18) for L can be, at least formally, computed. As a consequence, $\theta_i(t)$ and the coefficients $\beta_i(t)$ can be considered as generalized coordinates for the approximate modes. Denoting by $\beta(t) = (\beta_{2,1}, \ldots, \beta_{n_1,1}, \ldots, \beta_{n_N,N})^T$, the approximate model in the Hamiltonian form, when external forces are applied, is given by

$$\dot{\theta} = \frac{\partial H}{\partial p_\theta}, \qquad \dot{\beta} = \frac{\partial H}{\partial p_\beta}, \qquad -\dot{p}_\theta = \frac{\partial H}{\partial \theta} - u, \qquad -\dot{p}_\beta = \frac{\partial H}{\partial \beta} \qquad (22)$$

where the Hamiltonian function is $H = p_\theta^T \dot{\theta} + p_\beta^T \dot{\beta} - L$.

4   Application to a Single-Link Manipulator

A lot of applications of the flexible link manipulators exist and information about them may be found in the references (see for example [15]). Here we consider a mechanical system which consists of one elastic body with mass M and length l, which can rotate around one of its extremities by en external torque m. We suppose also that along the arm the modulus of elasticity E, the transverse area moment of inertia I and the mass per unit length ρ are constant. Two reference frames are defined in the plane of motion. The first frame (x, y) is inertial, has the origin in the joint and x - axis opposite to the gravity vector. The second one (x', y') is noninertial, has the same origin and x' - axis tangent in the joint to the flexed body. If the curve describing the body neutral line is sufficiently regular it can be presented, in the noninertial frame, by the parametric equations

$$x'(t, s) = s, \qquad y'(t, s) = \alpha(t, s), \qquad s \in [0, l] \qquad (23)$$

that in the inertial frame (x, y) take the form

$$x(t, s) = s \cos \theta(t) - \alpha(t, s) \sin \theta(t), \qquad y(t, s) = s \sin \theta(t) + \alpha(t, s) \cos \theta(t).$$

The Lagrangian function is then given by

$$L = \frac{M}{2l}[\alpha^2 \dot{\theta}^2 + (s\dot{\theta} + \dot{\alpha})^2] - \frac{Mg}{l}(s \cos \theta - \alpha \sin \theta) - \frac{EI}{2}(\frac{\partial^2 \alpha}{\partial s^2})^2. \qquad (24)$$

The momentum densities are expressed by

$$\pi_\theta = \frac{M}{l}(\alpha^2 \dot{\theta} + s^2 \dot{\theta} + s\dot{\alpha}) = \frac{\partial L}{\partial \dot{\theta}}, \qquad \pi_\alpha = \frac{M}{l}(s\dot{\theta} + \dot{\alpha}) = \frac{\partial L}{\partial \dot{\alpha}}. \qquad (25)$$

Taking into account the equation (20) for H_i, then from (19) and (21) we obtain

$$\dot{\pi}_\theta = \frac{Mg}{l}[s\sin\theta + \alpha\cos\theta)] + u\,\delta(s), \quad \dot{\pi}_\alpha = \frac{Mg}{l}\sin\theta + \frac{l}{\alpha^2 M}(\pi_\theta - s\,\pi_\alpha)EI\frac{\partial^4\alpha}{\partial s^4}$$

In this way we have constituted the exact model of the single-link arm. In order to derive a model with only ordinary differential equations, we substitute in (24) the generalized coordinates $\alpha(t, s)$ approximated by $\alpha(t, s_i) \cong \sum_{k=2}^{n}\beta_k(t)s_k$. After integrating along the link, the Lagrangian function can be derived. Finally, we can compute the generalized momenta

$$p_\theta = \frac{\partial L}{\partial\dot{\theta}} = M[\dot{\theta}(\frac{l^2}{3} + \sum_{k=2}^{n}\sum_{h=2}^{n}\beta_k\beta_h\frac{l^{k+h}}{k+h+1}) + \sum_{k=2}^{n}\dot{\beta}_k\frac{l^{k+1}}{k+2}]$$

$$p_{\beta_k} = \frac{\partial L}{\partial\dot{\beta}} = M[\sum_{h=2}^{n}\dot{\beta}_h\frac{l^{k+h}}{k+h+1} + \dot{\theta}\frac{l^{k+1}}{k+2}], \quad k = 2,\ldots,n. \tag{26}$$

Eqs.(26) can be rewritten in compact form $p = B\,\dot{q}$, $p = (p_\theta, p_{\beta_2}, \ldots, p_{\beta_n})^T$ and $q = (\theta, \beta_2, \ldots, \beta_n)^T$. The elements of the inertia matrix B are

$$b_{11} = [\frac{l^2}{3} + \sum_{k=2}^{n}\sum_{h=2}^{n}\beta_k\beta_h\frac{l^{k+h}}{k+h+1}]M, \quad b_{ij} = [\frac{l^{i+j}}{i+j+1}]M, \quad i, j \neq 1, 1.$$

Since the inertia matrix is nonsingular, we can derive the first equations of the Hamiltonian model $\dot{q} = B^{-1}p$. Substituting this equation into the Hamiltonian function $H = T+U$ and using the third and the fourth of Eq. (22), the remaining equations can be obtained. In particular, when the order of approximation $n = 2$, the motion equations are given by

$$\dot{\theta} = \frac{60\,(4\,l\,p_\theta - 5\,p_{\beta_2})}{M\,l^3\,(5 + 48\,\beta_2^2\,l^2)}, \quad \dot{\beta}_2 = \frac{20\,(20\,p_{\beta_2} + 12\,\beta_2^2\,l^2\,p_{\beta_2} - 15\,l\,p_\theta)}{M\,l^4\,(5 + 48\,\beta_2^2\,l^2)}$$

$$\dot{p}_\theta = g\,M\,(\frac{l}{2}\sin\theta + \frac{\beta_2\,l^2}{3}\cos\theta) + u \tag{27}$$

$$\dot{p}_{\beta_2} = \frac{720\,\beta_2}{M\,l}(\frac{5\,p_{\beta_2} - 4\,l\,p_\theta}{5 + 48\,\beta_2^2\,l^2})^2 + \frac{g\,M\,l^2}{3}\sin\theta - 4\,\beta_2\,E\,I\,l.$$

5   Conclusion

The paper treats the problem of dynamic modelling of flexible link manipulator using exact and approximate model based on Hamiltonian equations. As is known, the exact modelling of flexible manipulators leads to partial differential equations, which reflect the distributed nature of elasticity. However, a common practice is to use finite dimensional approximate models. The most popular are finite element method and the assumed modes method. Here, the adopted approximate model is obtained by using the Hamiltonian approach combined with the assumed modes method. The use of Hamiltonian equations allows us to get the dynamic model as a set of first-order nonlinear differential equations. This model is quite convenient for deriving nonlinear control law by using pseudo - linearization approach. In kinematical aspect, in presenting of the transformation matrices, a vector - parameterization of the rotation group is involved.

Acknowledgements. The author would like to thank the Alexander von Humboldt Foundation for donating the computer algebra system `Mathematica`® which was indispensable in realizing the above programme algorithm in symbolic form. It has to be noted also that this work is supported by Bulgarian NSF, Grant No. DO 02-262/2008 and Grant No. ID 02-14/2009.

References

1. Angeles, J.: Rational Kinematics. Springer, New York (1988)
2. Angeles, J., Kecskemethy, A.: Kinematics and Dynamics of Multi-Body Systems. In: CISM Courses and Lectures, vol. 360. Springer, New York (1995)
3. Bremer, H., Pfeiffer, F.: Elastic Multibody Systems (in German). Teubner, Stuttgart (1992)
4. Hassenpflug, W.: Rotation Angles. Computer Methods in Appl. Mechanics and Engineering 105, 111–124 (1993)
5. Ibrahimbegovic, A., Frey, F., Kozar, I.: Computational Aspects of Vector-like Parameterization of Three-Dimensional Finite Rotations. Int. J. Num. Methods in Engineering 38, 3653–3673 (1995)
6. Mathews, J.: Coordinate-free Rotation Formalism. Am. J. Phys. 44, 1210 (1976)
7. Mladenova, C.: An Approach to Description of a Rigid Body Motion. Comp. Rend. Bulg. Acad. Sci. 38, 1657–1660 (1985)
8. Mladenova, C.: Applications of a Lie Group Theory to the Modeling and Control of Multibody Systems. Multibody System Dynamics 4, 367–380 (1999)
9. Mladenova, C.: Group Theory in the Problems of Modeling and Control of Multi-Body Systems. J. Geometry and Symmetry in Physics 8, 17–121 (2006)
10. Mladenova, C.: An Approach for Computing the Euclidean Motions on the Base of Measurement Data. In: AIP Conf. Proc., vol. 1340, pp. 212–220 (2011), doi:10.1063/1.3567139
11. Mladenova, C.: The Rotation Group and its Mechanical Applications. International Book Market Service, Ltd. (2011)
12. Mladenova, C., Müller, P.: Dynamics and Control of Elastic Joint Manipulators. J. Intelligent & Robotic Systems 20, 23–44 (1997)
13. Rashkov, I., Mladenova, C.: Displacements of Elastic Link from Open-loop Kinematic Chain (manipulator). In: Proc. 36th Spring Conf. of the Union of Bulg. Mathematicians, Varna, Bulgaria, pp. 289–298 (2007)
14. Shabana, A.: Dynamics of Multibody Systems, 2nd edn. Cambridge Univ. Press, Cambridge (1998)
15. Tokhi, M.O., Azad, A.K.M.: Flexible Robot Manipulators: Modelling, Simulation and Control. Inst. of Engineering and Technology, London (2008)

An Outline for an Intelligent System Performing Peg-in-Hole Actions with Flexible Objects

Andreas Jordt[3], Andreas R. Fugl[1,2], Leon Bodenhagen[1], Morten Willatzen[2],
Reinhard Koch[3], Henrik G. Petersen[1], Knud A. Andersen[4],
Martin M. Olsen[4], and Norbert Krüger[1]

[1] The Maersk Mc-Kinney Moller Institute, University of Southern Denmark
{arf,lebo,hgp,norbert}@mmmi.sdu.dk
[2] Mads Clausen Institute, University of Southern Denmark
willatzen@mci.sdu.dk
[3] Institute of Computer Science, Christian-Albrechts-Universität Kiel, Germany
{jordt,rk}@mip.informatik.uni-kiel.de
[4] Centre for Robot Technology, Danish Technological Institute, Denmark
{kaa,mmo}@teknologisk.dk

Abstract. We describe the outline of an adaptable system which is able to perform grasping and peg-in-hole actions with flexible objects. The system makes use of visual tracking and shape reconstruction, physical modeling of flexible material and learning based on a kernel density approach. We show results for the different sub-modules in simulation as well as real world data.

1 Introduction

The manipulation of flexible objects in a dynamic and unconstrained situation poses a number of challenges on robotics. First, the configuration of the object shape needs to be sensed in 'real–time', i.e. computed fast enough to allow for a robot action. Second, properties of the material relevant for its deformation process must be sensed visually or haptically. Third, the deformation of the object under external forces is difficult to model and depends on the actual properties of the material. In addition, all sensing and actuating involves delays which requires to not only describe the current state of the object but at a future state (a usual offset is approx. 500ms) due to delays in the vision and robot processes. Fourth, the actual manipulation needs to be performed addressing the three challenges mentioned above. In this context it is unlikely that all parameters of the system can be estimated by analytic modeling only and hence it will be important to integrate some kind of learning in such a system.

In this paper, we outline a system which tackles all four problems mentioned above to perform grasping and peg-in-hole task with flexible objects (Fig. 1 shows the physical set-up and Fig. 2 the different steps of the process). More specifically, we address them in the following way:

1) Sensing of Object Shape: The acquisition process is split into two separate problems: (1) Capturing the 3D shape of the object in one stage and (2) tracking

S. Jeschke, H. Liu, and D. Schilberg (Eds.): ICIRA 2011, Part II, LNAI 7102, pp. 430–441, 2011.

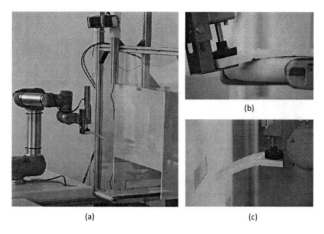

Fig. 1. a) Photo of whole set-up. b) Photo of grasping process. c) Photo of peg-in hole action.

its deformation and movement during the interaction with the robot in a second stage. This way, a capturing system with high spatial resolution can be applied while the object remains static on the conveyor, exploiting rigidity. Afterwards, a system of high temporal resolution can be employed tracking the object while it is manipulated, using the already known shape provided by the previous stage.

2) Sensing of Material properties: The material properties can be obtained by combining vision and haptic feedback together with physical modeling. Subject to given external forces acting on the surface of the body, the response of the material is acquired by vision tracking and force-displacement sensing from the robotic gripper. Knowing the deformed state of the body for a set of configurations allows the parameters of the physical model to be found by an inverse formulation.

3) Physical Modeling and Prediction: We use a mathematical representation of flexible objects based on the general linear elasticity equations of an isotropic medium. This requires us to solve three coupled partial differential equations (PDEs) in the three displacement components subject to boundary conditions that can be rigid, free, or forced. Given the PDE representation of the flexible object, it's form, external forces and knowledge of the material properties, we solve numerically for the displacements.

4) Manipulation and Learning: Learning needs to be applied in two contexts: First, in the grasping of the deformed objects (see Fig. 1b) and second the actual peg-in-hole action (see Fig. 1c). Both tasks are parametrized by extensions of the concept of grasp densities (see [4]) which is a kernel based learning method. This allows for an adaptation of the system based on experience gathered in simulation and real world execution.

In this paper, we will show results for the different sub-modules on real world data as well as simulation. Finding stable solutions for the first three problems and a successful integration into an embodied system opens possibilities

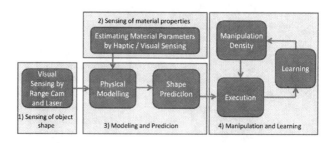

Fig. 2. Overview of the manipulation approach, for a detailed explanation see text

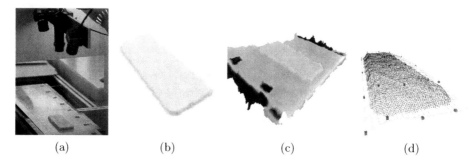

     (a)   (b)   (c)   (d)

Fig. 3. From left to right: Photo of the real object during the laser scan; The colored 3D scan of the object; 3D data from the Kinect camera showing the object; The object mesh (black) and the deformation surface (green)

in a number of application fields from industrial robotics (e.g., food production, manufacturing, etc.) to service robotics (e.g., feeding robots, helpers in kitchens, etc.). Earlier attempts have been made to create robot systems for the handling of flexible objects [1,8]. However, they were often restricted to a narrow class of elastic objects. We envision the ability to model and handle a much broader range of objects by the use of 3D vision, general continuum elasticity and learning.

2   State of the Art and Own Contributions

1) Sensing of Object Shape: Acquiring a 3D shape of a static object has been subject to research for a long time [13]. For the task at hand, a line structured light approach [3] provides the required quality and speed in 3D shape acquisition. We use a rig containing two cameras and one line laser (see Fig. 3a), where the second camera allows to increase the stability of the calibration [20].

Tracking the 3D deformation of objects is a task far more complex. The research performed in this area has been done with a wide range of applied hardware and algorithms. Incorporated sensors range from multi-projector[6] and multi-camera systems [17] [2], active range cameras [9] down to stereo [21] and even monocular camera systems [18], from which the deformation has to be computed. For the task at hand we will not be able to observe the object from all sides because of the interaction with the robot, hence we will stick to an approach similar to [9], based on the combination of range camera and color camera. In our test setup we use a PrimeSense Kinect to acquire color and depth information. The basic approach is to deform the high resolution scan received from the laser stage using NURBS functions [14], such that it fits the observations of range- and color camera.

2) Sensing of Material properties: In [23] they equipped a robot hand with strain gauges and performed haptic exploration of the environment. Soft and hard objects could be distinguished and classified. However, no estimation of material parameters was attempted. In [19] they performed tests by rolling indenters to locate and identify simulated tumors inside elastic material mimicking tissue. By gathering force and deformation data, the parameters for a hyperelastic model was found by the Newton-Rhapson method. For our task however, we do not have the boundary conditions as controlled and we must employ a full 3D model for approximation. [5] did experiments on determining the importance of controlling boundary conditions. They relied on using cylindrical samples and tightly controlled boundary conditions to allow for analytical solutions to the inverse problem. We instead rely on the numerical approximations by the finite difference method to handle complicated surface geometries and several free boundary conditions.

3) Physical Modeling and Prediction: The underlying elasticity equations for a general elastic material are well-known and their solutions to a general forced input [11,24]. However, a complete and numerically tractable PDE-based physical model of a flexible object subject to a comprehensive set of relevant boundary conditions, used in the context of robot-gripping dynamics, is not available in the literature today. Much work has been done however to tailor mass-spring models [15], to suit the physical parameters of real material. [12] used mass-spring models to mimic elasticity in cloth and thread handling using robots and in performing real-time surgery simulation. The approach however was manually tuned for both spring topology and spring constants and no track of modeling errors was presented. [8] outlined a system for the characteristics of grasping of flexible objects, modeled by mass-spring. The model was intended to supply estimates for the required grasping force, to reliably manipulate an object. However not many simulation results were presented, and no measure could be seen on modeling errors. The same approach to employ mass-spring models was used in [16]. They showed realistic contact behavior for pure compression, but admitted problems with handling shear strain due to their spring topology.

4) Manipulation and Learning: The different components of the system integrated in the setup shown in Fig. 1 represent a complex robot–vision system. It is known that a stable working of such systems is a challenging engineering task. To account for these complexities and to become more robust to exact calibrations of the different sub-components we apply learning from the experiments the robot system experiences by means of kernel density methods [22,4]. To our knowledge, there exist very few adaptable systems in such industrial settings and we think that the exploration of the potential of adaptable systems is an important step towards more intelligent systems in future production.

3   The Four Modules of the System

The overall architecture of our system is sketched in Fig. 2. Starting with the visual extraction process (as outlined in section 3.1) and the haptically estimation process (section 3.2), the physical modeling of the material is performed which then lead to the prediction of the state of the flexible object at the moment of manipulation (section 3.3). An appropriate action then is executed and evaluated as described in section 3.4. The evaluated action is then input for the learning of grasp and manipulation densities.

3.1   Sensing of Object Shape

There are multiple ways to describe the deformation of a 3D shape. The most intuitive and the most common way for shapes given as triangle meshes is to simply displace the vertices of a mesh in 3D space. It is widely used in deformation tracking (e.g. [2],[18],[21]). But as a side effect, this very high dimensional degree of freedom entails ambiguities and under-determined equation systems, so every approach fitting vertex positions directly to the data usually comes with a set of additional side constrains and regularization terms attached to it. For an approach aiming at producing results in real-time a search space of much lower dimension is required, containing regularization and side conditions implicitly in the domain reduction of the search space.

In our setup, NURBS surfaces [14] are used to approximate the object surface very roughly. For that matter, its degree of freedom does not accommodate the actual surface shape of the object but the ability to model its deformation, leading to a surface function described by only a few control points. The missing high-frequency information on the objects surface is added to the NURBS surface function for each mesh vertex separately with a displacement value. In fact, the initial NURBS surface does not have to match the objects surface shape at all, as long as its deformation along with the per-vertex displacement is able to describe the deformation of the actual object properly. For the proposed setting, the initial NURBS function is simply defined as a 2D bounding box to the scanned object (see Fig. 3d).

To register a set of vertices to a NURBS surface, for each vertex the parameter of the NURBS surface point closest to this vertex is saved, along with its offset from the surface. This registration can be seen as a conversion of the vertex coordinates from the world coordinate system (x, y, z) to the NURBS coordinate system (u, v, d), where u and v are the parameters of a NURBS surface point and d is the offset perpendicular to the surface . Given the projections of the calibrated [20] setup and the object position, the deformation tracking can be expressed as a minimization problem.

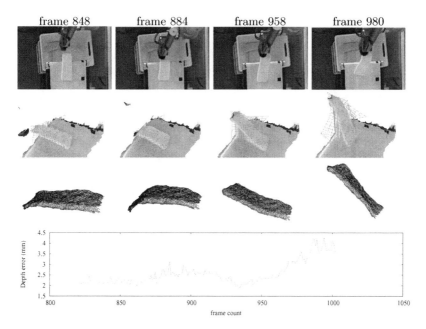

Fig. 4. Images from a deformation sequence recorded with the Kinect camera. From top to bottom: The actual color image from the Kinect camera; The colored 3D mesh from the Kinect data with deformation NURBS surface (green); Deformed high resolution mesh; The average vertex error for frames 820 - 1000 of the recording.

The control points of the NURBS surface can be adjusted to the color and depth data by evaluating a cost function in an analysis by synthesis like approach: For each configuration of control points, the corresponding surface function yields a set of vertex positions in the world coordinate system, which can be compared to the actual distances and color measurements by projecting the 3D position into the known color- and depth camera centers.

The minimization task is solved by the CMA-ES [7] optimization method (Covariance Matrix Adaptation - Evolution Strategy), a particle filter like algorithm which is able to circumvent possible local minima in the consistency costs. An example for such a deformed mesh is depicted in Fig. 4.

Results on Tracking of Flexible Objects. An appropriate way to measure the accuracy of an analysis by synthesis system is to simply compare the synthesis with the actual measurements. The tracking algorithm was tested with an image sequence from an interaction of robot and deformable material. An object of 8mm×60mm×150mm is tracked while grasped and lifted by the robot (Fig. 4).

The Kinect device has an quantization step size of approx. 2.5mm at the object distance (970 mm). Fig. 4 (bottom) depicts the average depth error (RMS) of the deformed object vertices during this interaction, i.e. the average difference between the measured distance and the calculated distance between vertex and camera center.

It shows that the reprojection error is below the quantization step size of the Kinect camera for the most part of the sequence. The increased error value at the end of the sequence (frame 970 and following) is due to the increased slope of the tracked object. Since the number of quantized measurements becomes less while the difference between these measurements increases due to the high slope, the quantization error increases as well, while the quality of the fit remains the same (apparent in Fig. 4, frame 980, second row).

3.2   Sensing of Material Properties

We propose two methods for determining the parameters of the elasticity model, applicable to the use in robotics work cells. Both methods rely on applying a known force distribution and measuring the resulting deformation to provide data for the inverse calculation of elasticity parameters.

Our first proposal is to observe the deformation of the elastic object by the means of 3D deformation tracking, using vision. In this case, the robot manipulator makes a preliminary grasp of the object and presents it to the vision system, hanging freely only under the influence of gravity. Sampling the resulting deformation for a wide range of poses, we construct an inverse formulation by the use of the numerical models of elasticity and estimate the model parameters.

Our second proposal employs the use of the force-controllable gripper mounted on the robot. This gives us the ability to apply accurately force distributions to the object and measure the resulting deformation.

To model both processes, we require accurate information on the effect of real-world boundary conditions and measurement errors. For this we have first investigated their effects on off-line experiments. Obtaining the stress-strain response of an elastic object is conceptually simple, but require careful considerations as to properly control and model boundary conditions. Should a boundary condition be improperly modeled, e.g. slipping of a surface point assumed to be fixed, considerable errors in estimating parameters will be present [5].

Results on Sensing Material Properties. The setup of an off-line experiment can be seen on Fig. 5. A large cylindrical piece of silicone rubber (15 cm in diameter) is deformed by a pressure bench capable of producing several hundred kilograms of load.

On Fig. 5 the relationship between the applied stress and the strain is for large part of the curve linear. Young's modulus may be directly determined by the slope of the curve. In this case, it is determined to be 930 kPa In the first part of the stress-strain curve, the effects of measuring resolution and indeterminate boundary conditions are evident as a non-linear response. As [5] we can only rely on the stress-strain curve, when we pre-load the sample (corresponds to discarding the first part of the curve).

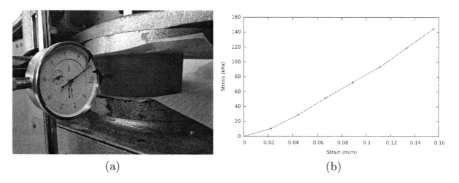

(a)   (b)

Fig. 5. (a) Offline estimation of material parameters. Putting material samples in a pressure testing machine is the classic way of estimating material parameters for a linearly elastic objects. (b) Stress-strain curve for the silicone rubber undergoing uniform compression.

3.3 Modeling and Prediction

In our approach we use a linear model for elasticity (for small deformations) which is the classical and most simple model of an elastic material [11]. The elastic model accommodates a linear relationship between stress and strain of a solid material; the coupling tensor is known as the stiffness tensor. Despite the limitations of a linear model, a linear approximation for many materials and for simple load-distributions and object geometries is sufficient to derive analytical and quantitative solutions. In particular, it is suitable in the context of our work since the full model involves dynamic solution of a system where vision and manipulation aspects are considered in conjunction with detailed equations-of-motion for the dynamic behavior.

An important case is for isotropic (i.e., material microstructure composition is directionally independent) and homogeneous materials (i.e., material properties are independent of position). Such materials are the simplest possible in terms of elasticity complexity and only two elastic parameters are needed: Young's modulus and Poisson's ratio. Together with the mass density of the object, this completely defines the model for the object. This is contained in the Navier-Cauchy PDE providing the motion of an elastic body:

$$\rho \frac{\partial^2 u}{\partial t^2} = (\lambda + \mu)\nabla(\nabla \cdot u) + \mu\nabla^2 u \tag{1}$$

where u is the local deformation and t is time; The material parameters are the two Lamé coefficients (μ and λ) and the mass density ρ.

Note that having very few material parameters is highly desirable to reduce the parameter estimation problem of section (3.2). It is the plan to implement an online estimation of these parameters in the near future.

We use the Finite Difference Method, for approximating the Navier-Cauchy PDE and solving for the objects as provided by the vision stage. As opposed

Fig. 6. Left: The real-life deformation of an elastic object, before a peg-in-hole task. **Right:** The deformation process of an elastic object, as predicted by the physical modeling.

to traditional regular grid methods, requiring uniforms grids we use adaptive grids which give us high spatial resolution near the object boundaries while maintaining a low resolution in the object interiors.

As an example for the modeling of a flexible object is given in Fig. 6 in which the deformation process before a peg-in-hole action is shown in the real image as well as predicted by the elasticity model. From the simulation, an estimated deflection angle of the object can be calculated and provided for motion planning to move the robot.

Results. For the test shown in Fig. 6 we use a cuboid piece of soft silicone rubber. The silicone rubber has an estimated value for Young's modulus of $E = 930$ kPa, mass density $\rho = 755$ g/cm^3 and a tabulated value for Poisson's ratio of $\sigma = 0.49$. These values constitute the model parameters, as used in the numerical method. We model the area of the object in contact with the gripper with fixed boundary conditions. The rest of the surface has no-stress boundary conditions and are thus free to move.

We get good correspondence in both shape and deflection angle. For the situation of Fig. 6 we calculate the maximum deflection angle to be 33 degrees from the horizontal plane in simulations, whereas it was measured in experiments to 31 degrees. We also capture the effects of edge singularities, with the material buckling slightly upwards toward, seen both real-world and simulations.

3.4   Execution and Learning

The mechanical part of the demonstrator for bundling all the technologies, is made in lightweight materials such as framework in aluminum profiles, which allows fast and easy changes and even fast dismantling and assembly moving the demonstrator to new facilities. The plates are glued together using square laths in the corners to increase the surfaces for the glue. This gives a lightweight strong construction which is in the same time anti-static and eliminate transmission of eventual mechanical noise from the robot.

The gripper is a special design using a SMAC-actuator [1]. The gripper has a force-feedback and can at the same time give very accurate information about its position, which allows us to measure the impact into the surface of the object compared to applied force. To make realistic testing on flexible objects on different sites at the same time having same properties on the objects we manufactured synthetic meat objects by means of casted silicone models.

The grasping knowledge, generated by each executed grasp, is encoded in grasp densities (see [4]). Given a set of evaluated grasps, where each grasp is represented as an object-relative 6D pose, grasp densities estimate the distribution of successful grasps $p\,(pose|success)$ using kernel density estimation (see also Fig. 7). If the distribution of grasps is uniform, the value of the density at a given pose will be proportional to success-likelihood $P\,(success|pose)$ of the corresponding grasp. If the grasps are not distributed uniformly two approaches are available: Importance sampling can be used to weight the samples according to their distribution (see [4]) or Bayes theorem can be applied to obtain $P\,(success|pose)$.

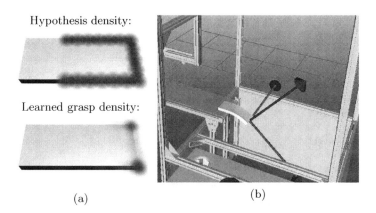

(a)   (b)

Fig. 7. (a) Projection of the grasp hypothesis density on the undeformed objects (top) and a projection of the learned density (bottom) – the more opaque the red color is, the higher the value of the density is. (b) View from the simulator. The coordinated frame for the grasps is defined based on the deflection of the object.

Once a density is learned it can be used to obtain grasps with a maximum likelihood for being successful. Future grasp knowledge can then be integrated to the density by a batch-learning approach. However, an initial exploratory learning strategy is costly to perform in a real world setup, as the majority of the grasps can be expected to fail. Therefore one aim of this project is to integrate the handling of flexible objects into a simulation environment (see [10]) enabling initial learning in the simulator. Subsequently the learned grasp density can be refined based on real world experiments.

---

[1] http://www.smac-mca.com

Results. An example of a learned density is visualized on Fig. 7. The hypothesis density has been defined for the undeformed object. As the gripper is designed to grasp an object at its borders (see Fig. 6), only the border of the object is considered for the hypothesis density. An projection of the hypothesis density integrating over all orientations is shown on Fig. 7a (top). From the hypothesis density random samples are drawn, transformed according to the maximum deflection angle of the object and evaluated based in a force-closure criteria in the simulator. Fig. 7b shows a screenshot from the simulator with the tilted coordinate frame highlighted. A projection of the grasp density, based on the succeeding examples, is shown on Fig. 7a (bottom). It is evident that most grasps succeeded at the corners of the object. This has been expected as a wider range of different orientations of the gripper will lead to successful grasps at the corners.

4 Discussion

We have outlined a robot system for the handing of flexible objects. The different submodules required for such a system have been described and evaluated. These evaluations indicate the feasibility of the integration of the sub–modules into one system on which we are currently working.

Previous robotics systems handling flexible objects, have been tailored to specific sub-classes. Often both visual sensing and physical modeling focus exclusively on an individual, specific task. We believe that by combining vision, general and accurate modelling, and learning techniques, our system design has a strong potential to cope with a broad range of different tasks in manipulating flexible objects. The peg-in-hole action with flexible objects is one such task with a number of challenges that we aim to solve with our system.

Acknowledgments. This work was co-financed by the INTERREG 4 program Syddanmark-Schleswig-K.E.R.N. by EU funds from the European Regional Development Fund.

References

1. Bell, M.: Flexible object manipulation. Ph.D. thesis, Dartmouth College Hanover, New Hampshire (2010)
2. Cagniart, C., Boyer, E., Ilic, S.: Probabilistic Deformable Surface Tracking from Multiple Videos. In: Daniilidis, K., Maragos, P., Paragios, N. (eds.) ECCV 2010. LNCS, vol. 6314, pp. 326–339. Springer, Heidelberg (2010)
3. Chen, C.H., Kak, A.C.: Modelling and calibration of a structured light scanner for 3d robot vision. In: IEEE Conf. on Robotics and Automation, pp. 807–815 (1987)
4. Detry, R., Kraft, D., Kroemer, O., Bodenhagen, L., Peters, J., Krüger, N., Piater, J.: Learning grasp affordance densities. Paladyn Journal of Behavioral Robotics (2011) (accepted)
5. Erkamp, R., Wiggins, P., Skovoroda, A., Emelianov, S., ODonnell, M.: Measuring the elastic modulus of small tissue samples. Ann Arbor 1001, 48109–2125 (1998)

6. Griesser, A., Koninckx, T.P., Gool, L.V.: Adaptive real-time 3d acquisition and contour tracking within a multiple structured light system. In: Proceedings of the Computer Graphics and Applications, 12th Pacific Conference, PG 2004 (2004)
7. Hansen, N.: The CMA evolution strategy: a comparing review. In: Towards a New Evolutionary Computation. Advances on Estimation of Distribution Algorithms. Springer, Heidelberg (2006)
8. Howard, A., Bekey, G.: Recursive learning for deformable object manipulation. In: Proceedings., 8th Int.l Conf. on Advanced Robotics, ICAR 1997 (1999)
9. Jordt, A., Schiller, I., Bruenger, J., Koch, R.: High-Resolution Object Deformation Reconstruction with Active Range Camera. In: Goesele, M., Roth, S., Kuijper, A., Schiele, B., Schindler, K. (eds.) Pattern Recognition. LNCS, vol. 6376, pp. 543–552. Springer, Heidelberg (2010)
10. Jørgensen, J.A., Ellekilde, L.-P., Petersen, H.G.: RobWorkSim - an open simulator for sensor based grasping. In: Joint 41st Int. Sym. on Robotics, ISR (2010)
11. Landau, L.D., Pitaevskii, L.P., Lifshitz, E.M., Kosevich, A.M.: Theory of Elasticity. Butterworth-Heinemann (1986)
12. Mosegaard, J.: Cardiac Surgery Simulation - Graphics Hardware meets Congenital Heart Disease. Ph.D. thesis, Department of Computer Science, University of Aarhus, Denmark (2006)
13. Nehab, D.: Advances in 3D Shape Acquisition. Ph.D. thesis, Princeton University (September 2007)
14. Piegl, L.: On nurbs: a survey. IEEE Comput. Graph. Appl. 11, 55–71 (1991)
15. Provot, X.: Deformation constraints in a mass-spring model to describe rigid cloth behaviour. Graphics Interface (1995)
16. Reznik, D., Laugier, C.: Dynamic simulation and virtual control of a deformable fingertip. In: Proceedings. IEEE International Conference on Robotics and Automation, vol. 2, pp. 1669–1674. IEEE (1996)
17. Rosenhahn, B., Kersting, U., Powell, K., Klette, R., Klette, G., Seidel, H.P.: A system for articulated tracking incorporating a clothing model. Machine Vision and Applications 18(1), 25–40 (2007)
18. Salzmann, M., Lepetit, V., Fua, P.: Deformable surface tracking ambiguities. In: CVPR. IEEE Computer Society (2007)
19. Sangpradit, K., Liu, H., Seneviratne, L., Althoefer, K.: Tissue identification using inverse finite element analysis of rolling indentation. In: IEEE International Conference on Robotics and Automation, ICRA 2009, pp. 1250–1255 (May 2009)
20. Schiller, I., Beder, C., Koch, R.: Calibration of a pmd camera using a planar calibration object together with a multi-camera setup. In: The International Archives of the Photogrammetry, Remote Sensing and Spatial Information Sciences, vol. XXXVII. Part B3a (2008)
21. Shen, S., Zheng, Y., Liu, Y.: Deformable surface stereo tracking-by-detection using second order cone programming. In: ICPR, pp. 1–4. IEEE (2008)
22. Silverman, B.W.: Density Estimation for Statistics and Data Analysis. Chapman and Hall/CRC (1986)
23. Takamuku, S., Gomez, G., Hosoda, K., Pfeifer, R.: Haptic discrimination of material properties by a robotic hand. In: IEEE 6th Int. Conf. on Development and Learning, ICDL (2007)
24. Willatzen, M., Wang, L.: Mathematical modelling of one-dimensional piezoelectric transducers based on monoclinic crystals. Acta Acustica united with Acustica 93(6), 716–721 (2007)

Framework for Use of Generalized Force
and Torque Data in Transitional Levels of Autonomy

Kyle Schroeder and Mitch Pryor

Kyle.a.schroeder@utexas.edu, mpryor@mail.utexas.edu

Abstract. Manipulation of hazardous materials requires the use of robotics to limit exposure of human operators to the danger. In order to improve manipulator effectiveness while ensuring reliability and redundancy, layers of control are implemented in increments. Each level of autonomy is established such that should a fault occur, the control system can be operated at a lower level of autonomy. Force and torque data can be used as both a structural element of a level of autonomy and for fault detection. This paper presents a framework for the use of generalized force and torque data for improving manipulator safety, operational effectiveness, and world model augmentation. The framework is applied to a demonstration of the automated door opening.

Keywords: force control, position based force control, autonomy.

1   Introduction

Robotics and automation are used to limit human exposure to hazardous materials and radiation. So far at the US National Laboratories, task sequences and environments have been strictly controlled for automation or, when the environment cannot be controlled, robots are used in a teleoperated mode[17][14] [12][15].

Fig. 1. National Laboratory Robotic Applications: Hot cells [12] ARIES [17] Mighty Mouse [15] and Pit Viper [14]

Fig. 2 illustrates the range of task- and environment-structure. The horizontal axis indicates the level of certainty in the knowledge of the environment. The extreme right side of the figure indicates environments in which everything is known to a high level of certainty, i.e. the contents of the environment and their locations. The left side indicates that the environment is completely unknown to robot and operator before

S. Jeschke, H. Liu, and D. Schilberg (Eds.): ICIRA 2011, Part II, LNAI 7102, pp. 442–451, 2011.
© Springer-Verlag Berlin Heidelberg 2011

beginning the tasks. The vertical axis indicates the level of structure in task specification. At the top of the figure are known operations with well-defined tasks and sequences for completion.

At the bottom of the figure are those goals for which the tasks and their sequences are not known. Surgical robots are near the bottom left of this figure because the interior of a human's body cannot be modeled with high accuracy before exploration (figure left). Similarly, surgery often requires feedback from that exploration before the tasks and their sequence can be confidently identified (figure bottom). Factory floor automation is near the upper right corner because the environment is highly-controlled (figure right) and the sequence of tasks is well defined (figure top). Similar instances at the US National Labs can be identified.[12][15] Efforts, such as the Sphere Cleanout project,[3] aim to automate the projects in the center region; semi-structured tasks in semi-structured environments.

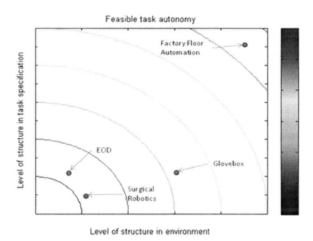

Fig. 2. Task and environment autonomy for robotic systems

Researchers have worked to develop algorithms which function in environments which are less structured. Many use vision, force, and other data to relax the environmental restrictions.[1][7] Some use the data to enhance the ability to perform a particular task.[11] Others use the data to increase the compliance of the manipulator, but a particular task is not explicitly defined.[19] Due to the large time commitments and investment costs required for deployment of the algorithms being demonstrated in research labs, many robots in industry still rely on position feedback.

Key to the evolution-instead-of-revolution approach to improving the dissemination of state-of-the-art robotic technologies is developing a framework that implements capabilities incrementally. With this approach, the objective is to not continually perform research on the elusive autonomous system of the future, but rather incrementally add features to a baseline system that improve the safety, performance, and/or efficiency. Additionally, such features must be easy to add and remove from the operational control loop so that they do not inhibit the command and control capabilities of a trained operator.

Our approach will focus on manipulation. It also recognizes that the primary intelligence in the control loop will continue to be the operator for the foreseeable future and yet the robotics development community has provided significant capabilities to ease the burden on that operator in most operational situations. Table 1 summarizes the proposed transitional levels from a purely directive mode (either tele-operation or the teaching of a rote, static process) to an idealized autonomous system.

Table 1. Transitional Levels of Autonomy

Level	Tele-operation → Autonomy...
1	Reduce operator's need to manage the robot's internal configuration.
2	Reduce operator's responsibility for avoiding contact with environment.
3	Reduce operator's need to move the robot to locations of interest.
4	Reduce operator's responsibility for selecting grasping configurations.
5	Allow the operator to quickly direct the system to complete tasks that involve subtasks (such as pick & place).
6	Reduce operator's responsibility to avoid threshold forces for contact tasks.
7	Reduce the levels of detail required for the operator to specify a task.
8	Integrate capability to complete task that require high levels of precision and/or the control a specific force profile
9	Reduce the need for the operator to be in the loop for tasks that respond to external events (i.e. timer on oven, low battery notification, etc.)
10	Based on prior tasks completed, the system anticipates future tasks.

For most operations at the National Labs, the lack of structure in the task or environment prevents the human from being completely removed from the loop. The high level control schemes for autonomy thus need to be applied in fault-tolerant transitional layers – so the robot can transition between levels of autonomy. The algorithms should incorporate the operator in decision making and provide information to the operator about the progress, success, or failure of the task. Feedback from any sensor can be useful for the development of these transitional levels of autonomy but this paper focuses on the use of generalized force data.

This framework provides a basis for implementation of kinematic control using generalized force feedback. The goal of the framework is to outline the near-term use of force data and facilitate automation in the region around the "Glovebox" point of Fig. 2. The framework addresses the challenges of a semi-unstructured environment and highly-unstructured task sequence. The framework facilitates the sharing of tasks and an environment (in space, if not in time) by humans and machines. Three areas are targeted by the framework:

- Safety
- Easing operator burden, and
- Task automation.

First, the generalized force data will be defined. Then generalized sensor types will be discussed. Then, the methods of force data usage will be presented. Then the framework will be implemented on a demonstration in which a serial manipulator will use force data to assist in the opening of a cabinet door given minimal *a priori* knowledge of the environment or input from other sensors. The opening of doors using force data has been demonstrated before [11][9][2], but this work applies the framework to this task with the goal of improving the safety of the task and of reducing the operator burden. Fault tolerance is implemented with online recovery in some cases, but with outlets to return control to the operator when necessary. A balance between algorithm development effort and task-completion effort is chosen for practicality in an industrial setting.

2   Generalized Force Data

Complete force data shall be defined as having three components.

— Detection of Contact Force

At the lowest level, a potential contact force is identified as a binary state; there is or is not an anomalous force. This level of data requires an expected value for the force. Methods for generating the expected values include biasing the sensor and modeling the manipulator dynamics.

— Location of Effective Force

The location of the force is a point in the frame of the manipulator. This is important for determining the magnitude and direction of force but may also be important to some collision detection algorithms or for ensuring the point of contact is in the desired location as in manipulation tasks. In some cases, multiple points of contact may be used.

— Magnitude and Direction of Force

The last force data, magnitude and direction, are coupled in collection and importance. They are generally represented in the form of a six-element vector. The magnitude of the force is obviously important for successful task completion and safety. In most cases, the direction of force is also important.

3   Force Data Collection

When designing a control algorithm to use force data, it is obviously necessary to identify the capabilities of the force sensor or to choose a sensor based on the requirements. Force data in robotics applications are collected by one of three means.

— Six-Axis Force/Torque Sensors

Six-axis force sensors measure all forces and torques relative to three orthogonal axes at a point. These sensors are capable of detecting forces outboard of the sensor. Sensors are often mounted at the wrist for convenient determination and control of contact and manipulation forces.[16] Demonstrations of contact detection over the entire length of the manipulator have been made using 2 six-axis sensors, one at the base and one at the end effector.[7]

— Actuation-Force Sensors

Sensors at the point of actuation, such as joint torque sensors, can detect forces over the entire body of the manipulator and have been used to demonstrate full-manipulator collision detection [13] and high-level torque control methods such as impedance control.[4] The ability of actuator force sensors to measure forces in particular directions is dependent upon the manipulator configuration.

— Contact Skins

Contact skins are very effective for the first and second modes of force data collection (Detection and Location). The large area covered by skins make them effective for detecting collisions. Because they are generally on the outside of the manipulator, they seldom require modeling of non-contact forces. Advanced skins are now capable of detecting forces in at least one direction and measuring magnitude making them effective inputs for tasks requiring control of contact forces in the task space. [10],[8]

4   Framework for Use of Generalized Force Data

Full teleoperation is an option for the "Glovebox" region of Fig. 2. However, the framework aims to improve the efficiency of the operator/robot task by improving manipulator safety and reducing operator burden. The framework does not exclude the developments by so many other researchers in the area of force and torque data usage,[1][16][7][13][4][19][6] but proposes a framework for the application of these algorithms in a strategy employing transitional levels of autonomy. The data are used for three aspects of controller design.

4.1   Safety

Force data can be monitored continuously to ensure manipulator safety. Data of only the lowest form (existence of anomalous force) is required for basic safety algorithms.[7][13] The simplest response is to stop the manipulator and return manual control to the operator. More advanced methods for response to collisions have also been realized. [1] Safe-force-monitoring applies to all levels of autonomy, from teleoperation to fully-autonomous behavior. At teleoperation levels, it may stop the manipulator and notify the operator or it may be used to guide teleoperation.

4.2   Task Completion

Force data are useful feedback for task completion. Compliance and impedance control have been successfully demonstrated many times.[4][19]   Much work has been done on the use of force data in specific areas of task completion.[11][9][2] The use of force data can be divided into five categories.

1. As a requirement for success, e.g., a particular force is required to fasten a rivet, tighten a screw, etc.
2. As a secondary requirement to achieve a task, e.g., a paint removal task may require a particular application of force.[6]
3. For alignment purposes such as assembly tasks.
4. For world model augmentation. Geometric constraints can be obtained from the position data collected while controlling the force in a particular direction. [11]
5. Serve as an indicator of algorithm success or failure, enhancing the effectiveness of the transitional levels of autonomy.

4.3   Operator Burden

In the glovebox task space, the operator chooses most of the actions to be performed, but at a higher level than teleoperation. Rather than choose the joint angles or even end effector location and orientation, these may be part of an automation unit. The automation of some tasks, by use of force data as outlined above or any other means is easier for the operator than full teleoperation. Force data can be used to assist the operator by indicating task success or failure and by providing additional information about the environment. From this, the operator can choose the next tasks to be completed.

4.4   Framework

The framework uses the generalized force data (anomalous force detection, contact location, and force magnitude/direction) and the methods of force data collection to define a method for implementing those methods in research using force feedback.

The first two steps are completed simultaneously. The task requirements are defined based on which data are provided by the available sensors. Concurrently, the sensors used are chosen based on the required data for task completion.

Next the anomalous force thresholds must be defined. From a system perspective, these thresholds may be determined by sensor noise, resolution, and range, model deficiencies, or robot payload. Task-specific thresholds are identified in the controller subsystems.

The controller subsystems are designed to complete portions of the overall task. The breaks between them should be where the control strategy changes, e.g. position-control changes to force-following, or significant data (vision-analysis, operator input, etc) must be collected to continue.

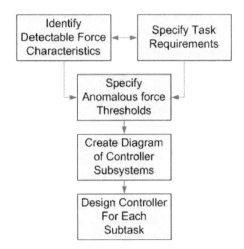

Fig. 3. Framework for the use of generalized force data

Lastly, these subtasks must be linked together in a meaningful way. Force data prepare the system to handle the next step. In the following demonstration, force data is collected while pulling the door ajar. This data is used to estimate the hinge location of the door, which is used in the final subtask, pushing the door completely open.

5   Demonstration and Implementation

The force data framework was applied to the task of remotely opening a cabinet door. The cabinet has a flat face and opens about a vertical hinge. The manipulator is a 7 degree of freedom Schunk LWA3 Lightweight Arm mounted on a mobile platform. The mobile platform is positioned in front of the cabinet before execution of the task. The system is shown in Fig. 4.

Fig. 4. System Configuration and Video Feedback for Door Opening Demonstration

Safety was improved by the sensing of force data during task execution. Operator burden was reduced by collecting world model data and automating the task. Transitional levels of autonomy were implemented in the form of task completion feedback to the operator. The algorithm checks its own progress for success throughout the course of the algorithm and provides a useful means for the operator to intervene, reinitiate the algorithm, or complete the task by teleoperation.

A three-fingered Barrett Hand grasper is mounted on the end effector. An ATI Gamma six-axis force/torque sensor is mounted at the wrist of the manipulator. The operator sees video feedback from a Swiss Ranger IR vision sensor mounted below the manipulator. The Swiss Ranger provides a 3-D point cloud representation of its field of view Fig. 4. The operator only has to identify the position of the latch from this video data and command the manipulator to open the door. Milestones for success incorporate force data and the operator is again brought into the loop if a milestone cannot be reached by automation alone.

Task: Identify and remove item from laboratory that may have triggered alarm.
Sub task: move system to area of interest in lab.
— System Autonomy: high. The mobile system knows the location of the alarm and moves to the area of interest.
— Possible operator intervention requests: Identify a new route or teleoperate the system around a difficult obstacle.
Sub task: Identify items of interest.
— System Autonomy: low. The system may recognize the containers outside but not inside the cabinet.
— Possible operator intervention requests: Designate the cabinet door to be opened.
Sub task: Open the latch.
— System Autonomy: moderate. The operator may identify using a vision sensor latch location and type. Latch is found and opened using force data.
— Possible operator intervention requests: For unfamiliar latches, system may request commands from the operator.
Sub task: Open the cabinet door.
— System Autonomy: high. The latch model is refined using force data. This data is also used to determine the door radius.
— Possible operator intervention requests: The cabinet is locked, latch fails, or forces exceed normal ranges.
Sub task: Inspect the cabinet.
— System Autonomy: high. Cylinder recognition and radiation detection allow task completion with high level of autonomy.
— Possible operator intervention requests: Unrecognized objects in the cabinet need to be inspected.
Sub task: Retrieve canister of interest.
— System Autonomy: variable. If the canister is identified, and the robot knows how to grasp it, the autonomy is high.
— Possible operator intervention requests: If the item of interest is obstructed, the operator may need to command other pick and place moves.

The framework presented deals specifically with the use of force data. In the demonstration, force data were used for detecting the location of the door and latch, actuation of the latch, and opening the door. Success was monitored in the form of positive contact forces during actuation tasks. For example, if the lifting force on the latch disappears, it is assumed the manipulator has lost contact with the latch and the operator regains control and can evaluate the system state and how to proceed. Additionally, world model data was collected through the use of the force data. The door hinge location and the radius of the door were estimated online in a manner similar to that presented by Petersson [11]. In Petersson, the door was pulled completely open. In this example, the door was opened in two steps, pulling ajar, then pushing completely open. While the door was pulled ajar, the lateral forces were minimized. The location of the end effector was recorded and a circle was fit to these points. (Fig. 5) The radius of the door and the location of the hinge is carried to the next stage where the door is pushed open about a circle centered at the hinge.

During the execution of the algorithm, the forces at the end effector are monitored to ensure they never exceed safe limits. If the algorithm is unable to maintain these forces below the safe threshold itself, the operator is brought back into the loop.

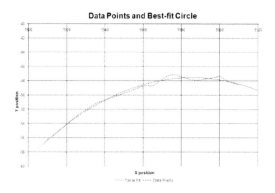

Fig. 3. Collected data points and best-fit circle for door hinge location

6   Conclusions

The generalized force framework presented in this paper is used as a guide for the development of the door-opening algorithm. The complicated multi-step task uses force data to automate each sub-task. Force data is used to determine the direction of motion or as a criterion for success. The algorithm is highly automated but does not completely remove the operator from the procedure. Faults introduced by the large tolerance of the vision data (on the order of a few mm) and by the operator (off-target selection of latch location) are detected by the interpretation of force data. This algorithm was developed in the course of a few working weeks, making it a feasible solution in an industrial setting. The use of the force data in a low-sophistication controller balances algorithm development requirements and operator burden.

References

1. De Luca, A., Albu-Schaeffer, A., Haddadin, S., Hirzinger, G.: Collision Detection and Safe Reaction with the DLR-III Lightweight Manipulator Arm. In: IEEE/RSJ International Conference on Intelligent Robots and Systems, pp. 1623–1630 (2006)
2. Hanebeck, U., Fischer, C., Schmidt, G.: Roman: A mobile robotic assistant for indoor service applications. In: IROS 1997, vol. 2, pp. 518–525. IEEE, CS Press, Grenoble (June 1997)
3. Harden, T., Pittman, P.: Development of a Robotic System to Clean Out Spherical Dynamic Experiment Containment Vessels. In: American Nuclear Society EP&R and RR&S Topical Meeting, pp. 358–364. American Nuclear Society, Albuquerque (2008)
4. Jung, S., Hsia, T.S., Bonitz, R.: Force Tracking Impedance Control of Robot Manipulators Under Unknown Environment. IEEE Transactions on Control Systems Technology, 474–483 (2004)
5. Kulkarni, A., Kapoor, C., Pryor, M., Kinoshita, R., Bruemmer, D.: Software framework for mobile manipulation. In: ANS 2nd International Joint topical Meeting on Emergency Preparedness & Response and Robotics & Remote Systems, Albuquerque, NM (March 2008)
6. Lee, J.: Apply Force/Torque Sensors to Robotic Applications. Robotics, 189–194 (1987)
7. Lu, S., Chung, J., Valinsky, S.: Human-Robot Collision Detection and Identification Based on Wrist and Base Force/Torque Sensors. In: IEEE International Conference on Robotics and Automation, Barcelona, Spain, pp. 3796–3801 (2005)
8. Marks, P.: Robots with Skin Enter Our Touchy-Feely World. New Scientist (April 19, 2010)
9. Nagatani, K., Yuta, S.: Designing strategy and implementation of mobile manipulator control system for opening door. In: Proc. Of International Conference on Robotics and Automation., vol. 3, pp. 2828–2834 (1996)
10. Papakostas, T., Lima, J., Lowe, M.: A Large Area Force Sensor for Smart Skin Applications. IEEE Sensors, 1620–1624 (2002)
11. Petersson, L., Austin, D., Kragic, D.: High-Level Control of a Mobile Manipulator for Door Opening. In: Proceedings of the 2000 IEEE/RSJ International Conference on Intelligent Robots and Systems, pp. 2333–2338 (2000)
12. Radioisotope handling facilities and automation of radioisotope production. Technical report for the International Atomic Energy Agency. IAEA-TECDOC-1430 (December 2004)
13. Ralph, S., Pai, D.: Detection and Localization of Unmodeled Manipulator Collisions. In: IEEE International Conference on Intelligent Robots and Systems, Pittsburgh, Pennsylvania, pp. 504–509 (1995)
14. Roeder-Smith, L.: Pit Viper Strikes at the Hanford Site: Pit Maintenance Using Robotics at the Hanford Tank Farms. Radwaste Solutions, 33–39 (May/June 2002)
15. Sandia National Laboratories. 'Mighty Mouse' robot frees stuck radiation source (December 14, 2005),
    http://www.sandia.gov/news-center/news-releases/2005/manuf-tech-robotics/mm-robot.html
16. Seraji, H., Lim, D., Steele, R.: Experiments in Contact Control. Journal of Robotic Systems, 53–73 (1996)
17. Turner, C., Lloyd, J.: Actinide Research Quarterly—Automating ARIES (July 2008),
    http://www.lanl.gov/source/orgs/nmt/nmtdo/AQarchive/1st_2ndQuarter08/page8.shtml
18. Yoshikawa, T.: Force Control of Robot Manipulators. In: IEEE International Conference on Robotics and Automation, pp. 220–226. IEEE, San Francisco (2000)
19. Zeng, G., Hemami, A.: An Overview of Robot Force Control. Robotica, 473–482 (1997)

A New Solution
for Stability Prediction in Flexible Part Milling

XiaoJian Zhang[1], Caihua Xiong[1,*], and Ye Ding[2]

[1] State Key Laboratory of Digital Manufacturing Equipment and Technology,
School of Mechanical Science and Engineering,
Huazhong University of Science and Technology, Wuhan 430074, China
chxiong@mail.hust.edu.cn
[2] State Key Laboratory of Mechanical System and Vibration,
School of Mechanical Engineering,
Shanghai Jiao Tong University, Shanghai 200240, China

Abstract. The machining instability (chatter phenomenon) easily occurs when flexible parts are machined. This paper predicts the milling stability domain of the flexible part with multiple structure mode interaction induced by the cutting force. First, the dynamic milling process of a flexible part is modeled as a multiple modal degree-of-freedom mechanical model. Then, the full-discretization method is employed to calculate the stability boundary and the cases with different factors are compared, the simulation shows that the cutting position has the dominating effect on the stability analysis of the flexible part milling. The chatter experiment verifies the validity of the proposed method. The proposed method can be used to improve the machining efficiency of flexible parts in aerospace and power industries.

Keywords: stability analysis, milling, flexible, modal, cutting force, full-discretization method.

1   Introduction

The flexible part machining is widely used in the aerospace and power industries. Due to the low stiffness of the part and un-proper cutting parameters, the phenomenon of strong vibration usually occurs, and regenerative mechanism is usually the explanation of the vibration. Regenerative chatter is a kind of self-excited vibrations and the cutting amount simultaneously depends on the paths left by the tooth tip of the current tooth and the previous tooth, so the cutting force varies as well as the chip thickness. To avoid such kind of chatter, there are vast researches on the milling stability analysis during the past years, and some of them are about the flexible part milling. Budak and Altintas [1] conducted the stability analysis of peripheral milling of a cantilevered thin plate. Bravo et al. [2] predicted the stability boundary by taking the frequency response functions of both the machine-tool stucture and workpiece into account, with the frequency domain method proposed in [3]. Vincent Thevenot et al. [4] presented three-dimension (3D)

---

* Corresponding author.

S. Jeschke, H. Liu, and D. Schilberg (Eds.): ICIRA 2011, Part II, LNAI 7102, pp. 452–464, 2011.
© Springer-Verlag Berlin Heidelberg 2011

lobes to determine optimal cutting conditions during the machining process, and the influence of material removal on stability alteration was investigated [5]. Li and Shin [6] investigated the stability of thin-walled part milling with large axial depth by using the standard peak-to-peak force criterion [7]. However, in the above works, only one mode of the structure is considered. Generally, in the flexible part milling, the first multiple modes of the flexible structure are of dominating effect on the machining stability and all of them should be included in the stability analysis.

In addition, some works about the flexible part milling and multiple modes of the structure are considered in the stability analysis [8-10]. Seguy et al. [8] examined the link between stability and variable surface roughness for thin wall milling, and the second and third modes were considered in the mechanic equation, and the modal weight functions are calculated by using the Matlab dde23 routine. Zhang et al. [10] conducted the experimental analysis between multiple structural modes and the chatter stability limits. Adetoro et al. [9] presented a numerical approach to obtaining the structures transfer function for thin wall milling stability prediction, etc. However, in most of these analyses the multiple-mode effect on the stability prediction is considered decoupled, and the stability prediction are usually conducted by using the frequency method [3] or the numerical method with long calculation time.

This paper focuses on the stability prediction of flexible part milling, and tries to analyze the stability prediction of the part with multiple modes coupled from the viewpoint of chatter stability, and such mode coupling is caused by the cutting force. The contribution of this paper lies in that the influence of cutting force inducing structure mode coupling on the stability prediction is investigated. A semi-analytical method is used for stability prediction and any multiple modes and helix angle effect can be included in the analysis and such problem can be easily calculated compared with previous analyses.

The remainder of this paper is summarized as follows. The dynamic equation of milling flexible thin-wall part is given in section 2. Then, the full-discretiztion method is briefly introduced in section 3 and the milling stability prediction of flexible part milling and experimental results are compared in section 4. The discussions and conclusions are drawn in the last section.

2   Mathematical Model of Milling Dynamics

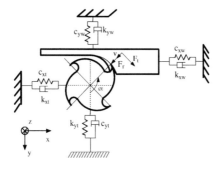

Fig. 1. Dynamic model of down milling

This work focuses on the peripheral milling of a flexible part. Without loss of generality, a down milling of two degree-of-freedom (DOF) system is adopted as in Fig.1. The flexible part is considered as compliant compared with the stiff tool, and the static deflection of the flexible part in cutting is neglected. According to the previous work [11], the cutting force acting on the cutter in two orthogonal directions are formulated as

$$
\left\{ \begin{matrix} F_x \\ F_y \end{matrix} \right\} = \frac{1}{2} a_p K_t \begin{bmatrix} \alpha_{xx} & \alpha_{xy} \\ \alpha_{yx} & \alpha_{yy} \end{bmatrix} \left\{ \begin{matrix} \Delta x \\ \Delta y \end{matrix} \right\},
$$

$$
with \quad \Delta x = x(t) - x(t-T), \quad \Delta y = y(t) - y(t-T) \tag{1}
$$

where

$$
\alpha_{xx} = \sum_{j=0}^{N-1} -g_j [\sin 2\phi_j + K_r (1-\cos 2\phi_j)],
$$

$$
\alpha_{xy} = \sum_{j=0}^{N-1} -g_j [1+\cos 2\phi_j + K_r \sin 2\phi_j],
$$

$$
\alpha_{yx} = \sum_{j=0}^{N-1} g_j [(1-\cos 2\phi_j) - K_r \sin 2\phi_j],
$$

$$
\alpha_{yy} = \sum_{j=0}^{N-1} g_j [\sin 2\phi_j - K_r (1+\cos 2\phi_j)]. \tag{2}
$$

When only the vibration in the y direction is concerned,

$$
F_y = \frac{1}{2} a_p K_t (\alpha_{yx} \Delta x + \alpha_{yy} \Delta y)
$$

$$
= \frac{1}{2} a_p K_t \alpha_{yy} [y(t) - y(t-T)]. \tag{3}
$$

On the other hand, the general dynamic equation (the motion equation of multiple DOFs system) in the y direction with the first n modes of the flexible structure considered can be described as

$$
\mathbf{M}_y \ddot{\mathbf{y}} + \mathbf{C}_y \dot{\mathbf{y}} + \mathbf{K}_y \mathbf{y} = \mathbf{f}_y. \tag{4}
$$

By the coordinate transformation $\mathbf{y} = \mathbf{\Phi q}$, the dynamic Eq.(4) can be rewritten as

$$
\mathbf{m}_y \ddot{\mathbf{q}} + \mathbf{c}_y \dot{\mathbf{q}} + \mathbf{k}_y \mathbf{q} = \mathbf{\Phi}^T \mathbf{f}_y, \tag{5}
$$

where

$$
\mathbf{m}_y = \mathbf{\Phi}^T \mathbf{M}_y \mathbf{\Phi}, \quad \mathbf{k}_y = \mathbf{\Phi}^T \mathbf{K}_y \mathbf{\Phi}, \quad \mathbf{c}_y = \mathbf{\Phi}^T \mathbf{C}_y \mathbf{\Phi}, \tag{6}
$$

where $\mathbf{m}_y$, $\mathbf{c}_y$, $\mathbf{k}_y$ are the modal mass matrix, modal damping matrix and modal stiffness matrix in y direction, respectively. The transforming matrix is $\mathbf{\Phi} = [\varphi_1 \ \varphi_2 \ \varphi_3 \ ... \varphi_n]$, where $\varphi_j (j = 1, 2, 3, ..., n)$ is the j-th normalized modal shape and here we designate $max(abs(\varphi_j))=1$. $\mathbf{f_y}$ is the external exciting force matrix. $\mathbf{y}$ is the displacement vector and the function of x and time t, which also can be presented as

$$\mathbf{y}(x,t) = \sum_{j=1}^{n} q_j(t)\boldsymbol{\varphi}_j(x), \tag{7}$$

where $q_j(t)$ is a time function representing the motion of y direction, and $\varphi_j(x)$ is the mode shape.

According to the assumption that different modes of the flexible structure (linear system) are decoupled, Eq.(5) can be expressed as below:

$$m_{jy}\ddot{q}_j + c_{jy}\dot{q}_j + k_{jy}q_j = \boldsymbol{\varphi}_j^T \mathbf{f}_y, \quad (j = 1, 2, ..., n). \tag{8}$$

It must be noted that in Eq.(8) the cutting force is in action on a single point (denoted by x_0) of the flexible part at a certain time actually, and multiplied by the corresponding mode shape value at the cutting position (x_0) ($\mathbf{f}_y$ in Eq.(4) is a matrix while F_y in Eq.(3) is a scalar quantity), then it is obtained

$$\boldsymbol{\varphi}_j^T \mathbf{f}_y \triangleq \boldsymbol{\varphi}_j^T(x_0) \cdot \mathbf{f}_y(x_0) = \boldsymbol{\varphi}_j^T(x_0) \cdot F_y = \varphi_{j, x_0} \cdot F_y, \quad (j = 1, 2, ..., n). \tag{9}$$

Substituting Eq. (3) and Eq. (9) into Eq. (8) and omitting the subscript 'y' to obtain

$$m_j\ddot{q}_j + c_j\dot{q}_j + k_j q_j = \frac{1}{2}a_p K_t \varphi_{j, x_0} \alpha_{yy} [\sum_{i=1}^{n} q_i(t)\varphi_{i, x_0}(t, x) - \sum_{i=1}^{n} q_i(t-T)\varphi_{i, x_0}(t-T, x)], \tag{10}$$

$$j = 1, 2, ..., n.$$

From Eq.(10), it is known that the different modes of the structure are coupled again, and such coupling is caused by the cutting force. It is difficult for the frequency domain method to solve Eq.(10), but as for the full-discretization method, it is convenient. When only one mode of the flexible structure is considered, Eq.(10) is degenerated into

$$m\ddot{q} + c\dot{q} + kq = \frac{1}{2}a_p K_t \varphi_{x_0} \alpha_{yy} [q(t)\varphi_{x_0}(t, x) - q(t-T)\varphi_{x_0}(t-T, x)], \tag{11}$$

and such case is analyzed in [1, 5] when

$$\varphi_{x_0}(t-T, x) = \varphi_{x_0}(t, x). \tag{12}$$

However, when multiple modes of the flexible part are considered, Eq.(10) is rewritten as

$$\mathbf{M\ddot{q}} + \mathbf{C\dot{q}} + \mathbf{Kq} = \frac{1}{2}a_p K_t \alpha_{yy} \mathbf{P_{x_0}} \mathbf{J} \mathbf{P_{x_0}} [\mathbf{q}(t) - \mathbf{q}(t-T)], \tag{13}$$

where $\mathbf{P}_{\mathbf{x}_0} = diag(\varphi_{1,x_0}, \varphi_{2,x_0}, \cdots, \varphi_{n,x_0})$, $\mathbf{J}$ is $n \times n$ matrix of ones, $i.e.$ $\mathbf{J} = \begin{bmatrix} 1 & \cdots & 1 \\ \vdots & \ddots & \vdots \\ 1 & \cdots & 1 \end{bmatrix}_{n \times n}$

$\mathbf{M} = diag(m_1, m_2, \cdots, m_n)$, $\mathbf{C} = diag(c_1, c_2, \cdots, c_n)$,

$\mathbf{K} = diag(k_1, k_2, \cdots, k_n)$, $\mathbf{q} = [q_1, q_2, \cdots, q_n]^T$

It must be noted that Eq.(13) is valid only when

$$\mathbf{P}_{\mathbf{x}_0}(t - T) = \mathbf{P}_{\mathbf{x}_0}(t), \tag{14}$$

which means that the normalized modal shape is unchanged during the machining process in a tooth passing period, which is easily satisfied. During the longer time when the tool cut at a time, such assumption is acceptable when the amount of cutting is small, especially during the finish process. It is noted that the matrix $\mathbf{P}_{\mathbf{x}_0}$ is the function of the tool position represented by x_0, when in cutting, the cutter is moving and the vibration characteristics of the part are varying, whether with the material removal being considered or not. It means that the variation of the vibration of the part is affected by the cutter position. Besides, the mode shape value at different position is different, the cutter position variation can be reflected in the mode shapes of the flexible structure.

The item of right-hand side in Eq.(13) is corresponding to the excitation with the regenerative effect which is related to the linear chatter stability prediction. Eq.(13) can be re-written as

$$\mathbf{M}\ddot{\mathbf{q}} + \mathbf{C}\dot{\mathbf{q}} + \mathbf{K}\mathbf{q} = a_p \mathbf{K}_c [\mathbf{q}(t) - \mathbf{q}(t - T)], \tag{15}$$

where $\mathbf{K}_c = \dfrac{1}{2} K_t \alpha_{yy} \mathbf{P}_{\mathbf{x}_0} \mathbf{J} \mathbf{P}_{\mathbf{x}_0}$ is periodic with T.

The mode coupling is reflected in the matrix $\mathbf{J}$. When $\mathbf{J}$ is an identity matrix, $i.e.$ the non-diagonal elements are zeros, the dynamic equation becomes uncoupled. When the helix angle β of the cutter is considered, the cutter can be modeled as a stack of differential disk elements along the depth of cut, and the angular position of the j-th cutting edge corresponding to the investigated differential element of the tool is related to the axial depth,

$$\varphi_j(t, z) = \frac{2\pi\Omega}{60}t - \frac{z \tan \beta}{R} + j\frac{2\pi}{N}.$$

The remainder analysis is similar to the above and is not detailed here.

3   Full-Discretization Method

By the transformation $\mathbf{p} = \mathbf{M}\dot{\mathbf{q}} + \mathbf{C}\mathbf{q}/2$ and $\mathbf{z}(t) = \begin{bmatrix} \mathbf{q}(t) \\ \mathbf{p}(t) \end{bmatrix}$, Eq.(15) becomes

$$\dot{\mathbf{z}}(t) = \mathbf{A}_0 \mathbf{z}(t) + \mathbf{A}(t)\big[\mathbf{z}(t) - \mathbf{z}(t - T)\big], \tag{16}$$

where $\mathbf{A}_0 = \begin{bmatrix} -\mathbf{M}^{-1}\mathbf{C}/2 & \mathbf{M}^{-1} \\ \mathbf{C}\mathbf{M}^{-1}\mathbf{C}/4 - \mathbf{K} & -\mathbf{C}\mathbf{M}^{-1}/2 \end{bmatrix}$, $\mathbf{A}(t) = \begin{bmatrix} 0 & 0 \\ a_p \mathbf{K}_c(t) & 0 \end{bmatrix}$.

Next, the full-discretization method (FDM) proposed by Ding et al. [12] is adopted to calculate the stability lobe diagram. The FDM is a numerical method based on the direct integration scheme to predict the milling stability, which has high computational efficiency [13] and the almost the same functions with semi-discretization method [14], and can simultaneously calculate the stability lobe diagrams and surface location error [15]. The FDM is briefly presented here only for completeness and clarity of this paper. First, the tooth passing period T is equally divided into m intervals, and the small interval $\tau = T/m$. On each time interval $k\tau \le t \le (k+1)\tau, (k = 0,\dots,m)$, the response of Eq.(16) with the initial value $\mathbf{z}_k = \mathbf{z}(k\tau)$ can be transformed as

$$\mathbf{z}_{k+1} = e^{\mathbf{A}_0 \tau}\mathbf{z}(k\tau) + \int_0^\tau \Big\{ e^{\mathbf{A}_0 \xi}\mathbf{A}(k\tau + \tau - \xi)\big[\mathbf{z}(k\tau + \tau - \xi) - \mathbf{z}(k\tau + \tau - \xi - T)\big]\Big\}d\xi. \tag{17}$$

Then, the state item, the time-periodic terms and the time-delay term are approximately linearized according to Ref. [12] and substituted into Eq.(17) to obtain

$$\mathbf{z}_{k+1} = \big(\mathbf{F}_0 + \mathbf{F}_{0,1}\big)\mathbf{z}_k + \mathbf{F}_{k+1}\mathbf{z}_{k+1} + \mathbf{F}_{m-1}\mathbf{z}_{k+1-m} + \mathbf{F}_m\mathbf{z}_{k-m}, \tag{18}$$

where

$$\mathbf{F}_0 = \mathbf{\Phi}_0, \tag{19}$$

$$\mathbf{F}_{0,1} = \big(\mathbf{\Phi}_2 / \tau\big)\mathbf{A}_0^{(k)} + \big(\mathbf{\Phi}_3 / \tau\big)\mathbf{A}_1^{(k)}, \tag{20}$$

$$\mathbf{F}_{k+1} = \big(\mathbf{\Phi}_1 - \mathbf{\Phi}_2 / \tau\big)\mathbf{A}_0^{(k)} + \big(\mathbf{\Phi}_2 - \mathbf{\Phi}_3 / \tau\big)\mathbf{A}_1^{(k)}, \tag{21}$$

$$\mathbf{F}_{m-1} = \big(\mathbf{\Phi}_1 - \mathbf{\Phi}_2 / \tau\big)\mathbf{B}_0^{(k)} + \big(\mathbf{\Phi}_2 - \mathbf{\Phi}_3 / \tau\big)\mathbf{B}_1^{(k)}, \tag{22}$$

$$\mathbf{F}_m = \big(\mathbf{\Phi}_2 / \tau\big)\mathbf{B}_0^{(k)} + \big(\mathbf{\Phi}_3 / \tau\big)\mathbf{B}_1^{(k)}, \tag{23}$$

and

$$\mathbf{\Phi}_0 = e^{\mathbf{A}_0 \tau}, \mathbf{\Phi}_1 = \int_0^\tau e^{\mathbf{A}_0 \xi}d\xi, \mathbf{\Phi}_2 = \int_0^\tau \xi e^{\mathbf{A}_0 \xi}d\xi, \mathbf{\Phi}_3 = \int_0^\tau \xi^2 e^{\mathbf{A}_0 \xi}d\xi,$$
$$\mathbf{A}_0^{(k)} = \mathbf{A}_{k+1}, \mathbf{A}_1^{(k)} = \big(\mathbf{A}_k - \mathbf{A}_{k+1}\big)/\tau, \text{ where } \mathbf{A}_k \text{ is short for } \mathbf{A}(k\tau), \tag{24}$$
$$\mathbf{B}_0^{(k)} = \mathbf{B}_{k+1}, \mathbf{B}_1^{(k)} = \big(\mathbf{B}_k - \mathbf{B}_{k+1}\big)/\tau, \text{ where } \mathbf{B}_k \text{ is short for } \mathbf{B}(k\tau).$$

The discrete map matrix $\mathbf{D}_k$ can be deduced as

$$\mathbf{D}_k = \begin{bmatrix} \left[\mathbf{I}-\mathbf{F}_{k+1}\right]^{-1}\left(\mathbf{F}_0+\mathbf{F}_{0,1}\right) & \mathbf{0} & \mathbf{0} & \cdots & \mathbf{0} & \left[\mathbf{I}-\mathbf{F}_{k+1}\right]^{-1}\mathbf{F}_{m-1} & \left[\mathbf{I}-\mathbf{F}_{k+1}\right]^{-1}\mathbf{F}_m \\ \mathbf{I} & \mathbf{0} & \mathbf{0} & \cdots & \mathbf{0} & \mathbf{0} & \mathbf{0} \\ \mathbf{0} & \mathbf{I} & \mathbf{0} & \cdots & \mathbf{0} & \mathbf{0} & \mathbf{0} \\ \vdots & \vdots & \vdots & \ddots & \vdots & \vdots & \vdots \\ \mathbf{0} & \mathbf{0} & \mathbf{0} & \cdots & \mathbf{0} & \mathbf{0} & \mathbf{0} \\ \mathbf{0} & \mathbf{0} & \mathbf{0} & \cdots & \mathbf{I} & \mathbf{0} & \mathbf{0} \\ \mathbf{0} & \mathbf{0} & \mathbf{0} & \cdots & \mathbf{0} & \mathbf{I} & \mathbf{0} \end{bmatrix}.$$

Finally, the transition matrix $\mathbf{\Psi}$ over one cutting tooth periodic time is

$$\mathbf{\Psi} = \mathbf{D}_{m-1}\mathbf{D}_{m-2}\cdots\mathbf{D}_1\mathbf{D}_0 \tag{25}$$

According to the *Floquet* theory[16], the stability of the system can be determined: if the moduluses of all the eigenvalues of $\mathbf{\Psi}$ are less than 1, the dynamic system is stable, otherwise, unstable.

4   Simulation and Experimental Verification

From the analysis above, it is known that to determine the stability diagram, the modal shapes of the flexible structure are needed, which can be obtained by the finite element analysis. The analysis of a flexible plate is conducted as follows. The plate dimension is 54mm×3mm×45mm and it is clamped at the bottom side. The material is 2A70 Al, Young's modulus is 7.2×10^9 m/N, Density is 2800kg/m^3 and the Poisson's ratio is 0.33. By using the finite analysis software, the first several of modes of the plate can be easily calculated, as shown in Fig. 2, the first three modes are plotted and all the mode shape value at each discretized nodes can be obtained.

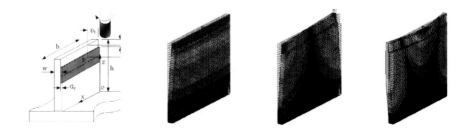

Fig. 2. Flexible plate and its first 3 modes

The modal frequencies of the structure can be approximated via the finite element analysis, but the modal damping can only be acquired from the experiment. The modal impact testing is performed to produce the structure frequency response function (FRF), then the rational fraction polynomials algorithm is adopted to fit the FRF curves to calculate the modal dampings [17]. The simulated frequencies can also be updated by the experimental results. The fitted modal parameters from the impact testing are listed in Table.1. The third modal frequency overpassing the measuring bandwidth (5120Hz) is not listed. The higher frequencies are neglected which have little influence on the stability.

Table 1. Modal parameters fitted

	Frequency (Hz)	Damping	Mass (kg)
1st mode	1197.7044	0.006 237	0.0597
2nd mode	2512.5076	0.003 347	0.0387

The cutting force coefficients are also needed in the stability analysis. Based on the end milling cutting force model [18], the tangential cutting coefficient and radial cutting coefficient are fitted as K_{tc}=1088MPa, K_{rc}=529MPa, K_{te}=7383N/m and K_{re}=7130N/m by the cutting experiment.

By using the FDM, the chatter stability diagram can be calculated with different cases, and only two different helix angles are plotted in Figs.3-4. Based on the predictions of the milling stability, it seems that the helix angle and mode coupling has little influence on the stability, while the cutting position has great effect on the stability prediction in the flexible part milling.

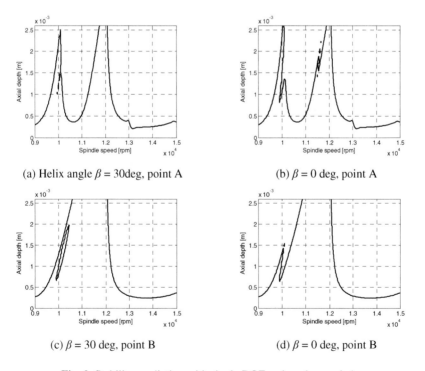

(a) Helix angle β = 30deg, point A

(b) β = 0 deg, point A

(c) β = 30 deg, point B

(d) β = 0 deg, point B

Fig. 3. Stability prediction with single DOF and mode-coupled

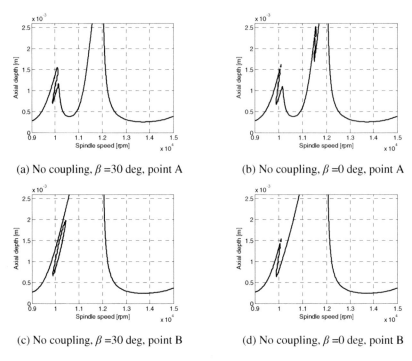

(a) No coupling, β =30 deg, point A

(b) No coupling, β =0 deg, point A

(c) No coupling, β =30 deg, point B

(d) No coupling, β =0 deg, point B

Fig. 4. Stability prediction with single DOF mode uncoupled

The 'point A' in Figs.4-5 is corresponding to the point 'A' in Fig.5 (a), and the 'point B' is corresponding to the point 'B' in Fig.5 (a). According to the modal shapes in Fig.2, it is shown that point A is affected by two modes of the plate, while point B is influenced by the first mode alone, because point B is at middle of the part and the mode shape value of the second mode is zero, *i.e.* the second mode doesn't influence the stability analysis. When the cutter moves from point A to point B, the variation of the stability boundaries is plotted in Fig.5 (b).

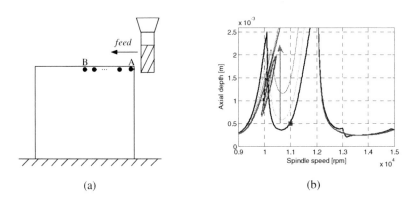

(a)

(b)

Fig. 5. Stability prediction with the moving cutting position

The milling chatter experiment is conducted to verify the method presented above. Peripheral milling of an aluminum alloy plate is carried out on the super high-speed machining centre HSM 600U, as shown in Fig.6. The tool technical parameters and the machining parameters are listed in Table.2. In the milling experiment, the sound pressure is recorded by using the microphone CHQ2255 as shown in Fig.6 and the sampling frequency is 40 kHz to record the entire possible high-frequency signals.

Fig. 6. Milling experiment set-up

Table 2. Cutter and machining parameters

Tool parameters		Milling parameters	
Diameter [mm]	8	Spindle speed [rpm]	11000
Teeth number	3	Feed per teeth [mm]	0.05
Helix angle [degree]	30	Axial depth [mm]	0.5
Material	carbide alloy	Radial depth [mm]	0.5

The experimental test is conducted and the parameter point (11000rpm, 0.5mm) in Fig.5(b) is tested to identify the chatter stability limit. The sound pressure signal is analyzed for the stability of cutting, and the time waves (Fig.7(a)) and the spectrums of the sound pressure (Fig.7(b)-(d)) are plotted. In Fig.7(a), the strong vibration appears when the cutter begins to cut (impact effect is neglected), the instability occurs via the spectrum analysis of the sound pressure as shown in Fig.7(b). At the cut-in point (Point A in Fig.5(a)), the parameter point is very close to the stability limit predicted in Fig.5(b), where the stability domain is affected by two modes simultaneously and the parameter point becomes easily unstable under the external disturbance. When the tool moves into the middle of the flexible part, the milling becomes stable, which can be seen from Fig.7(c), and the machining instability appears again when the cutter leaves from the middle to the side of the plate. The 'unstable–stable–unstable' vibration phenomenon can be explained by the effect of the modes of the structure, especially the second mode which is shown in Fig.2. At both sides of the plate, the second mode affects the predicted stability boundary which is closes to the testing point, so the chatter easily occurs. When in the middle of the plate, the second mode decreases to zero and the stability zone is influenced by the first mode alone, so the stable zone increases and the testing point is stable by a wide margin. It means when the cutter is in the middle of the plate, the cutting is stable, which is verified by the experiment.

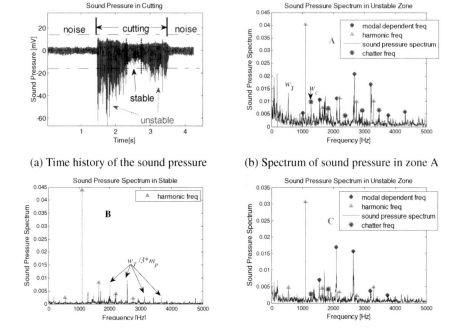

(a) Time history of the sound pressure   (b) Spectrum of sound pressure in zone A

(c) Spectrum of sound pressure in zone B   (d) Spectrum of sound pressure in zone C

Fig. 7. Time wave and spectrum of the sound pressure

By the analysis of the sound pressure signal, the experimental results agree with the prediction well, which verify the validity of the method proposed above. Additionally, in Fig.7, the harmonic frequency (1100Hz) is dominating in the spectrum analysis, which is close to the first natural frequency of the structure and leads to resonance. The second mode is also activated somewhat during the unstable zone where the chatter frequencies are actually not so obvious. The natural frequencies are easily activated due to the low stiffness of the plate and the low damping of the structure.

5   Discussion and Conclusions

Since flexible part milling is usually a kind of low radial immersion cases, the force excitation can be regarded as interrupted cutting, and the implicit assumption that the vibration response doesn't influence the cutting conditions of the next tooth seems reasonable. Actually, the assumption is hardly satisfied, due to the small structure damping and low stiffness. And the cutting force is also not like the assumed and changed with the vibration of the flexible structure, the feed per tooth, the entry and exit angles for each tooth all change.

In this work, the end milling dynamic model with multiple modes of the flexible structure at the compliant direction is developed, with multiple modes coupled induced by the cutting force, and the full-discretization method is employed to calculate the stability boundary. Such method is very suitable for thin-wall parts milling which have multiple low-frequency modes in action, and it can give a better prediction stability variation. However, the mode coupled originated from the cutting force has little effect on the stability domain. This paper tries to give the stability prediction of flexible part milling from the viewpoint of chatter stability, with multiple modes of the part being considered, while the resonance of the flexible part is neglected. In fact, the forced vibration of flexible part is more serious than regenerative effect. So simultaneously considering chatter and resonance avoidance is very necessary. The experimental results show that the large axial depth milling can reduce and even diminish the resonance. The future work will focus on this point.

Acknowledgments. This work is partially supported by the National Key Basic Research Program (grant 2011CB706804), the National Natural Science Foundation of China (Grant 50835004) and the National Funds for Distinguished Young Scientists of China (Grant No.51025518).

References

[1] Budak, E., Altintas, Y.: Analytical Prediction of Chatter Stability in Milling—Part II: Application of the General Formulation to Common Milling Systems. Journal of Dynamic Systems, Measurement and Control, Transactions of the ASME 120(1), 31–36 (1998)

[2] Bravo, U., Altuzarra, O., López de Lacalle, L.N., Sánchez, J.A., Campa, F.J.: Stability limits of milling considering the flexibility of the workpiece and the machine. International Journal of Machine Tools and Manufacture 45(15), 1669–1680 (2005)

[3] Altintas, Y., Budak, E.: Analytical Prediction of Stability Lobes in Milling. CIRP Annals-Manufacturing Technology 44(1), 357–362 (1995)

[4] Thevenot, V., Arnaud, L., Dessein, G., Cazenave-Larroche, G.: Integration of dynamic behaviour variations in the stability lobes method: 3D lobes construction and application to thin-walled structure milling. International Journal of Advanced Manufacturing Technology 27(7-8), 638–644 (2006)

[5] Thevenot, V., Arnaud, L., Dessein, G., Cazenave-Larroche, G.: Influence of Material Removal on the Dynamic Behavior of Thin-Walled Structures. Peripheral Milling. Machining Science and Technology. 10(3), 275–287 (2006)

[6] Li, H., Shin, Y.C.: A comprehensive dynamic end milling simulation model. Journal of Manufacturing Science and Engineering, Transactions of the ASME 128(1), 86–95 (2006)

[7] Smith, S., Tlusty, J.: Efficient simulation programs for chatter in milling. CIRP Annals 42(1), 463–466 (1993)

[8] Seguy, S., Dessein, G., Arnaud, L.: Surface roughness variation of thin wall milling, related to modal interactions. International Journal of Machine Tools and Manufacture 48(3-4), 261–274 (2008)

[9] Adetoro, O.B., Wen, P.H., Sim, W.M., Vepa, R.: Numerical and experimental investigation for stability lobes prediction in thin wall machining. Engineering Letters 17(4) (2009)

[10] Zhang, X., Xiong, C., Ding, Y., Zhang, X.: Stability analysis in milling of thin-walled workpieces with emphasis on the structural effect. Proceedings of the Institution of Mechanical Engineers, Part B: Journal of Engineering Manufacture 224(4), 589–608 (2010)

[11] Altintas, Y.: Manufacturing Automation: Metal Cutting Mechanics, Machine Tool Vibrations, and CNC Design. Cambridge University Press, Cambridge (2000)

[12] Ding, Y., Zhu, L., Zhang, X., Ding, H.: A full-discretization method for prediction of milling stability. International Journal of Machine Tools and Manufacture 50(5), 502–509 (2010)

[13] Insperger, T.: Full-discretization and semi-discretization for milling stability prediction: Some comments. International Journal of Machine Tools and Manufacture 50(7), 658–662 (2010)

[14] Insperger, T., Stepan, G.: Semi-discretization method for delayed systems. International Journal for Numerical Methods in Engineering 55(5), 503–518 (2002)

[15] Ding, Y., Zhu, L., Zhang, X., Ding, H.: On a Numerical Method for Simultaneous Prediction of Stability and Surface Location Error in Low Radial Immersion Milling. Journal of Dynamic Systems, Measurement, and Control 133(2), 24503 (2011)

[16] Farkas, M.: Periodic Motions. Springer, New York (1994)

[17] Richardson, M.H., Formenti, D.L.: Parameter estimation from frequency response measurements using rational fraction polynomials. In: Proc. 1st Int. Modal Anal. Conf., Orlando, FL, vol. 1, pp. 167–186 (1982)

[18] Budak, E., Altintas, Y., Armarego, E.J.A.: Prediction of milling force coefficients from orthogonal cutting data. Journal of Manufacturing Science and Engineering, Transactions of the ASME 118(2), 216–224 (1996)

A Practical Continuous-Curvature Bézier Transition Algorithm for High-Speed Machining of Linear Tool Path

Qingzhen Bi, Yuhan Wang, Limin Zhu, and Han Ding

Shanghai Jiaotong University, Shanghai 200240, P.R. China
{biqz,yhwang,zhulm,hding}@sjtu.edu.cn
http://www.sjtu.edu.cn

Abstract. A continuous-curvature smoothing algorithm is developed to approximate the linear tool path for high speed machining. The new tool path composed of cubic Bézier curves and lines, which is everywhere G^2 continuous, is obtained to replace the conventional linear tool path. Both the tangency and curvature discontinuities at the segment junctions of the linear tool path are avoided. The feed motion will be more stable since the discontinuities are the most important source of feed fluctuation. The algorithm is based upon the transition cubic Bézier curve that has closed-form expression. The approximation error at the segment junction can be accurately guaranteed. The maximal curvature in the transition curve, which is critical for velocity planning, is analytically computed and optimized. The curvature radii of all transition Bézier curves are also globally optimized to pursue the high feed speed by a linear programm model. Therefore, the algorithm is easy to implement and can be integrated into a post-process system.

Keywords: Bézier curve, continuous-curvature path, tool path smoothing, linear tool path, high-speed machining.

1 Introduction

Linear tool path (or G01 NC segment) is the widespread NC representation form. Linear segments provide an easy way to approximate the complex curve under a predefined tolerance. Many efficient algorithms have been developed to approximate the curve by line segments and generate the linear tool path [7]. Rapid development of 3-D scanning technology is the other reason to use the linear tool path. The digital model resulted from scanning technology is usually expressed by a point cloud or triangle mesh model. The linear tool path is the best NC represention form considering the computation efficiency and accuracy [13].

The linear tool path cannot achieve a higher feed rate in practice. The elementary tool path introduces both the tangency and curvature discontinuities at the segment junctions. The discontinuities are the most important source of feed fluctuation. Though lookahead scheme has been integrated in current CNC systems to alleviate the frequent start and stop, the discontinuous still cause the fluctuations of feed speed and acceleration. Replacing the linear tool path with smooth parametric curves is an important way to decrease the feed fluctuation and improve machining efficiency [6].

S. Jeschke, H. Liu, and D. Schilberg (Eds.): ICIRA 2011, Part II, LNAI 7102, pp. 465–476, 2011.

Many algorithms are developed to replace the linear tool path with parametric curves, such as Bézier [13] or Bspline curve [9]. A significant disadvantage of the parametric transition curve is that its point and curvature are complicated functions of its parameters. It is difficult to simultaneously consider the approximation error constraint and optimize the curvature profile in the approximation process. Yau and Wang [13] proposed a Bézier interpolation method to reduce the discontinuities. They defined a criterion to identify continuous short blocks and fit the blocks into cubic Bézier curves. This method only smoothes the linear paths with small corner angles; Furthermore, the resultant tool path cannot guarantee the tangency continuity at the Bézier curve junctions. Zhang et al. [14] proposed an transition algorithm for two linear segments based on the subsection parametrical cubic spline curve fitting approach. This algorithm guarantees the tangent continuity between the linear segment and the transition curve. Pateloup, Duc and Ray [9] developed an algorithm to blend the segment junction by a Bspline curve. The Bspline curve consists of eight control points that are symmetric with respect to the internal bisector of the two lines. Their study shows that the minimal control points, the avoidance of abrupt inversion of curvature direction, and the decreased sum of the squares of the curvature in the transition curve are the interesting geometrical criterions for tool path optimization. However, they did not give the algorithm to optimize the squares of the curvature.

The construction of smooth transition curve has also been actively investigated in mobile robot and highway design communities because unsmooth speed can cause slippage and overactuation [8]. Yang and Sukkarieh [12] proposed an interesting analytical continuous-curvature path-smoothing algorithm. They designed two symmetrical Bézier curves to blend the segment junction. The transition curves satisfy both curvature continuity and maximum curvature requirements. However, the method cannot be applied to smooth the tool path of NC machining because their algorithm does not consider the essential approximation error constraint.

In this paper, we develop an analytical transition Bézier curve defined by only four control points to smooth the segment junction of a linear tool path. The curvature continuity in the new tool path is also guaranteed. The inversion of curvature direction does not occur in the transition curve; Both the approximation error and maximal curvature of the transition curve can be analytically computed, which provides an easy way to globally optimize the curvature of the whole tool path.

This paper is organized as follows: Section II presents the definition of the G^2 continuous transition Bézier curve. The G^2 continuous path-smoothing algorithm for a linear tool path is presented in Section III and the curvature radii of the whole tool path are globally optimized in Section IV. Section V presents two computational examples and Section VI concludes the paper.

2   Definition of G^2 Continuous Transition Curve

DeRose and Barsky [3] defined the order of smoothness by parametric and geometric continuity. Geometric continuity has an advantage over parametric continuity because geometric continuity accommodates the differences of parameterizations. Here geometric continuity is selected to measure the smoothness of the tool path. G^1 continuity, the first-order geometric continuity, represents the continuity of the unit tangent vectors. G^2 continuity, the second-order geometric continuity, represents the continuity of the curvature vectors.

Assuming that the linear tool path is defined by a sequence of points $\{P_i = (x_i, y_i, z_i),$ $i = 1 \cdots n\}$, the objective of our algorithm is to fit the $n-1$ linear segments by G^2 continuous curves under the constraint of approximation error, while the curvature profile is optimized to tune the feed motion of the machine tool. A cubic Bézier curve, which is G^2 continuous, is adopted to blend the piecewise linear tool path together. The cubic Bézier curve is given by Farin [5] as

$$Q(t) = \sum_{i=0}^{3} \binom{3}{i} B_i (1-t)^{3-i} t^i, \tag{1}$$

where t is $0 \le t \le 1$ and B_i is the control points.

3 G^2 Continuous Blending of a Linear Tool Path

The cubic Bézier curve to smooth two neighboring line segments is first concerned. Fig. 1 shows the two line segments $P_1 V$ and $V P_2$, their unit directions T_1 and T_2, and the transition lengths $d_1 = \|D_1 V\|$ and $d_2 = \|D_2 V\|$. By the definition of G^2 continuity, at the points $Q(0)$ and $Q(1)$, the two unit tangent vectors are T_1 and T_2 respectively, and the curvatures are both zero.

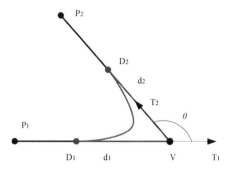

Fig. 1. The basic parameters of G^2 blending

3.1 G^2 Continuity Condition

In [11], a planar continuous cubic Bézier path-smoothing algorithm is suggested, which provides an elegant way to achieve G^2 continuous blending. The four control points of the cubic Bézier curve are simply given by

$$\begin{aligned} B_0 &= D_1, \\ B_1 &= B_2 = V, \\ B_3 &= D_2. \end{aligned} \tag{2}$$

Substitute (2) into (1), the G^2 continuous transition Bézier curve is simplified into

$$Q(t) = V - d_1(1-t)^3 T_1 + d_2 t^3 T_2. \tag{3}$$

The unsigned curvature of the cubic Bézier curve is given by

$$\kappa(t) = \frac{Q'(t) \times Q''(t)}{\|Q'(t)\|^3}$$

$$= \frac{2d_1 d_2 \sin\theta(1-t)t}{3\left[d_1^2(1-t)^4 + 2d_1 d_2 \cos\theta(1-t)^2 t^2 + d_2^2 t^4\right]^{\frac{3}{2}}}. \tag{4}$$

where θ is the angle between vector T_1 and vector T_2, as shown in Fig. 1. The notion $Q'(t) \times Q''(t)$ represents the scalar quantity $\|Q'(t)\|\|Q''(t)\|\sin\alpha$, where α is the angle between vector $Q'(t)$ and vector $Q''(t)$.

Its curvature derivative is given by

$$\kappa'(t) = \frac{g(t)}{[Q'(t) \cdot Q'(t)]^{\frac{3}{2}}}, \tag{5}$$

where

$$\begin{aligned}
g(t) &= [Q'(t) \times Q'''(t)][Q'(t) \cdot Q'(t)] \\
&\quad -3[Q'(t) \times Q''(t)][Q'(t) \cdot Q''(t)] \\
&= 162 d_1 d_2 \sin\theta [d_1^2(1-t)^5 + 5 d_1^2(1-t)^4 t - \\
&\quad 4 d_1 d_2 \cos\theta(1-t)^3 t^2 + 4 d_1 d_2 \cos\theta(1-t)^2 t^3 - \\
&\quad 5 d_2^2(1-t)t^4 - d_2^2 t^5].
\end{aligned} \tag{6}$$

3.2   Analytical Solution of the Maximal Curvature of the Transition Curve

The analytical solution of the maximal curvature of the transition cubic Bézier curve can be obtained if the two transition lengths are the same, $d = d_1 = d_2$. The analytical solution provides a simple way to optimize the curvature profile of the new tool path.

Theorem 1. *If $d_1 = d_2 = d$ and $\beta = \theta/2$, the maximal curvature of the G^2 transition Bézier curve is obtained as*

$$\kappa_{max} = \frac{8\sin\beta}{3d\cos^2\beta}. \tag{7}$$

Proof. Substituting $t = 0.5$ and $d = d_1 = d_2$ into (6), the numerator of the curvature derivative is simplified into

$$\begin{aligned}
g(0.5) &= 162 d^2 \sin\theta \left(0.5^5 d^2 + 5 d^2 0.5^5 - 4 d^2 \cos\theta 0.5^5 + \right. \\
&\quad \left. 4 d^2 \cos\theta 0.5^5 - 5 d^2 0.5^5 - d^2 0.5^5\right) \\
&= 0.
\end{aligned} \tag{8}$$

Therefore the curvature will be extremum when $t = 0.5$. This is the sole curvature extremum in the transition curve because there is exactly one curvature extremum between the two inflection points of a parametric cubic curve[10]. The curvature $\kappa(0.5)$ is maximal since the denominator of $\kappa'(t) > 0$,

$$g(0) = \frac{81}{16}d^4 \sin \theta \geq 0, \qquad (9)$$

and

$$g(1) = -\frac{81}{16}d^4 \sin \theta \leq 0. \qquad (10)$$

Substituting $t = 0.5$ and $d = d_1 = d_2$ into (4), the maximal curvature is calculated by

$$
\begin{aligned}
\kappa_{max} &= \kappa(0.5) \\
&= \frac{2d^2 \sin \theta 0.5^2}{3\left[d^2 0.5^4 + 2d^2 \cos \theta 0.5^4 + d^2 0.5^4\right]^{\frac{3}{2}}} \\
&= \frac{4 \sin \theta}{3d\left[0.5^2(2 + 2\cos \theta)\right]^{\frac{3}{2}}} \\
&= \frac{4 \sin \theta}{3d \cos^3 (\theta/2)} \\
&= \frac{8 \sin \beta}{3d \cos^2 \beta}.
\end{aligned}
\qquad (11)
$$

Another advantage of the method is that the oscillation does not occur in the transition Bézier curve. Oscillation avoidance is helpful to smooth feed motion of numerical controller. The abrupt inversion of the curvature sign, like abrupt curvature variation, will imply abrupt variations in acceleration and jerk [2]. In the transition curve, the curvature direction is fixed since the $\kappa(0.5)$ is the only curvature extremum and $\kappa(0) = \kappa(1) = 0$. This can also be found in Fig. 2.

3.3 Upper Bound Curvature under the Constraint of Approximation Error

The G^2 continuous path-smoothing algorithm of a linear tool path must satisfy the constraint of approximation error, and the curvature profile should also be optimized to improve the feed behavior of the machine tool. Therefore the transition length d should be decided by considering the predefined approximation error and the maximum curvature κ_{max}. The approximation error can be guaranteed by the following theorem.

Theorem 2. *The design variable d, the transition length, is analytically obtained as $d \leq 4\varepsilon \csc \beta$ if the predefined threshold of the approximation error is ε.*

Proof. Substitute $t = 0.5$ into (3), and the location closest to the vertex V is given by

$$
\begin{aligned}
Q(0.5) &= V - 0.5^3 dT_1 + 0.5^3 dT_2 \\
&= V - \frac{1}{8} d(T_2 - T_1) \\
&= V - \frac{1}{8} d \cdot 2\cos\left(\frac{\pi - \theta}{2}\right) \frac{T_2 - T_1}{\|T_2 - T_1\|} \\
&= V - \frac{d}{4} \sin\beta \frac{T_2 - T_1}{\|T_2 - T_1\|}.
\end{aligned}
\tag{12}
$$

The relationship between the maximal approximation error and the variable d can be represented

$$
\varepsilon = \|Q(0.5) - V\| = \left\| \frac{d}{4} \sin\beta \frac{T_2 - T_1}{\|T_2 - T_1\|} \right\| = \frac{d}{4} \sin\beta.
\tag{13}
$$

Therefore, the transition Bézier curve will satisfy the predefined approximation error ε if the variable d is selected by

$$
d \leq 4\varepsilon \csc\beta.
\tag{14}
$$

Usually the approximation error ε is predefined and the minimal κ_{max} of the transition Bézier curve is desired. Based on (14) and (11), the feasible κ_{max} is represented as

$$
\begin{aligned}
\kappa_{max} &\geq \frac{8\sin\beta}{3 \cdot 4\varepsilon \csc\beta \cdot \cos^2\beta} \\
&= \frac{2\tan^2\beta}{3\varepsilon}
\end{aligned}
\tag{15}
$$

Example 1. Fig. 2 demonstrates the method to smooth a linear tool path. The linear tool path is defined by four points, $P_1(1,0), P_2(0.9,0.3), P_3(0.2,0.6), P_4(0,1)$. The allowable approximation error is 0.02. The maximal transition lengths are 0.195 and 0.233. The two maximal unsigned curvatures of the two obtained transition curves are 6.722 and 4.473, respectively. The curvature combs show that the curvatures are continuous and there is only one curvature extremum in each transition curve.

4   Global Optimization of Curvature Radii in Transition Curves

The small and continuous curvature is helpful to tune the feed motion of the machine tool. If the ith transition cubic Bézier curve is used to blend the ith junction point, as shown in Fig. 4, the transitional velocity v_i in the ith transition curve is restricted by [14]

$$
v_i = \min.\left(\frac{2}{T}\sqrt{r_i^2 - (r_i^2 - \delta)^2}, \sqrt{r_i A_{max}} \right),
\tag{16}
$$

where T is the interpolation period, $r_i = 1/\kappa_{imax}$ is the minimal curvature radius in the ith transition curve, δ is the allowable chord error, and A_{max} is the maximum allowable

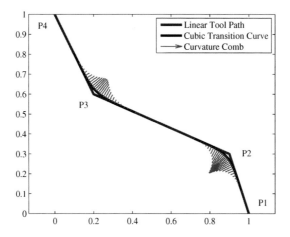

Fig. 2. Curvature combs of the G^2 continuous transition curves

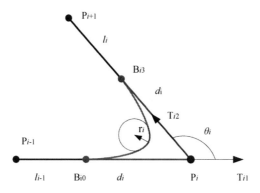

Fig. 3. The definition of the ith transition curve

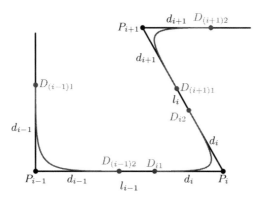

Fig. 4. The transition curves of a linear tool path

acceleration of the machine tool. It can be found that the curvature radii are critical to improve the feed velocity.

The minimal curvature radius r_i in the ith transition Bézier curve are mainly determined by the angle β_i and the transition length d_i, which can be found in (11). The angle β_i is fixed in the linear tool path. The transition length d_i is first restricted by the approximation error ε. The lengths of the two neighboring linear segments $l_i - 1$ and l_i also gives the constraints of d_i, $d_i + d_{i+1} \leq l_i$ and $d_i + d_{i-1} \leq l_{i-1}$. The minimal curvature radii $r_i (i = 2 \cdots n - 1)$ in the transition curves can then be globally optimized by the following model

$$
\begin{aligned}
\text{max.} \quad & (1 - \lambda)(n - 2) \min_{2 \leq i \leq n-1} r_i + \lambda \sum_{i=2}^{n-1} r_i \\
\text{s.t.} \quad & d_i \leq 4\varepsilon \csc \beta_i; \\
& d_i + d_{i-1} \leq l_{i-1}; \\
& d_1 = 0; \\
& d_{n-1} \leq l_{n-1}; \\
& d_i \geq 0; \\
& i = 2 \cdots n - 1
\end{aligned}
\tag{17}
$$

where r_i is the minimal curvature radius of the ith transition Bézier curve and λ is the weight factor. The minimal value and the sum of r_i are simultaneously optimized in the model. The weights of the two part are determined by λ. Usually $\lambda = 0.5$ is recommended and the obtained transition cubic Bézier curves will have moderate curvature radii variations.

Equation (11) shows

$$
r_i = \frac{1}{\kappa_{imax}} = d_i \frac{3 \cos^2 \beta_i}{8 \sin \beta_i}.
\tag{18}
$$

Let ξ be the minimal value of $r_i (2 \leq i \leq n - 1)$, the optimization model can be transformed into the following minimization problem:

$$
\begin{aligned}
\text{min.} \quad & -\xi(1 - \lambda)(n - 2) - \lambda \sum_{i=2}^{n-1} d_i \frac{3 \cos^2 \beta_i}{8 \sin \beta_i} \\
\text{s.t.} \quad & \xi - d_i \frac{3 \cos^2 \beta_i}{8 \sin \beta_i} \leq 0; \\
& d_i \leq 4\varepsilon \csc \beta_i; \\
& d_i + d_{i-1} \leq l_{i-1}; \\
& d_1 = 0; \\
& d_{n-1} \leq l_{n-1}; \\
& d_i \geq 0; \\
& \xi \geq 0; \\
& i = 2 \cdots n - 1.
\end{aligned}
\tag{19}
$$

Obviously, the optimization model in (19) is a linear program, that can be efficiently solved with a variety of algorithms, e.g. the well-known Simplex method or Interior-Points method [1].

Example 2. Fig. 5 shows the resultant G^2 continuous transition Bézier curves based on the optimized transition lengths. The linear tool path is defined by five points, $P_1(1,0)$, $P_2(0.9,0.3)$, $P_3(0.4,0.4)$, $P_4(0.2,0.9)$, $P_5(0,1)$. The predefined approximation error is 0.04. It can be found that the linear segment P_2P_3 is completely replaced by two transition Bézier curves to increase the maximal curvature radii r_2 and r_3. The resultant minimal curvature radii are $r_2 = r_3 = 0.149$. Another minimal curvature radius, $r_4 = 0.206$, is restricted by the length of l_4.

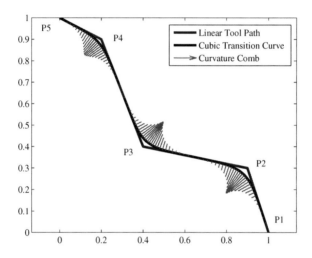

Fig. 5. Curvature combs of the optimized G^2 blending curves

5   Computational Example

Example 3. The proposed algorithm can apply to smooth 3D linear tool path. Generally it is not easy to realize the continuous-curvature path smoothing in 3D space. Since every two continuous linear segments form a plane, the transition algorithm is then applied after mapping the two linear segments to the 2D space.

In this example, the 3D linear tool path is defined by 4 points, $P_1(1,0,1)$, $P_2(0,0,1)$, $P_3(0,0,0)$ and $P_4(0,1,0)$, as shown in Fig. 6. The G^2 continuous tool path can be obtained by blending the segment connections, P_2 and P_3. The two connections are blended in the planes defined by the triangle $\Delta P_1P_2P_3$ and $\Delta P_2P_3P_4$. If the approximation error is set as 0.05 mm. The two transition lengths are both 0.2828 mm, and the minimal curvature radii are both 0.075 mm. The transition Bézier curves are marked with red in Fig. 6.

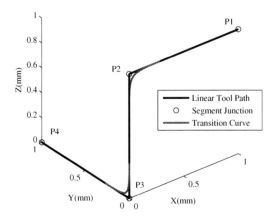

Fig. 6. G^2 transition curves of 3D linear tool path

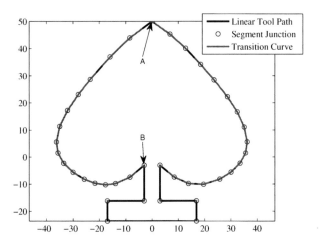

Fig. 7. Smoothed too path for machining the heart shape when $\varepsilon = 0.1$

Example 4. The linear path for machining a 2D complex shape is smoothed under the approximation error and G^2 continuity constraints in the example. The linear tool path for machining a heart shape is defined by 40 points, as shown in Fig. 7. The linear tool path consists of many abrupt variations of feed direction.

The smoothed tool path is shown in Fig. 7 when the maximal approximation error is set as 0.1. It can be observed that most of the linear tool path are replaced by the cubic Bézier curves and all the cusp points are blended. Two transition curves are illustrated in Fig. 8. Though the corner angles are large, cusp points are stilled to be avoided in the new tool path. The comparisons between the original linear tool path and transition curves indicate that the approximation errors are not greater than the predefined value 0.1.

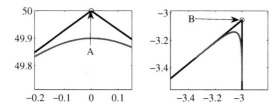

Fig. 8. Details of the smoothed too path when $\varepsilon = 0.1$

6   Conclusion

The proposed path-smoothing algorithm gives an analytical way to replace a piecewise linear tool path with G^2 continuous curves. The new tool path is composed of linear segments and cubic Bézier curves that are used to blend the segment junctions. Unlike the standard curve interpolation or approximation approaches, both the maximal approximation error and the maximal curvature in the transition cubic Bézier curve are analytically computed. Based on the analytical solutions, the linear path is smoothed under the approximation error and G^2 continuity constraints. The curvature radii of all transition Bézier curves are also globally optimized to pursue the high feed speed by a linear programm model. Therefore the algorithm is easy to implement. It can be integrated into a post-process system for high-speed NC machining.

The acceleration-continuous real-time interpolation algorithm will be studied in the future work. The proposed path-smoothing algorithm provides an novel method to replace a piecewise linear tool path with G^2 continuous transition curves. G^2 continuity is helpful to smooth the normal acceleration. Some existed speed-scheduling methods, such as S-curve acceleration&deceleration method [4], can guarantee the continuity of the tangential acceleration. The acceleration-continuous real-time interpolator may be designed by combining the two methods.

Acknowledgments. The authors gratefully acknowledge the financial support of the National Natural Science Foundation of China (No. 51005155 and No. 50875171), the National Basic Research Program of China (No. 2011CB706800) and and the China Postdoctoral Science Foundation (No. 00470687).

References

1. Boyd, S., Vandenberghe, L.: Convex optimization. Cambridge University Press (2004)
2. Cheng, M., Tsai, M., Kuo, J.: Real-time NURBS command generators for CNC servo controllers. International Journal of Machine Tools and Manufacture 42(7), 801–813 (2002)
3. DeRose, T.D., Barsky, B.A.: Geometric continuity, shape parameters, and geometric constructions for Catmull-Rom splines. ACM Transactions on Graphics (TOG) 7(1), 41 (1988)
4. Erkorkmaz, K., Altintas, Y.: High speed CNC system design. Part I: jerk limited trajectory generation and quintic spline interpolation. International Journal of Machine Tools and Manufacture 41(9), 1323–1345 (2001)

5. Farin, G.: Curves and Surfaces for Computer-Aided Geometric Design: A Practical Code. Academic Press, Inc., Orlando (1996)
6. Feng, J., Li, Y., Wang, Y., Chen, M.: Design of a real-time adaptive NURBS interpolator with axis acceleration limit. The International Journal of Advanced Manufacturing Technology 48(1), 227–241 (2010)
7. Lasemi, A., Xue, D., Gu, P.: Recent development in CNC machining of freeform surfaces: A state-of-the-art review. Computer-Aided Design 42(7), 641–654 (2010)
8. Magid, E., Keren, D., Rivlin, E., Yavneh, I.: Spline-based robot navigation. In: 2006 IEEE/RSJ International Conference on Intelligent Robots and Systems, pp. 2296–2301 (2006)
9. Pateloup, V., Duc, E., Ray, P.: Bspline approximation of circle arc and straight line for pocket machining. Computer-Aided Design 42(1), 817–827 (2010)
10. Walton, D., Meek, D.: Curvature extrema of planar parametric polynomial cubic curves. Journal of Computational and Applied Mathematics 134(1-2), 69–83 (2001)
11. Waltona, D., Meekb, D.: G2 blends of linear segments with cubics and Pythagorean-hodograph quintics. International Journal of Computer Mathematics 86(9), 1498–1511 (2009)
12. Yang, K., Sukkarieh, S.: An analytical continuous-curvature path-smoothing algorithm. IEEE Transactions on Robotics 26(3), 561–568 (2010)
13. Yau, H.T., Wang, J.B.: Fast Bezier interpolator with real-time lookahead function for high-accuracy machining. International Journal of Machine Tools and Manufacture 47(10), 1518–1529 (2007)
14. Zhang, L.B., You, Y.P., He, J., Yang, X.F.: The transition algorithm based on parametric spline curve for high-speed machining of continuous short line segments. The International Journal of Advanced Manufacturing Technology 52(1), 245–254 (2011)

Design of a FPGA-Based NURBS Interpolator

Huan Zhao, Limin Zhu, Zhenhua Xiong, and Han Ding

State Key Laboratory of Mechanical System and Vibration,
Shanghai Jiaotong University, Shanghai 200240, P.R. China
{huanzhao,zhulm,mexiong,hding}@sjtu.edu.cn
http://www.sjtu.edu.cn

Abstract. In this paper, a NURBS hardware interpolator based on FPGA is designed to perform the feedrate profile scheduling, de-Boor Cox calculation and second-order Talor expansion to realize real-time interpolation. Look-ahead algorithm including curve-scanning, feedrate adjustment and acceleration/deceleration planning is implemented in the computer to release the computational load of the interpolator, whereas a motion control card with DSP+FPGA architecture receives the pre-processed results from the look-ahead circuit through PCI bus, and sequently performs the interpolation task in the FPGA and position servo control in the DSP. Experiments are carried out to verify the feasibility of this interpolator. The results imply the FPGA can finish the interpolation within 0.5ms, meanwhile its resource utilization and the calculation speed can compromise to satisfy the practical application.

Keywords: NURBS interpolation, Hardware interpolator, Look-ahead algorithm, FPGA-based interpolator, Motion control card.

1 Introduction

In the modern machining, G2 continuity is always required so that the machine tool can move smoothly with high speed and high accuracy. For this reason, conventional linear or circular interpolation may not be suitable since the fluctuation of the feedrate may excite the natural modes of the mechanical structure or the servo control system, so spline trajectory based interpolator has been widely adopted when machining parts with complex geometry.

Non-uniform rational B-Spline (NURBS) has been employed as the standard geometry representation in CAD/CAM nowadays, and receives much attention in CNC systems due to its significant advantages: (1) smaller NC code size compared to that of linear or circular interpolation; (2) continuity between different segments can be controlled to reduce feedrate fluctuation or discontinuity; (3) feedrate can be adaptively adjusted according to the geometry feature of the curve. Due to these reasons, many researchers investigated NURBS to search efficient and reliable interpolation methods. Tsai et al. [7] proposed a real-time NURBS surface interpolator for three-axis CNC machining using the second-order Talor approximation method. Yau et al. [9] developed a FPGA-based real-time interpolator, which realized the de Boor-Cox algorithm utilizing the

S. Jeschke, H. Liu, and D. Schilberg (Eds.): ICIRA 2011, Part II, LNAI 7102, pp. 477–486, 2011.
© Springer-Verlag Berlin Heidelberg 2011

FPGA's high-speed parallel computational capability. Lin et al. [5] proposed a dynamics-based NURBS interpolator with real-time look-ahead algorithm in order to generate smooth and jerk-limited feedrate profile. Tsai et al. [8] also proposed an integrated look-ahead dynamics-based(ILD) algorithm which considers geometric and servo errors simultaneously. Lee et al. [4] developed an off-line curve-scanning and feedrate pre-processing method, which takes the constraints of chord error, acceleration and jerk limitations into account, and with this scheme, the burden in the real-time interpolation task can be released and the interpolation interval can be shortened significantly. Heng and Erkorkmaz [3] designed a NURBS interpolator and constructed a feed correction polynomial to map the arc-length to the spline parameter, so that speed fluctuation was eliminated and then smooth feedrate was realized by employing jerk-limited feedrate scheduling scheme.

However, the NURBS based interpolation also suffers from the following two problems: (1) the calculations of the interpolated points and their derivatives are time-consuming; (2) the difficulty to get the parametrization relationship between the arc-length and the spline parameter results in unwanted feedrate fluctuations. In our work, we focus on how to deal with the first problem. With respect to (1), microprocessor such as FPGA or DSP can be employed to realize hardware acceleration. Due to the FPGA's parallel computational capability and cost-effective feature, it has been employed to realize the NURBS interpolation [9]. Nevertheless, the main challenge in employing the FPGA is the floating-point computation. Actually, if higher computation speed is desired then more logical elements(LEs) should be sacrificed. So it is important to select a reasonable scheme to design the FPGA-based interpolator, such that the least resources will be cost and the NURBS calculation speed can satisfy our need.

In this paper, a DSP+FPGA based motion control card (MCC) is developed, which implements the NURBS interpolation in the NIOSII core that embedded in the FPGA, and the position servo control in the DSP. The look-ahead algorithm including curve-scanning, feedrate adjustment and pre-scheduling is implemented in the computer, then the pre-processed results are transferred to the MCC for real-time interpolation. Experiments on a biaxial table are carried out to demonstrate the feasibility of the proposed interpolator.

2   NURBS Interpolation Algorithm

The NURBS curve can be expressed as follows [6]:

$$C(u) = \frac{\sum\limits_{j=0}^{n} N_{j,p}(u)w_j P_j}{\sum\limits_{j=0}^{n} N_{j,p}(u)w_j} = \frac{\sum\limits_{j=i-p}^{i} N_{j,p}(u)w_j P_j}{\sum\limits_{j=i-p}^{i} N_{j,p}(u)w_j}, \qquad (1)$$

where $C(u)$, $N_{j,p}$, u, p, i, P_j and w_j represent the coordinates of the point on the NURBS curve, the basis function of the B-spline, the knot, the degree of the

B-spline, the knot span index that u lies in the knot vector, the control point and the corresponding weight, respectively.

Let $A(u) = \sum_{j=i-p}^{i} N_{j,p}(u) w_j P_j$, $B(u) = \sum_{j=i-p}^{i} N_{j,p}(u) w_j$, then the NURBS curve can be described as $C(u) = A(u)/B(u)$.

The main objective of NURBS interpolation is to determine the knot u to generate the profile of the NURBS curve. In order to reduce the feedrate fluctuations, the second-order Talor series expansion can be used to approximate the value of the next knot u_{i+1}, which is given as [10]

$$u_{i+1} = u_i + \frac{V(u_i)T_s + (T_s^2/2)Acc(u_i)}{|C'(u_i)|} - \frac{(V(u_i)T_s)^2 C'(u_i)C''(u_i)}{2|C'(u_i)|^4}, \qquad (2)$$

where $V(u_i)$, T_s, $Acc(u_i)$, $C'(u_i)$, $C''(u_i)$ are the feedrate, interpolation period, acceleration, the first- and second-order derivatives, respectively. Since $C(u) = A(u)/B(u)$, then $C'(u)$ and $C''(u)$ can be calculated by following expression:

$$C'(u) = \frac{A'(u) - B'(u)C(u)}{B(u)}, C''(u) = \frac{A''(u) - 2B'(u)C'(u) - B''(u)C(u)}{B(u)}. \quad (3)$$

$C(u)$, $C'(u)$ and $C''(u)$ can be computed based on the basis function, however, this method is very time-consuming. So de-Boor Cox algorithm can be used to compute the values due to its efficiency.

Considering a p-degree B-Spline $Q(u) = \sum_{j=0}^{n} N_{j,p}(u) P_j$, the value $Q(u)$ can be derived by following expression:

$$Q(u) = \sum_{j=i-p}^{i} N_{j,p}(u) P_j$$

$$= \sum_{j=i-p+1}^{i} N_{j,p-1}(u) P_j^1 = \cdots = \sum_{j=i}^{i} N_{j,0}(u) P_j^p = P_i^p \qquad (4)$$

where

$$P_j^h = \begin{cases} P_j, & h = 0, \\ (1-\alpha_j^h)P_{j-1}^{h-1} + \alpha_j^h P_j^{h-1}, & j = i-k+h, \cdots, i; h = 1, 2, \cdots, k. \end{cases} \qquad (5)$$

$$\alpha_j^h = \frac{u - u_j}{u_{j+p+1-h} - u_j}, \quad u \in [u_i, u_{i+1}]. \qquad (6)$$

Then the derivatives of $Q(u)$ can be expressed as follows,

$$Q(u)^{(r)} = \sum_{j=i-p}^{i} N_{j,p}^{(r)} P_j = \sum_{j=i-p+1}^{i} N_{j,p-1}^{(r-1)} S_j = \sum_{j=i-p+2}^{i} N_{j,p-2}^{(r-2)} T_j, \qquad (7)$$

where

$$S_j = \frac{p(P_j - P_{j-1})}{u_{j+p} - u_j}, T_j = \frac{(p-1)(S_j - S_{j-1})}{u_{j+p+1} - u_j}. \qquad (8)$$

So according to (4),

$$Q(u)^{(1)} = \sum_{j=i-p+1}^{i} N_{j,p-1}S_j = S_i^{p-1}, Q(u)^{(2)} = \sum_{j=i-p+2}^{i} N_{j,p-2}T_j = T_i^{p-2}. \quad (9)$$

Using the expressions above, $A(u)$, $B(u)$ and their derivatives can be calculated efficiently, consequently $C(u)$, $C'(u)$ and $C''(u)$ can be derived by substituting them into (3).

3   Look-Ahead Algorithm and Hardware-Interpolator

3.1   Look-Ahead Algorithm

Different from traditional linear or circular interpolation, the feedrate even in one NURBS block should be changed with respect to the curvature to ensure the confined chord error [11] and the kinematic constraints. So look-ahead algorithm can be performed to detect the sharp corners with local minimum feedrates in one NURBS block [9], and schedule the transition feedrate between two NURBS blocks. The look-ahead algorithm proposed in our work is separated into three stages: curve-scanning for sub-segments division, feedrate detection and adjustment, feedrate profile pre-scheduling using jerk-limited S-shape acc/dec scheme.

In the first stage, curve-scanning considering the confined chord error, curvature and kinematic characteristics is implemented. Feedrate V_i is determined by the following expression [4] [11],

$$V_{chord} = \frac{2}{T_s}\sqrt{2\rho_i\delta - \delta^2}, \; V_{curvature} = \frac{\kappa^* F}{\kappa_i + \kappa^*}, V_{acc} = \sqrt{\frac{A_{max}}{\kappa_i}}, \; V_{jerk} = \sqrt[3]{\frac{J_{max}}{\kappa_i^2}},$$
$$V_i = min\{F, V_{chord}, V_{curvature}, V_{acc}, V_{jerk}\}, \quad (10)$$

where ρ_i, δ, κ^*, κ_i, A_{max}, J_{max}, F, V_{chord}, $V_{curvature}$, V_{acc}, V_{jerk} are the radius of curvature, the chord error tolerance, the curvature that specified to maintain the derivative continuity of the feedrate [12], the curvature of the NURBS curve, the maximum acceleration, the maximum jerk, the specified feedrate from the CAM, the feedrate constrained by chord error, curvature, acceleration or jerk, respectively. By this means, the instantaneous feedrate can be derived, and according to de-Boor Cox algorithm and Talor approximation, u_{i+1} can be calculated. During the process of curve-scanning, the local minimum feedrates are acquired and the whole NURBS block curve is divided into several sub-segments with these critical points. Simultaneously, the local maximum feedrate in every sub-segment is stored into the buffer as well for the following feedrate profile pre-scheduling.

In the second stage, firstly, the arc-length of every sub-segment is calculated by adopting the adaptive Simpson rule [3], the concept of which is shown as follows,

$$l(u_i, u_{i+1}) = \int_{u_i}^{u_{i+1}} \sqrt{x'^2 + y'^2 + z'^2} du = \int_{u_i}^{u_{i+1}} f(u) du$$

$$\approx \frac{u_{i+1} - u_i}{6} [f(u_i) + f(\frac{u_i + u_{i+1}}{2}) + f(u_{i+1})], \qquad (11)$$

where $l(u_i, u_{i+1})$ is the arc-length of the sub-segment between the knots u_i and u_{i+1}, x', y' and z' are derivatives of the NURBS curve. Given the specified tolerance ε, let $a = u_i$, $b = u_{i+1}$, $c = (u_i + u_{i+1})/2$, then if $|l(a,c) + l(b,c) - l(a,b)| \le \varepsilon$, $l(a,b)$ can be considered as the approximation of $l(u_i, u_{i+1})$. With the recursive algorithm, the arc-lengths of all sub-segments are calculated by dividing into definited sub-parts to satisfy the inequation above.

Secondly, the local minimum/maxmum feedrates are modulated according to the kinematic constraints. In our work, five-phase jerk-limited S-shape acc/dec scheme is adopted. With regard to the first and last sub-segments in one NURBS block, the arc-lengths may be not long enough even for only acceleration or deceleration. In such case, the end velocity of the first sub-segment and the start velocity of the last sub-segment should be adjusted so that the kinematic constraints for acc/dec can be satisfied. Take the first sub-segment as an example: since $V_{start} = 0$, if the arc-length $l(u_0, u_1) < \sqrt{V_{end}^3/J_{max}}$, then the end velocity V_{end} should be modified to $\sqrt[3]{l(u_0, u_1)^2 J_{max}}$, where J_{max} is the absolute value of the jerk.

In the third stage, feedrate profile pre-scheduling is implemented in order to release the burden of the NURBS interpolator. After two stages above are performed, the arc-length, start or end velocity and the maximum velocity are known for every sub-segment. Then the feedrate profile pre-scheduling is implemented to obtain the acc/dec mode, the acceleration time, the constant-feedrate running time and the deceleration time in every sub-segment. The acc/dec modes consist of seven types [5]: (1) constant-feedrate running; (2) feedrate-accelerating; (3) feedrate-decelerating; (4) begin with feedrate-accelerating and then keep running with the maximum feedrate; (5) begin with constant-feedrate-running and then decelerate; (6) begin with feedrate-accelerating and then decelerate; (7) begin with feedrate-accelerating and then keep the maximum feedrate for some time, finally decelerate.

After the look-ahead algorithm is performed, the results of every sub-segment and the information of the NURBS curve are stored into the buffer, and then transferred to the MCC for NURBS interpolation.

3.2   Hardware-Interpolator

The task of the NURBS hardware interpolator is to implement S-shape feedrate profile planning and de-Boor Cox algorithm to provide the servo controller the reference commands, as well as performing the second-order Talor expansion to calculate the next knot. The task consists of three steps: (1) de Boor-Cox algorithm is performed using the knot which was computed in the last interpolation step, then the coordinates of the NURBS curve are sent to the servo controller for position control; (2) with the acc/dec mode of every sub-segment and the information of acc/dec time that transferred from the look-ahead processor, S-shape feedrate profile planning is performed to acquire the feedrate and the acceleration value in the current step; (3) substitute the derivatives derived in Step (1) and the feedrate, acceleration obtained in Step (2) into the the second-order Talor expansion, then the new knot can be calculated.

4   System Description

The block diagram of the system architecture is shown in Fig.1, which is constituted by three parts: the computer, the MCC and the biaxial table. Windows XP+RTX(real time extension) are running in the computer to construct a real-time environment for the look-ahead algorithm. After the look-ahead processing, the results are transferred through the PCI bus to the MCC, which has a $2K \times 16bit$ dual-port RAM (DPRAM) to exchange data with PCI bus, and a $512K \times 16bit$ RAM to store multi-NURBS blocks information. The MCC also provides four analog channels$(-10V \sim +10V)$ and four encoder feedback sampling channels so that it can control the X-Y table which is drived by two Yaskawa SGDV series servo drivers and SGMJV-motors.

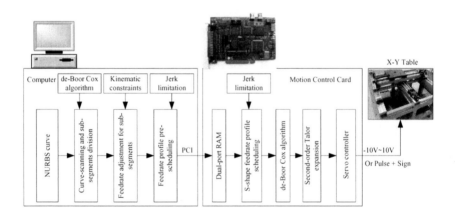

Fig. 1. Description of the system's architecture

Fig.2 shows the flowchart for the look-ahead algorithm. After the look-ahead processing, the DSP reads the results from the DPRAM, and stores them in the extended SRAM and sends one block information to the FPGA, which is performed as the hardware interpolator. Sequently, the FPGA starts NURBS interpolation that comprising feedrate scheduling, de-Boor Cox implementation and second-order Talor approximation.

The challenge encountered when the FPGA is utilized as the hardware interpolator is the floating-point calculation(FTP). There are two methods to perform FTP in the FPGA, the first of which realizes every FTP with a module

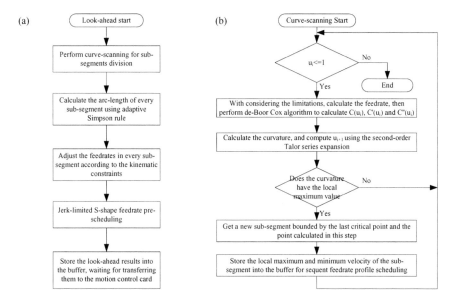

Fig. 2. Description of the look-ahead algorithm. (a) Describes the whole process of the look-ahead algorithm; (b) describes the first stage of the look-ahead algorithm in detail.

in the hardware description language, and the second calls for the user custom instructions in the NIOSII core to realize the FTP one by one.

With the first method, the whole computation time will be tiny since every FTP spends only a few clock cycles, and different FTPs can finish their tasks all in parallel. However, the resource cost will be large since hundreds of logical elements(LEs) have to be employed to construct one FTP module. Table 1 describes how many LEs are needed for the addition/subtration, division and multiplication operation [1] [2]. As shown in the table, LEs consumed in this scheme for the whole interpolation should be not less than 98530 for Altera-Cyclone II series FPGA. This requirement is impossible for the normal FPGAs so that the cost for this method is considerably high. In the second scheme, the NIOSII core is utilized in the FPGA and FTP is performed using the custom instructions, then the interpolation algorithm is implemented in serial mode but the FTP is hardware-accelerated. As a result, the whole computation time will be longer but the resource cost will be significantly reduced. In our work, CycloneII series FPGA-EP2C20F484C8N is selected to perform the NURBS interpolation, and one NIOSII core is embedded in the FPGA with 130MHz clock frequency. The LEs needed for the hardware interpolator are 9500, and the whole interpolation time can be less than $440\mu s$. Hence, with the second scheme, the resources of the FPGA can be considerably saved without sacrificing the interpolation speed too much.

Table 1. Resource utilization and time cost for FTP in the FPGA

Device Family	Floating Operation	Resource Utilization (LEs)	Implementation Time (Clock Cycles)	Feedrate Plan and de-Boor Cox
CycloneII	Add/Sub	785	7	88
CycloneII	Div	361	6	66
CycloneII	Mult	296	5	19

Remark: Resource Utilization-the minimum number of the LEs needed for one operation; Implementation Time-operation latency; Feedrate Plan and de-Boor Cox-the number of the FTPs to implement the S-shape feedrate scheduling and de-Boor Cox algorithm.

5   Experiments and Conclusions

5.1   Experiments

In this section, experiments are performed to verify the look-ahead algorithm and the feasibility of the NURBS hardware interpolator. Butterfly NURBS curve which is described by one NURBS block is taken as an example, and the corresponding limitations are: (1) chord error tolerance=1e-3mm; (2) the tolerance for arc-length computation=1e-6mm; (3) the interpolation period=0.5ms; (4) the desired feedrate=100mm/s; (5) the curvature limitation $\kappa^* = 1mm^{-1}$; (6) the maximum acceleration=$3000mm/s^2$; (7) the maximum jerk=$60000mm/s^3$.

The experiments are implemented with the following steps.

Step 1. Look-ahead algorithm implementation:

(1) Curve-scanning: after this operation, the whole NURBS curve is divided into 20 sub-segments, the start/end and maximum feedrates for every sub-segment are derived.

(2) Feedrates adjustment: then the feedrates obtained above are adjusted if the kinematic constraints are not satisfied. The feedrate limitation profile derived by chord-error-only constraint and all constraints are shown in Fig.3, respectively. In practical application, the chord-error constraint should be satisfied along the whole curve, however, the other constraints such as curvature, acceleration and jerk should be considered when the NURBS curve tends to be sharp coners.

(3) Feedrate pre-scheduling: jerk-limited S-shape based feedrate scheduling is implemented so that the acc/dec information for every sub-segment is obtained. After these operations, information of the NURBS curve and sub-segments is sent to the hardware interpolator.

Step 2. Hardware interpolation:

(1) Feedrate profile scheduling: the feedrate scheduling is carried out with the pre-processed results transferred from the computer, and the actual feedrate profile scheduled by the FPGA is shown as Fig.4(a).

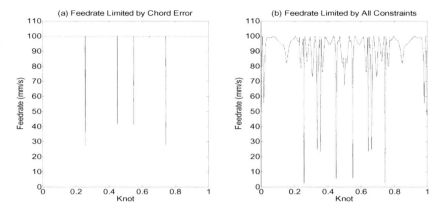

Fig. 3. Comparison of the feedrate limited by chord error and all constraints

(2) de-Boor Cox calculation and Talor approximation: the de-Boor Cox algorithm is implemented so that the reference commands for the position servo controller are acquired, and second-order Talor expansion is used to compute the next interpolated point. The actual position command sent to the DSP is shown in Fig.4(b).

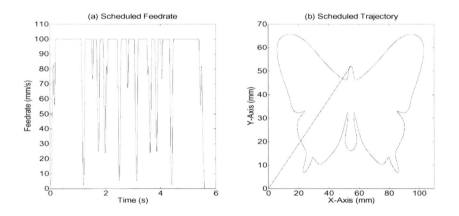

Fig. 4. The results of the interpolation implemented by the FPGA

5.2   Conclusions

Traditional NURBS interpolation is completed in the computer and the interval can not be tiny enough due to the computational power bottleneck and the problem of timer's precision. Hence, hardware interpolator based on FPGA is proposed by some researchers. Nevertheless, the resources utilization and the calculation speed must compromise to obtain the most cost-effective application scheme. In this paper, a hardware interpolator based on FPGA-NIOSII core is proposed, the real-time look-ahead algorithm is implemented in the computer to release the burden of the interpolator, and look-ahead results are transferred to the motion control card for interpolation. The experiments demonstrate that both high speed interpolation and low resource cost can be achieved simultaneously using the proposed hardware interpolator.

Acknowledgments. This work was partially supported by the National Key Basic Research Program under grant No. 2011CB706804, the Science & Technology Commission of Shanghai Municipality under Grant No. 11QH1401400, and the Research Project of State Key Laboratory of Mechanical System & Vibration MSVMS201102.

References

1. Altera: Floating-Point Divider Megafunctions User Guide (2008)
2. Altera: Floating-Point Megafunctions User Guide (2010)
3. Heng, M., Erkorkmaz, K.: Design of a NURBS interpolator with minimal feed fluctuation and continuous feed modulation capability. International Journal of Machine Tools and Manufacture 50(3), 281–293 (2010)
4. Lee, A.C., Lin, M.T., Pan, Y.R., Lin, W.Y.: The feedrate scheduling of NURBS interpolator for CNC machine tools. Computer-Aided Design (2011)
5. Lin, M., Tsai, M., Yau, H.: Development of a dynamics-based NURBS interpolator with real-time look-ahead algorithm. International Journal of Machine Tools and Manufacture 47(15), 2246–2262 (2007)
6. Piegl, L., Tiller, W.: The NURBS book. Springer, Heidelberg (1997)
7. Tsai, M.C., Cheng, C.W., Cheng, M.Y.: A real-time NURBS surface interpolator for precision three-axis CNC machining. International Journal of Machine Tools and Manufacture 43(12), 1217–1227 (2003)
8. Tsai, M.S., Nien, H.W., Yau, H.T.: Development of an integrated look-ahead dynamics-based NURBS interpolator for high precision machinery. Computer-Aided Design 40(5), 554–566 (2008)
9. Yau, H., Lin, M., Tsai, M.: Real-time NURBS interpolation using FPGA for high speed motion control. Computer-Aided Design 38(10), 1123–1133 (2006)
10. Yeh, S., Hsu, P.: The speed-controlled interpolator for machining parametric curves. Computer-Aided Design 31(5), 349–357 (1999)
11. Yeh, S., Hsu, P.: Adaptive-feedrate interpolation for parametric curves with a confined chord error. Computer-Aided Design 34(3), 229–237 (2002)
12. Zhiming, X., Jincheng, C., Zhengjin, F.: Performance evaluation of a real-time interpolation algorithm for NURBS curves. The International Journal of Advanced Manufacturing Technology 20(4), 270–276 (2002)

Iso-scallop Trajectory Generation
for the 5-Axis Machining of an Impeller

Xubing Chen[1], Jinbo Wang[1], and Youlun Xiong[2]

[1] School of Mechanical and Electrical Engineering, Wuhan Institute of Technology,
Wuhan 430073, P.R. China
`bluegif@gmail.com`
[2] State Key Laboratory of Digital Manufacturing Equipment and Technology, Huazhong
University of Science and Technology, Wuhan 430074, P.R. China
`famt@mail.hust.edu.cn`

Abstract. Iso-scallop trajectories, tool orientations and a tool swept volume for the 5-axis machining of an impeller have been developed in the paper. As the merits of ball end tools, the planning work has been done on the cutter location surface. Firstly, a boundary curve is selected as the master trajectory, and cutting intervals are calculated from the geodesic curvature on the blade surface to keep a constant scallop height. Secondly, tool orientation determinations are discussed to promise the trajectories interference-free. The determined tool orientations are starting from the trajectory point and pointing to a guide line located in the mid-plane between two neighbor blades. Finally, measurement results from a machining simulation and a produced tool swept volume are given to illustrate the feasibility and validity of the proposed method.

Keywords: impeller, 5-axis machining, iso-scallop trajectory, tool orientation, tool swept volume.

1   Introduction

Impellers are the typical parts used for the validation of 5-axis machining. They have complex geometries of thin blades, large distortions and small gaps between blades, which induce formidable machining processes and a lot of cutting work. For the 5-axis machining of impellers, ball end tools are usually employed for their merits of low milling load, stable machining process, and easy to transform from cutter location (CL) points to cutter contact (CC) points due to cutting ellipses degenerating to circles. The planning of CL points or CC points and determining their tool orientations lead to the blooming of the trajectory generation research in 5-axis machining.

Compared with iso-planar, iso-parametric and other traditional methods, iso-scallop trajectory generation provided more efficiency and better quality in the 5-axis machining, thus attracted many researchers. In 2002 and 2004, Feng and Li [1, 2] employed the scallop surface and the tool center surface to establish scallop curves and cutter-location tool paths. The results indicated that constant scallop-height

S. Jeschke, H. Liu, and D. Schilberg (Eds.): ICIRA 2011, Part II, LNAI 7102, pp. 487–494, 2011.

machining achieved the specified machining accuracy with fewer and shorter tool paths. In 2002 and 2005, Tournier and Due [3, 4] proposed the concept of the machining surface to computing iso-scallop tool paths in 5-axis milling. The approach was prominent in terms of precision and in particular its aptitude to treat curvature discontinuities. In 2003, Lee [5] developed a spiral-topology tool path with the minimum number of cutter retractions in high speed machining (HSM). In the contour offset procedure, the offset distance was determined such that the scallop height maintained a constant roughness. In 2003, Chen et al. [6] introduced the steepest-directed and iso-cusped (SDIC) tool path generation scheme for tool path generation in three-axis CNC milling. Their combination ensured high sculptured part productivity, less redundant milling, and good surface quality. In 2006, Agrawal et al. [7] optimized the orientation of the primary or master cutter path (MCP) through the application of a genetic algorithm while implementing iso-scallop machining. The results indicate a substantial reduction in total machining time. In 2007, Kim [8] introduced the generation of constant cusp-height tool paths as geodesic parallels on an abstract Riemannian manifold. He proved that a selection from a family of the constructed geodesic parallels constituted a rational approximation of accurate constant cusp-height tool paths. In 2008, Tournie and Lartigue [9] presented a new method of computing constant scallop height tool paths in 5-axis milling. The proposed approach consisted of parallel planes in 5-axis milling to avoid self-intersection of the tool path. In 2008, Lee et al. [10] developed a mesh-based tool path generation for obtaining constant scallop heights. The advantages of simple geometric computation and robust for mesh surface make it easy to check and remove interference in the process of tool path generation. In 2010, Ahmet and Ali [11] developed an iso-scallop tool-path generation strategy by adjusting the effective cutter radius to the surface curvature for the efficient 5-axis machining of free-form surfaces. According to the experimental results, the iso-scallop method reduced the total path length by about 22%–50%. In 2011, Chen et al. [12] developed a manifold approach to generating iso-scallop trajectories in three-axis machining. The proposed approach has appealing merits of dimensionality reduction, which decreases the algorithm complexity. According to the literature reviewed above, researches on iso-scallop trajectory generation are still hot topics, and further researches need to be carried out according to the detail machining processes.

The major motivation of this paper is to discuss the differential geometries and mathematical descriptions to maintain a constant scallop height in the 5-axis machining of an impeller. The rest of the paper is organized as follows. Tool path planning and tool orientation determination are introduced in section 2 and section 3, respectively. In Section 4, a blade case is developed for validating the iso-scallop trajectories. Finally, in Section 5, the contributions and limitations of the research are concluded with some suggestions for future work.

2   Tool Path Planning

The tool path planning of iso-scallop trajectories is based on the cutter location surface, which has a uniform distance from the blade surface, i.e. the radius of the ball end tool. Suppose a planning surface $M(u,v)$ is a smooth surface, and its Jacobian determinant has a non-zero values described as follows.

$$J(M) = \begin{vmatrix} \dfrac{\partial x}{\partial u} & \dfrac{\partial y}{\partial u} & \dfrac{\partial z}{\partial u} \\ \dfrac{\partial x}{\partial v} & \dfrac{\partial y}{\partial v} & \dfrac{\partial z}{\partial v} \end{vmatrix} \neq 0.$$ (1)

Therefore, the tool path planning on a smooth surface includes of six steps:

   i. Select a boundary curve as the master trajectory.
   ii. Extend the master trajectory long enough to promise the calculated trajectories touching the bounding box of the surface in both sides.
   iii. Discrete the trajectory in a specified accuracy and calculate the cutting interval for each discrete point to generate the discrete points of the next curve.
   iv. Fit the calculated discrete points into a smooth curve and project it into the planning surface, and treat the projection curve as the next trajectory.
   v. Repeat steps iii and iv to full cover the smooth surface.
   vi. Cut off the trajectories outside the surface, and the remained trajectories are iso-scalloped.

In step ii, extensions of the planning surface need to be done firstly for all the generated points having a parent object.

In step iii, the cutting interval L is a function of cutter radius r, scallop height h and geodesic curvature radius ρ at the cutter contact point of a ball-end cutter. For a given cutter radius and scallop height, the cutting interval L can be calculated as [13]

$$L = \frac{|\rho|}{(r+\rho)(h+\rho)} \times \sqrt{4(r+\rho)^2(h+\rho)^2 - [\rho^2 + 2r\rho + (h+\rho)^2]^2}.$$ (2)

There exists $\rho > 0$ for a convex surface and $\rho < 0$ for a concave surface. In practical machining, there usually exists $|\rho| >> h$, thus the cutting interval can be expressed as

$$L \approx 2\sqrt{2hr}\sqrt{\rho/(\rho+r)}.$$ (3)

In addition, the discrete point $(x(u,v), y(u,v), z(u,v))$ of the next curve can be treated as the intersection point of the smooth surface $M(u,v)$ and a circle with a radius L and a normal vector $r'(u_0,v_0)$ of the tangent direction at the discrete point $(x_0(u_0,v_0), y_0(u_0,v_0), z_0(u_0,v_0))$ of the first trajectory, as shown in Fig 1.

$$\begin{cases} M(u,v) = 0 \\ (x(u,v) - x_0(u_0,v_0), y(u,v) - y_0(u_0,v_0), z(u,v) - z_0(u_0,v_0)) \cdot r'(u_0,v_0) = 0 \end{cases}.$$ (4)

In step iv, although all the calculated discrete points are generated from the planning surface, the fitted curve may be not fully located in due to the fitting errors.

A projection is benefit for constraining the attribution relation between the next trajectory and the planning surface.

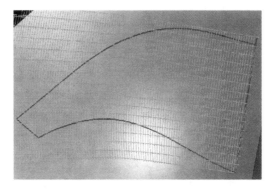

Fig. 1. Generated trajectories and their perpendicular circles on the extended blade surface

3   Tool Orientation Determination

To determine tool orientations of the generated trajectories, a guide line is established first. Suppose all the tool orientations are started from the trajectory points and ended at a guide line. The guide line is located in the mid-plane between two neighbor blades, which can be constructed from the two midpoints of the top boundary lines and a midpoint in the impeller hub surface, as shown in Fig 2(a). And there is a specified distance between the guide line and the projection line of the blade upper boundary line to keep the guide line a little far away from the impeller and promise interference-free tool orientations, as shown in Fig 2(b).

(a) Mid-plane between two neighbor blades   (b) Guide line of the tool orientations

Fig. 2. Constructions of the mid-plane and the guide line of tool orientations

Suppose the three midpoints are (x_1, y_1, z_1), (x_2, y_2, z_2) and (x_3, y_3, z_3), the mid plane can be described as follows.

$$\begin{vmatrix} x - x_1 & y - y_1 & z - z_1 \\ x_2 - x_1 & y_2 - y_1 & z_2 - z_1 \\ x_3 - x_1 & y_3 - y_1 & z_3 - z_1 \end{vmatrix} = 0 . \tag{5}$$

Suppose the projection line of the blade upper boundary line described as the following equations.

$$\frac{x - x_0}{m} = \frac{y - y_0}{n} = \frac{z - z_0}{p} . \tag{6}$$

where (x_0, y_0, z_0) is the starting point on the projection line, and (m, n, p) is the unit direction vector.

Then, the guide line can be described as:

$$\frac{x - x_0'}{m} = \frac{y - y_0'}{n} = \frac{z - z_0'}{p} . \tag{7}$$

where (x_0', y_0', z_0') is a point on the guide line and has a distance H from the point (x_0, y_0, z_0). Point (x_0', y_0', z_0') can be solved with the following equations.

$$\begin{cases} \sqrt{(x_0' - x_0)^2 + (y_0' - y_0)^2 + (z_0' - z_0)^2} = H \\ \begin{vmatrix} x_0' - x_1 & y_0' - y_1 & z_0' - z_1 \\ x_2 - x_1 & y_2 - y_1 & z_2 - z_1 \\ x_3 - x_1 & y_3 - y_1 & z_3 - z_1 \end{vmatrix} = 0 \\ (x_0' - x_0, y_0' - y_0, z_0' - z_0) \cdot (m, n, p) = 0 \end{cases} . \tag{8}$$

Up to now, the guide line is constructed. Cut the guide line into several segments of the same length, and keep the segment number the same as the trajectory element number. Therefore, assign the line segments to trajectory elements from right to left,

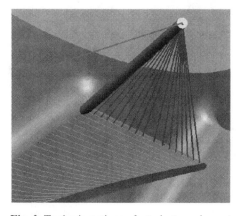

Fig. 3. Tool orientations of a trajectory element

one by one in sequence. The starting point of each line segment can be treated as the end point of tool orientations for the assigned trajectory element, as shown in Fig 3.

Suppose the starting point of an assigned line segment is point (x_i', y_i', z_i'), for a corresponding trajectory point $(x(t), y(t), z(t))$, the tool orientation can be described as follows.

$$T(\alpha, \beta) = (x_i', y_i', z_i') - (x(t), y(t), z(t)) .$$
(9)

where i is the sequential number of the line segment, α is the tilt angle of the tool orientation, i.e. the angle between the tool projection in the trajectory plane and the normal direction of the surface; and β is the yaw angle of the tool orientation, i.e. the angle between the tool projection in the perpendicular plane of the trajectory and the normal direction of the surface. Both the trajectory plane and the perpendicular plane are in parallel with the normal direction of trajectory point on the surface.

4   Case Study

To valid the proposed method, a tool swept volume of a selected impeller blade is produced, as shown in Fig 4(a). Fig 4(b) illustrates the results of machining simulation. And scallop heights of the simulated machining surface are measured to display in Fig 5 (a). The scallop heights are measured as the spatial distances between the cusp points and the objective surface. Obviously, the simulated surface has a constant cusp height with small vibrations in the figure and the root mean square value of cusp heights is 0.3533, while the set value of scallop height is 0.5. The small vibrations are mainly coming from the approximation errors, fitting errors, projection errors and computing errors. And the root mean square value includes of a remaining value of 0.1 to reduce the overcuts in the machined surface. Even then, a bit of overcuts are discovered in the tail of the blade, as shown in the circle of Fig 4(b).

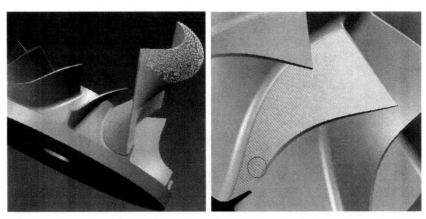

(a) Tool swept volume on the blade   (b) Machining simulation results on the blade

Fig. 4. Tool swept volume and machining simulation results of the generated iso-scallop trajectories

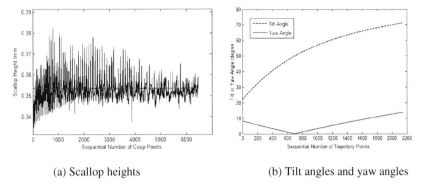

(a) Scallop heights   (b) Tilt angles and yaw angles

Fig. 5. Scallop heights, tilt angles and yaw angles of the generated iso-scallop trajectories

What is more, the tilt angles and yaw angles of the longest trajectory element are illustrated in Fig 5(b). It is easy to find that the tilt angle varies smoothly in $(22.0431°, 71.0577°)$, and the yaw angle varies in $(0.0057°, 13.8067°)$ with a turning point. The continuous property of the determined tool orientations is benefit from the merits of the smooth blade surface. Obviously, the tool swings are feasible and easy to be realized.

5   Conclusions and Future Work

Aiming at the 5-axis machining of an impeller, this paper presents a feasible method for iso-scallop trajectory generation. The proposed method is discussed in two steps: tool path planning and tool orientation determination. For tool path planning, a boundary curve is selected as the first trajectory, and cutting intervals are calculated at every discrete trajectory point to generate the next one. By this way, iso-scallop trajectories are generated one by one. For tool orientation determination, a guide line is constructed to promise interference-free trajectories at first. After that, the guide line is cut into several segments of the same length. And the line segments are assigned to trajectory elements in sequence. The tool orientation will be determined by the vector starting to the trajectory point and pointing to the endpoint of the line segment. The simulation results are implemented to verify the validity and efficiency of the proposed method.

However, there are some limitations with the proposed method and future work is required. The research is limited to the given impeller at present and not sure whether it is suitable for unsmooth surfaces including geometric mutations and cusps. Another aspect is that the selections of the first trajectory curve and the distance parameter H of the guide line are also an open issue in multi-axis machining, and it will be researched in the future work. Although different selections may be feasible, there should be certain rules existed to promise high efficient machining processes.

Acknowledgments. The work is supported by National Natural Science Foundation of China under Grant No. 50905131 and 50835004, and Natural Science Foundation of Hubei province under Grant No. 2009CDB251. The authors are also grateful to the editors and the anonymous reviewers for helpful comments.

References

1. Feng, H.Y., Li, H.W.: Constant scallop-height tool path generation for three-axis sculptured surface machining. Computer-Aided Design 34(9), 647–654 (2002)
2. Li, H.W., Feng, H.Y.: Efficient five-axis machining of free-form surfaces with constant scallop height tool paths. International Journal of Production Research 42(12), 2403–2417 (2004)
3. Tournier, C., Duc, E.: A surface based approach for constant scallop height tool-path generation. International Journal of Advanced Manufacturing Technology 19(5), 318–324 (2002)
4. Tournier, C., Duc, E.: Iso-scallop tool path generation in 5-axis milling. International Journal of Advanced Manufacturing Technology 25(9-10), 867–875 (2005)
5. Lee, E.: Contour offset approach to spiral toolpath generation with constant scallop height. Computer-Aided Design 35(6), 511–518 (2003)
6. Chen, Z.C., Vickers, G.W., Dong, Z.: Integrated steepest-directed and iso-cusped toolpath generation for three-axis CNC machining of sculptured parts. Journal of Manufacturing Systems 22(3), 190–201 (2003)
7. Agrawal, R.K., Pratihar, D.K., Choudhury, A.R.: Optimization of CNC isoscallop free form surface machining using a genetic algorithm. International Journal of Machine Tools and Manufacture 46(7-8), 811–819 (2006)
8. Kim, T.: Constant cusp height tool paths as geodesic parallels on an abstract Riemannian manifold. Computer-Aided Design 39(6), 477–489 (2007)
9. Tournie, C., Lartigue, C.: 5-axis Iso-scallop Tool Paths along Parallel Planes. Computer-Aided Design & Applications 5(1-4), 278–286 (2008)
10. Lee, S.G., Kim, H.C., Yang, M.Y.: Mesh-based tool path generation for constant scallop-height machining. International Journal of Advanced Manufacturing Technology 37(1-2), 15–22 (2008)
11. Ahmet, C., Ali, Ü.: A novel iso-scallop tool-path generation for efficient five-axis machining of free-form surfaces. International Journal of Advanced Manufacturing Technology 51(9-12), 1083–1098 (2010)
12. Chen, X.B., Li, W.L., Xiong, Y.L.: A manifold approach to generating iso-scallop trajectories in three-axis machining. Science in China Series E 54(1), 131–139 (2011)
13. Ren, B.Y., Tang, Y.Y.: Geometry Modeling Theories and Their Applications in NC Machining, pp. 120–124. Harbin Institute of Technology Press, Harbin (2000)

Swarm Robot Flocking: An Empirical Study

M. Fikret Ercan[1] and Xiang Li [2]

[1] Singapore Polytechnic, School of Electrical and Electronic Engineering, Singapore
[2] School of Information Science and Engineering, Central South University, China
mfercan@sp.edu.sg, xl_huse@126.com

Abstract. Robots can be used in exploration or investigation of unknown terrains especially if the environment is dangerous. It is customary to employ a sophisticated robot for such task. However, this approach is vulnerable since a failure of the robot means, failure of the entire mission. An emerging approach in robotics research is to employ many simple robots that can collectively achieve a demanding task. Even the failure of some robots should not affect the overall mission. Maneuvering such large systems poses new challenges in controlling them. In our earlier work, a control strategy, namely triangular formation algorithm (TFA), was developed and tested using simulation tools. The TFA is a local interaction strategy which basically makes three neighboring robots to form a regular triangular lattice. Simulation results show that swarm behaviors such as aggregation, flocking and obstacle avoidance can be achieved successfully. Here, we are concerned with implementing the algorithm in practice with real robots. We have developed a swarm of five robots and tested the performance of the algorithm in practice. This paper presents our initial findings.

Keywords: Swarm robots, swarm flocking, distributed control.

1 Introduction

Swarm robot studies deal with the problem of controlling and coordinating large number of simple robots to perform a task collectively. The type of task would be impossible, challenging or time consuming for a single robot to achieve. Swarm robotic is largely inspired by the observations made in social animals and their behavior. In a swarm, simple local behaviors of the individuals result in a complex global behavior of the group [1], [2]. Swarm behavior such as chain forming, aggregation, flocking, foraging are vastly studied in literature [1], [2]. Among these behaviors, flocking may found direct applications in practice such as surveillance, data acquisition and sensor networks. The flocking behavior in swarm robotics involves coordinating a group of robots to navigate towards a certain destination in an unknown environment. Members of the swarm are expected to achieve this goal while adapting to their environment. During the last decade, various control and planning strategies have been presented for flocking control. The earliest work on flocking of agents can be traced back to Reynolds, C.W., [3] who modeled the first flocking model. In his

S. Jeschke, H. Liu, and D. Schilberg (Eds.): ICIRA 2011, Part II, LNAI 7102, pp. 495–504, 2011.
© Springer-Verlag Berlin Heidelberg 2011

model, an agent possesses three elementary local behavior rules: separation for avoiding collision, cohesion for staying together and alignment towards a common velocity. Subsequently, Vicsek et al. [4] give a simple flocking model of autonomous agents, where a constant absolute velocity is assumed for all the agents. Jadbabie et al. [5] provided theoretical explanations for the observed behaviors in Vicsek's model. In another related research, Yang et al. [6], presented rules for flocking behavior in an unknown environment with obstacles where the nearest point on the obstacle is treated as a virtual agent. Potential field based methods are also studied extensively for distributed flocking behavior. For instance, Kim et al. [7] presented a set of analytical guidelines for designing potential functions to avoid local minima for group flocking of agents. All these works mentioned above have paid more attention to avoiding collision between the robots rather than the forming regular flocking networks among robots, which is relevant to many real world applications such as uniform sampling and data collection.

In our earlier study, we have developed a flocking algorithm, namely triangle formation algorithm (TFA), based on a geometric approach. The basic operation principle of the algorithm is to let three neighboring robots to form equilateral triangular configuration (ETC) [8]. Every robot is assigned with only two local behavior rules: formation and alignment. The control input of the robot dynamics consists of two forces: local formation and velocity alignment. Instead of providing a potential function to directly deal with the collision avoidance between members, the TF strategy achieves the collision avoidance by attempting to form a local lattice. The robots of the group maintain a uniform distance among each other and form a multi regular lattice network while flocking. A distinguishing advantage of the TF strategy is that behavior of an individual robot is determined by the local position of only two selected neighboring robots. This paper presents our experimental results in applying TF algorithm using simple identical robots.

2   Modeling and Realization of Robots

TF algorithm consider a swarm of N robots, denoted by r_1, r_2, ..., r_N, as mobile points in a plane. It is assumed that each robot is capable of sensing its neighbors and aware of its orientation. All the robots in a swarm execute the same algorithm. The actions of individual robots are asynchronous and independent from each other. Figure 1 shows the basic robot architecture. One of the sensors used in the robot structure is digital compass in order to detect robots' orientation. The arrow in the figure shows robots' forward direction. In addition, there are eight proximity sensors for detecting neighbors. There is no direct communication among the robots. The communication unit, Xbee module, is only used for sending data to a computer for recording robot motions. Texas instruments' TMS320C2407 DSP is the main controlling unit of the robot.

The other parameters used in TFA are s_r and s_a which represents a robot's sensing radius and the corresponding sensing area respectively. Sensing radius is about 80 cm in the experimental setup. The distance between the robots, or the lattice of an equidistant triangle, defined as d_u, that is $0 < d_u < s_r$. In the test robots, this distance is set to 25 cm. The distance between robots denoted as $dist(p_i, p_j)$ where p_i and p_j are the locations of the robots r_i and r_j. Robot r_i can detect the neighbors within s_a and then select two robots r_{s1} and r_{s2} among them as neighbors. p_{s1} and p_{s2} represent the positions of these two robots and defined as a position set $\{p_{s1}, p_{s2}\}$. Given p_i and $\{p_{s1}, p_{s2}\}$, C_i is *a configuration* determined by position set $\{p_i, p_{s1}, p_{s2}\}$ denoted as S_i. Initially, C_i is possibly an acute triangle, line segment or obtuse triangle. It is defined as *Equilateral Triangle* (E_i) when a triangle with equal side lengths of d_u is formed. Each robot in the swarm attempts to generate E_i together with its two other neighbors. Consequently, the entire swarm can form a uniform network with equal intervals between the members. To form E_i, each robot needs to know a goal position, p_g, to move towards. Triangular formation algorithm, run on every robot, produces the position p_g to achieve these motions.

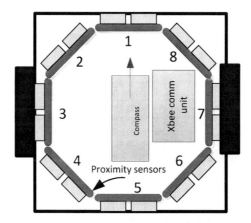

Fig. 1. Robots used in the experiments

3   Triangular Formation Algorithm (TFA)

At the beginning, the robots are distributed to the field arbitrarily and discretely, with random initial velocities. All the robots are assigned with the same behavior rules, (1) formation: steer to form isosceles triangle lattice with the two selective neighboring robots; (2) alignment: steer towards the average velocity of the three neighboring robots. It should be noted that, for a given robot, selection of two neighboring robots is dynamic at each time step and it is not fixed to neighbors selected at the initial stage. As a result, robots can flock with a common speed in an unknown environment while maintaining a multi Equilateral Triangular Configuration (ETC) network. The dynamics of each robot is defined as follows:

$$\ddot{x}_i = u_i \tag{1a}$$

$$u_i = - \underbrace{\sum_{j \in \{s_1, s_2\}} \left(v_i - v_j \right)}_{a_v} + \underbrace{p_g / \|p_g\|}_{a_f} \tag{1b}$$

Where x_i is the coordinates of robot r_i and u_i is the control input for robot r_i which can be refined as shown in equation (1b). In equation (1b), a_f is the formation acceleration, a_v is the alignment acceleration, v is the current velocity of the robot, p_g is the local goal position vector with respect to r_i. Here, we define the set $\{s_1, s_2\}$ which is the index set of the two neighboring robots selected by r_i. In order robot r_i to form an isosceles triangular configuration with two other robots, it needs to compute a goal position, p_g, with respect to its local coordinates.

We first consider the basic behavior of three neighboring robots. As each robot attempts to form isosceles triangle configuration with two other robots, an ETC will be constructed consequently regardless of their initial distribution. This basic behavior is the core of the group behavior. The group objective of three neighboring robots is to move at a common velocity and maintain an ETC with a side length of d_u. Reaching to a common velocity is easily achieved by averaging their velocities. However, our emphasis is to control three robots to autonomously to form an ETC regardless of their initial distribution. For simplicity, we assume that robots have no initial velocities. Instinctively, each robot should attempt to stay in an equal distant from the other two robots at any given time in order to form an ETC. Therefore, a robot needs to find a goal position and move towards it, such that distances between the goal position and the other two robots will be equal to d_u. In fact, for a given robot, the goal position satisfying the above requirement isn't always calculable, as it depends on the current three-point configuration constructed by them. If three-point configuration, constructed by the three neighboring robots, enables robot to locate two other neighbors, robot r_i can calculate the exact goal position p_g. If the initial three point configuration of three neighboring robots do not allow two other robots to be detected (such as a line formation), robot r_i calculates the local average position of them and takes it as approximate goal position p_g. In formation stage, there is an exact goal position for robot r_i, which has the equal distance, d_u, from the other two robots r_{s1} and r_{s2}. All the possible methods for calculating the goal position are given in our earlier study together with a detailed description of the algorithm and simulation studies [8]. When the number of robots in a swarm is more than three, a dynamic neighbor selection mechanism determines neighbors to be used in TF algorithm. In each time step, r_i selects the nearest robot as the first neighbor r_{s1}. When there is more than one candidate for r_{s1}, r_i uniquely determines its first neighbor by sorting the positions of the candidates in decreasing order. The second neighbor r_{s2} is selected such that r_{s1} and r_{s2} produces the minimal triangle perimeter. If there are multiple candidates, r_i determines r_{s2} by applying the same sorting rule [8].

4   Experiments and Discussion

Currently, our experimental robots only have proximity sensors hence the sensing is limited to detection of an object. By employing camera and image processing techniques, it is possible to identify objects as a peer robot or an obstacle. At this moment our robots do not have such feature. Therefore, our practical experiments are conducted in a controlled environment where there is no obstacle. That is, a positive sensor reading implies another robot at the vicinity. Hence, at this stage we are only able to test aggregation, formation and flocking behavior but not obstacle avoidance feature. During the experiments a central computer is used for data collection and recording coordinates of the robots. This method, though less accurate, is more cost effective and flexible compared to camera and image processing techniques commonly used in other reported studies. The experiments are conducted in a controlled environment. We use a platform of 2.3 x 2.3 meter with a uniform surface. It is coated with paint so that external disturbances, such as wheel slip, are minimized. Each robot performs TFA and moves accordingly while transmitting a block of data regularly containing robot orientation and coordinates. After aggregation, robots flock for a distance of 1.80 meters. The unit velocity for a robot is programmed as 2 cm/sec. The average performance deviation is then calculated and plotted by central computer. An important practical issue is the reliability of sonar sensors used in robots and interpretation of sensor readings. We have employed a Dempster-Shafer reliability model [9],

[10], [11] and adapted to dynamic environment. However, the robot hardware is not the main subject of this paper. The issues related to sensor fusion and interpretation is discussed separately [12].

The core algorithm TFA requires at least three robots in a swarm. For a larger swarm, a neighbor selection method is introduced to combine with TFA. During the experiments, the condition, $s_r > d_u$, must be satisfied. Also, each robot must have at least two robots located within its s_a at the beginning. Figure 2 shows snap shots of three robot aggregation and flocking behavior. Here, two different forms of initial robot configuration are tested. In Figure 2, all of the three robots are at the visual view of each other, whereas in Figure 3 initial positions of robots do not allow a clear view of neighbors for all three. Figure 4 shows snapshots of four robot flocking.

Fig. 2. Case of three robots: $N = 3$, $d_u = 25$ cm. Initial position of robots allow each robot to see neighbors (i.e. initial position forms a triangular)

Fig. 3. Case of three robots: $N = 3$, $d_u = 25$ cm. Robots have limited view initially (i.e. initial positions form a line)

Fig. 4. Case of three robots: $N = 4$, $d_u = 25$ cm. Robots aggregate first then flock

Initial robot positions and their orientations are generated randomly using a simple code written in Matlab. Robots are positioned at these random and distinct positions and their motions recorded. Starting from these random positions robots manage to form an ETC eventually. We use the average deviation (*adev*) of side lengths from the natural length d_u over time as a performance indicator and it is defined as following:

$$adev(n \cdot \Delta t) = \frac{\sum |d_{i,j}(n \cdot \Delta t) - d_u|}{3}, \ n \in N \quad (2)$$

In the above equation, Δt is the time step determined by data capturing rate from robots (which is approximately less than 3 sec intervals); $d_{i,j}$ is the distance between robots r_i and r_j at time instant $n \cdot \Delta t$.

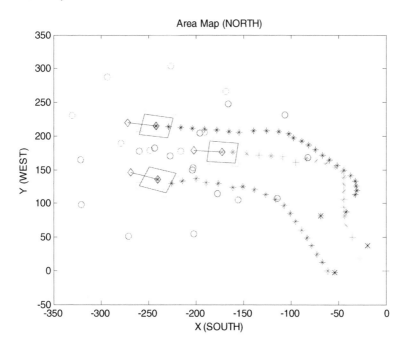

Fig. 5. Three robot motions captured in real-time

Figure 5 illustrates a plot of three robot flocking behavior. This plot is based on real time readings captured from the robots. Each robot sends a package of 15 bytes which contains robot ID, values of 8 proximity sensors, x and y coordinates of the robot, and compass readings. Current coordinate of robot is calculated by using the motor encoders and on board compass, therefore a controlled environment was essential for the experiments. In Figure 5, square boxes indicate a robots' current position, arrow indicates robot orientation based on compass reading and circles indicate the proximity sensor values of each robot. In the figure symbol '*' indicates robot position, based on its center of gravity, hence robot motions can be traced easily. The target of the flocking mission was to navigate towards the north-west corner of the experimental platform.

Figure 6 shows average deviation curve with 3, 4 and 5 robots. We observed a faster convergence rate with three robots. However, we did not observe any significant change for $N=4$ and 5 robots. In all the experiments, it is observed that robots approximately formed equidistant triangles with their neighbors within the first 100 seconds and then system began to fine tune. Table 1 shows a record of the experiments for various numbers of robots. Average convergence time, which is an average of first ten successful trials, the best and the worst convergence times and the maximum deviations are shown. Here, maximum deviation indicates the maximum deviation of the side lengths from the pre-set value, d_u, during the entire flocking process. For $N=4$ and $N=5$ the average convergence time and other performance indicators were similar. On the other hand for $N=3$ the average convergence time was significantly better.

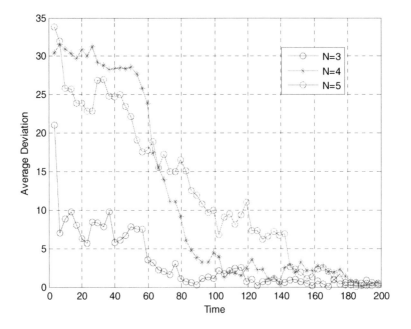

Fig. 6. Average deviations of side lengths over time (secs.)

In some trials we also observed failures, such as a robot being separated from the flock, or losing direction etc., mainly due to external factors such as wheel slippage, hardware/software failure, or simply due to mishaps of sensors. In Table 2, we present a list of failures as compared to number of trials performed as an indicator of overall performance of our experimental swarm robots. In the case of three robots with initial triangular configuration, we have observed minimum amount of failure. Intuitively, we expect a higher failure rate with increased robot population. The maximum failure rate was %19.04 in five robot case.

Table 1. Performance of TFA in practice (10 trials)

Configuration	Average convergence time (sec)	Best convergence time (sec)	Worst convergence time (sec)	Max deviation (cm)
n=3, initial formation triangular	73.02	63	115	19
n=3, initial formation line	78.3	59	145	22
n=4	136.7	114	190	26
n=5	142.1	107	212	22

Table 2. Performance of swarm in number of trials

Configuration	Number of trials recorded	Number of failures	Failure rate
n=3, initial formation triangular	18	1	%5.5
n=3, initial formation line	25	4	%16
n=4	22	3	%13.63
n=5	21	4	%19.04

5   Conclusions

This paper demonstrates an application of a distributed control algorithm, Triangular Formation Algorithm (TFA), for a swarm of robots to demonstrate aggregation and flocking behaviors. Robots negotiate the environment and dynamically adapt a collective behavior. TFA ensures three neighboring robots to form configuration E_i regardless of their arbitrarily distinct positions. There are only two requirements for TFA to operate properly. Firstly, at start each robot should be able to sense at least two other robots nearby and secondly the value of s_r should be set greater than d_u. By using neighbor selection strategy, TFA is extended to a larger swarm. Aggregation, via forming multi-E_i configurations, and flocking behavior are also achieved. Experiments with real robots demonstrated algorithm is effective in practice. Currently, we have an experimental set up made of five robots. The convergence of algorithm did not show a significant change with increased number of robots, however we intend to experiment with a large swarm (n>10) in near future.

Acknowledgments. This project is supported by Singapore Tote board fund 11-27801-36-M115 and 11-30012-36-M115. The authors are also grateful to Mr Lius Partawijaya for building robots and preparing the test platform.

References

1. Bayindir, L., Şahin, E.: A Review of Studies in Swarm Robotics. Turk. J. Elec. Engin. 15(2), 115–147 (2007)
2. Şahin, E.: Swarm Robotics: From Sources of Inspiration to Domains of Application. In: Şahin, E., Spears, W.M. (eds.) Swarm Robotics 2004. LNCS, vol. 3342, pp. 10–20. Springer, Heidelberg (2005)
3. Reynolds, C.W.: Flocks, Herds, and Schools: A Distributed Behavioral Model. Computer Graphics 21(4), 25–34 (1987)
4. Vicsek, T., Czirok, A., Jacob, E.B., Cohen, I., Schochet, O.: Novel Type of Phase Transitions in a System of Self-Driven Particles. Physical Review Letters 75, 1226–1229 (1995)
5. Jadbadaie, A., Lin, J., Morse, A.S.: Coordination of Groups of Mobile Autonomous Agents Using Nearest Neighbor Rules. IEEE Transactions on Automatic Control 48(6), 988–1001 (2003)
6. Yang, Y., Xiong, N., Chong, N.Y., Défago, X.: A Decentralized and Adaptive Flock-ing Algorithm for Autonomous Mobile Robots. In: the 3rd International Conference on Grid and Pervasive Computing Workshops, pp. 262–268. IEEE Press (2008)
7. Kim, D.H., Wang, H., Shin, S.: Decentralized Control of Autonomous Swarm Sys-tems Using Artificial Potential Function-Analytical Design Guidelines. J. Int. Robot Systems 45, 36–394 (2006)
8. Li, X., Ercan, M.F., Fung, Y.F.: A Triangular Formation Strategy for Collective Behaviors of Robot Swarm. In: Gervasi, O., Taniar, D., Murgante, B., Laganà, A., Mun, Y., Gavrilova, M.L. (eds.) ICCSA 2009. LNCS, vol. 5592, pp. 897–911. Springer, Heidelberg (2009)
9. Goren, A., Uyar, E., Baser, O., Dicle, Z.: Sensor Fusion Using Dempster-Shaffer The-ory of Evidence in Autonomous Robot Navigation. Automatic Control and Robotics 7(1), 133–144 (2008)
10. Jaafar, J., McKenzie, E.: Dempster-Shafer's Approach for Autonomous Virtual Agent Navigation in Virtual Environments. Engineering and Tech. (62), 389–393 (2010)
11. Wu, H., Siegel, M., Stiefelhagen, R., Yang, J.: Sensor Fusion Using Dempster-Shafer Theory. In: IEEE Instrumentation and Measurement Technology Conference (2002)
12. Li, X., Ercan, M.F.: Sensor Fusion and Interpretation for Swarm of Land Robots. Submitted to IEEE Int. Symposium on System Integration-SII2011 (2011)

Self-reconfiguration Path Planning Design
for M-Lattice Robot Based on Genetic Algorithm

Enguang Guan[1,2], Zhuang Fu[1,2,3], Weixin Yan[1,2],
Dongsheng Jiang[1,2], and Yanzheng Zhao[1,2]

[1] State Key Lab of Mechanical System and Vibration, Shanghai, P.R. China
{Enguangovo,ZhFu,WeixinYan,DongshengJiang,Yzh-Zhao}@Sjtu.edu.cn
[2] Shanghai Jiao Tong University, Shanghai, P.R. China
[3] State Key Laboratory of Robotics and System (HIT), Harbin, P.R. China

Abstract. M-Lattice is a kind of lattice modular robot, which can finish self-reconfiguration in three-dimensional plane. How to substitute the broken modules effectively is a critical question for modular robot system. In order to solve it, we introduce the topology structure of M-Lattice system and math representation for the reconfiguration question. An energy factor to illustrate the relationship between energy cost and moving path is defined. The non-real time path planning based on genetic algorithm is also given. From the results of simulation, the reliability and feasibility of the planning is demonstrated.

Keywords: Self-reconfigurable robot, Genetic algorithm, Path planning simulation.

1 Introduction

From 1980s the discrete robots system was presented, as an important branch of that theory, modular robot field has developed over 30 years. There are a lot of eximious research results in fields of line, lattice and mixed modular robots. The assumption that the modular robot system has the feature of independent movement, computation and communication [1-2], has been proved primarily.

In 1993, Mark Yim designed PolyPod, which is considered as the first modular robot. PolyPod and its second generation which was presented in 2000 are the classic line-modular robots[3]. M-TRAN, made by Yoshida etc from AIST[4], and Superbot, made by Wei-Min Shen etc from USC[5], are typical hybrid robots, which have the advantages of line-modular robots and lattice-modular robots. They are heuristic for our modular robot design.

M-Lattice is a novel kind of self-reconfigurable modular robot. As its multi degree of freedom, it is easy to realize three-dimensional movements. Every six modules can build a hexagon submodule. That reduces the motion constraint and increases the efficiency of space utilization.

During the application, how to replace the broken modules in the large modular robot array is not a trivial problem. In order to solve the question, we give the

S. Jeschke, H. Liu, and D. Schilberg (Eds.): ICIRA 2011, Part II, LNAI 7102, pp. 505–514, 2011.

math representation for the question. An energy factor is defined to show the tight coupling between energy cost and reconfiguration path. Then we try to use genetic algorithm to make a non-real time reconfigurable path planning design. At last, the reliability and feasibility of the planning is demonstrated, through the simulation experiments.

2   Analysis of Self-reconfiguration Progress in M-Lattice Modular Robot System

2.1   Introduction of M-Lattice Modular Robot System

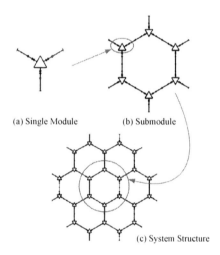

(a) Single Module   (b) Submodule

(c) System Structure

Fig. 1. Topology structure of M-Lattice system

The topology of M-Lattice module is lattice structure just as shown in Fig.1. Thus the self-reconfigurable system constituted by the modules looks like a mesh. Each node in the mesh represents a robot module and the changes of nodes` positions mean the system configuration transformations. This kind of lattice structure brings great convenience to realize the self-reconfigurable movements because a module in the mesh can move from one node to the neighbor node[6]. As illustrated in Fig.2, the robot is designed to be a center-symmetric three-arm mechanical. Three arms are installed on the three side walls of the center frame. Each mechanical arm contains two joints and one connection mechanism. The connection, separation and other movements of modules are completed by three arms [7]. In experiment, the weight of single modular robot is 2.2 kg, and the weight of a single arm is 0.7kg.

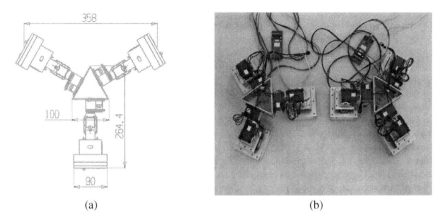

(a)   (b)

Fig. 2. A novel lattice self-reconfigurable robot module

2.2   Math Representation of Self-Reconfiguration Problem

When the system is working, some modules may be broken, and need to be substituted. The strategy of self-reconfigurable locomotion, including the order of connection, separation and rotation, is designed to solve this problem. First the broken modules are separated from the system, and the left vacancy can be seen as virtual modules. Then we can use the series of connection, separation and rotation to move the virtual modules in the known location to the places where good modules stay. The mathematic description can be shown in Fig.3: we assume the round area C1 is the system plane, and the centre is O1. There are m triangles which mean broken modules, and their locations are stochastic. There are also n good modules at the edge of C1, and their locations are known. The question is turned to find the optimal path between circles and triangles.

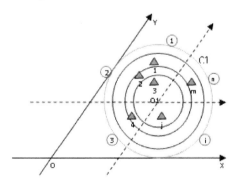

Fig. 3. The mathematic description of self-reconfiguration

As shown in Fig.4, the virtual module can change its position through the transformation of submodule, which includes the virtual module.

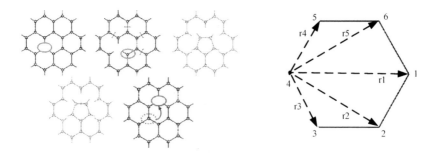

Fig. 4. Transformation of submodule   **Fig. 5.** Possible paths for the virtual module

It is easy to find that every step movement of virtual module is accomplished by the change of the arm joint angle. The motor on the rotating joint drives the unbroken modules in the submodule to finish the transformation. In one submodule, one virtual module has five paths to move, as shown in Fig.5. As the energy cost is in direct proportion with the angle variety. The target position of the virtual module determines the energy cost.

The energy factor is defined as follows:

1、 When an active module drives a passive module to rotate in angle θ, the energy cost can be count as e. Active module is the one which drives the connected modules to move, and active module will have energy cost. Passive module connected to the active module does not cost energy.

2、 If the number of passive modules is n and an active module drives them to rotate in angle θ, the energy cost is in direct proportion with n. And the step energy cost is $E_{step} = n \cdot e$. If a series of movements exist, the whole energy cost is $\sum E_{step}$.

3、 In hexagon submodule, energy cost of path rj is defined as E_{rj}. And E_{rj} is the minimum energy cost of all the possible paths, written as $E_{rj} = \min(\sum E_{step})$.

After calculation, the energy cost of all five possible paths for the virtual module movement can be written as:

$$\begin{cases} E_{r1} = 34e \\ E_{r2} = E_{r5} = 28e \\ E_{r3} = E_{r4} = 26e \end{cases} \tag{1}$$

Except that the broken modules are at the edge of the whole system, every broken module(virtual module) is the common node of three hexagon submodule. So every module has 12 paths to choose. Different path has different energy cost. It is obvious that the broken modules substitution process can be changed into the question that how to optimize the virtual modules path to the target position, written as:

$$\begin{cases} \min : g(X) = |(\sum_1^n x_i) - N| \\ s.t : \forall x_i \in \{26, 28, 34\} \end{cases} \tag{2}$$

Vector $X = (x_1, x_2, ..., x_n)^T$ is a solution space of energy cost, $x_i \in \{26, 28, 34\}$. As we want to find a series of path whose whole energy cost is approximate to the system energy threshold N, the target function $g(X) = |(\sum_1^n x_i) - N|$ is set to get the minimum value.

3   Path Planning Based on Genetic Algorithm

3.1   Introduction of Genetic Algorithm

In our representation, n dimensional vector $X = (x_1, x_2, ..., x_n)^T$ is discrete. The range of the solution searching space is 3^n. And the solution space is consisted of all the points which make the target function $g(X) = |(\sum_1^n x_i) - N|$ minimum. As a kind of heuristic algorithm, genetic algorithm is effective method to solve this problem. The working process is shown in Fig.6.

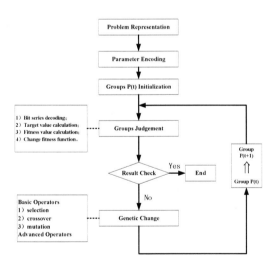

Fig. 6. Process of genetic algorithm

3.2   Application of Genetic Algorithm

Genetic Code

In our optimization model, the chromosome is n dimensional vector $X = (x_1, x_2, ..., x_n)^T$. x_i can only be one value of $\{26, 28, 34\}$. So we use decimal encoding method, and set $\{26, 28, 34\}$ as the range for chromosome bit series encoding. And the genetic code can be written as:

$$
\begin{cases}
S'' = \{X_1, X_2, ..., X_K\} \\
X_i = (x_{i1}, x_{i2}, ..., x_{in}), x_{ij} \in \{26, 28, 34\} \\
i = 1, 2, ..., K; j = 1, 2, ..., n; K = 3''
\end{cases}
\tag{3}
$$

Design of Fitness Function

Fitness function of solution searching space S'' can be formulated as $f(\bullet) = S'' \to R^+$. The return value of fitness function is real number. R^+ is a class of non-negative number. In optimal question $opt: g(x)(x \in [u, v])$, as the return value of target function may be negative, we need to set a map between fitness function and target function to make sure that the return value of fitness function is non-negative. And the trend of fitness function value must follow the optimal process. The fitness function can be set as:

$$
f(X) =
\begin{cases}
M - g(X) = M - |(\sum_1^n x_i) - N|, & if : g(X) < M \\
0 & , \quad otherwise
\end{cases}
\tag{4}
$$

M is a constant, which is larger than the maximum of $g(X)$. That makes $f(X)$ meet the requirement of fitness function.

Design of Genetic Operators

Basic genetic operators are selection, crossover and mutation. The new generation group follows use these operators to realize group evolution.

Selection

Selection means that the chromosome individuals whose fitness values are higher than others in one generation group are put into the mating pool. The mathematical expectation of whether an individual is chosen depends on the proportion between its fitness value and the group average fitness value. The roulette wheel method is used to pick individuals into mating pool.

In group $P = \{x_1, x_2, ..., x_n\}$, fitness value of $x_j \in P$ is $f(x_j)$. The opt probability is:

$$p_s(x_j) = \frac{f(x_j)}{\sum\limits_{i=1}^{n} f(x_i)} \quad , j = 1, 2, ..., n \tag{5}$$

Crossover

Crossover is a simulation of genetic rebuilding process which exists in sexual reproduction. It sends good gene to next generation, and makes the new genetic structure more complex. The crossover process is as follows:

(1) Choose two chromosomes from mating pool randomly.

(2) Choose one or several bits from $[1, L-1]$ as crossover positions. L is the length of the chromosome bit series.

(3) With the crossover probability $p_c (0 < p_c \leq 1)$, two chromosomes exchange their gene on the crossover positions. Generally, $p_c = 0.60 \sim 1.00$.

(4) The chromosomes in mating pool repeat the above process. And a new generation group is built.

Mutation

In natural world, genetic mutation always brings changes on structure and physics. In genetic algorithm, mutation operator randomly converts several bits of chromosome bit series with the probability p_m. Generally, $p_m = 0.005 \sim 0.01$. As the value range of chromosome code bit is small, in order to make the mutation process more effective, p_m can be set near to 0.01.

4   Simulation Experiments

The path planning method is simulated on Matlab platform. First, several functions are made to realize the genetic algorithm operators. Then a main program is designed to control the iteration process. Parameter initialization and terminal condition are also included in main program.

The number of chromosome in the mating pool is 10. The length of chromosome bit series is 10. In fitness function, $M = 100$, $N = 300$. Crossover probability $p_c = 0.60$. Mutation probability $p_m = 0.05$. The termination condition is the optimal solution is got or the number of generation reaches 50. The result is shown in Fig.7.

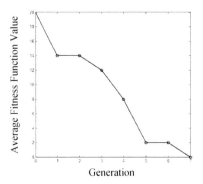

Fig. 7. Achieve the best solution in the evolution gradually

As shown in Fig.7, an optimal solution is get, when the generation number is 7. $X^* = [28,28,34,34,26,28,28,34,34,26]$ makes $g(X^*) = 0$. And the target function values decrease with the number of generation increases, rapidly. So the efficiency and accuracy are demonstrated.

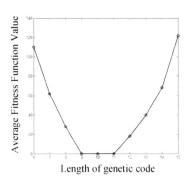

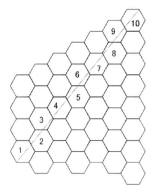

Fig. 8. Influence of code length L   **Fig. 9.** The physics meaning of code length L

If we change the length of chromosome bit series, the target function value of optimal solution will change with the length of chromosome bit series. As shown in Fig.8, if $L = 9,10,11$, the evolution will get the optimal solution that makes $g(X) = 0$, within 50 generations. In the rest situations, the target function value of optimal solution can't reach 0. And as the length of chromosome bit series far from $L = 9,10,11$, the target function value of optimal solution becomes higher, rapidly.

The relationship between the length of chromosome bit series and the final target function value can be explained by the characteristic of M-Lattice topology structure.

As shown in figure.9, if the initial position is in No.1 submodule and the target position is in No.10 submodule, we use a line l to connect the initial position and the target position. It is clear that the line l goes through 10 submodules, and l is the optimal solution for path planning. And if the virtual module is moved into the submodules which include the line l step by step, after 10 steps, it can reach the target position. So if the length of chromosome bit series is equal to the number of the submodules which include the optimal path, the optimal solution can be found with no doubt. And we can change the length of chromosome bit series to find the optimal solution, even though the distance between initial position and the target position is unknown.

Genetic algorithm is feasibility here, but it is not the perfect algorithm. If the length of chromosome bit series is chosen properly. The solution will not be found or have a lot redundancy. And if the scale of the modules is not big enough, the efficiency is also not evident. So in the future work, more attention will be taken on more efficient heuristic planning method. And the big scale modules simulations and real-time experiments will also be given.

5   Conclusions

This paper introduces the topology structure of M-Lattice modular robot. The math representation of broken module substitution problem is introduced. We try to use genetic algorithm to solve the virtual module path planning question. From the results of simulation experiments, the feasibility and accuracy are demonstrated.

Acknowledgments. This work was partially supported by the Research Fund of State Key Lab of MSV, China (under Grant No. MSV-MS-2010-03). the National Natural Science Foundation of China under Grant No. 60875058, 61075086, and the State Key Laboratory of Robotics and System (HIT) (Grant No. SKLRS-2010-ZD-06).

References

1. Wang, B., Jiang, Z.: Review on the status and development of modular reconfigurable robot technology. Mechanical & Electrical Engineering Magazine 25(5), 1–4 (2008)
2. Long, B., Mao, L.M., Sun, Z.H., Chen, G.: Existing state of development for overseas modular robot with self-variable structure. Journal of Machine Design 22(5), 1–4 (2005)
3. Yim, M., Duff, D., Roufas, K.D.: PolyBot: A modular reconfigurable robot. In: IEEE International Conference on Robotics and Automation, pp. 514–520. IEEE Press, San Francisco (2000)
4. Salemi, B., Moll, M., Shen, W.M.: SUPERBOT: A Deployable, Multi-functional, and Modular Self-Reconfigurable Robotic System. In: Proceedings of the 2006 IEEE/RSJ International Conference on Intelligent Robots and Systems, pp. 3636–3641. IEEE Press, Beijing (2006)

5. Murata, S., Yoshida, E., Kamimura, A.: M-TRAN : Self-Reconfigurable Modular Robotic System. IEEE/ASME Transactions on Mechatronics 7(4), 431–441 (2002)
6. Ding, Y., Zhu, J.Q., Quan, W., Fu, Z., Zhao, Y.Z.: Reconfigurable lattice modular robot with three connected arms. Chinese invention patent, No. 2009 1004 5065.7
7. Jiang, D.S., Guan, E.G., Fu, Z., Zhao, Y.Z.: Design of the Connection Mechanism for a Novel Self-reconfigurable Modular Robot. Journal of Shanghai Jiaotong University 44, 1026–1030 (2010)

Mobile Robot Controller Design by Evolutionary Multiobjective Optimization in Multiagent Environments

Yusuke Nojima and Hisao Ishibuchi

Graduate School of Engineering, Osaka Prefecture University,
1-1 Gakuen-cho, Naka-ku, Sakai, Osaka, 599-8531, Japan
{nojima,hisaoi}@cs.osakafu-u.ac.jp

Abstract. Evolutionary computation has been often used for the design of mobile robot controllers thanks to its flexibility and global search ability. A lot of studies have been done based on single-objective functions including weighted-sum scalarizing objective functions. For an example of mobile robot navigation, at least the minimization of the arrival time to the target and the minimization of dangerous situations should be considered. In this case, a weighted-sum of two objectives is always minimized. It is, however, difficult to specify an appropriate weight vector beforehand. This paper demonstrates the application of evolutionary multiobjective optimization to mobile robot navigation in order to optimize the conflicting objective simultaneously. We analyze the obtained non-dominated controllers through simulation experiments in multiagent environments. We also show the utilization of the obtained non-dominated controllers for situation change.

Keywords: Evolutionary multiobjective optimization, mobile robots, behavior coordination, multiagent environments.

1 Introduction

Mobile robot navigation is one of the most basic and important tasks in the field of robotics. Learning and/or evolutionary techniques have been often used for the design of robotic controllers because it is almost impossible to design well-suited robotic controllers to the facing environments [1-6]. These studies are often called evolutionary robotics. In conventional evolutionary robotics, single-objective evolutionary algorithms have been frequently used by means of a single-objective fitness function or a weighted-sum scalarizing fitness function. In general, for mobile robot navigation, we have to consider at least two objectives: 1) to minimize the travel time to the target point and 2) to avoid dangerous situations. These two objectives are conflicted. When a robot moves safely keeping large distances from obstacles, the robot goes a long way round. On the other hand, when a robot moves along a shortest path, the robot has to move very close to obstacles. For these conflicting objectives, the following scalarizing fitness function is used:

$$\text{Minimize } F = w_1 f_1 + w_2 f_2, \tag{1}$$

S. Jeschke, H. Liu, and D. Schilberg (Eds.): ICIRA 2011, Part II, LNAI 7102, pp. 515–524, 2011.
© Springer-Verlag Berlin Heidelberg 2011

where f_1 and f_2 are the travel time to the target and the degree of dangerous situations, respectively. w_1 and w_2 are weighted variables. One significant issue is how to define the weighted variables. It is very difficult to specify these variables beforehand.

Evolutionary multiobjective optimization (EMO) is currently one of the biggest research branches in evolutionary computation [7,8]. We can find some applications of EMO algorithms to the design of robotic controllers in the literature [9-11]. EMO algorithms can optimize several objective functions simultaneously like:

$$\text{Minimize } f_1 \text{ and minimize } f_2. \tag{2}$$

As a result, a number of solutions can be obtained with respect to the conflicting objectives (i.e., f_1 and f_2 in the above case). There are several advantages of the use of EMO algorithms. One is that we can analyze the tradeoff relationship among the objective functions. The other is that the search ability can be modified by the multiobjectivization of a single-objective function [12,13].

In this paper, we apply an EMO algorithm to mobile robot navigation problems in multiagent environments. Each robot moves toward own target while avoiding any collision with static obstacles and other robots. Two conflicting objectives are considered for the design of robotic controllers. One is to maximize the number of targets that robots arrived within a prespecified time-step. The other is to minimize the dangerous degree measured by distance sensors. Through computational experiments, we show that there exists a clear tradeoff relationship between two objectives. Then we analyze a number of non-dominated robotic controllers obtained by an EMO algorithm. Moreover, we also show the utilization of the non-dominated solutions for situation change.

This paper is organized as follows. In Section 2 we explains a mobile robot used in our simulation experiments. We explain the application of an EMO algorithm to the optimization of parameters in the robotic controller in Section 3. In Section 4, we explain our computational experiments and show the results. Finally we conclude this paper in Section 5.

2   Mobile Robots for Navigation

We utilize mobile robot simulation environments developed in [14]. Each robot has two basic behaviors and their coordination unit. As a preprocessing of raw sensor information, sensory network is also used. The overall architecture is shown in Fig. 1.

We assume that a mobile robot has eight distance sensors to measure distances from the robot to obstacles and four light sensors to detect the goal direction. The backside distance sensor is not used for control in this paper. We also assume that the robot does not know the exact layout and shapes of static obstacles in the environment. The objective of this task is to reach a target point while avoiding collisions with any obstacles. Subsequent subsections explain each module.

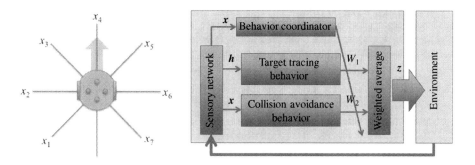

Fig. 1. A distance sensor configuration of mobile robots and the whole architecture

2.1   Basic Behaviors

We use simple if-then rules for the target tracing behavior that keeps the direction to
the target point. A fuzzy controller based on simplified fuzzy inference is used for the
collision avoidance behavior. Each controller independently decides the motor output
levels of two wheels of the mobile robot.

A fuzzy if-then rule for the collision avoidance behavior is described as follows,

> **If** x_1 is A_{i1} and ... and x_m is A_{im}
> 　　　**then** y_1 is w_{i1} and ... and y_n is w_{in}

where A_{ij} and w_{ik} are a Gaussian membership function for the jth input and a singleton
for the kth output of the ith rule, respectively. m and n are the numbers of inputs and
outputs, respectively. The simplified fuzzy inference is described by,

$$\mu_{A_{ij}}\left(x_j\right)=\exp\left(\frac{(x_j-a_{ij})^2}{b_{ij}^2}\right),\tag{3}$$

$$\mu_i=\prod_{j=1}^{m}\mu_{A_{ij}}(x_j),\tag{4}$$

$$y_k=\frac{\sum_{i=1}^{r}\mu_i w_{ik}}{\sum_{i=1}^{r}\mu_i},\tag{5}$$

where a_{ij} and b_{ij} are the central value and the width of the Gaussian membership
function A_{ij}, respectively. r is the number of rules. To simplify the control rules, two
linguistic labels of *dangerous* and *safe* are used to represent the degree of danger as a
function of the distance for each distance sensor input.

2.2   Behavior Coordination

In unknown environments, behavior-based switching architectures such as sub-sumption architecture are well-performed [15-17]. But its switching strategy may lead to breakdown due to the rapid change of control signals. To deal with such a problem, weighted average-based behavior coordination methods have been proposed [18-20].

By extending eq. (5), the final output; z_k is calculated by

$$z_k = \frac{\sum_{i=1}^{K} W_i(t) y_{ik}}{\sum_{i=1}^{K} W_i(t)}, \qquad (6)$$

where K is the number of basic behaviors. $W_i(t)$ is the behavior weight. y_{ik} is the kth output of the ith behavior. Now we assume only two basic behaviors. That is, K is 2. The behavior weights are updated by a behavior weight update function according to the time series of sensory inputs, and the robot can take a smooth action. We use the following simple behavior weight update function.

$$W_i(t+1) = W_i(t) + \Delta W_i, \qquad (7)$$

where ΔW_i is the update rate of the ith behavior weight. If the robot detects obstacles in the sensing range, the behavior weight of the collision avoidance behavior is updated. Otherwise, that of target tracing behavior is updated. After the update, each behavior weight is normalized in [0, 1]. Each update rate is specified independently.

2.3   Sensory Network

The mobile robot should concentrate on the surrounding area if there are many nearby obstacles, but the mobile robot should otherwise pay attention to the distant area. For this consideration, we apply sensory network with a scalable attention range [21] to adjust the shape of membership functions for the collision avoidance.

The attention range and velocity of the mobile robot should be changed according to the density of the obstacles. The attention range, $p(t)$, is changed as follows,

$$p(t) = q(t) \cdot S, \qquad (8)$$

$$q(t+1) = \begin{cases} \gamma^{-1} \cdot q(t) & \text{if all } x_i \geq p(t), \\ \gamma \cdot q(t) & \text{otherwise,} \end{cases} \qquad (9)$$

where $q(t)$ is the degree of sparseness of obstacles satisfying $0 < q_{min} \leq q(t) \leq q_{max} \leq 1.0$ for perception of the environment; S is the maximal sensing range, and $\gamma (0 < \gamma < 1.0)$ is a update rate for the attention range. Figure 2 shows the membership functions corresponding to the maximum and minimum attention ranges. Consequently, the internal state for the perception is updated by the time series of sensory inputs recursively.

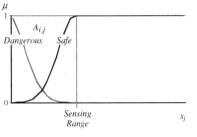
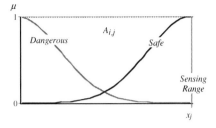

(a) Minimal attention range ($= q_{min} S$)   (b) Maximal attention range ($= q_{max} S$)

Fig. 2. Membership functions corresponding to linguistic variables of dangerous and safe based on the attention range

3   Application of an EMO Algorithm

In this paper, we apply an EMO algorithm to the optimization of the following parameters in the robotic controller explained in Section 2.

- The output variables of fuzzy if-then rules for collision avoidance,
- The update rate for each behavior weight.

We use NSGA-II of Deb et. al [22] which is one of the most well-known and powerful EMO algorithms. The outline of the NSGA-II is shown in Fig. 3. First an initial population P is generated in line 1. Pairs of parent solutions are chosen from the current population P in line 3. The set of the selected pairs of parent solutions is denoted by C in line 3. Crossover and mutation operations are applied to each pair in C to generate the offspring population C' in line 4. The next population is constructed by choosing good solutions from the merged population $P \cup C'$. The non-dominated ranking by the Pareto-dominance relation and a crowding measure are used to evaluate each solution in the current population P in line 3 and the merged population $P \cup C'$ in line 5. Elitism is implemented in line 5 by choosing good solutions as members in the next population from the merged population $P \cup C'$.

```
1:   P := Initialize (P)
2:   while stop_criterion not satisfied do
3:       C := SelectFrom (P)
4:       C':= Vary (C)
5:       P := Replace (P ∪ C')
6:   end while
7:   return (P)
```

Fig. 3. Outline of the NSGA-II

Since the variables optimized in NSGA-II are real numbers, a real number coding scheme is employed. We use blend crossover (BLX-α) with $\alpha = 0.5$ [23] and the uniform mutation with a certain range. If a real number becomes out of its range, it is repaired to be the minimum or maximum values of its range.

4   Computational Experiments

In this section, we explain the experimental settings and show some results for mobile robot navigation problems.

4.1   Experimental Setting

A simulation environment includes nine target points and five obstacles (squares). The number of mobile robots is four. Figure 4 shows a snapshot of the simulation. The size of the environment is 500 x 500 where the size of the robot is 6. Each robot selects a target point randomly and repeatedly after reaching the current target point. The minimum and maximum sensing ranges corresponding to q_{min} and q_{max} are 30 and 60, respectively. The length of a line from the robot in Fig. 4 is the maximum sensing range. The line from the robot becomes black when the robot detects obstacles in the attention range. A single run is 200,000 time steps.

In this paper, a collision avoidance behavior unit is composed of six fuzzy if-then rules shown in Table 1. The output values for each fuzzy rule are randomly initialized by adding small range of noise to the initial values in Table 1. In the same way, the update rates of behavior weights for target tracing behavior and collision avoidance behavior are randomly initialized by adding small range of noise to the initial values (0.2 for both weights). As mentioned earlier, the output values of fuzzy rules and the update rates of behavior weights are optimized by NSGA-II. It should be mentioned that all the robots have the same consequent values in fuzzy rules and the update rates.

In NSGA-II, the population size and the total number of generations are 20 and 100, respectively. The crossover rate is 1.0. The mutation rate is 1/8 (i.e., 1/(number of variables)). Binary tournament selection is used for parent selection. The above parameters would be not the best. The sensitivity analysis is necessary in future work.

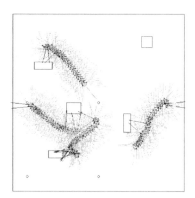

Fig. 4. A snapshot of our computational experiment. Each mobile robot moves toward own target point. Each trajectory and sensor ranges show how to avoid any collision with static obstacles and other mobile robots. Small circles are target points.

We calculated the average number of targets that four robots arrived and the average value of the dangerous degree over four robots within a single run. Each solution was evaluated by the above two values.

Table 1. Fuzzy rule sets for collision avoidance. The combination of fuzzy membership functions and the base values of the output angle and speed for each rule. S represents the membership "safe". D represents the membership "dangerous".

Rule	Distance sensors x_i							Outputs y	
	1	2	3	4	5	6	7	Angle	Speed
1	S	S	S	S	S	D	D	-2.0	3.0
2	S	S	S	S	D	D	S	-3.0	2.0
3	S	S	S	D	D	S	S	-4.5	1.0
4	S	S	D	D	S	S	S	4.5	1.0
5	S	D	D	S	S	S	S	3.0	2.0
6	D	D	D	D	D	D	D	2.0	3.0

4.2   Experimental Results for Four Mobile Robots

Figure 5 shows the non-dominated solutions with respect to the two objective functions at initial, middle, and final generations of a single run. It is clearly shown that there exists a tradeoff relationship between the two objectives. For example, mobile robots with Solution A could not pass a lot of target points but took a very safety action. On the other hand, mobile robots with Solution E could pass a lot of target points at the risk of collisions with obstacles. The user can choose one of the obtained solutions according to his/her preference.

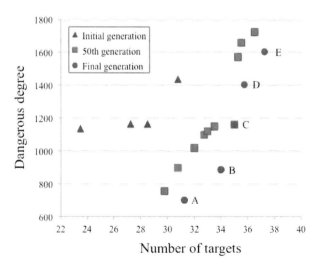

Fig. 5. Non-dominated solutions with respect to the two objective functions: the average number of targets that robots arrived and the average dangerous degree over four mobile robots

Let us analyze more details of the obtained solutions. Table 3 shows the output values for three non-dominated solutions. The angles were not symmetry for all the solutions especially rule 3 and 4. The robots tend to turn left when the robots detect obstacles in front of own body. Comparing three representative solutions, Solution E has the highest values of speed for all the if-then rules. This caused that the robots with Solution E could pass a lot of target points. But even when obstacles existed in front of the body, those robots did not decrease their speed. So that, those robots faced dangerous situations a lot.

Table 2. The output values of if-then rules for the collision avoidance behavior in three representative solutions

Rule	Solution A		Solution C		Solution E	
	Angle	Speed	Angle	Speed	Angle	Speed
1	-2.19	**3.50**	-1.80	**3.50**	-1.35	**3.50**
2	-2.93	1.21	-2.65	2.70	-2.64	**2.77**
3	-4.80	1.18	-4.72	2.21	-4.68	**3.50**
4	4.11	1.23	4.23	2.03	4.28	**2.35**
5	3.01	1.90	2.40	2.18	3.40	**3.50**
6	2.37	3.07	2.75	**3.13**	2.69	**3.13**

Table 3 shows the update rates of behavior weights in behavior coordination in (7). The robots with Solution A changed the behavior weights gradually and took a smooth action. The robots with Solution C updated the behavior weight for collision avoidance behavior quicker than those with Solution A. The robots with Solution E rapidly changed the main behavior like sub-sumption architecture.

Table 3. The update rates of behavior weights in behavior coordination in (7)

Solution A		Solution C		Solution E	
Target	Collision	Target	Collision	Target	Collision
0.25	0.45	0.71	0.36	**1.00**	**1.00**

4.3   Experimental Results for Situation Change

We performed the additional simulations for showing the utilization of the obtained non-dominated solutions. We used each solution in more complicated environments with more than four robots (i.e., five, six, and seven robots in each case). Each run was 1,000,000 time steps. We calculated the number of targets and the dangerous degree as the previous experiments.

Figure 6 shows the results for more complicated environments. Due to the increase of the number of robots in the environments, the number of targets decreased and the dangerous degree was deteriorated.

Let us assume the following preference. The user wants to use robots within a certain degree of dangerous (say 8,000) but wants to maximize the number of targets.

In the case that four robots are available, Solution D must be the best controller. But when five or six robots are available, Solution C is the best. Besides, in the case of seven robots, Solution B is the best choice.

According to the facing environments, we can choose one of the non-dominated solutions obtained by a single execution of an EMO algorithm. That is, we can eliminate additional optimization process for the different environments.

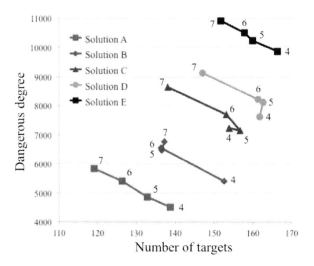

Fig. 6. The results for more complicated environments. Each number near symbols represents the number of robots used in the simulation.

5   Conclusions

In this paper, we applied evolutionary multiobjective optimization to mobile robot navigation problems in multiagent environments. We analyzed the obtained non-dominated controllers with respect to the number of passed targets and the dangerous degree in the simulation experiments. We also showed the utilization of the obtained non-dominated controllers for the situation change in which the number of available robots was changed.

As future research topics, additional objectives should be considered for multiagent environments (e.g., the degree of cooperation with other robots, energy consumption). The applicability of the obtained controllers to different environmental conditions should be also examined. Moreover, we have to incorporate the detection mechanism for situation change in the practical use of the non-dominated controllers.

References

1. Cliff, D., Harvey, I., Husband, P.: Explorations in Evolutionary Robotics. Adaptive Behavior 2, 73–110 (1993)
2. Nolfi, S., Floreano, D.: Evolutionary Robotics: The Biology, Intelligence, and Technology of Self-Organizing Machines. The MIT Press (2000)

3. Hoffmann, F., Pfister, G.: Evolutionary Design of a Fuzzy Knowledge Base for Mobile Robot. International Journal of Approximate Reasoning 17, 447–460 (1997)
4. Kubota, N., Morioka, T., Kojima, F., Fukuda, T.: Learning of Mobile Robots using Perception-based Genetic Algorithm. Measurement 29, 237–248 (2001)
5. Hoffmann, F., Schauten, D., Holemann, S.: Incremental Evolutionary Design of TSK Fuzzy Controllers. IEEE Trans. on Fuzzy Systems 15(4) (August 2007)
6. Vadakkepat, P., Peng, X., Kiat, Q.B., Heng, L.T.: Evolution of Fuzzy Behaviors for Multi-robotic Systems. Robotics and Autonomous Systems 55, 146–161 (2007)
7. Deb, K.: Multi-Objective Optimization Using Evolutionary Algorithms. John Wiley & Sons, Chichester (2001)
8. Coello, C.A.C., van Veldhuizen, D.A., Lamont, G.B.: Evolutionary Algorithms for Solving Multi-Objective Problems. Kluwer, Boston (2002)
9. Capi, G.: Multiobjective Evolution of Neural Controllers and Task Complexity. IEEE Trans. on Robotics 23(6) (December 2007)
10. Kim, J.-H., Kim, Y.-H., Choi, S.-H., Park, I.-W.: Evolutionary Multi-objective Optimization in Robot Soccer System for Education. IEEE Computational Intelligence Magazin, 31–41 (February 2009)
11. Katada, Y.: Distribution of Non-dominated Solutions and Preferred Solutions in the Objective Function Space for an Evolutionary Multi-objective Mobile Robot. In: Proc. of Joint 5th International Conference on Soft Computing and Intelligent Systems and 11th International Symposium on Advanced Intelligent Systems, pp. 710–715 (2010)
12. Knowles, J.D., Watson, R.A., Corne, D.W.: Reducing Local Optima in Single-Objective Problems by Multi-Objectivization. In: Zitzler, E., Deb, K., Thiele, L., Coello Coello, C.A., Corne, D.W. (eds.) EMO 2001. LNCS, vol. 1993, pp. 269–283. Springer, Heidelberg (2001)
13. Jensen, M.T.: Guiding Single-Objective Optimization Using Multi-objective Methods. In: Raidl, G.R., Cagnoni, S., Cardalda, J.J.R., Corne, D.W., Gottlieb, J., Guillot, A., Hart, E., Johnson, C.G., Marchiori, E., Meyer, J.-A., Middendorf, M. (eds.) EvoIASP 2003, EvoWorkshops 2003, EvoSTIM 2003, EvoROB/EvoRobot 2003, EvoCOP 2003, EvoBIO 2003, and EvoMUSART 2003. LNCS, vol. 2611, pp. 268–279. Springer, Heidelberg (2003)
14. Nojima, Y.: Multi-objective Behavior Coordination based on Sensory Network for Multiple Mobile Robots. In: Proc. of 2009 IEEE Workshop on Robotic Intelligence in Informationally Structured Space, pp. 66–72 (2009)
15. Brooks, R.A.: A Robust Layered Control System for a Mobile Robot. IEEE Journal of Robotics and Automation RA-2, 14–23 (1986)
16. Brooks, R.A.: Cambrian Intelligence. The MIT Press (1999)
17. Arkin, R.C.: Behavior-Based Robotics. The MIT Press (1998)
18. Saffiotti, A.: The Use of Fuzzy Logic in Autonomous Robot Navigation. Soft Computing 1, 180–197 (1997)
19. Bonarini, A., Invernizzi, G., Labella, T.H., Matteucci, M.: An Architecture to Coordinate Fuzzy Behaviors to Control an Autonomous Robot. Fuzzy Sets and Systems 134, 101–115 (2003)
20. Nojima, Y., Kubota, N., Kojima, F., Fukuda, T.: Control of Behavior Dimension for Mobile Robots. In: Proc. of The Forth Asian Fuzzy Systems Symposium, pp. 652–657 (2003)
21. Fukuda, T., Kubota, N.: An Intelligent Robotic System based on a Fuzzy Approach. Proceedings of IEEE 87(9), 1448–1470 (1999)
22. Deb, K., Pratap, A., Agarwal, S., Meyarivan, T.: A Fast and Elitist Multiobjective Genetic Algorithm: NSGA-II. IEEE Trans. on Evolutionary Computation 6(2), 182–197 (2002)
23. Eshelman, L.J., Schaffer, J.D.: Real-coded Genetic Algorithms and Interval-Schemata. In: Foundations of Genetic Algorithms, vol. 2, pp. 187–202. Morgan Kaufman, San Mateo (1993)

Learning Intelligent Controllers
for Path-Following Skills on Snake-Like Robots

Francisco Javier Marín[1], Jorge Casillas[1], Manuel Mucientes[2],
Aksel Andreas Transeth[3], Sigurd Aksnes Fjerdingen[3], and Ingrid Schjølberg[3]

[1] University of Granada, Granada, Spain
[2] University of Santiago de Compostela, Santiago de Compostela, Spain
[3] SINTEF ICT Applied Cybernetics, Trondheim, Norway

Abstract. Multi-link wheeled robots provide interesting opportunities within many areas such as inspection and maintenance of pipes or vents. A key functionality in order to perform such operations, is that the robot can follow a predefined path fast and accurately. In this paper we present an algorithm to learn the path-following behavior for a set of motion primitives. These primitives could then be used by a planner in order to construct longer paths. The algorithm is divided into two steps: an example-based stage for controller learning, and a controller tuning stage, based on an objective function and simulations of the path-following process. The path-following controllers have been tested with a simulator of a multi-link robot in several complex paths, showing an excellent performance.

Keywords: Path-following, snake-like robot, multi-link mobile robot, fuzzy control.

1 Introduction

Mobile robots constitute versatile platforms for a vast range of operations. In particular, multi-link mobile robots have the potential of traversing complex structures and narrow and confined spaces, which can be either too difficult or too dangerous for people to operate in. A key functionality in order to perform such operations, is that the robot can follow a predefined path fast and accurately. Moreover, the robot should also be able to recover to the path even in the case of large deviations (e.g. after avoiding an obstacle that was placed on the path).

The field of path-following for mobile robots is vast, but much of the focus has been limited to wheeled robots [1,2,3,4,5]. These robots have restrictions in their movements, as most of them are nonholonomic, but their kinematics are not as complex as for snake-like robots and, therefore, the complexity for path-following is lower.

In this paper we present an algorithm for learning a path-following behavior for multi-link mobile robots. Unlike in [4], the multi-link robot tries to reduce heading and deviation errors jointly at each step (and not independently), adjusting velocity and turning angle properly. Also, in our approach, the learning

S. Jeschke, H. Liu, and D. Schilberg (Eds.): ICIRA 2011, Part II, LNAI 7102, pp. 525–535, 2011.

complexity of the path-following behavior is reduced, as long paths are divided into a set of small motion primitives [6] (Fig. 1a) that can reach almost any point in the neighborhood. These primitives can be used for forward and reverse motion, but the latter have been omitted in Fig. 1a for clarity. Thus, a set controllers are learned (one for each motion primitive), instead a single one. The combination of these motion primitives allows to construct longer paths from any two points in the environment (Fig. 1b). This method favors accuracy because a single controller is dedicated to a single primitive. The learned controllers can be used with a planner that permits the coupling of the path-following behavior with an obstacle avoidance behavior, but this planner is not implemented for this paper.

(a)   (b)

Fig. 1. a) A set of motion primitives. b) A repeated and regular pattern of motion primitives that constructs the overall motion plan (bold curve).

A nonholonomic multi-link wheeled robot called PIKo (Pipe Inspection Konda) is used as a basis for simulation trials of the algorithm presented in this paper. The simulation results show that this robot is able to follow the paths with great accuracy. Moreover, it is able to quickly move onto its path when it is initially placed with a large deviation. The presented approach can be applied to other mobile robots just replacing the kinematics model.

The kinematic model of PIKo makes the reverse motion controllability difficult, only with information of the first link. So, only controllers for forward motion have been learned. For this reason, has been assumed that in case of a dead end, the snake will replan the path so that it can turn around.

This paper is arranged as follows: Sec. 2 presents the multi-link robot used for the simulation trials, while Sec. 3 details the controller learning algorithm for the path-following behavior. Sec. 4 analyzes the obtained results and, finally Sec. 5 points out the conclusions.

2 Description of PIKo Robot

The approach presented in this paper has been validated with a snake-like robot with active wheels (Fig. 2), called PIKo (Pipe Inspection Konda). PIKo is a nonholonomic robot developed by the Norwegian research organization SINTEF [7]. The robot currently consists of five interconnected modules, each with joints with two degrees of freedom. The wheels provide for a third degree of freedom per module. Each module has a measured maximum joint moment of 11 Nm and a weight of 1.2 kg. Current sensors include angle encoders for all joints, wheel encoders, and a 3D time-of-flight (TOF) camera system. The advantages of this robot are:

– The long and articulated body of snake-like robots make them ideal for internal inspection of complex pipe structures or other confined spaces. PIKo, moreover, can move through these narrow spaces, while maintaining the direct motion of wheeled vehicles. The direct motion is a great advantage against passive wheeled robots motion because it is less complex.
– The robot has many degrees of freedom (speed, horizontal and vertical angles for each module) but its movement can simulate the n-trailer problem [9] through a set of kinematic equations (with good accuracy), reducing the number of parameters needed to control it[8].
– A PIKo simulator based on an open-source physics engine called Open Dynamics Engine [12] has been developed by SINTEF and the Norwegian University of Science and Technology (NTNU). We have used this simulator for controller tests and for the tuning stage of the learning method presented in this paper.

Fig. 2. The snake-like robot PIKo

3   Path-Following Learning Algorithm

A two step method is proposed to learn path-following behavior. This technique combines inductive and deductive learning in optimization methods, with a first example-based learning stage and a second tuning stage with data from a simulator, which improves the accuracy of the obtained controllers. The proposal is valid for any learning algorithm based on the optimization of an objective funcion (e.g. genetic algorithms or artificial neural networks).

The example-based learning stage is based on the algorithm proposed in [10]. It has been used in problems like wall-following or moving object following with differential steering robots. In this paper, the different steps of this algorithm have been adapted to be applied to the path-following behavior for multilink robots, from the selection of variables to the scoring function.

3.1   Example-Based Learning Stage

In this stage, a general fuzzy controller that will seed the tuning stage is learned through a set of path-following examples. Each example of the training set consists of a combination of state and action values. The examples are generated in the space of the input (state) variables, starting from the minimum value of each variable and increasing the value in a quantity p_i until the maximum value is reached. The set of examples is created combining these values for all the input variables. On the other hand, the action values are determined testing all the posible combinations of the output variables (discretized with precision p_i), and selecting those values that place the robot in the state closest to the ideal state according to a score function. These examples are used as the training dataset of an advanced algorithm that learns the fuzzy controller (database and rulebase) that best fits the data.

In order to perform this stage, we need to define: the kinematics model of the robot, the input and output variables, the universe of discourse and precision p_i for the example generation, the scoring function (SF) and the test function.

Kinematics Model. The kinematics model of the robot PIKo is described in [7,8]. This model is used to describe the motion of the robot for the evaluation of the examples. In order to calculate the next position of the head of the robot, the following equations are needed:

$$\theta_1(t+1) = \theta_1(t) + \frac{V_{P1}}{L_{PJ}} \cdot tan(\delta_1) \cdot \Delta t \tag{1}$$

$$x_1(t+1) = x_1(t) + V_{P1} \cdot sin(\theta_1) \cdot \Delta t, \ y_1(t+1) = y_1(t) + V_{P1} \cdot sin(\theta_1) \cdot \Delta t \tag{2}$$

$$\phi_2(t+1) = \phi_2(t) - \frac{V_{P1}}{L_{PJ}} \cdot \left[sin(\phi_2(t)) + \left(\frac{L_{JP}}{L_{PJ}} \cdot cos(\phi_2(t)) + 1 \right) \cdot tan(\delta_1) \right] \cdot \Delta t \tag{3}$$

where x_1, y_1 and θ_1 are the position and heading of the first link of the robot, ϕ_2 is the angle between the first and second links of the robot, V_{P1} and δ_1 are the linear speed and angular speed of the first link and L_{PJ} and L_{JP} are the lengths of the segment $P_i \ J_i$ and $P_i \ J_i$ being P_i the center point of the wheel shaft of link i and J_i the location of the front end of link i.

Input and Output Variables. For the path-following behavior, the deviation of the robot from the path must be minimal at each step. We can use Frenet frames to find the deviation in position and orientation of the robot head with respect to the expected path. Therefore, two of input variables will be the distance from the robot position to the closest point of the path (Δz) and the heading error ($\Delta\theta$). Instead of using the closest point heading to estimate the heading error, the closest point heading in the next step is picked. This approach has some advantages:

- The robot can control both deviation and heading at the same time.
- The recovery process is stable and soft, especially at curves.

The other two input variables are the current linear speed (v), and $\phi_2(t)$ (Eq. 3). Finally, the output variables are the linear aceleration (a) and the turning angle (δ_1).

Universe of Discourse. In order to generate the training dataset, the limits and precisions of the values of the variables have to be stablished. Some of the variables have very large universes of discourse ($\Delta z \in [-\infty, \infty]$, $\Delta\theta \in [-180°, 180°]$). For these variables, the universe of discourse must be a reduced version of the real universe, and it should contain those values of the variable that are meaningful for learning (high values of distances are not useful for learning, as for all of them the robot will execute the same action).

Taking into account the kinematic equations, and assuming that $\delta_1 \in [-20, 20]$, a maximum speed v (V_{P1}) of 0.2 m/s and time step $\Delta t = 0.1s$, the values for the different variables are: $\Delta z = 0.003m$, $\Delta\theta = 6°$, and $\phi_2 = 15°$. Although higher values for the limits are not really significant, the ranges have been extended for precision discretization. The final universes of discourse and precisions for each variable are: $\Delta z \in [-0.0042, 0.0042]$ (negative values are used on left deviation, positive on right), $p_{\Delta z} = 0.0007$; $\Delta\theta \in [-6, 6]$, $p_{\Delta\theta} = 1$; $\phi_2 \in [-15, 15]$, $p_{\phi_2} = 5$; $v \in [0, 0.2]$, $p_v = 0.1$; $a \in [-0.2, 0.2]$, $p_a = 0.05$; $\delta_1 \in [-20, 20]$, $p_{\delta_1} = 1$.

Scoring Function. An important aspect of the proposed example set generation technique is the definition of the *SF*, a function that evaluates the action of the fuzzy controller over an example. The role of *SF* is to measure the deviation of each variable from the desired value (the one associated to the ideal state). For the path-following behavior, the robot needs to reach the closest point of the desired path, but keeping a low heading error. This causes two major problems:

- If the robot is located at a point on the path, the best action is to stay in the same place, because other actions may increase heading or distance error.
- It is crucial to find a good balance between heading and distance error improvements because these two variables are hardly coupled: if we want to reduce the distance error, the heading error must be increased.

The solution for the first issue is to penalize low speeds, including the speed as a parameter with high weight on the score function. The second issue can be partially solved with dynamic weights: the weights of deviation and heading errors depend on their respective initial errors. When the initial distance error is small, its weight is lower, increasing the importance of heading and speed weights. Then, the score function is defined as:

$$SF(RB(e^l)) = \alpha_1 + \alpha_2 + \alpha_3, \tag{4}$$

where e^l is the l-th example and *SF* is the score of the state reached by the robot, starting at the state defined by e^l and applying the control action proposed by the combination of the output values of the rulebase (RB). α_1, α_2 and α_3 are computed as follows:

$$\alpha_1 = \omega_1 \cdot \frac{e^l_{\Delta z}}{max_{\Delta z}} \cdot \frac{\Delta z}{p_{\Delta z}}, \quad \Delta z = \sqrt{(x_{robot} - x_{path})^2 + (y_{robot} - y_{path})^2} \tag{5}$$

$$\alpha_2 = \omega_2 \cdot \frac{e_{\Delta\theta}^l}{max_\theta} \cdot \frac{\Delta\theta}{p_{\Delta\theta}}, \quad \Delta\theta = |\theta_{robot} - \theta_{path}| \tag{6}$$

$$\alpha_3 = \omega_3 \cdot \frac{(max_v - v)}{p_v} \tag{7}$$

ω_1, ω_2 and ω_3 are three weights used for balancing the importance of each variable in the scoring function. These weights depend on the universe of discourse and the precision of the variables. $\frac{e_{\Delta z}^l}{max_{\Delta z}}$ is the dynamic weight for distance. $\frac{\Delta z}{p_{\Delta z}}$ determines the score of the action, divided by the precision of the variable. This makes possible the comparison of the deviations of different variables. The heading score is estimated in the same way and, finally, lower speeds are penalized on α_3, using the maximum speed (max_v) as limit. Thus, the best actions are those that set the speed closest to the maximum value and with the lowest distance and heading error. Therefore, the scoring function has to be minimized.

Test Function. After the learning process is performed, the quality of the fuzzy controllers has to be evaluated. This is done with the test function. This function simulates the path-following process in a path using the fuzzy controller that will be evaluated and the PIKo simulator. Deviation error (Δz) and current speed (v) are registered at each step until the robot reaches the final point or a maximum step limit. After that, average deviation and speed are calculated and presented together with the success flag: 1 if the robot reaches the final point, 0 in other case. Each controller is tested with several different paths.

3.2   Tuning Stage

Learning the whole fuzzy controller (database and rulebase) with examples is faster and easier than learning it with an objective function and the simulator. This is a quite theoretical learning and the generated controllers are not perfect, but they are a good starting point for the tuning stage. In this phase, the seed controller (obtained in the previous stage) is tuned based on several motion primitives, creating a set of fuzzy controllers (one for each primitive). For this task, a learning algorithm has to be used. It is run once for each motion primitive. This algorithm uses the previous generated controller rulebase and tries to improve the fuzzy database through an objective function. Also, this stage tries to improve the recovery process from large deviations. For this reason, the universe of discourse needs to be expanded for the variables Δz and $\Delta\theta$.

For this stage, we need to define: the set of motion primitives (Fig. 1a) and the objective function.

Objective Function. In the tuning stage we need to improve both deviation and recovering behaviors: the former by minimizing the distance error while maintaining a good average speed, and the latter by reducing the number of steps necessary to reach the path in a stable state (which does not generate future large deviations). The objective function (which has to be minimized) considers all this requirements:

$$ObjF = \omega_{dev} \cdot dev + \omega_{rec} \cdot rec \qquad (8)$$

where ω_{dev} and ω_{rec} are the weights that determine the importance of deviation and recovering and dev and rec are the variables that measure the quality of the controller on both behaviors:

$$dev = \omega_{\Delta z} \cdot \overline{\Delta z} + \omega_v \cdot (max_v - \overline{v}) \qquad (9)$$

$$rec = \omega_{\Delta z_r} \cdot \overline{\Delta z_r} + \omega_{rv} \cdot (max_{rv} - rv) \qquad (10)$$

Eq. 9 uses the same parameters of the test function: average distance error $(\overline{\Delta z})$ and average speed $(\overline{v})$ during a controller full test (until the robot reaches the final point or a maximum limit of steps). These values are weighted with $\omega_{\Delta z}$ and ω_v respectively.

Eq. 10 uses the number of steps necessary to reach a point close to the desired path (rv), and the average deviation from the time instant the point was reached until the end of the controller test $(\overline{\Delta z_r})$. rv is calculated as:

$$rv = \frac{n_r}{n_{steps}} \qquad (11)$$

where n_r is the number of steps needed to reach a point of the path, and n_{steps} represents the steps needed to complete the full test.

4 Results

4.1 Simulation Setup

Three different values for ω_1, ω_2 and ω_3 for the dataset generation have been tested, with five different seeds. Learned controllers have been tested on the PIKo simulator, with several paths of varying complexity. It is important to remark that these paths have not been used during training. In the first stage, the training set is only composed of a list of examples that have been chosen covering the input space with an adequate precision. Nine evaluations have been made for each controller: one without initial deviation and eight more with different initial offsets (for recovery testing), and average distance error, average speed and steps needed for recovering have been recorded (Table 1).

Controller learning and tuning have been realized with an advanced genetic fuzzy system called EGLFP [11], especially developed for fuzzy learning. We have used the following parameter values for this algorithm in both stages: 50,000 evaluations for learning and 5,000 for tuning, 50 individuals, 0.8 as crossover probability and 0.3 as mutation probability.

The set of motion primitives presented on Fig. 1 has been used in the tuning phase. It consists of 11 different primitives, so 11 different controllers have been learned. We have used a modified version of EGLFP for this task, replacing example learning with the objective function defined in Eq. 8 and data from the PIKo simulator. The weights that have been used on this phase are the following: $\omega_{dev} = 0.6$, $\omega_{rec} = 0.4$, $\omega_{\Delta z} = 0.99$, $\omega_v = 0.01$, $\omega_{\Delta z_r} = 0.95$ and $\omega_{rv} = 0.05$. Five seeds have been used for each pattern and each controller has been evaluated 9 times, like in the first stage. Average speed, steps needed for recovering and average deviation after recovering are presented at Table 2.

4.2   Path-Following

In this section we present the results of the different learned controllers, from the first and second stages, and a short study of the three weights of the score function of the first stage. Table 1 collects the results of these weights for the path-following problem with and without initial offset.

Table 1. Path-following deviation data. Deviation values are in meters and speed in m/s.

Weights (ω_1, ω_2, ω_3)	Right (2,2,90)	Left (1,2,0)	Left (1,1,90)	Right (2,2,45)
	Dev/Spd/Rec	Dev/Spd/Rec	Dev/Spd/Rec	Dev/Spd/Rec
(0.8, 0.2, 1)	0.092/0.17/0.69	0.102/0.13/0.72	0.025/0.13/0.80	0.88/0.16/0.68
(0.775, 0.225, 1)	0.022/ 0.2 /0.74	0.011/ 0.2 /0.71	0.022/ 0.2 /0.84	0.018/ 0.2 /0.69
(0.7, 0.3, 1)	0.024/ 0.2 /0.80	0.016/ 0.2 /0.77	0.022/ 0.2 /0.90	0.037/ 0.2 /0.79

Some of the tests with the weight combination of the first row have not reached the final position in the maximum number of steps, some of them were blocked at some point (first issue described in the score function subsection) and others caused for extreme heading deviation (second issue). These problems are represented in Fig. 3 (a and b). On the other hand, when the heading error has greater importance, the recovering process is slower or the robot never recovers (we can see this in the *rec* column of second and third rows). Without dynamic weights, a valid balance is never found. We can select any controller generated with the weights of the second row to be the seed of the tuning stage (Figure 3c).

Table 2 presents the deviation error, speed, and necessary steps for recovering after the tuning phase. Each motion primitive is identified with its direction, x and y displacements, and heading change. Each controller was tested with its corresponding motion primitive.

As we can see in Table 2, the proccess is very accurate: only a few millimeters of average deviation for all the patterns, with good speed. The recovering process is also improved: only a 15-30% of the total steps are needed for recovering offsets of 0.2 m (around 40% in the shortest paths). Fig. 4 shows other tests of different primitives.

Figs. 3c and 4c present the same paths with the same initial deviation. We can see that the tuning phase has greatly improved both recovery speed and deviation error.

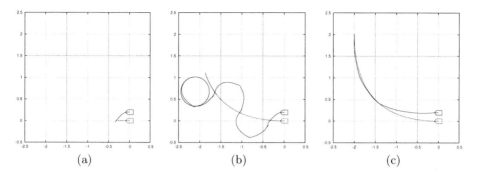

(a)   (b)   (c)

Fig. 3. Examples of controller tests. a) Blocked. b) Extreme heading error. c) One test of the controller selected as seed. The dotted curves are the ideal paths, continuous curves are the robot steps.

Table 2. Path-following deviation data after the tuning stage. Deviation values are in meters and speed in m/s.

Path	Dev/Rec/Spd	Path	Dev/Rec/Spd
Line (2,0,0)	0.002/0.24/0.13	Right (2,2,45)	0.006/0.21/0.14
Left (1,1,90)	0.009/0.41/0.16	Left (1,2,45)	0.005/0.31/0.16
Right (1,1,90)	0.007/0.36/0.15	Right (1,2,45)	0.002/0.21/0.13
Left (2,2,90)	0.001/0.16/0.14	Left (1,2,0)	0.007/0.33/0.15
Right (2,2,90)	0.002/0.16/0.13	Right (1,2,0)	0.008/0.25/0.13
Left (2,2,45)	0.004/0.20/0.14		

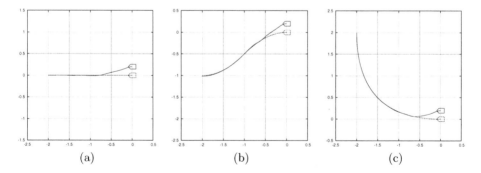

(a)   (b)   (c)

Fig. 4. Examples of controller tests. a) Line (2, 0, 0), b) Left (1, 2, 0), c) Right (2, 2, 90).

5   Conclusions

A two stage learning method for the path-following problem has been presented. It consists of a example based learning phase and a subsequent tuning phase for accuracy improvement. This process is applied to a set of motion primitives, obtaining a set of fuzzy controllers that could be combined in order to build longer paths. A tuning stage for the controllers is used to produce a very accurate path-following behavior: distance errors are reduced from various centimeters to several millimeters in this stage. This is very important for snake-like robots, as they can move in narrow spaces like pipes or vents where large path deviations must be avoided. In addition, the methodology also steers the robot quickly onto its desired path even for large initial deviations. Reverse motion controllers can also be learned with this method, but the kinematic function of the robot makes the reverse motion controllability difficult using only head information. This will be a topic for future work.

The use of motion primitives allows the robot to reach all the points of the lattice space with the combination of a few primitives. This facilitates the design of a planner, and reduces the path complexity for the learning algorithm. The areas of robot learning and multi-link robots are rapidly expanding and will eventually provide systems for autonomous inspection and maintenance operations. The results provided in this paper are steps toward such robot functionality.

References

1. Lapierre, L., Zapata, R., Lepinay, P.: Combined Path-following and Obstacle Avoidance Control of a Wheeled Robot. The International Journal of Robotics Research 26(4), 361–375 (2007)
2. Ashoorirad, M., Barzamini, R., Afshar, A., Jouzdani, J.: Model Reference Adaptive Path Following for Wheeled Mobile Robots. In: International Conference on Information and Automation (ICIA 2006), pp. 289–294 (December 2006)
3. Campani, M., Capezio, F., Rebora, A., Sgorbissa, A., Zaccaria, R.: A Minimalist Approach to Path Following among Unknown Obstacles. In: IEEE/RSJ International Conference on Intelligent Robotics and Systems (IROS 2010), pp. 3604–3610 (October 2010)
4. Liu, N.: Intelligent Path Following Method for Nonholonomic Robot Using Fuzzy Control. In: Second International Conference on Intelligent Networks and Intelligent Systems, ICINIS 2009, pp. 282–285 (November 2009)
5. Fierro, R., Lewis, F.L.: Control of A Nonholonomic Mobile Robot Using Neural Networks. IEEE Transactions on Neural Networks 9(4), 589–600 (1998)
6. Pivtoraiko, M., Knepper, R.A., Kelly, A.: Differentially Constrained Mobile Robot Motion Planning in State Lattices. Journal of Field Robotics 26(3), 308–333 (2009)
7. Fjerdingen, S.A., Liljebäck, P., Transeth, A.A.: A Snake-Like Robot for Internal Inspection of Complex Pipe Structures. In: Proceedings of the 2009 IEEE/RSJ International Conference on Intelligent Robots and Systems, IROS 2009, St. Louis, USA, pp. 5665–5671 (October 2009)
8. Murugendran, B., Transeth, A.A., Fjerdingen, S.A.: Modeling and Path-Following for a Snake-Robot with Active Wheels. In: Proceedings of the 2009 IEEE/RSJ International Conference on Intelligent Robots and Systems, IROS 2009, St. Louis, USA, pp. 3643–3650 (October 2009)
9. Altafini, C.: Some properties of the general n-trailer. International Journal of Control 74(4), 409–424 (2001)

10. Mucientes, M., Casillas, J.: Quick Design of Fuzzy Controllers With Good Interpretability in Mobile Robotics. IEEE Transactions on Fuzzy Systems 15(4), 636–651 (2007)
11. Casillas, J.: Embedded genetic learning of highly interpretable fuzzy partitions. In: Joint 2009 International Fuzzy Systems Association World Congress and 2009 European Society of Fuzzy Logic and Technology Conference (IFSA-EUSFLAT 2009), Lisbon, Portugal, pp. 1631–1636 (2009)
12. Open Dynamics Engine, http://www.ode.org

Modular Behavior Controller for Underwater Robot Teams: A Biologically Inspired Concept for Advanced Tasks

Dong-Uck Kong and Jinung An

Daegu Gyeongbuk Institute of Science & Technology
50-1 Sang-Ri, Hyeonpung-Myeon, Dalseong-Gun
711-873 Daegu, Republic of Korea
{kong,robot}@dgist.ac.kr
http://www.dgist.ac.kr

Abstract. In ambition to give subaqueous robot groups more robustness and behavioral flexibility for real applications, this paper proposes a modularized behavior control architecture. Schools of naval mammals provide the proof that also individual members of the group can achieve higher leveled intelligence independent of the simplicity of their collective behavior. Due to their structurally and functionally modularized brain organization, dolphins are capable of language based communication and learning complex motions by human training. Inspired by dolphins, 3 modules for the behavior controller can be conceptualized. The swarming module optimized by evolutionary methods represents the basic behavior given in the natural environment. The mission module includes extendable sets of behavior primitives that can be structured by reinforcement learning. A knowledge based sensing module can be implemented separately to increase the information reliability. With this approach, subaqueous robot schools can be expected to perform more advanced tasks than just moving as a swarm.

Keywords: Collective Robotics, Swarm Intelligence, Behavior Controller, Underwater Robots.

1 Introduction

Robotic multi-agent teams are meaningful for many reasons. A group of robots could cover a larger area than a single robot so that tasks as explorations or measurements can be done much more efficiently. It brings not only temporal benefits in performing certain tasks, but also the accuracy and the reliability of the collected information increase significantly. In the exemplary case of Icelandic volcanic eruptions in 2010, a representation of the global ash dispersion was almost impossible due to the punctual and selective measurement method. A large number of drones in a coordinated manner could have brought better

S. Jeschke, H. Liu, and D. Schilberg (Eds.): ICIRA 2011, Part II, LNAI 7102, pp. 536–547, 2011.

results. Furthermore, biological role models as ant colonies or bee colonies show impressive performance in more complicated tasks, e.g. in cooperative foraging or cooperative building tasks, what would be simply impossible for a single member of the colony. Also, homogeneous decentralized systems in particular present another important advantage. Such systems are redundant so that damage or failure of one or few other members may not influence the global performance of the group much negatively. Thus, there were a lot of approaches to transfer all those benefits to robotics in the past years.

1.1   Recent Research Directions

Most existing multi-robot systems are homogeneous decentrally controlled groups like their biological role models. Already since the late 1980s, engineers have presented many of remarkable results in collective robotics. Many researchers implemented various algorithms in common simple mission scenarios like foraging, box pushing and coordinated motions. Using reactive, behavior-based or learning controller architectures they show how decentralized controllers using simple local communication lead to an efficient collective performance in mentioned tasks by small and large robotic groups [1],[2],[3],[4].

This research trend leaded to a new subdomain of collective robotics, so called swarm robotics. Dorigo and Sahin provide summarizing criteria to characterize swarm robotics. As first, the study should be relevant for the control of a large number of robots. The benefit of working in cooperation compared with working alone should be cognizable. Furthermore, the homogeneity or rather the high redundancy, but also the locality of sensing and communication abilities belongs to swarm robotics. The most recent representative research in swarm robotics is introduced by Vito Trianni in [5]. In this work, Trianni, Nolfi and Dorigo propose the artificial evolution as a tool to synthesize self-organizing behaviors. Parameters of a black-box-Controller are updated with evolutionary method with certain quality criteria to generate individual behaviors. The simulation results show that it produces efficient individual behaviors that lead to the desired collective behaviors, even to simple collective decision making behaviors.

The common focus of recent researches in swarm robotics lies on the self-organizing phenomenon based on the simplicity of individual behaviors that can lead to execution of complex collective tasks. The evolutionary approach in particular shows the trend to solve the typical design problem of swarm robotics. It eliminates the arbitrary decompositions at the level of finding the mechanisms that lead to the emergent global behavior, and at the level of implementing those mechanisms into a controller for the robots [5]. The resulting performance is impressive indeed.

1.2   Goal of the Work

However, we would like to seize more practically oriented questions at this point. We believe that they are essential for developing a robust physical robot platform for real applications. Suppose that a group of robots have to operate in a

3-dimensional space, for example in a subaqueous environment. Simple collective motion coordination might be feasible using conventional collective behavior algorithms that are mostly developed and tested in an 2-dimensional space. But regarding more sophisticated operations, there would be a lot of challenging issues even if the behavior rules and the communication of the individual swarm members should be rather simple. In a underwater environment, disturbances such as varying lighting conditions, diverse particles in the water, attenuation of signals, dynamic obstacles and also gas bubbles have to be considered. Even in an aerial environment, especially in disaster zones, clouds of chemical smokes e.g. would be very disturbing. A high capability of generalization is necessary for the controller in order to correctly sense the direction, the intensity and the type of signals from neighbor robots during a dynamic 3-dimensional motion. Expandability, flexibility and adaptability of the behavior controller are also relevant issues for us so that the controller doesn't has to be completely redesigned once new tasks shall be added. Thus, the goal and the ambition of this work is to propose a pragmatic concept for homogeneous decentralized robot groups for various real-world applications in a 3-dimensional subaqueous environment.

2   Biological Inspiration

Bottlenose dolphin is the most well known species of Delphinidae family (oceanic dolphins) for human. Bottlenose dolphins are as known social animals living in a group, even when they are rather flexible regarding to leaving or reorganizing their groups.

Fig. 1. Collective movement of a dolphin school(*left, source: www.fotocommunity.de*) and one of their typical hunting scenes(*right, source: www.wdr.de*)

This social behavior is amongst others described in [6] and [7]: In their natural environment, dolphins live in a so called school typically consisting of around 20-50 members(Fig. 1), where they can build a group of over 1000 animals if needed. Although they are mammals, they represent, in contrast to herds and prides, a swarm-typical behavior without any central leader. However, dolphins social behavior is characterized not only by simply moving collectively. They furthermore seem to be able to act strategically. Dolphins are even able to surround the entire group of prey and hunt strategically(Fig. 1). Dolphins are also capable of communicating by a kind of language with each other. For this purpose they use clicking sounds, chatter and other noises with specific patterns for each purpose [8],[10]. Hawkins[9][10] claims that the animals exchange context-specific information in this way and assign significant sounds to activities such as resting or eating. Such coded signals represent an important basis for the intelligent behavior of the group.

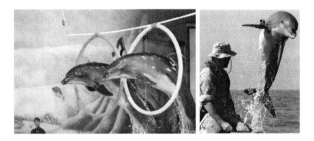

Fig. 2. Dolphins in artificial environments: a dolphinarium circus(*left, source: www.in-dubai.com*) and a dolphin trained for naval mine detection(*right, source: www.wikipedia.com*)

Dolphins high intelligence gives them the opportunity to live in an artificial environment and to acquire additional skills they cannot learn in their natural environment(Fig. 2). In dolphinariums the animals are trained by human. Performing an aimed motion correctly, dolphins will be fed, in other cases, they will be forced to stay hungry. In this way, dolphins can be trained for certain motions even when they do not really understand what they do and wherefore they do it. Dolphins are applied not only for entertainment purpose but also in the military use to detect naval mines or even to install those.

It is obvious that the fact that naval mammals have a structurally and functionally modularized brain organization plays an important role in such extremely high level of collective intelligence. Baars [11] explains how evolution and individual history are expressed in the brain. The brain grew and evolved from lower to higher regions. Basic survival and behavioral functions are controlled in the more ancient lower brainstem, while the large prefrontal cortex is a lately added higher region for decision-making, self-control, personality and other sophisticated behavioral abilities. It is also remarkable that a local damage to prefrontal cortex has little impact on the basic functions taking place in the lower regions what shows the clear functional mapping of mammal brains. Cruse et al. explains in a similar work [12] that there are two different types of intelligence: In addition to phylogenetic *species intelligence* given by a long term evolution of the species, one can note *individual intelligence* obtained by learning in a comparatively short period. On the other side, Cruse et al. furthermore point the importance of symbolic representation of things for the intelligence to manage all brain mechanisms efficiently.

3   3-Layer Behavior Control Architecture

The functional development of the mammal intelligence described above might be sketched as the structure shown on the left side of Fig. 3. Here, we would like to clearly separate the phylogenetic species intelligence such as sensing and interpreting abilities and swarming habit of dolphins from the individual intelligence which can represent skills achieved in artificial training environment. The top of left shows a number of possible tasks once the individual skills are successfully learned as in the second layer.

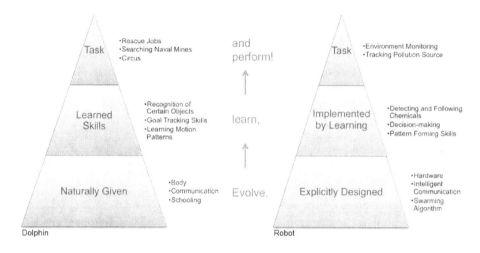

Fig. 3. Transfer from biological model to robotic behavior architecture

The right side of Fig. 3 presents how the principle of *evolve, learn and perform* can be transferred to an individual member of an robot team. Implementing basic behavior patterns of a swarm member explicitly as the first step, a robot team platform can be simply created which will be able to imitate basic swarm movements of their role models. The second step is to afford the robot team members higher intelligence level to achieve additional skills by learning methods. Each of the layers can be advantageously modularized in the next progression. The right pyramid of Fig. 3 also shows considerable practical applications. As an example case as shown in Fig. 4, the underwater robot team could swim as a swarm in a river and measure the water quality forming an array of sensor nodes, for example. Once they detect any polluting substances, the team could also disperse the formation and track the concentration gradients of the substances in a cooperative manner to find the emitting source.

From practical point of view, the main benefit of breaking down the goal system into a number of subsystems is obvious. Replacing one complex system by several clearly defined simple subsystems, a higher flexibility and higher plasticity can be achieved. Above all, the subsystems can be independently analyzed

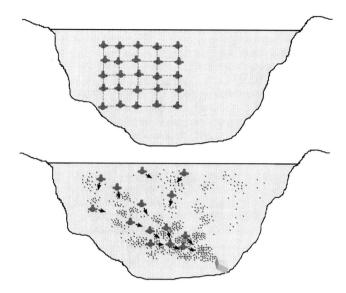

Fig. 4. A possible mission scenario for the aimed robot team. Formation of a sensor array(*above*) and tracking of polluting substances(*below*)

and optimized which cannot be taken for granted for systems consisting of various reciprocally linked functions. This gives the opportunity to design a system with minimal prejudicing, which implicates a large freedom for other combinations and extensions. In the case that a robot system has to handle a new task, for example, it would be not necessary to redesign the entire system. Also in case of problems, the failure can be located and corrected more efficiently. Modification or addition of one subsystem can often suffice for this purpose. With this objective, the following discussion will show how such a system can be realized.

3.1   Sensing Module

A swarm robot system is usually based on local interaction and communication so that the communication system has to overcome only a few meters. In addition, the distances between the individual robots in a swarm of robots would anyway be only at most few meters. Nevertheless, conventional communications methods such as electromagnetic data transmission are strongly limited by a lot of factors in an underwater environment. Even for acoustic and optical sensors will very quickly reach their limits as the signals are attenuated in the water and additionally disturbed by numerous particles floating around. Exposure conditions or unforeseen phenomena like air bubbles should be also considered. During dynamic movements in a three-dimensional space, this can easily lead to wrong interpretation or missing of sensor signals. Since the successful emergent behavior depends on reliable local communications, a robust communication strategy is essential.

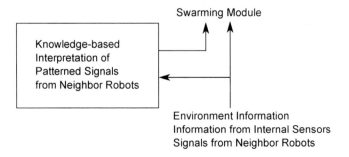

Fig. 5. Information flow in sensing module based on knowledge driven signal interpretation

To correctly interpret the signals sent by neighbor robots or percepted from the environment, a context-dependent symbolic language is to be used which express complex informations by a small number of characters. The proposed sensing module (Fig. 5) is an independent system that perceives its environment by signals, translates those by a priori stored context knowledge and transmits them to other modules of the behavior controller. The module is also capable of forwarding unprocessed raw data, e.g. signals from the internal position sensor for mechanical control. A more reliable communication can be ensured in this way.

3.2 Swarming Module

The swarming module represents an explicit implementation of basic skills observed on schools of dolphins or other fish. Reynolds [13],[14]demonstrated in 1987 with the aid of artificial birds named "boids" that the flocking behavior of birds can be realistically simulated using only three simple local rules. These are:

1. collision avoidance and separation: pull away before they crash into one another or against an obstacle
2. Velocity matching and heading alignment: try to go about the same velocity as their neighbors
3. flock centering: try to move toward the center of the flock

A number of scientists slightly modified this algorithm since Reynolds study. Kwong and Jacob [15] for example added two more rules to the reynolds ones to show the variety of possible behaviors such as ring and figure-eight formations. Movements of a robot team as a swarm in a three-dimensional space can be easily realized by such simple algorithms. The swarming module responds using the local sensor data feedbacked from the sensing module and outputs a resulting control command(Fig. 6).

However, to ensure the stability of the swarm during a collective movement in an highly dynamic underwater environment may be very difficult. In order

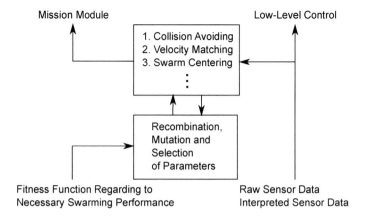

Fig. 6. Functional principle of swarming module

to optimize internal parameters of the algorithm, evolutionary method with an a priori defined fitness function depending on the swarm stability is considered instead of manual parameter setting. With such an optimization algorithm, not only the optimal distance for the collision avoidance rule can be found, but also parameters for the reaction agility of the individuals can be adjusted, which can be compared with mechanical impedance. Furthermore, the response speed of the velocity matching rule can also be a relevant parameter for the swarm stability and can be adjusted by the same optimization algorithm.

3.3   Mission Module

The mission module is based on the behavior-based scheme of Arkin [16] and includes a set of behavior primitives, a context selector, a learning algorithm, and a conflict resolution unit. The set of behavioral primitives includes any number of simple behavioral components that are combined and result in a more complex behavior. This traditional concept enables us to reuse and recombine primitive to build a highly adaptable system and provides opportunities for learning algorithms to be applied. The context selector consists of different state modes that are responsible for each mission context and can be trained by reinforcement learning algorithm to perform the given mission. The goal of the learning process is to select and weight the appropriate behavior primitives depending on the actual given mission. However, reinforcement learning for an underwater environment is a challenging issue, because there are a lot of constraints as the complexity of the environment, need of multi-robot interaction and limited information about the environment etc.. In order to apply the classical reinforcement learning in such an complex environment, different methods can be used as introduced in e.g. [17]: Breaking down mission contexts in part missions and part situations can reduce the complexity of decision problem. Not only such hierarchical modularization of the strategy, but also simplification of the state space, abstractions and avoidance of redundant information may be helpful. They also suggest to approximate a parametric function as evaluating function instead of representing the evaluation for each single state. That means generalization of the experience of agents.

Once the learning algorithm is successfully applied, the responsible state mode for each mission context can be activated, which in turn generates appropriate action commands combined from several weighted behavior primitives. Furthermore, a conflict resolution unit is needed that combines the command from the swarming module with those from the mission module and resolve any inconsistency and interferences if necessary(Fig. 7).

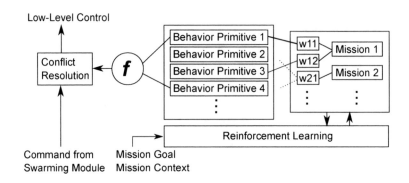

Fig. 7. A model of mission module based on reinforcement learning method

3.4   Hierarchical Allocation of the Modules

Fig. 8 shows the resulting modular architecture of the behavior controller. The right side of the diagram shows the sensory information flow from the environment of a single robot through its sensors to each modules. As already mentioned, the sensory data flow includes not only the interpreted informations from external sensors but also raw signals from internal sensors for mechanical control purpose. The left side of the diagram visualizes the flow of control signals. The mission context including information about necessary formation parameters will be given to the swarming module and mission module to be processed by the behavioral algorithm of both modules. The resulting control command will be given to the actuating system of the single robot.

This hierarchical disposition of the designed modules clearly exhibits the analogy to the three-level representation of our biological role model introduced at the beginning of this section. The sensing module and the swarming module build the first intelligence layer *evolve*. This level implicates abilities of a robot that can be assumed as naturally given. The mission module builds the second layer of the robot intelligence *learn*. It affords a framework for robots to be able to learn how to combine single behavior assemblages to perform a certain sophisticated behavior pattern successfully. Last but not least, the actuating unit of the robot hardware and its interaction with the environment and the neighbor robots represent the third layer *perform*.

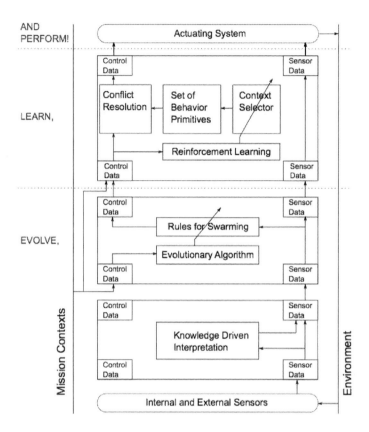

Fig. 8. Hierarchical allocation of the designed modules to the three intelligence layers

4   Conclusion and Outlook

The aim of this study is to figure out a concept that can be applied to a homogeneous team of robots to execute advanced tasks in a real three-dimensional dynamic environment with reduced signal transmission capability. On the one hand, a robot swarm with highly robust algorithm is needed that is suitable not only for simple flocking or schooling behavior, but also for practical operations in the real world. The system should also have a certain flexibility to be able to add new missions or to modify the algorithm modularly. On the other hand, a robust sensor system for reliable communication and interaction has to be created in order to cope with highly dynamic changing environment parameters and various disturbances.

The result of this work is a modular architecture that takes the intelligence development of dolphins as role model. First, a robot system is designed and equipped with a priori given certain skills. The sensory system based on symbolic communication ensures that the exchange of information is reliable. Based on few simple behavioral rules, the robot team is capable of moving around in a three-dimensional space like a swarm of its natural role model. By adding a small number of additional behaviors, the swarm can also vary the shape of the formation. To make an additional level of intelligence available which allows to learn complex unnatural actions as dolphins do, another module has been designed. This module is a behavior-based subsystem which can be extended and modified with little effort. Fig. 3 shows diverse considerable applications.

In next steps of our research, implementing approaches based on experimental work should motivate and help us to find the answers to the following remaining questions: How can the conflict resolution unit of the mission module be designed so that the resulting behavior is stable and robust? What is the real potential of reinforcement learning and evolutionary optimization regarding to this specific robot design problem? How can the control system be tuned or modified during execution of tasks? How effective is the performance of the resulting robot team? It is of great importance to study in future research both advantages and disadvantages of such hierarchical modular behavior controller in comparison with other methods unifying all behavioral and sensory mechanisms in a single controller unit. We believe that research in this direction could probably make a significant contribution to solving complex engineering problems in subaqueous environment.

Acknowledgments. This paper resulted during the collaboration research with the German Research Center for Artificial Intelligence(DFKI) Bremen. This work was supported by the DGIST R&D Program of the Ministry of Education, Science and Technology of Korea.

References

1. Balch, T., Arkin, R.C.: Behavior-Based Formation Control For Multirobot Teams. IEEE Transactions on Robotics and Automation 14(6), 27–52 (1998)
2. Mataric, M.J.: Learning Social Behavior. Robotics and Autonomous Systems 20, 191–204 (1997)
3. Parker, L.E.: ALLIANCE: An Architecture for Fault Toleratnt Multi-Robot Co-operation. IEEE Transactions on Robotics and Automation 14(2), 220–240 (1998)
4. Groß, R., Dorigo, M.: Group Transport of an Object to a Target That Only Some Group Members May Sense. In: Yao, X., Burke, E.K., Lozano, J.A., Smith, J., Merelo-Guervós, J.J., Bullinaria, J.A., Rowe, J.E., Tiño, P., Kabán, A., Schwefel, H.-P. (eds.) PPSN VIII. LNCS, vol. 3242, pp. 852–861. Springer, Heidelberg (2004)
5. Trianni, V.: Evolutionary Swarm Robotics: Evolving Self-Organising Behaviours in Groups of Autonomous Robots. Springer, Berlin (2008)
6. Shirihai, H., Jarrett, B.: Whales Dolphins and Other Marine Mammals of the World, pp. 155–158. Princeton Univ. Press (2006)

7. Perrin, W.F., Wuersig, B., Thewissen, J.G.M.: Encyclopedia of Marine Mammals. American Press (2009)
8. Au, W.: The Sonar of Dolphins. Springer, New York (1993)
9. Hawkins, E., Gartside, D.: Association of acoustics and behaviour of provisioned Inshore Bottlenose Dolphins (Tursiops aduncus) at Tangalooma, Moreton Island, Queensland, Australia. In: Proceedings of the 16th Biennial Conference on the Biology of Marine Mammals, San Diego (2005)
10. Hawkins, E., Gartside, D.: Contextual Use of Whistles by Wild Bottlenose Dolphins. In: Proceedings of the 17th Biennial Conference on the Biology of Marine Mammals, Cape Town (2007)
11. Baars, B.J., Gage, N.M.: Cognition, Brain, and Consciousness: Introduction to Cognitive Neuroscience. Academic Press (2007)
12. Cruse, H., Dean, J., Ritter, H.: Die Entdeckung der Intelligenz oder Koennen Ameisen denken? C.H. Beck oHG, Munich (1998)
13. Reynolds, C.W.: Flocks, Herds, and Schools: A Distributed Behavioral Model. In: Proccedings of ACM SIGGRAPH, Anaheim, pp. 25–34 (1987)
14. Kennedy, J., Eberhart, R.C., Shi, Y.: Swarm Intelligence. Morgan Kaufmann, San Francisco (2001)
15. Kwong, H., Jacob, C.: Evolutionary Exploration of Dynamic Swarm Behaviour. In: Proceedings of the IEEE Congress on Evolutionary Computation, pp. 662–669 (2003)
16. Arkin, R.C.: Behavior-Based Robotics. MIT Press, Cambridge (2000)
17. Knabe, J.: Kooperatives Reinforcement Lernen in Multiagentensystemen. Universitaet Osnabrueck (2005)

BioMotionBot – A New 3D Robotic Manipulandum with End-Point Force Control

Volker Bartenbach[1], Klaus Wilging[1], Wolfgang Burger[1], and Thorsten Stein[2,3]

[1] IPEK – Institute of Product Engineering
[2] Department of Sport and Sport Science, BioMotion Center
[3] YIG "Computational Motor Control and Learning"
Karlsruhe Institute of Technology (KIT), Germany
{volker.bartenbach,wolfgang.burger,thorsten.stein}@kit.edu

Abstract. In this paper we present the design of a new 3D robotic manipulandum that will be used in human motor-control research and additionally enables physiotherapists to design tailor-made robotic therapies. Moreover, it offers the opportunity to develop completely new types of movement-specific coordination and condition training programs in sports. The presented manipulandum has a special designed 3D kinematics that allows movements in 3D space while maintaining its orientation. The paper contains an overview of the mechanical design, the electronic components, the user interface, the design of the control system as well as a first performance test.

Keywords: robotic manipulandum, motor learning, rehabilitation.

1 Introduction

A fundamental understanding of human motor control and learning is a prerequisite in order to design safer workplaces, better tools, smarter robots, better prostheses and more effective learning and training strategies in sports and rehabilitation. Today, it is generally accepted that the human Central Nervous System (CNS) implements neural representations of the biomechanics of the musculoskeletal system and the objects in the environment and uses this information to control movements [1]. These representations are called "internal models". Results of several studies support the existence of internal models [2]. Thereby, subjects have to adapt to dynamic perturbations during goal directed movements induced by a robot manipulandum. By allowing a period for training, the CNS can adapt the internal model to the inverse of the combined arm dynamics and the dynamic perturbation. The robot manipulanda used in these studies can generate physical objects that have novel dynamical properties and change these properties in real time and thereby confront subjects with highly novel situations unlikely to have been experienced outside the lab.

Additionally, the use of the concept of internal models and robotic devices provide a tremendous opportunity for rehabilitation [3]. To assess subtle deficits in motor function novel tasks involving mechanical loads induced by a robot

S. Jeschke, H. Liu, and D. Schilberg (Eds.): ICIRA 2011, Part II, LNAI 7102, pp. 548–557, 2011.

manipulandum can be used to stress the motor system and may reveal specific anomalies in motor performance. A study by Smith et al. [4] revealed that subjects with genetically confirmed Huntington's disease's but with not yet any clinically documented impairments exhibited deficits in adapting to novel mechanical loads. Stroke induced abrupt losses of neural functions can result in a large range of different movement dysfunctions. Often, some degree of improvement occurs spontaneously and can be enhanced by individually-designed rehabilitation programs [3]. Thereby, the application of robotic manipulanda is a new promising development [5]. Moreover, the complexity of the motor task to be learned can be controlled precisely with a robot which enables an objective testing of different therapies. Besides that robotic manipulanda could also be used to design tailor-made training programs for athletes in sports.

The concept of internal models is extensively used in the study of human motor control and learning. However, the majority of results are based on the analysis of rather simple and restricted 2D movements. It is currently unknown if the current state of research is also valid for more complex and realistic movement tasks. More complex movement tasks in three dimensions in combination with a larger workspace also provide new opportunities for rehabilitation programs. Moreover, to be able to design tailor-made training programs for athletes in sports the device should be able to exert large forces at its endpoint (more than 200 N). An analysis of the technical literature [6] revealed that currently no device meets these demands. Accordingly, we developed a new 3D robotic manipulandum with end-point force control called "BioMotionBot" that is presented in this paper.

2 Design

2.1 Specification

The following requirements and specifications for the BioMotionBot were defined at the beginning of the project:

1. Designed as a manipulandum where the human keeps contact with the machine by means of a handle;
2. Movements in all three Cartesian directions with a fixed orientation of the handle during the movement;
3. Possibility to change the orientation of the handle manually (not during usage);
4. High Cartesian forces (over 200 N) in each Cartesian direction;
5. 6D Force-Torque measurement at the Handle;
6. Large workspace that enables a wide variety of tasks (800x500x700 mm);
7. Availability of force control and the ability to define different types of force fields;
8. Ability to reduce the workspace to a two dimensional plane or a freely definable trajectory in space;

9. A simple user interface to control the BioMotionBot, log the measured values, and give a visual feedback to the subject;

10. A safe handling and minimization of risks by offering different levels of safety features;

2.2 Design Overview

To meet the required specification, different kinds of standard robotic designs including SCARA robots, articulated robots, parallel robots and gantry robots have been evaluated. Because none of these designs met the requirements of the BioMotionBot, we developed a special kind of hybrid serial-parallel kinematics that is presented in chapter 2.3. The overview of the design of the BioMotionBot can be seen in figure 1. The BioMotionBot has a handle for the user that can be

Fig. 1. Picture of the BioMotionBot

seen on the left side of the picture. Underneath the handle a six DOF force-torque sensor is situated to measure the reaction force between the BioMotionBot and the subject. The handle is connected via the kinematic structure to a wagon that consists mainly of 2D aluminum parts. This wagon sits on top of a base frame that is assembled out of extruded aluminum sheaths. Two actuators and drive units are situated on the wagon, while a third one is integrated in the base frame and moves the wagon in the Z-direction (figure 2). The microcontroller that is used for the control system, (section 2.4) and the amplifier for the analog signals of the force-torque sensor, are situated on the wagon, while the rest of the electronic components and the power supply system are situated in the box underneath the base frame.

2.3   Kinematics and Actuation

The kinematics of the BioMotionBot consists of three prismatic joints. The first joint moves the wagon, and the other two move separate slides located on top of the wagon. All three joints are connected to the handle via two rods that are arranged as a parallelogram, with each rod having a ball joint at both of its ends. This kinematic arrangement ensures that the handle has only translational degrees of freedom and has a fixed orientation in space during motion. The orientation of the handle can be varied manually in 45 degree steps around the Z-axis by mounting it in a different orientation on the manipulandum. The overview of the kinematics is shown in figure 2. The figure also shows the standard coordinate system with its X-, Y- and Z-Axes that is used for the BioMotionBot and for all descriptions and results presented in this paper. The shown kinematics is

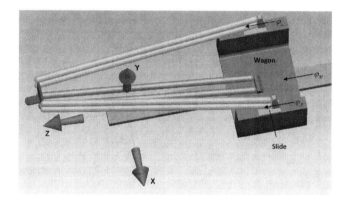

Fig. 2. Kinematics of the BioMotionBot

a combination of a parallel and a serial kinematics, where φ_L and φ_R are serially connected to φ_M. To calculate the forward and inverse kinematics a standard algorithm for parallel robots with three prismatic joints can be used with this arrangement (compare [8]). The value of φ_M simply needs to be added to φ_L and φ_R to get the "absolute position" of these joints. This special arrangement was chosen because it provides the demanded large workspace as well as the required high forces and stiffness. Moreover, it ensures that the orientation of the handle is fixed in three dimensional space with only three joints, which would not be possible using an articulated robot. Additionally, this design has the advantage that the user never enters the kinematic structure of the BioMotionBot with his arm, which is an important safety feature. For actuation three EC-Motors (EBM Papst ECI 24.80) are used. The two motors on the wagon are combined with a ball screw and a slide that moves on a linear bearing to form a prismatic joint, while the third EC-Motor is situated in the base frame and combined with a planet gear to move the entire wagon with a belt drive. The wagon itself moves on the base frame on a linear bearing.

2.4   Sensor and Electronics

A simplified overview over the electronic components of the BioMotionBot is given in figure 3. Its main parts are the identical electronic components of the three prismatic joints (only one of them is shown in detail): the microcontroller on which the control system runs, the force sensor and an amplifier for the sensor signals. For the axis electronics we used motor control units (MCUs) from

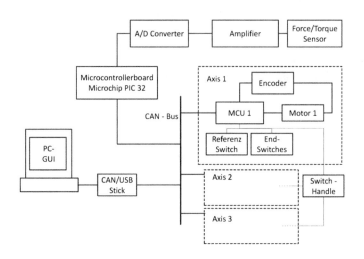

Fig. 3. Electronic components of the BioMotionBot

a supplier (miControl type mcDSA-E3). They are directly connected to the EC Motors and to the encoders. The MCUs have an integrated three loop cascaded control system. The outer loop is for position control, the second one for speed control and the inner one for electric current control. The motor control units can be programmed in Python. Since the encoders work incrementally, reference switches are integrated at each axis and are directly connected to the MCUs. After one reference drive at the beginning, the absolute position in increments is available at the MCU and is sent via the CAN-Bus to the PIC 32 microcontroller where it is converted into mm for the control system and the kinematic calculations. As a safety feature, a dead man switch is integrated into the handle that has to be pressed by the subject during the operation of the BioMotioBot. Otherwise the MCUs keep the BioMotionBot at a fixed position. The 6 DOF force torque sensor is situated directly underneath the handle and it is connected directly to the the the amplifier situated on the wagon. The amplifier is connected to a 24 bit analog-digital converter that transmits the digitalized signals directly to the microcontroller. For the control system we used a Microchip PIC 32 microcontroller starter kit that was extended with an additional self developed board that includes modules for the CAN-communication, and an additional serial interface, and houses the 24 bit A/D converter. The communication between the microcontroller and the MCUs is done over a CAN-bus system, while the user interface on the PC is connected to the BioMotionBot using a CAN/USB stick. As a last safety feature, an emergency stop switch is available to the operator to shutdown the MCUs as soon as it is pressed. Afterwards a manual release and a reference drive is necessary to reactivate the BioMotionBot.

2.5   Control System

For the separated position control of every individual axis, the position control system of the motor control units is used (PID controller). The parameter of the PID-controllers were systematically adjusted in order to achieve good performance. It is notable that this position control is the only part of the control system that works in local axis coordinates in the configuration space, therefore forward and inverse kinematics were implemented on the microcontroller to transform between the control modules in real time. On top of this position control loop, the self designed and implemented control loop is situated. The control system consists of two components, a force control system and a "force field generator" (figure 4). The force control system has a given force and con-

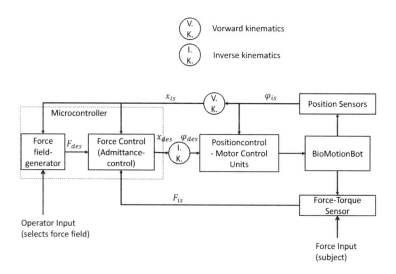

Fig. 4. Control system of the BioMotionBot

trols the movement of the BioMotionBot accordingly. The concept is that of an admittance control system like the one that is presented in [9]. The force control module measures the actual force at the handle, comparing it with the desired force given by the force field generator and reacts accordingly with a motion towards or away from the desired force direction. In addition to the force control, the possibility of a hybrid force position control is given. This enables the operator to constrain the movement to a certain area or plane by using position control, and only in the defined space the force control applies. The second component of the BioMotionBot control system is the "force field generator". This part of the system simulates different behaviors. It contains all the mathematical rules to generate the desired force at the handle of the BioMotionBot as specified in advance by the user. This can be a constant force in one direction, a force proportional to the current velocity, or a force that simulates the behavior of a spring to a fixed point in space. For the first tests of the system (section 3), we used a force field that is similar to that presented in [7]. The forces in the X- and Z-directions are calculated from the velocities in the X- and Z-directions. In this scenario the movement is limited to a two dimensional horizontal plane, and the movement along the Y-axis is restricted by the control system. The formula of the force field is given in equation 1 (force in N, velocity in $\frac{m}{s}$).

$$\begin{pmatrix} F_x \\ F_z \end{pmatrix} = \begin{pmatrix} 50 & 56 \\ 56 & -56 \end{pmatrix} \cdot \begin{pmatrix} v_x \\ v_z \end{pmatrix} \tag{1}$$

The shape of the resulting forcefield is shown in figure 5.

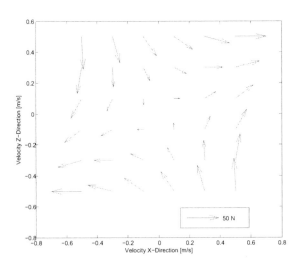

Fig. 5. The environment (2D) as described by the force field in equation 1

2.6   User Interface

The user interface that is used to adjust the settings of the BioMotionBot, and to visualize the different movement tasks for the subject, runs on a standard Windows PC. It is written in C# and consists of two windows. The first window is called the "Manipulandum Control Pannel (MCP)" and enables the control of the settings, and the selection of the active control system for the BioMotion-Bot. Additionally, predefined movement tasks can be selected. The position and angle of the camera can also be changed using the MCP with a fixed set of existing scenarios that can be chosen according to the movement task. The second

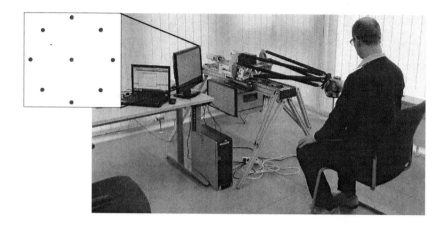

Fig. 6. The setting of the BioMotionBot with an enhanced view of the classical center-out movement task in the upper left corner. Red are passive targets, blue is the active target and the small black sphere represents the actual X-Z- position of the handle.

window, which is called the "Manipulandum User Interface (MUI)", contains a 3D representation of the selected workspace of the BioMotionBot (shown in the upper left corner in figure 6). In this 3D representation, the position of the handle is shown as a small black sphere. In figure 6 the classical center-out movement task is shown. Thereby one sphere is situated in the center and eight spheres are arranged in a circle around the center with a distance of 10 cm. During the test one target is activated and the color is changed from red to blue. The subject has to move the handle from the center sphere to the blue sphere and thereby the trajectory of the handle is recorded. The active force field can be selected separately so that a number of experiments with the same movement task but different force fields can be conducted and the resulting data can be analyzed.

3   Results

So far we conducted two types of experiments. First, we analyzed the behavior of the different components of the BioMotionBot. Because these tests provided satisfactory results, we the examined in a second step, if it is possible to reproduce the findings from the motor-control literature with the BioMotionBot. Selected results of these tests are shown below.

We conducted a couple of tests similar to the study of [7] using the force field described in section 2.5 and the center-out task shown in figure 6. First, the subject conducted five trials under null-field condition to each of the eight targets around the center resulting in 40 trials. Because the handle had to be moved to the target and back to the center the subject conducted a total of 80 trials. We only recorded the trajectories from the center to the targets but not the way back. After these 80 trials the force field illustrated in figure 5 was activated. Then, the subject conducted 400 trials under the force field condition (50 trials to each target). As before we only recorded the trajectories from the center to the targets. The trajectories in figure 7 represent mean trajectories (N = 5). Under the null-field condition, the subject produced nearly straight hand trajectories (figure 7, left). After the force field was turned on, the hand trajectories deviated significantly from the roughly straight-line hand paths (figure 7, middle). With practice, the trajectories of the hand in the force fields converged toward a path very similar to that produced before the perturbation (figure 7, right). The findings are consistent with the results in the literature [7,2]. In other words, the BioMotionBot has the ability to cause an adaptation of the inverse dynamics model of the arm to the applied dynamic perturbation in the subject [1].

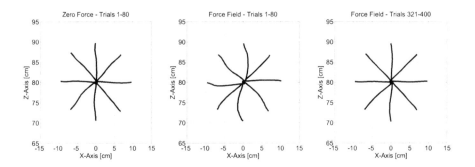

Fig. 7. Mean trajectories of one subject under null-field condition (left) and force field condition (middle and right)

4   Conclusion

This paper presented the general design of all the components of the BioMotion-Bot.

In the following, an enhanced performance evaluation and system identification of the BioMotionBot will be conducted to gain more data for further improvements of the BioMotionBot. To provide a tool for safe testing of a changed control system and to perform structural optimization processes as shown in [10], a co-simulation model consisting of a multibody simulation and a control system simulation block will be created and used for further improvement of the mechanical design and control system of the BioMotionBot.

The selected results presented in this paper indicate that the BioMotionBot can be used in the context of motor-control research. Next, different force fields will be implemented and various two and three-dimensional movement tasks will be tested. Based on these implementations, force field studies as described in [7] can be conducted. In the future established therapy programs for the treatment of neurological and orthopedic injuries will implemented and tested on the BioMotionBot.

Acknowledgments. The Young Investigator Group (YIG) "Computational Motor Control and Learning" received financial support by the "Concept for the Future" of Karlsruhe Institute of Technology within the framework of the German Excellence Initiative.

References

1. Kawato, M.: Internal models for motor control and trajectory planning. Current Opinion in Neurobiology 9, 718–727 (1999)
2. Lackner, J.R., DiZio, P.: Motor control and learning in altered dynamic environments. Current Opinion in Neurobiology 15, 653–659 (2005)
3. Scott, S.H., Norman, K.E.: Computational approaches to motor control and their potential role for interpreting motor dysfunction. Current Opinion in Neurology 16, 693–698
4. Smith, M.A., Brandt, J., Shadmehr, R.: Motor disorder in Huntington's disease begins as a dysfunction in error feedback control. Nature 403, 544–549 (2000)
5. Kwakkel, G., Kollen, B., Krebs, H.: Effects of Robot-Assisted Therapy on Upper Limb Recovery After Stroke: A Systematic Review. Neurorehabilitation and Neural Repair 22, 111–121 (2008)
6. Howard, I.S., Ingram, J.N., Wolpert, D.M.: A modular planar robotic manipulandum with end-point torque control. Journal of Neuroscience Methods 181, 199–211 (2009)
7. Shadmehr, R., Mussa-Ivaldi, F.A.: Adaptive representation of dynamics during learning of a motor task. The Journal of Neuroscience 14(5), 3208–3224 (1994)
8. Stock, M., Miller, K.: Optimal kinematic design of spatial parallel manipulators: application to linear delta robot. Journal of Mechanical Design 125, 292–301 (2003)
9. Van Der Linde, R.Q., Lammertse, P.: HapticMaster–a generic force controlled robot for human interaction. Industrial Robot: An International Journal 30(6), 515–524 (2003)
10. Ottnad, J.: Topologieoptimierung von Bauteilen in dynamischen und geregelten Systemen, Dissertation (2009)

Adaptive Control Scheme with Parameter Adaptation - From Human Motor Control to Humanoid Robot Locomotion Control

Haiwei Dong[1] and Zhiwei Luo[2]

[1] Japan Society for the Promotion of Science and Kobe University
1-8 Chiyoda-ku, 1028472 Tokyo, Japan
[2] Department of Computational Science, School of System Informatics
1-1, Rokkodai-cho, Nada-ku, 6578501 Kobe, Japan
{haiwei,luo}@gold.kobe-u.ac.jp

Abstract. As the origin intention of humanoid robot is showing the possibility of the biped walking and explaining the principle, there are many common issues between human motor control and humanoid robot locomotion. This paper considers two major common issues of the two researches. First is modeling. Both in human dynamics simplification and humanoid dynamics modeling, we actively or passively choose parts of the variable states because of dynamics simplification and unmodeled dynamics. In these cases, it is questionable that the dynamics represented by the partial variables states still corresponds to a physical system. In this paper, we discuss this problem and prove that the partial dynamics satisfies the conditions of a physical system, which is the basis of control scheme design. Second is control. To tolerate all the errors or perturbations, we design a control scheme which is composed of variable state control and parameter adaptation. The former can tolerate modeling error; the latter can identify the dynamic system in real time. Finally, we apply the proposed control scheme into a humanoid robot control case, which shows the effectiveness of the proposed control scheme.

Keywords: Unmodeled dynamics, model simplification, adaptive control.

1   Introduction

From the viewpoint of biomechanics, human body can be seen as a multi-rigid-object with numerous joints. Adding muscles and tensors, human body can move as desired by the neural system. The whole system is called neural-skeleton-muscle system [1,2]. One of the features of this system is that there are much more muscles than required to generate movement. Hence, the human body is an over redundant system [3]. One of the important roles of neural system is to control these muscles, which is called human motor control [4]. While in the research area of robotics, there is one research filed focusing on locomotion control of the humanoid robot [5,6]. As the origin intention of humanoid robot is showing the possibility of the biped walking and explaining the principle, there are many common issues between the two research areas.

S. Jeschke, H. Liu, and D. Schilberg (Eds.): ICIRA 2011, Part II, LNAI 7102, pp. 558–568, 2011.

In this paper, we address the common problems of human motor control and humanoid robot locomotion and give solution.

Specifically, this paper considers two issues in common. First is modeling. As we all know, human body has about 206 bones and numerous joints connecting adjacent bones. Based on the classification criteria of human joints, the joints can be mainly divided into hinge (1 DOF), pivot (2 DOF), saddle (2 DOF), gliding (2 DOF) and ball socket (3 DOF). In dynamic equations, each DOF is expressed as one differential equation. Hence, the overall human dynamics is too large to handle. It is necessary to pick up some state variables which are crucial [7]. The same case is with humanoid robot. To model a humanoid robot, we can not model all the dynamics. The unmodeled dynamics is inevitable. These unmodeled dynamics shows the dynamics corresponding with the omitted state variables. Thus, both in human dynamics simplification and humanoid dynamics modeling, we actively or passively choose parts of the variable states. In these cases, it is questionable that these dynamics represented by the partial variables states corresponds to a physical system. In Part II, we discuss this problem and prove that the partial dynamics satisfies conditions of a physical system, which is the basis of control scheme design.

The second issue is control. For simplified human dynamics, the variable states which are not picked up as crucial variable state also influence the total human dynamics in the form of disturbance. On the other hand, the humanoid model does not only have unmodeled dynamics, but also have many perturbations and modeling errors because of measurement error. To accomplish human motor control or humanoid robot locomotion control, we have to make sure that the designed control scheme is able to tolerate the mentioned disturbances, perturbations and modeling error. In Part III, we design a control scheme consisting of variable state control and parameter adaptation. The former can tolerate modeling error; the latter can identify the dynamic system in real time. The proposed control scheme is verified by applying it into a humanoid robot control case.

2   Dynamic Reduction in Modeling

Consider the general form of a dynamic system

$$H(q)\ddot{q} + C(q,\dot{q})\dot{q} + G(q) = \tau_{pass} + \tau_{rob} \tag{1}$$

where τ_{rob} is an active torque which is the power to drive the system and τ_{pass} is a passive torque which can not be controlled. From previous research [8], in Hamiltonian form we can write conservation of energy in the form

$$\dot{q}^T(\tau_{pass} + \tau_{rob} - G) = \frac{1}{2}\frac{d}{dt}(\dot{q}^T H\dot{q}) = \dot{q}^T H\ddot{q} + \frac{1}{2}\dot{q}^T \dot{H}\dot{q} \tag{2}$$

From equation (1), we have

$$H\ddot{q} = \tau_{pass} + \tau_{rob} - G - C\dot{q} \tag{3}$$

Taking equation (3) into equation (2), we obtain

$$\dot{q}^T(\tau_{pass} + \tau_{rob} - G) = \dot{q}^T(\tau_{pass} + \tau_{rob} - G - C\dot{q}) + \frac{1}{2}\dot{q}^T \dot{H}\dot{q} \tag{4}$$

After simplification, the result is

$$\dot{q}^T (\dot{H} - 2C)\dot{q} = 0 \tag{5}$$

i.e. the matrix of $\dot{H} - 2C$ is a skew-symmetric matrix. Specifically, for any mechanical system in the form

$$\begin{bmatrix} H_{11} & H_{12} & \cdots & H_{1n} \\ \vdots & \vdots & \cdots & \vdots \\ H_{n1} & H_{n2} & \cdots & H_{nn} \end{bmatrix}\begin{bmatrix} \ddot{q}_1 \\ \vdots \\ \ddot{q}_n \end{bmatrix} + \begin{bmatrix} C_{11} & C_{12} & \cdots & C_{1n} \\ \vdots & \vdots & \cdots & \vdots \\ C_{n1} & C_{n2} & \cdots & C_{nn} \end{bmatrix}\begin{bmatrix} \dot{q}_1 \\ \vdots \\ \dot{q}_n \end{bmatrix} + \begin{bmatrix} G_1 \\ \vdots \\ G_n \end{bmatrix} = \begin{bmatrix} \tau_1 \\ \vdots \\ \tau_n \end{bmatrix} \tag{6}$$

it holds that $\dot{H} - 2C$ is a skew-symmetric matrix. Hence, the following relation satisfies

$$\dot{H}_{ij} - 2C_{ij} = \begin{cases} 0 & \text{if } i = j \\ -\left(\dot{H}_{ji} - 2C_{ji}\right) & \text{otherwise} \end{cases} \tag{7}$$

During modeling process, without loss of generality, we choose $q_s = [q_{i,1} \quad q_{i,2} \quad \cdots \quad q_{i,m}]$ as new state vector which we are interested in. Thus, we generate a new system with dynamic reduction

$$H_s(t)\ddot{q}_s + C_s(t)\dot{q}_s + G_s(t) = \tau_s(t) \tag{8}$$

Following the same system simplification procedures, the dynamics equation of the new system is

$$\begin{bmatrix} H_{i1,i1}^s & H_{i1,i2}^s & \cdots & H_{i1,im}^s \\ \vdots & \vdots & \cdots & \vdots \\ H_{im,i1}^s & H_{im,i2}^s & \cdots & H_{im,im}^s \end{bmatrix}\begin{bmatrix} \ddot{q}_{i1}^s \\ \vdots \\ \ddot{q}_{im}^s \end{bmatrix} + \begin{bmatrix} C_{i1,i1}^s & C_{i1,i2}^s & \cdots & C_{i1,im}^s \\ \vdots & \vdots & \cdots & \vdots \\ C_{im,i1}^s & C_{im,i2}^s & \cdots & C_{im,im}^s \end{bmatrix}\begin{bmatrix} \dot{q}_{i1}^s \\ \vdots \\ \dot{q}_{im}^s \end{bmatrix} + \begin{bmatrix} G_{i1}^s \\ \vdots \\ G_{im}^s \end{bmatrix} = \begin{bmatrix} \tau_{i1}^s \\ \vdots \\ \tau_{im}^s \end{bmatrix} \tag{9}$$

According to the relation of equation (7), the new system satisfies

$$\dot{H}_{iu,iv} - 2C_{iu,iv} = \begin{cases} 0 & \text{if } iu = iv \\ -\left(\dot{H}_{iv,iu} - 2C_{iv,iu}\right) & \text{otherwise} \end{cases} \tag{10}$$

Therefore,

$$\dot{H}_s - 2C_s \text{ is a skew symmetric matrix} \tag{11}$$

which means the new system after dynamic reduction satisfies conditions of a physical system. Based on it, we design an adaptive control scheme as follows.

3   Control Scheme Design

From now on, we consider the system after dynamic reduction (equation (8)). For the convince of derivation, we define some parameter variables as follows. The actual parameter vector is $P = \begin{bmatrix} P_H & P_C & P_G \end{bmatrix}^T$, where

$$P_H = \begin{bmatrix} H^s_{11} & H^s_{12} & \cdots & H^s_{1n} & \cdots & H^s_{n1} & H^s_{n2} & H^s_{nn} \end{bmatrix}^T$$

$$P_C = \begin{bmatrix} C^s_{11} & C^s_{12} & \cdots & C^s_{1n} & \cdots & C^s_{n1} & C^s_{n2} & C^s_{nn} \end{bmatrix}^T, P_G = \begin{bmatrix} G^s_1 & G^s_2 & \cdots & G^s_n \end{bmatrix}^T$$

estimate parameter vector is $\hat{P} = \begin{bmatrix} \hat{P}_H & \hat{P}_C & \hat{P}_G \end{bmatrix}^T$, where

$$\hat{P}_H = \begin{bmatrix} \hat{H}^s_{11} & \hat{H}^s_{12} & \cdots & \hat{H}^s_{1n} & \cdots & \hat{H}^s_{n1} & \hat{H}^s_{n2} & \hat{H}^s_{nn} \end{bmatrix}^T$$

$$\hat{P}_C = \begin{bmatrix} \hat{C}^s_{11} & \hat{C}^s_{12} & \cdots & \hat{C}^s_{1n} & \cdots & \hat{C}^s_{n1} & \hat{C}^s_{n2} & \hat{C}^s_{nn} \end{bmatrix}^T, \hat{P}_G = \begin{bmatrix} \hat{G}^s_1 & \hat{G}^s_2 & \cdots & \hat{G}^s_n \end{bmatrix}^T$$

and estimate error vector is $\tilde{P} = \hat{P} - P$.

3.1   Basic Control Scheme

Define a Lyapunov function candidate

$$V_1(t) = \frac{1}{2} s^T H_s s + \frac{1}{2} \tilde{P}^T \Gamma \tilde{P} \tag{12}$$

where Γ is a symmetric positive definite matrix. A tracking error vector s is defined as

$$s = \dot{\tilde{q}}_s + \Lambda \tilde{q}_s = (q_s - q_{s,d})' + \Lambda(q_s - q_{s,d}) \tag{13}$$

where Λ is a symmetric positive definite matrix. $q_{s,d}$ is the desired value of q_s. In addition, a velocity-reference vector is defined as

$$\dot{q}_{s,r} = \dot{q}_s - s \tag{14}$$

Then the first part of $V_1(t)$ can be written as

$$\left(\frac{1}{2} s^T H_s s \right)' = s^T H_s \dot{s} + \frac{1}{2} s^T \dot{H}_s s = s^T H_s (\ddot{q}_s - \ddot{q}_{s,r}) + \frac{1}{2} s^T \dot{H}_s s$$

$$= s^T (H_s \ddot{q}_s - H_s \ddot{q}_{s,r}) + \frac{1}{2} s^T \dot{H}_s s \tag{15}$$

From equation (8), $H_s \ddot{q}_s = \tau_s - C_s \dot{q}_s - G_s$, then

$$\left(\frac{1}{2} s^T H_s s \right)' = s^T \left(\tau_s - C_s(s + \dot{q}_{s,r}) - G_s - H_s \ddot{q}_{s,r} \right) + \frac{1}{2} s^T \dot{H}_s s$$

$$= s^T (\tau_s - H_s \ddot{q}_{s,r} - C_s \dot{q}_{s,r} - G_s) + \frac{1}{2} s^T (\dot{H}_s - 2C_s) s \tag{16}$$

According to equation (11), $\dot{H}_s - 2C_s$ is a skew-symmetric matrix. Hence,

$$\left(\frac{1}{2} s^T H_s s \right)' = s^T (\tau_s - H_s \ddot{q}_{s,r} - C_s \dot{q}_{s,r} - G_s) \tag{17}$$

Therefore, $V_1(t)$ can be simplified as

$$\dot{V}_1(t) = \left(\frac{1}{2}s^T H_s s\right)' + \left(\frac{1}{2}\tilde{P}^T \Gamma \tilde{P}\right)' = s^T(\tau_s - H_s \ddot{q}_{s,r} - C_s \dot{q}_{s,r} - G_s) + \dot{\hat{P}}^T \Gamma \tilde{P} \qquad (18)$$

Taking the control law as

$$\tau_s = \hat{H}_s(t)\ddot{q}_{s,r} + \hat{C}_s(t)\dot{q}_{s,r} + \hat{G}_s(t) - k \cdot \text{sgn}(s) \qquad (19)$$

where k is a symmetric positive matrix and $\text{sgn}(\cdot)$ is a signal function. Applying the control law into $\dot{V}_1(t)$, which leads to

$$\dot{V}_1(t) = s^T\left(\tilde{H}_s(t)\ddot{q}_{s,r} + \tilde{C}_s(t)\dot{q}_{s,r} + \tilde{G}_s(t)\right) - k \cdot \text{sgn}(s) + \dot{\hat{P}}^T \Gamma \tilde{P}$$
$$= [s_1 \ddot{q}_{s,r}^{\ T} \ \cdots \ s_n \ddot{q}_{s,r}^{\ T}]\tilde{P}_H + [s_1 \dot{q}_{s,r}^{\ T} \ \cdots \ s_n \dot{q}_{s,r}^{\ T}]\tilde{P}_C + s^T \tilde{P}_G - k \cdot \text{sgn}(s) + \dot{\hat{P}}^T \Gamma \tilde{P} \qquad (20)$$

where

$$\ddot{q}_{s,r} = \left[\ddot{q}_{r,1}^s \ \ddot{q}_{r,2}^s \ \cdots \ \ddot{q}_{r,n}^s\right]^T, \dot{q}_{s,r} = \left[\dot{q}_{r,1}^s \ \dot{q}_{r,2}^s \ \cdots \ \dot{q}_{r,n}^s\right]^T$$

Therefore,

$$\dot{V}_1(t) = \left[s_1 \ddot{q}_{s,r}^{\ T} \ \cdots \ s_n \ddot{q}_{s,r}^{\ T} \ s_1 \dot{q}_{s,r}^{\ T} \ \cdots \ s_n \dot{q}_{s,r}^{\ T} \ s_1 \ \cdots \ s_n\right]\tilde{P} - k \cdot \text{sgn}(s) + \dot{\hat{P}}^T \Gamma \tilde{P} \quad (21)$$

Taking the parameter adaptation law

$$\dot{\hat{P}}^T = -\left[s_1 \ddot{q}_{s,r}^{\ T} \ \cdots \ s_n \ddot{q}_{s,r}^{\ T} \ s_1 \dot{q}_{s,r}^{\ T} \ \cdots \ s_n \dot{q}_{s,r}^{\ T} \ s_1 \ \cdots \ s_n\right]\Gamma^{-1} \qquad (22)$$

Then

$$\dot{V}_1(t) = -k \cdot \text{sgn}(s) \le 0 \qquad (23)$$

Hence, the state q_s converges to $q_{s,d}$ and meanwhile the estimate parameter $\hat{P}$ converges to the actual parameter P.

3.2   Additional Parameter Adaptation

In practical application, when the modeled system has large dynamic reduction, it is of great importance to have quick convergence speed of parameter. Here we add additional adaptation law into basic control scheme. Considering the normal usage of system identification, we rewrite the dynamics of the modeled system as

$$\tau_s(t) = H_s(t)\ddot{q}_s + C_s(t)\dot{q} + G_s(t) \qquad (24)$$

In practice, $\ddot{q}_s$ is hard to measure. To avoid the joint acceleration in equation (24), we use filtering technique. Specifically, multiply both sides of equation (24) with $e^{-\lambda(t-r)}$ where λ and r are positive number. By integrating equation (24), we get

$$\int_0^t e^{-\lambda(t-r)} \tau_s(r)dr = \int_0^t e^{-\lambda(t-r)} \begin{bmatrix} \ddot{q}_s^T & 0 & \cdots & 0 & \dot{q}_s^T & 0 & \cdots & 0 & 1 & 0 & \cdots & 0 \\ 0 & \ddot{q}_s^T & \cdots & 0 & 0 & \dot{q}_s^T & \cdots & 0 & 0 & 1 & \cdots & 0 \\ \vdots & & \ddots & \vdots & \vdots & & \ddots & \vdots & \vdots & & \ddots & \vdots \\ 0 & 0 & \cdots & \ddot{q}_s^T & 0 & 0 & \cdots & \dot{q}_s^T & 0 & 0 & \cdots & 1 \end{bmatrix} dr \cdot \begin{bmatrix} P_H \\ P_C \\ P_G \end{bmatrix}$$

(25)

where $\ddot{q}_s = \begin{bmatrix} \ddot{q}_{s,1} & \ddot{q}_{s,2} & \cdots & \ddot{q}_{s,n} \end{bmatrix}^T, \dot{q}_s = \begin{bmatrix} \dot{q}_{s,1} & \dot{q}_{s,2} & \cdots & \dot{q}_{s,n} \end{bmatrix}^T$.

By using partial integration, the term consisting of $\ddot{q}_s^T$ on the right side can be rewritten as

$$\int_0^t e^{-\lambda(t-r)} \begin{bmatrix} \ddot{q}_s^T & 0 & \cdots & 0 \\ 0 & \ddot{q}_s^T & \cdots & 0 \\ \vdots & & \ddots & \vdots \\ 0 & 0 & \cdots & \ddot{q}_s^T \end{bmatrix} dr$$

(26)

$$= e^{-\lambda(t-r)} \begin{bmatrix} \dot{q}_s^T & 0 & \cdots & 0 \\ 0 & \dot{q}_s^T & \cdots & 0 \\ \vdots & & \ddots & \vdots \\ 0 & 0 & \cdots & \dot{q}_s^T \end{bmatrix}\Bigg|_0^t - \int_0^t \frac{d}{dr}\left(e^{-\lambda(t-r)} \begin{bmatrix} \dot{q}_s^T & 0 & \cdots & 0 \\ 0 & \dot{q}_s^T & \cdots & 0 \\ \vdots & & \ddots & \vdots \\ 0 & 0 & \cdots & \dot{q}_s^T \end{bmatrix}\right) dr$$

Therefore, equation (25) can be written in the form

$$T(t) = W(t, q_s, \dot{q}_s)P \tag{27}$$

In fact, from this view, we consider $T(t)$ as "output" of the system; $W(t, q_s, \dot{q}_s)$ as signal matrix; P as real parameters, respectively. We can predict the value of the output $T(t)$ based on the parameter estimate. The prediction model is

$$\hat{T} = W \cdot \hat{P} \tag{28}$$

Then the prediction error e is defined as

$$e(t) = \hat{T}(t) - T(t) = W \cdot \hat{P} - W \cdot P = W \cdot \tilde{P} \tag{29}$$

The basic idea to update the unknown parameters is that the parameters should be updated so that the prediction error is reduced.

$$\dot{\hat{P}} = -\Xi \frac{\partial(e^T e)}{\partial \hat{P}} = -\Xi \frac{\partial\left((W\hat{p} - Wp)' \cdot (W\hat{p} - Wp)\right)}{\partial \hat{P}} \tag{30}$$

where Ξ is a diagonal matrix gain with positive number. Hence,

$$\dot{\hat{P}} = -2\Xi W^T (W\hat{P} - WP) = -2\Xi W^T e = -2\Xi W^T \left(\hat{T}(t) - T(t)\right) \tag{31}$$

If we consider the parameter change much slower with respect to the parameter identification, we have

$$\dot{\tilde{P}} = \dot{\hat{P}} - \dot{P} = -2\Xi W^T W \tilde{P} \tag{32}$$

Choose a Lyapunov candidate

$$V_2(t) = \frac{1}{4}\tilde{P}^T \tilde{P} \tag{33}$$

then the derivative of $V_2(t)$ is

$$\dot{V}_2(t) = \frac{1}{2}\tilde{P}^T \dot{\tilde{P}} = \frac{1}{2}\tilde{P}^T \left(-2\Xi W^T W \tilde{P}\right) = -\Xi \left(W\tilde{P}\right)^T \left(W\tilde{P}\right) \le 0 \tag{34}$$

which means the estimate error of parameters converge to zero. In all, considering the Lyapunov function candidate in equation (12), we choose the Lyapunov candidate as

$$V(t) = V_1(t) + V_2(t) = \frac{1}{2}s^T H_s s + \frac{1}{4}\tilde{P}^T \left(2\Gamma + I\right)\tilde{P} \tag{35}$$

Thus, in all, the control law and parameter adaptation law are chosen as

$$\tau_s = \hat{H}_s(t)\ddot{q}_{s,r} + \hat{C}_s(t)\dot{q}_{s,r} + \hat{G}_s(t) - k \cdot \mathrm{sgn}(s)$$
$$\dot{\hat{P}}^T = -\left[s_1\ddot{q}_{s,r}^{\ T} \quad \cdots \quad s_n\ddot{q}_{s,r}^{\ T} \quad s_1\dot{q}_{s,r}^{\ T} \quad \cdots \quad s_n\dot{q}_{s,r}^{\ T} \quad s_1 \quad \cdots \quad s_n\right]\Gamma - 2\Xi W^T \left(\hat{T}(t) - T(t)\right) \tag{36}$$

From equation (23) and equation (34), it is easy to prove $\dot{V}(t) \le 0$, which indicates the tracking error as well as parameter estimate error converge to zero. In the total control scheme, we use two kinds of errors to adjust the estimate parameters. One is tracking error s and the other is prediction error e, both of which contain the parameter information. Such an adaptation scheme leads to fast parameter convergence and finally smaller tracking error.

4   Humanoid Robot Control Application

We apply the proposed control scheme into postural control of a humanoid robot (Fig. 1). The robot is composed of torso, upper legs, lower legs and feet. For this

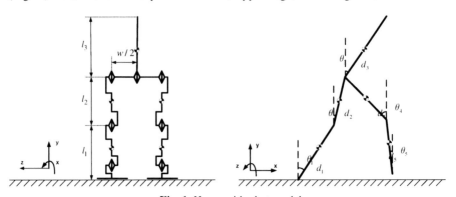

Fig. 1. Humanoid robot model

humanoid robot model, all the body parts are modeled as cylinder and the material is aluminum. As foot is considered as a cube whose thickness is infinite small, the mass of the foot is set as zero. The parameter settings of the robot are shown in Table 1. It is noted that as the material is aluminum, the mass and moment of inertia are small.

Table 1. Parameter of the humanoid robot

link	mass m_i (kg)	moment of inertia I_i (kg m)	length l_i (m)	location of center of mass d_i (m)	Width of robot w (m)
1, 5	0.0211	1.787×10^{-5}	0.1	0.05	
2, 4	0.0211	1.787×10^{-5}	0.1	0.05	
3	0.0211	1.787×10^{-5}	0.1	0.05	
					0.1

In this application, we use a software package AUTOLEV to model the humanoid robot and output it in MATLAB code. Considering the unmodeled dynamics and consequence from modeling error, we picked up parts of the variable states $q_s = [\theta_1 \ \theta_2 \ \theta_3 \ \theta_4 \ \theta_5]^T$. The dynamic equation is as follows.

$$H_s(t)\ddot{q}_s + C_s(t)\dot{q}_s + G_s(t) = \tau_s(t) \tag{37}$$

Then we apply the control scheme into the dynamic equation (37). Specifically, the initial state is $q_s(0) = [0 \ 0 \ 0 \ 0 \ 0]^T$ and the desired state values are

$$q_{s,d} = \sin(t)\begin{bmatrix} 1 & 1 & 1 & 1 & 1 \end{bmatrix}^T$$
$$\dot{q}_{s,d} = \cos(t)\begin{bmatrix} 1 & 1 & 1 & 1 & 1 \end{bmatrix}^T \tag{38}$$
$$\ddot{q}_{s,d} = -\sin(t)\begin{bmatrix} 1 & 1 & 1 & 1 & 1 \end{bmatrix}^T$$

The parameters in the control scheme are shown in Table 2. To show the adaptivity of the proposed control scheme, we just initial the estimation of dynamics equation parameters at the beginning of simulation as

$$\hat{H}_s = H(0), \quad \hat{C}_s = C(0), \quad \hat{G}_s = G(0) \tag{39}$$

As $H_s(t)$, $C_s(t)$, $G_s(t)$ are time-variant, the $\hat{H}_s(t)$, $\hat{C}_s(t)$, $\hat{G}_s(t)$ adapt values to the actual ones by the parameter adaptation law.

Table 2. Parameter values for the control scheme

Λ	k	Γ	Ξ
$\begin{bmatrix} 1 & & & & \\ & 1 & & & \\ & & 1 & & \\ & & & 1 & \\ & & & & 1 \end{bmatrix}$	$\begin{bmatrix} 0.08 & & & & \\ & 0.08 & & & \\ & & 0.01 & & \\ & & & 0.01 & \\ & & & & 0.01 \end{bmatrix}$	$\begin{bmatrix} 0.01 & & \\ & 0.01 & \\ & & 0.01 \end{bmatrix}^T$	$\begin{bmatrix} 0.01 & & \\ & 0.01 & \\ & & 0.01 \end{bmatrix}$

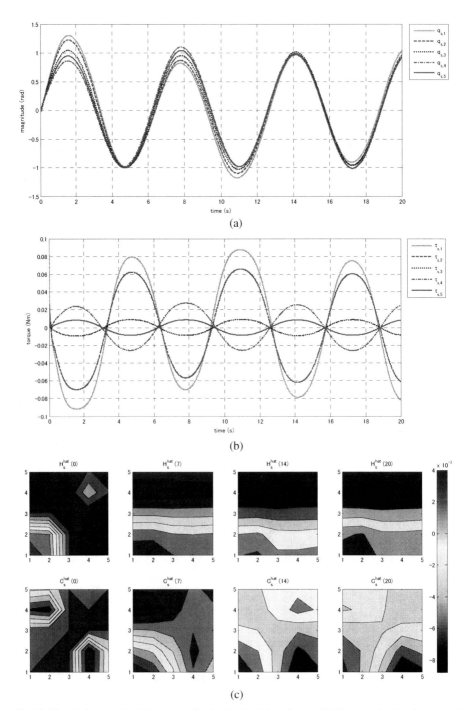

Fig. 2. Simulation results. (a) q_s tracks the desired sine signal. (b) Torques during the control process. (c) Snapshots of $\hat{H}_s(t)$ and $\hat{C}_s(t)$ in initial time (0s), 7s, 14s, 20s.

The simulation results are shown in Fig. 2. It is shown that the q_s converges to the desired states with time. Considering $\hat{H}_s(t)$, $\hat{C}_s(t)$, $\hat{G}_s(t)$ are completely updated by the parameter adaptation law (equation (36)), the tracking performance is satisfactory (Fig. 2 (a)). There is no torque with extremely large value, which indicates that proposed control scheme has advantage in energy expenditure (Fig. 2 (b)). The snapshots of $\hat{H}_s(t)$, $\hat{C}_s(t)$, (shown in the form of contour plot) during the whole dynamics are shown in Fig. 2 (c). One obvious fact is that $\hat{H}_s(t)$, $\hat{C}_s(t)$, change all the time verifying they are time-varying. Another important phenomena is that the patterns of $\hat{H}_s(t)$ and $\hat{C}_s(t)$ do not coincide with the initial values. The explanation is that these estimated values can also have the same state output although they are not equal to the real values. When the dynamics gets more variety, the estimated values converge to the real ones.

5   Conclusion

This paper considered the human motor control and humanoid robot locomotion control together as one topic. Human motor control has to deal with the redundancy of the human movement system while humanoid robot locomotion control is influenced by unmodeled dynamics and modeling error. The two issue can be seen as one together, i.e., actively or passively selection of state variables. After proving the simplified dynamics also corresponds with a physical system, we designed a control scheme. One feature of the proposed scheme is adaptivity, which is verified by the simulation. For a time-varying system (i.e. dynamic process of humanoid robot), the system can track the desired signal very well under the condition that the time-varying parameters are given only in the initial moment. The contribution of this paper is giving an explanation on dynamic reduction in modeling process by a mathematical proof and further more, designing an adaptive control scheme for the model with reduced dynamics.

Acknowledgement. This work was supported in part by Japan Society for the Promotion of Science.

References

1. Ivancevic, V.G., Ivancevic, T.T.: Natural Biodynamics. World Scientific Publishing Co. Pte. Ltd. (2005)
2. Crago, P.E.: Creating Neuromusculoskeletal Models. In: Biomechanics and Neural Control of Posture and Movement, pp. 119–133. Springer, Heidelberg (2000)
3. Manal, K., Gonzalez, R.V., Lloyd, D.G., Buchanan, T.S.: A Real-time EMG-driven Virtual Arm. Computers in Biology and Medicine 32, 25–36 (2002)
4. Winter, D.A.: Biomechanics and Motor Control of Human Movement. John Wiley & Sons, Inc. (1990)

5. Tzafestas, S., Raibert, M., Tzafestas, C.: Robust Sliding-mode Control Applied to a 5-Link Biped Robot. Journal of Intelligent and Robotic System 15, 67–133 (1996)
6. Kogakkai, S., Kumamoto, M.: Revolution in Humanoid Robotics: Evolution of Motion Control. Tokyo Denki University Publisher (2006)
7. Dong, H., Luo, Z., Nagano, A.: Adaptive Attitude Control of Redundant Time-Varying Complex Model of Human Body in the Nursing Activity. Journal of Robotics and Mechatronics 22, 418–429 (2010)
8. Slotine, J.J.E., Li, W.: Applied Nonlinear Control. Prentice Hall (1991)

Online Walking Gait Generation with Predefined Variable Height of the Center of Mass

Johannes Mayr, Hubert Gattringer, and Hartmut Bremer

Johannes Kepler University Linz
Altenbergerstr. 69, 4040 Linz, Austria
{joh.mayr,hubert.gattringer,hartmut.bremer}@jku.at
http://www.robotik.jku.at

Abstract. For biped robots one main issue is the generation of stable trajectories for the center of mass (CoM). Several different approaches based on the zero moment point (ZMP) scheme have been presented in the past. Due to the complex dynamic structure of bipedal robots, most of the considered algorithms use a simplified time invariant linear model to approximate the dynamics of the system. This model is extended to a time variant one and then used to generate stable CoM trajectories with variable predefined CoM height. This allows to generate trajectories online for walking underneath obstacles with more accuracy. It is shown that using this extended scheme it is possible to overcome some kinematic limits as joint speed in the knee or the maximum step length for common walking.

Keywords: Biped Walking, Online Gait Generation.

1 Introduction

Stable motion of a humanoid robot without tripping over entirely relies on the contact forces between the robot and the environment. Due to the fact that feet can only push on the ground, the amount of feasible motions is strictly limited. Therefore, the generation of stable trajectories is one main issues in humanoid robotics. Different offline approaches have been proposed in [1] [8] [3]. The main limitation of these methods is the lack of possibilities to react on external influences as for example when unknown forces are applied to the robot or when the next foot landing position or time is changed. In order to overcome these limitations it is worthwhile to generate trajectories in realtime and continuously adapt them as needed.

For the generation of stable trajectories it is necessary to consider the dynamics of the robot. Due to the high number of degrees of freedom and the complex structure of most walking machines, the description of their dynamical behavior is quite extensive and results in highly nonlinear equations of motion. This makes it necessary to find simplified representations for humanoid robots which approximate the multi body system by a model that can be handled more easily. To be able to apply the attained results to the real system, the approximation

S. Jeschke, H. Liu, and D. Schilberg (Eds.): ICIRA 2011, Part II, LNAI 7102, pp. 569–578, 2011.

has to be as accurate as possible. A quite common approximation, called Three-Dimensional Linear Inverted Pendulum Mode (3D-LIPM) [5], uses a single point mass kept at a constant height to approximate the dynamics. Due to the use of a point mass, the angular momentum of the robot, and therefore of every single component, is neglected. An alternative view called cart-table model, resulting in the same approximation as the 3D-LIPM, was shown in [4]. An other approach making use of three point masses, one for the upper body and one for each leg, has been suggested in [7].

These simplified models are then used for gait generation. Most offline as well as online gait generation methods make use of the 3D-LIPM. An other approach for generating trajectories online uses an extension of the well known Linear Quadratic Regulator theory (LQR) [4]. Integral and preview action are added to the ordinary LQR scheme, which leads to the so called preview control scheme [9] [6]. This method seems to perform quite well, but does not allow the consideration of any constraints on the position of the ZMP, nor the use of variable height of the CoM. Parts of these limitations have been overcome in [11] and [2] by using a linear model predictive control scheme.

The paper is organized as follows: First, the the cart-table model, which is used to approximate the dynamic behavior of the biped robot, is modified to allow variable CoM heights in Section 2. This model is then used in Section 3 to derive a gait generation scheme that takes a predefined vertical CoM movement into account. Section 4 shows up some simulation results and ideas of how to gain benefits out of a variable CoM height.

2 Dynamical Modeling

In general humanoid robots are described by a quite complex nonlinear equation of motion. For gait generation it is therefore worthwhile to reduce this complexity by using approximations as the 3D-LIPM [5] or the equivalent cart-table model [4]. Both approximations do not consider inertia effects due to rotations of the single rigid bodies. Instead, the whole dynamic is reduced to a single concentrated mass located at the CoM of the overall system. A further assumption is that the CoM has to be kept on a horizontal plane with constant height. These simplifications result in a completely decoupled relationship between the movement of the CoM and the position of the ZMP in lateral and forward direction. Therefore the generation of the CoM trajectory can be split up into two identical tasks.

This limitation to constant CoM height, as mentioned above, can be overcome by extending the cart-table model and allowing a vertical movement of the CoM. Figure 1 shows a schematic of the extended cart-table model with variable CoM height. One degree of freedom is added to the original model to allow the top of the table, and therefore the CoM, to move in vertical direction. The resulting torque τ_y at a random point ξ in the support area is

$$\tau_y(\xi, t) = m(g + \ddot{c}_z(t))(c_x(t) - \xi) - mc_z(t)\ddot{c}_x(t), \qquad (1)$$

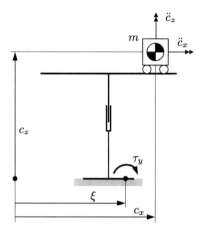

Fig. 1. Extended cart-table model: Additional degree of freedom is added to allow vertical movement of the CoM

where m is the mass of the robot, c_x and $\ddot{c}_x$ are the horizontal position and acceleration of the CoM, c_z and $\ddot{c}_z$ are the vertical position and acceleration of the CoM and g is the gravity acceleration. Regarding the definition in [10], the distributed floor reaction force can be replaced by a single force at the ZMP. This definition is equivalent to a resulting moment vector of the form $\tau_{ZMP} = \begin{bmatrix} 0 & 0 & \tau_z \end{bmatrix}^T$. With this definition and Eqn. 1 one can easily calculate the position of the ZMP in forward direction as

$$p_x(t) = c_x(t) - \frac{c_z(t)}{g + \ddot{c}_z(t)} \ddot{c}_x(t) \ . \tag{2}$$

The corresponding relation for the position of the ZMP in lateral direction can be derived the same way. Compared to the original ZMP equation from [4], the vertical acceleration of the CoM is now considered and makes Eqn. 2 non-linear in $c_z(t)$ and $\ddot{c}_z(t)$. To get a linear time variant system in $c_x(t)$ and $\ddot{c}_x(t)$, the vertical movement needs to be given beforehand. Due to the similar treatment of the forward and lateral motion, the latter one will be neglected in the further explanations. Choosing the jerk of the CoM as input $u = \dddot{c}_x$, the ZMP as output $y = p_x$ and the state vector as $\mathbf{x} = \begin{bmatrix} c_x & \dot{c}_x & \ddot{c}_x \end{bmatrix}$, Eqn. 2 can be rewritten as a time variant state space model of the form

$$\dot{\mathbf{x}}(t) = \mathbf{A}_c \mathbf{x}(t) + \mathbf{B}_c u(t) \tag{3}$$
$$y(t) = \mathbf{C}_c(t) \mathbf{x}(t) \ . \tag{4}$$

Keeping the input u and the vertical acceleration of the CoM $\ddot{c}_z$ constant during the sample time intervals of length T_A, gives the recursive discrete representation of Eqn. 4

$$\mathbf{x}_{k+1} = \mathbf{A}_d \mathbf{x}_k + \mathbf{B}_d u_k \tag{5}$$
$$y_k = \mathbf{C}_{d,k} \mathbf{x}_k \tag{6}$$

at times $t = kT_A, \quad k \in \mathbb{N}$ with

$$\mathbf{A}_d = \begin{bmatrix} 1 & T_a & \frac{T_a^2}{2} \\ 0 & 1 & T_a \\ 0 & 0 & 1 \end{bmatrix}, \quad \mathbf{B}_d = \begin{bmatrix} \frac{T_a^3}{6} \\ \frac{T_a^2}{2} \\ T_a \end{bmatrix}, \quad \mathbf{C}_{d,k} = \begin{bmatrix} 1 & 0 & -\frac{c_z(kTa)}{g+\ddot{c}_z(kT_a)} \end{bmatrix}.$$

3   Gait Generation

As already mentioned, several different online gait generation schemes have been proposed in the past. A meanwhile well known one is the ZMP preview control scheme, first proposed in [4]. The general idea behind this scheme is to minimize a discrete linear quadratic cost function with infinite horizon of the form

$$J = \sum_{i=k}^{\infty} \frac{1}{2}[Q(y_i - y_i^d)^2 + R\Delta u_i^2], \tag{7}$$

in every sample kT_A with $Q \geq 0, R > 0$ to gain the optimal incremental control inputs $\Delta u_i, i \in \mathbb{N} \setminus [1, k[$ with $\Delta u_i = u_i - u_{i-1}$. The superscript d refers to desired reference values. This leads to an extension of the well known linear quadratic regulator (LQR) by an integral and a preview action, first proposed in [9]. The first value of the optimal incremental control inputs Δu_k is then applied to the system, before the same quadratic cost function is minimized again in the next sample. The solution to this problem can be found by the discrete-time algebraic Ricatti equation and leads to a simple linear control law. One main disadvantage of this regulator is that the controlled system has to be time invariant whereas a variable height of the CoM leads to the time variant system from Eqn. 6. To overcome this restriction, the original cost function from Eqn. 7 is adopted by just taking N_p future reference values and $N_c \leq N_p$ future incremental control inputs into account. This gives the new cost function

$$J = \sum_{i=k}^{k+N_d-1} \frac{1}{2}Q_i(y_{i+1} - y_{i+1}^d)^2 + \sum_{i=k}^{k+N_c-1} \frac{1}{2}R_i\Delta u_i^2, \quad Q_i \geq 0, R_i > 0. \tag{8}$$

As before, this cost function is minimized in every sample to get the optimal control input. The first value Δu_k is then applied to the system before minimizing the cost function again one sample later.

As a result of the finite prediction horizon time, the variant system can now be handled. It is worth mentioning that the parameters Q_i and R_i can be different for every addend, which gives further possibilities to adopt the control scheme.

3.1   Model Predictive Control

For the design of the model predictive controller N_p future outputs y_k need to be calculated. This can be done by evaluating Eqn. 6 recursively, giving N_p future states of the system based on the state $\mathbf{x}_k$ at time kT_A and the sum over previous inputs $u_{k-1} = \sum_{i=0}^{k-1} \Delta u_i$

$$\mathbf{X}_{k+1} = \mathbf{S}_A \mathbf{x}_k + \mathbf{S}_B u_{k-1} + \mathbf{S}_U \Delta \mathbf{U}_k \tag{9}$$

where

$$\mathbf{X}_{k+1} = \begin{bmatrix} \mathbf{x}_{k+1} \\ \vdots \\ \mathbf{x}_{k+N} \end{bmatrix}, \quad \mathbf{S}_A = \begin{bmatrix} \mathbf{A} \\ \vdots \\ \mathbf{A}^N \end{bmatrix}, \quad \mathbf{S}_B = \begin{bmatrix} \mathbf{B} \\ \vdots \\ (\mathbf{A}^{N-1} + \ldots + \mathbf{I})\mathbf{B} \end{bmatrix},$$

$$\mathbf{S}_U = \begin{bmatrix} \mathbf{B} & \cdots & \mathbf{0} \\ \vdots & \ddots & \vdots \\ (\mathbf{A}^{N_c-1} + \ldots + \mathbf{I})\mathbf{B} & \cdots & \mathbf{B} \\ \vdots & \ddots & \vdots \\ (\mathbf{A}^{N_p-1} + \ldots + \mathbf{I})\mathbf{B} & \cdots & (\mathbf{A}^{N_p-N_c} + \ldots + \mathbf{I})\mathbf{B} \end{bmatrix}, \quad \Delta \mathbf{U}_k = \begin{bmatrix} \Delta u_k \\ \vdots \\ \Delta u_{k+N-1} \end{bmatrix}.$$

The future outputs are given by

$$\mathbf{Y}_{k+1} = \mathbf{S}_{\mathbf{C},k} \mathbf{X}_{k+1} \tag{10}$$

with

$$\mathbf{Y}_k = \begin{bmatrix} y_k \\ \vdots \\ y_{k+N_p-1} \end{bmatrix}, \quad \mathbf{S}_{C,k} = \begin{bmatrix} \mathbf{C}_k & \cdots & 0 \\ \vdots & \ddots & \vdots \\ 0 & \cdots & \mathbf{C}_{k+N_p} \end{bmatrix}.$$

One can see that the matrices $\mathbf{S}_A$, $\mathbf{S}_B$ and $\mathbf{S}_U$ are constant and can be pre-calculated to save up computing time, whereas $\mathbf{S}_{C,k}$ contains the vertical CoM trajectory and needs to be calculated online. Due to the finite prediction horizon Eqn. 8 can be rewritten to

$$J = \frac{1}{2}[(\mathbf{Y}_{k+1} - \mathbf{Y}_{k+1}^d)^T \mathbf{Q}_k (\mathbf{Y}_{k+1} - \mathbf{Y}_{k+1}^d) + \Delta \mathbf{U}_k^T \mathbf{R}_k \Delta \mathbf{U}_k] \tag{11}$$

with the future reference vector $\mathbf{Y}_k^d$ and the weighting matrices $\mathbf{Q}_k$ and $\mathbf{R}_k$

$$\mathbf{Y}_k^d = \begin{bmatrix} y_k^d \\ \vdots \\ y_{k+N_p-1}^d \end{bmatrix}, \quad \mathbf{Q}_k = \begin{bmatrix} Q_k & \cdots & 0 \\ \vdots & \ddots & \vdots \\ 0 & \cdots & Q_{k+N_p-1} \end{bmatrix}, \quad \mathbf{R}_k = \begin{bmatrix} R_k & \cdots & 0 \\ \vdots & \ddots & \vdots \\ 0 & \cdots & R_{k+N_c-1} \end{bmatrix}.$$

This corresponds to the standard quadratic programming formulation

$$\min_{\Delta \mathbf{U}_k} \frac{1}{2}[\Delta \mathbf{U}_k^T \mathbf{H}_k \Delta \mathbf{U}_k + \Delta \mathbf{U}_k^T \mathbf{g}_k] \tag{12}$$

where

$$\mathbf{H}_k = (\mathbf{S}_{C,k} \mathbf{S}_U)^T \mathbf{Q}_k (\mathbf{S}_{C,k} \mathbf{S}_U) + \mathbf{R}_k,$$
$$\mathbf{g}_k = (\mathbf{S}_{C,k} \mathbf{S}_U)^T \mathbf{Q}_k (\mathbf{S}_{C,k} \mathbf{S}_A \mathbf{x}_k + \mathbf{S}_{C,k} \mathbf{S}_B u_{k-1} - \mathbf{Y}_k^d)$$

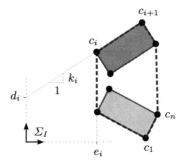

Fig. 2. Convex hull during the double support phase consisting of c points ordered clockwise

leading to the analytic optimal control vector

$$\Delta \mathbf{U}_k = -\mathbf{H}_k^{-1}\mathbf{g}_k^T .\tag{13}$$

For model predictive control only the first entry of the optimal control vector is used, so the next input for the system is given by

$$\Delta u_k = \begin{bmatrix} 1 & 0 & \dots & 0 \end{bmatrix} \Delta \mathbf{U}_k .\tag{14}$$

3.2   Constraints

Another advantage compared to the infinite horizon LQR is the possibility to extend the minimization problem to a Quadratic Program (QP) so that constraints on the ZMP can be considered. In this case the QP is given by

$$\min_{\Delta \mathbf{U}_k} J \tag{15}$$

$$\text{s.t.}\quad \mathbf{b} \le \mathbf{A}\tilde{\mathbf{Y}}_k \tag{16}$$

with $\tilde{\mathbf{Y}}_k = \begin{bmatrix} \mathbf{Y}_{x,k}^T, \mathbf{Y}_{y,k}^T \end{bmatrix}^T$ as the ZMP position in forward and lateral direction, the cost function J from Eqn. 11 and $\mathbf{A}$ and $\mathbf{b}$ to limit the valid ZMP position inside the support polygon. Also further constraints, like for the velocity, acceleration or jerk of the CoM, can be considered.

If the double support phase is neglected and feet are kept parallel, the calculation of $\mathbf{A}$ and $\mathbf{b}$ is straightforward. In general, some more effort need to be done to gain $\mathbf{A}$ and $\mathbf{b}$. First, the convex hull of the support area is calculated. During the single support phase this is straightforward and can be precalculated. In the double support phase algorithms like the Grahams Scan algorithm return an ordered list of points of the convex hull. Figure 2 shows the convex hull during the double support phase for two rectangular feet. Points are numbered clockwise. Every pair of neighboring points builds a line with the valid area for the ZMP either on the left or on the right hand side. Due to the fact that the points are in clockwise order, the correct side can be determined by the sign of $\Delta x_j = c_{x,j+1} - c_{x,j}$. In case of a vertical line Δx is equal to zero and the right inequality constraint is given by the sign of $\Delta y_j = c_{y,j+1} - c_{y,j}$. At each time

$t = kT_A$ the convex hull consists of c points $\mathbf{c}_j \in \mathbb{R}^2$ which gives c inequality constraints of the form $b_{k,j} \leq \mathbf{A}_{k,j}\mathbf{y}_k, \quad j \in [1, c]$

$$
\begin{aligned}
\Delta x_j > 0 &\Rightarrow -d \leq \begin{bmatrix} k & -1 \end{bmatrix} \mathbf{y}_k \\
\Delta x_j < 0 &\Rightarrow d \leq \begin{bmatrix} -k & 1 \end{bmatrix} \mathbf{y}_k \\
\Delta x_j = 0 &\Rightarrow \begin{cases} \Delta y_j > 0 & \Rightarrow e \leq \begin{bmatrix} 1 & 0 \end{bmatrix} \mathbf{y}_k \\ \Delta y_j < 0 & \Rightarrow -e \leq \begin{bmatrix} -1 & 0 \end{bmatrix} \mathbf{y}_k \\ \Delta y_j = 0 & \Rightarrow \text{no constraints} \end{cases}
\end{aligned}
\tag{17}
$$

where $k = \Delta y_j / \Delta x_j$, $d = c_{y,j} - k c_{x,j}$, $e = c_{x,j}$ (see Fig. 2) and $\mathbf{y}_k = \begin{bmatrix} y_{x,k} & y_{y,k} \end{bmatrix}^T$. All constraints for one sample kT_A can be combined to

$$
\bar{\mathbf{b}}_k = \begin{bmatrix} b_{k,1} & b_{k,2} & \cdots & b_{k,c} \end{bmatrix}^T
\tag{18}
$$

$$
\bar{\mathbf{A}}_k = \begin{bmatrix} \mathbf{A}_{k,1}^T & \mathbf{A}_{k,2}^T & \cdots & \mathbf{A}_{k,c}^T \end{bmatrix}^T .
\tag{19}
$$

Combining constraints for N_p future samples finally results in

$$
\mathbf{d} \leq \mathbf{A}\tilde{\mathbf{Y}}_{k+1}
\tag{20}
$$

with $\mathbf{e}_1 = \begin{bmatrix} 1 & 0 \end{bmatrix}^T$, $\mathbf{e}_2 = \begin{bmatrix} 0 & 1 \end{bmatrix}^T$ and

$$
\mathbf{A} = \begin{bmatrix} \bar{\mathbf{A}}_k \mathbf{e}_1 \cdots & 0 & \bar{\mathbf{A}}_k \mathbf{e}_2 \cdots & 0 \\ \vdots & \ddots & \vdots & \vdots & \ddots & \vdots \\ 0 & \cdots \bar{\mathbf{A}}_{k+N_p}\mathbf{e}_1 & 0 & \cdots \bar{\mathbf{A}}_{k+N_p}\mathbf{e}_2 \end{bmatrix}, \quad \mathbf{b} = \begin{bmatrix} \bar{\mathbf{b}}_k \\ \vdots \\ \bar{\mathbf{b}}_{k+N_p} \end{bmatrix}.
$$

4 Results

4.1 Walking Underneath an Obstacle

For the evaluation of the extended control scheme a trajectory for a sample robot, walking underneath a beam, as in Fig. 3, was generated. The position of the beam is known relative to the start position, so there is no online perception of the environment. The robot lowers his CoM by 25 cm at time $t = 3.5$ s and bends his upper body forward by 1 rad. After passing the beam at time $t = 10.5$ s the robot returns to its original CoM height and upper body posture.

Two different scenarios have been simulated. Figure 4 shows the CoM trajectory generated by the model predictive control scheme from Eqn. 14 but with a constant height of CoM. This corresponds to the original LQR from Eqn. 7, but with finite prediction horizon. The used parameters are $g = 9.81 \, \text{ms}^{-2}$, $c_z = 0.7 \, \text{m}$, $T_A = 20 \, \text{ms}$, $N_p = 100$, $N_c = 75$ $Q_k = 10^{10}$ and $R_k = 10^{-3}$. The reference trajectory for the ZMP is generated by using a step length of 20 cm, a stance width of 24 cm and a step time of 1 s with a double support time of 0.1 s. As one can see, the ZMP trajectory in lateral direction still stays within the support polygon but has a quite large deviation to the reference trajectory.

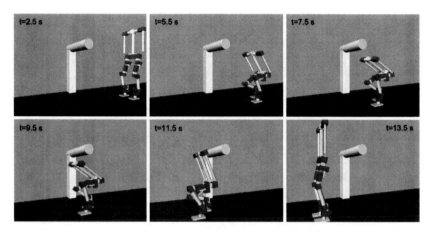

Fig. 3. Humanoid Robot (size 1.6 m) walking underneath a beam (gap width 1.1 m)

Due to the fact that the full body dynamic is approximated by a single concentrated mass, the neglected angular momentum, especially that of the upper body, can drive the real ZMP outside the stable region. In the second simulation the CoM trajectory was generated with the same model predictive control scheme for the ZMP but considering the vertical CoM movement. Figure 5 shows that now the tracking error for the ZMP is minimal.

4.2   Extending Kinematic Limits

A vertically variable CoM is not just useful for walking underneath obstacles, it can also be used to extend kinematic limits. Lowering the CoM position results in a joint configuration that is further away from a stretched knee and accordingly from the main limiting singularity. Hence, the valid range of footsteps that can be reached without violating kinematic constraints is extended. This goes along with a reduction of joint speed in the knee because the farther away from a singularity, the lower the joint speed for a given Cartesian speed.

Reducing the CoM height permanently has two main disadvantages. On the one hand, it results in a walking gait that does not really look like that of a human because knees are always bended quite much. On the other hand, this leads to a minimal larger lateral movement of the hip for dynamic walking. This can be deduced from Eqn. 2 with $\ddot{c}_z = 0$. The lower the CoM position, the smaller the weighting term for horizontal acceleration. Therefore, either the horizontal acceleration or the lateral movement of the hip increases. This fact can be noticed in Fig. 4 and 5 between $t = 4.5\,\text{s}$ and $t = 10.5\,\text{s}$. In the first figure the lower CoM position is not considered. In the second figure the lower CoM position is considered and therefore the peak to peak motion of the CoM is around 2.5 cm higher. Both side effects can be reduced by varying the CoM height depending on the progress of a step. A straight step forward is considered. If both feet are on the ground, the CoM should be so low that there are no kinematic

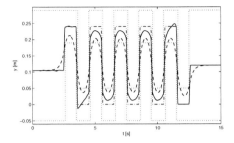

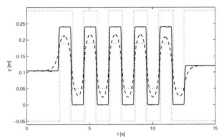

Fig. 4. Lateral position of the CoM (dashed line) for a humanoid robot walking underneath a beam when a change in height of the CoM is neglected. The solid line represents the approximated ZMP for the shown CoM if vertical movement is considered.

Fig. 5. Same result as in Fig. 4 but this time the vertical CoM movement is taken into account for the generation of the lateral CoM position. Dotted lines represent the borders of the stability area.

singularities because of widely opened legs. This means that in this phase the CoM is at its lowest position. If the swing leg is next to the supporting leg, the joint configuration is farthest away from knee singularities, so the CoM can be chosen higher. Getting closer to the final position of the swing leg, the knees are getting more straightend again, so the CoM has to be lowered. Figure 6 shows a sample movement of the CoM for such a step. Looking at Eqn. 2, one can see that if the CoM is accelerated downwards, both numerator and denominator get smaller and therefore the decrease of the horizontal acceleration weight is reduced. For the CoM trajectory shown in Fig. 6 the lateral movement could nearly be kept constant by this technique. Also the knees are more stretched in average, so that the generated gait is more human-like.

For the used start configuration a step length of 30 cm is not possible without lowering the CoM by at least 4 cm in double support due to stretched knees.

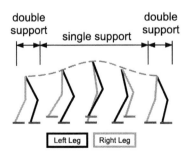

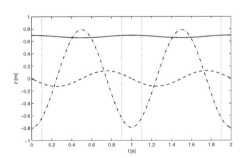

Fig. 6. Sample trajectory of vertical CoM movement for a wide step forward. CoM position (solid line) is lowered by 4 cm during double support ($t = \in [0.1, 0.9] \vee [1.1, 1.9]$ s) with a cosine function. Corresponding speed is shown with dashed and acceleration with dashdoted line.

Therefore the step length is reduced to 20 cm to be able to compare the knee joint speeds for constant and varying CoM height. For the reduced step length the absolute maximal joint speed in the knee could be reduced by around 25 % by lowering the CoM by 4 cm in double support.

Acknowledgments. Support of the present work in the framework of the peer-reviewed Austrian Center of Competence in Mechatronics (ACCM) is gratefully acknowledged.

References

1. Choi, Y., Bum-Jae, Y., Doik, K.: On the walking control for humanoid robot based on the kinematic resolution of com jacobian with embedded motion. In: Proceedings of the IEEE International Conference on Robotics and Automation, pp. 2655–2660 (2006)
2. Diedam, H., Dimitrov, D., Wieber, P., Mombaur, K., Diehl, M.: Online walking gait generation with adaptive foot positioning through linear model predictive control. In: Proceedings of the IEEE/RSJ International Conference on Intelligent Robots and Systems (2008)
3. Huang, Q., Yokoi, K., Kajita, S., Kaneko, K., Arai, H., Koyachi, N., Tanie, K.: Planning walking patterns for a biped robot. IEEE Transactions on Robotics and Automation 17, 280–289 (2001)
4. Kajita, S., Kanehiro, F., Kaneko, K., Fujiwara, K., Harada, K., Yokoi, K., Hirukawa, H.: Biped walking pattern generation by using preview control of zero-moment point. In: Proceedings of the IEEE International Conference on Robotics and Automation, pp. 1620–1626 (2003)
5. Kajita, S., Kanehiro, F., Kaneko, K., Yokoi, K., Hirukawa, H.: The 3d linear inverted pendulum mode: a simple modeling for a biped walking pattern generation. In: Proceedings of the IEEE/RSJ International Conference on Intelligent Robots and Systems, pp. 239–246 (2001)
6. Katayama, T., Ohki, T., Inoue, T., Kato, T.: Design of an optimal controller for a discrete-time system subject to previewable demand. International Journal of Control 41, 677–699 (1985)
7. Feng, S., Sun, Z.: Biped robot walking using three-mass linear inverted pendulum model. In: Proceedings of the First International Conference on Intelligent Robotics and Applications, pp. 371–380 (2008)
8. Takanishi, A., ok Lim, H., Tsuda, M., Kato, I.: Realization of dynamic biped walking stabilized by trunk motion on a sagittally uneven surface. In: Proceedings of the IEEE/RSJ International Workshop on Intelligent Robots and Systems, vol. 1, pp. 323–330 (1990)
9. Tomizuka, M., Rosenthal, D.E.: On the optimal digital state vector feedback controller with integral and preview actions. Journal of Dynamic Systems Measurement and Control 101, Transactions of the ASME, 172–178 (1979)
10. Vukobratovi'c, M., Stepanenko, J.: On the stability of anthropomorphic systems. In: Mathematical Biosciences, pp. 1–37 (1972)
11. Wieber, P.: Trajectory free linear model predictive control for stable walking in the presence of strong perturbations. In: Proceedings of the IEEE/RAS International Conference on Humanoid Robots (2006)

Visual Control of a Remote Vehicle

David Sanchez-Benitez[1], Jesus M. de la Cruz[1],
Gonzalo Pajares[1], and Dawei Gu[2]

[1] Department of Computer Architecture and Automatics
Universidad Complutense de Madrid, Spain
{davisanc,jmcruz}@fis.ucm.es, pajares@dacya.ucm.es
[2] Engineering Department, Leicester University, UK
dag@le.ac.uk

Abstract. We present a method for locating and determining the six degrees of freedom through a simple algorithm based on artificial vision. This algorithm can estimate the relative orientation of the camera with respect to a precise figure, it gives, roll, pitch and yaw, as well as the distance to the figure. We make use of the Euler number of a set of figures with a given distribution. We use the system to drive a small radio controlled car with the only assistant of the information gathered by a standard web-cam.

Keywords: Artificial Vision, Computer Vision, Control, Autonomous Vehicles, six Degrees Of Freedom (6DOF).

1 Introduction

In recent years there has been a huge increase in the study and manufacturing of autonomous aerial vehicles [1][2]. Of special civil interest are those aerial vehicles with hovering capability, for their possible use in search, locating and rescue. Part of the project in which the ISCAR group, from UCM, is involved, is the co-operation of several aerial and marine autonomous vehicles for the use in rescue missions, minimizing the risks for human teams. Among the qualities these aerial vehicles should have, is the autonomous vertical take off and landing (VTOL) on the ships, even when these are not stabilized or halted. When an Unmanned Aerial Vehicle (UAV) has to land, it has to recognise the touch-down spot somehow. Thus, it is necessary that some kind of system based on artificial vision is present onboard to help in the manoeuvre. Starting with the detection of a two-dimensional figure, which is easily reproducible, a small commercial web-cam detects its state, that is, the respective angles of inclination the web-cam has with respect to the figure (roll, pitch and yaw) and the distance to this figure, enabling the projection of the spatial coordinates on the plane to locate the camera in the three-dimensional world. This extends the applicability of the system to the reader's imagination. There are several publications regarding the same problem but taking a different perspective to solve the problem ([5][6][3][7][9][10]). None of them determine the whole state of the camera, i.e. the vehicle carring it, relative to the landing pad.

S. Jeschke, H. Liu, and D. Schilberg (Eds.): ICIRA 2011, Part II, LNAI 7102, pp. 579–588, 2011.

2   The Vision System

2.1   Why Euler?

To use the vision system as a locating system, the properties or characteristics that are going to be used to distinguish the target from the surroundings of the image have to be selected. From the beginning, it was decided not to use stereo vision (as done in [11]) to simplify the algorithm. We decided to test geometrical characteristics of some patterns, instead of colour analysis or the matching with a base figure, processes that are huge system-resource consumers, slowing down the process, and also noise sensitive being affected by the changing illumination conditions. In our case, we opted for distinguishing precise figures through their Euler number (number of connected regions or objects minus number of holes within the figures ([4])). The determination of this geometrical property is comfortably integrated within the package software we used for this study (MATLAB 2007b), its calculation requires very little computational time and allows us to distinguish and catalogue different figures in a picture rapidly. The implementation of the algorithm shown in [8] for calculating this property was considered first and later discarded for practical reasons, since the software mentioned above gave us more than sufficient processing speed.

2.2   The Figure and Its Raison d'être

Another factor to decide in our identification system is which pattern to use. As mentioned previously, the geometrical property used for identification is the Euler number. When we take and analyse images around us, randomly, it can be observed that regions with Euler numbers -2, -1, 0, 1 are normal, whereas, those with an Euler number smaller than -3 are quite unusual. For that reason, a pattern whose Euler number is -4 is chosen. This pattern is made out of three elements: the main element is a circle with five inner regions (holes) symmetrically distributed. The main property of this element is that its Euler number equals -4, which makes it easily distinguishable in the picture, since it is unusual for a geometrical entity to possess that property. The area of this part of the pattern is used in the calibration of the camera, for a latter determination of the distance from the camera to the target figure. The second element is situated inside one of the peripheral holes of the first element. It is an ellipse with two circular holes inside, thus it has an Euler number of -1. Finally, at the centre of the main element, a ring is included (with an Euler number of 0). The final pattern is represented in figure 1. For each element, besides the mentioned Euler number, the centre of mass (CM) is computed. The coordinates of the CMs of each one of the elements is the main information used for the calculation of the state variables. With these coordinates, we calculate the yaw angle as follows: Set an imaginary vertical line from top to bottom of the picture's plane, crossing the centre of the figure, given by the coordinates of the CMs of the main element, with Euler number equal to -4, which we will call CM_4 from now on for clarity. Next, draw the line connecting CM_4 with the CM of the ellipse (CM_1).

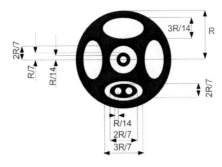

Fig. 1. Pattern used for detection and its proportions

Fig. 2. Determination of the yaw angle

The angle formed by these two lines is the yaw angle of the camera with respect to the figure. (See figure 2) For the calculation of the pitch and roll we make use of the following: When a figure is observed it forms a certain angle with respect to its vertical, the figure appears distorted to the beholder, in a way such that the closest region will seem to have more mass than the farthest region (figure 3).

This distortion makes the CMs of the observed figure move closer to the position of the observer. Then. the greater the angle of observance, the greater the distortion and subsequently, the greater the displacement of the CMs. This way, since the images are captured under perspective projection, the main figure, when it is not observed exactly from its vertical, will present its CM displaced to the observer. The difference between the main region and the central ring is quite significant (in terms of area), hence, when the whole pattern is observed, the CM of the ring (CM_0) will barely alter its position, while the CM_4 will be seen clearly displaced from its centre, as much as the point of view. Thus, once we have the coordinates of both points, (CM_0 and CM_4) we will be able to obtain two distances: a vertical separation (what we call D_{ry} in the algorithm) and an horizontal one (D_{rx}, see figure 3). The horizontal distance between both CM of the main element and the small central ring will be proportional to the lateral inclination of the camera (roll) and the vertical distance between them will be proportional to pitch angle.

Fig. 3. D_{ry} and D_{ry}: the vertical and horizontal distance between CM_4 and CM_0

3   Algorithm

3.1   Relative Pose

Processing images is a very system-demanding task. It is important to proceed efficiently and to accelerate the process it is recommended to analyse the smallest portion of the image as possible. When the analysis starts, the whole image is analysed searching the figure in the largest possible region. If the target is found (region with Euler number -4), the region of interest (roi) is reduced to a region slightly bigger than the target itself. If the target is lost, the search restarts using the whole frame again. Once the target is located, the region of interest is extracted. This roi is centred on the target figure and wraps it so that in the next image the target will be inside this roi. This section of the picture that includes our target, is transformed into its complementary image- an image where the value of each pixel is 255 minus the value of the original pixel. The complementary image is then filtered and converted into a binary. The algorithm is similar to that used in [5]. The time invested by the system (CORE2 DUO T7700, 2GB RAM, MATLAB 2007b) was studied in taking and analysing one hundred images for different configurations in the sequence of the process. Table 1 synthesizes our results. Therefore, the first sequence of analysis, will provide an algorithm capable of taking and analysing 25 images per second. In the processed image, we will only have the characteristic figure of our platform (the pattern may be used as taking off/landing platform), which contain the three regions that interest us (figure 4). For another series of measurements, 519 images were taken from which the our pattern was detected in 492 ocasions (95%). Keeping the relative pose of the camera (fixed angles and distance), the standard deviation for the yaw angle was 0.1 degrees, and for the distance to the pattern, 0.03 cm.

Table 1. Invested time for every sequence of analysis

Sequence	Invested Time/100 frames (s)
Image - roi - complementary - binary	3.9
Image - complementary - binary	6.3
Image - roi - binary -complementary	7.2
Image - binary - complementary	8.3

(a)   (b)

Fig. 4. a) Image taken by the camera and b) after being processed

3.2 Spatial Location

In order to locate the pattern spacially we use the position of the centre of mass (CM(1),CM(2)) of the main element of the pattern within the frame taken by the camera, whose origin lies on the upper left corner. We have to bear in mind that the algorithm analyses only a part of the frame taken by the camera, the region of interest, to which the position of this region of interest has to be added to the coordinates of the centre of mass in question. If the position of the region of interest inside the global image is given by the coordinates [lim1 lim2 lim3 lim4], where lim1 and lim2 indicate the position of the upper left corner of the region of interes in the global image, and lim3 and lim4 are, respectively, the height and width of this region of interest (see figure 5 for clarity). Then, we can assign the following values to the position of the figure: X = CM(1) + lim1 and Y = CM(2) + lim2. The drawback in the preceding method lies in the aberration introduced by the camera lens, which produces a distortion in the field of vision, rounding the edged of the image. This aberration might be ignored in cases where huge precision is not needed, as ours. Furthermore, for each variable, the rate of change is obtained from the time used in every iteration of capture-analysis and the previous measurement of the variable. With this, we are able to estimate the twelve state variables of the system under observance: three Euler angles, three spatial coordinates and all their rate of change.

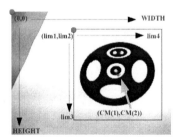

Fig. 5. Image of the platform showing the CMs

4 Constrains

Certain conditions are introduced in the detection process to insert robustness in the determination of the pattern. The first limitation introduced is the minimum area the pattern can present in the image taken by the camera. Experimentally, it has been determined that if that area (number of pixels) is smaller than 800 (pixels), the different elements that make up the pattern can not be distinguished within it by the lost of sharpness, from which, an object whose Euler number is -4 but presents an area smaller than 800, is not considered as our pattern. This case is presented when the camera is too far from the pattern.

The second restriction imposed over the location process deals with the possible distance between CM_4 and CM_1, the main element and the ellipse fitted in one of the ellipse-like holes. This distance must be smaller than the radius of the main element, otherwise, the element with Euler number -1 could not lie inside the pattern. The big issue here (not that big) is to obtain the area of the pattern. To do this, we can concentrate in figure 1 that presents the proportions of our pattern. Firstly, we consider the figure-pattern as a disk of radius R from which four ellipses and another smaller disk are extracted. The semimajor and semiminor axis of these ellipses are $3R/7$ and $3R/14$ respectively. These apparently strange proportions loose any strangeness and become whole numbers when R equals 7, the original radius used in the first test run with the algorithm. Following basic mathematics:

$$area_{pattern} = \pi R^2 - 4\pi \frac{3R}{7} \frac{3R}{14} - \pi \left(\frac{2R}{7}\right)^2. \tag{1}$$

from which the following constrain is obtained:

$$dist(CM_4, CM_1) < R = \sqrt{\frac{49 area_{pattern}}{27\pi}} \tag{2}$$

A third condition is imposed in the distance between the center of mass of the central ring and that of the main element. Experimentally, it is determined that this distance can not be bigger than 20 pixels, case presented when the pattern is observed at close range uncer a huge observation angle, from which if a bigger distance is measured during the location proccess. Thus, the camera focuses on objects alien to our pattern which consequently will be discarded from the search.

Another constrain is introduced to the rate between the area of the main element, $area_4$, and the area of the ellipselike element, $area_4$. This rate has been determined for small angles, and it always lies within the interval [15, 25]. Then, if the calculated rate between the areas of these objects does not lie between the given values, we do not consider those elements part of our pattern.

The fifth and last constrain deals with the area of the ellipselike element, $area_1$, and that of the hollow central ring, $area_0$. Again, from basic mathematics, it can be shown that

$$\frac{area_{disk}}{area_{disk}} = 2. \tag{3}$$

This relation depends on the point of view, but it does not diverge much under small angles. Hence, to avoid being absolutist and battle with possible oscillations of the measurements, we restrict the value of the mentioned relation to values within the interval $[1.5, 2.5]$[1].

---

[1] Videos showing the algorithm at work can be watched in the following links:
    http://www.youtube.com/watch?v=6upOLBCXDtO
    http://www.youtube.com/watch?v=NnRikxv9A8Q

5   Practical Application

5.1   The Vehicle

To test the applications of our system, we use a small radio controlled car (figure 6) in which we attach a copy of our figure-pattern. We want to drive the vehicle with the only assistance of the camera, that will be pointed to the car, taking images of the scene that will be then processed by an external computer, which is also in charge of producing the control signals and send them through radio to the car.

Fig. 6. The vehicle

5.2   Filtering the Data

Like any other sensor, information gathered by the camera is subject to certain grade of errors. To overcome the slightly deviations of the measurements, a simple and first order fast filter is applied to the estimation of angles and distance. This filter takes the actual measurement and the previous one, weighting each one by a constant factor, so that if a huge discrepancy is found between them, this would be smoothed, avoiding abrupt changes in the control signals. Then, for the angles and the distance, the filter applied is:

$$value_{new} = (1 - K_{filter})value_{old} + K_{filter}value_{measured} \qquad (4)$$

In figure 7, the effect of the filter is visible. It shows the evolution taken by the data when K_{filter} takes the values 0.1, 0.4, 0.7 and 0.9. It clearly shows how it smooths the values of the measurements taken by the camera. 0.Similar results are obtained for the distance. We use a value of $K_{filter} = 0.7$ in our tests.

5.3   Car Control

From the state estimation, it is expected to drive a vehicle with the only information obtained by the vision algorithm. As a first approach, we use the distance between the camera and the pattern to decide wether the car moves either forward or backward. Bearing in mind that our goal is testing the usefulness of the vision system, a simple control law is implemented which makes the vehicle moves at slow constant speed in both senses. The distance to the vehicle is divided into three zones: when de vehicle is closer than a certain threshold distance, this moves forward; when it is farther than another threshold distance,

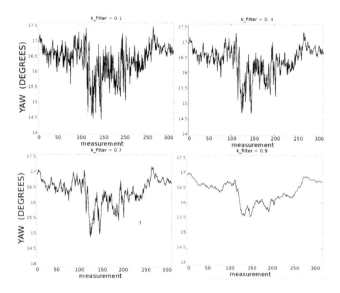

Fig. 7. Evolution of yaw with the value of the filter constant

it moves backward; there is a zone between both thresholds where the vehicle stops. Besides, the estimation of the yaw angle is used to steer the vehicle. For this variable, we use a proportional control, saturating the signal to fit it to the actuator limitations (the servo motor driving our small RC car can steer to angles up to 30 degrees).

5.4   The Hardware

Our system would be uncompleted without some electronics in charge of the vehicle control. The microcontroller Atmega 328 has been chosen, which come integrated in a arduino board ([12] offers extensive and useful information on the use of such development platform, as well as numerous practical examples). This development board is known for for its programming easiness, independently of the operating system used. Even when the programming is performed in C, there are plenty of implemented libraries that make easier the use of external sensors, both analogue and digital. They are developed under the open source philosophy, from which there is a extent community of users keeping them updated and rendering the solution of problems fast and feasible. The essential accompaniment for a wire-free application is an Xbee radio ([13]). We make a radio connection between the PC and the arduino board mounted on the vehicle, what will allow us to send control signals once the vision algorithm is run on the PC. Figure 8 caricatures the layout used to run our test. On the one hand, a printing of the pattern is attached to the vehicle, whose motor speed controller and steering servo are connected to the arduino board, that receives control signal by radio. On the other hand, a handhold camera plugged to a external PC points to the pattern on the vehicle. The PC performs the visual analysis following the

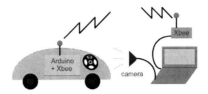

Fig. 8. The experimental layout

described algorithm; with the estimation of the relative position between the camera and the pattern, it sends control signals by radio to the vehicle (the PC is attached with an radio serial adapter [14]).

5.5 The Results

A test is run where a small RC car is driven with the only help of the visual analysis. The pattern is attached to the vehicle and the handhold camera is pointed to it (QuickCam Deluxe from Logitech). The algorithm in test detects the relative position of the camera relative to the pattern, as well as its distance. Measuring the time taken during the capture and anaylis of the image and previous values, states change rates are estimated. After analysing the data gathered for the filtering test, we are confident in the usability of our algorithm. The vehicle steers left and right following the movement of the camera. Equally, forward movement seems to be quite smooth due to the speed limitation. We have to remember the speed is kept constant in both sense of directions and stopped in a rank of distances, to make sure we are able to manoeuvre to vehicle within the boundaries of our test room[2]. During the tests, the vehicle is placed in a room illuminated by both natural and artificial light; there is a white, black and grey fleck carpet on the floor room; furniture is present and the vehicle itself offers numerous surfaces that could muddled up the location of our pattern. Besides all these factors, the algorithm is able to extract the pattern out of the frame, estimating the state of the camera relative to it. There are moments when the location is not achieved, probably due to changes in the room light that camouflage the different elements that built up our pattern, and obviously, when the pattern falls out of the field of vision of the camera.

References

1. Pounds, P., Mahony, R., Corke, P.: Modelling and control of a quad-rotor robot. Aerospace Science and Technology 11, 183–193 (2007)
2. Bouabdallah, S.: Design and control of quadrotors with application to autonomous flying. PhD Thesis, Ecole Polytechnique Féderale Lausanne (2007)

[2] Tests run with the algorithm and vehicle can be watched in the following links:
  http://www.youtube.com/watch?v=uA8xjLpx2Xk
  http://www.youtube.com/watch?v=AA1Fo3pBjj0
  http://www.youtube.com/watch?v=6sYSHvmqqRs

3. Bagen, W., Hu, J., Xu, Y.: School of Aeronautics Science and Engineering, Beijing University, China (2009)
4. Berthold, P.K.: Horn: Robot Vision. McGraw-Hill, New York (1986)
5. Saripalli, S., Montgomery, J.F., Sukhtatme, G.S.: Vision-based landing of an unmaned aerial vehicle. IEEE Transactions on Robotics and Automation 19(3), 371–381 (2003)
6. Sharp, C., Shakernia, O., Sastry, S.: A Vision System for Landing an Unmanned Aerial Vehicle. In: IEEE Int. Conf. on Robotics and Automation (2001)
7. Cesetti, A., Frontoni, E., Mancini, A., Zingaretti, P.: A Vision-based guidance system for UAV Navigation and safe landing using natural landmarks. J. Intell Robot Syst. (57), 233–257 (2009)
8. Dey, S., Bhargab, B., Malay, K., Tinku, A.: A fast algorithm for computing the Euler number of an image and its VTSI implementation. Indian Statistical Institute, Calcuta, India (2000)
9. Xu, G., Zhang, Y., Ji, S., Cheng, Y.: Research on computer vision-based for UAV autonomous landing on a ship. Pattern Recognition Letters (30), 600–605 (2009)
10. Lange, S., Snderhauf, N., Protzel, P.: Autonomous Landing for a Multirotor UAV Using Vision. In: Workshop Proceedings of Intl. Conf. on Simulation, Modeling and Programming for Autonomous Robots, SIMPAR 2008, Venice, Italy, November 3-4, pp. 482–491 (2008)
11. Petruszka, A., Stentz, A.: Stereo vision automaticlanding of VTOL UAVS. In: Proceedings of Assoc. Unmanned Vehicle Syst. Int., pages 24563 (1996)
12. Arduino, http://www.arduino.cc
13. DIGI International, http://www.digi.com/products/wireless-wired-embedd
14. Sparkfun Electronics, http://www.sparkfun.com

Longitudinal and Lateral Control in Automated Highway Systems: Their Past, Present and Future

Mohammad Alfraheed, Alicia Dröge, Max Klingender,
Daniel Schilberg, and Sabina Jeschke

Institute of Information Management in Mechanical Engineering & Center of Learning
and Knowledge Management. Dennewartstr. 27, D-52068 Aachen, Germany
{Mohammad.Alfraheed,Alicia.Droege,Max.Klingender,
Daniel.Schilberg,Sabina.Jeschke}@ima-zlw-ifu.rwth-aachen.de

Abstract. Due to the increase in road transportation by 35% over the last years in Europe it is essential to find solutions to optimize highway traffic. Therefore, several projects involving automated highway systems were initiated. In these systems, the longitudinal and lateral controls enable (with the help of other components) vehicles to be coupled electronically to form a platoon. Here, just the first vehicle is driven actively and the following vehicles are controlled automatically. Several projects were initiated to develop systems for different environments (i.e. Urban, Motorway). However, the developed techniques still are limited in their application range and e.g. cannot be applied in unstructured environment (i.e. rural or dirty areas). Furthermore, they were not tested for many different heterogeneous vehicles like trucks or passenger cars. This paper presents the past and present of automated highway systems and discusses solutions for future developments, e.g. how existing technologies can be adapted for a wider application range.

Keywords: Automated Highway System, Unstructured Environment, Heterogeneous Platoon, Longitudinal and Lateral Control.

1   Introduction

The optimization of national highway traffic has captured the attention of many governments, especially the European Union, for the reduction of the increasing number of the traffic jams and congestions. In 2003 the European Commission stated that every day 7500 kilometers of the European road system are being blocked by traffic jams [1]. Furthermore, an increase of 55% in road transportation is expected between the years 2000 and 2020 [2]. To optimize highway traffic, vehicles are driven closely to each other with just the necessary safety distance. Each vehicle (except the first vehicle) is thus able to drive with a low air resistance, which saves energy and fuel. Moreover the number of congestions, the CO_2 emission and the global warming are reduced. [3].

Several projects concerning Automated Highway Systems (AHS) therefore were initiated to optimize the highway capacity [4] [5]. With AHS two homogenous vehicles are coupled electronically, meaning that each automobile is automatically con-

S. Jeschke, H. Liu, and D. Schilberg (Eds.): ICRA 2011, Part II, LNAI 7102, pp. 589–598, 2011.
© Springer-Verlag Berlin Heidelberg 2011

trolled and driven at the same speed and safety distance [6][7]. The longitudinal and lateral controls of AHS enable - with the help of other AHS components - vehicles to be coupled electronically and to form a semi-autonomous platoon. Therein the first vehicle is driven actively and the following vehicles automatically.

The longitudinal control's essential function is the measurement of the distance between the preceding and following vehicle to maintain the safety distance. For the latter, the relatively constant speed of the preceding vehicle also has to be considered [8].

The lateral control's essential function is to keep the following vehicle behind the preceding vehicle. Two approaches are used for this task. The first is called "lane keeping", where the lane markings are considered as a reference point for the lateral guidance. The second is called "Electronic Two Bar", meaning that the relative position of each vehicle in the platoon is used to keep the following vehicle in the same track as preceding vehicle [9].

As an example, the system developed within the research project KONVOI (Development and analysis of electronically coupled truck platoons) [5][4] is used to demonstrate the main components of AHS and the mechanism of the longitudinal and lateral controls.

1.1   The Platoon System Based on the Project KONVOI

The project KONVOI was funded by German's Federal Ministry of Economics and Technology as an interdisciplinary research project with partners of RWTH Aachen University, industry and public institutions. Generally KONVOI is established to optimize traffic flow with driver assistance systems.

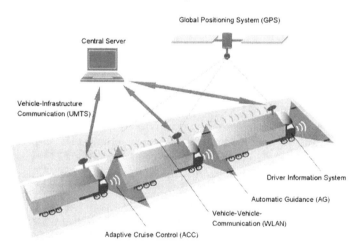

Fig. 1. The main components of the project KONVOI

In Fig. 1 the main components of the platoon system KONVOI are shown. An Advanced Driver Assistance System (ADAS) was developed to automatically control the longitudinal and lateral movement of the vehicles behind the actively driven preceding vehicle [4]. A Light Detection and Ranging (LIDAR) distance sensor is used to measure the distance in longitudinal direction and the lateral offset to the preceding vehicle. The latter's track position, which is detected using a Complementary Metal Oxide Semiconductor (CMOS) image processing system, is used for the lateral control of the ADAS [5].

Within the Adaptive Cruise Control (ACC) the target distance of 10 meters is realized. In addition, the ACC functionality has been improved based on the analysis of the data flow from the vehicle-vehicle communication via WLAN [10]. Therefore, a target acceleration interface is implemented in all platoon vehicles to automatically calculate the drive-train and the management of the different brakes. An automated guidance of vehicles is realized for the necessary steering moment based on a steering actuator which is established on the base of an electric motor and is built as a dual circuit with detached energy supply [11].

The Driver Information System (DIS) enables the vehicle driver to plan his route, select economic platoon participants as well as to initializes and confirms the platoon maneuvers. Moreover, the DIS sends the time schedule, route plan and GPS position of the vehicle with a vehicle-infrastructure-communication (G3) to the central server. The latter, in turn, organizes the platoon based on a data-mining-algorithm under consideration of economic aspects [12].

Within this paper a survey of AHSs is presented, which aims to give an overview about longitudinal and lateral control in different projects of AHS. Furthermore, the paper discusses possible solutions for future developments.

An overview about the past and the present of AHS in section 2 is given. The future developments of the AHS and what has prevented them so far for being used in non-highway environment are discussed in section 3. The proposed solution for homogeneous vehicles and unstructured environment is given in the section 4. Finally, the conclusion is presented in the last section.

2   The Past and Present of Automated Highway Systems

The PATH (Partners for Advanced Transit and Highways) project [6][7] was initiated in California in 1986. Here, an automated platoon consisting of 4 cars was tested. The solution depended on radar sensors and one result was the reliable measurement of the lateral vehicle position. Another key result was that the cars maintained a fixed spacing of 6.5 meters between themselves while driving the platoon at highway speed.

Within the DEMO 2000 project (the Demonstration 2000 Cooperative driving) [13][14], which was established by the Japanese Ministry of Economy, Trade and Industry in 2000, a system for obstacle detection was developed for longitudinal and lateral control. Within this development, the platoon is able to distinguish between small (i.e. small rocks) and big obstacles to drive around them. The development consisted of a dead reckoning vision system based on odometers [13]. The localization, heading and speed of each vehicle were transmitted via inter-vehicle communication based on 5.8 GHz DSRC (dedicated short-range communications).

Recently, the DEMO 2000 project has developed the Energy ITS (Intelligent Transport System) which aims for the reduction of energy as well as of CO_2 emission [3]. Therein, three automated vehicles (25-ton trucks) are driven at 80km/h with a 20 m inter-vehicle-distance. The longitudinal and lateral control depends on the vehicle-to-vehicle communication to transmit vehicle driving data (i.e. emergency braking and speed to other vehicles) as well as to enable merging and lane changing. In addition, the distance between vehicles is measured using triangulation between a pair of infrared markers on the top of the preceding vehicle.

In the European project CHAUFFEUR I [9], which was established in Germany in 1999, two homogeneous heavy vehicles were coupled. An onboard image processing system was used to determine the relative position of the preceding vehicle. This system depended on the detection of infrared light (IR) coming from IR emitters, which were attached to the back view of the leading vehicle.

To avoid the requirement of special equipment in the preceding vehicle, the CHAUFFEUR II project (Germany, 2004) [15] developed the CHAUFFEUR assistant application. The longitudinal control system was provided by a radar system with data about the acceleration, distance and relative velocity of the preceding vehicle. The lateral control depended on lane markings, which were captured by a monocular camera [15].

The research project KONVOI [5][4][10][11], supervised by the Institute of Information Management in Mechanical Engineering at the RWTH, was started in 2005 in Germany. In KONVOI, an Advanced Driver Assistance System (ADAS) replaced the CHAUFFEUR assistant application to increase the efficiency and accuracy of the longitudinal and lateral controls [16][17] Based on a requirement sheet [17] [18], which was developed especially for electronically coupled trucks, the developed ADAS had LIDAR distance sensors, CMOS-cameras and RADAR sensors incorporated. Four homogeneous trucks were equipped and electronically coupled so that a platoon was successfully formed at highway speed on a highway with a distance of 10 m between the vehicles. In KONVOI the coupled trucks were tested and realized in highway traffic for over 3000 km.

Within the project PRAXITELE (Preliminary Results From the Saint-Quentin Station-Car Experiment) [19][20] a concept for individual public transport for urban environment was developed in France in 1999. Here a platoon of empty homogenous electric cars was realized. A heterogeneous scenario was not tested. The distance between the cars, the speed of every car and the angle between the preceding (the car in front) and the following car was determined for longitudinal and lateral control by a distance measuring sensor, velocity sensors and a vision approach that worked with a target located at the rear of each vehicle [19][20].

In 2004 the INRIA (Institut National de Recherche en Informatique et Automatismes) [20] [21][22] patented a platoon technique with more advanced vision sensors, which did not depend on any additional equipment e.g. identical markers. This technique was developed in the CyberCar project [20] [21] [22] and depended on urban infrastructure. A heterogeneous scenario was not tested. Three approaches were demonstrated to achieve the longitudinal and lateral control of the vehicles. The first approach depended on a camera technique that extracted features from images of the preceding vehicle. The second approach used a laser scanner with reflective beacons. The third approach used a camera technique with IR emitters [20][21][22].

In 2009 the SARTRE (Social Attitudes to Road Traffic Risks in Europe) [23] project has been started by the Ricardo UK Ltd company. It uses a navigation system and transmitter/receiver unit that communicates with the preceding vehicle. First results are expected at the beginning of 2011.The system is to be developed for highways and heterogeneous vehicles.

3   Future: The Automated Highway System to Be Developed

Traffic jam, congestion, $CO2$ emission and the global warming do not only arise on highways, but also on unstructured environment (i.e. rural or dirty areas). Also, different shapes and types of vehicles are present on highway and unstructured environment. As shown in Table 1, all techniques developed within the projects discussed, were based on structured environment like a highway (see Chapter 2). In the future, the results of these projects should be also applicable to unstructured environment like e.g. for unpaved roads. Furthermore, these results should be adaptable for heterogeneous vehicles like passenger cars and trucks. Consequently, there is a need to apply the AHS on those environments without motorways.. In addition, the need to merge different shapes of vehicles in the platoon for improving the optimization of the highway capacity.

Table 1. Limitations of the significant projects of automated highway system

Project Name	Limitations
PATH	Limited to highway environment, since obstacles like rocks would deflect most of the sensors signals away from the follower.
DEMO 2000	Limited to short vehicle distances since platoon vehicles have to be in sight of each other to avoid the dissolution of the platoon.
CHAUFFEUR I	Limited to homogeneous vehicles, since the back view is not large enough to attach a large circular pattern of emitters to it.
CHAUFFEUR II	Limited to lane markings as reference points for the longitudinal and lateral control. No heterogeneous scenario was tested.
KONVOI	Limited to lane markings as reference points for the longitudinal and lateral control. No heterogeneous scenario was tested.
PRAXITELE	Limited to a short distance (around 5m) between the cars.
CyberCar	Limited to expensive sensors and a short vehicle distance (2-15 m).
SARTRE	Limited to highway environment.

In Fig. 2 the challenges, which need to be addressed to make AHS applicable in unstructured environment and for heterogeneous platoon are shown. They include the challenge (Weather Conditions), which arises due to in the proposed solution used equipment.

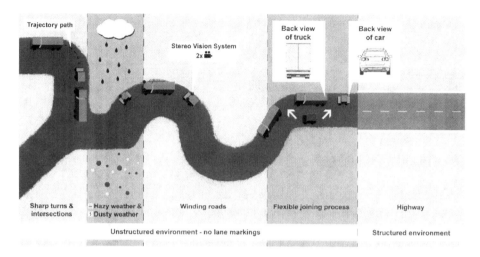

Fig. 2. Challenges to be addressed to apply the AHS in unstructured environment

Challenge 1: Independence of Lane Marking

There are no lane markings in the unstructured environment (Fig. 2), but most AHS systems use lane markings as reference points for the lateral control in highway environment.

Challenge 2: Flexible Joining Process

To realize heterogeneous vehicle convoys and to minimize the inter-vehicle-distance a flexible joining process is necessary. For example, in Germany the required maximum distance between cars relates to two tenths of their velocity [24] e.g. 20 m for 100 km/h. The minimum distance from a truck to any kind of vehicle is 50 m. It therefore is much more efficient to drive passenger cars in a row, with smaller distances and the trucks in a row with a fixed distance of 50 m. Most developed AHS however only allow that a new vehicle can join the platoon at its front or end but not in the middle, which then would prevent the sorting of the vehicles by type.

Challenge 3: Platoon Dissolution in Winding Roads and Sharp Turns

Most of the AHS have dissolving problems, meaning that the platoon dissolves in winding roads because the preceding vehicle is just partly in sight of the following vehicle. Most of the signals therefore do not reach the sensors and thus the longitudinal control cannot work efficiently. Most systems are therefore limited to short distances between the vehicles. A similar challenge is the complete loss of the signal in sharp turns or when driving over a hill top or through a valley

Challenge 4: Weather Conditions

Due to the proposed solution (see Chapter 4), the dusty and hazy weather conditions reduce the image quality. Consequently, this challenge affects the efficiency of the distance measurement in the system because the appearance of the features of captured images is distorted.

4   Possible Solutions for Heterogeneous Platoons and Unstructured Environment

Within this work several solutions are proposed (Table 2) to overcome the addressed challenges (Chapter 3). An algorithm is proposed here, which is a combination of machine learning algorithm and tracking algorithm. The algorithm provides the longitudinal and lateral controls with the necessary parameters without using expensive equipment and infrastructure. For the controls the detection and tracking of the preceding vehicle is necessary, where the detection task depends on a machine learning algorithm. In contrast, for the tracking task a new mechanism is used to follow the preceding vehicle instead of detecting it again. Further, a stereo vision system (SVS) [24][25] is applied to measure the distance between vehicles.

Table 2. Proposed solutions to overcome the challenges addressed for heterogeneous platoon and unstructured environment

Challenge ID	Solutions Proposed to Overcome the Challenges
Challenge 1	Solving the lane marking dependency by using the back view of the preceding vehicle (BVPV) as a reference point.
Challenge 2	Realizing a heterogeneous platoon and the highway capacity optimization by the joining of a new vehicle where it fits best.
Challenge 3	Generating and saving the path of the preceding vehicle while driving the AHS on winding roads.
Challenge 4	Enhancement of the appearance of the captured back view.

Based on five issues, the proposed solution collection (SVS + BVPV) is compared to other available technical solutions, as shown in Table 3. These issues are the financial costs (Costs), the performance of the distance measurement (Performance), applicable under real time constraint (Reliability), robustness against hazy and dusty weather effects (Robustness) and compatibility with heterogeneous platoons and

Table 3. Comparison with technical solution based on Costs, Performance, Reliability, Robustness and Compatibility

Tools	Costs	Performance	Reliability	Robustness	Compatibility
SVS + BVPV	Cheap	Very Good	No	No	Yes
On Board IP System with IR	Cheap	Good	Yes	No	No
Distance Measuring Sensors	Expensive	Excellent	Yes	Yes	No
Advanced Vision Sensors	Expensive	Excellent	Yes	Yes	No
Navigation System	Expensive	Excellent	Yes	Yes	Yes

unstructured environment (Compatibility). Four available technical solutions are used for the comparison, which are an On Board Image Processing (IP) System with Infrared Lights (IR) [7] [11][15] [18][20], Distance Measuring Sensors [21] [22], Advanced Vision Sensors [21] [22] and a Navigation System [3][23]. The here proposed solution is thus cheaper and shows a stable performance. The proposed solution still faces the challenge to be applied under real time constraints and to be robust enough in hazy and dusty weather. Furthermore, the solution has to prove its quality to be adaptable with the heterogeneous platoon and in unstructured environment.

5   Conclusion

The longitudinal and lateral movement of a platoon of vehicles can be controlled and automated with suitable equipment ("Automated Highway Systems"). However, existing approaches are based on the capture and evaluation of lane markings and therefore are not applicable in an unstructured environment. Also, they are optimized for homogeneous convoys. Based solely on the information acquired by a Stereo Vision System a solution is proposed which controls the longitudinal and lateral steerage for unstructured routes as well as heterogeneous convoys. The central challenges are: 1) Independence from lane markings, 2) Handling of signal loss in sharp turns, 3) Stability with reduced image quality (weather conditions), 4) Control of heterogeneous convoys (vehicles of different type), 5) Capability to integrate further vehicles into the platoon flexibly. The back view of the preceding vehicle is used as a starting point for the solution: Based on vehicle distances and deviation angles of different reference points of the preceding vehicle, its further trajectory path is calculated and the steerage of the vehicle automatically adapted. The solution thus allows the extension of automated highway systems to a manifold of additional application scenarios.

References

1. Commision of the European Communities. Europe at a crossroad - The need for sustainable transport. Manuscript of the European Commission, Brussels (2003)
2. Commission of the European Communities. Keep Europe Moving – Sustainable Mobility for our Continent, Brussels (2006)
3. Tsugawa, S., Kato, S.: Energy ITS: another application of vehicular communications. IEEE Communications Magazine 48, 120–126 (2010)
4. Kunze, R., Ramakers, R., Henning, K., Jeschke, S.: Organization and Operation of Electronically Coupled Truck Platoons on German Motorways. In: Xie, M., Xiong, Y., Xiong, C., Liu, H., Hu, Z. (eds.) ICIRA 2009. LNCS, vol. 5928, pp. 135–146. Springer, Heidelberg (2009)
5. Kunze, R., Tummel, C., Henning, K.: Determination of the order of electronically coupled trucks on German motorways. In: 2009 2nd International Conference on Power Electronics and Intelligent Transportation System (PEITS), pp. S.41–S.46 (2009)
6. Shladover, S.: AHS research at the California PATH program and future AHS research needs. In: IEEE International Conference on Vehicular Electronics and Safety, ICVES 2008, pp. S.4– S.5 (2008)

7. Vehicle Platooning and Automated Highways,
   http://www.path.berkeley.edu/PATH/Publications/Media/FactShe
   et/VPlatooning.pdf
8. Khodayari, A., Ghaffari, A., Ameli, S., Flahatgar, J.: A historical review on lateral and
   longitudinal control of autonomous vehicle motions. In: 2010 2nd International Conference on Mechanical and Electrical Technology (ICMET), pp. S.421–S.429 (2010)
9. Fritz, H.: Longitudinal and lateral control of heavy duty trucks for automated vehicle
   following in mixed traffic: experimental results from the CHAUFFEUR project. In: Proceedings of the IEEE International Conference on Control Applications, vol. 2, pp.
   S.1348–S.1352 (1999)
10. Kunze, R., Haberstroh, M., Ramakers, R., Henning, K., Jeschke, S.: Automated truck pla-
    toons on motorways - a contribution to the safety on roads. In: Procceedings of 15th Inter-
    national Conference Road Safety on Four Continents, RS4C, Abu Dhabi, United Arab
    Emirates (2010)
11. Ramakers, R., Henning, K., Gies, S., Abel, D., Max, H.: Electronically coupled truck pla-
    toons on German highways. In: IEEE International Conference on Systems, Man and Cy-
    bernetics, SMC 2009, pp. S.2409–S.2414 (2009)
12. Philipp, M., Thomas, S., Klaus, H.: A Data-Mining Technique for the Planning and Organ-
    ization of Truck Platoons. In: Gehalten auf der International Conference on Heavy Vehicle
    Transport Technology
13. Tsugawa, S.: A history of automated highway systems in Japan and future issues. In: IEEE
    International Conference on Vehicular Electronics and Safety, ICVES 2008, pp. S.2–S.3
    (2008)
14. Kato, S., Tsugawa, S., Tokuda, K., Matsui, T., Fujii, H.: Vehicle control algorithms for
    cooperative driving with automated vehicles and intervehicle communications. IEEE
    Transactions on Intelligent Transportation Systems 3, 155–161 (2002)
15. Fritz, H., Gern, A., Schiemenz, H., Bonnet, C.: CHAUFFEUR Assistant: a driver assis-
    tance system for commercial vehicles based on fusion of advanced ACC and lane keeping.
    In: 2004 IEEE Intelligent Vehicles Symposium, pp. S.495–S.500 (2004)
16. Happe, J., Leonie, P., Eva, P.: Drei Einsatzszenarien für elektronisch gekoppelte Lkw-
    Konvois auf Autobahnen. In: Einsatzszenarien für Fahrerassistenzsysteme im Güterver-
    kehr und deren Bewertung, Fortschritt- Berichte VDI, pp. S.146–S.185. VDI: Düsseldorf:
    VDI Verlag (2003)
17. Klaus, H., Eva, P., Johannes, H.: Einsatzszenarien für Fahrerassistenzsysteme im Güter-
    verkehr. In: Fortschritt-Bericht VDI. VDI: Düsseldorf: VDI Verlag (2003)
18. Petry, L.: Einschränkungsfreie Mobilitätspraktiken? In: Möglichkeiten zur Realisierung am
    Beispiel der Familie. wvb Wissenschaftlicher Verlag, Berlin (2006)
19. Daviet, P., Parent, M.: Longitudinal and lateral servoing of vehicles in a platoon. In: Pro-
    ceedings of the 1996 IEEE Intelligent Vehicles Symposium, pp. S.41–S.46 (1996)
20. Lapierre, E., Massot, M.: Praxitele: the missing link. World Transit Research (1999)
21. Parent, M.: Automated urban vehicles: state of the art and future directions. In: 8th Con-
    trol, Automation, Robotics and Vision Conference, ICARCV 2004, vol. 1, pp. S.138–
    S.142 (2004)
22. Parent, M., De La Fortelle, A.: Cybercars: Past, Present and Future of the Technology.
    cs/0510059 (2005)
23. Car_Trains_press_release_ENG.pdf,
    http://www.sartre-
    project.eu/en/press/Documents/Car_Trains_press_release_ENG.pdf
24. StVO §4: Abstand, http://www.verkehrsportal.de/stvo/stvo_04.php

25. Leibe, B., Schindler, K., Cornelis, N., Van Gool, L.: Coupled Object Detection and Tracking from Static Cameras and Moving Vehicles. IEEE Transactions on Pattern Analysis and Machine Intelligence 30, 1683–1698 (2008)
26. Robert, K.: Video-based traffic monitoring at day and night vehicle features detection tracking. In: 12th International IEEE Conference on Intelligent Transportation Systems, ITSC 2009, pp. S.1–S.6 (2009)
27. Lin, S., Tang, J., Zhang, X., Lv, Y.: Research on traffic moving object detection, tracking and track-generating. In: IEEE International Conference on Automation and Logistics, ICAL 2009, pp. S.783–S.788 (2009)
28. Bradski, G.R., Kaehler, A.: Learning OpenCV. O'Reilly Media (2008)
29. Grabner, H., Bischof, H.: On-line Boosting and Vision. In: 2006 IEEE Computer Society Conference on Computer Vision and Pattern Recognition, pp. S.260–S.267 (2006)
30. Avidan, S.: Ensemble Tracking. IEEE Transactions on Pattern Analysis and Machine Intelligence 29, 261–271 (2007)
31. Okuma, K., Taleghani, A., de Freitas, N., Little, J.J., Lowe, D.G.: A Boosted Particle Filter: Multitarget Detection and Tracking. In: Pajdla, T., Matas, J(G.) (eds.) ECCV 2004, Part I. LNCS, vol. 3021, pp. 28–39. Springer, Heidelberg (2004)
32. Han, M., Xu, W., Tao, H., Gong, Y.: An algorithm for multiple object trajectory tracking. In: Proceedings of the 2004 IEEE Computer Society Conference on Computer Vision and Pattern Recognition, CVPR 2004, vol. 1, pp. S.I-864–S.I-871 (2004)
33. Wu, B., Nevatia, R.: Detection and Tracking of Multiple, Partially Occluded Humans by Bayesian Combination of Edgelet based Part Detectors. International Journal of Computer Vision 75, 247–266 (2007)
34. Bay, H., Ess, A., Tuytelaars, T., Van Gool, L.: Speeded-Up Robust Features (SURF). Computer Vision and Image Understanding 110, 346–359 (2008)
35. Seemann, E., Leibe, B., Schiele, B.: Multi-Aspect Detection of Articulated Objects. In: 2006 IEEE Computer Society Conference on Computer Vision and Pattern Recognition, pp. S.1582–S.1588 (2006)
36. Leibe, B., Schindler, K., Van Gool, L.: Coupled Detection and Trajectory Estimation for Multi-Object Tracking. In: IEEE 11th International Conference on Computer Vision, ICCV 2007, pp. S.1–S.8 (2007)
37. Leibe, B., Cornelis, N., Cornelis, K., Van Gool, L.: Dynamic 3D Scene Analysis from a Moving Vehicle. In: IEEE Conference on Computer Vision and Pattern Recognition, CVPR 2007, pp. S.1–S.8 (2007)
38. Xianqiao, C., Qing, W., Xinping, Y., Xiuming, C.: The Enhancement for Foggy Traffic Image Based on EM Algorithm. In: Proceedings of the 2009 International Conference on Computational Intelligence and Natural Computing, vol. 02, pp. 261–264. IEEE Computer Society, Washington, DC (2009)
39. Shwartz, S., Namer, E., Schechner, Y.: Blind Haze Separation. In: 2006 IEEE Computer Society Conference on Computer Vision and Pattern Recognition, pp. S.1984–S.1991 (2006)
40. Nayar, S., Narasimhan, S.: Vision in bad weather. In: 1999. The Proceedings of the Seventh IEEE International Conference on Computer Vision, vol. 2, pp. S.820–S.827 (1999)
41. Tan, R.: Visibility in bad weather from a single image. In: IEEE Conference on Computer Vision and Pattern Recognition, CVPR 2008, pp. S.1–S.8 (2008)
42. Fattal, R.: Single image dehazing. ACM Transactions on Graphics (TOG), S.72:1–S.72:9 (2008)
43. Carr, P., Hartley, R.: Improved Single Image Dehazing Using Geometry. In: Digital Image Computing: Techniques and Applications, pp. S.103–S.110. IEEE Computer Society, Los Alamitos (2009)

Surface Defects Classification Using Artificial Neural Networks in Vision Based Polishing Robot

Anton Satria Prabuwono[1], Adnan Rachmat Anom Besari[2],
Ruzaidi Zamri[3], Md Dan Md Palil[3], and Taufik[4]

[1] Universiti Kebangsaan Malaysia, 43600 UKM Bangi, Selangor D.E., Malaysia
[2] Electronic Engineering Polytechnic Institute of Surabaya, Surabaya 60111, Indonesia
[3] Universiti Teknikal Malaysia Melaka, Durian Tunggal, 76109 Melaka, Malaysia
[4] California Polytechnic State University, San Luis Obispo, CA 93407, USA
antonsatria@ftsm.ukm.my, anom@pens.its.ac.id,
{ruzaidi,drdan}@utem.edu.my, taufik@calpoly.edu

Abstract. One of the highly skilled tasks in manufacturing is the polishing process. The purpose of polishing is to get uniform surface roughness. In order to reduce the polishing time and to cope with the shortage of skilled workers, robotic polishing technology has been investigated. This paper proposes a vision system to measure surface defects that have been classified to some level of surface roughness. Artificial neural networks are used to classify surface defects and to give a decision in order to drive the actuator of the arm robot. Force and rotation time have been chosen as output parameters of artificial neural networks. The results show that although there is a considerable change in both parameter values acquired from vision data compared to real data, it is still possible to obtain surface defects classification using a vision sensor to a certain limit of accuracy. The overall results of this research would encourage further developments in this area to achieve robust computer vision based surface measurement systems for industrial robotics, especially in the polishing process.

Keywords: polishing robot, vision sensor, surface defects, and artificial neural networks.

1 Introduction

Polishing is the finishing process that is widely used in many manufacturing industries including the aerospace, automobile, dies and mould industries. It is a process that uses abrasives to smooth the part surface without affecting its geometry. In general, the purpose of polishing is to get the uniform surface roughness distributed evenly throughout the part's surface [1]. Traditionally, polishing has largely been a manual operation. It is very labor intensive, highly skill dependent, inefficient with long process time, high cost, error prone, and hazardous due to abrasive dust. Automation is a solution to overcome the above-mentioned problems of the manual operation. The importance of polishing automation has drawn many researchers to investigate

S. Jeschke, H. Liu, and D. Schilberg (Eds.): ICIRA 2011, Part II, LNAI 7102, pp. 599–608, 2011.

polishing robotic technology. The major goal is to improve time efficiency together with surface quality [2].

The surface roughness measured by a computer vision system over a wide range could be obtained with a reasonable degree of accuracy compared with those measured by traditional contact methods. Researches in surface roughness inspection and defects detection are usually developed and improved with artificial intelligent (AI) techniques [3]. One of the artificial intelligent techniques that can model human reasoning in solving this polishing problem is artificial neural networks (ANN). It is used to train the system to get the best polishing pattern. The goal of this research is to build the system to act like human beings and with the ability to learn. The capability of such a skilled polishing worker is developed by using a vision based intelligent robot with two-dimensional specimens using artificial neural networks.

2   Related Works

Successful implementation of an automated polishing system requires in-depth studies of the polishing process. In the past, many researches have been carried out to investigate prospective methods for designing and implementing automated polishing systems. Researchers should decide what kinds of sensors are required to realize the ideas. The method usually used in a polishing robot sensor system can be divided into contact methods and non-contact methods [4]. Presently, contact-methods occupy a large volume in researches of practical polishing robots. Many researchers develop contact-methods like force sensors [5], ultrasonic vibration [6], and the touch trigger probe [7] due to the fact that these methods are easy to implement. In contrast this process is still inefficient, because it takes much sensing time in the polishing process.

In contradiction to contact methods, non-contact methods are rarely used for polishing robots. It is often used for surface roughness and defect inspection for evaluation in the final manufacturing process. The non-contact methods may present an alternative to allow the surface defects to be measured rapidly with an acceptable accuracy. One of the most promising non-contact methods in terms of speed and accuracy is the computer vision technique [8]. Compared to the contact method, the computer vision system is a useful method for measuring the surface defects with higher speed, lower price, and lower environmental noise in the manufacturing process [9]. Automatic surface defect detection with vision systems can bring manufacturers a number of significant benefits, especially when used on-line.

An experimental robotics based on a die polishing set-up using multiple vision sensors and fuzzy ANN has been developed to recognize new surfaces and plan an appropriate strategy for the polishing process [10]. A highly complex non-linear optimal problem in path planning optimization is proposed based on an improved genetic algorithm for a polishing robot [11]. The latest vision localization method for a micro-polishing robot has been presented, which is restricted within a certain working space [12,13]. Researchers usually improve time efficiency in the polishing process by optimizing path planning. Therefore this research tries to use force adapted based on surface defects classification to reduce polishing time and cope with the shortage of skilled workers.

3   System Design

In general, the system design was built as shown in Figure 1.

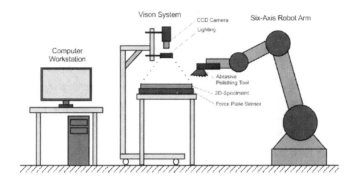

Fig. 1. The general system design

3.1   Material and Defects Classification

The material used in the experiment is aluminum steel plate. The material is mostly used in the automotive industry. A survey of surface defect classification was carried out including for scratches and corrosion. Scratches happen due to physical contact between materials and solid and rough objects.

3.2   Sensor and Actuator

OMRON F500 Vision System with 1 mega pixel resolution that enables high-precision inspections and measurements was used to grab surface image details. This camera has a standard image resolution for inspection of 512x484 (247.808 pixels). Furthermore, ring lighting was applied for illumination in surface inspection. The performance of the vision sensor depends on the combination of camera, lens, and lighting to create an appropriate combination for inspection purposes. To take force data during the polishing process, the Logic Pro LP342i force plate sensor (Texas Instrument) was used. This system was used as an actuator of a six-axis arm robot with an abrasive polishing tool as end-effectors. The model of arm robot in this research was the SMART NS 16-1.65 (COMAU Robotic Italia). The robot consists of an anthropomorphic structure with six degrees of freedom. Implementation of the polishing robot system is shown in Figure 2 and a block diagram of hardware and software is shown in Figure 3.

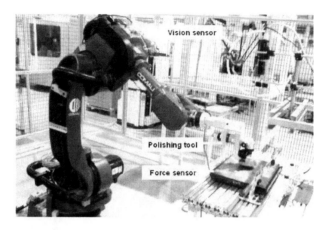

Fig. 2. Implementation of the polishing robot system

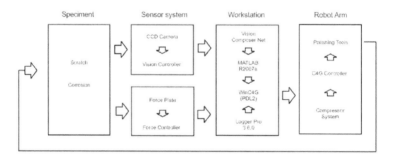

Fig. 3. Hardware and software block diagram

4   Surface Defects Classification

This section basically defines a surface defects classification using the image processing technique. The basic idea is to find an optimal gray-level threshold value for separating objects of interest in an image from the background. The method is based on gray-level distribution. There are two steps in surface defects classification. The first step is image acquisition that involves image capturing, image adjusting and noise removing by a filtering technique. The second step is multilevel threshold and image classification with contour levels to get features of the surface defects.

4.1   Image Acquisition

The color of the specimen is silver. It causes the light to be reflected directly. This condition causes the camera to be unable to get a good surface image of the specimen.

An extra lighting system with red color is used for the gray scale camera. Figure 4 shows the vision system in defects classification with direct vertical reflected light.

Fig. 4. Image acquisition using vision system

4.2   Image Adjusting and Filtering

There are two limitations with the grabbed image. The first is the characteristic of a material with non-uniform texture of surface. It makes features in the image to be covered by a lot of noise. The second is the use of direct lighting which generates noise in the centre of the specimen image. The noise has a circle form based on the shape of the lighting. A lot of noise in the image prevents further processes from being carried out. In the preliminary process, contrast was used to make the defects segmentation brighten up from the whole image. Then a Gaussian filter was used to remove the noise, so that noise and defects can be differentiated in order to get features of defects.

4.3   Multilevel Threshold and Contour Region

One of the segmentation techniques often used is the multilevel threshold. This technique is a process of segmenting a gray-level image into several distinct regions. The multilevel threshold technique determines more than one threshold for a given image and segments the image into certain brightness regions. It corresponds to one background and several objects. A variant of the classification algorithm by the clustering method is used to compute optimal values and to threshold the image into a number of classes [14].

After getting features of defects by performing some multilevel thresholds, simplifying the defects into some gray-level regions (image editing application known as gray-slice) has been done. The contour level is used to indicate the roughness level on surface defects. Based on the multilevel threshold image, the system can classify images in a simple manner. This method divides the surface defects features into some contour regions as shown in Figure 5.

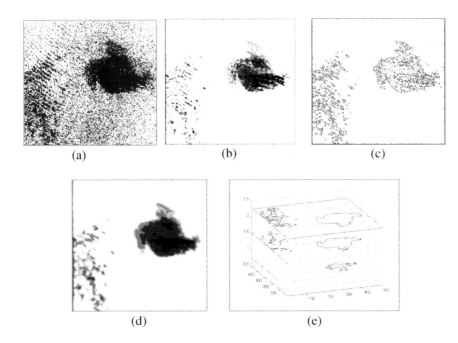

(a)   (b)   (c)

(d)   (e)

Fig. 5. Surface defects classification process (a) Defects image with non-uniform noise (b) Defects filtering from the noise (c) Defects segmentation from image (d) Multi-level threshold of defects (e) Contour region in some levels of defects.

5   Classification Using Artificial Neural Networks (ANN)

An artificial neural network was used to model input data from a variety of surface conditions of material. The aim is to obtain a pattern by finding the relationship between input parameters and output parameters.

5.1   Parameters Selection

In the polishing process, there are several parameters which can be changed such as abrasive value (u), force (F), rotation speed (ω) and polishing time (t) as shown in Figure 6. There are several levels of abrasiveness (roughness) in polishing tools, where those with a large abrasive value will effect significant surface changes as well. Given a good surface condition, these may even cause a new surface defect.

Normally, with a good surface condition it is sufficient if it is given a little bit of force due to the fact that the value of the desired changes is not significant. On the contrary, when the surface condition is bad, desired changes must be large, so large force values are required.

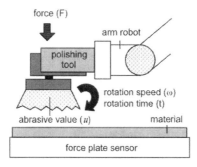

Fig. 6. System parameters

Table 1. Surface defects classification process

Experiment	Original Image	Enhanced Image	Characterized Image	Surface Defects Level
Force : 0 N Time : 0 sec				D1 : 11.11 % D2 : 7.85 %
Force : 2 N Time : 10 sec				D1 : 10.17 % D2 : 7.12 %
Force : 5N Time : 20 sec				D1 : 6.47 % D2 : 3.19 %
Force : 10 N Time : 30 sec				D1 : 3.51 % D2 : 2.61 %

Rotation speed means the rotational speed of the polishing tool, and rotation time means the time required to improve surface quality. It is not possible to provide a very high speed due to some limitations of a compressor drive system. A possible parameter for representing rotation speed (ω) is rotation time (t). For abrasive values, the parameter will be compared to the significance of surface quality change. Some levels of surface defects are easy to remove and some levels are hard to remove. From image classification, surface defects that are easy to remove are referred as D1 (Defect Lv.1) while the part that is hard to remove is called D2 (Defect Lv.2). In the next experiment, D1 will be associated with the rotation time (t) parameter, while D2 will be associated with the force (F) parameter. From this, the relationship between surface defects classification and output parameters can be determined. Table 1 illustrates some classification results with several parameter changes.

5.2   Network Architecture

Back-propagation neural network has been chosen to develop the defects classification. A supervised learning was used as a method of neural networks training. This research has considered a simple three layers of ANN with two input nodes, one hidden layer with seven nodes and one output node. Input means the data have surface defects classification with one parameter: force (F) or rotation time (t). Comparison of results between surface defects level (D1 and D2) and force or rotation time will be obtained from the new surface defects classification. Then a significant value of changes will be obtained. Changes in the surface defects classification before the polishing process are compared to the results. Output data is force (F) or rotation time (t). Each used as a target in the design of ANN. Those two parameters are divided into several discrete levels with the aim of simplifying the parameters.

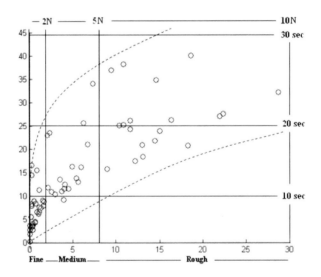

Fig. 7. Distribution of surface defects data (D1 and D2) compared to output parameter: force (N) and rotation time (sec)

The section focused on combining two main parameters of force (F) and rotation time (t). Many samples of data representing surface conditions are used to model the relationship between surface defects level with force and rotation time. D1 and D2 are described in Cartesian coordinates, and then made to determine boundaries of force and rotation time. The relationship between D1 and t is described in x coordinates, while D2 and F are described in y coordinates. Data can be classified into nine clusters. In data distribution, there are three clusters which are fully filled with data, four clusters are half-filled with data, and two clusters are not filled by the data (empty cluster). From this condition, seven clusters (three fully-filled clusters and four half-filled clusters) will be used for grouping the data. Artificial neural networks will be modeled to get the classification from the data as shown in Figure 7.

6   Result and Discussion

Some experiments have been done in the Robotic Laboratory of UTeM. However the maximum value of force is 10N. It means when the force value reaches 10N the polishing tool will be stopped immediately. Besides the maximum value of rotation time parameter is 30sec. This happened due to the fact that changes of surface defects values are not significant when rotation time increased to more than 30sec. Experiments have been conducted 66 times, in detail 30 times with force parameters of 2N, 4N, 6N, 8N and 10N respectively. Each condition is done with five different surface defects. Furthermore the 36 experiments have been done with rotation time parameters of 5sec, 10sec, 15sec, 20sec, 25sec and 30sec respectively. Each made five different surface defect conditions.

Supervised learning was used for data classification. For each class, the values of classification have been given. Values for the fine class are 1 & 1.3, for the medium class are 1.7, 2 & 2.3, while for the rough class they are 2.7 & 3. The purpose of this experiment is to classify the data into several groups by using a simple three layers of ANN. To achieve an error value = 0.05, ANN training has been done with 534 epochs. This training is experienced enough to teach the network forming groups of data. Learning error from this network is about 0.18; this value is assessed according to stages of the supervised learning method. The surface defect can be classified in order to get features and details of defects especially for scratches and corrosion.

7   Conclusion

This paper presents preliminary research in vision based polishing robots. The system is based on images taken by a CCD camera. Lighting and image pre-processing have been developed to divide surface defects into two levels. Polishing tasks require force control adapting to current levels of surface defects. The greater magnitude of unidirectional force normal to the surface polishing force must be adjusted for a rougher surface, while a lighter magnitude must be regulated for a smoother surface.

Artificial neural networks were used to train the robotic system to emulate a human's example in the polishing process. However defining the rules for the polishing process from image data which has natural variations would be a very difficult task. By using neural networks, any explicit classification rules do not need to be understood. Another advantage is, if the errors happened it can be retrained by using a larger training set. Besides, the system can be easily modified to inspect the different surface defect types. In future, several intelligent methods called hybrid technology will be combined to minimize the learning time of neural networks. It can increase the system's ability to be adaptive in dealing with various defects in a variety of surface conditions.

Acknowledgments. This research is supported by Ministry of Higher Education Malaysia under Fundamental Research Grant Scheme No. FRGS/2007/FKP(8)-F0033, UKM-TT-03-FRGS0131-2010 and UKM-OUP-ICT-36-186/2011.

References

1. Liao, L., Xi, F., Liu, K.: Modeling and Control of Automated Polishing-Deburring Process using a Dual-Purpose Compliant Toolhead. Int. J. Machine Tools & Manufacture 48, 1454–1463 (2008)
2. Tam, H., Lui, O.C., Mok, A.C.K.: Robotic Polishing of Free Form Surfaces using Scanning Paths. J. Materials Processing Technology 95, 191–200 (1999)
3. Kuo, R.J.: Intelligent Robotic Die Polishing System Through Fuzzy Neural Networks and Multi-Sensor Fusion. In: Int. Joint Conf. on Neural Networks, pp. 2925–2928 (1993)
4. Besari, A.R.A., Palil, M.D.M., Zamri, R., Prabuwono, A.S.: A Review of Novel Sensing Techniques for Automatic Polishing Robot System. In: Nat. Conf. on Design and Concurrent Engineering, pp. 353–358 (2008)
5. Nagata, F., Kusumoto, Y., Fujimoto, Y., Watanabe, K.: Robotic Sanding System for New Designed Furniture with Free-Formed Surface. Robotics and Computer-Integrated Manufacturing 23, 371–379 (2007)
6. Zhao, J., Zhan, J., Jin, R., Tao, M.: An Oblique Ultrasonic Polishing Method by Robot for Free Form Surfaces. Int. J. Machine Tools & Manufacture 40, 795–808 (2000)
7. Yang, Z., Xi, F., Wu, B.: A Shape Adaptive Motion Control System with Application to Robotic Polishing. In: Robotics and Computer-Integrated Manufacturing, vol. 21, pp. 355–367 (2005)
8. Li, X., Wang, L., Cai, N.: Machine-Vision-Based Surface Finish Inspection for Cutting Tool Replacement in Production. Int. J. Production Research 42(11), 2279–2287 (2004)
9. Lee, B.Y., Yu, S.F., Juan, H.: The Model of Surface Roughness Inspection. Mechatronics 14, 129–141 (2004)
10. Kuo, R.J.: A Robotic Die Polishing System Through Fuzzy Neural Networks. Computers in Industry 32, 273–280 (1997)
11. Tong-Ying, G., Dao-Kui, Q., Zai-Li, D.: Research of Path Planning for Polishing Robot Based on Improved Genetic Algorithm. In: IEEE Int. Conf. on Robotics and Biomimetics, pp. 334–338 (2004)
12. Yang, Z., Chen, F., Zhao, J., Wu, X.: A Novel Vision Localization Method of Automated Micro-Polishing Robot. J. Bionic Engineering 6, 46–54 (2009)
13. Liu, Z., Zhao, J., Zhang, L., Chen, G., Li, D.: Realization of Mobile Robot Trajectory Tracking Control Based on Interpolation. In: IEEE Int. Symp. on Industrial Electronics, pp. 648–651 (2009)
14. Besari, A.R.A., Zamri, R., Rahman, K.A.A., Palil, M.D.M., Prabuwono, A.S.: Surface Defects Characterization in Polishing Process using Contour Dispersion. In: Int. Conf. on Soft Computing and Pattern Recognition, pp. 707–710 (2009)

Efficient Skin Detection
under Severe Illumination Changes and Shadows

Bishesh Khanal and Désiré Sidibé

Université de Bourgogne, Laboratoire LE2I - UMR CNRS 5158
12 rue de la fonderie, 71200 Le Creusot, France

Abstract. This paper presents an efficient method for human skin color detection with a mobile platform. The proposed method is based on modeling the skin distribution in a log-chromaticity color space which shows good invariance properties to changing illumination. The method is easy to implement and can cope with the requirements of real-world tasks such as illumination variations, shadows and moving camera. Extensive experiments show the good performance of the proposed method and its robustness against abrupt changes of illumination and shadows.

Keywords: Skin detection, Invariance to illumination, Log-chromaticity color space, Face detection.

1 Introduction

Detecting human skin color is an important step in various applications including video surveillance, visual tracking, content-based image retrieval systems, human computer interaction and robots interaction. In the context of interacting robots, advanced robots should be able to reliably find people in their vicinity and interpret their motion without any a priori knowledge about the environment. Among many visual cues, skin color has proved to be a very useful cue for person detection and for faces or hands detection and tracking.

Color as a low-level feature offers many advantages such as robustness to occlusions, scale variation and geometric transformations. However, the color of an object depends on the illumination conditions, the camera parameters and the reflectance properties of the object. A good skin color detector must be robust against illumination variations and must be able to cope with the great variability of skin color between ethnic groups. Another challenge in detecting human skin color is the fact that many objects in the real world can have skin-tone colors. For example, wood, leather, skin-colored clothing, hair, etc. This produces a high number of false detections in uncontrolled environment.

Skin color detection can be viewed as a classification problem and the primary step is the selection of a suitable color space, i.e. a color space in which one can easily discriminate between skin and nonskin pixels. Several color spaces have been employed in literature and the choice of the color space affects the performance of any skin detector and its sensitivity to changes in illumination conditions [1,2]. In most approaches, a color space that de-correlate luminance

S. Jeschke, H. Liu, and D. Schilberg (Eds.): ICIRA 2011, Part II, LNAI 7102, pp. 609–618, 2011.

and chromatic components is adopted, since it is assumed that chromatic components are less sensitive to lighting conditions [3]. However, Cheddad et al. [4] have shown that luminance can be useful in finding skin pixels in color images.

In this paper, we propose the use of a log-chromaticity color space for skin color detection. The log-chromaticity color space shows two important properties. Firstly, a surface color seen under different illuminant colors tends to lie on a straight line in this space. Secondly, for a given camera, the lines corresponding to different surface colors are parallel to each other. Thus an illumination invariant representation of images can be obtained in log-chromaticity color space [5]. We take advantage of this invariant property to develop an efficient skin color detector robust against severe illumination variations and shadows. This robust and fast skin detection algorithm can be used as main input for a module of the software architecture controlling a mobile robot for finding people.

The rest of the paper is organized as follows: previous work on skin detection are described in Section 2, the proposed method is presented in Section 3, experimental and comparative results are shown in Section 4, and conclusions are given in Section 5.

2   Related Work

Human skin color is a very effective feature for persons, faces or hands detection and extensive research has been carried out in developing skin segmentation methods. Most existing techniques involve the classification of image pixels into skin and nonskin categories based on the pixels intensity values. The basic idea behind these techniques is that human skin pixels tend to occupy a small cluster in various color spaces. Therefore, in order to discriminate between skin and nonskin pixels, a color transformation is performed. Skin color detection algorithms are then applied in the new color space.

Many different color spaces are employed in literature including RGB, normalized RGB, HSI, HSV, YCbCr, YES, YUV, CIE Lab [1,2]. Many authors use chrominance color spaces that de-correlate luminance and chromatic components, assuming that chromatic components are less sensitive to lighting conditions than the luminance. In a comparative study of nine chrominance color spaces, Terrillon et al. [3] shows that the tint-saturation-luminance (TSL) space and the normalized RGB space provide best results for Gaussian models. However, it was also shown that discarding the luminance component degrades skin color segmentation results. For example, Cheddad et al. [4] propose a luminance based skin detection method based on deriving an error signal from the grayscale map and the non-red encoded grayscale version of the image. A comprehensive survey of skin color detection in different color spaces can be found in [1,2].

Albiol et al. [6] show that the performance of a skin detection algorithm is largely unaffected by the color space choice, i.e. if an optimal skin detector is designed for every color space, then the performances will be same. Therefore, the classification rules are of most importance. The simplest classification methods are classifiers which define cluster boundaries in terms of single or multiple thresholds in the color space. For example, Chai and Ngan [7] propose a facial region segmentation algorithm in the CbCr plane of the YCbCr color space. Pixels falling within $Cb = [77, 127]$ and $Cr = [133, 173]$ are classified as skin pixels. Sobottka and Pitas [8] propose a set of fixed skin thresholds in the HS plane. The obvious advantage of using explicit thresholding methods is the simplicity of detection rules that leads to a very fast classifier.

Another approach is to use Bayesian classification techniques based on skin color distributions. This family of methods can be divided into parametric and nonparametric methods. Parametric methods assume that skin color distribution follows a known probability density function whose parameters are to be estimated. The parameters are estimated using a training set of skin pixels and a unimodal Gaussian pdf is often adopted [9]. A more sophisticated model, a mixture model, can also be employed [10,3]. However as shown by Caetano et al. [11] the advantage of using a multimodal representation over a unimodal one is limited. The performance of mixture models exceeds single models performance only when a high true positive rate is needed. But a high true positive rate in this case is obtained at the cost of a high false positive rate. In the case of nonparametric methods, the skin color distribution is represented by a lookup table or a histogram. Jones and Rehg [12] use a histogram representation in RGB color space and report better performance in comparison with Gaussian models. Nonparametric methods have the advantage of being independent of the distribution shape. Thus, they can adapt to arbitrary distributions.

A very important aspect of any skin detection algorithm is the robustness against illumination variations since radically changing lighting conditions greatly affect the skin color distribution in an image. Most of the skin detection methods described above can deal only with slight variations in lighting conditions. To achieve robustness against illumination changes, a color constancy algorithm can be used as a preprocessing step. Hsu et al. [9] use the Gray World algorithm to normalize images prior to skin detection while Kakumanu et al. [13] use a neural network based constancy technique. A physics-based approach can also be used to solve the problem of color constancy for skin detection. This approach is based on finding a skin locus, i.e. an area occupied by skin pixels in chromaticity space under certain illuminations. Soriano et al. [14] find the locus directly from images taken under four representative light sources, Horizon (2300K), Incandescent A (2856K), Fluorescent TL84, and daylight 6500K, and use the obtained locus for skin pixels classification.

3   Proposed Method

3.1   Log-Chromaticity Color Space Properties

The log-chromaticity color space (LCCS) is a 2D space obtained by taking the logarithm of ratios of color channels. For example, log(R/G) and log(B/G) form a 2D LCCS. The illumination invariance property is based on the image formation model governed by Eq. 1:

$$I_c = \sigma \int_\Omega E(\lambda)S(\lambda)Q_c(\lambda)d\lambda, \ c \in \{R, G, B\}; \tag{1}$$

where, I_c is the color intensity at a pixel for the color channel c, σ is the Lambertian shading, E is the illumination power spectral distribution, S is the surface spectral reflectance function and, Q_c is the camera sensor sensitivity function. The integral is computed over the visible spectrum Ω.

Under the assumptions of Planckian lighting, Lambertian surface and a narrowband camera, Finlayson et al. [5,15] shows that the color of a pixel in the LCCS move in a straight line when the illumination is varied. For a given camera, different pixels color in this space are found to be moving in lines parallel to each other, and therefore projecting the pixels in a line perpendicular to these parallel lines, an illumination invariant image can be obtained. To see why this is the case let analyse the implications of the different assumptions.

The narrowband assumption states that the sensor sensitivity functions are exactly Dirac functions $Q_c(\lambda) = q_c\delta(\lambda - \lambda_c)$ centered at wavelength λ_c. Under this assumption, Eq. 1 becomes:

$$I_c = \sigma E(\lambda_c)S(\lambda_c)q_c. \tag{2}$$

The Planckian assumption implies that lighting can be approximated by Planck's law, in Wien's approximation [5,16]:

$$E(\lambda, T) = Ik_1\lambda^{-5}\exp\left(-\frac{k_2}{T\lambda}\right), \tag{3}$$

where T is the illuminant temperature and k_1 and k_2 are constants containing the Planck constant, the Boltzman constant and the speed of light in vacuum.

With these assumptions, the color intensity at a pixel is then given by:

$$I_c = \sigma Ik_1\lambda_c^{-5}e^{-\frac{k_2}{T\lambda_c}}S(\lambda_c)q_c. \tag{4}$$

If, we now form the chromatic components by taking the ratios, for example, of Red and Blue channels w.r.t. Green channel, it is clear from Eq. 4 that intensity and shading information are removed. To remove the nonlinearity, we take the natural logarithm of the ratios and obtain:

$$\rho_c = log(I_c/I_G) = log(s_c/s_G) + (e_c - e_G)/T, \ c \in \{R, B\}; \tag{5}$$

with $s_c = k_1\lambda_c^{-5}S(\lambda_c)q_c$ and $e_c = -k_2/\lambda_c$.

Eq. 5 shows that in the LCCS all the color values of a surface seen under different illuminants fall on in straigt line. The direction of this line, given by the vector$(e_c - e_G)$, is independent of the surface reflectance function. As a consequence, different surface characteristics will produce different lines in the LCCS. However, all these lines are parallel, since they share the same slope (independent from the surface). An invariant image can be formed by projecting the chromatic components into a direction orthogonal to these parallel lines. The result of this projection is a scalar image which is called *intrinsic image* [5].

3.2 Skin Detection in Log-Chromaticity Color Space

As stated in Section 2, an important aspect of any skin detection algorithm is its ability to achieve correct classification in the presence of varying illumination conditions. A good skin color detector must be robust against illumination changes and must be able to deal with the great variability of skin color between ethnic groups.

The invariance properties of the log-chromaticity color space can be exploited to develop a robust skin detector. The motivation of our approach is that the skin pixels under different lighting conditions tend to form a distinct cluster in the LCCS. We can thus define a simple classification rule based on the skin cluster boundaries in LCCS. Though other classification techniques such as parametric and nonparametric estimation methods can be used, we have found in our experiments that an explicit thresholding method gives better results (see Section 4.1). Another advantage of using explicit boundaries for classification is the simplicity of detection that leads to a very fast classifier. The boundaries are obtained from a training set of pixels that are manually selected from various images. The images are chosen in order to represent different skin tones, ranging from dark to brownish and whitish, seen under different illumination conditions.

A pixel in an image is classified as a skin pixel if its projection in the LCCS lies in the region defined by: $log(R/G) \in [0.15; 1.1]$ and $log(B/G) \in [-4; 0.3]$. The experiments described in Section 4 show that this simple rule leads to very good detection results in various conditions, providing an efficient solution for human skin color detection.

4 Experimental Results

To evaluate the performance of the proposed skin detection method we apply it to a large dataset of images. This dataset used in [17] contains 846 images collected from different existing datasets and is composed of 4.9 million skin pixels and 13.7 million nonskin pixels. We use this dataset for skin detection methods evaluation because it contains ground truth images, i.e. manually segmented skin areas in the images containing humans. With the ground truth images available, it is possible to perform a quantitative analysis of the results. The performances are evaluated in terms of correct detection rate (CDR), false detection rate (FDR) and overall classification rate (CR) [1]. CDR, FDR and CR are, respectively, the percentage of skin pixels correctly classified, the percentage of nonskin pixels incorrectly classified and the percentage of pixels correctly classified.

4.1 Skin Detection in Log-Chromatic Color Space

Different classification rules can be employed to detect skin pixels in the LCCS. In this section, we compare a simple direct thresholding method and a parametric method using a Gaussian model (GM). The parameters, mean and covariance, of the GM in LCCS are obtained from the same training set of pixels used to find the ranges for the fixed threshold method. Since classification with a GM requires setting a threshold on the probabilities, we vary the threshold from 0 to 1 and find for each value of the threshold the corresponding CDR and FDR. In Table 1, we show the classification performance of the GM in LCCS obtained with different thresholds and the performance of the proposed method with fixed explicit thresholds. As we can see, the fixed thresholds method outperforms the parametric GM approach which, for the same CDR, gives a lot of false positive detection. Moreover, using explicit ranges in LCSS avoid the computation of probabilities or distances, making the detection faster. This justifies our use of explicit threshold ranges for skin detection in LCCS.

Table 1. Comparison of parametric Gaussian model(GM) and explicit thresholds values for skin detection in LCCS

	GM with varying thresholds T								Proposed method with fixed threshold
	T_1	T_2	T_3	T_4	T_5	T_6	T_7	T_8	
CDR	92.30	85.08	80.09	74.48	68.33	60.88	50.93	38.28	89.96
FDR	61.68	21.68	15.32	11.23	8.45	6.30	4.54	2.93	16.40

4.2 Comparative Results

We compared the proposed skin detection method (LCCS) with other popular methods which also use explicit thresholding for classification. The methods considered are the skin locus approach in normalized RGB (NRGB) [18], the use of hue and saturation components in HSV color space (HS) [8], the combination of normalized RGB with hue and saturation (NRGB-HS) [19], the use of chromatic components in YCbCr color space (CbCr) [7], and the luminance based method described by Cheddad et al. [4]. For all these methods we use the thresholds given by authors.

Testing on a large dataset showing both indoor and outdoor environments with varying lighting conditions provide an objective comparison of the different methods. Figure 1 shows a few images from the dataset and the detection results using the different methods. The detection results with the entire dataset are summarized in Table 2. We can see that the proposed method compare very well against other opproaches. LCSS leads to an overall classification rate (CR) of about 85% and is outperformed only by the luminance method which achieves a CR of 90.45%. On the other hand, the luminance method gives a correct detection rate (CDR) of 68.89% which much less than 89.96% given by LCCS. This means that the luminance method misses much more skin pixels than LLCS as can be observed in Figure 1.f and Figure 1.g. The proposed LCCS skin detection method outperforms NRGB, HS and CbCr in terms of CDR, FDR and CR. It achieves the best tradeoff between high CDR, detecting as many skin pixels as possible in the images, and low FDR, producing few incorrect detection of nonskin pixels.

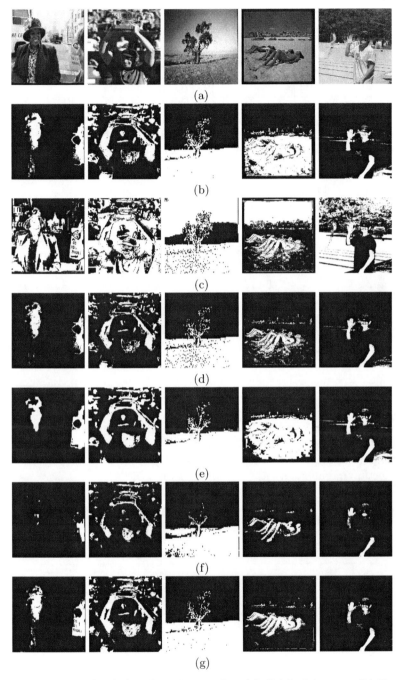

Fig. 1. Some example of skin detection results. (a) Original images. (b) Detection results with NRGB [18]. (c) Detection results with HS [8]. (d) Detection results with NRGB-HS [19]. (e) Detection results with CbCr [7]. (f) Detection results with the luminance method [4]. (g) Detection results with the proposed LCCS method.

Table 2. Comparison of detection results with the entire dataset

	NRGB [18]	HS [8]	NRGB-HS [19]	CbCr [7]	Luminance [4]	LCCS (proposed)
CDR	70.58	63.78	47.55	89.84	68.89	89.96
FDR	17.26	29.57	11.55	22.72	5.32	16.40
CR	80.75	63.34	81.75	84.04	90.45	84.64

4.3 Robustness against Illumination Variation and Shadow

In this section we evaluate the proposed method in the case of severe illumination changes and shadow. This experiment is performed because detecting people with a camera mounted on a mobile robot is one of our future applications. We use a video consisting of three people moving from outdoor bright sunlight to the inside of a building with darker regions. The persons are followed with a hand-held camera. The images of the video contain various lighting conditions, from bright sunlight to artificial fluorescent light, and also contains some shadowed areas.

Figure 2 shows some of the results obtained with the video. As can be seen, the proposed method operates well for skin under shadows and abrupt changes in illumination in comparison to other methods. In the third and fourth columns of Figure 2 for example, we can see that the luminance and the CbCr methods can hardly detect skin pixels and mainly detect the red color of clothing. On the contrary, the proposed LCCS method performs extremely well in such difficult cases. Note how the visible skin areas of the persons are correctly segmented with few false positive detection. Correct classification and false positive rates for this dataset are given in Table 3. The results are obtained using fifty frames taken from the video for which the ground truth images were obtained manually. It contained in total 15.04 million pixels with 0.68 million skin pixels and 14.46 non-skin pixels. As can be seen, the proposed LCCS method outperforms other skin detection methods for this difficult dataset.

Table 3. Detection results with severe illumination changes and shadows

	NRGB [18]	HS [8]	NRGB-HS [19]	CbCr [7]	Luminance [4]	LCCS (proposed)
CDR	35.03	41.93	22.07	40.94	29.76	64.84
FDR	4.01	32.30	1.87	6.17	4.18	4.50

5 Conclusion

In this paper an efficient and robust skin detection method is proposed. The method is based on finding human skin locus in the log-chromaticity color space. Based on invariant properties of this color space, a skin detection method is developed and extensive experiments with a large dataset show that the proposed method is particularly robust against severe illumination changes and shadows for images under natural sunlight. Comparison with many other approaches show

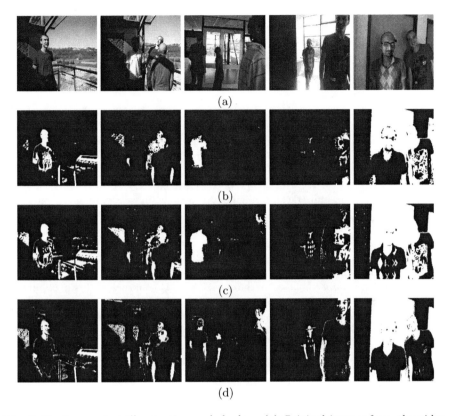

Fig. 2. Testing against illumination and shadow. (a) Original images from the video. (b) Detection results with the luminance method [4]. (c) Detection result with CbCr [7]. (d) Detection results with LCCS (proposed).

that the proposed method achieves the best tradeoff between correct classification of skin pixels and false detection of nonskin pixels. The simplicity and the robustness of the method make it suitable for real-world robotic applications. Our future work include using the proposed method for person detection and tracking with a mobile robot.

References

1. Phung, S.L., Bouzerdoum, A., Chai, D.: Skin segmentation using color pixel classification: analysis and comparison. IEEE Trans. on Pattern Analysis and Machine Intelligence 27(1), 148–154 (2005)
2. Kakumanu, K., Makrogiannis, S., Bourbakis, N.: A survey of skin color modeling and detection methods. Pattern Recognition 40(3), 1106–1122 (2007)
3. Terrillon, J., Shirazi, M.N., Fukamachi, H., Akamatsu, S.: Comparative performance of different skin chrominance models and chrominance spaces for the automatic detection of human faces in color images. In: IEEE International Conference on Face and Gesture Recognition, pp. 54–61 (2000)

4. Cheddad, A., Condell, J., Curran, V., Mc Kevitt, P.: A skin tone detection algorithm for an adaptive approach to steganography. Signal Processing 89(12), 2465–2478 (2009)
5. Finlayson, G.D., Drew, M.S., Lu, C.: Intrinsic Images by Entropy Minimization. In: Pajdla, T., Matas, J(G.) (eds.) ECCV 2004. LNCS, vol. 3023, pp. 582–595. Springer, Heidelberg (2004)
6. Albiol, A., Torres, L., Delp, E.J.: Optimum color spaces for skin detection. In: IEEE International Conference on Image Processing, pp. pp. 122–124 (2001)
7. Chai, D., Ngan, K.N.: Face segmentation using skin color map in videophone applications. IEEE Trans. on Circuits and Systems for Video Technology 9(4), 551–564 (1999)
8. Sobottka, K., Pitas, I.: A novel method for automatic face segmentation, facial feature extraction and tracking. Signal Processing: Image Communication 12(3), 263–281 (1998)
9. Hsu, R., Abdel-Mottaleb, M., Jain, A.K.: Face detecting in color images. IEEE Trans. on Pattern Analysis and Machine Intelligence 24, 696–706 (2002)
10. Greenspan, H., Goldberger, J., Eshet, I.: Mixture model for face-color modeling and segmentation. Pattern Recognition Letters 22, 1525–1536 (2001)
11. Caetano, T.S., Olabarriaga, S.D., Barone, D.A.C.: Do mixture models in chromaticity space improve skin detection? Pattern Recognition (36), 3019–3021 (2003)
12. Jones, M., Rehg, J.M.: Statistical color models with application to skin detection. International Journal of Computer Vision 46(1), 81–96 (2002)
13. Kakumanu, P., Makrogiannis, S., Bryll, R., Panchanathan, S., Bourbakis, V.: Image chromatic adaptation using ANNs for skin color adaptation. In: 16th IEEE International Conference on Tools with Artificial Intelligence, pp. 478–485 (2004)
14. Soriano, M., MartinKauppi, J.B., Huovinen, S., Lksonen, M.: Adaptive skin color modeling using the skin locus for selecting training pixels. Pattern Recognition 36(3), 681–690 (2003)
15. Finlayson, G., Drew, M., Lu, C.: Entropy minimization for shadow removal. International Journal of Computer Vision 85, 35–57 (2009)
16. Eibenberger, E., Angelopoulou, E.: The narrow-band assumption in log-chromaticity space. In: Color and Reflectance in Imaging and Computer Vision Workshop, in Conjunction with ECCV (2010)
17. Schmugge, S.J., Jayaram, S., Shin, M.C., Tsap, L.V.: Objective evaluation of approaches of skin detection using ROC analysis. Computer Vision and Image Understanding 108, 41–51 (2007)
18. Ali, M.R., Morris, T.: Skin locus based skin detection for gesture recognition. In: BMVC UK Postgrad. Workshop - British Machine Vision Conference, pp. 10.1–10.11 (2010)
19. Wang, Y., Yuan, B.: A novel approach for human face detection from color images under complex background. Pattern Recognition 34(10), 1983–1992 (2001)

Author Index